Financial Statement Analysis

Visit the *Financial Statement Analysis* Companion Website at **www.pearsoned.co.uk/Petersen** to find valuable **student** learning material including:

- Multiple choice questions to test your understanding
- Annotated weblinks to accounting information, credit rating agencies, company information, and financial data for companies referenced in the text
- A glossary and flashcards to focus your study of key terms

WITHDRAWN FROM THE LIBRARY

UNIVERSITY OF WINCHESTER

D1323471

PEARSON

We work with leading authors to develop the
strongest educational materials in Accounting,
bringing cutting-edge thinking and best
learning practice to a global market.

Under a range of well-known imprints, including
Prentice Hall, we craft high quality print and
electronic publications which help readers to understand
and apply their content, whether studying or at work.

To find out more about the complete range of our
publishing, please visit us on the World Wide Web at:
www.pearson.com/uk

Financial Statement Analysis
Valuation · Credit analysis · Executive compensation

Christian V. Petersen
and
Thomas Plenborg

**Financial Times
Prentice Hall
is an imprint of**

PEARSON

Harlow, England • London • New York • Boston • San Francisco • Toronto • Sydney • Singapore • Hong Kong
Tokyo • Seoul • Taipei • New Delhi • Cape Town • Madrid • Mexico City • Amsterdam • Munich • Paris • Milan

UNIVERSITY OF WINCHESTER
LIBRARY

Pearson Education Limited

Edinburgh Gate
Harlow
Essex CM20 2JE
England

and Associated Companies throughout the world

Visit us on the World Wide Web at:
www.pearson.com/uk

First published 2012

UNIVERSITY OF WINCHESTER
7-day
04277694   657.3
PET

© Christian V. Petersen and Thomas Plenborg 2012

The rights of Christian V. Petersen and Thomas Plenborg to be identified as authors of this work have been asserted by them in accordance with the Copyright, Designs and Patents Act 1988.

All rights reserved. No part of this publication may be reproduced, stored in a retrieval system, or transmitted in any form or by any means, electronic, mechanical, photocopying, recording or otherwise, without either the prior written permission of the publisher or a licence permitting restricted copying in the United Kingdom issued by the Copyright Licensing Agency Ltd, Saffron House, 6–10 Kirby Street, London EC1N 8TS.

All trademarks used herein are the property of their respective owners. The use of any trademark in this text does not vest in the author or publisher any trademark ownership rights in such trademarks, nor does the use of such trademarks imply any affiliation with or endorsement of this book by such owners.

Pearson Education is not responsible for the content of third-party internet sites.

ISBN: 978-0-273-75235-6

British Library Cataloguing-in-Publication Data
A catalogue record for this book is available from the British Library

Library of Congress Cataloging-in-Publication Data

Petersen, Christian V.
  Financial statement analysis : valuation, credit analysis and executive compensation / Christian V. Petersen and Thomas Plenborg.
      p. cm.
  Includes bibliographical references and index.
  ISBN 978-0-273-75235-6 (pbk.)
  1. Financial statements. 2. Corporations—Finance. I. Plenborg, Thomas. II. Title.
  HG4028.B2P48 2012
  657′.3—dc23
                                        2011030723

ARP impression 98

Typeset in 10/12pt Sabon by 73
Printed and bound by Ashford Colour Press Ltd., Gosport.

This book is dedicated to our families

Thomas: my wife, Susanne, and children, Peter, Frederikke and Karl Emil

Christian: my wife, Susanne, and children, Sofie, Katrine and Sebastian

We love you!

Contents

Preface

Financial statement analysis has proven to be useful in a wide range of business decisions. Equity analysts use it as a foundation for their projection of the earnings potential of a company. Credit analysts use it as a tool to analyse operating and financial risks and to determine whether loans should be extended. Consultants apply it as part of their strategic analysis. Management uses it in monitoring competitors and in establishing a 'best practice' in an/their industry. Investment bankers and private equity funds apply financial statement analysis as basis for analysing potential mergers and acquisitions.

The course 'financial statement analysis' is therefore in demand at business schools worldwide. It provides business students with a framework for analysing financial statements for different analytical purposes. It is our ambition that the framework laid out in this book will provide business students and practitioners with a unique insight into financial statement analysis.

Vision of the book

Most textbooks on financial statement analysis primarily focus on investors. This implies that the analysis aims at supporting a valuation perspective. This book differs from other books by introducing and developing a framework for financial statement analysis that takes a wider user perspective. In addition to valuation we also focus on credit analysis and design of accounting-based bonus plans for executives. This implies that the book takes the view point of an equity analyst, credit analyst and compensation analyst, respectively. This book recognises that these three users make decisions in different contexts using different aspects of financial statements. So, to make optimum decisions, we focus on each of these contexts separately using different accounting information and applying different sets of ratios.

Overview

An important premise when reading this textbook is that although a firm's financial statement serves as an important source of information it is crucial that additional information is collected and analysed. This includes an understanding of the firm's strategy and its competitors and the markets which it serves. Thereby it is possible to analyse the financials much more intelligently and generate more powerful analyses.

The book is divided into four parts which, when combined, give you an excellent insight into financial statement analysis. Each part represents a theme that includes information on:

- Part 1 – Accounting data
- Part 2 – Financial analysis
- Part 3 – Decision making
- Part 4 – Assessment of accounting data

In **Part 1 – Accounting data** we present the different financial statements in the annual report. Needless to say, familiarity with the components of the annual report is an essential prerequisite for understanding the other parts of this book. Based on our experience many students as well as practitioners have only limited knowledge on how firms record (double-entry bookkeeping) transactions and enter them into different financial statements. We therefore also revisit the double-entry bookkeeping system.

In **Part 2 – Financial analysis** we discuss in details how to measure and analyse a firm's profitability, growth and risk. Good *profitability* is important for a company's future survival and to ensure a satisfactory return to shareholders. The historical profitability is also an important element in defining the future expectations for a company. *Growth* is seen by many as the driving force for future progress in companies. It is therefore essential to measure growth and ensure that it is profitable. The monitoring of the *liquidity risk* is central to any business. Without liquidity a company cannot pay its bills or carry out profitable investments and in extreme cases lack of liquidity leads to bankruptcy. An analysis of short- and long-term liquidity risk is therefore crucial.

In **Part 3 – Decision making** we apply the financial analysis on different decision contexts:

- Forecasting
- Valuation
- Cost of capital
- Credit analysis
- Accounting-based bonus plans for executives

Forecasting (pro forma statements) serves as the foundation for many business decisions. An understanding of how to build pro forma statements and ensuring that they are based on reasonable assumptions is therefore essential. The chapter on *valuation* gives an overview of the valuation techniques available and we discuss in detail how to apply the most popular valuation techniques including the present value approaches such as the discounted cash flow model and the economic value added model, multiples such as the P/E ratio and EV/EBIT ratio and the liquidation approach. *Cost of capital* is a concept used across different decision contexts. For example, cost of capital serves as the discount factor in valuation and as a performance standard (threshold) in compensation schemes. Consequently, we discuss how to estimate the cost of capital. The chapter on *credit analysis* aims at assessing a company's ability and willingness to pay its financial obligations in a timely manner. It also examines the probability that a company defaults and the potential loss in case of a default. Finally, the chapter on *accounting-based bonus plans for executives* addresses some of the financial issues when designing an executive's compensation contract.

In the first three parts we have taken reported financial data at face value. In the final part, **Part 4 – Assessment of accounting data,** we challenge the accounting data used in the financial analysis. The concept of 'accounting quality' is defined, and we document that management has some flexibility and discretion in producing financial statements. We therefore discuss accounting policies and flexibility and how they have an impact on firm valuation, credit analysis and the design of accounting-based bonus plans for executives.

Target group

This book is intended for people interested in financial statement analysis. Many of the techniques discussed in this book can be used in relation to valuation of companies, assessment of creditworthiness and the design of accounting-based bonus plans for executives. However, people interested in related matters such as financial management and risk management may also find inspiration in this book. The book is designed so that it can be used in financial statement analysis for a variety of settings including MBA, Master in Accounting and Finance, executive courses, and undergraduate courses in Accounting and Finance. Furthermore, the book is suitable for practitioners with an interest in financial statement analysis.

Prerequisites

Since financial statements typically serve as the primary source of data in financial statement analysis, it is important that students and practitioners have a basic knowledge of financial accounting. Although the book can be read with minor or with no prior knowledge of financial accounting and reporting, to gain full benefit from reading the text, we do recommend that students as well as practitioners, have a basic understanding of financial accounting. Furthermore, knowledge of financial and strategic issues is also useful as we draw on both disciplines throughout our book.

Acknowledgement

We are grateful to the following colleagues who gave us valuable feedback in writing this book: Rune Dalgaard, Jens Østrup and Morten Jensen.

Publisher's acknowledgements

We are grateful to the following for permission to reproduce copyright material:

Figures
Figures 6.5, 6.6 and 6.7 from Data Source: Compustat®, Copyright © 2011 The McGraw-Hill Companies, Inc. Standard & Poor's, including its subsidiary corporations (S&P), is a division of The McGraw-Hill Companies, Inc. Figures 8.5 and 8.6 from *Competitive Advantage: Creating and Sustaining Superior Performance* (Porter, Michael E.) Copyright © 1985, 1998 by Michael E. Porter, reprinted with the permission of Free Press, a Division of Simon & Schuster, Inc. All rights reserved; Figure 9.3 from Issues in valuation of privately-held firms, *Journal of Private Equity*, Vol. 10 (1), pp. 34–48 (Petersen, C., Plenborg, T. and Schøler, F., 2006), reproduced with permission of Euromoney Institutional Investor plc in the format textbook via Copyright Clearance Center; Figure 11.2 from Financial ratios as predictors of failure, *Journal of Accounting Research, Supplemental, Empirical Research in Accounting: Selected Studies*, p. 82 (Beaver, W., 1966), Copyright © 1966 Blackwell Publishing, reproduced with permission of Blackwell Publishing Ltd; Figure 13.2 from GAAP versus the street: An empirical assessment of two alternative definitions of earnings, *Journal of Accounting Research*, 1, pp. 41–66 (Bradshaw, M.T. and Sloan, R.G., 2002), with permission of John Wiley & Sons via Copyright Clearance Center.

Tables
Tables 2.2, 2.4, 2.5, 2.6 and 2.7 from *Annual Report 2008*, Ericsson, used with permission of Telefonaktiebolaget L. M. Ericsson; Table 3.2 from *Annual Report 2008*, Carlsberg Group, p. 77; Table 4.1 from *Annual Report 2008*, Carlsberg Group p. 72; Table 4.2 from *Annual Report 2008*, Carlsberg Group, p. 74; Tables 4.3, 4.8 from Annual Reports, Carlsberg Breweries A/S; Tables 4.9 and 4.12 from *Annual Report 2008*, Carlsberg Group, p. 85; Table 4.10 from *Annual Report 2008*, Carlsberg Group, p. 98; Table 4.13 from *Annual Report 2008*, Carlsberg Group, p. 99; Table 4.14 from *Annual Report 2008*, Carlsberg Group, p. 112; Table 4.15 from *Annual Report 2008*, Carlsberg Group, p. 118; Table 6.6 from Data Source: Compustat®, Copyright © 2011 The McGraw-Hill Companies, Inc. Standard & Poor's including its subsidiary corporations (S&P), is a division of The McGraw-Hill Companies, Inc. Table 7.4 from William Demant Holding's Annual Reports, http://www.demant.com/annuals.cfm; Table 8.7 from FactSet Estimates; Table 9.16 from Annual Reports, http://www.ab-inbev.com/go/investors.cfm; Table 10.2 from *Betas used by professors: a survey with 2,500 answers*, Working Paper, IESE Business School (Fernandez, P., 2009) May, Table 5, used with permission of the author; Table 10.6 from *Betas used by professors:*

a survey with 2,500 answers, Working Paper, IESE Business School (Fernandez, P., 2009) May, Table 7, used with permission of the author; Table 10.7 from *Market risk premium used in 2008 by professors: a survey with 1,400 answers*, Working Paper, IESE Business School (Fernandez, P., 2009) April, Table 2, used with permission of the author; Table 10.8 from *Market risk premium used in 2008 by professors: a survey with 1,400 answers*, Working Paper, IESE Business School (Fernandez, P., 2009) April, Table 7, used with permission of the author; Table 11.9 from *Fundamentals of Corporate Credit Analysis*, McGraw-Hill (Ganguin, B. and Bilardello, J., 2004) p. 302, Table 11.4, reproduced with permission of McGraw-Hill Companies, Inc. – Books in the format tradebook via Copyright Clearance Center; Table 11.12 from *Fundamentals of Corporate Credit Analysis*, McGraw-Hill (Ganguin, B. and Bilardello, J., 2004) p. 298, Table 11.2, reproduced with permission of McGraw-Hill Companies, Inc. – Books in the format tradebook via Copyright Clearance Center; Table 11.14 from Financial ratios as predictors of failure, *Journal of Accounting Research, Supplemental, Empirical Research in Accounting: Selected Studies*, p. 90 (Beaver, W., 1966), Copyright © 1966 Blackwell Publishing, reproduced with permission of Blackwell Publishing Ltd; Table 13.2 from *Geschäftsbericht 2009, Annual Report 2009*, Bayer Group, p. 273, Table 1.2; Table 13.4 from *Geschäftsbericht 2009, Annual Report 2009*, Bayer Group, p. 74, Table 3.16; Table 13.5 from *Annual Report 2009*, Wolseley plc, p. 94; Table 13.6 from *Annual Report 2009*, Wolseley plc, p. 139; Table 13.8 from *Annual Report 2006*, SABMiller plc, p. 129; Table 13.9 from *Annual Report 2006*, SABMiller plc, p. 142; Table 13.12 from DSV A/S; Table 14.2 from *Annual Report 2009*, Carlsberg Group, p. 72; Table 15.15 from *Annual Report 2008*, E.ON AG, p. 115.

Text

Appendix 2.1 from *International Financial Reporting and Analysis*, 4th ed., Cengage Learning (Alexander, D., Britton, A. and Jorissen, A., 2009) p. 16; Appendix 5.1 from Annual Reports, www.heineken.com, © Heineken N.V., Tweede Weteringplantsoen 21, 1017 ZD Amsterdam; Appendix 14.1 from PricewaterhouseCoopers, http://www.pwc.com/gx/en/ifrs-reporting/ifrs-local-gaap-similarities-and-diferrences.jhtml; Appendix 14.2 from *The Financial Numbers Game: Detecting Creative Accounting Practices*, John Wiley & Sons, Inc. (Mulford, C.W. and Comiskey, E.E., 2002) p. 65, Copyright © John Wiley & Sons, Inc. 2002, reproduced with permission of John Wiley & Sons, Inc.

In some instances we have been unable to trace the owners of copyright material, and we would appreciate any information that would enable us to do so.

CHAPTER 1

Introduction to financial statement analysis

Learning outcomes

After reading this chapter you should be able to:

- Understand the three user perspectives applied in this book
- Identify the different decision models available for valuation and credit analysis
- Identify the financial performance measures available in executives' compensation schemes
- Recognise that accounting information is treated differently in different decision contexts
- Understand the structure of this book

Introduction to financial statement analysis

Consider this scenario:

A company's inventory is destroyed in a fire and the company recognises a substantial loss on its income statement because it was under-insured. How should this loss influence a financial statement analysis? Would you deduct this loss when determining the income of the company? Why or why not?

These sorts of decisions are at the heart of financial statement analysis. In fact, the purpose for financial statement analysis is to help people make better decisions. But it is not always as straightforward as it initially appears.

For instance, if we continue with the above scenario and add a bit of context, your decision about how the loss should influence a financial statement analysis might change:

First, assume that the purpose of the analysis is to determine the market value of equity. If management corrects the under-insurance problem, then, for equity valuation purposes, the loss can be considered transitory – in other words 'noise' – and should be excluded when extrapolating from past income in order to forecast future income.

On the other hand, if the objective is to determine the amount that management will receive in bonus income, then it probably makes sense to include the loss when determining the income. This is because management has failed adequately to insure inventory and this failure caused a loss to the owners as a consequence of the fire.

The case above demonstrates that the decision – the reason for doing the analysis – drives the information needed and used in the analysis.

There are many different decision contexts and types of decision makers, but this book focuses on three important groups: **equity-oriented stakeholders**, **debt-capital-oriented stakeholders** and **compensation-oriented stakeholders**. To get a sense of who might be in each group, take a look at Table 1.1.

Table 1.1

Equity-oriented stakeholders	Debt-capital-oriented stakeholders	Compensation-oriented stakeholders
• Investors	• Banks	• Management
• Companies	• Mortgage-credit institutes	• The board
• Corporate finance analysts	• Companies	• Investors
• Pension funds	• Providers of mezzanine capital	
• Venture capital providers		
• Private equity providers		

These groups receive guidance from analysts. **Equity analysts** value the residual return in a company after all other claims have been satisfied, with the goal of determining the level of investment in the firm. **Credit analysts** assess a company's ability to repay its existing or new debts, with goals pertaining to the amount and terms of credit to be extended to the firm. **Compensation analysts**, including company board members, use a company's financial statements to determine performance-based management compensation.

These three groups make decisions in different contexts using different aspects of financial statements. Therefore, we treat these analytical contexts separately. We will introduce different decision models for each group and show what accounting information is required in each instance.

International Financial Reporting Standards

This book is written for users of financial statements prepared under different sets of **accounting standards**. However, we primarily rely on International Financial Reporting Standards (**IFRS**) and only to a minor extent on the US accounting standards (US GAAP). As we consider specific topics, we mainly discuss definitions, recognition issues, measurement criteria and classification issues as set forth under IFRS as developed by the International Accounting Standards Board (**IASB**). IFRS are used in many parts of the world, including the European Union, Hong Kong, Australia, Malaysia, Pakistan, GCC countries, Russia, South Africa, Singapore and Turkey. More than 110 countries around the world, including all of Europe, currently require or permit IFRS reporting. Approximately 85 of those countries require IFRS reporting for all domestic, listed companies.

More recently, the US Securities and Exchange Commission (SEC) has begun to accept the IFRS financial statements of non-US companies, thus allowing these companies to issue stocks and bonds in American capital markets. American companies are not yet required to apply IFRS. In fact, initially, non-US companies may apply either IFRS or US accounting standards, whereas American companies are allowed to report under US standards only. The US accounting standards are often referred to as generally accepted accounting principles, or '**GAAP**', as the Financial Accounting Standards Board (**FASB**) calls them.

It has become increasingly challenging to analyse financial statements because of the trend toward measuring assets and liabilities at **fair value**. Clearly, the objective of fair value financial statements is admirable: to measure company assets and liabilities at their economic value. But with fair value, both the producer (i.e. management of the firm) and the user of the information take on additional responsibilities. With fair value, managers must look beyond simplistic historical cost accounting methods to choose among the measurement techniques allowed by IFRS (and other standard setters). Users, on the other hand, read the financial disclosures with an eye toward discerning the 'truth'. The truth, it turns out, depends on the context of the question being asked. For instance:

1 What is the value of the residual equity in the business?
2 Can the firm repay new or existing debt?
3 What is the firm's performance for management compensation purposes?

IFRS standards require both producers and users to exercise considerable judgement. Consider, for example, the IFRS standard that requires assets to be tested for impairment. An impairment test essentially requires that management estimate the value of an asset or group of assets (a cash generating unit, or CGU). If the value of an asset or group of assets is below the carrying value, they need to be written down. The result of the impairment test can have a large impact on the firm's earnings and financial ratios. However, there is plenty of room for management discretion in this decision, since outsiders cannot see all inputs that management uses. Both management and the user know that the quality of accounting information depends on management faithfully to convey useful information. Because of this, the user will ask key questions like: 'To what extent do I trust the information provided by management?' and 'Is there any need to make adjustment to the reported accounting data?'

Facing this situation, management's reporting decision is likely to depend on the relative importance of existing and future contracts based on financial statement information. Managers of firms with stringent contracts, such as debt covenants, are likely to choose measurements that avoid breach of such covenants. On the other hand, managers are more likely to be truthful if the financial information is being provided to informed users who are not bound by existing long-term contracts based on financial information. Ultimately, whether the financial statements faithfully reflect firm economics depends on these contractual incentives, management's innate integrity, and the firm's internal and external control systems.

Decisions and decision models

Users should keep focused on the reason for the financial analysis – the decision at hand. In the midst of information overload, users can lose sight of the purpose of their analysis, and this often results in a well-informed answer to the wrong question. For this reason we encourage analysts to specify, and write down, the decision at hand before digging into the data and analysis. Here are a few examples of business decisions:

1 Should our bank lend a firm €10 million at 7% per annum for three years?
2 Determine comparable returns on equity in a recent accounting period for two firms in the same industry in order to allocate €5 million in equity capital.
3 In the most recent quarter, how much profit was generated from operations under the authority of the executive responsible for Asian operations?

By clearly defining the decision from the outset, the analyst will be able to stay focused on the relevant information and will be more likely to make the right choice.

Now let's explore in more depth the three sets of decision makers mentioned earlier: equity-oriented stakeholders, debt-capital-oriented stakeholders and compensation-oriented stakeholders.

Equity-oriented stakeholders

In general, equity-oriented stakeholders use financial information to assess the intrinsic value of a company. Investors decide whether to buy, hold or sell residual equity (e.g. shares of stock). Stock analysts tend to work within specific industry segments in order to gain superior knowledge of an industry and therefore a competitive advantage. For instance, analysts often specialise in segments such as biotech, information technology or food and beverages. A stock analyst typically gathers information based on an industry's history and expected performance prior to focusing on a specific firm. Once an industry's outlook has been assessed, the analyst will assess a firm's historical performance and form an opinion of the expected earnings potential of the company. Conversely, an analyst in a corporate finance department advises the company concerning financial matters of a company such as merger and acquisitions, issues concerning initial public offerings (IPOs), choice of capital structure and the achievement of debt capital. From both sides of the coin, there are similarities between the work carried out by a stock analyst and an analyst in a corporate finance department – both aim to assess the value of the company.

Investors who buy the analyses from the stock analysts often invest according to some predefined criteria. For instance, they may invest in certain industries such as biotech or information technology or within a specific country or region (e.g. Russia, South America or Asia). Investors may also self-select into clienteles based on the desire for 'value' or 'growth' investing. Though investors and their analysts work in different ways and spend different amounts of time on valuation, they all try to assess the future earnings potential of a company.

The techniques used to value **equity** are increasingly being employed outside of traditional stock analysis. In the mid-1980s Professor Alfred Rappaport popularised the concept of value-based management. The concept was soon followed by a large number of consultancy firms including Stern Stewart (the EVA concept), McKinsey & Co., Boston Consulting Group and PA Consulting. The basic principle of the concept of value-based management is to systematise, quantify and evaluate strategic action plans. The concept is therefore an extension of the strategy literature since it quantifies the economic values of different strategic plans of action.

Stock-based compensation schemes are popular throughout the world as a means of aligning the interests of management and shareholders, while conserving cash available for managers to invest. In addition, a large number of unlisted companies, especially within the biotech and information technology industries, compensate key employees with promises of 'a share of the action', or equity. In deciding whether to enter into these contracts, both employees and management need to assess the value of the compensation contract.

Impairment test of goodwill is one of the latest examples of an area in which the techniques of valuation are applicable. The accountant has to reassess the value of goodwill in order to identify a possible impairment loss. This requires knowledge of the market value of the cash generating unit being assessed.

As the above examples illustrate, valuation of companies are used in a number of contexts.

Valuation models

Equity-oriented stakeholders focus on determining the 'true' value of firms' equity since investors who correctly value a firm's stock can make money if the market value is different. Underpriced shares can be purchased to return a profit when the market value corrects. Conversely, overpriced shares can be sold short, and the investor will make money as long as the market value reflects the true potential of the firm during the period in which the investor holds the position.[1]

There are a number of different valuation models. Figure 1.1 categorises valuation models into four distinct groups. We will now briefly elaborate on each approach, in order to show that the different valuation approaches require different inputs, which affect how we design our financial statement analysis. In Chapter 9 we will explain in more detail how to use each approach for valuation purposes.

Present value models

The first group of valuation models is named **present value approaches**. These models share the same characteristics: the value of a firm (or asset) is estimated as the present value of future cash flows. The estimated market value of equity is found by discounting expected cash flows by the owners' required rate of return taking into account the time value of money and the underlying risk of the income streams.

With the dividend models as the point of departure, the market value of the equity of a company can be calculated as:

$$P_0 = \sum_{t=1}^{\infty} \frac{\text{div}_t}{(1 + r_e)^t}$$

where

P_0 = Estimated market price of equity at time 0

div_t = Dividends at time t

r_e = Investors' required rate of return

In order to apply the present value models, information about future profitability, growth rates and risk is needed. It is therefore necessary to estimate the future economic potential of a company to be able to apply a present value model. The financial statement analysis is in this context an important element since it gives an insight into the historical profitability, growth rates and risk. The financial statement analysis thus establishes (historical) levels and trends in the economic performance of the firm, which is a good starting point for making forecasts.

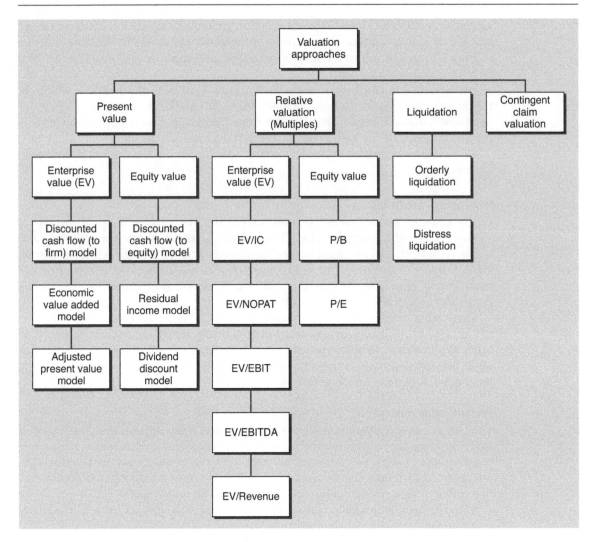

Figure 1.1 Overview of valuation approaches

As part of a historical financial statement analysis the analysts will consider the quality of the reported accounting data. For example, the analysts need to distinguish between permanent (recurring) and transitory (non-recurring) accounting items. Transitory items, for example gains or losses on the sale of **non-current assets**, are those that are not likely to recur; or only with large time intervals. Therefore, when predicting the future earnings potential of a company, analysts will typically exclude transitory items from the historical data and analyses. Furthermore, it is important to check that historical data is based on unchanged accounting policies. This ensures that any observed trend is caused by underlying changes in operations rather than by changes in accounting policies.

Relative valuation models
Relative valuation models are often referred to as multiples. In these models the value of a company is estimated by comparing with the price of comparable (peer group) companies based on reported or expected accounting earnings, equity, turnover or cash flows. Example 1.1 illustrates the application of multiples.

Example 1.1 Assume that a pharmaceutical company located in Europe is planning to buy an Australian competitor which is doing research within the central nervous system (CNS). The Australian competitor which is not listed has announced that the outlook for the coming fiscal year are favourable. Thus, a 20% increase in earnings is expected. As a result net earnings increase to €200 million. Currently, most pharmaceutical companies, specialising in CNS, are traded at a P/E multiple[2] around 17. Assuming that it is fair to pay €17 per every euro of net income for a company within the CNS industry, the value of the Australian competitor can be estimated to be €3.4 billion (€200 million × 17). ■

The example demonstrates that the use of multiples assumes that accounting data can be compared across firms. Thus, the use of multiples makes significant constraints on the data. First, the accounting policies for the companies that are compared have to be identical. Second, earnings of the companies which are compared have to have the same 'quality'. This implies that a distinction between permanent (recurring) or transitory (non-recurring) earnings have to be made. Finally, applying the same multiple across different companies implies that they have the same expectation about future profitability, growth and risk.

Liquidation models

In **liquidation models** the value of a company is estimated by assessing the value of the assets and the liabilities if the firm is liquidated. The **liquidation value** (break-up value) is calculated by subtracting the liquidation value of all liabilities from the liquidation value of all assets.

The data requirements of the liquidation approach are rather substantial since all (economic) assets and liabilities have to be recognised in the balance sheet. Furthermore, the book value of assets and liabilities has to be a reasonable proxy for the proceeds obtainable through a liquidated sale. This is only rarely the case. For instance the annual report is prepared assuming a 'going concern', i.e. assuming continuing operations. This raises a measurement problem that the analyst has to overcome. The analyst, thus, has a considerable amount of work in identifying and reassessing the value of all assets and liabilities when using the liquidation model, as illustrated in Table 1.2.

The first step in applying the liquidation approach is to recognise assets and liabilities that have not previously been identified. The second step is to measure each asset and liability as if the firm liquidates. In the example in Table 1.2 non-recognised liabilities of 50 are now included. This could be, for instance, a possible loss related to an unsettled lawsuit or an obligation to clean up a piece of polluted land. Furthermore, all assets and liabilities are measured at liquidation value which reduces the value of assets by 245 and increases the value of liabilities by 5. Thus, the impact on net assets is minus 250 (245 + 5). The example shows that in the case of liquidation all equity is lost.

Contingent claim valuation models

Contingent claim models, **contingency models**, also defined as real option models, are the fourth and last group of models. They are related to the present value models. Present value models can be thought of as static as they value only one scenario at a time. Contingent claim models also include the value of flexibility. The method is applicable to companies and assets that share the same characteristics as options. Biotech companies, for instance, are free to abandon research projects if they do not turn out to be commercially viable. This flexibility is valuable and should have a

Table 1.2 Valuation based on the liquidation approach

Liquidation model (example)

	Book value	Liquidation value		Book value	Liquidation value
Intangible assets	100	10	**Equity**	300	0
Tangible assets	250	195	Provisions	20	20
Financial assets	50	0	Interest-bearing debt	290	295
Non-current assets	**400**	**205**	Operating liabilities	95	95
			Non-recognised liabilities	0	50
Inventories	150	120	**Liabilities**	**405**	**460**
Receivables	140	120			
Cash and securities	15	15			
Current assets	**305**	**255**			
Assets	**705**	**460**	**Equity and liabilities**	**705**	**460**

positive effect on the estimated value of the firm. Since contingent claim models simply add the value of flexibility to the firm value estimate based on the present value models, the requirements for the accounting data are identical for the two types of valuation models.

In order to understand the equity-oriented stakeholders' need for information, it is necessary to learn the methods applied for valuation of companies. Each set of valuation methods requires its own set of assumptions and input.

Debt-capital-oriented stakeholders

Debt-capital-oriented stakeholders aim to value the creditworthiness of a company as well as the possible extension of business relations with that company. The assessment of the creditworthiness of companies enjoys increasing attention by financial institutions as a consequence of the financial crisis as well as rules that entail that banks and mortgage-credit institutions have to weight their loans by risk.

Banks and mortgage-credit institutions have an economic interest in developing enhanced models for assessment of creditworthiness, as, ultimately, they are expected to lead to:

- More efficient credit processing
- Better forecasting of possibly bad loans
- More correct pricing of credit contracts
- Better allocation of capital through a better registration of risk.

Companies make assessments of the creditworthiness of both customers and suppliers. The creditworthiness of the customer is estimated in order to be able to assess the customer's ability to pay its bills. In the same way, assessing the creditworthiness of suppliers helps firms to avoid doing business with firms that may not be able to deliver according to their contractual terms.

Methods for assessment of creditworthiness of companies

To understand the information needs of the providers of debt, an understanding of the models that are used for assessment of creditworthiness is required. There are several methods for judging creditworthiness. Financial institutions often have their own way of assessing credit risk, and therefore it is difficult to codify current practice. In Figure 1.2 the most prevalent methods for assessing creditworthiness are shown.

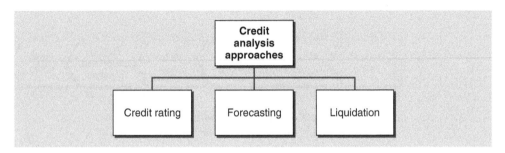

Figure 1.2 Grouping of methods for creditworthiness of companies

We will now briefly elaborate on each method. Again, you will see that the different credit approaches require different inputs, which affect how we design our financial statement analysis. In Chapter 11 we will explain in more detail how to use each approach for assessment of a company's creditworthiness simultaneously.

Credit rating models

Credit rating models have long been used by rating agencies such as Moody's and Standard & Poor's. Among banks and credit institutions, credit rating models are used as an operational tool for assessing the creditworthiness of a large number of companies.

Table 1.3 is a simplified example of a credit rating model. The example shows the credit rating model tailored to industrials and various financial ratios are used for assessing the creditworthiness and ranking the companies. AAA is the highest rating

Table 1.3 Credit rating of industrials

Adjusted key industrial financial ratios
US industrial long-term debt

Three years median	AAA	AA	A	BBB	BB	B	CCC
EBIT interest cover (x)	21.4	10.1	6.1	3.7	2.1	0.8	0.1
EBITDA interest cover (x)	26.5	12.9	9.1	5.8	3.4	1.8	1.3
Free operating cash flow/total debt (%)	84.2	25.2	15.0	8.5	2.6	−3.2	−12.9
FFO/total debt (%)	128.8	55.4	43.2	30.8	18.8	7.8	1.6
Return on capital (%)	34.9	21.7	19.4	13.6	11.6	6.6	1.0
Operating income/revenue (%)	27.0	22.1	18.6	15.4	15.9	11.9	11.9
Long-term debt/capital (%)	13.3	28.2	33.9	42.5	57.2	69.7	68.8
Total debt/capital (%)	22.9	37.7	42.5	48.2	62.6	74.8	87.7
Number of companies	8	29	136	218	273	281	22

while CCC is the lowest rating in the example. A risk premium based on the rating is added to the risk-free interest rate so that the rate of interest firms have to pay on their debt (risk-free rate of return + risk premium) reflects the risk of the individual company. In relation to the final credit rating other factors are included as well. Among these are the strategic positioning of the company, the attractiveness of the industry and the quality of management. The structure of credit rating procedure is shown in Figure 1.3.

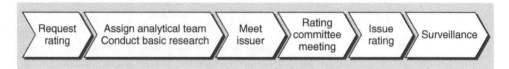

Figure 1.3 Example of steps in a credit analysis process
Source: Adapted and based on data from Standard & Poor's website

The annual report and the financial ratios form an essential base in a typical credit rating model. It is therefore important that past financial ratios are good indicators of future trends. It is necessary that the annual report provides the relevant information, so that the quality of the annual report can be assessed. Since credit rating models compare companies within the same industry, there is an underlying data requirement that the companies apply the same accounting policies.

Forecasting models

An alternative, but more time consuming, method for assessment of creditworthiness is **forecasting**. The forecasting method assesses the ability for firms to repay debt. In contrast to the credit rating models that are more oriented towards the past, the forecasting method is oriented towards the future. As for the present value approaches the analyst prepares a budget (pro forma statements), including an estimate of the free cash flow, to assess the analysed firm's ability to service its debt. The data requirements are therefore the same as for present value approaches detailed in earlier paragraphs.

Modifications of the forecasting method are the so-called **value at risk** (VaR) analyses. The forecasting method, as described above, operates with only one scenario. In value at risk analyses a budget is made up for every scenario in order to estimate the likelihood of default of payments. This idea is illustrated in Figure 1.4 where three scenarios are shown in which the cash flows for supporting debt fall short of interest payments and instalments. The likelihood of default of payments is thus in this example estimated as being 4% (1% + 1% + 2%).

Liquidation models

The liquidation method is typically used to estimate the ability of a firm to repay its debt assuming that the company is not able to continue operations (worst case scenario). The methodology and the data requirement therefore resemble those previously described. In the example in Table 1.2 this method was illustrated and it was shown that while the owners lost their investment, banks and mortgage-credit institutions and other creditors would have their outstanding claims covered in case of liquidation.

While the credit rating method and the forecasting method are used for estimating the likelihood of suspension of payments the liquidation method is used for estimating the likelihood of a loss in case of defaults of payments.

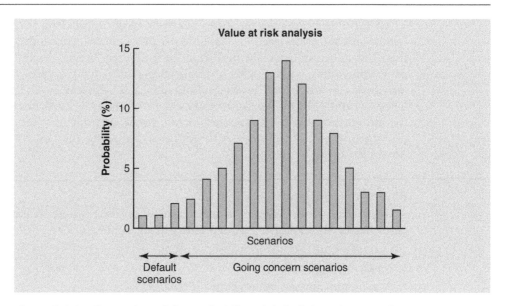

Figure 1.4 An illustration of the probability of default based on simulations

Remuneration-oriented stakeholders

Performance-related pay makes up an increasing part of total management remuneration. Examples of performance-related pay include stock options and cash bonuses. The interesting aspects of this subject are: (a) which measure of performance triggers the bonus or the stock option scheme, (b) the relation between performance measures and bonuses, (c) which performance standard to apply (bonus threshold), and in case of accounting-based bonus plans, (d) how to address transitory items and changes in applied accounting policies and tax rates (accounting quality).

We will now elaborate on each aspect to illustrate some of the analytical accounting issues when designing an accounting-based bonus plan. In Chapter 12 we discuss the topic in greater detail.

Performance measures

As for models for assessment of creditworthiness there is no complete list of the decision models used in relation to performance-based remuneration. However, most frequently one of the three categories of performance measures shown in Figure 1.5 are used in compensation contracts.

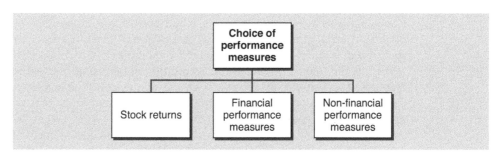

Figure 1.5 Performance measures used in compensation contracts

All three performance measures are frequently applied by listed firms. Since quoted market prices are not available for privately held firms they tend to apply financial and non-financial performance measures in performance-related compensation contracts. Examples of financial performance measures include revenue (growth), earnings before interest and taxes (EBIT), net earnings (E) and return on invested capital (ROIC). Customer satisfaction, employee satisfaction, service quality and market share are examples of non-financial measures. Ideally, the chosen performance measure(s) support the firm's strategy and the underlying value creation of the firm.

Pay-to-performance relation

An open question in designing a compensation contract is how should pay be tied to performance. The following list represents likely candidates:

- Linearity between performance and pay
- Lump-sum bonuses
- A minimum and maximum bonus (floors/caps).

The compensation literature generally favours a linear pay-to-performance structure since it mitigates the incentive to manage the performance measure (Holmstrom and Milgrom 1987). Non-linear bonus plans such as a lump-sum bonus or a minimum and maximum bonus provide the executives with an incentive to manage earnings. For example, if the year-to-date performance indicates that annual performance will exceed that required to achieve the bonus cap, executives have incentives to either withhold effort or 'move' current earnings to future periods.

Performance standards

An important aspect of a compensation contract is the threshold of performance; i.e. what level of performance that triggers a bonus. Generally, a distinction is made between internal and external performance standards. Examples of internal performance standards are last year's performance and internal budgets. Peers' performance is an example of an external performance standard. There are pros and cons to each performance standard. For example, Murphy (2000) finds support for the use of external standards. He finds that income smoothing is prevalent in companies using internal standards (e.g. budgets and last year's result), but not in companies using external standards.

Accounting quality

Bonus plans that rely on accounting-based performance measures must consider the quality of accounting data. For instance, earnings generated from the core business (permanent earnings) are regarded as more valuable than earnings based on transitory items (i.e. the impact of changes in accounting policies and unusual accounting items recognised as part of core earnings). The consequences of changes in accounting policies and tax rates on earnings also need to be eliminated in order to capture the 'true' underlying value creation.

It is clear, based on the above discussion, that financial statement analysis needs to be modified according to (a) the purpose of the analysis and (b) the decision model applied.

Outline of the book

The purpose of this book is to provide you with an insight into how financial statement analysis can be used by decision makers in valuing firms, assessing a firm's creditworthiness and designing accounting-based bonus contracts (executive compensation).

The book is divided into four parts as follows (and as shown in Table 1.4):

- Part 1 provides an overview of the content of the annual report (accounting data).
- Part 2 discusses how a firm's profitability, growth and risk can be assessed and measured by the use of various financial ratios.
- Part 3 presents the different decision models used in equity valuation, credit analysis and compensation.
- Part 4 elaborates on the concept of accounting quality.

Table 1.4 **Contents of the book**

Part 1 Accounting data	Part 2 Financial analysis	Part 3 Decision making	Part 4 Assessment of accounting data
Chapter 2 Introduction to financial statements and bookkeeping	Chapter 4 The analytical income statement and balance sheet	Chapter 8 Forecasting	Chapter 13 Accounting quality
		Chapter 9 Valuation	Chapter 14 Accounting flexibility in the income statement
Chapter 3 Accrual-based versus cash-flow-based performance measures	Chapter 5 Profitability analysis	Chapter 10 Cost of capital	
	Chapter 6 Growth analysis	Chapter 11 Credit analysis	Chapter 15 Accounting flexibility in the balance sheet
	Chapter 7 Liquidity risk analysis	Chapter 12 Accounting-based bonus plans for executives	

The contents of each of these four parts are briefly described below.

Part 1 – Accounting data

In the first part of the book the purpose of financial statement analysis is discussed. For readers with no or little accounting background, the chapter on recording transactions and preparing financial statements based on those transactions will be helpful. The advantages and disadvantages of cash-flow-based and accounting-based performance measures are discussed in the subsequent chapter and provides an insight into how these two measures deviate.

Chapter 2 – Introduction to financial statements and bookkeeping

This chapter is intended for students with little or no background in accounting. The chapter highlights how transactions are recorded (essentially, basic debit–credit entries) and how these transactions enter into the financial statements. The income statement, balance sheet, statement of changes of equity, and cash flow statement is presented alongside other essential aspects of the annual reports. Finally, it is shown how these different statements articulate (i.e. relate to each other).

This chapter is crucially important, as the annual report contains the primary data used in financial statement analysis. The familiarity with the components of the annual report is therefore an essential prerequisite for understanding the other chapters of this book.

Chapter 3 – Accrual-based versus cash-flow-based performance measures

This chapter focuses on various measures of performance derived from the income statement and cash flow statement. It discusses whether cash-flow-based measures of performance give a better estimation of a firm's underlying performance than the ones based on accounting data. Furthermore, other analytical contexts where cash flows can be used are addressed.

Part 2 · Financial analysis

Part 2 covers a cornerstone in financial statement analysis. Before carrying out an analysis, the financial statements must be reformulated for analytical purposes. Having prepared the analytical financial statements, the analyst is ready to assess a firm's profitability, growth and risk. A common way of assessing profitability, growth and risk is to calculate a variety of financial ratios. This part of the book provides numerous examples of how to define, calculate and interpret such financial ratios.

Chapter 4 – The analytical income statement and balance sheet

This chapter discusses how the income statement and the balance sheet can be prepared for analytical purposes. Specifically there is a distinction between accounting items related to operations and accounting items related to financing activities. This distinction is relevant when the financial statement analysis of past performance is used as an input to the development of pro forma statements. By distinguishing sharply between accounting items related to operations and those related to financing it is also possible to identify value generating and value destroying operating activities of a company.

Chapter 5 – Profitability analysis

Financial ratios describing the profitability of companies are presented. The chapter distinguishes between financial ratios measuring the profitability of operating and financing activities, respectively. Measuring the profitability of a company is one of the most important subjects of financial statement analysis. Superior profitability is crucial in generating value for shareholders and ensures the survival of the company. It signals economic health and strengthens the possibilities for contracting with the company's stakeholders such as customers, suppliers and banks. Moreover, the level and trend in the historical profitability are important elements when forecasting future earnings of the company.

Chapter 6 – Growth analysis

This chapter distinguishes between different ways to assess growth and introduces financial growth measures which are aligned with shareholder value creation. It also focuses on important growth issues such as (a) how fast a company can grow while ensuring that the financial balance is maintained, (b) the quality of growth and (c) the association between growth and liquidity. Analyses of growth appear in a number of analytical contexts. For instance, investors use analyses of growth in relation to making forecasts, while creditors use them for assessing the need for liquidity.

Chapter 7 – Liquidity risk analysis

This chapter focuses on liquidity risk. Analysis of liquidity risk is relevant for instance in assessing a firm's creditworthiness and the risk of default on its outstanding debt. The difficulties of estimating risk stem from the fact that in most cases (the majority of firms are privately held) there is not an active market for trading a firm's equity and liabilities. Risk is therefore not measured on a continuous basis (e.g. on a stock market). The individual stakeholders (and analysts) are, thus, left to measuring risk on their own, which creates considerable uncertainty.

Part 3 – Decision making

The third part of the book concerns decision making. In this part of the book it is demonstrated how financial statement analysis supports forecasting and valuation (Chapters 8 and 9). Since risk plays a major role in valuing a firm or measuring whether value has been created within a period, a separate chapter is devoted to calculating the cost of capital (Chapter 10). The application of credit analysis is the topic of Chapter 11. Finally, issues in the design of accounting-based bonus plans for executives are discussed in Chapter 12. Thus, Part 3 gives you the opportunity to apply what you have learned from Parts 1 and 2 to real-life business situations.

Chapter 8 – Forecasting

Valuation of firms and credit analysis are often based on a forecast of *future* earnings or cash flows. Therefore, in order to value a firm or conduct a proper credit analysis, future earnings and cash flows must be forecasted. Chapter 8 addresses three core issues in forecasting. The first issue is how to technically develop pro forma statements (i.e. how to ensure that the forecasted income statement, balance sheet and cash flow statement articulate). The second issue concerns how to add realism into the projected earnings and cash flow measures. Obviously, financial statement analysis as laid out in previous chapters will be drawn upon as well as a strategic analysis of the industry, the market and the target firm and its peers. The third issue concerns the use of budget control and sensitivity analyses in order to evaluate the quality (realism) of the pro forma statements. The chapter is rich in examples of forecasting.

Chapter 9 – Valuation

This chapter discusses different types of valuation models with an emphasis on present value approaches (e.g. the DCF model), multiples (e.g. P/E), and the liquidation approach. The chapter highlights similarities and differences between each of the valuation approaches and the merits and demerits of each type. In addition, the chapter illustrates the different valuation techniques through a number of examples.

Chapter 10 – Cost of capital

Cost of capital is used in a variety of contexts in financial statement analysis. For instance, cost of capital must be estimated in order to value companies using present value approaches. Since the value of a firm is quite sensitive to the discount factor (cost of capital), it's important that resources are devoted to estimating risk.

Furthermore, cost of capital is an important factor when evaluating the performance of a firm within a short period of time (e.g. 12 months). The board can use the cost of capital as a threshold for good performance. The management may be rewarded bonuses based on its ability to create economic value (i.e. returns on invested capital that exceed cost of capital).

Chapter 11 – Credit analysis

This chapter demonstrates different models for credit analysis including forecasting and financial ratio analysis. The advantages and disadvantages of each approach are discussed. For instance, ratio analysis (i.e. rating a firm's economic well-being based on financial ratios) is simple to apply and less costly than other methods. On the other hand, the method is based on past performance and depends upon a number of underlying assumptions which must be fulfilled for the method to be useful. The chapter contains a list of illustrative examples.

Chapter 12 – Accounting-based bonus plans for executives

Executives, among others, may receive bonuses based on stock prices, financial performance measures and non-financial measures. This chapter focuses on accounting-based bonus plans and discusses the choice of performance measure, the pay-to-performance relation and the choice of performance standard. In addition, accounting issues like the treatment of transitory items and changes in accounting policies are addressed in relation to accounting-based bonus plans.

Part 4 – Assessment of accounting data

The final part of the book covers accounting quality. So far the book has used reported accounting figures without assessing the realism of those figures. However, as will be clear from this part of the book, it is important to look into the quality of the reported accounting figures. Recognition, measurement and classification of accounting items are highly subjective, even within IFRS, leaving room for earnings management. A proper assessment of accounting data and accounting policies is a must. In this way the analyst makes sure that possible changes in a firm's performance and financial ratios are caused by changes in the underlying operations of the firm and not by changes in accounting policies.

Chapter 13 – Accounting quality

'Good accounting quality' is defined and a number of issues in assessing accounting quality are listed and discussed. Specifically the following subjects are addressed:

- Management's incentives for manipulating reported financial data
- The quality (realism) of applied accounting policies
- Permanent (recurring) versus transitory (non-recurring) items
- The information level in the annual reports
- Identification of 'red flags'.

The concept of accounting quality is thoroughly analysed with respect to the different users (decision makers) of accounting information.

Chapter 14 – Accounting flexibility in the income statement

In the previous chapters reported financial data was taken at face value. However, reported financial statements may be noisy measures of the underlying 'true' revenues, expenses, assets or liabilities. This is so because there is inherent flexibility in reported accounting numbers, as these are based on a firm's accounting policies and estimates made by management.

In Chapter 14 accounting flexibility in the income statement is discussed in order to identify specific areas where accounting noise may appear frequently. The accounting issues which are analysed are:

- Changes in accounting policies
- Revenue recognition criteria
- Non-recurring and special items
- Non-capitalisation of expenses.

In addition, the chapter specifically explores the impact of accounting flexibility on valuation, credit analysis and executive compensation.

Chapter 15 – Accounting flexibility in the balance sheet

This chapter explores accounting flexibility in the balance sheet. More specifically, the following items are discussed:

- Inventory accounting
- Intangible and tangible assets
- Lease accounting
- Provisions
- Deferred tax liabilities.

As in Chapter 14 the potential economic consequences of accounting flexibility are discussed.

Conclusions

The aim of this chapter has been to introduce you to the world of 'financial statement analysis'. We have emphasised that the annual report is used in a number of analytical contexts as an important source of data, and the use of different decision models entails different requirements to the financial statement analysis. It is therefore a fundamental principle in this book that the financial statement analysis should be interpreted with the purpose of the analysis in mind. Depending on the objective of the analysis a number of different decision models are available. We hope that by the time you have worked your way through this book, you will have gained the confidence and knowledge to analyse and look for data that best support the requirements of the underlying decision model which you use. Good luck!

Review questions

- Who are the users of financial statements?

- What kinds of approaches are available for valuation?

- Is the data requirement identical across the different valuation approaches?

- What kinds of approaches are available for credit evaluation?

- Is the data requirement identical across the different approaches available for credit analysis?

- What are the challenges in designing an accounting-based bonus plan?

- What are the four parts of this book?

Notes

1 'Sold short' refers to the practice of borrowing shares, selling them, and subsequently repurchasing the shares and returning the repurchased shares to the lender.
2 The multiple P/E expresses the current share price as a number of times of its earnings per share. That is how many euros investors are willing to pay for one euro in earnings.

References

Holmstrom, B. and P. Milgrom (1987) Aggregation and linearity in the provision of intertemporal incentives, *Econometrica*, **55**, 303–28.

Murphy, K. (2000) Performance standards in executive contracts. *Journal of Accounting and Economics*, **30**, 245–78.

PART 1

Accounting data

Introduction to Part 1

Introduction to Part 1

The annual report is the primary document in financial statement analysis. Chapters 2 and 3 discuss the accounting information available in the annual report.

Chapter 2 highlights how transactions are recorded and financial statements are prepared based on those bookkeeping transactions. The income statement recognises a firm's revenues, and expenses gains and losses. The balance sheet represents a firm's assets, liabilities and equity. Statement of changes in equity highlights how equity changes from the beginning of the period to the end of the period. Finally, the cash flow statement shows cash flows from operating, investing and financing activities (transactions) and how those cash flows are related to the income statement and balance sheet.

Chapter 3 elaborates on the accrual accounting concept and explains the difference between accrual and cash-flow-based performance measures. The chapter discusses whether the accrual or the cash-flow-based performance measures appear more informative from an investor perspective. The chapter also considers under which analytical circumstances the cash-flow-based performance measures appear most useful.

CHAPTER 2

Introduction to financial statements and bookkeeping

Learning outcomes

After reading this chapter you should be able to:

- Understand the purpose of the income statement and identify its parts
- Understand the purpose of the balance sheet and identify its parts
- Understand the purpose of the statement of changes in owners' equity and identify its parts
- Understand the purpose of the cash flow statement and identify its parts
- Record business transactions
- Produce financial statements based on recorded transactions
- Make adjustments to financial statements

Introduction to financial statements and bookkeeping

This chapter introduces the different **financial statements** which firms must produce and gives an overview of how transactions are recorded (**double-entry bookkeeping**) and entered into the different financial statements.

The annual report contains the primary data used in the financial statements, enabling users to estimate a firm's growth, profitability and risk. It provides information about the following accounting elements:

Revenues and expenses Gains and losses	Income statement Statement of comprehensive income
Assets Liabilities Equity	Balance sheet
Cash inflows and outflows	Cash flow statement

The annual report will also include a management's review, and potential supplementary reports.

In addition to the annual report, firms must supply a **statement of changes in owners' equity**. To give a fuller financial picture, firms provide notes alongside this statement. This includes a summary of significant accounting policies, estimates and other explanatory information.

The key elements of financial statements – consisting of the **income statement** and statement of comprehensive income, **balance sheet, cash flow statement** and statement of changes in owners' equity – are discussed below.

The income statement and statement of comprehensive income

The income statement discloses a firm's earnings for a predefined period, which in the annual report is 12 months. In its basic form the income statement includes a firm's earnings, calculated as the difference between revenue and expenses. Revenues are income from selling a firm's products or services, while expenses consist of a variety of items including depreciation and amortisation:

Revenue

− Expenses

= Earnings (for the period)

But simply calculating earnings as above – the difference between revenues and expenses – tells us very little about the financial health of a company. This is because there is no story behind the figures. We do not know, for example, whether development costs are recognised as **expenses** or **assets** (i.e. costs are capitalised).

Thus, financial statement users want to know *how* the earnings figure has been produced. This includes in particular:

- Which revenues and expenses are recognised?   } **Recognition criteria**
- When are revenues and expenses recognised?   }
- How are revenues and expenses measured?   } **Measurement attributes**
- How are revenues and expenses presented?   } **Classification issues**

As we mentioned in Chapter 1, international financial reporting standards reflect this need to standardise how a company recognises, measures and classifies expenses and revenues. The delimitation of which revenues and expenses must be recognised in the income statement can be found in IASB's Conceptual Framework (paragraph F70):

*Income is increases in economic benefits during the accounting period in the form of inflows or enhancements of assets or decreases of **liabilities** that result in increases in equity, other than those relating to contributions from equity participants.*

Expenses are decreases in economic benefits during the accounting period in the form of outflows or depletions of assets or incurrences of liabilities that result in decreases in equity, other than those relating to distributions to equity participants.

According to IAS 1: 'Presentation of Financial Statements' all income and expenses recognised in a period shall be included in the income statement unless a Standard or an Interpretation requires otherwise (paragraph 78).

The income statement shall include as a minimum the following items:

- Revenues
- Finance costs
- Share of the profit or loss of associates and joint ventures accounted for using the equity method
- Post tax profit or loss of discontinued operations
- Tax expenses.

Yet, these minimum requirements are hardly, if ever, sufficient. IASB acknowledges this by requiring that additional line items shall be added when such a presentation is relevant to an understanding of the firm's financial performance. Certain items must be disclosed either on the face of the income statement or in the notes, if material, including:

- Write-downs of inventories to net realisable value or of property, plant and equipment to recoverable amount, as well as reversals of such write-downs
- Restructurings of the activities of an entity and reversals of any provisions for the costs of restructuring
- Disposals of items of property, plant and equipment
- Disposals of investments
- Discontinuing operations
- Litigation settlements
- Other reversals of provisions.

An enterprise shall present an *analysis* of expenses, classifying them either by nature (raw materials, staff costs, depreciation, etc.) or by function (cost of goods sold, distribution costs, administrative expenses, etc.), whichever provides information that is reliable and relevant. It is not a prerequisite that the information (analysis) is presented on the face of the income statement, but it is encouraged (IAS 1.88). An example of classification comparing the **nature of expense method** and **function of expense method** is provided in Table 2.1.

Table 2.1 Income statement nature of expense vs function of expense method

Nature of expense method		Function of expense method	
Revenue	X	Revenue	X
Other income	X	Cost of sales	X
Changes in inventories of finished goods and work in progress	X	Gross profit	X
Employee benefits expenses	X	Selling and distribution costs	X
Depreciation and amortisation expenses	X	Administrative expenses	X
Other expenses	X	Other income	X
Total expenses	X	Other expenses	X
Profit (net earnings)	X	Profit (net earnings)	X

Enterprises that classify items by function shall disclose additional information on the nature of expenses, including depreciation, amortisation and employee benefits expenses. This is to ensure that there is sufficient information for users to make accurate assessments of the financial state of a company.

To illustrate how firms report income statements, an extract of Ericsson's consolidated income statement is provided in Table 2.2. It shows that Ericsson classifies expenses based on their function (e.g. selling and administrative expenses). This is a common method – using the expense by function method – but other firms choose the alternative way of classifying expenses, as shown in Table 2.3.

Table 2.2 **Consolidated income statement for Ericsson**

SEK million	Year 8	Year 7	Year 6
Net sales	208,930	187,780	179,821
Cost of sales	−134,661	−114,059	−104,875
Gross income	**74,269**	73,721	74,946
Gross margin %	35.50%	39.30%	41.70%
Research and development expenses	−33,584	−28,842	−27,533
Selling and administrative expenses	−26,974	−23,199	−21,422
Operating expenses	**−60,558**	−52,041	−48,955
Other operating income and expenses	2,977	1,734	3,903
Share in earnings of joint ventures and associated companies	−436	7,232	5,934
Operating income	**16,252**	30,646	35,828
Operating margin %	7.80%	16.30%	19.90%
Financial income	3,458	1,778	1,954
Financial expenses	−2,484	−1,695	−1,789
Income after financial items	17,226	30,729	35,993
Taxes	−5,559	−8,594	−9,557
Net income	**11,667**	22,135	26,436

Table 2.3 **Consolidated income statement for Cosmo Pharmaceuticals S.p.A.**

EUR (1,000)	Year 7	Year 6
Revenue	21,900	15,158
Other income	516	4,934
Changes in inventories of finished goods and work in progress	380	−110
Raw materials and consumables used	−6,642	−5,387
Personnel expenses	−6,629	−4,910
Depreciation and amortisation	−1,460	−1,492 .
Other operating expenses	−8,313	−6,818
Operating result	**−248**	**1,375**
Financial income	870	112
Financial expenses	−469	−983
Profit before taxes	**153**	**504**
Income tax expenses	−37	−848
Profit for the period	**116**	**−344**

The example shows that Cosmo Pharmaceuticals has separate line items for each (major) type of expense. For instance personnel expenses (salaries and pensions) and depreciation and amortisation are shown separately. Since depreciation and amortisation expenses are non-cash flows items, an analyst may wish to separate these items from other items. However, if the expense by function method is applied, the analyst must look in the notes for information about depreciation and amortisation, since these items are included in several accounting items (cost of sales, research and development expenses and selling and administrative expenses).

Even though reported profit is unaffected by the choice of classification (by nature or function), it plays an important role how a firm specifies its revenues, expenses, assets and liabilities. The level of detail may have an impact on, for example, the degree of detail an analyst uses in preparing budgets for valuation purposes. For instance, a specification of costs into variable and fixed costs will enable the analysts to use the contribution ratio as a key value driver. In addition, time-series and cross-sectional analyses are difficult to make when items are classified differently. Finally, note that it would be more difficult and time consuming to carry out a time-series analysis if a firm switches from one method of classification to the other.

The **statement of comprehensive income** presents all income and expense items, whether or not these are recognised in the income statement. Elements of comprehensive income include:

- Changes in revaluation surplus
- Actuarial gains and losses on defined benefit plans
- Exchange differences (gains and losses) on translating the financial statements of foreign operations
- Gains and losses on re-measuring available-for-sale financial assets
- The effective portion of gains and losses on hedging instruments in a cash flow hedge
- Income tax relating to other comprehensive income.

Firms may either present a statement of comprehensive income separately or as part of two linked statements. If the firm uses two linked statements, one must display the income statement and the other statement must begin with profit or loss for the year (bottom line in the income statement) and then show all items included in 'other comprehensive income'.

Table 2.4 shows Ericsson's comprehensive income. Ericsson labels the statement of comprehensive income for the period 'Consolidated Statement of Recognised Income and Expense'. Total income and expense recognised for the period amount to SEK 14,615 million of which SEK 11,667 million has been recognised in the income statement (net income) and SEK 2,948 million as transactions reported directly in equity.

Table 2.4 Consolidated statement of recognised income and expense, Ericsson

SEK million	Year 8	Year 7	Year 6
Income and expense recognised directly in equity			
Actuarial gains and losses related to pensions	−4,015	1,208	440
Revaluation of other investments in shares and participations			
Fair value re-measurement reported in equity	−7	2	−1 ▶

SEK million	Year 8	Year 7	Year 6
Cash flow hedges			
Fair value re-measurement of derivatives reported in equity	−5,080	584	4,100
Transferred to income statement for the period	1,192	−1,390	−1,990
Transferred to balance sheet for the period	–	–	99
Changes in cumulative translation adjustments	8,528	−797	−3,119
Tax on items reported directly in/or transferred from equity	2,330	−73	−769
Total transactions reported directly in equity	**2,948**	−466	−1,240
Net income	11,667	22,135	26,436
Total income and expense recognised for the period	**14,615**	21,669	25,196
Attributable to:			
Stockholders of the parent company	13,988	21,371	25,101
Minority interest	627	298	95

Balance sheet

A balance sheet is a summary of a company's financial position at a specific point in time and shows a summary of a firm's total investments (assets) and how these assets have been financed (liabilities and equity). In its simplest form, the balance sheet looks like this:

> Assets
> − Liabilities
> = Equity capital

Similarly to what we saw above, this formula without any context is of little use to users. To understand the real story, financial statement users need insight into which assets and liabilities are recognised, how those items are measured, and how they are presented.

Assets and liabilities are classified into current and non-current assets, and current and non-current liabilities, respectively. **Current assets** are those that satisfy one or more of the following criteria:

- It is expected to be realised in, or is intended for sale or consumption within a normal operating cycle
- It is held primarily for the purpose of being traded
- It is expected to be realised within 12 months after the reporting date
- It is cash or a cash equivalent.

Assets that do not meet any of these criteria shall be classified as **non-current assets**. **Current liabilities** are those that satisfy any of the following criteria:

- It is expected to be settled within a normal operation cycle
- It is held primarily for the purpose of being traded
- It is due to be settled within 12 months after the reporting date
- The firm does not have an unconditional right to defer settlement of the liability for at least 12 months after the reporting date.

All other liabilities shall be classified as **non-current liabilities.**

IAS 1 does not prescribe the order or format in which items must be presented. It does, however, stipulate that as a minimum, the face of the balance sheet should include line items which present each of the amounts shown in Table 2.5. In addition the balance sheet shall also include line items that present the following amounts:

- The total of assets classified as held for sale and assets included in disposal groups
- Liabilities included in disposal groups.

Table 2.5 Classification of assets and liabilities

Assets

Property, plant and equipment

Investment property

Intangible assets

Financial assets

Investments accounted for using the equity method

Biological assets

Inventories

Trade and other receivables

Cash and cash equivalents

Liabilities and shareholders' equity

Trade and other payables

Provisions

Current interest-bearing liabilities

Tax liabilities and tax assets

Deferred tax liabilities

Non-current interest-bearing liabilities

Minority interests

Issued capital and reserves

As illustrated in Table 2.5 the balance sheet is fairly detailed – despite the basic formula outlined above. An entity must disclose further sub-classifications of the line items presented in a manner appropriate to the entity's operations. This reflects that various industries may need to present information differently. An accountant must choose whether to present additional items separately based on:

- The nature and liquidity of assets
- The function of the assets within the entity
- The amounts, nature and timing of liabilities.

The use of different measurement bases for different classes of assets suggest that their nature or function differs and, therefore, that classes of assets should be presented as separate line items. For example, different classes of property, plant and equipment can be carried at cost or revalued amounts in accordance with IAS 16 Property, Plant and Equipment.

Ericsson's balance sheet is shown in Table 2.6. Assets as well as liabilities are classified as current and non-current, respectively. This makes it possible for analysts to separate items that generate cash inflows (assets) and cash outflows (liabilities) within a firm's operating cycle from items that do not.

Table 2.6 **Consolidated balance sheet for Ericsson**

SEK million	Year 8	Year 7
ASSETS		
Non-current assets		
Intangible assets		
Capitalised development expenses	2,782	3,661
Goodwill	24,877	22,826
Intellectual property rights, brands and other intangible assets	20,587	23,958
Property, plant and equipment	9,995	9,304
Financial assets		
Equity in joint ventures and associated companies	7,988	10,903
Other investments in shares and participations	309	738
Customer finance, non-current	846	1,012
Other financial assets, non-current	4,917	2,918
Deferred tax assets	14,858	11,690
Total non-current assets	**87,159**	**87,010**
Current assets		
Inventories	27,836	22,475
Trade receivables	75,891	60,492
Customer finance, current	1,975	2,362
Other current receivables	17,818	15,062
Short-term investments	37,192	29,406
Cash and cash equivalents	37,813	28,310
Total current assets	**198,525**	**158,107**
Total assets	**285,684**	**245,117**

▶

Table 2.6 (*continued*)

Equity and liabilities	Year 8	Year 7
Equity		
Stockholders' equity	140,823	134,112
Minority interest in equity of subsidiaries	1,261	940
	142,084	**135,052**
Non-current liabilities		
Post-employment benefits	9,873	6,188
Provisions, non-current	311	368
Deferred tax liabilities	2,738	2,799
Borrowings, non-current	24,939	21,320
Other non-current liabilities	1,622	1,714
	39,483	**32,389**
Current liabilities		
Provisions, current	14,039	9,358
Borrowings, current	5,542	5,896
Trade payables	23,504	17,427
Other current liabilities	61,032	44,995
	104,117	**77,676**
Total equity and liabilities	**285,684**	**245,117**

Cash flow statement

Cash flow statements report a company's cash receipts, cash payments, and the net change in the company's cash resulting from a company's operating, investing and financing activities for the period it is prepared for. Cash flow statements provide users of financial statements the basis for assessing a company's ability to generate cash and how cash is used.

Cash flow statements can be used in many contexts, for example in credit analysis, in valuation, and in assessing a firm's financial resources – all issues which will be addressed in later chapters. In the financial statement analysis cash flow statements can be used to gauge the quality of earnings, as earnings and cash flows should be correlated if measured over an extended period of time.

Ericsson's cash flow statement is shown in Table 2.7. As the table illustrates, Ericsson's cash in year 8 amounted to SEK 37,813 million compared to SEK 28,310 million at the beginning of the year. Thus, during the year Ericsson's cash balance increased by SEK 9,503 million (37,813 − 28,310).

Table 2.7 **Consolidated statement of cash flows for Ericsson**

SEK million	Year 8	Year 7	Year 6
Operating activities			
Net income	11,667	22,135	26,436
Adjustments to reconcile net income to cash	14,318	7,172	6,060
	25,985	**29,307**	**32,496**
Changes in operating net assets			
Inventories	−3,927	−445	−2,553
Customer finance, current and non-current	549	365	1,186
Trade receivables	−11,434	−7,467	−10,563
Provisions and post-employment benefits	3,830	−4,401	−3,729
Other operating assets and liabilities, net	8,997	1,851	1,652
	−1,985	**−10,097**	**−14,007**
Cash flow from operating activities	**24,000**	**19,210**	**18,489**
Investing activities			
Investments in property, plant and equipment	−4,133	−4,319	−3,827
Sales of property, plant and equipment	1,373	152	185
Acquisitions of subsidiaries and other operations	−74	−26,292	−18,078
Divestments of subsidiaries and other operations	1,910	84	3,086
Product development	−1,409	−1,053	−1,353
Other investing activities	944	396	−1,070
Short-term investments	−7,155	3,499	6,180
Cash flow from investing activities	**−8,544**	**−27,533**	**−14,877**
Cash flow before financing activities	**15,456**	**−8,323**	**3,612**
Financing activities			
Proceeds from issuance of borrowings	5,245	15,587	1,290
Repayment of borrowings	−4,216	−1,291	−9,510
Sale of own stock and options exercised	3	94	124
Dividends paid	−8,240	−8,132	−7,343
Cash flow from financing activities	**−7,208**	**6,258**	**−15,439**
Effect of exchange rate changes on cash	1,255	406	58
Net change in cash	**9,503**	**−1,659**	**−11,769**
Cash and cash equivalents, beginning of period	**28,310**	29,969	41,738
Cash and cash equivalents, end of period	**37,813**	28,310	29,969

Statement of changes in owners' equity

The statement of changes in equity reconciles equity at the beginning of the period with equity at the end of the period. The change in equity consists of a number of significant items. Usually the most significant item is retained earnings, i.e. the accumulation of profit (and losses) over time net of dividends. Another item is revaluation reserves (for instance caused by revaluing property to fair value). In addition, other items which bypass the income statement like certain currency translations and fair value adjustments are recognised as part of (changes in) equity. Finally, changes in equity includes items which are not part of operations but which are only a matter between shareholders, such as increases in share capital and share repurchase.

In relation to financial statement analysis, changes in equity are relevant because they show to what extent equity includes items that violate the so-called clean surplus assumption. That is, some items may bypass the income statement and be recognised directly as equity. Such items may have to be reclassified as part of operating income. Furthermore, scrutiny of the changes in equity reveals whether the development in equity and the market value of the company can be assigned to operations (retained earnings) or if it is due to transactions with the owners.

In Table 2.8, Ericsson includes transactions in the changes in shareholders' equity, which have not been recognised as part of earnings. For instance, cash flow hedges have a positive effect on reported equity by SEK 569 million.

Ericsson's financial statements are based on an enormous number of transactions, which are recorded in Ericsson's bookkeeping system. Every item in the financial statements is, thus, the sum of a vast number of underlying transactions. For example, revenue (the top line in the income statement) includes the total amount of every single sales (or services) transaction Ericsson's has made during a one-year period.

In the next section, we provide a short introduction to the double-entry bookkeeping system. We show how transactions are recorded and how they ultimately enter into the financial statements. If you are unfamiliar with bookkeeping, you may find it useful to consult introductory financial accounting textbooks.

A simple example (Example 2.1, From transactions to financial statements (page 37)) is provided to show how financial statements may be reformulated so they can be used for analytical purposes. If you, as an analyst, find it difficult to carry out the analysis at hand, you might find it valuable to go back to the simplified example to get a picture of the link the entire way from recording transactions to calculating financial ratios based on the analytical financial statements.

Recording transactions and preparing financial statements

Financial statements – the income statement, balance sheet, statement of cash flows, and statement of changes in owners' equity – are based on a firm's transactions (economic events) during a period of time. The number of transactions may be few for privately owned firms, whereas conglomerates with subsidiaries scattered around the world may report financial statements based on millions of economic events.

All transactions are recorded in the double-entry bookkeeping system, which dates back to 1494. The system is based on the principle of duality – the idea is that *every* recorded economic event has two aspects which offset or balance each other. Every transaction that is recorded consists of at least one debit and one credit

Table 2.8 Changes in stockholders' equity, Ericsson

SEK million Year 8	Capital stock	Additional paid in capital	Investments in shares and participations	Cash flow hedges	Cumulative translation adjustments	Retained earnings	Stock-holders' equity	Minority interests	Total equity
1 January, Year 8	16,132	24,731	5	307	−6,345	99,282	134,112	940	135,052
Actuarial gains and losses related to pensions									
Group						−4,019	−4,019	–	−4,019
Joint ventures and associates						4	4	–	4
Revaluation of other investments in shares and participations									
Fair value measurement reported in equity									
Group			−6			–	−6	–	−6
Joint ventures and associates			−1			–	−1	–	−1
Cash flow hedges									
Fair value remeasurement of derivatives reported in equity									
Group				−5,116		–	−5,116	–	−5,116
Joint ventures and associates				36		–	36	–	36
Transferred to income statement for the period				1,192		–	1,192	–	1,192
Changes in cumulative translation adjustments									
Group				–	7,081	–	7,081	233	7,314
Joint ventures and associates				–	1,214	–	1,214	–	1,214
Tax on items reported directly in/or transferred from equity			1	1,225	174	930	2,330	–	2,330
Total transactions reported directly in equity	–	–	−6	−2,663	8,469	−3,085	2,715	233	2,948
Net income									
Group						11,564	11,564	394	11,958
Joint ventures and associates						−291	−291	–	−291
Total income and expenses recognised for the period	–	–	−6	−2,663	8,469	8,188	13,988	627	14,615
Stock issue	100					–	100	–	100
Sale of own shares						88	88	–	88
Repurchase of own shares						−100	−100	–	−100
Stock purchase and stock option plans									
Group						589	589	–	589
Joint ventures and associates						–	–	–	–
Dividends paid						−7,954	−7,954	−286	−8,240
Business combinations						–	–	−20	−20
31 December, Year 8	16,232	24,731	−1	−2,356	2,124	100,093	140,823	1,261	142,084

record, and the total amount of debits must equal the total amount of credits for each transaction.

Financial statement analysis often requires adjustments to the financial statements (e.g. converting operating leases to financial leases) in order to eliminate 'noise' or to make accounting data comparable over time or across firms. Thus, analysts need to have a basic knowledge of the double-entry bookkeeping system.

In this section, we describes overall rules for recording transactions and illustrate how these transactions enter into the different financial statements. In addition, we include a simple example, which shows how financial statements relate to underlying business transactions and how the financial statements interrelate (articulate). We will use this same example in later chapters as an ongoing case. The idea is that this basic example makes it easier for the reader to understand more complicated issues, which naturally arise when we introduce real-life firms such as Carlsberg and Heineken and their financial statements.

Recording transactions

The general rules for recording transactions, in the double-entry bookkeeping system, can be illustrated by using the so-called 'T-accounts'. Each T account has a name that describes the types of transactions, which is recorded on the account, and a debit (left side) and credit (right side) as shown below:

Title of account	
Debit side	Credit side
(left side)	(right side)
Dr.	Cr.

In the balance sheet, the left side represents resources owned by the firm, whereas the right side represents claims from owners or third parties (e.g. banks) on these resources. In contrast, the income statement shows revenues on the right (credit) side and represents increases in owners' equity arising from increases in assets received in exchange for delivery of goods or services to customers. Items on the left hand (debit) side are expenses, and represent decreases in owners' equity that arise as goods or services are delivered (sold) to customers.

The following simple examples illustrate how transactions are recorded:

- *Transaction 1*: The firm incurs insurance expenses and pay on account

Expense		Accounts payable	
200			200

The firm records an increase in expenses of 200 (insurance account is debited) and a related increase in the amount owed to suppliers (accounts payable is credited by 200).

- *Transaction 2*: The firm sells its product and the customer pays in cash:

Revenues		Cash	
	1,000	1,000	

The firm records revenues of 1,000 (revenues account is credited) and a related increase of the cash balance (cash is debited by 1,000).

General rules illustrated

The following example highlights how typical transactions enter into the income statement and balance sheet, respectively.

- Recording expenses or assets:
  A firm rents an office for 100 and pays either in cash (a) or alternatively on account (b). The recording becomes:

Expense	Cash	Accounts payable
100 (a/b)		100 (a)		100 (b)

Whether rents are paid in cash (a) or on account (b), the firm recognises an expense of 100 (debit transaction). The corresponding credit transaction is either (a) a draw on a cash account (decrease in an asset account) or (b) an increase in amounts owed to creditors (an increase in a liability account). Thus, it should be clear (we hope) that an expense is followed by a decrease in assets or an increase in liabilities. In both cases net assets (equity), decrease by 100. This is hardly surprising, as it is a concept that most of us encounter in our personal lives. For instance, if you pay rent on your flat, either your cash balance decreases or you owe more money to your bank. In any case your equity, i.e. your financial fortune, suffers.

- Similarly, if a firm buys inventory, it may do so by paying in cash (a) or on account (b). If the firm purchase inventory for 400, the records become:

Inventory	Cash	Accounts payable
400 (a/b)		400 (a)		400 (b)

Thus, inventory increases (an increase in an asset account). As with the expense example above, the corresponding credit transaction is either (a) a draw on a cash account (a decrease in an asset account) or (b) an increase in amounts owed to creditors (an increase in a liability account).

- Recording income (revenues, other income, gains etc.), liabilities and owners' equity:

  A firm sells a product for 200 to a customer, who either pays in cash (a) or alternatively on account (b). The recording becomes:

Revenues	Cash	Accounts receivable
	200 (a/b)	200 (a)		200 (b)	

Whether customers pay in cash (a) or buy on account (b), the firm recognises revenue of 200 (credit transaction). The corresponding debit transaction is either (a) an increase in cash (increase in an asset account) or (b) an increase in amounts owed by customers (an increase in an asset account). Thus, it should be clear that income is followed by an increase in assets.

UNIVERSITY OF WINCHESTER
LIBRARY

- If the firm borrows 50 in order to have cash in hand, the transaction is recorded as follows:

Cash			Loan
50			50

In this case cash increases by 50 (debit to an asset account), while the firm borrows (additional) 50 (credit to a liability account). Net assets from this transaction is zero ($50 - 50 = 0$). The firm's equity remains unchanged. Please notice that in this case, the transaction has no effect on the income statement. The firm's net worth is not affected.

- Finally, if the investors pay-in additional share capital of 100, the recording becomes (disregarding transaction costs):

Cash			Share capital
100			100

In this case cash increases by 100 (debit to an asset account), while share capital increases by the same amount (credit to an equity account). The firm's net assets and equity increases by 100.

Summarising

Based on the above, simple transactions, the rules for using T accounts may be summarised as follows:

Income statement		Balance sheet	
Income	**Expenses**	**Assets**	**Liabilities and owners' equity**
− | +	+ | −	+ | −	− | +
Dr. | Cr.	Dr. | Cr.	Dr. | Cr.	Dr. | Cr.

Thus, an increase in *expenses* (costs and losses) and *assets* are debit entries, while an increase in *income* (revenues and gains) and *liabilities and owners' equity* are credit entries. These general rules *always* hold true. For example, *any* increase in assets, say, purchase of inventory is debited to an asset account.

The above rules are summarised in the table below:

	Increases recorded by	
Accounting item	Debit	Credit
Revenues (or income)		√
Expenses (or losses)	√	
Assets	√	
Liabilities and owners' equity		√

Transaction analysis illustrated

In the previous section, we shared general guidelines for recording transactions. In this section, we demonstrate how a number of transactions, which typically occur in a retail company, are recorded. Based on those transactions the firm's financial statements are prepared. We also illustrate the relation between the different statements – income statement, balance sheet, statement of owners' equity and cash flow statement. These statements must, as Example 2.1 shows, *always* relate in a certain way. That is they must articulate. For instance, equity at the beginning of the year plus comprehensive income minus dividends must equal equity at year end.

Example 2.1	From transactions to financial statements

For simplicity reasons, value added tax (VAT), sales tax etc. are disregarded in the following example. These taxes are collected on behalf of public authorities and paid back at different intervals (depending on the country). VAT and similar duties have no effect on the income statement.

The example is illustrative and the basic principles for recording the transactions can be applied to other transactions and firms in different industries.

A number of investors start a business in the retail industry as of 1 January, year 1. The firm is named Goods4U. The investors paid-in share capital amounts to 365; with the addition of a bank loan of 100, invested capital becomes 465. The bank loan includes a bank overdraft account. The capital invested in the firm at start-up is used to buy the following assets:

- Purchase of warehouse: 200
- Purchase of equipment: 50
- Purchase of inventory: 200
- Cash in hand: 5
- Cash deposited in a banking account: 10

The opening balance sheet becomes:

Balance sheet, 1 January, year 1 for Goods4U

Assets	
Warehouse	200
Equipment	50
Inventories	200
Cash and cash equivalents	15
Total assets	**465**
Liabilities and shareholders' equity	
Equity	365
Loans and borrowings	100
Total liabilities and shareholders' equity	**465**

During year 1 a huge number of transactions are recorded. Those transactions can be summarised as follows (numbers in the first column refer to the transaction numbers):

No.	Transactions*	
1	Sales paid in cash	80
2	Sales on account	120
3	Salaries to employees paid by increasing bank loan	10
4	Advertising and promotion expenses paid in cash	6
5	Utility expenses paid in cash	2
6	Maintenance expenses paid in cash	4
7	Insurance expenses paid by increasing bank loan	1
8	Other operating expenses paid in cash	3
9	Purchase of equipment paid on account	50
10	Purchase of inventory paid by increasing bank loan (130) and on account (170)	300
11	Interest income	5
12	Interest expenses paid by increasing bank loan	15
13	Payments made by customers, who bought on account (payment reduces bank loan)	6
14	Payments made to suppliers for purchases made on account (paid by increasing bank loan)	50
	Adjusting and closing entries at year end:	
15	Inventory at year end	450
16	Depreciation of warehouse (4) and equipment (10)	14
17	Corporation tax	30

*Each transaction shall be regarded as the total (sum) of all similar transactions. For instance, Goods4U may have had a large number of sales transactions, which have been paid in cash by customers, amounting to a total of 80.

The bookkeeping of the above transactions (items 1–17) is as follows:

1 Sales paid in cash		80
Recording of item 1	**Debit**	**Credit**
Net revenue (income statement, increase in income)		80
Cash/bank account (balance sheet, increase in assets)	80	

Sales constitute a firm's income from its core business. As shown above an increase in revenues is a credit. Since customers pay in cash, the cash balance increases by 80.

2 Sales on account		120
Recording of item 2	**Debit**	**Credit**
Net revenue (income statement, increase in income)		120
Accounts receivable (balance sheet, increase in assets)	120	

Even though customers pay on account, Goods4U still recognises 120 as revenue. This highlights that financial statements (in this case the income statement) differ from cash flow statements. Revenues and expenses are recognised even if payment has not been made. Since customers pay on account, accounts receivable increases by 120.

3 Salaries to employees paid by increasing bank loan		10
Recording of item 3	**Debit**	**Credit**
Personnel expenses (income statement, increase in expenses)	10	
Bank loan (balance sheet, increase liability)		10

Employees are paid cash (often on a monthly basis, thus, transaction 3 could in reality be 12 transactions of approximately 0.83 each). This, of course, represents an expense, with a relating increase in liabilities.

4 Advertising and promotion expenses paid in cash		6
Recording of item 4	**Debit**	**Credit**
Advertising expenses (income statement, increase in expenses)	6	
Cash/bank account (balance sheet, decrease in assets)		6

Advertising and promotion are expenses. Since they are paid in cash, the relating entry is a decrease in assets.

Utility, maintenance, insurance and other operating expenses all represent expenses. The corresponding entries depend on whether the expenses are (a) paid in cash (or similarly deducted from a bank account) or (b) paid on account.

5	Utility expenses paid in cash	2
6	Maintenance expenses paid in cash	4
7	Insurance expenses paid by increasing bank loan	1
8	Other operating expenses paid in cash	3

The entries are shown below:

Recording of items 5–8	Debit	Credit
Utility expenses (income statement, increase in expenses)	2	
Cash/bank account (balance sheet, decrease in assets)		2
Maintenance expenses (income statement, increase in expenses)	4	
Cash/bank account (balance sheet, decrease in assets)		4
Insurance expenses (income statement, increase in expenses)	1	
Bank loan (balance sheet, increase in liability)		1
Other operating expenses (income statement, increase in expenses)	3	
Cash/bank account (balance sheet, decrease in assets)		3

All the above expenses are operating expenses.

9 Purchase of equipment paid on account		50
Recording of item 9	**Debit**	**Credit**
Equipment (balance sheet, increase in assets)	50	
Accounts payable (balance sheet, increase in liabilities)		50

Purchase of equipment represents two entries to the balance sheet. First, equipment increases, while Goods4U at the same time must recognise a liability as the equipment has not yet been paid for.

Since assets and liabilities increase by the same amount, equity is unchanged (equity = assets − liabilities).

10 Purchase of inventory paid by increasing bank loan (130) and on account (170)		300
Recording of item 10	**Debit**	**Credit**
Inventory (balance sheet, increase in assets)	300	
Accounts payable (balance sheet, increase in liabilities)		170
Bank loan (balance sheet, increase in liabilities)		130

Purchase of inventories represents three entries in this particular case. First, inventory increases by 300. This entry is perfectly offset by an increase in accounts payable (170) and an increase in borrowing (130). Thus, as a result of transaction 10, Goods4U recognises a simultaneous increase in an asset account and an increase in two liability accounts by the same amount. Equity remains unchanged. Note that the income statement is not affected. Recognition in the income statement will not happen until the goods are sold or written-off if impaired (e.g. due to obsolescence).

11 Interest income		5
Recording of item 11	**Debit**	**Credit**
Interest received (income statement, increase in financial income)		5
Cash/bank account (balance sheet, increase in assets)	5	

Goods4U earns interests on its deposits in the bank (and on securities such as bonds). Interest income is recognised as financial income. Interest received have nothing to do with Goods4U core business – selling various products – and should not be recognised as revenue.

12 Interest expenses paid by increasing bank loan		15
Recording of item 12	**Debit**	**Credit**
Interest paid (income statement, increase in financial expenses)	15	
Bank loan (balance sheet, increase in liability)		15

Goods4U pays interests on its bank loans. Interest expenses are recognised as financial expenses. Just like interest received, interest paid is not related to Goods4U's core business and should, consequently, be recognised as financial expenses.

13 Payment made by customers, who bought on account		6
Recording of item 13	**Debit**	**Credit**
Bank loan (balance sheet, decrease in liabilities)	6	
Accounts receivable (balance sheet, decrease in assets)		6

Some of the customers who did not pay cash on delivery have paid subsequently (by bank transfer) during the financial year. Due to this the balance on Goods4U's bank loan decreases, while accounts receivable decreases. Customers owe less to Goods4U.

Again, Goods4U's equity remains unchanged. The firm has just converted one asset (accounts receivable) to another fully liquid asset (increase in a bank balance). Naturally, the risk associated with the fully liquid asset is less than the risk on the amount owed by the firm's customers. We will discuss the concept of risk later in the text.

14 Payment made to suppliers for purchases made on account		50
Recording of item 14	**Debit**	**Credit**
Accounts payable (balance sheet, decrease in liabilities)	50	
Cash/bank loan (balance sheet, decrease in assets)		50

Some suppliers are paid during the financial year. Due to this the balance on Goods4U's bank account decreases, while accounts payable decrease. The net worth (equity) of Goods4U is unaffected. The firm reduced its liabilities (accounts payable) and assets (bank account) by the exact same amount.

Adjusting transactions

At year end there will almost always be a number of adjusting and closing entries. Therefore, before preparing the financial statements, Goods4U need to make some final entries into the bookkeeping system. We describe the closing entries for Goods4U below.

First, Goods4U needs to calculate cost of goods sold. In other words, they must determine the costs of the inventory which have been sold to customers. Usually, Goods4U would do this by physically counting inventory in hand at year end. Each piece of inventory is valued at cost. So if a firm has, say, 4 pieces in hand at a price of 10 per piece, and 12 pieces in hand at a price of 5 per piece, the carrying amount of inventory amounts to 100 ($4 \times 10 + 12 \times 5 = 100$).

Cost of goods sold is calculated as:

15	Ending inventory at 31 December	450
	Beginning inventory at 1 January	200
10	+ Inventory purchased during the year	300
	= Inventory available for sale	500
15	− Ending inventory at 31 December	−450
	− Cost of goods sold (COGS)	50

COGS are the costs associated with the sales of Goods4U's products. This represents an expense in the income statement, with a corresponding decrease in inventory in hand. Note, however, that a firm's COGS is often known even if inventory has not been counted at year end, since at the point of sales the goods, which have been sold, are automatically recognised by a bar code.

The recording of transaction 15 becomes:

Recording of item 15	Debit	Credit
Cost of goods sold (income statement, increase in expenses)	50	
Inventory (balance sheet, decrease in assets)		50

Second, tangible assets need to be depreciated. Warehouses, machinery, equipment, automobiles and other tangible assets are prone to wear and tear. Eventually those assets are worn out, or technological obsolete, so they must be depreciated. Warehouses (and property in general) has fairly long estimated useful lifetimes, whereas machinery and equipment mostly have a much shorter lifetime.

16 Depreciation of warehouse and equipment		14
Recording of item 16	**Debit**	**Credit**
Depreciation of warehouse (income statement, increase in expenses)	4	
Warehouse, depreciated (balance sheet, decrease in assets)		4
Depreciation of equipment (income statement, increase in expenses)	10	
Equipment, depreciated (balance sheet, decrease in assets)		10

Goods4U estimates the lifetime of the warehouse to be 50 years, and the useful lifetime of equipment to be 10 years on average. The depreciation method is straight-line. Depreciation is calculated as:

Initial book value/useful lifetime (years) = Depreciation expense per year
Warehouse: $200/50 = 4$
Equipment: $(50 + 50)/10 = 10$

Equipment amounted to 50 at the beginning of the year. With a purchase during the year of 50, total costs for equipment amounts to 100. In practice, purchases during the year are only depreciated proportionally. For instance, if equipment of 50 was bought at mid-year the depreciation of these costs would only be $50/10 \times \frac{1}{2} = 2.5$ in Year 1 and $50/10 = 5$ in subsequent years. The example assumes that the assets have no salvage value.

Furthermore, Goods4U needs to pay tax on its income. A firm's taxable income differs in several respects from the accounting income as reported in the annual report. Tax payable (and deferred taxes) cannot be calculated until the annual report has been finalised. For the sake of simplicity, assume that Goods4U reported accounting earnings equal its taxable income. This means that there are no deferred taxes (for a discussion of deferred taxes please refer to Chapter 15). Assuming a tax rate of 30%, the tax expense becomes:

Corporation tax = earnings before tax $\times$ corporate tax rate = $100 \times 30\% = 30$

17 Corporation tax		30
Recording of item 17	**Debit**	**Credit**
Corporation tax (income statement, increase in expenses)	30	
Tax payable (balance sheet, increase in liabilities)		30

■

As illustrated in the above example, tax is an expense like any other expense. Since tax has not been paid yet, it becomes a liability. In reality, firms may have to pay tax during the year. In this case, tax payable is reduced accordingly.

In reality, the number of *actual* transactions would normally be much higher than 17 as in the example. For instance, employees would generally receive salaries (at least) 12 times per year. But the principles are the same regardless of the number of transactions, so you should be confident that these concepts of double-entry bookkeeping apply regardless of the size of the company – or the number of transactions.

Based on the transactions, accountants prepare financial statements. We illustrate these statements below in a condensed form.

Financial statements

After the above transactions have been recorded, accountants enter them into the financial statements as shown below. After each item in the financial statements, we show the transaction number(s) associated with that item. This should make it easy for you to see how transactions and financial statement items are linked.

Income statement in condensed form	Total	Transaction(s)
Net revenue	200	1, 2
Cost of goods sold	–50	15
Gross profit	**150**	
Operating expenses (excluding depreciation and amortisation)	–26	3, 4, 5, 6, 7, 8
Earnings before interest, tax, depreciation and amortisation (EBITDA)	**124**	
Depreciation	–14	16
Earnings before interest and tax (EBIT)	**110**	
Financial income	5	11
Financial expenses	–15	12
Earnings before tax (EBT)	**100**	
Corporation tax	–30	17
Net earnings (E)[1]	**70**	

[1] Sometimes labelled net profit. See glossary in Appendix 2.1 for commonly used accounting terms or expressions.

Balance sheet in condensed form

Assets	1 Jan., year 1	Dr.	Cr.	31 Dec., year 1	Transaction(s)
Warehouse	200	0	4	196	16
Equipment	50	50	10	90	9, 16
Inventories	200	300	50	450	10, 15
Accounts receivable	0	120	6	114	2, 13
Cash and cash equivalents[1]	15	85	15	85	1, 4, 5, 6, 8, 11
Total assets	**465**	**555**	**85**	**935**	

▶

43

(continued)

Liabilities and shareholders' equity	1 Jan., year 1	Dr.	Cr.	31 Dec., year 1	Transaction(s)
Equity	365		70	435	
Tax payable	0		30	30	17
Accounts payable	0	50	220	170	9, 10, 14
Loans and borrowings (bank accounts)	100	6	206	300	3, 7, 10, 12, 13,14
Total liabilities	465			500	
Total liabilities and shareholders' equity	465	56	526	935	

[1]By the end of the day cash sales are deposited in a savings account. A little cash (petty cash) is left over. Cash and cash equivalents include petty cash and cash deposited in a savings account.

To see how these statements articulate, the cash flow statement is provided below.

Cash flow statement in condensed form	
Cash flow from operating activities	
Net earnings	70
Depreciation of non-current assets *(Note 1)*	14
Movements in working capital (Note 2):	
(Increase)/decrease in accounts receivable	−114
(Increase)/decrease in inventories	−250
Increase/(decrease) in accounts payable	170
Increase/(decrease) in tax payables	30
Net cash generated by operating activities (A)	−80
Cash flow from investing activities	
Purchase of equipment (B)	−50
Cash flow from financing activities	
Proceeds from borrowing (C)	200
Net increase in cash and cash equivalents (A + B + C)	70
Cash and cash equivalents at the beginning of the year	15
Cash and cash equivalents at the end of the year	**85**

Note 1

Depreciation (and amortisation and impairment losses) of assets are added to net earnings, as these expenses have been subtracted from earnings but have no cash flow consequences.

Note 2

In order to calculate the total cash flow from operations, changes in net working capital must be taken into account. An increase in assets (e.g. inventory and accounts receivable) has a negative effect on the cash flow. Likewise, a decrease in liabilities (e.g. accounts payable) has a negative effect on the cash flow.

For instance, in the above example, inventories increase from 200 at the beginning of the year to 450 at year end. The difference (increase of an asset) of 250 reduces the cash flow by this amount.

The different financial statements as shown above must articulate (be related to one another in a certain way). As the example demonstrates:

Equity at the beginning of the financial year	365
+ Net earnings	70
= **Equity at the end of the financial year**	**435**
Total assets at year end	935
− Total liabilities at year end	500
= **Equity at year end**	**435**

Equity calculated in these two different ways must match. Likewise, cash and cash equivalents at financial year end must equal cash in hand at the beginning of the financial year plus all cash flows related to operating, investing and financing activities during the financial year:

Cash and cash equivalents at the beginning of the financial year	15
+/− Cash flow from operating activities	−80
+/− Cash flow from investing activities	−50
+/− Cash flow from financing activities	200
= **Cash and cash equivalents at the end of the financial year**	**85**

Analysts often need to prepare pro forma financial statement – for instance, in valuing companies – using **present value approaches**. In such valuation tasks, the analyst should make sure those pro forma financial statements (including cash flow statements) articulate as described in this chapter. We discuss this issue further in Chapters 8 and 9.

Conclusions

In this chapter, we have highlighted how transactions are recorded and financial statements are prepared based on bookkeeping transactions. All transactions must include (at least) one debit and (at least) one credit record. Each transaction must balance in the sense that the amount(s) debited must match the amount(s) credited. Income (revenues, other income and gains), liabilities and equity are credit transactions. Expenses (costs and losses) and assets are debit transactions.

Financial statements summarise all recorded transactions. The income statement measures a firm's earnings capacity over a period of time: the difference between income and expenses. The balance sheet represents a firm's assets, liabilities and equity at a point in time. Statement of changes in equity highlights how equity changes from the beginning of the period to the end of the period. Finally, the cash flow statement shows cash flows from operating, investing and financing activities (transactions) and how those cash flows are related to the income statement and balance sheet. Just as all transactions must balance, that is debit entries equal credit entries, the financial statements must relate to each other in a certain way. The statements must articulate.

We included examples of how to record transactions and how these transactions entered into the different financial statements. However, we disregarded certain items.

For example, when customers buy a firm's product, they pay value added tax (VAT), but the firm only recognises sales net of VAT. The VAT is simply collected on behalf of a third party and does not become part of sales.

A thorough knowledge of bookkeeping is paramount in order to carry out a financial statements analysis. In later chapters, we discuss how analysts may need to make adjustments to the financial statements before carrying out the analysis. These adjustments are essentially bookkeeping records. Without knowing, say, how capitalising rather than expensing development costs affects the financial statements, the analyst will not be able to make such adjustments, and will, therefore, not be able to make proper decisions.

Review questions

- How many formats of the income statement does IASB allow?

- What are the main components of an income statement?

- What is the distinction between current and non-current assets?

- What is the distinction between current and non-current liabilities?

- What are the three main categories of a cash flow statement?

- Why is knowledge of bookkeeping a useful skill for an analyst?

- A payment from a customer must be credited to the bank account – true or false?

- An investment in property, plant and equipment must be debited assets – true or false?

APPENDIX 2.1

Accounting terms: IASB, UK and USA (see Alexander et al. (2009) *International Financial Reporting and Analysis*, 4th edn, page 16).

IASB	UK	USA
Inventory	Stock	Inventory
Shares	Shares	Stock
Treasury shares	Own shares	Treasury stock
Receivables	Debtors	Receivables
Payables	Creditors	Payables
Finance lease	Finance lease	Capital lease
Sales (or revenue)	Turnover	Sales (or revenue)
Acquisitions	Purchase	Purchase
Uniting of interest	Merger	Pooling of interest
Non-current assets	Fixed assets	Non-current assets
Income statement	Profit and loss account	Income statement

CHAPTER 3

Accrual-based versus cash-flow-based performance measures

Learning outcomes

After reading this chapter you should be able to:

- **Make a distinction between common accrual- and cash-flow-based performance measures**
- **Explain the differences between accrual- and cash-flow-based performance measures**
- **Understand the differences between single-period and multi-period performance measures**
- **Understand the concept of a firm's earnings capacity**
- **Discuss the information content of accrual- and cash-flow-based performance measures**
- **Understand in which analytical contexts that cash-flow measures can be used**

Accrual-based versus cash-flow-based performance measures

Financial statement analysis helps you identify a company's ability to create value for its shareholders. In this context it is often debatable whether **accrual-based performance measures** like EBIT and net earnings give a good description of a company's underlying operations and, thus, is a good starting point for forecasting future performance. Arguments like 'historically oriented' and 'prone to manipulation' are used against accrual-based performance measures. The finance literature recommends valuations based on cash flows, rather than accrual-based performance measures. Cash flows are perceived as an objective outcome that cannot be manipulated and some even argue that 'cash is king'. The following sections discuss to what extent the two types of performance measures are suitable for measuring the value creation in a company.

Both North American (FASB) and international accounting regulation (IASB) argue that information on cash inflows and cash outflows enhances users' ability to assess the following aspects of a company:

- Future cash flows
- Liquidity (short-term liquidity risk)
- Solvency (long-term liquidity risk)
- Financial flexibility.

While the FASB was among the first to implement the cash flow statement as an integrated part of financial statements, FASB still sees the (accrual) income statement as being superior to the cash flow statement for measuring a company's value creation (**earnings capacity**) within a given period.

Many researchers and practitioners disagree with the above view. In the past few decades, advocates have focused on cash flows as an alternative way to measure a firm's earnings capacity; i.e. its ability to create value within a given period such as a financial year. The most eager proponents of 'cash is king' in this debate are a group of people who suggest that the cash flow statement should replace the traditional financial statements (income statement and balance sheet). Ijiri (1978), Lawson (1985) and Lee (1985) have all developed systems of alternative cash flow statements to replace the traditional financial statements. The management literature has advocated for the measurement of value creation through cash flows. Among stock analysts there has also been an increased focus on measuring earnings capacity through cash flows. As a result, there is some conflict between researchers and practitioners, as to whether accrual-based or **cash-flow-based performance measures** are best at estimating a firm's value creation.

The distinction between accrual-based and cash-flow-based performance measures

In the following section, we demonstrate the distinction between accrual- and cash-flow-based performance measures. To help you understand the conceptual difference between the two, consider a firm which must record the following seven transactions in period 0 (P0):

	P − 1	P0	P1
1		−1000 (P) −1000 (PCR) +2600 (S) +26000 (PCU)	
2	−100 (P) −100 (PCR) +200 (S)	+200 (PCU)	
3	−2,500 (P) −2,500 (PCR)	+4,800 (S) +4,800 (PCU)	
4	−3,100 (P)	−3,100 (PCR) +6,000 (S) +6,000 (PCU)	
5		−1,000 (P) −1,000 (PCR) +1,400 (S) +1,400 (PCU)	
6		−3,000 (P) −3,000 (PCR) +5,700 (S) +5,700 (PCU)	
7		−3,900 (P)	−3,900 (PCR) +5,500 (S) +5,500 (PCU)

P = Purchase, PCR = Payment to creditor, S = Sales, PCU = Payment from customer

Based on the seven transactions, we have measured the performance of the company in P0 using both accrual and cash flow accounting.

The accrual-based earnings generated in P0 can be calculated as follows:

Revenue (transactions 1, 3, 4, 5)	2,600 + 4,800 + 6,000 + 1,400	14,800
Cost of goods sold (transactions 1, 3, 4, 5)	1,000 + 2,500 + 3,100 + 1,000	7,600
Accrual based earnings		**7,200**

The cash flow generated in period P0 is calculated as follows:

Cash inflow (transactions 1, 2, 3, 4)	2,600 + 200 + 4,800 + 6,000	13,600
Cash outflow (transactions 1, 4, 5, 6)	1,000 + 3,100 + 1,000 + 3,000	8,100
Cash flow P0		**5,500**

As you can see from this example, accrual-based earnings is 7,200, while net cash inflow amounts to 5,500. Although accrual accounting matches revenue and expenses from the same transaction, a similar match is not made in the cash flow statement. This is because in an accrual accounting regime unused purchases at the end of a financial year is recognised as inventory. Thus, inventory serves as a 'parking place' for unused purchases waiting to be recognised in the income statement as cost of goods sold. Cash flow accounting, on the other hand, recognises purchases in the cash flow statement in the year that the purchase has been paid for. Therefore, the same transaction can be treated differently in the income statement and cash flow statement.

To help make the difference between the accrual- (accounting) based earnings of 7,200 and the net cash inflows of 5,500 more explicit, we have calculated a traditional cash flow statement based on the seven transactions:

	Begin	End	
Accrual-based earnings in period P0			7,200
Inventory	5,600	6,900	–1,300
Accounts receivable	200	1,400	–1,200
Accounts payable (creditors)	3,100	3,900	800
Cash flow P0			**5,500**

In the above example, the differences between accrual-based earnings and cash flows are made up by changes in net working capital, i.e. inventory, accounts receivable and **accounts payable**. As noted above, inventory helps matching revenue with expenses from the same transaction. In the example, accrual accounting is moving purchases of 1,300 to future periods where the sales will take place. On the other hand, cash flow accounting recognises all 1,300 as a cash outflow in P0. Accounts receivable are growing by 1,200 indicating that accrual-based earnings recognises 1,200 as sales in P0 that is still not recognised in the cash flow statement (since no cash has been received). As you can see from the example, accrual accounting recognises a transaction at the time when a sale is made rather than when cash is received from the customer. In contrast, cash flow accounting is more prudent as it does not recognise a transaction until cash has been received from customers, i.e. when a transaction results in an inflow of cash. Finally, accounts payable are growing by 800. Cash flow accounting acknowledges that not all purchases are paid in P0.

Different accrual- and cash-flow-based performance measures are reported by companies and used by analysts. In Table 3.1 we have highlighted the most important ones in bold.

Table 3.1 Various accrual-based performance measures

Revenue
− Operating costs excluding depreciations and write-downs
= Operating earnings before depreciation, amortisation and impairment losses (EBITDA)
− Depreciation, amortisation and impairment losses
= Operating earnings (EBIT)
+/− Net financial items
= Ordinary earnings before tax (EBT)
+/− Tax on ordinary profit
= Ordinary earnings after tax
+/− Extraordinary items, discontinued operations and change in accounting policies
= Net earnings (E)
+/− Transactions recognised directly in equity
= Comprehensive income

As Table 3.1 illustrates, four accrual-based performance measures are typically disclosed: operating earnings (before and after depreciation, amortisation and impairment losses), ordinary earnings, net earnings and comprehensive income. Operating earnings and comprehensive income are considered as two extremes among the accrual-based performance measures. Essentially, operating earnings measure the part of earnings which are likely to recur from period to period (permanent portion of earnings), while comprehensive income measures both the permanent part of earnings as well as the part of earnings that do not occur often or regularly. Net earnings are in between operating earnings and comprehensive income.

Table 3.2 shows each accrual-based performance measure on Carlsberg – one of the world's largest breweries. Looking at the table it is interesting to note the deviation between comprehensive income and net income. While net earnings equal DKK 3.2 billion, comprehensive income equals DKK 9.2 billion. A closer look at Carlsberg's net amount recognised directly in equity reveals that value adjustment on acquisition of

Table 3.2 The accrual-based performance measures of Carlsberg

DKKm	Year 8
Net revenue	59,944
Operating expenses excluding depreciation and amortisation	−49,815
Operating earnings before depreciation and amortisation (EBITDA)	**10,129**
Depreciation and amortisation	−3.771
Earnings before interest and tax (EBIT)	**6,358**
Net financial expenses	−3,456
Earnings before tax (EBT)	**2,902**
Corporation tax	304
Net earnings (E)	**3,206**
Net amount recognised directly in equity	6,000
Comprehensive income	**9,206**

subsidiaries, foreign exchange adjustments and value adjustments of hedging instruments and securities explain the difference.

The most widespread cash-flow-based performance measures (marked in bold), and the relationship between them, are shown in Table 3.3.

Table 3.3 The relationship between cash-flow-based performance measures

Operating income (EBIT)
$+/-$ Adjustment for items with no cash flow effects (depreciation, provision, etc.)
$+/-$ Change in net working capital (inventories, receivables and operating liabilities)
$+/-$ Corporate tax
= Cash flow from operating activities
$+/-$ Investments in non-current assets, net
= Cash flow after investments (free cash flow, FCF)
$+/-$ Financing items
= Net cash flow for the period (change in cash)

Cash flow from operations and free cash flows are the most frequently used cash flow measures by analysts. Net cash for the period are rarely used as a stand-alone performance measure. The cash-flow-based performance measures shown for Carlsberg are shown in Table 3.4. Carlsberg's cash flow from operation is clearly not sufficient to cover investments in non-current assets of DKK 57.2 billion. Carlsberg, therefore, has to rely on cash flow from financing activities (borrowing) to support the heavy investments made in non-current assets.

Table 3.4 Cash-flow-based performance measures for Carlsberg

DKKm	Year 8
Cash flow from operating activities	**7,812**
Cash flow from investing activities (non-current assets)	−57,153
Free cash flow	**−49,341**
Cash flow from financing activities	50,084
Net cash flow	743

Measuring earnings capacity

It is important to distinguish between the measurement of a firm's earnings capacity in the short term and long term when comparing accrual- and cash-flow-based performance measures. As we cannot predict what is going to happen in the future, it is not possible for us to measure earnings capacity over the entire lifetime of a company. Therefore, measurement of earnings capacity changes from being forward looking to being (partly) backward looking. Typically, earnings capacity is measured over relative short time intervals (on a quarterly, semi-annual or annual basis) because users of financial statements in a world of uncertainty need continuous updates of a firm's performance and financial position. Users, thus, have opportunities constantly to revise their view of a company. Among certain cash flow proponents there is a tendency to confuse the concepts of short- and long-term earnings capacity, i.e. comparing single-period performance measures measuring short-term performance with multi-period performance measures measuring long-term performance. For example, accrual-based **earnings per share** (EPS) has been compared to a cash-flow-based multi-period **shareholder value added** (SVA) measure.

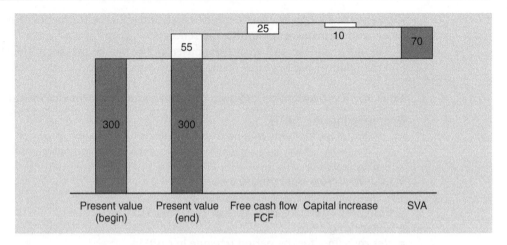

Figure 3.1 Example on the use of a multi-period performance measure (SVA)

Figure 3.1 illustrates the SVA concept and how it is measured. The present value of future cash flows is measured at the beginning and at the end of the measurement period. In this example, the present value of cash flows increases by 55. Moreover, in the period a free cash flow of 25 has been generated, which added to the increase in present value gives 80. If there were no transactions with owners, the 80 would reflect value created during the period. However, the owners contributed 10 in the period, so the real value creation (SVA) is only 70.

Obviously, comparing an ex-post single-period performance measure as EPS with a (forward looking) multi-period performance measure as SVA is not very useful. EPS and SVA serve two very distinct and different purposes. While EPS is a short-term performance measure of last year's performance SVA is multi-period performance measure measuring the long-term earnings capacity of a company.

The distinction between EPS and SVA is highlighted in Figure 3.2. The single-period accrual-based EPS is (partly) backward looking and measures value creation for short-term intervals. This is in contrast to the cash-flow-based SVA-concept, which is forward looking, takes growth and risk into consideration and measures value creation throughout a firm's lifetime. Thus, the cash-flow-based SVA concept will appear to be a superior performance measure of earnings capacity in the long term compared to the accrual-based EPS. However, to make a real comparison of accrual- and cash-flow-based performance measures requires a separation of the short- and long-term earnings capacity.

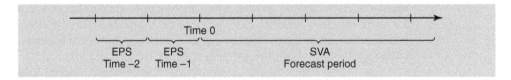

Figure 3.2 Single-period versus multi-period performance measure

Shortcomings of accrual-based and cash-flow-based performance concepts

As shown above, there is some disagreement about the usefulness of accrual- and cash-flow-based performance measures. Part of the explanation for this divergence is that both accrual- and cash-flow-based performance measures suffer from shortcomings when measuring the earnings capacity in the *short term*. Overall, the criticism of the accrual-based performance measures can be summarised into the following points:

- Accrual problems:
  - Arbitrary cost allocation and accounting estimates
  - Alternative accounting policies
- Time value of money is ignored.

One of the main disadvantages of accrual-based performance measures is the introduction of concepts such as (arbitrary) cost allocation (e.g. amortisation of intangible assets), accounting estimates (e.g. estimating uncollectible accounts receivable) and alternative accounting policies (e.g. first in, first out (FIFO) versus average costs for inventory accounting). As a consequence of these concepts the preparer of financial statements (management) obtain some flexibility in reported earnings numbers. In accounting literature it is well documented that when accruals are abnormally high, the quality of reported earnings is generally low and less suitable for predictive purposes (Sloan 1996). The concepts of abnormal accruals and earnings quality are discussed in further detail in Chapter 13. Another potential disadvantage of accrual-based performance measures is that they do not take into account the time value of money. This problem is particularly prone during periods of rapid price changes (inflation). Since revenue is measured at current prices and operating expenses are measured at historical prices (costs), a firm's earnings capacity will generally be overvalued in times of (large) inflation.

However, cash-flow-based performance measures are also problematic. Criticism of cash-flow-based performance measures can be summarised as follows:

- Failure to account for uncompleted transactions
- Cash flows can be manipulated.

One of the main problems with cash-flow-based performance measures is that they do not match cash inflows with cash outflows from the same transactions. While cash outflows are significant at times of new investments cash inflows from those investments are typically significant in subsequent periods. The magnitude of this problem typically increases with the number of uncompleted transactions in a given period. For example, engineering, consultancy firms, and shipyards are all characterised by transactions that may span several periods. Thus, the proportion of uncompleted transactions within the measurement period is typically significant for these types of companies. Conversely, supermarkets are characterised by many completed transactions and the proportion of uncompleted transactions within the measurement period is modest. Thus, the information content of cash flows is expected to decrease with the length of a firm's transactions (operating cycle).

Based on data from commercial, service and manufacturing industries we examine the accrual- and cash-flow-based performance measures' ability to measure a firm's earnings capacity for different length of operating cycles. In this context an operating cycle is defined as the number of days it takes from the purchase of raw materials until the customer pays for the finished good. As an estimate for earnings capacity stock returns are used. The analysis is carried out in a two-step process. In the first step, each performance measure (accrual- and cash-flow-based performance measures, respectively) are correlated with stock returns for the same period. The correlation coefficient describes the individual performance measure's ability to gauge a firm's earnings capacity. In the second step, the correlation coefficient (i.e. the proxy for a firm's earnings capacity) of each performance measure is correlated with the length of the operating cycle. If the correlation coefficient from this test is close to zero and insignificant, the performance measure's ability to measure a firm's earnings capacity is not affected by the length of the operating cycle. However, if the correlation coefficient is negative (and significant) it indicates that the longer the operating cycle (in days), the poorer the performance measure's ability to gauge the earnings capacity of a firm. The correlation coefficients are presented in Table 3.5. As is clear from the table the correlation coefficient for net earnings is close to zero and insignificant. However, there is a significant negative correlation between the ability to measure the earnings capacity and the length of the operating cycle for the two cash-flow-based performance measures. That is, the longer the period from the purchase of raw materials and until the customer pays in cash, the worse the cash-flow-based performance measures ability to gauge the underlying economic performance.

Table 3.5 **The correlation between a firm's earnings capacity and the length of the operating cycle**

Net earnings	Cash flow from operations	Free cash flow
4%	−27%	−43%
(Insignificant)	(Significant at the 5% level)	(Significant at the 5% level)

A commonly overlooked problem with cash-flow-based performance measures is that they can be manipulated by management just as the accrual-based performance measures can be manipulated. For example, cash flows from operations increase if a firm sells some of its accounts receivable (factoring) or defer purchases of inventory. However, from an economic point of view, factoring may be expensive and a shortage of inventory may make customers look for alternative products. Cash flow from operations also increases by cuts in research and development activities or marketing expenses. Cash flow measured net of investments can be improved by postponing investments. Again, this may improve short-term cash flows at the expense of long-term earnings and cash flows. Cash-flow-based performance measures are, thus, in many respects like accrual-based performance measures not a perfect measure of a firm's earnings capacity. In the following section, we explore the information content of accrual- and cash-flow-based performance measures in greater detail.

The information content of accrual-based and cash-flow-based performance measures

As shown above, it is not possible to infer the performance measure which seems to be most suitable for measuring profitability for any given measurement period. A number of studies, however, have been designed to assess the information content of accrual-based as well as cash-flow-based performance measures; i.e. how useful they are in explaining the earnings capacity of a firm. If a performance measure is valuable to investors, it means that the performance measure is able to measure the entire earnings capacity, or portions thereof. In these studies the information content of accrual- and cash-flow-based performance measures are assessed as changes in investors' assessment of the probability distribution of future returns (measured by stock returns).

These studies can be divided into two groups. The first group considers accrual- and cash-flow-based performance measures as competing measures and examines which is best suited to measuring earnings capacity for a given period – typically one year. The second group considers accrual- and cash-flow-based performance measures as complementary performance measures, and examines whether the use of both performance measures simultaneously increases the ability to measure the earnings capacity as opposed to only using one of the two measures. Figure 3.3 illustrates some of the possible outcomes of such studies.

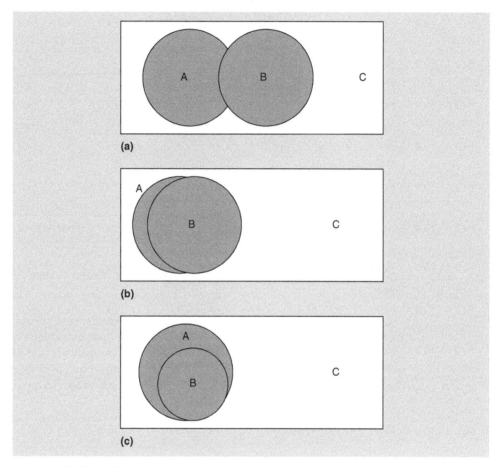

Figure 3.3 **The information content of accrual- and cash-flow-based performance measures. (A) Accrual-based performance measure. (B) Cash-flow-based performance measure. (C) The market's total set of information**

The rectangular boxes labelled C in Figure 3.3 represent the total information available on the market at any given time. In Figure 3.3(a) both types of performance measures are equally informative and the information content is increased by using both of them. Figure 3.3(b) shows a case where both measures are equally informative, but where information content is not increased by using both of them. Finally, Figure 3.3(c) shows a case where the accrual-based performance measure is relatively more informative than the cash-flow-based performance measure and the value of information does not increase by using the cash-flow-based performance measure together with the accrual-based performance measure.

The investigation shows that accrual-based performance measures is better at measuring the earnings capacity of a firm (see Dechow (1994), Ali and Pope (1995) and

Plenborg (1999)). In Figure 3.4 we show some of the results from these studies. As illustrated in the figure, net earnings are able to explain about 11% of the price movements within a year, while operating cash flows are only able to explain about 4%. In the same measurement period, there is no correlation between stock returns and the free cash flow. These results support that accrual-based performance measures gauge earnings capacity better than the cash-flow-based performance measures.

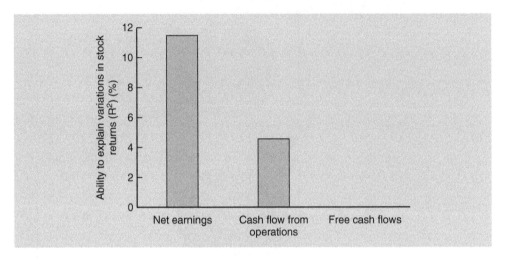

Figure 3.4 The information content of performance measures (measurement period: 1 year)

Generally, it is expected that the longer the measurement period, the better the accrual- and cash-flow-based performance measures are at explaining a firm's earnings capacity. This is due to the fact that more transactions are completed within the measurement period. In Figure 3.5, the above findings have been reproduced with a change to the measurement period, which has been adjusted to four years. As shown,

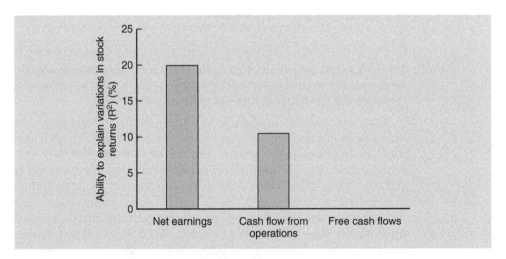

Figure 3.5 The information content of performance measures (measurement period: four years)

the performance measures net earnings and operating cash flow improve the ability to measure a firm's earnings capacity. However, there is no correlation between stock returns and free cash flows over a four-year measurement period. This suggests that the measurement window should be expanded significantly until the free cash flow measure is able to gauge a firm's earnings capacity. This finding is elaborated on when we discuss firm valuation in Chapter 9.

The empirical results support the illustration in Figure 3.3(c). The findings also contradict the cash flow proponents, who suggest that cash-flow-based performance measures are superior at explaining a firm's earnings capacity compared to accrual-based performance measures.

Based on the empirical results it cannot be ruled out that cash-flow-based performance measures contain information on important aspects of a firm's earnings capacity not included in accrual-based performance measures. As mentioned above standard-setting bodies find that the cash flow statement contains important information about long- and short-term liquidity risk. Empirical studies (see for example Livnat and Zarowin (1990), Plenborg (1999) and Charitou et al. (2000)) support this assumption. They find that cash flows are useful together with the accrual-based performance measures. These results support the illustration in Figure 3.3(a).

The above empirical findings indicate that while cash flows are less informative than accrual-based performance measures they do provide useful information for the analyst. Below we move on to discuss areas where reported cash flow numbers are expected to be useful in financial statement analysis:

1 Assessment of earnings quality
2 Assessment of financial flexibility
3 Assessment of short- and long-term liquidity risk.

Assessment of earnings quality

Accounting earnings are characterised by a greater degree of subjectivity than cash flows. This means that in some cases analysts may doubt the credibility of reported figures. By comparison, there is a greater degree of credibility to reported cash flow numbers. Over a longer period of time, there should be a closer association between accumulated accounting profit and cumulative cash flow. If it is not possible to identify this association, analysts must question the quality of the reported accounting figures. In Chapter 13 the method is discussed in further detail.

Assessment of financial flexibility

Cash flow statements are also useful for assessing a company's financial flexibility. Questions that can be answered by analysing the cash flow statement include (a) whether a company generates sufficient cash to finance its growth or whether it needs additional capital and (b) what sources of financing (debt or equity) that a company relies on when additional capital is needed.

Assessment of short- and long-term liquidity risk

Cash flow statements are often used as input for calculation of financial ratios used to assessing short- and long-term liquidity risk. Analysts can also choose to forecast future cash flows in order to assess the short- and long-term liquidity risk. Financial ratios and forecasting of future cash flows are discussed in greater details in subsequent chapters.

Approximations to cash flows

In recent years it has become popular to focus on accounting concepts such as EBITDA (earnings before interest, taxes, depreciation and amortisation) and EBITA (earnings before interest, taxes and amortisation) when making a credit rating or a firm valuation. For example, the multiple EV/EBITDA is often used to valuing companies. The rationale for the use of EBITDA and EBITA is that both accounting measures are believed to be closer to a firm's cash flows from operations than for instance net earnings. At the same time as a result of not including depreciation (and amortisation), differences in depreciation policies do not affect the performance measure. The same is true with regard to tax. By excluding tax analysts avoid the impact of estimates related to deferred tax. In conclusion, concepts like EBITDA and EBITA are used in an attempt to eliminate differences in accounting policies between companies and across national borders.

Using EBITDA as a measure of cash flow is, however, problematic. First, it is difficult to justify that a significant portion of a firm's costs is excluded from operations. Depreciation is a proxy for the use of resources (e.g. property, plant and equipment) that is needed in generating earnings. Thus, EBITDA includes the benefits (revenue) from those resources but excludes the related costs.

Second, if EBITDA is used as a performance measure it will be difficult to compare businesses which grow organically and businesses which are growing through acquisitions. For example, businesses that generate goodwill internally must expense those goodwill outlays due to measurement problems. Companies which acquire other businesses or activities, on the other hand, must capitalise goodwill, while the consumption of goodwill (goodwill impairment losses) is not recognised in EBITDA.

Third, there has been a change in accounting regulation from expensing investment in intangible assets to the capitalisation of intangible assets. For example, development costs, as a general rule, must be capitalised. Previously, this accounting item was expensed as incurred. This also implies that development costs, which used to be included in EBITDA, are now excluded. A further problem in this context is that some companies fail to capitalise development costs. The following example of Novo Nordisk, which is a healthcare company and a world leader in diabetes care, illustrates this. The extract is taken from Novo Nordisk's Annual Report (note 1 – summary of significant accounting policies).

Research and development

Due to the long development period and significant uncertainties relating to the development of new products, including risks regarding clinical trials and regulatory approval, it is concluded that the Group's internal development costs in general do not meet the capitalisation criteria in IAS 38 'Intangible Assets'. Consequently, the technical feasibility criteria of IAS 38 are not considered fulfilled before regulatory approval is obtained. Therefore, all internal research and development costs are expensed in the Income statement as incurred.

Novo Nordisk chooses to expense development costs using the argument that the group's development costs do not meet the requirements for capitalisation. When analysts compare EBITDA across firms, which treat development costs differently, they face the risk of drawing wrong conclusions; unless these differences are adjusted for. Examples of wrong conclusions are misleading credit ratings or share price estimates.

Finally, even if it were possible to take into account the above points, EBITDA and EBITA are far from ideal cash flow measures. Neither of the two measures account for investments in non-current assets nor for investments in working capital. Furthermore, they do not take into account non-cash items included in operating earnings such as provisions relating to restructuring, etc.

This shows that you should be cautious in applying approximations to cash flow measures such as EBITDA and EBITA. It seems more natural to use real cash flow measures; especially bearing in mind that these must be reported by companies.

Conclusions

There has been much debate about the use of accrual- and cash-flow-based performance measures as proxies for a firm's earnings capacity within a given period. Despite the fact that accrual-based performance measures are historically oriented and prone to manipulation, they seem to be better at measuring value creation in a given period than cash-flow-based performance measures.

However, you should also bear in mind that cash flows offer value relevant information in addition to the information contained in reported accrual-based earnings measures. For example, cash-flow-based performance measures are often used in determining the short- and long-term liquidity risk, the assessment of accounting quality and financial flexibility. Some of these aspects will be further elucidated in subsequent chapters.

Review questions

- What is the distinction between accrual-based and cash-flow-based performance measures?

- What are the most important subtotals from the income statement?

- What are the most important subtotals from the cash flow statement?

- How is shareholder value added measured?

- What is the distinction between a multi-period and a single-period performance measure?

- What are the advantages and disadvantages of accrual-based and cash-flow-based performance measures?

- Do the cash-flow-based performance measures appear more useful than accrual-based performance measures?

- In which analytical settings does the cash flow appear useful?

- Is EBITDA a useful proxy of cash flow from operation?

References

Ali, A. and P. Pope (1995) 'The incremental information content of earnings, working capital from operations, and cash flows: The UK evidence', *Journal of Business, Finance and Accounting*, Vol. 22, 19–34.

Charitou, A., C. Clubb and A. Andreou (2000) 'The value relevance of earnings and cash flows: Empirical evidence for Japan', *Journal of International Financial Management and Accounting*, Vol. 11, No. 1, Spring, 1–22.

Dechow, P. (1994) 'Accounting earnings and cash flow as measures of firm performance: The role of accounting accruals', *Journal of Accounting and Economics*, Vol. 18, 3–42.

Ijiri, Y. (1978) 'Cash flow accounting and its structure', *Journal of Accounting, Auditing and Finance*, Summer, 331–48.

Lawson, G.H. (1985) 'The measurement of corporate performance on a cash flow basis: A reply to Mr. Egginton', *Accounting and Business Research*, Spring, 99–108.

Lee, T.A. (1985) 'Cash flow accounting, profit and performance measurement: A response to a challenge', *Accounting and Business Research*, Spring, 93–7.

Livnat, J. and P. Zarowin (1990) 'The incremental information content of cash flow components', *Journal of Accounting and Economics*, Vol. 13, 25–46.

Plenborg, T. (1999) 'An examination of the information content of Danish earnings and cash flows', *Accounting and Business Research*, Vol. 30, No. 1, 43–55.

Sloan, R. (1996) 'Do stock prices reflect information in accruals and cash flows about future earnings', *Accounting Review*, Vol. 71, No. 3, 289–315.

PART 2

Financial analysis

Introduction to Part 2

Introduction to Part 2

The previous chapters outlined the information available in the annual reports. Chapters 4 to 7 discuss how a firm's financial performance and position can be analysed using a number of different financial ratios.

Chapter 4 describes how the income statement and balance sheet can be reformulated for analytical purposes. Chapter 5 presents financial ratios which illustrate a firm's profitability. Chapter 6 discusses different methods for measuring growth. Chapter 7 focuses on short- and long-term liquidity risk.

Introduction to financial ratio analysis

Financial ratio analysis is a useful tool for mapping a firm's economic well-being, and uncovering different aspects of its performance and financial position, for example:

- Profitability
- Growth
- Risk.

The primary tool for evaluating a firm's financial health is the calculation of a variety of financial ratios, which are important *indicators of* a firm's financial performance. Financial ratios help you to identify areas that may require additional analysis. A financial ratio analysis enables you to compare a firm's financial ratios:

- Across multiple periods (time-series analysis)
- Across firms within the same industry (cross-sectional analysis, benchmarking)
- With the proper required rate of return (e.g. WACC).

Financial ratios describe the level and trend in a firm's profitability, growth and risk. It is therefore possible to evaluate if there is a positive trend in profitability as a consequence of, for example, an improved profit margin.

In financial statement analysis a time-series analysis or a cross-sectional analysis is usually employed. In a time-series analysis the efficiency of a firm's strategy across time can be measured. Time-series analysis is an important tool in forecasting as the historical levels and trends in financial ratios (value drivers) are used as input to forecasting.

The purpose of cross-sectional analysis is to examine the relative performance of a firm within an industry. Cross-sectional analysis is used as inspirational analysis in examining operating performance. Valuable information can be found by analysing the most profitable firms within an industry. Gathering information from competitors in order to identify 'best practice' in the industry may prove beneficial.

An alternative way to benchmark is to compare financial ratios with the appropriate required rate of return. Obvious examples include return on invested capital (ROIC) and return on equity (ROE). For both of these ratios it is possible to estimate a required rate of return from primary financial data. If a firm generates returns in excess of the required rate of return, it achieves above normal profit (economic profit). This is illustrated below by benchmarking return on invested capital (ROIC) with the weighted average cost of capital (WACC) and return on equity (ROE) with investors' required rate of return (r_e), respectively:

Excess return $= (\text{ROIC} - \text{WACC}) \times \text{Invested capital}$

Excess return $= (\text{ROE} - r_e) \times \text{Shareholders' equity}$

where

$\text{ROIC} = \text{Return on invested capital}$

$\text{ROE} = \text{Return on equity}$

$\text{WACC} = \text{Weighted average cost of capital (Company's required return)}$

$r_e = \text{Investors' required rate of return}$

Some consulting firms provide advice on using these financial ratios. Stern Stewart uses the term 'Economic Value Added' (EVA™), while the Boston Consulting Group labels it 'Economic Profit' (EP). Both concepts are equivalent to excess return.

Pitfalls in financial ratio analysis

A major premise in a time-series and cross-sectional analysis is that financial ratios provide signals and pieces of information that the decision maker can act upon. Consequently, it is important that information obtained from these financial ratios do not contain 'noise' that is that they faithfully represent a firm's underlying performance. Sources of noise should be controlled prior to calculating and analysing financial data and ratios since not doing so could lead to misinterpretations and false conclusions. The following table lists sources of noise that should be considered when carrying out time-series and cross-sectional analyses, respectively.

Sources of noise in time-series and cross-sectional analysis

Time-series analysis	Cross-sectional analysis
1 Different accounting policies across time	1 Different accounting policies across firms
2 Special and unusual items	2 Special and unusual items
3 Acquisitions and disposing of lines of business, SBUs etc.	3 Comparison of different types of firms (differences in risk)
4 New products/markets (change in risk profile)	4 Different definitions of financial ratios across firms

The purpose of a time-series analysis is to analyse the level and trend in a firm's operating performance. It is, therefore, important to eliminate any noise in the signals from the time-series analysis.

Accounting policies over time

One source of noise is the impact of changes in accounting policies. In analysing key financial ratios, it is important to separate the effect of changes in accounting policies from changes in the underlying operations across time.

Impact of special and unusual items

A second source of noise is the impact of special and unusual items on performance. A key issue is whether to include or exclude special and unusual items from the analysis. As pointed out earlier, this depends upon the purpose of the analysis. For example, if the objective of the analysis is to forecast financial statements, those items are likely to be excluded in calculating financial ratios, while in assessing management's performance (in the past) they are more likely to be included.

Acquisition and disposal of business units

A third source of noise in a time-series analysis is the impact of acquisitions and disposal of business units on financial ratios. In the case that a firm has changed its operational characteristics in the analysed period, financial ratios may have limited relevance if compared across time. For instance, if a firm has acquired a new line of business with another risk profile than the existing business, changes in profitability may be due to the acquired business segment and/or changes in the original business, which reduces the information content of the financial ratios considerably. For example, consider that the risk in the new line of business is much higher than in the existing business, the required rate of return would therefore be higher.

Change in underling risk

A similar type of noise in a time-series analysis is the impact of an introduction of new products, or introduction of existing products on new markets, on financial ratios. Carlsberg's operation in Eastern Europe may increase profitability, but the focus on markets in Eastern Europe may also increase total risk in Carlsberg, as investments take place in countries with less political stability (for instance Russia). Thus, if the risk profile of the company has changed over time it is necessary to adjust the required rate of return accordingly.

Peer group companies

Cross-sectional analyses involve many of the same considerations. In comparing financial ratios across firms, it is important that financial statements are based on the same accounting policies and special and unusual items must be treated uniformly across firms. A further requirement in cross-sectional analyses is that firms that are benchmarked are comparable. A cross-sectional analysis of Carlsberg, therefore, should be based on comparing Carlsberg with other breweries and not with firms from other industries. If Carlsberg is compared with firms from other industries, with a different risk profile, a comparison of the firms' return on invested capital (ROIC), or similar performance measures, will not be appropriate. Alternative interpretations will reduce the relevance of financial ratios. It should be pointed out that even within the same industry the risk can be quite different across firms; for instance, if they operate on different markets.

Different terminology of financial ratios

An additional source of noise in cross-sectional studies is that firms may define financial ratios differently. As illustrated in subsequent chapters, the same financial ratio may be calculated differently, as there are no uniform definitions of financial ratios. If a financial ratio from two comparable firms has been defined differently, they might have different interpretations, which reduces the value of the information inherent in the key ratio. This issue is often problematic in using financial ratios from industry reports and databases, where definitions are not made public.

Requirements for financial ratio analysis

In order to analyse the trend in the financial ratios, data from the last three to seven years will be required. The length of the time period examined will be determined by:

- The availability of data
- The continuity in the analysed firm
- The length of a typical business cycle.

In deciding how long a period to include in the analysis, the analysts would ideally have access to data that covers an entire business cycle, but may be restricted to fewer data, for instance because the firm has only existed for a few years.

Over time growth, profitability and risk often vary substantially. To get a sense of those fluctuations and an assessment of the underlying level of profitability a longer time-series is needed; an entire business cycle is recommended as the historic analysis thereby covers upturns as well as downturns. This provides the analysts with valuable information about the analysed firm's ability to adapt to changes in the economic climate. It further prevents a wrong basis for forecasting. This point is illustrated in Figure P.2.1, where the example shows realised earnings and budgeted earnings for two hypothetical firms. If analysts or potential investors are not aware that firms have a business cycle, they risk forecasting earnings that are either too high (Company 1) or too low (Company 2).

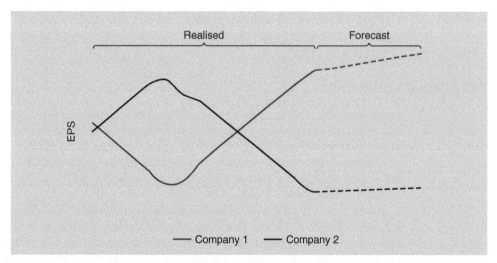

Figure P.2.1 **Example of two otherwise identical firms in different stages of a business cycle**

By studying the performance of a firm over a business cycle the analyst obtains useful information about the firm's ability to adapt to upturns as well as downturns. Furthermore, it gives some insights as to where in the business cycle the firm is currently located. If analysts ignore these aspects they may draw incorrect conclusions as to the earnings potential of the firm being analysed.

A short time-series may prove more useful in cases where the structure of the firm has changed significantly. A spin-off of a business unit or the acquisition of a new business unit may imply that historical accounting data are of limited use. Sometimes financial information is only available for a few years. For start-up firms with no or little history, financial ratios can be calculated for a short time period only; as financial information may not be avaliable.

In the following chapters a number of financial ratios, which illustrate a firm's growth, profitability and risk, are presented. An important premise in Chapters 4 to 7 is that data quality, including accounting policies, is not questioned. Thus, the examples are based on raw, unadjusted accounting figures. Assessment of the quality of financial data is an issue that is dealt with separately in Chapters 13 to 15.

CHAPTER 4

The analytical income statement and balance sheet

Learning outcomes

After reading this chapter you should be able to:

- Understand that operations is the primary driving force behind the value creation in a firm
- Separate operating income and expenses from financial income and expenses
- Make a distinction between operating and financial assets and liabilities
- Prepare an income statement and balance sheet for analytical purposes
- Define and measure net operating profit after tax (NOPAT) and invested capital, respectively

The analytical income statement and balance sheet

A firm consists of operating, investing and financing activities. When you calculate financial ratios to measure a firm's profitability, it is beneficial to separate 'operations' and 'investments in operations' from financing activities. For example, property, plant and equipment and inventory are *operating items*, while bank loans and equity are *financing items*.

The reason why operating items should be separated from financing items is that the company's operations is the primary driving force behind value creation and therefore important to isolate. Furthermore, a company's operation is what makes the company unique and difficult to 'copy', whereas the financial composition is much easier to replicate. Financial items, on the other hand, convey how operations (including investments in operations) are financed. In financial statements, the distinction between operating items and financial items is not always easy to see due to several factors:

- The definition of operations is not clear-cut
- The classification of items in the income statement and the balance sheet do not clearly distinguish between operating and financing items
- The notes are not sufficiently informative.

To determine which activities to include in operations depends on the business model and the characteristics of the firm. Items that are sometimes categorised as belonging to 'operations' may at other times be classified as belonging to 'financing'. Example 4.1 illustrates this issue.

Example 4.1   The NTR Group, a listed company at OMX NASDAQ, stated in their annual report for year 1 that the associated firm Bahrain Precast Concrete (BPC) was outside the group's focus. This indicates that the associated company might be divested in the future. It is, thus, relevant to discuss whether the ownership interest should be classified as part of financial assets. If so the share of profit from BPC shall be reclassified as part of financial income and the investments in BPC as a financing activity.

In the following period the NTR Group undergoes significant changes with disposal of nearly all its core lines of businesses.

In the annual report for year 5, the chairman of the board of directors stated that:

Over the last few years, the NTR group has implemented a number of adjustments, dispos-ing of various activities to focus on one single, clearly defined business area. The board of directors is gratified to find that this aim has now been achieved, and NTR will in future concentrate on developing and extending the precast concrete panel activities in the coun-tries around the Arabian Gulf. The respective countries are still seeing substantial growth, and by virtue of heavy oil and gas reserves this growth would seem secured for many years hence. For a number of years, the group results have been adversely affected by the dis-continuation of the previous contractor activities in Germany. The winding up has not yet been finished but this year did carry us a solid step in the right direction and through the adjustments of the group, NTR has secured a good basis for continuing and completing the winding up . . .

Within a period of five years, the associated firm (BPC) in the Middle East has changed status from being outside the scope of NTR's core business to become the group's only core busi-ness. There is no doubt that today the associated company BPC Group is the primary activity in the NTR Group. ■

As noted in Chapter 2, IAS 1 does not require a detailed income statement; only a few items must be included. In most cases, however, the income statement pro-vided by companies is fairly detailed. Carlsberg, as shown in Table 4.1, is a case in point. If a comparison is made between Carlsberg's income statement and the mini-mum requirement as laid out in IAS 1, it is obvious that Carlsberg provides a much more detailed income statement. It includes subtotals such as gross profit and operat-ing profit and also provides information on 'special items'.

As shown in Chapter 2, an entity must normally present a classified balance sheet, separating current assets and liabilities from non-current assets and liabilities. The current/non-current split may only be disregarded if a presentation based on liquidity provides information that is reliable and more relevant. In either case, notes that sepa-rate the non-current assets and liabilities (above 12 months) from the current assets and liabilities (maximum 12 months) are required.

Current assets include cash, cash equivalents, accounts receivable and inventories. All other assets are non-current. Examples include property, plant and equipment.

Current liabilities are to be settled within the enterprise's normal operating cycle, or which are due within 12 months, those held for trading, and those for which the entity does not have an unconditional right to defer payment beyond 12 months. Other liabilities are non-current. Examples include borrowings and provisions.

In the balance sheet non-current assets are classified separately from current assets and non-current liabilities are separated from current liabilities. Thus, the balance

Table 4.1 Carlsberg Group's consolidated income statement

Income statement (DKKm)	Year 7	Year 8
Revenue	60,111	76,557
Excise duties on beer and soft drinks etc.	−15,361	−16,613
Net revenue	**44,750**	**59,944**
Cost of sales	−22,423	−31,248
Gross profit	**22,327**	**28,696**
Sales and distribution costs	−14,528	−17,592
Administrative expenses	−3,123	−3,934
Other operating income	933	1,178
Other operating expenses	−448	−450
Share of profit after tax, associates	101	81
Operating profit before special items	**5,262**	**7,979**
Special items, income	0	0
Special items, costs	−427	−1,641
Operating profit	**4,835**	**6,338**
Financial income	651	1,310
Financial expenses	−1,852	−4,766
Profit before tax	**3,634**	**2,882**
Corporation tax	−1,038	324
Consolidated profit	**2,596**	**3,206**

sheet does not specifically distinguish between operating assets and financial assets nor does it separate operating liabilities from financial liabilities. To illustrate this point, Carlsberg's balance sheet is shown in Table 4.2. Carlsberg's non-current assets, current assets, non-current liabilities and current liabilities may all contain operating as well as financing items. For example, current liabilities include operating (e.g. trade payables) as well as financing activities (e.g. borrowings).

The analytical income statement

The **analytical income statement** requires every accounting item to be classified as belonging to either 'operations' or 'finance'. The purpose of dividing the accounting items in this way is to obtain a better knowledge of the different sources of value creation in a firm. For example, investors consider operating profit as the primary source of value creation and in most cases they value operations separately from finance activities. Lenders consider operating profit as the primary source to support servicing of debt. Thus, analysts spend time on reformulating the income statement and balance

Table 4.2 Carlsberg Group's balance sheet

Assets (DKKm)	Year 7	Year 8
Non-current assets		
Intangible assets	21,205	84,678
Property, plant and equipment	22,109	34,043
Investments in associates	622	2,224
Securities	123	118
Receivables	1,476	1,707
Deferred tax assets	733	1,254
Retirement benefit plan assets	11	2
Total non-current assets	**46,279**	**124,026**
Current assets		
Inventories	3,818	5,317
Trade receivables	6,341	6,369
Tax receivables	62	262
Other receivables	1,453	3,095
Prepayments	950	1,211
Securities	34	7
Cash and cash equivalents	2,249	2,857
Receivables from associates		
Total current assets	**14,907**	**19,118**
Assets held for sale	34	162
Total assets	**61,220**	**143,306**
Equity and liabilities (DKKm)		
Equity		
Share capital	1,526	3,051
Reserves	17,095	52,470
Equity, shareholders in Carlsberg A/S	**18,621**	**55,521**
Minority interests	1,323	5,230
Total equity	**19,944**	**60,751**

▶

Table 4.2 (*continued*)

Equity and liabilities (DKKm)	Year 7	Year 8
Non-current liabilities		
Borrowings	19,385	43,230
Retirement benefit obligations	2,220	1,793
Deferred tax liabilities	2,191	9,803
Provisions	249	1,498
Other liabilities	20	263
Total non-current liabilities	**24,065**	**56,587**
Current liabilities		
Borrowings	3,869	5,291
Borrowings from associates		
Trade payables	5,833	7,993
Deposits on returnable packaging	1,207	1,455
Provisions	494	677
Corporation tax	197	279
Other liabilities etc.	5,611	9,905
Total current liabilities	**17,211**	**25,600**
Liabilities, assets held for sale		368
Total liabilities	**41,276**	**82,555**
Total equity and liabilities	**61,220**	**143,306**

sheet so that they reflect the contribution from operating and financing activities, respectively. This idea is illustrated in Table 4.3. The financial data in the tabulation is also used in Chapter 2 (see page 43) and the analytical income statement and balance sheet can be followed all the way back to the bookkeeping transactions shown there.

Table 4.3

Income statement	
Revenues	200
Operating expenses	−90
Earnings before interest and taxes (EBIT)	**110**
Financial income	5
Financial expenses	−15
Earnings before tax (EBT)	**100**
Corporation tax	−30
Net earnings	**70**

Operating earnings is a key performance measure, as it shows a firm's profit from its core business regardless of how it has been financed. Generally, operating earnings can be measured both before and after tax. While earnings before interest and tax (EBIT) measures operating profit before tax, **net operating profit after tax (NOPAT)** is an after tax measure.

While EBIT is reported in the example, NOPAT is not disclosed. This implies that the analyst has to deduct tax on EBIT to obtain NOPAT. Since reported tax is positively affected by net financial expenses (i.e. a firm pays less in taxes as financial expenses are tax deductible) it is necessary to add back the tax advantage that the net financial expenses offer (tax shield). This is highlighted in Table 4.4. The effective corporate tax rate is calculated as

$$\text{Tax rate} = \frac{\text{Corporation tax} \times 100}{\text{Earnings before tax}} = 30 \times \frac{100}{100} = 30\%$$

Table 4.4

Effective corporate tax rate, t	30.0%
Revenues	200
Operating expenses	−90
EBIT	**110**
Taxes on EBIT	−33
NOPAT	**77**
Net financial expenses	−10
Tax savings from debt financing	3
Net financial expenses after tax	**−7**
Net earnings (operating earnings after tax + net financial expenses after tax)	**70**

As illustrated in the example, tax savings from net financial expenses amounts to 3 (tax rate × net financial expenses). Thus, taxes on EBIT equal 33 (30 + 3). Alternatively, tax on operating earnings can be calculated as 110 × 30% = 33.

The analytical balance sheet

In order to match the items in the analytical income statement with the related items in the **analytical balance sheet**, items marked as operating ('O') and financing ('F') activities, in the income statement, must be marked the same way in the balance sheet. For example, if earnings from 'share of profit of associates' are labelled as 'operations' in the income statement the matching item 'investments in associates' in the balance sheet must also be classified as an operating activity.

The combined investment in a company's operating activities is denoted 'invested capital' or 'net operating assets' and equals the sum of operating assets minus operating liabilities. Operating liabilities such as trade payables reduce the need for (interest-bearing) debt and are therefore deducted from operating assets. **Invested capital** is defined as follows:

Invested capital represents the amount a firm has invested in its operating activities and which requires a return.

The calculation of invested capital is illustrated in Table 4.5. You can see from the example that the accounting item 'cash and cash equivalents' is treated as finance, while the remaining assets are considered as operating assets. Furthermore, 'accounts

Table 4.5

Assets (average figures)		Type
Intangible and tangible assets	268	O
Total non-current assets	268	
Inventories	325	O
Accounts receivables	57	O
Cash and cash equivalents	50	F
Total current assets	432	
Total assets	**700**	
Equity and liabilities (average figures)		
Equity	400	F
Loans and borrowings	100	F
Total non-current liabilities	100	
Loans and borrowings	100	F
Tax payable	15	O
Accounts payable	85	O
Total current liabilities	200	
Total equity and liabilities	**700**	
Invested capital		
Total assets	700	
Cash and cash equivalents	−50	
Accounts payables and tax payable	−100	
Invested capital (net operating assets)	**550**	
Invested capital		
Equity	400	
Loans and borrowings (non-current)	100	
Loans and borrowings (current)	100	
Cash and cash equivalents	−50	
Interest-bearing debt, net	150	
Invested capital (financing)	**550**	

Note: O = operations, F = financing

payable' and 'tax payable' are operating liabilities that are considered as 'interest free loans', which can be subtracted from the operating assets. The deduction of operating liabilities from operating assets envision that the need for financing is reduced; the higher the amount of operating liabilities the less a firm needs to borrow to finance its activities. This is also reflected when examining the two sources used to financing invested capital. Only shareholders equity and (net) interest-bearing debt are included as financing items – both sources of financing that require a return. In summary, invested capital may either be regarded as net operating assets or funds used to finance operations, which is the sum of equity and net interest-bearing debt.

Classification of accounting items when defining invested capital

While the majority of accounting items are easily classified as either being part of operations or part of financing, a number of accounting items need to be carefully considered before you can decide whether they belong to operations or finance. Those items include:

- Special items
- Tax on ordinary activities
- Investment in associates and related income and expenses from associates
- Receivables and payables to group enterprises and associated firms
- Cash and cash equivalents
- Prepayment and financial income as part of core operation
- Exchange rate differences
- Derivative financial instruments
- Minority interests
- Retirement benefits
- Tax payable.

In practice, a number of different accounting items fall within the categories just listed. However, at the same time, similar deliberations can be applied to other accounting items not included in the list.

We will now look at the accounting items individually and discuss the classification issues below.

Special items (other income and expenses)

This accounting item includes activities that are indirectly part of a firm's core business. A study of accounting practices shows that special items typically contain a number of different sources of income and expenses including:

- Gains and losses from sale of non-current assets
- Royalty/licence income
- Restructuring costs
- Rent income and expenses from property (lease income and expenses)
- Write-down (impairment) of assets
- Other (unspecified).

From an analytical point of view special items raise two fundamental issues. First, it must be decided whether an item should be categorised as part of operations or finance. In most cases, we believe, special items should be categorised under operations. However, there are examples where special items should be treated as a financing activity. For example, if property is not regarded as part of a firm's core business, it could be argued that an alternative to investing in this property is to invest in securities, in which case the accounting item 'lease income' should be classified as a financing activity.

Second, the analyst must decide whether the accounting item is unusual or if it is part of the firm's normal operations. Analysts should ask themselves if, for example, gains of disposal of assets and restructuring costs are a necessary part of a firm's day-to-day operations. It's hard to imagine that a firm does not have to adjust its organisation to changing market conditions, general upturns and downturns etc. This explains why restructuring costs must be expected to recur frequently; although not necessarily every year. From this point of view it seems reasonable to classify (most) 'special items' as part of core operation. This issue is discussed further in Chapter 13.

Tax on ordinary activities (operating profit)

The accounting item corporation tax (income tax expense) relates to operating as well as financing items. Since accounting practice does not distinguish between tax on operations and tax on financial items, there is a need to divide income tax expenses into tax on operations and tax on financing. This segregation may be accomplished by estimating the tax shield from net financial expenses. Tax benefits from net financial expenses can be calculated as follows:

$$\text{Tax benefits (shield)} = \text{Net financial expenses} \times \text{Corporate tax rate}$$

In determining the tax shield the analyst has to decide whether to use the marginal tax rate or the effective tax rate as a proxy for the corporate tax rate. Since the tax shield is based on the marginal tax rate it is tempting to suggest the marginal tax rate. However, borrowing in a subsidiary in a foreign country with a different local tax rate will affect the value of the tax shield. In this case it may be relevant to use the local marginal tax rate on the part of debt belonging to the foreign subsidiary. Information about debt in foreign entities is hardly ever available for outsiders (analysts) and the analysts have to accept the inaccuracy by using the home country's corporate tax rate. Alternatively the effective tax rate may be used. It expresses the average tax rate levied on all income in the firm and reflects different tax rates within the group. Therefore, if the effective tax rate is used the analyst assumes that operating income as well as financial income are taxed by the same rate.

Investment in associates and related income and expenses from associates

If investments in associates are regarded as part of a firm's core business, the related income and expenses should be included in operating income. Furthermore, investments in associates should be included in invested capital. This may be the case if, for example, the associated company is a subcontractor or a sales unit that sells the group's products. To the contrary, if an investment in an associate is not regarded as a part of the core business, it should be considered as a financial item (excess cash not needed to operate the firm) and it should be subtracted in calculating net interest-bearing debt.

Receivables and payables to group enterprises and associated firms

Loans provided by associated firms are often interest-bearing and should be classified as part of financing activities. However, if debt is part of usual intercompany trading, the accounting item should be classified as capital invested in operations.

Cash and cash equivalents

Cash and cash equivalents are often considered as excess cash, which in reality can either be paid out as dividends, used to buy back own shares, or used to repay debt without affecting the underlying operations. Reported cash (and cash equivalents), however, may include cash that is needed in day-to-day operations (i.e. operating cash). Thus, cash can be separated into operating cash and excess cash. Cash and cash equivalents reported in firms' balance sheets do not distinguish between operating cash and excess cash. In practice, different rules of thumbs are used to estimate operating cash. However, it must be acknowledged that these rules lead to imprecise and vast different results. The analysts must rely on their own knowledge, and on any additional information supplied by the firm in question, to estimate operating cash in practice.

We argue that the consequences of reclassification of operating cash are likely to be modest in most cases. If the cash position remains stable across time it seems fair to treat cash and cash equivalents as excess cash.

Prepayment and financial income as part of core operation

Some firms like insurance companies and travel agents are characterised by receiving prepayment for their services. Likewise, their products are priced to reflect the return on the prepaid cash. Their ability to earn a return on prepayments is an important element in assessing operations of such companies.

Some firms within trade, service and manufacturing use a similar model. As part of their business model they receive large prepayments. Since the 'cost' of prepayment (if any) is already reflected in the reported operating profit (through lower margins) we classify prepayment as an operating liability. In addition, we consider reclassifying financial income (if any) from prepayment as part of operating income. However, typically prepayment will be tied up in inventories and operating expenses.

In a similar vein, in the car industry cheap loans are offered to customers supporting the sale of their products. Since these loans are offered to stimulate sales it seems reasonable to classify these receivables as part of invested capital and the related interest income as part of operating profit, given that it is a part of their core and ongoing business model.

Exchange rate differences

IAS 21 'The Effects of Changes in Foreign Exchange Rates' states that:

> *Exchange differences arising on the settlement of monetary items or on translating monetary items at rates different from those at which they were translated on initial recognition during the period or in previous financial statements shall be recognised in profit or loss in the period in which they arise.*

Exchange rate differences are mostly recognised in the income statement as part of financial income and expenses. Since exchange rate differences are related to both operating and financing activities it could be argued that exchange rate differences should be separated into an operating and a financial component, respectively. Exchange rate differences from operations are not reported separately from exchange rate differences related to finance, which makes it difficult to make such a distinction.

If a firm faces a currency risk it may choose to hedge the risk using financial instruments. Alternatively, the firm may choose not to hedge the currency risk. In this case, the firm 'net' that the underlying exchange rate is moving in a favourable direction from the time of the transaction and until the date of the payment. Whether a firm hedges the currency risk depends upon its financial policies. In this light it seems reasonable to classify exchange rate gains and losses as a finance activity. As exchange rate gains and losses are already classified as financial items, there is no need to make reclassifications.

Derivative financial instruments

A further issue related to financial items is gains – and losses on derivative financial instruments. Derivative financial instruments are used to hedge financial risks including exchange rate risks, as noted above, and interest rate risks. Derivatives are measured at cost at first recognition. Subsequently, they are measured at fair value, and value adjustments are primarily recognised in the income statement. (An exception is hedge accounting (IAS 39 'Financial Instruments: Recognition and Measurement'). IAS 39.46 lists the exceptions to using fair value as the measurement attribute.)

Often gains and losses from financial instruments (derivatives and debt instruments) are tied to hedging of financial risks. Hedging of operating risks may occur by, for example, hedging price movements on raw materials or hedging of next year's sales revenues in foreign currencies. It's open to discussion whether gains and losses from using derivatives should be divided into operating- and finance-related hedges, respectively. Such a separation, however, is not recommended in practice. First, all operating and finance hedges are regarded as being financial decisions. For the same reason, gains and losses from derivatives should also be treated as part of financing activities. Second, the accounting item 'gains and losses from hedging financial instruments' hardly ever separate operating from financing activities, making it impossible to divide the item in practice.

Minority interests

Minority interests represent the investment in subsidiaries not fully owned by the parent company; that is the parent company owns less than 100% of the subsidiaries. Minority interests share of profit or loss is reported on an after tax basis.

Minority interests must be recognised in the group accounts in some form or another, as all assets and liabilities shall be recognised in full. From an analytical perspective it is not the question if the accounting item is linked to operations, but rather if minority interests should be included in interest-bearing debt or as a part of equity.

There are strong arguments in favour of treating minority interests as equity capital. In valuation of firms the required rate of return from minority interests will be different from the interest rate on debt, but likely to be close to the return required by the other investors. In credit analysis minority interests are ranked alongside investors in the parent company, and in case the firm goes bankrupt they will split the remaining cash (after debt has been repaid) with investors in the parent company. Thus, minority interests are treated as equity capital. This view is modified in Chapter 9.

Retirement benefits

For defined benefit plans an actuarial calculation is made of the present value of future benefits under such a plan. The present value is determined on the basis of assumptions about the future development in variables such as salary, interest rates, inflation and mortality. The actuarial present value less the fair value of any plan assets is recognised in the balance sheet. For example, if a firm's defined benefit plan is underfunded, the underfunded part must be recognised as a liability. Since recognised retirement benefits are interest bearing (discounted to present value) it seems reasonable to treat retirement benefits as a financing activity, i.e. as interest-bearing debt.

Tax payable

In the analytical example above, tax payable is regarded as an operating liability. Tax payable arises because a firm pays too little in tax on account (for example, because realised earnings are higher than expected) during the fiscal year. If the tax authorities impose an interest charge on tax payable, when tax payable should be regarded as a financial item.

Carlsberg's NOPAT and invested capital

In this section, Carlsberg Group's annual accounts for a six-year period are reformulated based on the above considerations. To help show this, Carlsberg Group's reported income statements and balance sheets for the period are shown in Table 4.6.

Table 4.6 **Carlsberg Group's income statements and balance sheets**

Income statement (DKKm)	Year 3	Year 4	Year 5	Year 6	Year 7	Year 8
Revenue	47,345	49,690	51,847	55,753	60,111	76,557
Excise duties on beer and soft drinks etc.	−12,719	−13,406	−13,800	−14,670	−15,361	−16,613
Net revenue	**34,626**	**36,284**	**38,047**	**41,083**	**44,750**	**59,944**
Cost of sales	−16,989	−18,065	−18,879	−20,151	−22,423	−31,248
Gross profit	**17,637**	**18,219**	**19,168**	**20,932**	**22,327**	**28,696**
Sales and distribution costs	−12,172	−12,833	−13,332	−14,173	−14,528	−17,592
Administrative expenses	−2,712	−2,807	−2,961	−3,065	−3,123	−3,934
Other operating income	575	612	876	660	933	1,178
Other operating expenses			−465	−393	−448	−450
Share of profit after tax, associates	236	210	232	85	101	81
Operating profit before special items	**3,564**	**3,401**	**3,518**	**4,046**	**5,262**	**7,979**
Special items, income	0	0	0	602	0	0
Special items, costs	−401	−598	−386	−762	−427	−1,641
Operating profit	**3,163**	**2,803**	**3,132**	**3,886**	**4,835**	**6,338**
Financial income	416	666	548	725	651	1,310
Financial expenses	−891	−1,818	−1,788	−1,582	−1,852	−4,766
Profit before tax	**2,688**	**1,651**	**1,892**	**3,029**	**3,634**	**2,882**
Corporation tax	−590	−382	−521	−858	−1,038	324
Consolidated profit	**2,098**	**1,269**	**1,371**	**2,171**	**2,596**	**3,206**

Table 4.6 (*continued*)

Assets (DKKm)	Year 3	Year 4	Year 5	Year 6	Year 7	Year 8
Non-current assets						
Intangible assets	5,661	19,489	20,672	21,279	21,205	84,678
Property, plant and equipment	19,131	20,435	20,355	20,367	22,109	34,043
Investments in associates	1,630	1,750	1,105	579	622	2,224
Securities	672	524	2,710	170	123	118
Receivables	2,136	1,290	1,235	1,139	1,476	1,707
Deferred tax assets	732	867	1,005	822	733	1,254
Retirement benefit plan assets	0	0	21	14	11	2
Total non-current assets	**29,962**	**44,355**	**47,103**	**44,370**	**46,279**	**124,026**
Current assets						
Inventories	2,675	2,883	2,866	3,220	3,818	5,317
Trade receivables	6,212	6,290	5,979	6,108	6,341	6,369
Tax receivables		82	132	84	62	262
Other receivables	1,751	1,370	3,015	1,145	1,453	3,095
Prepayments	620	610	587	917	950	1,211
Securities		71	109	8	34	7
Cash and cash equivalents	5,165	1,758	2,240	2,490	2,249	2,857
Receivables from associates	327					
Total current assets	**16,750**	**13,064**	**14,928**	**13,972**	**14,907**	**19,118**
Assets held for sale	0	279	328	109	34	162
Total assets	**46,712**	**57,698**	**62,359**	**58,451**	**61,220**	**143,306**
Equity and liabilities (DKKm)	Year 3	Year 4	Year 5	Year 6	Year 7	Year 8
Equity						
Share capital	1,278	1,526	1,526	1,526	1,526	3,051
Reserves	9,998	13,558	16,442	16,071	17,095	52,470
Equity, shareholders in Carlsberg A/S	**11,276**	**15,084**	**17,968**	**17,597**	**18,621**	**55,521**
Minority interests	6,630	1,708	1,528	1,390	1,323	5,230
Total equity	**17,906**	**16,792**	**19,496**	**18,987**	**19,944**	**60,751**
Non-current liabilities						
Borrowings	10,883	21,708	17,765	16,241	19,385	43,230
Retirement benefit obligations	600	1,889	2,061	2,006	2,220	1,793
Deferred tax liabilities	1,167	2,334	2,362	2,425	2,191	9,803

▶

Equity and liabilities (DKKm)	Year 3	Year 4	Year 5	Year 6	Year 7	Year 8
Provisions	360	189	195	366	249	1,498
Other liabilities	212	18	65	54	20	263
Total non-current liabilities	**13,222**	**26,138**	**22,448**	**21,092**	**24,065**	**56,587**
Current liabilities						
Borrowings	4,985	3,357	8,213	6,556	3,869	5,291
Borrowings from associates	14					
Trade payables	4,173	4,074	4,513	5,147	5,833	7,993
Deposits on returnable packaging	1,234	1,260	1,224	1,159	1,207	1,455
Provisions	141	481	561	466	494	677
Corporation tax	464	710	720	187	197	279
Other liabilities etc.	4,573	4,886	5,174	4,856	5,611	9,905
Total current liabilities	**15,584**	**14,768**	**20,405**	**18,371**	**17,211**	**25,600**
Liabilities, assets held for sale			10	1		368
Total liabilities	**28,806**	**40,906**	**42,863**	**39,464**	**41,276**	**82,555**
Total equity and liabilities	**46,712**	**57,698**	**62,359**	**58,451**	**61,220**	**143,306**

You can see from Table 4.6 that Carlsberg's classification of accounting items in the income statement and balance sheet, does to a large extent, separate operating items from financing items, but adjustments still need to be made. For example, total corporation tax relates to operating as well as financing activities. Also, provisions and other liabilities etc. may be classified as operating debt and/or interest-bearing debt depending on the actual content of those accounting items.

In Table 4.7 we have presented the reformulated income statement and balance sheet for Carlsberg Group are provided. The notes next to selected accounting items are references to the discussion that follows.

Table 4.7 Carlsberg Group's analytical income statement and balance sheet

Notes	Analytical income statement Income statement (DKKm)	Year 3	Year 4	Year 5	Year 6	Year 7	Year 8
	Revenue	47,345	49,690	51,847	55,753	60,111	76,557
	Excise duties on beer and soft drinks etc.	−12,719	−13,406	−13,800	−14,670	−15,361	−16,613
	Net revenue	**34,626**	**36,284**	**38,047**	**41,083**	**44,750**	**59,944**
1	Cost of sales	−15,527	−16,465	−17,218	−18,426	−20,787	−28,756
	Gross profit	**19,099**	**19,819**	**20,829**	**22,657**	**23,963**	**31,188**
1	Sales and distribution costs	−11,298	−12,095	−12,623	−13,317	−13,668	−16,814

▶

Table 4.7 (*continued*)

Notes	Analytical income statement Income statement (DKKm)	Year 3	Year 4	Year 5	Year 6	Year 7	Year 8
1	Administrative expenses	−2,533	−2,596	−2,777	−2,913	−2,969	−3,765
	Other operating income	575	612	876	660	933	1,178
	Other operating expenses	0	0	−465	−393	−448	−450
3	Share of profit after tax, associates	236	210	232	85	101	81
3	Tax on profit from associates	101	90	90	33	34	27
	Operating profit before special items	**6,180**	**6,040**	**6,162**	**6,812**	**7,946**	**11,445**
2	Special items, income	0	0	0	602	0	0
1,2	Special items, costs	−382	−583	−386	−560	−324	−1,309
	EBITDA	**5,798**	**5,457**	**5,776**	**6,854**	**7,622**	**10,136**
1	Depreciation and amortisation	−2,534	−2,564	−2,554	−2,935	−2,753	−3,771
	EBIT	**3,264**	**2,893**	**3,222**	**3,919**	**4,869**	**6,365**
	Corporation tax	−590	−382	−521	−858	−1,038	324
3	Tax on profit from associates	−101	−90	−90	−33	−34	−27
4	Tax shield, net financial expenses	−143	−346	−347	−240	−300	−864
	NOPAT	**2,431**	**2,075**	**2,264**	**2,788**	**3,497**	**5,798**
	Financial income	416	666	548	725	651	1,310
	Financial expenses	−891	−1,818	−1,788	−1,582	−1,852	−4,766
4	Tax on net financial expenses	143	346	347	240	300	864
	Net financial expenses	**−333**	**−806**	**−893**	**−617**	**−901**	**−2,592**
	Group profit after tax	**2,098**	**1,269**	**1,371**	**2,171**	**2,596**	**3,206**
	Invested capital (DKKm)						
	Non-current assets						
	Intangible assets	5,661	19,489	20,672	21,279	21,205	84,678
	Property, plant and equipment	19,131	20,435	20,355	20,367	22,109	34,043
3	Investments in associates	1,630	1,750	1,105	579	622	2,224
	Receivables	2,136	1,290	1,235	1,139	1,476	1,707
4	Deferred tax assets	732	867	1,005	822	733	1,254
	Total non-current assets	**29,290**	**43,831**	**44,372**	**44,186**	**46,145**	**123,906**
	Current assets						
	Inventories	2,675	2,883	2,866	3,220	3,818	5,317
6	Trade receivables	6,212	6,290	5,979	6,108	6,341	6,369
4	Tax receivables	0	82	132	84	62	262

▶

Notes	Analytical income statement Invested capital (DKKm)	Year 3	Year 4	Year 5	Year 6	Year 7	Year 8
6	Other receivables	1,751	1,370	3,015	1,145	1,453	3,095
3	Receivables from associates	327	0	0	0	0	0
	Prepayments	620	610	587	917	950	1,211
	Total current assets	**11,585**	**11,235**	**12,579**	**11,474**	**12,624**	**16,254**
	Non-interest-bearing debt						
4	Deferred tax liabilities	1,167	2,334	2,362	2,425	2,191	9,803
	Provisions	360	189	195	366	249	1,498
	Other liabilities	212	18	65	54	20	263
	Trade payables	4,173	4,074	4,513	5,147	5,833	7,993
	Deposits on returnable packaging	1,234	1,260	1,224	1,159	1,207	1,455
	Provisions	141	481	561	466	494	677
	Corporation tax	464	710	720	187	197	279
7	Other liabilities etc.	4,374	3,828	4,043	4,157	4,687	6,497
3	Borrowings from associates	14	0	0	0	0	0
	Total non-interest-bearing debt	**12,139**	**12,894**	**13,683**	**13,961**	**14,878**	**28,465**
	Invested capital (net operating assets)	**28,736**	**42,172**	**43,268**	**41,699**	**43,891**	**111,695**
	Total equity	**17,906**	**16,792**	**19,496**	**18,987**	**19,944**	**60,751**
	Net-interest-bearing debt						
	Borrowings	10,883	21,708	17,765	16,241	19,385	43,230
8	Retirement benefit plan obligations	600	1,889	2,061	2,006	2,220	1,793
	Borrowings	4,985	3,357	8,213	6,556	3,869	5,291
9	Liabilities, assets held for sale	–	–	10	1	–	368
7	Interest payable	199	425	526	337	321	681
7	Derivatives	–	633	605	362	603	2,727
	Interest-bearing debt	**16,667**	**28,012**	**29,180**	**25,503**	**26,398**	**54,090**
	Securities	672	524	2,710	170	123	118
8	Retirement benefit plan assets	–	–	21	14	11	2
	Securities	–	71	109	8	34	7
5	Cash and cash equivalents	5,165	1,758	2,240	2,490	2,249	2,857
9	Assets held for sale	–	279	328	109	34	162
	Interest-bearing assets	**5,837**	**2,632**	**5,408**	**2,791**	**2,451**	**3,146**
	Net-interest-bearing debt	**10,830**	**25,380**	**23,772**	**22,712**	**23,947**	**50,944**
	Invested capital	**28,736**	**42,172**	**43,268**	**41,699**	**43,891**	**111,695**

Note 1: Depreciation, amortisation and impairment losses – property, plant and equipment and intangible assets

In the Carlsberg Group's income statement depreciation, amortisation and impairment losses are recognised in the function to which they belong. In the notes depreciation and impairment losses are specified for a six-year period as shown in Table 4.8. By reclassifying depreciation, amortisation and impairment losses (in the analytical income statements) it is possible to calculate earnings before interests, taxes, depreciations and amortisation (EBITDA). This earnings measure is useful in calculating the cash flow statement. Likewise, EBITDA is a popular earnings measure in valuation of firms and credit analysis. Thus, cost of sales, sales and distribution costs, administrative expenses and special items in the *analytical income statement* are exclusive of depreciation, amortisation and impairment losses.

Table 4.8 Carlsberg Group's annual report – note on depreciation, amortisation and impairment

DKKm	Year 3	Year 4	Year 5	Year 6	Year 7	Year 8
Cost of sales	1,462	1,600	1,661	1,725	1,636	2,492
Sales and distribution expenses	874	738	709	856	860	778
Administrative expenses	179	211	184	152	154	169
Special items	19	15	0	202	103	332
Total	**2,534**	**2,564**	**2,554**	**2,935**	**2,753**	**3,771**

Note 2: Special items, net

Special items vary substantially across time. In year 7 special items amounted to minus DKK 427 million (DKK 324 million exclusive of depreciation and impairment losses), while in year 8 special items represented a net expense of DKK 1,641 million (net expense of DKK 1,309 million exclusive of depreciation and impairment losses). In accounting policies applied Carlsberg states that:

> The use of special items entails Management judgement in the separation from other items in the income statement, cf. the accounting policies. When using special items, it is crucial that these constitute significant items of income and expenses which cannot be attributed directly to the Group's ordinary operating activities but concern fundamental structural or process-related changes in the Group and any associated gains or losses on disposal. Management carefully considers such changes in order to ensure the correct distinction between the Group's operating activities and restructuring of the Group made to enhance the Group's future earnings potential. Special items also include other significant non-recurring items, such as impairment of goodwill.

Special items are specified in Carlsberg Group's annual report as shown in Table 4.9, and, as shown in the notes, special items in year 7 and year 8 include impairment expenses and restructuring costs. It could be argued that those items should be included in earnings from operations and not separately classified as special items. For instance, every firm needs to adjust its organisation and restructure, in order to stay competitive. This suggests that restructuring should be classified as an operating expense. Accordingly, none of the items classified as special items should be classified as part of financial income or expenses.

The note for special items provides information about which function those special items relate to. Thus, in year 8, cost of goods sold would be negatively affected by DKK 919 million if special items were reclassified as part of recurring operation. This issue will be further discussed in the chapters concerning accounting quality.

Table 4.9 Carlsberg Group's annual report – note on special items

NOTE 7 SPECIAL ITEMS

DKKm	Year 8	Year 7
Impairment, Türk Tuborg	–	–100
Impairment of Leeds Brewery, Carlsberg UK	–197	–
Impairment of Braunschweig Brewery, Carlsberg Deutschland	–135	–
Impairment losses and expenses relating to withdrawal from the market for discount soft drinks in Denmark (year 7: reversal of provision)	–	7
Loss on disposal of Türk Tuborg	–232	–
Provision for onerous malt contracts	–245	–
Relocation costs, termination benefits and impairment of non-current assets in connection with new production structure in Denmark (year 7: reversal of provision)	–19	14
Termination benefits and impairment of non-current assets in connection with new production structure at Sinebrychoff, Finland	–30	–3
Termination benefits etc. in connection with Operational Excellence programmes	–150	–190
Termination benefits and expenses, transfer of activities to Accounting Shared Service Centre in Poland	–16	–29
Restructuring, Carlsberg Italia	–93	–67
Restructuring, Brasseries Kronenbourg, France	–291	–
Restructuring, Ringnes, Norway	–26	–
Costs in connection with outsourcing of distribution, Carlsberg Sverige	–	–26
Other restructuring costs etc., other entities	–138	–33
Integration costs related to acquisition of part of the activities in S&N	–69	–
Special items, net	**–1,641**	**–427**
If special items had been recognised in operating profit before special items, they would have been included in the following items:		
Cost of sales	–919	–145
Sales and distribution expenses	–114	–135
Administrative expenses	–226	–44
Other operating income	27	29
Other operating expenses	–409	–126
	–1,641	–421
Impairment of goodwill	–	–6
Special items, net	**–1,641**	**–427**

Special items constitute significant items that cannot be attributed directly to the Group's ordinary operating activities and are significant over time

Note 3: Investments in associates (including tax on profits)

Based on Carlsberg Group's financial reporting most *associated companies* seem to be involved in brewery-related activities. Carlsberg also classify 'share of profit after tax, associates' as part of operating profit before special items. This supports the idea that income from associates (Table 4.10) should be classified as part of operating profit. Accordingly, investments in associated firms, from the balance sheet, should be classified as part of operation.

Table 4.10 Carlsberg Group's annual report – note on associates

NOTE 18 ASSOCIATES

DKKm	Revenue	Profit for the year after tax	Assets	Liabilities	Carlsberg Group share, Year 8 Ownership interest	Profit for the year after tax	Equity
Key figures for associates:							
Tibet Lhasa Brewery Co.	217	50	375	23	33%	16	127
Lanzhou Huanghe Jianjiang Brewery Company	333	18	377	118	30%	5	82
Hanoi Beer Company	–	–	–	–	16.00%	11	578
Chongqing Brewery	–	–	–	–	17.50%	–	1,013
Other associates, Asia	382	44	351	155	30–49.8%	21	85
International Breweries	342	–60	671	449	16%	–11	35
Nuuk Imeq A/S	153	27	230	85	31.90%	9	16
Other	941	195	1,857	1,347	20–25%	30	288
						81	**2,224**

Since Carlsberg's share of profit from associates is measured after tax we need to calculate 'tax on profit from associates'. This allows us to calculate operating profit before and after tax, respectively, on income from associates. In Table 4.11 we use the marginal corporate tax rate for Carlsberg from year 3 to year 8.

Table 4.11 Carlsberg's share of profit, associates

DKKm	Year 3	Year 4	Year 5	Year 6	Year 7	Year 8
Corporation tax, marginal	30%	30%	28%	28%	25%	25%
Share of profit after tax, associates	236	210	232	85	101	81
Tax on profit from associates	101	90	90	33	34	27
Share of profit before tax, associates	**337**	**300**	**322**	**118**	**135**	**108**

Note 4: Taxes

In Carlsberg's annual report *corporation tax* (income tax) is recognised as a single item in the income statement. Corporate tax is related to operating as well as financial items (financial income and financial expenses). The analysts must therefore estimate taxes from operating income and net financial expenses. As mentioned above, this estimate may be based on different assumptions. Typically the analyst must choose between using the effective tax rate and the marginal tax rate. Since Carlsberg's taxable income is sufficiently large to cover net financial expenses, the marginal tax rate seems to be the right choice. However, there are some caveats in the case of Carlsberg. First, the company may have borrowed in countries with tax rates that differ from Carlsberg's domestic corporate tax rate (25% in recent years). Second, financial items include income and expenses other than just interest expenses (or income).

As seen from the notes on financial income and financial expenses (Table 4.12), accounting items such as dividends, foreign exchange gains (and losses), fair value adjustments, impairment of financial assets and other financial income and expenses are also recognised as financial items. The notes do not disclose whether such financial items are taxable, and if so

Table 4.12 Carlsberg's financial income and expenses

NOTE 8   FINANCIAL INCOME

DKKm	Year 8	Year 7
Interest income[1]	249	186
Dividends from securities	21	19
Fair value adjustments of financial instruments, net, cf. note 36	556	–
Foreign exchange gains, net	–	55
Realised gains on disposal of associates and securities	126	43
Expected return on plan assets, defined benefit plans	308	321
Other financial income	50	27
Total	**1,310**	**651**

[1]Interest income relates to interest from cash and cash equivalents.

NOTE 9   FINANCIAL EXPENSES

DKKm	Year 8	Year 7
Interest expenses	2,635	1,262
Fair value adjustments of financial instruments, net, cf. note 36	–	65
Realised foreign exchange losses, net	1,358	–
Realised losses on disposal of securities	5	20
Impairment of financial assets	3	4
Interest cost on obligations, defined benefit plans	340	323
Loss on other financial instruments	–	73
Other financial expenses	425	105
Total	**4,766**	**1,852**

In addition, fair value adjustments of financial instruments were affected by DKK 110 million related to the inefficient part of the currency options acquired to hedge the GBP exposure on the S&N transaction.

Other financial expenses consist mainly of payment to establish credit facilities and fees for unutilised draws on these facilities. Approximately DKK 315 million relates to up-front and commitment fees etc. from establishing of financing related to the acquisition of part of the activities in S&N.

at which tax rate. As no other information is provided in the financial statements, we use the marginal tax rate when estimating the tax shield.

Generally, *deferred tax assets* arise from tax loss carry forwards or assets (liabilities) that are recognised at a lower (higher) value in the balance sheet than for tax purposes. According to the annual report, DKK 3,106 million out of DKK 3,590 million relates to tax loss carry forwards.

Carlsberg does not provide information that enables the analyst to decide if tax loss carry forwards are linked to operations or financing. In most cases, however, tax assets are directly related to operations (differences between valuing assets and liabilities for accounting purposes and tax purposes), even though tax deficits may arise from financial activities like losses from disposal of securities or financial expenses that cannot be contained within positive earnings from operation. Deferred tax assets will be classified as operations. Notice, however, that Carlsberg do not include deferred tax assets in their definition of invested capital.

Deferred tax liabilities are likewise treated as operating items, arising as a consequence of temporary differences between book values and tax values. If we refer to the consolidated financial statements in Carlsberg's annual report, it is evident that deferred tax liabilities relate to intangible and tangible assets, and, thus, should be treated as an operating liability.

Note 5:   Cash and cash equivalents
Firms need *operating cash* that can be used to finance upcoming investments, build up inventories or to pay unforeseen bills. The share of cash holdings that is needed for operations is not disclosed. However, Carlsberg treats cash and cash equivalent as excess cash when defining their invested capital for reporting purposes. This indicates that cash and cash equivalents should be treated as excess cash.

A closer look at Carlsberg's cash and cash equivalents reveal that they remain lower at year-end (fourth quarter) than in most other quarters. This indicates that cash and cash equivalents at year end are not invested in operating assets during the financial year. It seems, therefore, reasonable to classify all cash and cash equivalents at year-end as excess cash.

Note 6:   Trade receivables and other receivables
Receivables are specified in Carlsberg Group's annual report, note 20 (Table 4.13).

Table 4.13 **Group's annual report year 8 – note on receivables**

NOTE 20 RECEIVABLES		
DKKm	**Year 8**	**Year 7**
Receivables are included in the balance sheet as follows:		
Trade receivables	6,369	6,341
Other receivables	3,095	1,453
Total current receivables	9,464	7,794
Non-current receivables	1,707	1,476
Total	**11,171**	**9,270**

Trade receivables comprise invoiced goods and services as well as short-term loans to customers in the on-trade.

Other receivables comprise VAT receivables, loans to associates, interest receivables and other financial receivables.

Non-current receivables consist mainly of on-trade loans. Non-current receivables fall due more than one year from the balance sheet date, of which DKK 171 million (year 7: DKK 478 million) falls due more than five years from the balance sheet date.

Trade receivables comprise invoiced goods and services plus short-term loans to customers. *Non-current receivables* consist mainly of on-trade loans falling due more than one year from the balance sheet date. When studying the applied accounting policies more closely it becomes clear that Carlsberg considers on-trade loans as operating in nature. This implies that the interest on these loans should be recognised in (other) operating income. However, this piece of information is not disclosed in the annual report.

Other receivables comprise VAT receivables, loans to associates, interest receivables and other financial receivables. While VAT receivables are part of operations, loans to associates, interest receivables, and other financial receivables are likely candidates for being treated as interest bearing (i.e. financial items). However, without further notes on other receivables it is not possible to separate VAT receivables from loans to associates, interest receivables, and other financial receivables. In this case, analysts must make their own assumptions. In the example, we treat other receivables as operating assets.

Note 7: Other liabilities, etc.
The accounting item *other liabilities* consists of excise duties and VAT payable, staff costs payable, interest payable, fair value of hedging instruments, liabilities related to the acquisition of entities, amounts owed to associates, deferred income and 'other' (see Table 4.14).

Table 4.14 **Group's annual report – note on other liabilities**

NOTE 29   OTHER LIABILITIES ETC.

DKKm	Year 8	Year 7
Other liabilities are recognised in the balance sheet as follows:		
Non-current liabilities	263	20
Current liabilities	9,905	5,611
Total	**10,168**	**5,631**
Other liabilities by origin:		
Excise duties and VAT payable	1,953	1,889
Staff costs payable	1,434	980
Interest payable	681	321
Fair value of hedging instruments (derivatives)	2,727	603
Liabilities related to the acquisition of entities	215	90
Amounts owed to associates	2	2
Deferred income	1,172	171
Other	1,984	1,575
Total	**10,168**	**5,631**

Interest payable and fair value of hedging instruments are financial liabilities (i.e. included in interest-bearing debt). The remaining other liabilities are classified as capital invested in operations. This implies that we treat 'other liabilities' under this heading as operating liabilities.

Note 8: Retirement benefit plan assets and obligations
Retirement benefit plans relate to defined benefit plans. For those plans Carlsberg bears the risk associated with future developments in inflation, interest rates, mortality and disability.

Retirement benefit costs from defined benefit plans are recognised in the income statement as staff costs (amounting to DKK 139 million in year 8 and DKK 162 million in year 7).

Ideally, if the benefit plans were fully funded, net obligations (present value of funded plans less fair value of plan assets) should amount to zero. As benefit plan assets is a way of funding Carlsberg's pension obligations and the pension liabilities are interest bearing (discounted to present value), it is logical to treat benefit plan assets and obligations as part of financing activities.

Note 9: Assets held for sale

Carlsberg classifies assets held for sale and the associated liabilities as separate items in the balance sheet.

We would classify assets held for sale as a financial item (reduction of net interest-bearing debt), as the disposal of those assets will reduce Carlsberg's borrowings (or increase cash and cash equivalents). Therefore, we exclude assets held for sale and related liabilities from operation and treat them as part of financing.

Carlsberg's invested capital

For comparison purposes invested capital as reported by Carlsberg in year 8 is compared with our calculation of invested capital for the same year (Table 4.15). As can be seen we calculate a lower invested capital than Carlsberg. Roughly three accounting items explain the difference: (a) deferred tax, (b) other receivables, and (c) provisions.

(a) Carlsberg excludes deferred tax assets from invested capital while we regard deferred tax assets as operating assets. Furthermore, they do not treat deferred tax liabilities as an operating liability as we do. One explanation for these differences can be that Carlsberg considers deferred tax assets and liabilities as equity equivalents. The basic idea is that deferred taxes will never have to be paid and as such should not be considered as an asset or liability but rather as an equity equivalent item. This issue will be further discussed in Chapters 14 and 15.

(b) As may be recalled we did not have the information necessary to separate *other receivables* into operating and financing activities, respectively. According to Carlsberg's calculation of invested capital loan to associates (6) and interest income from receivables (1,470) make up 1,476. In our calculation of invested capital we did not exclude these assets from other receivables.

(c) Carlsberg excludes restructuring from provisions (603). From an analytical standpoint is it not clear why restructuring is treated differently from other types of provisions such as losses in connection with Carlsberg UK's outsourcing of the servicing of draught beer equipment, warranty obligations, onerous contracts, ongoing disputes, lawsuits etc.

On the whole, reformulating financial statements for analytical purposes can be a daunting task. As shown in the above example, invested capital (and the split between operating earnings after tax (NOPAT) and net financial expenses after tax for that matter) may be different depending upon the underlying assumptions. In the case of Carlsberg, the notes were relatively detailed and Carlsberg did calculate and specify invested capital. Such detailed information is often not available, and analysts are left to make judgements based on their own knowledge.

Table 4.15 Carlsberg Group's invested capital

Carlsberg Group's invested capital year 8

DKKm	Carlsberg's calculation	Our calculations	Differences
Total assets	143,306	143,306	0
Deferred tax	–1,254		–1,254
Loan to associates	–6		–6
Interest income receivables etc.	–1,470		–1,470
Securities	–125	–125	0
Cash and cash equivalents	–2,857	–2,857	0
Assets held for sale	–162	–162	0
Retirement benefit plan assets		–2	2
Total operating assets	**137,432**	**140,160**	**–2,728**
Trade payables	–7,993	–7,993	0
Deposits on returning packaging	–1,455	–1,455	0
Provisions, excluding restructuring	–1,572	–2,175	603
Corporation tax	–279	–279	0
Deferred income	–1,172	–1,172	0
Finance lease liabilities, in borrowings	–47		–47
Other liabilities	–5,588	–5,588	0
Deferred tax liabilities		–9,803	9,803
Total operating liabilities	**–18,106**	**–28,465**	**10,359**
Invested capital	**119,326**	**111,695**	**7,631**

Conclusions

The purpose of separating accounting items into operation and financing is to highlight the sources of value creation, which will be useful to most of a firm's stakeholders. For equity – and debt capital providers – forecasting will be easier and the board of directors will be able to measure value creation in a given period in order to determine performance related bonuses etc.

The most important problems in dividing accounting items into operation and financing are:

- The definition of core operation is not unequivocal
- The income statement and balance sheet do not distinguish clearly between operating and financing activities
- The notes are not sufficiently informative.

The two basic rules to remember are:

1 Items in the income statements should match the items in the balance sheet. For example, if 'investments in associates' are classified as an operating activity, so must 'profit from associates'.
2 Invested capital should be defined consistently over time and across firms.

It is worth noting here that additional matters of dispute may arise in relation to dividing accounting items into operating and financing activities. As with any adjustments to the accounts, a reclassification should only be made if the analyst experiences higher information content as a result.

Review questions

- What are the three analytical areas where ratio analysis appears useful?

- What are the typical sources of noise in a time-series analysis?

- What are the typical sources of noise in a cross-sectional analysis?

- Why is it important to make a distinction between operating and financing activities?

- What is NOPAT?

- How is invested capital defined?

- What challenges does an analyst typically face when measuring NOPAT and invested capital?

CHAPTER 5

Profitability analysis

After reading this chapter you should be able to:

- **Understand the structure of the profitability analysis**
- **Define, calculate and interpret key financial ratios such as return on invested capital, profit margin and turnover rate of invested capital**
- **Identify the limitations in using return on invested capital**
- **Understand the importance of trends and levels in key financial ratios**
- **Recognise that benchmarking is typically based on a comparison with the required rate of return or competitors**
- **Prepare a common-size analysis as well as a trend analysis (index numbers)**
- **Understand the impact of financial leverage on profitability**
- **Recognise when financial ratios should be measured before and after tax**

Profitability analysis

Measuring a company's profitability is one of the key areas of financial analysis. Profitability is important for a company's future survival and to ensure a satisfactory return to shareholders. Sound profitability is a signal of economic strength and helps a firm maintain positive relationships with both customers and suppliers. The historical profitability is an important element in defining the future expectations for a company.

This chapter presents a number of key figures and tables used to illustrate and measure profitability. We will consider the following areas:

- Measurement of operating profitability
- Alternative interpretations of the return on invested capital
- Decomposition of return on invested capital
- Analysis of profit margin and turnover rate of invested capital
- Return on equity.

Measurement of operating profitability

The structure for profitability analysis and inter-relationships of ratios linked to operation is illustrated in Figure 5.1. In the following section, the profitability ratios will be defined and their inter-relationships described. The definitions of profitability ratios linked to operation are based on the analytical income statement and balance sheet as described in the previous chapter.

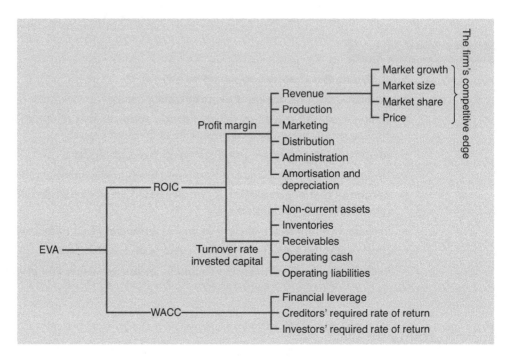

Figure 5.1 **Structure of profitability analysis – Du Pont model**

Return on invested capital (ROIC) is the overall profitability measure for operations. The ratio expresses the return on capital invested in a firm's net operating assets as a percentage; and should be compared with returns from alternative investments with a similar risk profile. ROIC measured after tax is defined as:

$$\text{ROIC} = \frac{\text{Net operating profit after tax (NOPAT)}}{\text{Invested capital}} \times 100$$

ROIC before tax is measured as:

$$\text{ROIC} = \frac{\text{EBIT}}{\text{Invested capital}} \times 100$$

Return on invested capital is an important ratio. In a valuation context it is a significant factor, since a higher rate of return will lead, *ceteris paribus*, to a higher (estimated) value. In connection with lending it will be more attractive to provide loans to a company with a high ROIC. The company will accordingly be able to obtain cheaper financing.

Below we use the simple numerical example outlined in Chapters 2 and 4 to show how ROIC (after tax) is calculated.

Example 5.1

Revenues	200	**Invested capital (net operating assets)**	
Operating expenses	−90	Total assets	700
EBIT	110	Cash and cash equivalents	−50
Taxes on EBIT	−33	Accounts payables and tax payable	−100
NOPAT	**77**	**Invested capital (net operating assets)**	**550**
Net financial expenses	−10		
Tax savings from debt financing	3	**Invested capital (financing)**	
Net financial expenses after tax	**−7**	Equity	400
Net earnings	70	Loans and borrowings (non-current)	100
		Loans and borrowings (current)	100
		Cash and cash equivalents	−50
		Interest bearing debt, net	150
		Invested capital (financing)	**550**

$$\text{ROIC} = \frac{77}{550} \times 100 = 14.0\%$$

A ROIC of 14.0% indicates that the business is able to generate a return of 14 cents for each euro invested in operations. ∎

To see how it works in real-life cases, we have calculated Carlsberg's rate of return on invested capital for the past five years. The results are shown in Figure 5.2. The

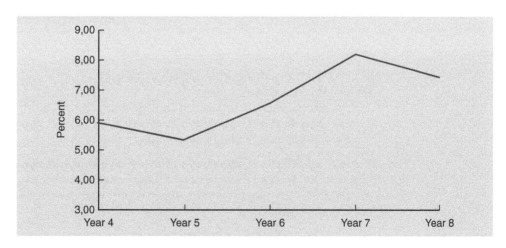

Figure 5.2 **Return on invested capital for Carlsberg**

calculation is based on the reformulated income statement and balance sheet as described in Chapter 4. It should be noted that the calculations are based on averages for invested capital. This calculation works best if there is a steady development in invested capital over the year. It is considered the most accurate method. However, it may provide a noisy measure of ROIC, if there is an extraordinary high activity. For example, a divestiture of business units at year-end means that average invested capital would be too low.

When interpreting the return on invested capital, and other key ratios in general, it is important to address the following issues:

- The *level* of returns
- The *development* of returns over time.

Assessment of the level of returns

An important element in evaluating the return on invested capital is whether the ratio is at a satisfactory level. There are two ways to determine this:

- An estimation of the required rate of return (WACC)
- A comparison with competitors (**benchmarking**).

As you can see from the analytical balance sheet, invested capital consists of net operating assets or alternatively net interest-bearing debt plus shareholders' equity. In order to estimate cost of capital, which reflects the required (expected) return on invested capital, it is necessary to know the

- net interest-bearing debt
- shareholders' equity
- interest rate on debt after tax
- shareholders' required rate of return.

This total required rate of return is called the **weighted average cost of capital (WACC)** and is calculated as:

$$ \text{WACC} = \frac{\text{NIBD}}{\text{NIBD} + \text{MVE}} \times r_\text{d} \times (1 - t) + \frac{\text{MVE}}{\text{NIBD} + \text{MVE}} \times r_\text{e} $$

where

$$
\begin{aligned}
\text{NIBD} &= \text{Market value of net interest-bearing debt} \\
\text{MVE} &= \text{Market value of equity} \\
r_\text{d} &= \text{Interest rate on net interest-bearing debt} \\
r_\text{e} &= \text{Shareholders' required rate of return} \\
t &= \text{The company's marginal tax rate}
\end{aligned}
$$

The calculation of WACC is addressed in further details in Chapter 10. Subtracting WACC from ROIC leaves an expression of **Economic Value Added (EVA)**. As mentioned earlier, EVA is synonymous with super profit, economic rents, above normal profit and economic profits:

$$ \text{EVA} = (\text{ROIC} - \text{WACC}) \times \text{Invested capital} $$

WACC is the expected return on invested capital. If ROIC exceeds WACC a company creates excess return or Economic Value Added; i.e. value for its shareholders. Accounting profit (operating profit) is not necessarily value creating. It requires that accounting (operating) profit, measured as a percentage of invested capital (ROIC) exceeds the average cost of capital to debt-holders and equity-holders (WACC).

Assuming that Carlsberg's WACC was 8% in the past, it is clear that Carlsberg is only creating value for its shareholders in year 7. This is illustrated in Figure 5.3.

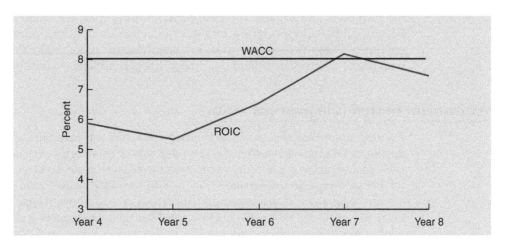

Figure 5.3 Return on invested capital versus WACC for Carlsberg

An alternative method of assessing the level of return on invested capital is to compare it with the competitors' performance. Such a comparison is called cross-sectional analysis and must take into account the issues referred to in the Introduction to Part 2 about cross-sectional analysis.

To illustrate how a cross-sectional analysis may be carried out, a comparison of Carlsberg and Heineken is provided in Figure 5.4. Both companies focus on the

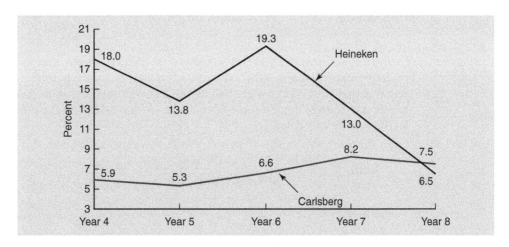

Figure 5.4 Comparison of the return on invested capital for Carlsberg and Heineken

production and sale of beverages and they are among the top-five players in the brewery sector worldwide. From this perspective, they are comparable. Heineken's reformulated income statements and balance sheets are shown in Appendix 5.1 on page 122.

Carlsberg is only able to generate a ROIC that exceeds Heineken's in year 8. This indicates that Carlsberg's level of profitability is generally below Heineken's in the period examined.

The comparison of profitability between Carlsberg and Heineken illustrates that the method is also suitable for identification of best practice. Some companies take advantage of the opportunity to gather information and inspiration by analysing competitors' ability to create value. By identifying the most profitable businesses and understand the strategy behind their success, it is possible to find inspiration.

Assessment of trends in financial ratios

Another important element in evaluating the return on invested capital, and other key financial ratios is whether the ratio develops satisfactorily over time. In practice, such an assessment is primarily carried out by measuring the development of the ratio relative to comparable companies. Figure 5.4 illustrates the evolution of the return on invested capital for Carlsberg and Heineken. As noted above, Heineken is generally more profitable than Carlsberg. However, Heineken experiences a decreasing ROIC while Carlsberg is able to improve ROIC from year 4 to year 8. In fact, in year 8 Carlsberg's ROIC exceeds Heineken's. To summarise, while Carlsberg's profitability is generally below Heineken's, Carlsberg are able to improve ROIC over time.

For listed companies where the market value of the company is known, the implicit forecast (expectation) of the development of profitability can be calculated. This kind of analysis provides management with guidance about the market's outlook of the company's future profitability. This method is illustrated based on Carlsberg's annual reports and market value. To calculate the stock market's implicit ROIC, a valuation model is required. The EVA model is applied as follows:

$$\text{Market value of equity} = \text{Book value of equity} + \frac{(\text{ROIC} - \text{WACC}) \times \text{invested capital}}{(\text{WACC} - g)}$$

In the above formula, g denotes growth in EVA. It shows that the market value of equity exceeds book value, if value is created in future periods (EVA > 0); this requires that ROIC is greater than WACC. Assuming a constant growth rate and a constant required rate of return (WACC) the stock market's implicit (forward looking) ROIC may be calculated as:

$$\text{ROIC} = \frac{(\text{MVE} - \text{BVE}) \times (\text{WACC} - g)}{\text{Invested capital}} + \text{WACC}$$

where

MVE = market value of equity
BVE = book value of equity

Both market capitalisation and the book value of equity are available for Carlsberg:

Market value of equity (MVE) = DKK 53.2 billion

Book value of equity (BVE) = DKK 55.5 billion

Invested capital = DKK 111.7 billion

Carlsberg's organic growth has been moderate in recent years. We assume a growth rate of between 0% and 3% and a required rate of return (WACC) of between 8% and 9%. Based on the above assumptions the stock market's implicit expectations for return on invested capital for Carlsberg are calculated.

This is illustrated in Table 5.1. For instance, with an assumed growth rate of 2% and a WACC of 8%, the market expects Carlsberg to earn a return on invested capital (ROIC) of 7.9% in perpetuity. With a ROIC of 7.9% in perpetuity, the market value of equity would amount to DKK 53.2 billion. As shown in the figure the market's implicit expectations for return on invested capital for Carlsberg is in the range 7.8–8.9%.

Table 5.1

		WACC		
		8.0%	8.5%	9.0%
	0%	7.8%	8.3%	8.8%
Growth	1%	7.9%	8.3%	8.8%
	2%	7.9%	8.4%	8.9%
	3%	7.9%	8.4%	8.9%

This should be compared with an average realised return (ROIC) of 6.7% in years 4 to 8. Carlsberg's return shows an increasing trend. The return on invested capital is 7.5% in the last financial year 8. Thus, the market expects a slight improvement in return on invested capital in the coming years. Please note that since Carlsberg's market value of equity is almost identical to the book value of equity, growth does not matter. This explains the lack of variation of implicit ROIC across different growth rates.

Analysts may find it beneficial to estimate the implicit rate of return because it clarifies the implicit expectations about future profitability. In the case of Carlsberg the analyst must assess whether it is likely that Carlsberg will be able to improve ROIC from 7.5% to 7.8%–8.9%. A firm's management may use the information embedded in the implicit rate of return to assess whether the chosen strategy is appropriate and/ or if they need to improve information to the stock market so that there is a higher degree of coherence between the stock market's and the company's own outlook for the future.

Alternative interpretations of the return on invested capital

When evaluating the return on invested capital, it is important to understand the information that can be inferred from the ratio. Many analysts associate high and positive developments in the return on invested capital as attractive, because it signals increasing value creation in the company. In practice it will often be true, but there are circumstances with alternative interpretations. For example, ROIC is affected by:

- Differences in accounting policies
- The average age of assets
- Differences in operating risks
- Product lifecycle.

Each of these issues is now discussed in turn.

Differences in accounting policies

It is important that accounting policies are the same over time (time-series analysis) and across firms (cross-sectional analysis). This ensures that differences in return on invested capital over time or across firms are not attributed to changes in accounting policies but rather to changes in the underlying profitability of operation.

In Chapters 13 to 15 we discuss the concept of earnings quality and selected accounting items. These chapters examine the quality of data available for analyses and explore the analytical problems of changes in accounting policies.

The average age of assets

In financial theory the **internal rate of return (IRR)** is used as a financial ratio for measuring return on invested capital. The IRR shows what investors can expect to earn on average each year (expressed as a percentage) during the entire lifetime of the project. In order to calculate IRR, all future cash flows must be estimated by the analyst (since they are unknown) and, thus, IRR changes from being known and sure to being an estimate. The method is shown in the following example.

An investor intends to invest in a wind turbine. The total investment amounts to €100 million and the expected lifetime of the wind turbine is 20 years. The annual net payments from the investment are expected to be €11.75 million. Based on this data, it is possible to estimate IRR to 10%:

$$\sum_{t=1}^{20} \frac{11.75}{(1 + IRR)^t} - 100 = 0 \rightarrow IRR = 10\%$$

The formula demonstrates that the wind turbine investment in each of the next 20 years will provide an annual return of 10%. ROIC is the accounting equivalent to the IRR. In practice, ROIC is often used because the IRR is based on prospects, while the ROIC is based on realised figures, making the ratio more reliable and easier to estimate. It does not, however, mean that ROIC is necessarily a good indicator of the IRR. By using the above information from the wind turbine project, it is actually possible to estimate the annual rate of return (ROIC) so it matches the IRR (Table 5.2).

As shown in the example, depreciation must increase over time. To ensure that IRR equals ROIC, a progressive depreciation scheme must be adopted. In reality, most firms use linear depreciation for external reporting purposes. Changing from progressive to straight-line depreciation gives a more realistic picture of actual reporting

Table 5.2 Estimation of IRR

Year	1 Net-cash inflow	2 Depreciation	3 (1–2) EBIT	4 (4–2) Invested capital (end of year)	5 (3/4) ROIC = IRR
0				100	
1	11.75	1.7	10.0	98	10.0%
2	11.75	1.9	9.8	96	10.0%
3	11.75	2.1	9.6	94	10.0%
4	11.75	2.3	9.4	92	10.0%
5	11.75	2.6	9.2	89	10.0%
6	11.75	2.8	8.9	87	10.0%
7	11.75	3.1	8.7	83	10.0%
8	11.75	3.4	8.3	80	10.0%
9	11.75	3.7	8.0	76	10.0%
10	11.75	4.1	7.6	72	10.0%
11	11.75	4.5	7.2	68	10.0%
12	11.75	5.0	6.8	63	10.0%
13	11.75	5.5	6.3	57	10.0%
14	11.75	6.0	5.7	51	10.0%
15	11.75	6.6	5.1	45	10.0%
16	11.75	7.3	4.5	37	10.0%
17	11.75	8.0	3.7	29	10.0%
18	11.75	8.8	2.9	20	10.0%
19	11.75	9.7	2.0	11	10.0%
20	11.75	10.7	1.1	0	10.0%

practices. Using straight-line depreciation ROIC increases over time as shown in Table 5.3.

The difference between the IRR and ROIC (the accounting equivalent to the IRR), is illustrated in Figure 5.5.

At the beginning of the project ROIC is typically below the 'true' return (IRR), while the opposite is true at the end of the project. Apart from the period between year 6 and year 10, where ROIC is a reasonable indicator of the underlying IRR of 10%, the decision maker risks making irrational decisions. The information which can be inferred from ROIC for additional periods, i.e. in years 1–5 and 11–20, is quite simply misleading.

The above example fits well for start-up firms or firms under liquidation. Other companies which have been in business for some time will find that depreciation is superseded by new investments, so for these companies ROIC is often a reasonable indicator of the underlying IRR.

Table 5.3 **Estimation of the return on invested capital**

	1	2	3	4	5
			(1–2)	(4–2)	(3/4)
Year	Net-cash inflows	Depreciation	EBIT	Invested capital (end of year)	ROIC
0				100	
1	11.75	5.0	6.7	95	6.7%
2	11.75	5.0	6.7	90	7.1%
3	11.75	5.0	6.7	85	7.5%
4	11.75	5.0	6.7	80	7.9%
5	11.75	5.0	6.7	75	8.4%
6	11.75	5.0	6.7	70	9.0%
7	11.75	5.0	6.7	65	9.6%
8	11.75	5.0	6.7	60	10.4%
9	11.75	5.0	6.7	55	11.2%
10	11.75	5.0	6.7	50	12.3%
11	11.75	5.0	6.7	45	13.5%
12	11.75	5.0	6.7	40	15.0%
13	11.75	5.0	6.7	35	16.9%
14	11.75	5.0	6.7	30	19.3%
15	11.75	5.0	6.7	25	22.5%
16	11.75	5.0	6.7	20	27.0%
17	11.75	5.0	6.7	15	33.7%
18	11.75	5.0	6.7	10	45.0%
19	11.75	5.0	6.7	5	67.5%
20	11.75	5.0	6.7	0	134.9%

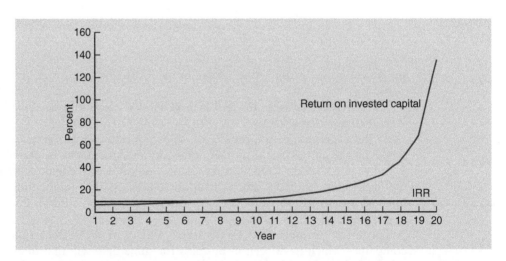

Figure 5.5 **A comparison of the IRR and return on invested capital for a project with finite lifetime**

Differences in operating risks

A further explanation for alternative interpretations of return on invested capital is differences in operating risk. According to economic theory investors require compensation for bearing greater risks. In Table 5.4 the expected rate of return from the operation for a significant number of different industries is shown. Assuming no financial leverage the expected, return is estimated by using the following relationship:

Expected return $= r_f + \beta_a \times$ risk premium

where

r_f = Risk-free interest rate
β_a = Systematic risk on assets; i.e. operating risk (unlevered beta)

Table 5.4 **Projected operating earnings in different industries based on European data**

Industry name	Number of firms	Unlevered β	Expected operating returns
Financial Svcs. (Div.)	294	0.44	6.0%
Bank	504	0.48	6.2%
Thrift	234	0.49	6.2%
Natural Gas Utility	26	0.52	6.3%
Oil/Gas Distribution	15	0.52	6.3%
Property Management	12	0.52	6.4%
Water Utility	16	0.58	6.6%
Maritime	52	0.59	6.7%
Food Wholesalers	19	0.60	6.7%
Electric Utility (Central)	25	0.61	6.7%
Electric Utility (West)	17	0.62	6.8%
Electric Utility (East)	27	0.63	6.9%
Bank (Canadian)	8	0.64	6.9%
R.E.I.T.	147	0.64	6.9%
Bank (Midwest)	38	0.66	7.0%
Tobacco	11	0.66	7.0%
Food Processing	123	0.67	7.0%
Paper/Forest Products	39	0.69	7.1%
Investment Co.	18	0.71	7.2%
Environmental	89	0.71	7.2%
Canadian Energy	13	0.71	7.2%
Natural Gas (Div.)	31	0.75	7.4%
Toiletries/Cosmetics	21	0.75	7.4%
Apparel	57	0.76	7.4%
Trucking	32	0.78	7.5%
Packaging & Container	35	0.79	7.6%

Table 5.4 (*continued*)

Industry name	Number of firms	Unlevered β	Expected operating returns
Household Products	28	0.80	7.6%
Electrical Equipment	86	0.80	7.6%
Home Appliance	11	0.81	7.6%
Beverage	44	0.81	7.6%
Grocery	15	0.81	7.7%
Healthcare Information	38	0.82	7.7%
Homebuilding	36	0.83	7.7%
Restaurant	75	0.83	7.8%
Securities Brokerage	31	0.85	7.8%
Petroleum (Producing)	186	0.86	7.9%
Building Materials	49	0.87	7.9%
Newspaper	18	0.87	7.9%
Auto & Truck	28	0.88	8.0%
Insurance (Prop/Cas.)	87	0.88	8.0%
Furn/Home Furnishings	39	0.89	8.0%
Insurance (Life)	40	0.89	8.0%
Diversified Co.	107	0.92	8.1%
Office Equip/Supplies	25	0.92	8.1%
Chemical (Specialty)	90	0.93	8.2%
Medical Services	178	0.95	8.3%
Foreign Electronics	10	0.95	8.3%
Hotel/Gaming	75	0.96	8.3%
Reinsurance	11	0.96	8.3%
Petroleum (Integrated)	26	0.97	8.4%
Information Services	38	0.97	8.4%
Utility (Foreign)	6	0.98	8.4%
Retail Store	42	0.98	8.4%
Pharmacy Services	19	0.99	8.5%
Metals & Mining (Div.)	78	0.99	8.5%
Air Transport	49	1.00	8.5%
Machinery	126	1.01	8.5%
Oilfield Svcs/Equip.	113	1.01	8.5%
Industrial Services	196	1.02	8.6%
Telecom Services	152	1.03	8.6%
Precious Metals	84	1.04	8.7%
Railroad	16	1.04	8.7%
Auto Parts	56	1.05	8.7%

▶

Industry name	Number of firms	Unlevered β	Expected operating returns
Publishing	40	1.05	8.7%
Chemical (Diversified)	37	1.05	8.7%
Cable TV	23	1.06	8.8%
Aerospace/Defence	69	1.06	8.8%
Retail Building Supply	9	1.10	8.9%
Metal Fabricating	37	1.10	8.9%
Retail (Special Lines)	164	1.15	9.2%
Entertainment	93	1.17	9.3%
Electronics	179	1.17	9.3%
Advertising	40	1.19	9.4%
Heavy Construction	12	1.21	9.5%
Retail Automotive	16	1.24	9.6%
Recreation	73	1.25	9.6%
Educational Services	39	1.26	9.7%
Human Resources	35	1.30	9.9%
Investment Co. (Foreign)	15	1.31	9.9%
Medical Supplies	274	1.34	10.0%
Chemical (Basic)	19	1.35	10.1%
Biotechnology	103	1.38	10.2%
Shoe	20	1.44	10.5%
Computer Software/Svcs	376	1.51	10.8%
Coal	18	1.52	10.8%
Precision Instrument	103	1.53	10.9%
Steel (General)	26	1.59	11.1%
Drug	368	1.66	11.5%
Power	58	1.69	11.6%
Manuf. Housing/RV	18	1.71	11.7%
Steel (Integrated)	14	1.73	11.8%
Computers/Peripherals	144	1.77	12.0%
Telecom Equipment	124	1.89	12.5%
Internet	266	1.94	12.7%
Wireless Networking	74	1.96	12.8%
Entertainment Tech	38	2.01	13.0%
E-Commerce	56	2.02	13.1%
Semiconductor Equip	16	2.35	14.6%
Semiconductor	138	2.49	15.2%
Market	**7,364**	**1.03**	8.6%

(*Source:* Damodaran, NYU)

Under the assumption that operating risk is (fairly) identical within industries, the expected return on operation can be calculated for any company within an industry. With a risk-free interest rate of 4% and a risk premium of 4.5% the required rate of return on the operation may be calculated. In Chapter 10, the methodology behind the estimation of the required rate of return on operation is looked at in greater detail.

As shown in Table 5.4, there is a large gap between the return which will satisfy investors. Within the energy sector (water and electricity) the expected required rate of return is around 6.5%. In contrast, investors find there is significant risk involved in investing in the semiconductor industry (semiconductor). An investment in this sector will result in a required rate of return on operations of 15%. A comparison of the profitability of the two industries would be meaningless due to significant differences in operating risks.

Product lifecycle

Products undergo various stages of time, and similar considerations can be made for businesses in general. The following description illustrates the lifecycle at the product level, but the considerations can be used at the enterprise level as well.

Products undergo roughly four stages in their lifecycle: introduction, growth, maturity and decline. At the launch of the product the focus is on investment in research and development, marketing, building sales organisations, etc. In the growth phase the organisation is geared to handle the growth, which is usually capital intensive. In both the introductory and growth stage, there is uncertainty as to whether the product will be accepted by customers in the market and if the organisation can handle the transition from introduction to growth. When the product passes into a more moderate growth pace, and has been accepted in the market, the product 'matures'. At this stage companies are reaping the gains of the previous phases of investments. There is often no need for greater investments and there is potential for a nice return on invested capital. Often the lower growth in the mature phase of a product's lifecycle initiates increased competition. As the organic growth is modest at this stage, it is often possible to achieve further growth only by capturing market shares from competitors. An often used parameter to achieve this goal is to reduce the price of the product or offer more features on the product. This increased competition will gradually lead to pressure on profit margins and thus the return on invested capital. As the technological development makes products obsolete in the mature stage, the demand decreases and the products will be phased out gradually as they become unprofitable.

The above ideas are illustrated in Figure 5.6 and, as shown, return on invested capital develops from being negative in the early stage of the product lifecycle to peak in the last part of the growth phase and in the first part of the mature phase. Then, return on invested capital decreases over time and becomes negative, unless the product has been phased out in time and replaced by a newer product with more attractive features.

If this philosophy is transferred to company level, it is clear that companies in the early stage of their lifecycle are not directly comparable with those companies later in their lifecycle. This applies even if firms are within the same industry. Although a comparison of return on invested capital for companies at different stages in their lifecycle does not immediately make sense, an analyst might often find inspiration by

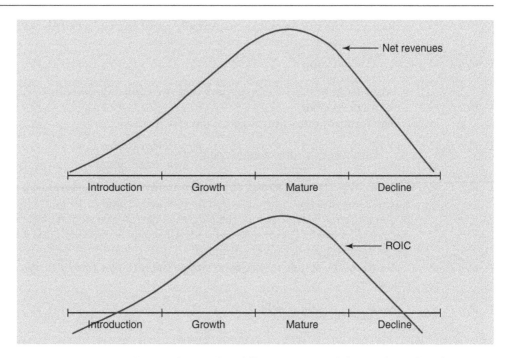

Figure 5.6 Return on invested capital at different stages of the product lifecycle

examining the profitability level of firms later in their lifecycle. For an assessment of an early stage firm it would be appropriate to look at companies later in their lifecycle in order to assess the future earnings potential.

Decomposition of return on invested capital

Return on invested capital measures a firm's return on capital invested in operation. ROIC, however, is not able to explain whether profitability is driven by a better revenue and expense relation or an improved capital utilisation. To be able to answer this question, it is necessary to decompose the ratio into (a) the **profit margin** and (b) the **turnover rate of invested capital**:

ROIC = Profit margin × Turnover rate of invested capital

Profit margin after tax is defined as:

$$\text{Profit margin} = \frac{\text{Net operating profit after tax (NOPAT)}}{\text{Net revenues}} \times 100$$

Profit margin before tax is defined as:

$$\text{Profit margin} = \frac{\text{Earnings before interests and taxes (EBIT)}}{\text{Net revenues}} \times 100$$

The profit margin is sometimes named the operating profit margin.

Profit margin describes the revenue and expense relation and expresses, operating income as a percentage of net revenue. All things being equal, it is attractive with a high profit margin.

107

Based on the simple numerical example profit margin is calculated as:

$$PM = \frac{77 \times 100}{200} = 38.5\%$$

A profit margin of 38.5% expresses that the company generates 38.5 cents on each euro of net revenue.

The turnover rate of invested capital is defined as:

$$\text{Turnover rate of invested capital} = \frac{\text{Net revenue}}{\text{Invested capital}}$$

The turnover rate expresses a company's ability to utilise invested capital. A turnover rate of 2 conveys that a firm has tied up invested capital in 180 days (360 days divided by 2) or alternatively, that for each euro the firm has invested in operation (net operating assets), a sale of 2 euro is generated. All things being equal, it is attractive to have a high turnover rate of invested capital.

Based on the simple numerical example the turnover rate of invested capital is calculated as:

$$\text{Turnover rate} = \frac{200}{550} = 0.36$$

A turnover rate of 0.36 indicates that invested capital is tied up in two years and 280 days on average (360/0.36). (You may apply 365 days in the numerator as this is the number of days in a year.)

The level of the profit margin and turnover rate describes quite well the type of business being analysed. Service industries are typically characterised by having few investments and a high turnover rate. On the other hand, it is difficult to maintain a high profit margin because the price is often a major competitive parameter. Pharmaceutical companies are investing heavily and characterised by relatively low turnover rates. In contrast, the price is not in the same way an important competitive parameter. Here the product's ability to help patients with life threatening illnesses is the decisive competitive factor. Therefore, it is possible to maintain a high profit margin. These considerations are generalised in Figure 5.7.

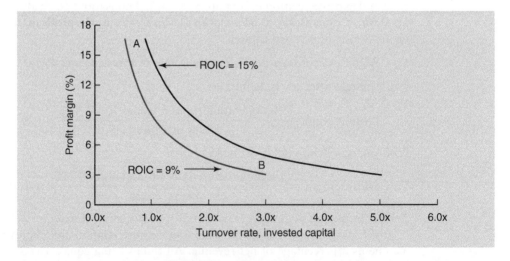

Figure 5.7 **Decomposition of ROIC in profit margin and turnover rate**

Heavy investment companies like pharmaceutical companies, which are characterised by a high proportion of fixed costs, often have low turnover rates. To be able to attract capital to the industry, it is necessary to generate higher profit margins to compensate for the low turnover rate. The higher profit is achieved usually because the product has special properties that are difficult to imitate or other competitive advantages which affect the market share positively. These companies are located in area A in Figure 5.7.

Companies that offer standard services (commodities), often operate in areas affected by significant competition. Within these industries, there is an upper limit to the profit margin. Price is typically the most important parameter, as the products or services do not differ significantly among competitors. To be able to attract capital for such undertakings, they need to generate high turnover rates. A high turnover rate is achieved by tight cost control throughout the value chain, while invested capital is held at a minimum. These companies are located in area B in Figure 5.7.

Most enterprises or industries lie in between A and B on the curve. The above examples are some of the extremities. The same arguments as presented above can apply to any other industry or firm. The lower the operating profit margin (turnover rate) achieved in an industry, the higher the turnover rate (profit margin) would have to be to maintain a satisfactory return on invested capital. In practice, there are industries where it is difficult to achieve a satisfactory return (ROIC). It is typical mature industries where demand is waning.

The following example illustrates the link between the profit margin and turnover rate and how changes in these ratios affect the value creation. The example rests on the following assumptions:

Invested capital = 1,000
Revenue   = 1,000
Profit margin = 10%
WACC   = 10%

Based on these figures it is possible to calculate various financial ratios. In addition, the economic consequences of good or poor cash management (i.e. cash tied up in invested capital) can be calculated. The starting point, based on the above assumptions, is a turnover rate of 1.0 (revenue/invested capital), which corresponds to a firm having invested capital tied up for one year on average (360/1).

To see how management may improve value creation have a look at Table 5.5. The example illustrates the points made in Figure 5.7. Suppose the company is able to reduce cash tied up in invested capital by 60 days from 360 to 300 days. This would improve the overall profitability, as measured by EVA, from 0 to 16.7, as shown in Table 5.5. The calculations behind the example are:

$$\text{Required invested capital} = \frac{1{,}000 \times 300}{360} = 833.3$$

$$\text{ROIC} = \frac{\text{NOPAT}}{\text{Invested capital}} = \frac{100 \times 100}{833.3} = 12\%$$

Thus, EVA becomes: (ROIC − WACC) × Invested capital = (12% − 10%) × 833.3 = 16.7.

It is also possible to calculate how much the operating margin needs to improve by, to have the same effect on profitability (EVA) as the reduction of 60 days in cash tied up in invested capital. In this example, a reduction in cash tied up by 60 days is equivalent to an improvement in the operating margin from 10.0 to 11.7% – an increase of close to 17%. The underlying calculations are:

Invested capital   = 1,000 (unchanged)
EVA   = 16.7 (as calculated above)
Invested capital turnover   = 1.0
Profit margin   = ?
ROIC   = ?

$$EVA = 16.7 = (ROIC - 10\%) \times 1{,}000 \Rightarrow ROIC = 11.7\%$$

Therefore, profit margin (PM) becomes:

$$ROIC = 11.7\% = PM \times Invested\ capital\ turnover = PM \times 1.0 \Rightarrow Profit\ margin = 11.7\%$$

In other words, an improvement in the profit margin from 10.0% to 11.7% has the same effect on value creation (i.e. EVA improves by 16.7) as a reduction in cash tied up in invested capital by 60 days. This is illustrated in Table 5.5.

Table 5.5 The relationship between financial ratios and value added (EVA)

Invested capital tied-up No. of days	Revenue	NOPAT	Profit margin	Invested capital	Turnover rate, invested capital	Cost of capital (WACC)	EVA	Effect on profit margin	Change in profit margin
60	1000.0	100.0	10.0%	167	6.00	16.7	83.3	18.3%	83.3%
120	1000.0	100.0	10.0%	333	3.00	33.3	66.7	16.7%	66.7%
180	1000.0	100.0	10.0%	500	2.00	50.0	50.0	15.0%	50.0%
240	1000.0	100.0	10.0%	667	1.50	66.7	33.3	13.3%	33.3%
300	1000.0	100.0	10.0%	833	1.20	83.3	16.7	11.7%	16.7%
360	**1000.0**	**100.0**	**10.0%**	**1000**	**1**	**100.0**	**0.0**	**10.0%**	**0.0%**
420	1000.0	100.0	10.0%	1167	0.86	116.7	−16.7	8.3%	−16.7%
480	1000.0	100.0	10.0%	1333	0.75	133.3	−33.3	6.7%	−33.3%
540	1000.0	100.0	10.0%	1500	0.67	150.0	−50.0	5.0%	−50.0%
600	1000.0	100.0	10.0%	1667	0.60	166.7	−66.7	3.3%	−66.7%
660	1000.0	100.0	10.0%	1833	0.55	183.3	−83.3	1.7%	−83.3%
720	1000.0	100.0	10.0%	2000	0.50	200.0	−100.0	0.0%	−100.0%

The example in Table 5.5 illustrates how the profit margin and the turnover rate on invested capital affect value creation of a firm.

In Figure 5.8 the profit margin is calculated for Carlsberg and Heineken. As shown by the comparison in Figure 5.8, Carlsberg's profit margin increases from 5.7% to 9.7% from year 4 to year 8. On the other hand, Heineken experiences a decreasing profit margin. By year 8 Carlsberg's profit margin exceeds Heineken's.

Figure 5.9 compares the turnover rate of invested capital for the two breweries. While both breweries experience a decreasing turnover rate, Heineken's consistently exceeds Carlsberg's. However, the differences in turnover rate diminish over time.

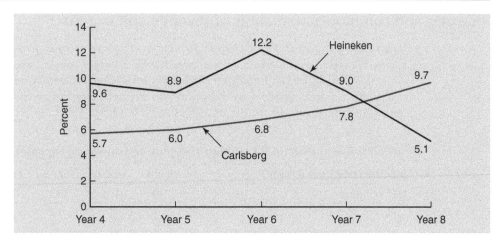

Figure 5.8 Comparison of profit margin of Heineken and Carlsberg

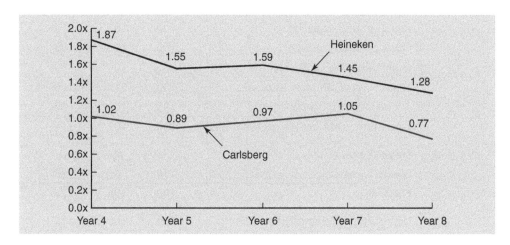

Figure 5.9 Comparison of turnover rate for Heineken and Carlsberg

The decomposition of ROIC into the profit margin and the turnover rate reveals that Carlsberg's increase in ROIC is purely driven by an improvement in the revenue and expense relation (profit margin). On the other hand, Heineken's declining ROIC is explained by a reduced revenue and expense relation as well as a reduced utilisation of invested capital (turnover rate).

Analysis of profit margin and turnover rate of invested capital

An analysis of the profit margin and turnover rate of capital helps to explain whether the revenue/expense relation and the capital utilisation efficiency have improved or deteriorated over time. The analysis of the two ratios is, however, vague in their description of why the ratios have evolved as they have. In order to deepen our understanding of the evolution of the revenue/expense relation and the capital utilisation efficiency, it is necessary to decompose the two ratios further. This can be done in two ways:

- Indexing (trend analysis)
- Common-size analysis.

Indexing and common-size analysis of revenue and expenses

Indexing is a suitable method to quickly identify trends in various revenue and expense items. We have calculated index numbers for Carlsberg. From an analytical point of view, it would be useful if comparable figures for Heineken were available. However, Carlsberg reports expenses by function and Heineken reports expenses by nature making a comparison of the expenses less suitable (Table 5.6).

Table 5.6 Trend analysis of Carlsberg's revenue and operating expenses

Income statement (DKKm)	Year 4	Year 5	Year 6	Year 7	Year 8
Net revenue	**100**	**105**	**113**	**123**	**165**
Cost of sales	100	105	112	126	175
Gross profit	**100**	**105**	**114**	**121**	**157**
Sales and distribution costs	100	104	110	113	139
Administrative expenses	100	107	112	114	145
Other operating income	100	143	108	152	192
Other operating expenses	na	100	85	96	97
Share of profit after tax, associates	100	110	40	48	39
Tax on profit from associates	100	100	37	37	30
Operating profit before special items	**100**	**102**	**113**	**132**	**189**
Special items, income	na	na	na	na	na
Special items, costs	100	66	96	56	225
EBITDA	**100**	**106**	**126**	**140**	**186**
Depreciation and amortisation	100	100	114	107	147
EBIT	**100**	**111**	**135**	**168**	**220**
Corporation tax	100	136	225	272	−85
Tax on profit from associates	100	100	37	37	30
Tax shield, net financial expenses	100	100	69	87	250
NOPAT	**100**	**109**	**134**	**168**	**279**

Carlsberg's net revenue increases by 65% from year 4 to year 8. In the same period, cost of sales increases by 75%, and this affects Carlsberg's profit margin negatively. Other operating expenses such as sales and distribution costs, administrative expenses and depreciation and amortisation expenses all increase at a lower rate than growth in revenues. This indicates that Carlsberg is able to manage these expenses relatively tightly.

Index numbers show the trend in important operating items. However, index numbers do not reveal the *relative size* of each item. For this purpose, common size analysis is more useful. **Common-size analysis** scales each item as a percentage of revenue and is demonstrated using Carlsberg as an example (Table 5.7).

The common-size analysis shows that cost of sales as a percentage of net revenue has grown from 45% in year 4 to 48% in year 8. In comparison sales and distribution

Table 5.7 Common-size analysis of Carlsberg's revenue and operating expenses

Income statement (DKKm)	Year 4	Year 5	Year 6	Year 7	Year 8
Net revenue	**100%**	**100%**	**100%**	**100%**	**100%**
Cost of sales	−45%	−45%	−45%	−46%	−48%
Gross profit	**55%**	**55%**	**55%**	**54%**	**52%**
Sales and distribution costs	−33%	−33%	−32%	−31%	−28%
Administrative expenses	−7%	−7%	−7%	−7%	−6%
Other operating income	2%	2%	2%	2%	2%
Other operating expenses	0%	−1%	−1%	−1%	−1%
Share of profit after tax, associates	1%	1%	0%	0%	0%
Tax on profit from associates	0%	0%	0%	0%	0%
Operating profit before special items	**17%**	**16%**	**17%**	**18%**	**19%**
	0%	0%	0%	0%	0%
Special items, income	0%	0%	1%	0%	0%
Special items, costs	−2%	−1%	−1%	−1%	−2%
EBITDA	**15%**	**15%**	**17%**	**17%**	**17%**
	0%	0%	0%	0%	0%
Depreciation and amortisation	−7%	−7%	−7%	−6%	−6%
EBIT	**8%**	**8%**	**10%**	**11%**	**11%**
	0%	0%	0%	0%	0%
Corporation tax	−1%	−1%	−2%	−2%	1%
Tax on profit from associates	0%	0%	0%	0%	0%
Tax shield, net financial expenses	−1%	−1%	−1%	−1%	−1%
NOPAT	**6%**	**6%**	**7%**	**8%**	**10%**

costs, administrative expenses and depreciation and amortisation expenses together make up 47% of revenue in year 4 and 40% in year 8. Thus, even though the most influential expense, cost of sales, is growing at a faster rate than net revenue Carlsberg is able to improve profit margin through an efficient control of other operating expenses. However, the analysis clearly highlights a cost saving potential by managing cost of sales more efficiently.

Indexing and common-size analysis of invested capital

The analysis of the turnover rate of invested capital (see Figure 5.9 above) revealed a decrease over time from 1.02 in year 4 to 0.77 in year 8. This implies that Carlsberg has tied up invested capital in an additional 117 days or, alternatively, Carlsberg needs to finance €1 of invested capital in 474 days in year 8 in comparison to 357 days in year 4. (Days on hand is defined as follows: 360/turnover rate of invested capital.)

We apply both index numbers and common size analysis to gain a better understanding of the development in capital utilisation. Since both breweries use roughly the same classification of assets and liabilities in the balance sheet, we include both companies in the analyses. This allows us to compare the efficiency in utilising invested capital across the two breweries (see Table 5.8).

Table 5.8 Trend analysis of invested capital for Carlsberg and Heineken, respectively

	Carlsberg				Index numbers	Heineken				
Year 4	Year 5	Year 6	Year 7	Year 8	Invested capital	Year 4	Year 5	Year 6	Year 7	Year 8
					Non-current assets					
100	160	167	169	421	Intangible assets	100	141	162	153	309
					Tangible assets	100	0	0	0	0
100	103	103	107	142	Property, plant and equipment	100	206	210	201	230
100	84	50	36	84	Investments in associates	100	228	267	804	1,520
100	74	69	76	93	Receivables					
					Loans to customers	0	0	100	149	143
					Advances to customers	0	0	0	100	266
100	117	114	97	124	Deferred tax assets	100	206	253	264	214
100	**121**	**121**	**124**	**233**	**Total non-current assets**	**100**	**113**	**123**	**127**	**181**
					Current assets					
100	103	109	127	164	Inventories	100	103	110	110	132
100	98	97	100	102	Trade receivables	100	113	122	122	141
100	261	263	178	395	Tax receivables					
100	140	133	83	146	Other receivables					
100	0	0	0	0	Receivables from associates					
100	97	122	152	176	Prepayments	0	0	0	100	310
100	**104**	**105**	**106**	**127**	**Total current assets**	**100**	**110**	**118**	**120**	**145**
					Non-interest-bearing debt					
100	134	137	132	343	Deferred tax liabilities	100	202	225	234	277
100	70	102	112	318	Provisions	100	34	31	24	30
100	36	52	32	123	Other liabilities					
					Current liabilities	100	0	0	0	0
100	104	117	133	168	Trade payables	100	218	241	246	309
100	100	96	95	107	Deposits on returnable packaging					
100	168	165	154	188	Provisions	100	333	516	616	700
100	122	77	33	41	Corporation tax	100	570	967	733	520
100	96	100	108	136	Other liabilities etc.					
100	0	0	0	0	Borrowings from associates					
100	**106**	**110**	**115**	**173**	**Total non-interest-bearing debt**	**100**	**86**	**96**	**96**	**117**
100	**120**	**120**	**121**	**219**	**Invested capital**	**100**	**130**	**139**	**144**	**208**

Both Carlsberg and Heineken have more than doubled the size of invested capital over the analysed period. Carlsberg's invested capital increases by 119% from year 4 to year 8, which is on par with an increase of 108% for Heineken. As noted above, Carlsberg's net revenue only increases by 65% in the same period leading to a lower turnover rate of invested capital. Heineken's net revenue grows by 42% also leading to a lower turnover rate. For Carlsberg, investments in intangible assets (primarily goodwill) seem to be the main explanation for the increase in invested capital. Investments in associates and intangible assets seem to explain the increase in invested capital for Heineken. A drawback of using index numbers, when analysing invested capital, is that the importance of each item is not obvious.

We generally prefer to apply a variation of common-size analysis to address this issue. By calculating the number of **days on hand** for each item making up invested capital, we obtain useful information on both the relative importance (weight) and the trend of each item. This is attractive from an analytical perspective. In Table 5.9 we report the days on hand for each item making up invested capital for both breweries. The days on hand is found by using the following ratio:

Days on hand (for each item): 360/turnover rate (of each item)

Days on hand express the number of days that an accounting item is consuming cash. For example, in year 8 trade receivables in Carlsberg equal 39 days. This implies that Carlsberg is offering customers on average 39 days of credit which increases working capital and invested capital. On the other hand, in year 8 trade payables are negative by 42 days. This indicates that Carlsberg obtains 42 days of credit from its suppliers reducing the need for invested capital. Days on hand indicate how well invested capital and its components have been managed.

A comparison of days on hand for both breweries reveals some interesting findings. First, Carlsberg has made significant investments in intangible assets. In year 4 intangible assets explain 126 days of the 357 days that Carlsberg has invested capital in hand. In year 8 intangible assets explain 322 days of the 474 days that Carlsberg has invested capital on hand. Alternatively, while invested capital increases by 117 days intangible assets increase by 196 days. This indicates that investments in intangible assets are the sole explanation for the deterioration in the turnover rate of invested capital for Carlsberg. In fact, the days on hand for other items such as property, plant and equipment, receivables, trade receivables, and deferred tax liabilities improve significantly. For example, the days that trade receivables are on hand in Carlsberg are reduced by 24 days (63 days minus 39 days) from year 4 to year 8. Therefore, despite the negative trend in days on hand for invested capital, Carlsberg seems to manage most of its capital more efficiently over time. After analysing the data, we believe that the main concern for an analyst is whether the acquisitions (and thereby the related intangible assets such as goodwill) made by Carlsberg are too expensive. Only time will show if this is the case.

Second, Carlsberg has invested capital tied up for 474 days in comparison to Heineken's 284 days. Differences in the level of investments in intangible assets explain this gap. While Carlsberg has intangible assets 322 days on hand in year 8 Heineken only has intangible assets tied up for 117. If we analyse other items of invested capital than intangible assets, we find that Carlsberg is generally performing worse than Heineken in year 4. For example, current assets are 115 days on hand in Carlsberg as compared to Heineken's 84 days. In spite of this, over time Carlsberg is able to utilise other items of invested capital than intangible assets more efficiently. In fact, if we ignore intangible assets Carlsberg is able to improve the number of days that other

UNIVERSITY OF WINCHESTER
LIBRARY

Table 5.9 Days on hand of invested capital for Carlsberg and Heineken, respectively

Carlsberg					Days on hand	Heineken				
Year 4	Year 5	Year 6	Year 7	Year 8	Invested capital	Year 4	Year 5	Year 6	Year 7	Year 8
					Non-current assets					
126	193	186	173	322	Intangible assets	54	71	75	74	117
					Tangible assets	91	0	0	0	0
199	196	181	173	171	Property, plant and equipment	87	166	154	156	140
17	14	7	5	9	Investments in associates	2	5	6	17	26
17	12	11	11	10	Receivables					
					Loans to customers	0	0	5	8	6
					Advances to customers	0	0	0	3	7
8	9	8	6	6	Deferred tax assets	5	9	11	12	7
368	423	393	368	518	**Total non-current assets**	239	252	250	270	304
					Current assets					
28	28	27	29	28	Inventories	29	28	27	29	27
63	59	54	51	39	Trade receivables	55	58	57	60	54
0	1	1	1	1	Tax receivables					
16	21	18	11	14	Other receivables					
2	0	0	0	0	Receivables from associates					
6	6	7	8	7	Prepayments	0	0	0	2	4
115	114	107	98	88	**Total current assets**	84	86	85	90	86
					Non-interest-bearing debt					
−18	−23	−21	−19	−37	Deferred tax liabilities	−7	−13	−13	−15	−14
−3	−2	−2	−3	−5	Provisions	−30	−10	−8	−6	−6
−1	0	−1	0	−1	Other liabilities					
					Current liabilities	−53	0	0	0	0
−41	−41	−43	−45	−42	Trade payables	−37	−75	−75	−81	−80
−13	−12	−11	−10	−8	Deposits on returnable packaging					
−3	−5	−5	−4	−4	Provisions	−1	−2	−3	−4	−4
−6	−7	−4	−2	−1	Corporation tax	−1	−3	−4	−4	−2
−41	−38	−36	−36	−34	Other liabilities etc.					
0	0	0	0	0	Borrowings from associates					
−126	−127	−123	−118	−132	**Total non-interest-bearing debt**	−128	−103	−104	−110	−106
357	410	377	349	474	**Invested capital**	195	236	230	251	284

items of invested capital are on hand by 79 days (231 days in year 4 minus 151 days in year 8). In comparison, Heineken increases the number of days that other items of invested capital than intangible assets are on hand by 16 days (141 days in year 4 minus 167 days in year 8). Therefore, over time Carlsberg seems to manage invested capital (except for intangible assets) more efficiently.

Return on equity

In the previous sections, the focus was on measurement of operating profitability. In this section we examine the impact of **financial leverage** on profitability. **Return on equity (ROE)** measures the profitability taking into account both operating and financial leverage:

$$\text{Return on equity} = \frac{\text{Net earnings after tax}}{\text{Book value of equity}} \times 100$$

Return on equity measures owners' accounting return on their investments in a company. Based on the simple numerical example from Chapter 2 (page 43) and Chapter 4 (page 74) we calculate ROE as follows:

$$\text{ROE} = \frac{70}{400} = 17.5\%$$

The following factors affect the level and trend in ROE:

- Operating profitability
- Net borrowing interest rate after tax
- Financial leverage.

This can be shown by a relationship, which will always apply:

$$\text{Return on equity} = \text{ROIC} + (\text{ROIC} - \text{NBC}) \times \frac{\text{NIBD}}{\text{BVE}}$$

where

ROIC = Return on invested capital after tax
BVE = Book value of equity
NIBD = (Book value of) net interest-bearing debt
NBC = Net borrowing cost after tax in per cent

Net borrowing cost (NBC) is defined as:

$$\text{NBC} = \frac{\text{Net financial expenses after tax}}{\text{Net interest-bearing debt}} \times 100$$

NBC rarely matches a firm's borrowing rate. First, NBC will be affected by the difference between deposit and lending rates. Second, other financial items such as currency gains and losses on securities are included in financial income and expenses. Thus, from an analytical point of view NBC should be interpreted with care.

Financial leverage is defined as:

$$\frac{\text{NIBD}}{\text{BVE}} = \frac{\text{Net interest-bearing debt}}{\text{Book value of equity}}$$

Net interest-bearing debt is measured as the difference between interest-bearing debt and interest-bearing assets (e.g. cash and securities) pursuant to Chapter 4. Based on the simple numerical example the various components of the ROE relation are calculated as follows:

$$\text{ROE} = 14.0\% + (14.0\% - 4.7\%) \times \frac{150}{400} = 17.5\% \text{ (allow for rounding errors)}$$

The first step in determining ROE is ROIC, which expresses the overall profitability of operations. The second part shows the effect of financial leverage on overall profitability. If the difference between ROIC and NBC is positive, an increase in financial leverage will improve ROE. However, financial leverage has a negative impact on ROE if ROIC is lower than NBC. The difference between ROIC and NBC is often defined as 'the interest margin' or 'spread'. The effect of financial leverage on return to shareholders (ROE) can be shown, as illustrated in Figure 5.10.

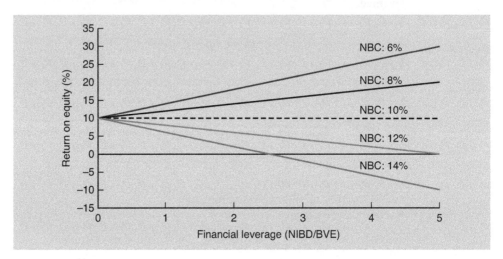

Figure 5.10 The relationship between financial leverage and return on equity

The graph is depicting changes in return on equity assuming a constant ROIC of 10%, varying interest rates (net) at 6–14% and an increasing financial leverage. With a fixed spread between ROIC and NBC, ROE develops linearly as a function of financial leverage. For example, if the spread between ROIC and NBC is positive, ROE increases linearly with financial leverage. Further, the variation in ROE increases as financial leverage goes up. However, this also indicates that risk escalates as financial leverage goes up. We elaborate on this point in Chapter 10.

Effect of minority interests on return on equity

A minority interest arises when the parent company does not own 100% of the shares in a subsidiary. In calculating invested capital, minority interests were classified together with the remaining equity. Investors in the parent company do not, however, benefit from the value creation which belongs to the minority interests. Thus, a distinction should be made between return on equity measured at the group level and return on equity measured at the parent level:

$$\text{Return on equity, group} = \frac{\text{Net earnings before minority interests}}{\text{Equity, group}} \times 100$$

$$\text{Return on equity, parent} = \frac{\text{Net earnings after minority interests}}{\text{Equity, parent}} \times 100$$

The ROE relation can also be expanded to accommodate for minority shareholders' share of return.

$$\text{Return on equity, parent} = \text{ROIC} + (\text{ROIC} - \text{NFE}) \times \frac{\text{NIBD}}{\text{BVE}} \times \text{parent's share of return}$$

where parent's share of return is calculated as:

$$\frac{\text{Net earnings after minority interests/Net earnings before minority interests}}{\text{Equity, parent/Equity, group}}$$

The following simple example illustrates the interpretation of the parent's share of return. The example is based on the following assumptions:

Net earnings before minority interest = 100
Group equity   = 1,000
Equity, parent   = 900

Based on these figures, it is shown how the parent's ROE varies according to different shares of return belonging to minority interests and the parent, respectively:

Net earnings after minority interests	100	95	90	85	80
Minority interests' share of profit	**0**	**5**	**10**	**15**	**20**
Parent's share of return	1.11	1.06	1.00	0.94	0.89
Return on equity, group	**10.0%**	**10.0%**	**10.0%**	**10.0%**	**10.0%**
Return on equity, parent	11.1%	10.6%	10.0%	9.4%	8.9%
Return on equity, minority interests	**0.0%**	**5.0%**	**10.0%**	**15.0%**	**20.0%**

A parent's share of 1.0 implies that the minority shareholders and the parent's shareholders receive the same rate of return on their invested capital. A ratio greater than 1.0 indicates that the parent's shareholders receive a higher ROE than the minority shareholders.

An assessment of the level and development of ROE can be made using the same criteria as for ROIC. The measure of the level of equity should not be based on a comparison with WACC, but with the owners' required rate of return; i.e. cost of equity. This is due to the fact that the cost of debt capital has already been taken into consideration when calculating ROE. By deducting owners' required rate (r_e) from ROE it is possible to calculate value added for the owners (also defined as **residual income (RI)**):

$$\text{Residual income} = (\text{ROE} - r_e) \times \text{BVE}$$

In order to accommodate for financial leverage, the structure of profitability, originally shown in Figure 5.1 above, must be modified as shown in Figure 5.11.

The natural starting point is the value added that owners achieve (residual income). Furthermore, ROE is shown as a function of ROIC, NBC and financial leverage. The remaining structure of profitability analysis is the same as shown in Figure 5.1.

In Table 5.10 we calculate ROE and its components for Carlsberg and Heineken. Carlsberg's ROE is significantly lower than Heineken's in the first four years (years 1–3 not shown). This applies at both group and parent level. A decomposition of ROE shows that the higher return in Heineken can be attributed to a higher ROIC. In fact, if Heineken adopted a financial leverage similar to Carlsberg in year 4 to year 7 it would experience a significantly higher ROE than actually realised. In year 8 Heineken's ROE is suffering due to a sharp decline in ROIC.

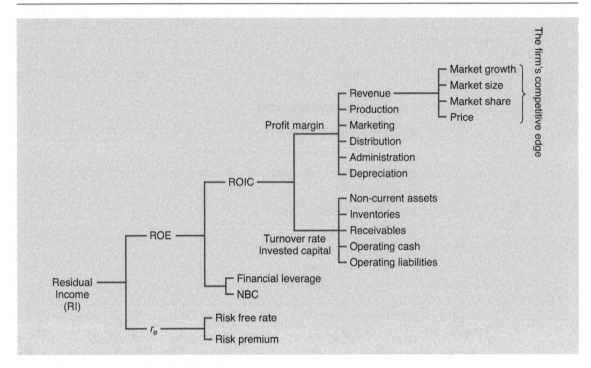

Figure 5.11 Structure of profitability analysis

Table 5.10 The decomposition of ROE for Carlsberg and Heineken

Carlsberg						Heineken				
Year 4	Year 5	Year 6	Year 7	Year 8	Ratios	Year 4	Year 5	Year 6	Year 7	Year 8
5.9%	5.3%	6.6%	8.2%	7.5%	Return on invested capital (ROIC)	18.0%	13.8%	19.3%	13.0%	6.5%
1.04	1.35	1.21	1.20	0.93	Financial leverage (NIBD/BVE)	0.41	0.69	0.49	0.38	1.13
4.5%	3.6%	2.7%	3.9%	6.9%	Net borrowing cost after tax (NBC)	15.0%	3.2%	4.0%	3.7%	6.4%
7.3%	7.6%	11.3%	13.3%	7.9%	Return on equity (ROE), group	19.2%	21.1%	26.8%	16.5%	6.6%
1.14	0.89	0.94	0.95	0.89	Parent's share of return	1.04	1.00	1.01	0.94	0.64
8.3%	6.7%	10.6%	12.7%	7.1%	Return on equity (ROE), parent	20.0%	21.1%	27.0%	15.5%	4.2%

Conclusions

Monitoring a firm's profitability is a key issue in financial statement analysis. The profitability analysis reveals important information about the trend and level of key ratios describing different aspects of a firm's profitability. This is useful information if you want to evaluate the performance of the management or develop your own assumptions about the future profitability.

The chapter introduces a number of key figures to describe profitability and presents a structure for a profound profitability analysis. Table 5.11 defines and summarises all the significant financial ratios that have been discussed in this chapter.

Table 5.11

Overview of financial ratios describing profitability

Level of analysis	Financial ratio	Definition	Information about
Level I	Value added (EVA)	$(\text{ROIC} - \text{WACC}) \times \text{invested capital}$	Economic profit
Financial ratios describing operating profitability			
Level II	Return on invested capital (ROIC)	$\dfrac{\text{NOPAT}}{\text{Invested capital}} \times 100$	Return on net operating assets
	WACC	$\dfrac{\text{NIBD}}{\text{NIBD} + \text{MVE}} \times r_d \times (1 - t) + \dfrac{\text{MVE}}{\text{NIBD} + \text{MVE}} \times r_e$	Weighted average cost of capital
Level III	Profit margin (PM)	$\dfrac{\text{NOPAT}}{\text{Revenue}} \times 100$	Revenue/expense relation
	Turnover rate, invested capital	$\dfrac{\text{Net revenue}}{\text{Invested capital}}$	Utilisation of invested capital (capital intensity)
Level IV	Indexing Common-size analysis		Identification of trends and levels for: – Revenue – Costs – Invested capital
The impact of financial leverage on profitability (owner's perspective)			
Level V	Value added (RI)	$(\text{ROE} - r_e) \times \text{BVE}$	Owners' economic profit
Level VI	Return on equity, group (ROE, group)	$\dfrac{\text{Net earnings before minority interests}}{\text{Group equity}} \times 100$ Which can be expressed as: $\text{ROIC} + (\text{ROIC} - \text{NBC}) \times \dfrac{\text{NIBD}}{\text{Group equity}}$	Return on equity before adjusting for minority interests' share of return
	Return on equity, parent (ROE, parent)	$\dfrac{\text{Net earnings after minority interests}}{\text{Equity, parent}} \times 100$ Which can be expressed as: $\text{ROIC} + (\text{ROIC} - \text{NBC}) \times \dfrac{\text{NIBD}}{\text{Group, parent}} \times \text{MI share}$	Return on equity to parent; i.e. after adjusting for minority interests' share of return
	Cost of equity (r_e)	Risk free rate + company's risk premium	Owners' cost of capital
Level VII	Financial leverage	$\dfrac{\text{NIBD}}{\text{BVE}}$	Financial leverage (risk)
	Net borrowing cost after tax (NBC)	$\dfrac{\text{Net financial expenses after tax}}{\text{NIBD}}$	Net borrowing rate (after tax)
	Minority interests' share (MI share)	$\dfrac{\text{Net earnings after MI/net earnings before MI}}{\text{Equity, parent/group equity}}$	Minority interests' share of profit

121

Review questions

- Explain the structure in a profitability analysis.

- What is the definition of ROIC, profit margin and turnover rate of invested capital?

- When is it useful to define ROIC before and after tax, respectively?

- A company experiences a drop in ROIC from 12% in year 1 to 5% in year 4. Provide potential explanations for the drop in ROIC of 7 percentage points.

- What is the appropriate benchmark for ROIC?

- What actions can a management take to improve the profit margin?

- A company that realises a turnover rate of invested capital of 4 has invested capital 180 days on hand – true or false?

- What actions can the management take to improve the turnover rate of invested capital?

- Explain the similarities and differences of indexing and common-size analyses.

- What is the definition of ROE?

- How does financial leverage affect the return to shareholders?

- What is the appropriate benchmark for ROE?

APPENDIX 5.1

Heineken original and reformulated financial statements

Reported financial statements

Income statement (€m)	Year 3	Year 4	Year 5	Year 6	Year 7	Year 8
Net turnover	9,255	10,062	10,796	11,829	11,245	14,319
Other income				379	28	32
Raw materials, consumables and services	−5,557	−6,101	−6,657	−7,376	−7,320	−9,548
Staff costs	−1,832	−1,957	−2,180	−2,241	−1,951	−2,415
Amortisation/depreciation and value adjustments	−644	−656	−710	−786	−638	−1,206
Total operating expenses	**−8,033**	**−8,714**	**−9,547**	**−10,403**	**−9,909**	**−13,169**
Operating profit	**1,222**	**1,348**	**1,249**	**1,805**	**1,364**	**1,182**

▶

Income statement (€m)	Year 3	Year 4	Year 5	Year 6	Year 7	Year 8
Share of profit of associates and joint ventures after tax	101	21	34	27	54	−102
Interests expenses	−140	−243	−199	−185	−155	−469
Interests income		78		52	64	91
Other net financing income (expenses)		−165	60	11		−107
			25		−4	
Profit before tax	**1,183**	**1,039**	**1,169**	**1,710**	**1,323**	**595**
Corporation tax	−319	−306	−300	−365	−394	−248
Group profit after tax	**864**	**733**	**869**	**1,345**	**929**	**347**
Minority interests	−66	−91	−108	−134	−122	−138
Net profit to parent's shareholders	**798**	**642**	**761**	**1,211**	**807**	**209**

Assets (€m)	Year 3	Year 4	Year 5	Year 6	Year 7	Year 8
Non-current assets						
Intangible assets	1,151	1,837	2,380	2,449	2,110	7,109
Tangible assets	4,995					
Financial assets	1,122					
Property, plant and equipment		4,773	5,067	4,944	4,673	6,314
Investments in associates		134	172	186	892	1,145
Other investments		632	646	786	397	641
Deferred tax assets		269	286	395	316	259
Advances to customers					209	346
Total non-current assets	**7,268**	**7,645**	**8,551**	**8,760**	**8,597**	**15,814**
Short-term assets						
Inventories	834	782	883	893	883	1,246
Trade and other receivables	1,379	1,646	1,787	1,917	1,769	2,504
Investments/securities	76	26	23	12	14	14
Cash	1,340	678	585	1,374	560	698
Payments and accrued income					110	231
Assets classified for sale				41	21	56
Total current assets	**3,629**	**3,132**	**3,278**	**4,237**	**3,357**	**4,749**
Total assets	**10,897**	**10,777**	**11,829**	**12,997**	**11,954**	**20,563**
Equity & liabilities (€m)						
Group equity						
Shareholder's equity	3,167					
Issued capital		784	784	784	784	784
Reserves		354	568	666	692	−74

▶

123

(continued)

Equity & liabilities (€m)	Year 3	Year 4	Year 5	Year 6	Year 7	Year 8
Retained earnings		2,118	2,617	3,559	3,928	3,761
Minority interests in other group companies	732	477	545	511	307	281
Total group equity	**3,899**	**3,733**	**4,514**	**5,520**	**5,711**	**4,752**
Liabilities						
Non-current liabilities						
Long-term borrowings	2,721					
Interest bearing loans and borrowings		2,615	2,195	2,091	1,295	9,084
Other non-current liabilities		23	38			
Employee benefits		680	664	665	586	688
Provisions long-term	1,367	298	273	242	158	344
Deferred tax liabilities		384	393	471	427	637
Total non-current liabilities	**4,088**	**4,000**	**3,563**	**3,469**	**2,466**	**10,753**
Current liabilities						
Bank overdraft		517	351	747	251	94
Interest bearing loans and borrowings		429	709	494	787	875
Trade and other payables		2,025	2,451	2,496	2,525	3,846
Income tax payable		30	141	149	71	85
Provisions short-term		43	100	122	143	158
Total current liabilities	**2,910**	**3,044**	**3,752**	**4,008**	**3,777**	**5,058**
Total liabilities	**6,998**	**7,044**	**7,315**	**7,477**	**6,243**	**15,811**
Total equity and liabilities	**10,897**	**10,777**	**11,829**	**12,997**	**11,954**	**20,563**

Analytical financial statements

Analytical income statement (€m)	Year 3	Year 4	Year 5	Year 6	Year 7	Year 8
Net turnover	9,255	10,062	10,796	11,829	11,245	14,319
Other income	0	0	0	379	28	32
Raw materials, consumables and services	−5,557	−6,101	−6,657	−7,376	−7,320	−9,548
Staff costs	−1,832	−1,931	−2,161	−2,234	−1,947	−2,398
Income from loans to customers less impairment losses				11	5	6
Share of profit of associates and joint ventures after tax	101	21	34	27	54	−102

▶

Analytical income statement (€m)	Year 3	Year 4	Year 5	Year 6	Year 7	Year 8
Tax on profit from associates and joint ventures	53	11	16	11	18	−35
EBITDA	**2,020**	**2,062**	**2,028**	**2,647**	**2,083**	**2,274**
Amortisation/depreciation and value adjustments	−644	−656	−710	−786	−638	−1,206
Operating profit (EBIT)	**1,376**	**1,406**	**1,318**	**1,861**	**1,445**	**1,068**
Corporation tax	−319	−306	−300	−365	−394	−248
Tax shield, net financial expenses	−48	−123	−42	−41	−27	−130
Tax on profit from associates and joint ventures	−53	−11	−16	−11	−18	35
Net operating profit after tax (NOPAT)	**956**	**966**	**960**	**1,444**	**1,006**	**725**
Interests expenses	−140	−243	−199	−185	−155	−468
Interests income	0	78	60	41	59	84
Other net financing income (expenses)	0	−191	6	4	−8	−124
Net financial expenses	−140	−356	−133	−140	−104	−508
Tax on net financial expenses	48	123	42	41	27	130
Group profit after tax	**864**	**733**	**869**	**1,345**	**929**	**347**
Minority interests	**−66**	**−91**	**−108**	**−134**	**−122**	**−138**
Net profit to parent's shareholders	**798**	**642**	**761**	**1,211**	**807**	**209**
Analytical balance sheet (€m)						
Assets						
Intangible assets	1,151	1,837	2,380	2,449	2,110	7,109
Tangible assets	4,995					
Property, plant and equipment		4,773	5,067	4,944	4,673	6,314
Loans to customers				329	161	310
Deferred tax asset		269	286	395	316	259
Investments in associates		134	172	186	892	1,145
Total non-current assets	**6,146**	**7,013**	**7,905**	**8,303**	**8,152**	**15,137**
Current assets						
Inventories	834	782	883	893	883	1,246
Trade and other receivables	1,379	1,646	1,787	1,917	1,769	2,504
Payments and accrued income					110	231
Total current assets	**2,213**	**2,428**	**2,670**	**2,810**	**2,762**	**3,981**
Provisions						
Provisions long-term	1,367	298	273	242	158	344
Total provisions	**1,367**	**341**	**373**	**364**	**301**	**502**

▶

(*continued*)

Analytical balance sheet (€m)	Year 3	Year 4	Year 5	Year 6	Year 7	Year 8
Non-interest-bearing debt						
Current liabilities	2,910					
Trade and other payables		2,025	2,389	2,486	2,504	3,759
Provisions short-term		43	100	122	143	158
Income tax payable		30	141	149	71	85
Deferred tax liabilities		384	393	471	427	637
Total non-interest-bearing debt	**2,910**	**2,482**	**3,023**	**3,228**	**3,145**	**4,639**
Invested capital	**4,082**	**6,661**	**7,279**	**7,643**	**7,611**	**14,135**
Group equity						
Shareholder's equity	3,167					
Issued capital		784	784	784	784	784
Reserves		354	568	666	692	−74
Retained earnings		2,118	2,617	3,559	3,928	3,761
Minority interests in other group companies	732	477	545	511	307	281
Total group equity	**3,899**	**3,733**	**4,514**	**5,520**	**5,711**	**4,752**
Interest-bearing liabilities						
Long-term borrowings	2,721					
Interest-bearing loans and borrowings		2,615	2,195	2,091	1,295	9,084
Other non-current liabilities		23	38			
Employee benefits		680	664	665	586	688
Bank overdraft		517	351	747	251	94
Derivatives used for hedging	–	–	62	10	21	87
Interest-bearing loans and borrowings		429	709	494	787	875
Total interest-bearing liabilities	**2,721**	**4,264**	**4,019**	**4,007**	**2,940**	**10,828**
Interest-bearing assets						
Financial assets	1,122					
Other Investments		632	646	457	236	331
Advances to customers					209	346
Investments/securities	76	26	23	12	14	14
Cash	1,340	678	585	1,374	560	698
Assets classified for sale				41	21	56
Total interest-bearing assets	**2,538**	**1,336**	**1,254**	**1,884**	**1,040**	**1,445**
Total invested capital	**4,082**	**6,661**	**7,279**	**7,643**	**7,611**	**14,135**

Growth analysis

Learning outcomes

After reading this chapter you should be able to:

- Measure how fast a company can grow while maintaining the financial risk at the same level
- Recognise that there are many ways to measure growth but only one way to measure if growth is value creating
- Evaluate the quality of growth
- Assess if growth is sustainable
- Understand whether growth induced by share buy-back adds value
- Understand the importance of liquidity when growing a business

Growth

Growth in sales is seen by many as the driving force of future progress in enterprises. Growth is associated with value creation, but as shown in this chapter, it is not always the case. However, it is clear that growth in businesses has secondary effects that influence a company's stakeholders, for example:

- Shareholders perceive growth to be attractive as it allegedly creates value
- Lenders are interested as growth creates a need for liquidity
- Suppliers are keen to sell their products to growth companies
- Employees see growth companies as dynamic and challenging: an appealing work environment.

A company can make a comparison with competitors' growth rates. This is done to assess its relative performance, identify major competitors and to recognise future growth opportunities. It is therefore no surprise that growth analysis is a key concept in the accounting literature.

A firm's growth is a function of many factors including market growth and intensity of competition. Measurement of growth in key financial data is therefore a mirror image of how a company performs relative to its competitors. For the same reason, growth-related financial ratios should never stand alone, but should be supplemented with information on strategy, competitor information, information on market growth and market share, etc.

This chapter focuses on the measurement of growth from a financial perspective. Specifically, the chapter aims at answering the following key questions about growth:

- How fast can a company grow, while maintaining the financial risk at the same level (sustainable growth rate)?
- Is growth always value creating?
- What is the quality of growth?
- Is growth sustainable?
- Is growth in earnings per share (EPS) always value creating?
- Does growth in financial ratios caused by share buy-back always add value?
- What is the relationship between growth and liquidity?

We will discuss each of these issues in further detail below.

Sustainable growth rate

Companies may have set strategic objectives for market share and growth, but may be unable to fund these objectives through internally generated cash. In this case, a firm has a number of ways to finance its strategy. It can issue new shares, increase financial leverage (borrow) or reduce dividends payments. Alternatively, a firm may reduce its ambitions and adjust its strategy to reflect the firm's financial capacity.

A firm's **sustainable growth rate** is a useful growth measure. It indicates at what pace a company can grow its revenues while preserving its financial risk; i.e. maintaining its financial leverage at the same level despite growth. Knowledge about the sustainable growth rate is also important in valuing companies and credit rating. Analysis of the sustainable growth rate can also be used to identify the different sources of growth, including operating and financial factors. This knowledge is important when assessing the quality of growth.

The sustainable growth rate is calculated as:

$$g = \left[\text{ROIC} + (\text{ROIC} - \text{NBC}) \times \frac{\text{NIBD}}{\text{E}} \right] \times \text{Minority interests share} \times (1 - \text{PO})$$

where

g	Sustainable growth rate
ROIC	Return on invested capital after tax (based on the beginning of the year balance sheet)
NBC	Net borrowing cost after tax in per cent (based on the beginning of year balance sheet)
NIBD	Net interest-bearing debt
E	Equity
PO	Payout ratio (dividend as a percentage of net profit)

As shown in the formula for the sustainable growth rate, return on equity and the **payout ratio** comes into play:

$$g = \underbrace{\left[\text{ROIC} + (\text{ROIC} - \text{NBC}) \times \frac{\text{NIBD}}{\text{E}} \right] \times \text{Minority interests share}}_{\text{Return on equity (ROE)}} \times (1 - \text{PO})$$

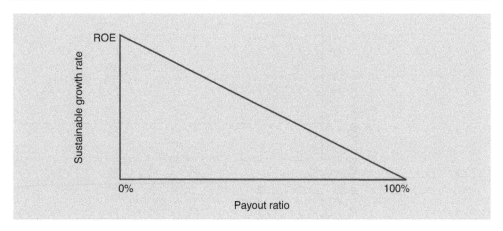

Figure 6.1 The relationship between the payout ratio and the sustainable growth rate

Return on equity is further dealt with in Chapter 5. The payout ratio is calculated as the proportion of net earnings that is distributed to shareholders. From the above equation it is evident that a company's dividend policy affects the sustainable growth rate. Figure 6.1 illustrates how this is the case. Suppose a company's return on equity is 20%. Based on this, it can be shown that the company's sustainable growth rate is a function of a firm's dividend policy (payout ratio).

As shown in Figure 6.1 the sustainable growth rate decreases as the payout ratio increases. In the extreme case where the entire profits are distributed to shareholders, the sustainable growth rate becomes 0%. The example also shows that a company that relies on a constant debt to equity ratio cannot grow faster than return on equity.

Based on the equation for the sustainable growth rate another point can be made. Improved profitability allows for a higher sustainable growth rate. Suppose a company has the following characteristics:

Financial leverage = 1
Net borrowing cost after tax in per cent = 5%
Payout ratio = 0%

Based on these assumptions, the company's sustainable growth rate can be shown as a function of operating profitability (return on invested capital after tax) as illustrated in Figure 6.2. For example, if ROIC is 5% or alternatively 10%, the sustainable growth rate becomes:

$$g = \left[\text{ROIC} + (\text{ROIC} - \text{NBC}) \times \frac{\text{NIBD}}{\text{E}} \right] \times (1 - \text{PO})$$
$$= \left[5\% + (5\% - 5\%) \times 1 \right] \times (1 - 0) = 5\%$$

$$g = \left[\text{ROIC} + (\text{ROIC} - \text{NBC}) \times \frac{\text{NIBD}}{\text{E}} \right] \times (1 - \text{PO})$$
$$= \left[10\% + (10\% - 5\%) \times 1 \right] \times (1 - 0) = 15\%$$

As shown in Figure 6.2, there is a positive association between the return on invested capital and a firm's sustainable growth rate.

The impact of financial leverage on the sustainable growth rate depends upon a firm's ability to earn a return on invested capital in excess of its net borrowing rate.

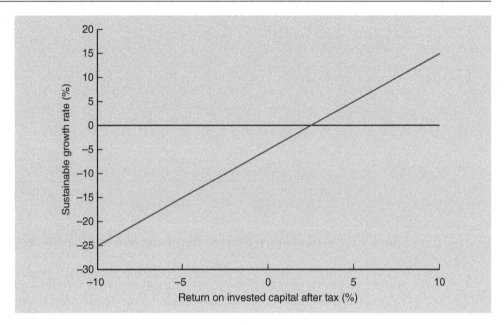

Figure 6.2 The relationship between return on invested capital and sustainable growth rate

To the extent that the spread between return on invested capital and the net borrowing rate is positive, financial leverage contributes positively to the sustainable growth rate. This is illustrated in Example 6.1.

Example 6.1 Two companies within the same industry have the following characteristics:

Financial ratio	Company 1	Company 2
Return on invested capital after tax	3%	7%
Net borrowing cost after tax	5%	5%
Minority interests share	1.0	1.0
Payout ratio	0%	0%

Based on these assumptions, the sustainable growth rate is a function of financial leverage as illustrated in Figure 6.3. When the return on invested capital exceeds the net borrowing rate, financial leverage contributes positively to the sustainable growth rate. On the other hand financial leverage has a negative effect on the sustainable growth rate if the net borrowing rate exceeds the return on invested capital.

$$g = \left[\underbrace{\text{ROIC}}_{\text{Operations}} + \underbrace{(\text{ROIC} - \text{NBC}) \times \frac{\text{NIBD}}{\text{E}}}_{\text{Financial leverage}} \right] \times \text{Minority interests share} \times \underbrace{(1 - \text{PO})}_{\text{Dividend policy}}$$

For the two companies, the sustainable growth rate is calculated as:

Company 1: $g = [3\% + (3\% - 5\%) \times 1 \times (1 - 0)] = 1\%$

Company 2: $g = [7\% + (7\% - 5\%) \times 1 \times (1 - 0)] = 9\%$

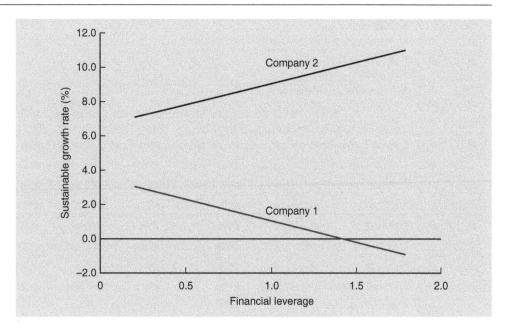

Figure 6.3 The relationship between financial leverage and sustainable growth rate

As Company 1 has a negative spread (ROIC − NBC < 0), financial leverage has a negative impact on the sustainable growth rate. For example, had financial leverage been 2.0, the sustainable growth would have been −1%.

In summary, we have identified three sources that affect the sustainable growth rate: operating profitability, financial leverage and dividend policies. Now, take a moment to consider the following question:

> Should companies always strive to obtain a high sustainable growth rate? ■

A high sustainable growth rate indicates that a company has chosen to reinvest most of its accounting profit and thus decided not to distribute it to its shareholders as dividends or share buy-backs. From a shareholder's perspective, this is only attractive if reinvestments derived from the accounting profit will be invested in profitable projects, i.e. projects which create value. From the lender's standpoint, a high sustainable growth rate, *ceteris paribus*, decrease the risk of the existing loan arrangements, since a larger share of net profit remains in the company. Conversely, it reduces a firm's need for borrowing, and thus banks' market for loans. Often a firm's dividend policy becomes part of the loan terms (debt covenants). If a firm violates the debt covenants – for example, exceeds some pre-defined limits for selected financial ratios – the banks can influence a firm's dividend policy in order to increase the available collaterals in their lending commitments.

Is growth always value creating?

In addition to sustainable growth rate, many other growth measures are used, for example, growth in:

- Revenue
- Operating profit (EBIT)

131

- Net earnings
- Free cash flows
- Dividends
- Invested capital
- Economic value added (EVA).

In Table 6.1 Satair has been used to illustrate the effect of growth in selected accounting items, which are often used by analysts. Satair is one of the world's leading distributors of spare parts for aircraft and is listed on the OMX Nasdaq Stock Exchange.

Table 6.1 **Satair: Growth in selected accounting items and performance measures**

	Year 1	Year 2	Year 3	Year 4	Avg
Revenue	20%	2%	3%	17%	10%
EBIT	34%	−40%	−21%	−6%	**−8%**
Net earnings	34%	−65%	22%	−24%	−8%
Invested capital	69%	0%	−12%	26%	21%
Owners' equity	29%	8%	−8%	19%	12%
Free cash flow	−199%	−126%	368%	−186%	−36%
Sustainable growth rate	33%	7%	9%	6%	**14%**

A comparison of Satair's different growth rates reveals a disparate picture of growth. Revenues, invested capital and equity increase on average by 10–21% annually, although growth is slowing. Moreover, the sustainable growth rate averaged **14%**. These figures indicate that Satair is a growth business. Another picture of Satair appears when growth in accounting-based performance measures are analysed. The average growth rate of net earnings and operating profit amount to **minus 8%**. Similarly, there is a significant negative growth rate in the free cash flows, partly due to investment in non-current assets. Therefore, based on the above, is Satair a growth business?

The increase in accounting numbers such as revenue and invested capital demonstrate that this is apparently the case. On the other hand, the trends in the performance measures indicate that Satair is rather a company with negative growth.

Chapter 5 shows that from a shareholder's perspective it is not sufficient that accounting earnings are positive. Value creation is only obtained if accounting returns (ROIC) exceed the required rate of return (WACC) or alternatively if return on equity (ROE) exceeds investors required rate of return (r_e). As noted earlier this can be shown in one of two ways:

$$\text{Value added (EVA)} = (\text{ROIC} - \text{WACC}) \times \text{Invested capital}$$

or

$$\text{Value added (residual income)} = (\text{ROE} - r_e) \times \text{Equity}$$

These two measures provide the same results. A positive value added measure is a sufficient condition to ensure that value is created from a shareholder's perspective. In a growth context, it means that growth is only interesting if EVA (or residual income) increases.

Satair's EVA develops as shown in Table 6.2. WACC is assumed to be a constant at 9% in all years. As shown, the development of EVA is negative in years 1 to 4. From generating DKK 43.6 million in EVA in year 1, EVA becomes negative in each of the following years. Satair, therefore, destroys value for its shareholders over the period years 2–4. It is clear from the above calculations that growth in revenue and invested capital has not created value. On the contrary, in contrast to the growth in Satair's revenue and invested capital, EVA has become negative. From a shareholder's perspective, Satair is not a growth business. The company seems to experience negative growth based on the development in EVA. Shareholders have also reacted negatively. The share price has almost dropped by 50% during the four-year period.

Table 6.2 Satair: EVA calculations based on annual reports

DKKm	Year 1	Year 2	Year 3	Year 4
Return on invested capital after tax	24.7%	8.9%	6.9%	7.4%
WACC	9.0%	9.0%	9.0%	9.0%
Invested capital	276.7	466.5	468.6	412.6
EVA	43.6	−0.6	−9.6	−6.5
Growth in EVA		−101%	−1,465%	32%
Share price	220	133	108	119

In general growth in EVA can be obtained by:

- Optimising existing operations (improving return on invested capital)
- Growth in invested capital if growth is profitable (ROIC > WACC)
- Reducing the cost of capital (WACC).

The actions a company can take to reduce its cost of capital are rather limited. Both lenders and owners operate in a competitive market and are likely to offer financing on market terms, i.e. at competitive rates that reflect the underlying risk of the company. This means that a firm can reduce the required rate of return from capital providers (WACC) only by changing the capital structure. Both theoretically and in practice, it is questionable whether changes in the capital structure reduce the costs of capital (Parum 2001). In most cases, a company is therefore left to focus on optimising existing operations and invest in profitable business projects.

In the short term, optimisation of operations contributes to the growth in EVA. There is, however, a limit as to how much companies can optimise operations. Accordingly, long-term growth in EVA must come from investments in profitable business projects.

Suppose Satair in years 2–4 had been able to maintain the same rate of return on invested capital (24.7%) as in year 1. Under this assumption Satair's EVA would have been positive and have grown, as shown in Table 6.3.

EVA would grow from DKK 43.6 million to DKK 64.9 million just like invested capital increase during the period. The example illustrates that long-term growth in EVA must come from investments in profitable projects.

Table 6.3 Satair: EVA calculation at a constant ROIC

DKKm	Year 1	Year 2	Year 3	Year 4
ROIC (beginning)	24.7%	24.7%	24.7%	24.7%
WACC	9.0%	9.0%	9.0%	9.0%
Invested capital, beginning	276.7	466.5	468.6	412.6
EVA	**43.6**	73.4	73.8	**64.9**
Growth in EVA		69%	0%	−12%

What is the quality of growth?

An analysis of growth in EVA is important to prevent any faulty reasoning. It is appropriate to ask the question:

What is the underlying reason for the growth in EVA?

In this section, we present and discuss some of the financial factors that drive growth.
    To provide a structure for growth analysis, the DuPont model introduced in Chapter 5 comes into play. This model is shown in a modified form in Figure 6.4.

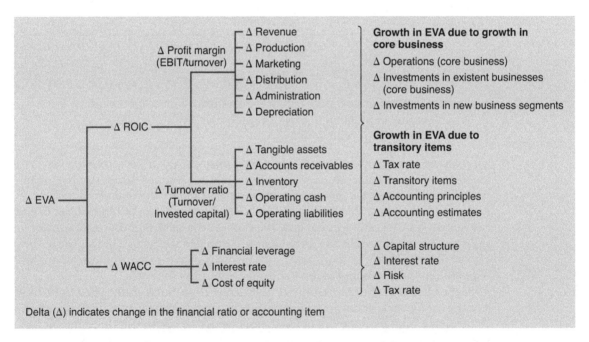

Delta (Δ) indicates change in the financial ratio or accounting item

Figure 6.4 Structure of the analysis of growth in EVA – DuPont model

The modified model demonstrates that it is changes in profitability (return on invested capital) and cost of capital (WACC), which affects the growth in EVA. As pointed out in the previous section, a company has few opportunities to affect the cost of capital. Therefore, this section focuses on changes in operating profitability. Furthest to right in Figure 6.4 several possible explanations for improvements in operating ratios, and hence growth in EVA, are provided. In this context it is important to assess the sustainability of growth. It is more attractive if changes (improvements) in financial ratios are persistent, i.e. recurring.

Growth in EVA due to growth in core business

Generally, it is assumed that earnings from a firm's core business are more attractive than earnings of transitory nature, as earnings from core business to a greater extent are expected to be recurring. Optimisation of earnings from core business may be obtained in several ways:

- Introducing a more profitable pricing policy
- Selling fewer but more profitable products
- Using more efficient production methods, including outsourcing to countries with low wages
- Changing the marketing approach
- Optimising administration
- Optimising invested capital (e.g. a reduction in inventories).

As shown in the Satair example, investments in *existing businesses* or *new businesses* may lead to growth in EVA if the return on new investments exceeds the required rate of return.

A change in the tax rate will have a lasting impact on future EVAs. For example, in many countries the corporate tax rate is substantially lower today than just a few decades ago. The lower tax rate has had a positive effect on EVA.

Growth in EVA due to transitory items

Accounting items, which all directly contribute to the growth in EVA, but which are either **transitory** in nature, or merely reflective of an artificial increase in the underlying operations, include:

- Gains and losses on sale of non-current assets
- Restructuring costs
- Discontinued operations
- Change in the corporate tax rate
- Changes in accounting estimates
- Changes in accounting policies.

Gains and losses on disposal of non-current assets, *restructuring cost* and *discontinued operations* are accounting entries that are transitory by nature. The effect is not long-lasting and the change in EVA attributable to these items is only temporary.

The impact of *changes in the tax rate* on earnings contains elements that are both recurring and transitory by nature. On the one hand, a change in the tax rate will have an impact on future earnings and the effect is therefore recurring in nature. On the other hand, a change in the tax rate will affect the value of deferred tax liabilities (deferred tax assets) which results in a gain if the tax rate decreases and a loss if the tax rate increases. These gains and losses are non-recurring and therefore transitory.

At first sight *changes in accounting policies* and *accounting estimates* express a sustained change, as it can be assumed that changes in accounting policies apply in the future. A closer analysis, however, demonstrates that this is not the case. First, changes in EVA caused by changes in accounting policies or accounting estimates do not add value as such. There is no association between the change in EVA and trends in the underlying performance of the business. Second, it can be shown that any progress in EVA prompted by, say, an expansion of the estimated lifetime of depreciable, non-current assets is only temporary. This is illustrated in Example 6.2.

<table>
<tr><td>Example 6.2</td><td></td></tr>
</table>

Change of accounting estimate

An entity is characterised by the following financial characteristics:

$$
\begin{aligned}
\text{Annual investments} &= 1{,}000 \\
\text{Lifetime of investments} &= 2 \text{ years} \\
\text{Profit margin (EBITDA)} &= 1{,}200 \\
\text{Corporate tax rate} &= 50\% \\
\text{WACC} &= 10\%
\end{aligned}
$$

Other assumptions:

- Non-current assets are identical to invested capital
- No growth in investments

Based on these assumptions NOPAT becomes:

EBITDA	1,200
Depreciation and amortisation	−1,000
EBIT	200
Taxes (50%)	−100
NOPAT	100

Assuming that the above assumptions remain constant in future periods, growth in the company's EVA can be calculated as shown in Table 6.4, and, as shown, there is no growth in EVA. Operating profit after tax and costs of capital are constant over time.

Table 6.4 Growth in EVA before change in accounting estimates

Year	1	2	3	4	5	6
NOPAT	100	100	100	100	100	100
Non-current assets, end of year	500	500	500	500	500	500
Cost of capital	−50	−50	−50	−50	−50	−50
EVA	50	50	50	50	50	50
Growth in EVA		0%	0%	0%	0%	0%

Now assume that the company changes its accounting estimates in year 4 *for new investments*, so that the expected useful life of its non-current (tangible and intangible) assets is extended from two years to three years for all future investments. It affects in the short run the accounting figures used to calculate EVA. This is shown in Table 6.5, and, as is evident, depreciation is lower in years 4 and 5 due to the change in the estimated lifetime for non-current assets. Also, the cost of capital increases due to the increase in book value of invested

Table 6.5 Growth in EVA after change in accounting estimates

	Changes in estimates						
Year	1	2	3	4	5	6	7
WACC	10%						
EBITDA	1,200	1,200	1,200	**1,200**	1,200	1,200	1,200
Depreciation and amortisation	−1,000	−1,000	−1,000	**−833**	−667	−1,000	−1,000
EBIT	200	200	200	**367**	533	200	200
Taxes (50%)	−100	−100	−100	**−183**	−267	−100	−100
NOPAT	100	100	100	**183**	267	100	100
Non-current assets	500	500	500	**667**	1,000	1,000	1,000
Cost of capital	−50	−50	−50	**−67**	−100	−100	−100
EVA	**50**	50	50	117	167	0	0
Growth in EVA		0%	0%	133%	43%	−100%	0%

capital (non-current assets). The total effect is that EVA changes from 50 in year 1 to 167 in year 5. Looking further ahead EVA reverses to a 'permanent' level of 0 (zero). Growth in EVA caused by changes in accounting estimates is, hence, non-lasting. It fades away, when changes in applied accounting policies (accounting estimates) are fully normalised. Value creation is – not surprisingly – unaffected as changes in accounting estimates have no cash flow effects. ∎

In conclusion, growth in EVA caused by an improvement in the core business is preferable. This is so because it must be expected that such an improvement is more likely to continue (recurring) than improvements based on the disposal of assets or changes in accounting estimates (i.e. transitory items). The above example illustrates the importance of analysing the quality of growth in EVA. The concept of accounting quality will be discussed further in Chapter 13.

Is growth sustainable?

One of the purposes of a growth analysis is to estimate future growth. This is done by comparing the historical growth rate in revenues with future growth opportunities in the industry. The potential growth will be affected by the underlying market growth, for example, rivalry among competitors, threats from potential entrants and the relative competitive strengths.

It was argued above that growth caused by an improvement in the core business is longer lasting than growth based on transitory accounting items. The question is how stable each accounting item and financial ratio is over time. Stability in accounting items makes it easier to forecast future earnings. Below, we examine the stability in a number of financial ratios for US firms over a 50-year period. Specifically, we examine how accounting items and financial ratios correlate over time. For example, in Table 6.6 we show how growth in revenue in year 0 is correlated with growth in revenue in the following five years. The higher the correlation, the more stable the growth in revenue.

Table 6.6 Measurement of the stability of selected financial ratios (correlation coefficients)

Year relative to first year (year 0)	1	2	3	4	5
Growth in revenue	**32.30**	15.44	12.53	10.90	11.87
EBITDA margin	97.25	93.91	90.64	89.01	85.75
EBIT margin	96.90	92.06	88.59	86.41	83.40
Special items/revenue	47.07	36.25	29.48	23.17	20.96
Tangible assets/revenue	89.14	80.82	78.68	77.68	74.71
ROIC	77.19	65.04	58.39	54.20	51.00

Source: Compustat®, Copyright © 2011 The McGraw-Hill Companies, Inc. Standard & Poor's, including its subsidiary corporations (S&P), is a division of The McGraw-Hill Companies, Inc. Reproduction of this Work in any form is prohibited without S&P's prior written permission.

As shown in Table 6.6, the correlation between growth in revenue last year and this year (1) is only 32.3%. This shows a limited stability. This is also supported by the development of growth in revenue as illustrated in Figure 6.5, where all companies are divided into 10 portfolios in year 1 based on their growth in revenue. Thus, each line in the figure represents one portfolio of companies with similar growth rates. Each company remains in the same portfolio in the five subsequent years. As shown, there is a clear tendency that an atypically high or low revenue growth rate for a portfolio of companies is quickly followed by more normal growth rates. After no more than three or four years, sales growth converges towards a long-term average value.

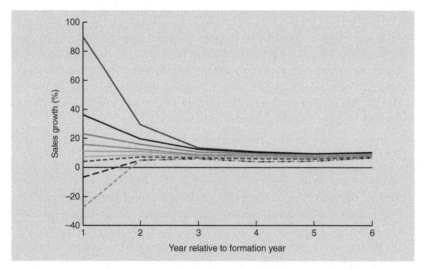

Figure 6.5 Stability (sustainability) in sales growth
Source: Compustat®, Copyright © 2011 The McGraw-Hill Companies, Inc. Standard & Poor's, including its subsidiary corporations (S&P), is a division of The McGraw-Hill Companies, Inc. Reproduction of this Work in any form is prohibited without S&P's prior written permission.

Table 6.6 also reports the correlation coefficients for margins, (the inverse of) turnover rate of tangible assets and ROIC. These correlation coefficients reveal that margins and turnover rates remain stable and at a high level over time. For example, the correlation coefficient between the EBIT margin today and six years ago is 83%. We have also calculated a margin that only consists of special items; i.e. primarily transitory items. The correlation coefficient between that margin today and six years ago was only 21%.

A comparison of ROIC inclusive of permanent and transitory accounting items and transitory accounting items only, reveals larger correlation coefficients for ROIC when calculated on both permanent and transitory accounting items together. To illustrate these results the relative development of the return on invested capital (including both permanent and transitory items) and return on invested capital calculated solely on transitory items are shown in Figures 6.6 and 6.7.

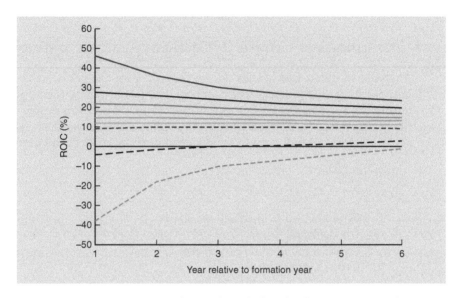

Figure 6.6 Return on invested capital (including both permanent and transitory items)
Source: Compustat®, Copyright © 2011 The McGraw-Hill Companies, Inc. Standard & Poor's, including its subsidiary corporations (S&P), is a division of The McGraw-Hill Companies, Inc. Reproduction of this Work in any form is prohibited without S&P's prior written permission.

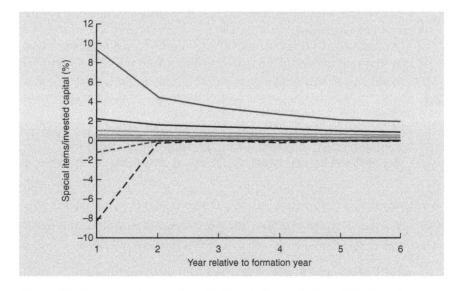

Figure 6.7 Return on invested capital (including only transitory items)
Source: Compustat®, Copyright © 2011 The McGraw-Hill Companies, Inc. Standard & Poor's, including its subsidiary corporations (S&P), is a division of The McGraw-Hill Companies, Inc. Reproduction of this Work in any form is prohibited without S&P's prior written permission.

As shown, both ratios converge towards a long-term average value. This pattern is particularly noticeable for return on invested capital which is based on transitory items only. The above findings support the importance of distinguishing between transitory and permanent items. The results also support economic theory. For example, it seems impossible to maintain high growth rates in the long run. There is a tendency for accounting items to converge towards a long-term mean value. This is a crucial point when we discuss forecasting in Chapter 8.

Is growth in earnings per share (EPS) always value creating?

Analysts, managers and boards of directors often use the performance measure earnings per share (EPS) in different contexts. Analysts use the growth in EPS in valuing businesses. Presumably, there is a positive correlation between the growth in EPS and firm value. This is illustrated by reference to the dividend discount model. Under the assumption of constant growth the dividend discount model can be expressed as:

$$P = \frac{\text{Div}}{r_e - g}$$

where

P = Estimated value of equity per share
Div = Dividends per share
r_e = Owners' required rate of return
g = Growth in dividends

Since dividends equals EPS × Payout ratio, the dividend model can be rewritten as follows:

$$P = \frac{\text{EPS} \times \text{Payout ratio}}{r_e - g}$$

Therefore, from the modified dividend discount model it seems that higher EPS will lead to higher firm value. This implies that analysts will value a company at a higher rate if EPS is growing.

Accordingly, boards may use EPS to determine management's bonus based on the idea that an improved EPS will lead to higher firm value. Consider Example 6.3.

Example 6.3 Marks and Spencer has given a hint of the tough High Street environment, lowering the profits the firm has to make for directors to earn bonuses.

Top executives will achieve a maximum payout if earnings per share grow by more than 8% above inflation, compared with a 12% target the previous year.

But M&S said the new target was 'at least as challenging' in the current economic climate.

Source: BBC News, 6 June 2008

As shown in the example, the top executives of Marks and Spencer are awarded bonuses depending on the growth rate in earnings per share (EPS). Last year EPS had to grow by more than 12% above inflation, while this year growth in EPS had to exceed inflation by at least 8% for executives to earn bonuses.

However, it is not unproblematic to use the growth in EPS as a performance measure in bonus contracts. As illustrated in Example 6.4, it is possible to obtain growth in EPS while destroying value at the same time, which makes accounting figures like EPS questionable to use as performance measures.

| Example 6.4 | **Earnings per share** |

In Table 6.7 it is assumed that the company is 100% equity financed and the number of shares is constant. This implies that operating profit after tax equals net earnings. Furthermore, investors' required rate of return is assumed to be 10%.

Table 6.7 Example of the growth in EPS and EVA

Year	1	2	3	4	5	6
Net operating profit after tax (NOPAT)	100.0	115.0	132.3	152.1	174.9	201.1
Growth in EPS		15%	15%	15%	15%	15%
Invested capital	1,000.0	1,250.0	1,562.5	1,953.1	2,441.4	3,051.8
Growth in invested capital		25%	25%	25%	25%	25%
Cost of capital	100.0	125.0	156.3	195.3	244.1	305.2
Economic Value Added (EVA)	0.0	−10.0	−24.0	−43.2	−69.2	−104.0
Growth in Economic Value Added (EVA)		n.a.	−140%	−80%	−60%	−50%

As shown in Table 6.7, EPS grows by 15% annually. This immediately indicates a strong progress and if the figures represented earnings' trends in Marks and Spencer, the company's top executives would be awarded a bonus (unless inflation is above 15% − 8% = 7%). However, growth in EPS (15%) is less than growth in invested capital (25%). This reduces the overall profitability of the company. Apart from the starting point (year 1), EVA is negative and increasingly so. The example illustrates that economic decisions, which are based on EPS, and ignores investments, may lead to irrational behaviour. In the above example top executives would have received a bonus, despite the fact that they destroy value throughout the analysed period. It is therefore essential to be cautious in applying growth in EPS as an indicator of management's performance. ∎

Does growth in financial ratios caused by share buy-back always add value?

It has become increasingly common for companies to buy back their own shares, rather than using excess cash to pay out dividends. An argument for **share buy-backs** is that it improves financial ratios, including EPS, and thereby supposedly increases the value of the company.

Consider share buy-backs in Holland in recent years. As listed in Table 6.8 a number of Dutch firms have had share buy-back programmes. Philips, for example, bought back their own shares five times during a four-year period. Similar share buy-back programmes are also prevalent in many other countries.

Figure 6.8 provides additional evidence on the increased use of share buy-back programmes. Based on US data in the period from 1977 to 2004, it is evident that investors in the beginning of the period earned a return almost entirely by means of dividends (and price appreciation of the shares). In later years, however, the pay-off to investors is almost equally split between dividends and share buy-backs. In fact, in 2004 share buy-backs represented a larger part of pay-off than dividends.

Table 6.8 **Share buy-back in the Netherlands over a four-year period**

Company	Date	Amount (EUR m)	% of market cap
ABN AMRO	28 Jun 05	2,200	3.00%
ABN AMRO	8 Feb 07	1,000	1.40%
Aegon	10 Aug 06	170.7	0.70%
Aegon	1 Mar 07	117.4	0.50%
ASML	19 Apr 06	400	5.25%
ASML	9 Oct 06	180	3.00%
ASML	14 Feb 07	152	1.65%
ASML	28 Mar 07		30.00%
BE Semiconductor	27 Feb 07	5	3.00%
Beter Bed Holding	9 Mar 07	5	1.00%
CSM	17 May 05	90	5.00%
CSM	29 Sep 06	190	9.00–10.00%
DSM	27 Sep 06	750	10.00%
Fugro	28 Jun 05	12.2	0.50%
Hagemeyer	29 Jun 05	10.8	0.50%
Heineken	28 Jun 05	20.4	
Heineken	1 Jan 07	8.74	
Hunter Douglas	25 Nov 03	65.8	4.00%
ING	28 Jun 05	142	0.21%
KPN	28 Jun 04	500	3.00%
KPN	26 Jun 05	500	3.00%
KPN	1 Mar 05	985	6.70%
KPN	9 Aug 05	250	1.60%
KPN	7 Feb 06	1,515	6.5–7.0%
KPN	6 Feb 07	1,000	4.50%
Macintosh	28 Jun 05	7.4	1.13%
New skies satellites	1 May 03	49.8	6.67%
Nutreco	22 Jun 06	50	2.77%
Philips	27 Jan 05	500	2.00%
Philips	15 Aug 05	1,500	5.00%
Philips	17 Jul 06	1,500	4.0–4.5%
Philips	16 Oct 06	2,320	7.0–7.5%
Philips	9 Jan 07	1,630	5.00%
Reed Elsevier	16 Feb 06	870	5.00%
Royal Dutch Shell	29 Apr 04	1,300	1.90%
Royal Dutch Shell	4 Feb 05	5,000	2.5–4.5%
Stork	26 Jul 06	70	5.45%
Telegraaf	16 Mar 06	54.4	5.00%
TNT	6 Dec 05	1,000	10.00%
TNT	6 Nov 06	415	4.15%
TNT	6 Nov 06	585	5.85%
Unilever	10 Feb 05	500	1.80%
Unilever	8 Feb 07	750	2.03%
Vastned Offices/Industrial	15 Dec 05	16.6	3.87%
Vastned Retail	13 Sep 06	15.7	1.23%
Wereldhave	28 Jun 05	39.32	2.00%
Wolters Kluwer	27 Mar 07	475	

Source: Annual reports, Bloomberg, Thomson OneBanker and Dealogic M&A analytics

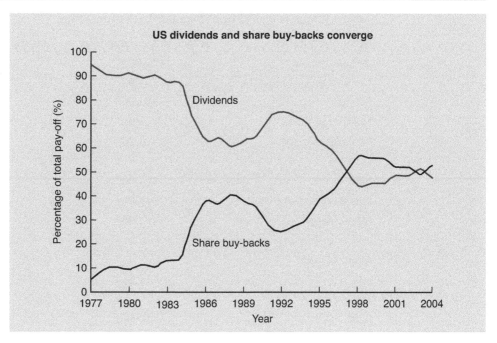

Figure 6.8 Dividends *vs* share buy-backs in the USA
Source: Mauboussin, 2006

On the face of it, it seems illogical that share buy-backs increase the value of a company. The shares are purchased in free trade, i.e. at the current market price and financed by drawing on cash balances or increasing interest-bearing debt. The effect should be value-neutral. Net interest-bearing debt increases by exactly the same amount as the reduction in equity due to the share buy-back. The investors have therefore not gained any value from the share buy-back. Example 6.5 clarifies this issue further.

Example 6.5 **Effect of share buy-back on earnings per share (EPS)**

This example is based on a firm that operates on a mature market without growth. Competition is moderate, which ensures that return on invested capital equals cost of capital. Due to lack of growth opportunities the firm is overcapitalised. As a consequence, equity amounts to four times net interest bearing debt. During a board meeting it is decided to buy back 300 shares. The share repurchase is financed by issuing new debt equivalent to 30,000. The motive for the share repurchase programme is that the CFO of the firm has announced that EPS and ROE will grow considerably, which is expected to have a positive impact on the market value of the firm.

To make calculations simpler taxes are ignored. In Table 6.9 accounting items and financial ratios are provided both before and after the share repurchase programme.

As shown in Table 6.10, the company buys back 300 of their own shares by issuing new debt (increasing from 20,000 to 50,000). Consequently, EPS grows from 11.25 (9,000/800) to 15.00 (7,500/500) representing a growth rate of 33.3%. Likewise, return on equity (ROE) increases from 11.3% to 15.0%. After the share buy-back programme, EPS and ROE will remain at 15.0% and 15.0%, respectively. As a result, there is a permanent change in the level of EPS and ROE – evidence that firm value should increase.

143

Table 6.9 **Impact on EPS by a share buy-back programme**

Accounting items	Before share repurchase	After share repurchase
Invested capital	100,000	100,000
Net interest bearing debt	20,000	50,000
Equity	80,000	50,000
Number of shares	800	500
Financial leverage	0.25	1.00
EBIT	10,000	10,000
Interest expenses (5%)	−1,000	−2,500
Net earnings	9,000	7,500
Financial ratios		
EPS	11.25	15.00
EPS growth		33.3%
ROIC	10.0%	10.0%
ROE	11.3%	15.0%

Table 6.10 **The impact of share buy-back on the required rate of return, EVA, P/E and firm value**

Cost of capital	Before share repurchase	After share repurchase
Risk free interest rate	4.0%	4.0%
β assets (business risk)	1.5	1.5
β debt (financial risk)	0.25	0.25
β equity	1.8	2.75
Risk premium	4.0%	4.0%
Equity cost of capital	11.3%	15.0%
WACC	10.0%	10.0%
Financial leverage	0.25	1.00
Valuation:		
Invested capital	100,000	100,000
EVA	0	0
Enterprise value	100,000	100,000
Net interest bearing debt	20,000	50,000
Estimated value of equity	80,000	50,000
Estimated price per share	100	100
P/E	8.9	6.7

However, ROIC remains at 10%, which is not surprising, as share buy-backs only affect the capital structure not the firm's underlying operations and performance. This shows that the firm value remains unchanged. In order to gain a deeper understanding of a share buy-back's potential impact on firm value, consider the required rate of return both before and after the share buy-back programme to show potential effects. The calculations follow.

They show that WACC remains constant at 10% (taxes and risk of bankruptcy are not considered). For instance, before the repurchase WACC is calculated as:

$$\text{WACC} = 80{,}000/100{,}000 \times 11.3\% + 20{,}000/100{,}000 \times 5.0\% = 10\%$$

An unchanged WACC signals that a change in the capital structure does not create value for shareholders.

As a consequence of the increased financial leverage (changes from 0.25 to 1.0) equity owners require further compensation. The adjustment to equity cost of capital is calculated as follows:[1]

Before repurchase:

$$\beta_e = \beta_a + (\beta_a - \beta_d) \times \frac{\text{NIBD}}{\text{E}} = 1.5 + (1.5 - 0.25) \times 0.25 = 1.81$$

After repurchase:

$$\beta_e = \beta_a + (\beta_a - \beta_d) \times \frac{\text{NIBD}}{\text{E}} = 1.5 + (1.5 - 0.25) \times 1 = 2.75$$

where

β_a = Systematic risk on assets; i.e. operating risk (unlevered beta)
β_d = Systematic risk on debt
NIBD/E = Target firm's capital structure based on market values (net interest-bearing debt to equity ratio)

With a higher systematic risk on equity (β_e) of 2.75, cost of equity based on CAPM can be calculated as:

Before repurchase:

$$r_e = r_f + \beta_e \times \text{risk premium} = 4\% + 1.81 \times 4\% = 11.3\%$$

After repurchase:

$$r_e = r_f + \beta_e \times \text{risk premium} = 4\% + 2.75 \times 4\% = 15\%$$

Therefore, with the change in capital structure the equity cost of capital increases from 11.3% to 15.0%. Cost of capital on the remaining equity, thus, neutralises the improvement in return on equity. As a result, the firm does not create additional value due to changes in the capital structure:

$$\text{Value added (EVA)} = (10\% - 10\%) \times 100{,}000 = 0$$

$$\text{Value added (residual income)} = (15\% - 15\%) \times 50{,}000 = 0$$

Enterprise value is left at 100,000 and the value of equity is 50,000 (enterprise value of 100,000 minus net interest bearing debt of 50,000).

If the firm is valued based on the P/E ratio, the firm appears cheap. This is further supported by the fact that ROE has grown to 15%. The lower P/E, however, simply expresses the increased risk in investing in the firm. As noted above, shareholders demand a higher return as a compensation for the higher financial leverage. It can also be shown by the following P/E relation:[2]

Before share buy-back:

$$\frac{P}{E} = \frac{ROE - g}{ROE \times (r_e - g)} = \frac{0.113 - 0.0}{0.113 \times (0.113 - 0.0)} = 8.9$$

After share buy-back:

$$\frac{P}{E} = \frac{ROE - g}{ROE \times (r_e - g)} = \frac{0.15 - 0.0}{0.15 \times (0.15 - 0.0)} = 6.7$$

P/E decreases from 8.9 to 6.7 due to the higher cost of capital of 15%. The market value of equity based on the P/E relation equals 50,000 (6.7 × 7,500). Before share buy-backs the market value of equity was 8.9 × 9,000 = 80,000.

In conclusion, share repurchases are equivalent to a change in the capital structure. The underlying business is not affected by share repurchases.[3] ∎

In Example 6.5 EPS grows by 33%. It is, however, not certain that EPS increases as a result of share buy-backs. Share buy-backs only lead to growth in EPS when return on invested capital exceeds the net borrowing rate. Likewise, the consequences of share buy-backs on EPS are negative if the net borrowing rate is higher than ROIC. This is illustrated in Table 6.11 which exemplifies that a positive growth in financial

Table 6.11 The impact of share buy-backs on EPS assuming different relations between ROIC and the net borrowing rate

	ROIC Interest rate	ROIC = Interest rate	ROIC > Interest rate
Before share buy-back			
EBIT	3,000	5,000	7,000
Financial expenses	−1,000	−1,000	−1,000
Net result	2,000	4,000	6,000
Number shares	800	800	800
EPS	2.5	5.0	7.5
Equity	80,000	80,000	80,000
Net interest-bearing debt	20,000	20,000	20,000
Invested capital	100,000	100,000	100,000
ROIC	3%	5%	7%
After share buy-back			
EBIT	3,000	5,000	7,000
Financial expenses	−2,500	−2,500	−2,500
Net earnings	500	2,500	4,500
Number of shares	500	500	500
EPS	1.0	5.0	9.0
Equity	50,000	50,000	50,000
Net interest-bearing debt	50,000	50,000	50,000
Invested capital	100,000	100,000	100,000
ROIC	3%	5%	7%
Growth in EPS	−60%	0%	20%

ratios, including EPS, caused by share buy-backs requires a ROIC that exceeds the net borrowing rate. The example further demonstrates that firms where management is compensated based on EPS, or similar financial measures, may find it advantageous to change the dividend policy so that dividends are paid to shareholders by means of the firm buying back their own shares. This may explain why more firms buy back shares as opposed to paying out dividends to shareholders.

The relationship between growth and liquidity

Growth is often associated with cash consumption, as it requires investment in non-current assets such as property, plant and equipment. Moreover, working capital usually increases with growth. Finally, higher sales are typically associated with higher accounts receivable and inventories.

An examination of the correlation between sales growth and the free cash flow to the firm for a large sample of European firms shows that it is highly negative. This supports that sales growth is associated with cash consumption. It is therefore important that growth is accompanied by close monitoring of cash flows. If there is a lack of cash management, growth companies may eventually have to suspend their payments.

Table 6.12 illustrates what happens when a growth company runs short of cash. Bioscan used to develop and manufacture bio-refineries, which collate and convert organic waste such as manure, municipal waste, waste from food industry, organic sludge and wastewater to:

* Clean water
* Green energy
* Fertiliser.

Table 6.12 **The development in key financial data for Bioscan**

	Year 1	Year 2	Year 3	Year 4	Year 5	Accumulated
Revenue	2,748	17,976	23,396	32,422	16,247	92,789
Operating earnings (EBIT)	−5,935	−23,245	−41,396	2,408	−29,466	−97,634
FCF	−18,356	−35,894	−25,725	−10,838	−10,293	−101,106
Market value of equity	339,015	417,782	57,669	42,733	98,502	

At first sight it seemed like a good idea to convert waste to clean water, energy and fertiliser. The trend in Bioscan's revenue also supports this view. Bioscan is growing from modest revenue of barely DKK 3 million in year 1 to revenues of DKK 32 million in year 4. However, despite strong sales growth, earnings cannot keep pace and with the exception of year 4, operating earnings are negative. At the same time, cash flow after investments (the free cash flow) is negative in all years, and overall there is a financing gap (negative cash flows) of approximately DKK 101 million. The above figures indicate that this is a company with a serious liquidity problem. In year 3, Bioscan had to let its German subsidiary suspend payments. Already at this point of time Bioscan's future survival was questioned. The share price of Bioscan also fell sharply during the period. The market value dropped from DKK 339 million in year 1 to barely DKK

43 million in year 4. The market value, however, increased to approximately DKK 99 million in year 5. The stock market was seemed to be sceptical of Bioscan's business model. The stock market was proved right. Bioscan suspended payments a few years later and went bankrupt shortly thereafter.

As the example of Bioscan shows it is not sufficient to generate growth in revenue. If growth does not generate sufficient profit (and ultimately) cash and management of non-current assets and net working capital (invested capital) is inadequate, the consequences on the firm's liquidity are negative.

Conclusions

The main points to remember are as follows:

- A company cannot grow faster than the sustainable growth rate if it wants to preserve its financial risk. The company may affect the sustainable growth rate in three ways. It may improve operating performance, enhance earnings from debt capital (increase the interest spread and/or financial leverage) or reduce the payout ratio.
- Growth is not always value creating. For instance, growth in EPS and growth in financial ratios induced by the purchase of own shares are not necessarily value creating.
- It is rare that high sales growth can be maintained in the long run. Empirical evidence supports that sales growth converges towards a long-term average after four to five years. In this context it is important to distinguish between growth based on recurrent (permanent) and non-recurring (transitory) items. Growth based on the former has considerably longer sustainability.
- Growth firms often consume cash and therefore it is important to closely monitor the liquidity of these firms. Firms can generally improve liquidity by improving the income-expense relation (profit margin) and the utilisation of invested capital (invested capital turnover).

While this chapter primarily focuses on the historical growth, it is important to note that the purpose of the historical growth analysis is often to predict future growth. The historical growth analysis in this context provides valuable insight about future growth, but will never stand alone. The historical analysis should be combined with an in-depth knowledge of the market, the industry and the firm being analysed in order to determine the future growth potential. Finally, we note that growth shall not be maximised but optimised.

Review questions

- How is a firm's sustainable growth rate measured?
- What types of information can be retrieved from the sustainable growth rate?
- What factors affect a firm's sustainable growth rate?
- A firm's sustainable growth rate should be as high as possible – true or false?
- How should a firm's growth rate be measured if value creation is a key objective?
- Growth is always of the same quality – true or false?

- Growth in EPS is always value creating – true or false?

- Does a share buy-back programme always result in an improved EPS?

- What is the relation between a firm's growth rate and its liquidity?

Notes

1 In Chapter 10 we elaborate in further details on the beta relations applied in this chapter.
2 Please refer to Chapter 9 for an elaboration of the applied P/E relation.
3 In the literature and among practitioners other arguments support share repurchases. Jensen (1986) argues that firms that are high on cash may be tempted to carry out investments that might often prove unprofitable. By paying out excess cash, firms (management) do not have this option. It is also argued that share buy-back improves the underlying liquidity in the stock. This argument seems, however, to be short sighted, as the number of shares after share buy-back and cancellation of shares is fewer than before the share buy-back programme.

References

Jensen, M.C. (1986) 'Agency costs of Free Cash Flow, Corporate Finance and Takeovers', *The American Economic Review*, Vol. 76, 323–9.

Mauboussin, M. J. (2006) 'Clear Thinking about Share Repurchase', Legg Mason Capital Management, 10 January 2006.

Parum, C. (2001) 'Corporate Finance', Lawyer and Økonomforbundets Publishing.

CHAPTER 7

Liquidity risk analysis

Learning outcomes

After reading this chapter you should be able to:

- **Recognise the importance of liquidity (cash)**
- **Understand the concept of short-term and long-term liquidity risk**
- **Calculate and interpret financial ratios used to measure short-term and long-term liquidity risk**
- **Understand the merits and demerits of the financial ratios used to calculate liquidity risk**
- **Recognise that using financial ratios is one of several ways of measuring liquidity risk**

Liquidity risk

Liquidity is a crucial subject for any business. Without liquidity a company cannot pay its bills or carry out profitable investments and in certain cases lack of liquidity leads to bankruptcy. Therefore, it is important to analyse short- and long-term liquidity risk. Analysis of the **short-term liquidity risk** uncovers a company's ability to satisfy (pay) all short-term obligations as they fall due. The **long-term liquidity risk**, also defined as the solvency risk, refers to the company's long-term financial health and ability to satisfy (pay) all future obligations. The short- and long-term liquidity risk also serve as important input when evaluating the credit risk of a company.

A firm's liquidity risk is influenced by its ability to generate positive net cash flows in both the short- and long-term. The ability to meet all short- and long-term commitments is essential for any company to be able to act freely and exploit profitable business opportunities.

Lack of liquidity may:

- Limit management's freedom of action
- Reduce the potential for profitable investment opportunities
- Force managers to divest profitable businesses with a substantial discount
- Increase financial expenses
- Lead to suspension of payment and possible bankruptcy.

As you can see, the lack of liquidity often affects a company's profitability negatively. It is particularly damaging for shareholders because of their (bad) standing in the priority order in case of bankruptcy. Other stakeholders are also affected by a bankruptcy, for example, creditors lose on loan commitments and miss out on future business opportunities, suppliers experience losses on their receivables and a potential lack of sales outlets, customers face the risk of a shortage of supply and employees may lose their jobs. Consequently, stakeholders have an interest in conducting a proper analysis to identify both the short- and long-term liquidity risk.

A quantitative assessment of the short- and long-term liquidity risk can generally be based on *financial ratios*, which rely on historical accounting figures, and various forecasting techniques that predict the short- and long-term cash flows. In this chapter, we purely focus on calculating and interpreting financial ratios measuring the short- and long-term liquidity risk. In Chapter 8, we expand the analysis and explore how cash flows can be forecast and in Chapter 11 we examine in further detail the credit risk relying on both financial ratios and forecasting.

Financial ratios are often used to predict a company's short- and long-term liquidity risk. For example, rating agencies rely on financial ratios when determining the credit risk of a firm. Financial institutions often include financial ratios as covenants in debt contracts and many companies evaluate their customers and suppliers based on only a few financial ratios. While financial ratios are based on historical figures and often describe parts of a company's profitability and financial position only, they offer the advantage of being easy to calculate. This implies that many companies can be analysed with only modest effort. Financial ratios have, therefore, proven to be a cost-efficient way to rank businesses based on their liquidity risk.

In this chapter we use Rörvik Timber AB (Rörvik Timber) to illustrate the abilities of financial ratios in predicting the short- and long-term liquidity risk. Rörvik Timber is a Swedish company involved in the processing of wood. It is a spinoff of the former RörvikGruppen and used to be listed on the Stockholm Stock Exchange. A short description of Rörvik Timber including abstracts of management commentaries from the latest annual reports and a summary of key financial figures and ratios is provided in Example 7.1. In Appendix 7.1 at the end of this chapter you will find comprehensive income statements, balance sheets and cash flow statements from year 1 to year 6.

| Example 7.1 | Rörvik Timber AB |

Previously Rörvik Timber was involved in other business areas within the foresting and wood industry and owned power and heating plants. Eight years ago a new strategy emerged and the new long-term focus for the company should be the sawmill operations. Unrelated business areas were divested and extensive structural programmes were initiated. The new strategy focused on increased processing of products in order to create greater value for the customers and the development of products should be made in close cooperation with the customers. These initiatives and an expansion of the enterprise should make Rörvik Timber a preferred long-term partner for other companies within the industry. Despite these initiatives Rörvik Timber suspended its payments in year 7. The following abstracts from the annual report from year 3 to year 6 briefly describe the management view of the business.

Management commentary year 3

Year 3 was overwhelmingly influenced by the hurricane that hit southern Sweden in January. The hurricane Gudrun hit southern Sweden with extensive damage as a consequence. In total, it is estimated that approximately 70 million forest cubic metres fell or were damaged. The group industries moved up previously planned production increases. These in order, to the fullest extent possible, utilise the increased inward shipments of storm-felled timber and to minimise the significant financial damage that the storm caused. The average price level on the timber products supplied was approximately 3% lower than the previous year. The large quantity of timber on offer due to the storm meant substantially lower price levels for raw material. The cost level for purchased timber during the year fell by 25%. The saw production during the year increased to 678 timber cubic metres, largely due to the storm.

Management commentary year 4

Year 4 was characterised by a continued strong market and increased prices for sawn wood products. The year's profit is the best in the group's history. Demand gradually increased during the year. The market for sawn wood products has been strong in Europe, North Africa and Asia. The market in the US has, on the other hand, weakened, primarily because of the decreased pace of housing construction. During the year, Swedish export prices have risen by approximately 18%.

Management commentary year 5

Profits after financial gains/losses increased by SEK 146 million to SEK 237 million. This is the best net income in the history of the group. The profit was influenced in a positive manner during the year by increased volumes and higher prices for sawn wood products and by-products. The business segment 'Timber' has, thanks to this, shown an improvement in operating profits to SEK 273 million . . . Year 6 has started with continued weak deliveries. We expect to see a gradual seasonal recovery and a reduction in warehouse stores during the second quarter. In a longer-term perspective, the market prospects for wood products look quite positive.

Management commentary year 6

Year 6 is a year that is heavily affected by the financial crisis . . . For a long time many thought that Europe would not be affected by the financial crisis that the United States had already experienced in year 5. Today, we know the consequences of the financial crisis that has proven to be both dramatic and have severe consequences . . . Profit before tax amounted to negative SEK 293 million (237) . . . The weak market conditions have affected the sales negatively and worsen the payment conditions. These difficulties have affected the cash flow negatively and consequently, the company is facing difficulties in meeting future obligations . . . 29 April year 7, the company suspended its payments . . . The company has developed a reconstruction plan that aims at improving the company's result and financial position.

Since the restructuring plan has not been completed, the auditor cannot confirm that Rörvik Timber has sufficient liquidity to support its business. The auditor, therefore, questions the going concern of Rörvik Timber in the annual report from year 6. The verbal description retrieved from the management commentary and audit report from year 6 show that Rörvik Timber has severe financial problems.

Table 7.1 gives a summary of the key financial figures and ratios for Rörvik Timber are disclosed. These financial figures and ratios indicate that Rörvik Timber is doing quite well until year 5. In fact, growth rates are two-digits in most years and ROIC continuously improves from year 1 to year 5 indicating that the company is generating more profit from operations. However, a dramatic change is taking place in year 6. ROIC is negative and Rörvik Timber's equity decreases by almost 50%. Net interest-bearing debt (interest-bearing debt minus excess cash) is peaking that year and equals SEK 885 million.

Table 7.1 Key financial figures and ratios (end of year balances) of Rörvik Timber, year 1 to year 6

Income statement (SEKm)	Year 1	Year 2	Year 3	Year 4	Year 5	Year 6
Revenue	1,306.9	1,434.0	1,879.1	2,113.0	2,641.8	2,390.4
Net operating profit after tax	17.2	20.7	52.1	77.1	191.5	−167.9
Net income	7.6	2.3	42.6	65.2	169.4	−211.2
Balance sheet (SEKm)	**Year 1**	**Year 2**	**Year 3**	**Year 4**	**Year 5**	**Year 6**
Invested capital	535	521	574	697	1,203	1,109
Book value of equity	201	205	243	314	466	215
Net interest bearing debt	334	316	331	383	737	895
Cash flow statement (SEKm)	**Year 1**	**Year 2**	**Year 3**	**Year 4**	**Year 5**	**Year 6**
Cash flow from operations	10.1	61.3	75.5	14.0	−112.1	47.4
Cash flow from investments	−65.1	−18.7	−55.2	−59.0	−166.8	−83.7
Cash flow from financing	51.5	−47.8	−3.4	24.9	278.3	36.1
Financial ratios	**Year 1**	**Year 2**	**Year 3**	**Year 4**	**Year 5**	**Year 6**
Revenue growth	7.8%	9.7%	31.0%	12.4%	25.0%	−9.5%
ROIC	3.2%	4.0%	9.1%	11.1%	15.9%	−15.1%
Turnover ratio (invested capital)	2.4	2.8	3.3	3.0	2.2	2.2
NOPAT margin	1.3%	1.4%	2.8%	3.6%	7.2%	−7.0%
Financial leverage	1.7	1.5	1.4	1.2	1.6	4.2
Return on equity	3.8%	1.1%	17.5%	20.7%	36.4%	−98.3%

We will now examine whether financial ratios would have revealed that Rörvik Timber eventually had to suspend payments.

Measuring short-term liquidity risk

In the following section, we describe some of the key financial ratios that can be used to assess short-term liquidity risk. To help illustrate this, we use Rörvik Timber and other firms as examples.

Liquidity cycle

An indicator of the short-term liquidity risk is the number of days it takes to convert working capital to cash, also defined as the **liquidity cycle** or cash cycle. The basic idea is that inventory and accounts receivable consume cash while accounts payable generate cash. The fewer days it takes to convert working capital into cash the better the cash flow. The liquidity cycle is calculated as follows:

$$\text{Liquidity cycle} = \frac{365}{\dfrac{\text{Costs of good sold}}{\text{inventory}}} + \frac{365}{\dfrac{\text{Revenue}}{\text{Accounts receivable}}} - \frac{365}{\dfrac{\text{Purchase, material}}{\text{Accounts payable}}}$$

UNIVERSITY OF WINCHESTER LIBRARY

Consider a company with the following funds tied-up in working capital:

Days inventory in hand	35 days
Days accounts receivable in hand	42 days
Days accounts payable in hand	−27 days
Liquidity cycle (measured in days)	50 days

Based on this simple numerical example, the liquidity cycle is 50 days. This indicates that it takes 50 days to convert working capital into cash and that the turnover rate for **net working capital** is approximately 7.3 (365/50). All other things being equal, companies should strive to reduce the length of the liquidity cycle since it improves its cash flows. This can be done by a tight control of inventory and receivables, or by obtaining further credit from the company's suppliers.

By dividing the number of days in a year (365) with the **turnover rate of net working capital** we obtain an approximate value of the liquidity cycle:

$$\text{Liquidity cycle} = \frac{365}{\text{Turnover rate of net working capital}}$$

Turnover rate of net working capital is defined as:

$$\frac{\text{Revenue}}{\text{Inventory} + \text{receivables} + \text{prepaid expenses} - \text{operating liabilities}}$$

In Table 7.2 Rörvik Timber's liquidity cycle (days) is calculated for year 1 to year 6. For instance, in year 1 net working capital consists of:

Accounting item	Amount (SEKm)
Stocks on hand (i.e. inventory)	296.1
Short-term receivables (i.e. accounts receivable)	163.3
Accounts payable	−126.7
Other liabilities, short-term	−9.4
Accrued expenses and prepaid income	−54.5
Net working capital	268.8

Table 7.2 Rörvik Timber's liquidity cycle (end of year balances)[1]

Rörvik Timber (SEKm)	Year 1	Year 2	Year 3	Year 4	Year 5	Year 6
Net turnover	1,307	1,434	1,879	2,113	2,642	2,390
Net working capital	269	233	258	355	682	355
Liquidity cycle (days)	75	59	50	61	94	54
Net working capital, liquidity cycle = 50 days	180	197	258	290	363	328

[1]Since we want the latest possible data, the financial ratios are based on end of year balances.

In year 1, the turnover rate for net working capital becomes $1,307/269 = 4.86$ and the liquidity is therefore $365/4.86 = 75$ days.

As shown, Rörvik Timber's liquidity cycle improves from year 1 to year 3 by 25 days (75 days minus 50 days). From year 3, Rörvik Timber's liquidity cycle worsens and in year 5 the liquidity cycle is 94 days. The development in the liquidity cycle from year 3 to year 5 affects the cash flow negatively. If Rörvik Timber had been able to maintain its liquidity cycle of 50 days from year 3 until year 5 the net working capital would equal SEK 363 million (682 × 50/94) compared to a realised net working capital equal to SEK 682 million in year 5. This difference corresponds to a negative cash impact of SEK 319 million in year 5, which Rörvik Timber needs to get funded from other sources, such as financial institutions and shareholders. Assuming a funding rate of 8%, the funding cost of SEK 319 million equals SEK 25.5 million annually.

It is important to stress that the liquidity cycle only describes a fraction of a company's overall liquidity. Important elements, for example, operating income and expenses and capital expenditures are not included in the financial ratio. Furthermore, an appropriate benchmark is needed to fully utilise the potential of the liquidity cycle. Despite these shortcomings the analysis of Rörvik Timber's liquidity cycle indicates potential liquidity problems.

| Example 7.2 | **End of year versus average balances** |

Financial ratios, which rely on data from the balance sheets, are based on ending balances rather than the average of the beginning and ending balances. This is motivated by a desire to work with the most updated data. To illustrate the point we have calculated the financial leverage of Rörvik Timber in year 6 based on ending balance and the average of the beginning and ending balances.

Rörvik Timber	Year 6
Financial leverage, book values, end	6.45
Financial leverage, book values, average	3.96

Calculating financial leverage based on an ending balance provides a more accurate picture of current financial leverage. Financial leverage based on average balances tends to even out changes in the balance sheet. We acknowledge, however, that financial ratios based on average balances may also serve a purpose when measuring liquidity risk as it evens out temporarily events on the balance sheet. ∎

Current ratio

The current ratio is an alternative measure for the short-term liquidity risk:

$$\text{Current ratio} = \frac{\text{Current assets}}{\text{Current liabilities}}$$

The **current ratio** sometimes excludes the impact of inventory. This variation of the current ratio is also defined as the **quick ratio**. The basic idea of the quick ratio is that only the most liquid current assets are included.

$$\text{Quick ratio} = \frac{\text{Cash} + \text{securities} + \text{receivables}}{\text{Current liabilities}}$$

Since the quick ratio includes only the most liquid current assets, it is perceived to be a relatively more conservative indicator of the short-term liquidity risk than the current ratio. Even so, both ratios attempt to answer the following question:

What is the likelihood that current assets cover current liabilities in the event of liquidaion?

The basic idea is that the larger the ratio, the greater the likelihood that the sale of current assets are able to cover current liabilities. Different rules of thumb are used to assess the level of the current ratio. Some argue that a current ratio greater than 2.0 is an indication of low (short-term) liquidity risk. However, as we illustrate below, it is difficult to apply these rules of thumb across different industries and firms.

The usefulness of the current ratio (and quick ratio) depends on its ability to predict future cash flow needs. As with the liquidity cycle, the current ratio relies on financial data describing the net working capital position. Many aspects of a company's financial position are, therefore, not covered by the ratio. Moreover, it is doubtful whether current net working capital is able to predict the development of future cash tied up in working capital. The level of activities in an enterprise seems to be a much better indicator of the development in working capital. For example, accounts receivable is a function of revenue (and credit terms). Furthermore, greater activity leads to greater purchases of materials (and thus a higher level of accounts payable) and inventories.

In the event of liquidation, it is doubtful whether assets can be realised at book value. For example, inventory is recognised in the balance sheet at costs, which is rarely a good indicator of the liquidation value. Assume that the inventory consists of IT equipment, where (1) rapid obsolescence is inherent and (2) prices tend to fall sharply for the same, or similar, products over time. In such cases, the purchase price is typically a poor indicator of the actual realisable value and most likely overestimates the realisable value. Furthermore, the realisation of accounts receivable is in some ways equivalent to factoring. In case of factoring, financial institutions require a discount to reflect the risk (bad debt) and the time value of money. In summary, the book value of current assets often does not reflect the realisation value.

Finally, it may be difficult to estimate when the current ratio is at an adequate level. As mentioned above, it is argued that a current ratio greater than 2.0 signals low short-term liquidity risk. It is, however, not possible to operate with a general rule of thumb across different business types or industries. Manufacturing firms often have large inventories and accounts receivable, which substantially exceed operating liabilities. Conversely, service companies are typically characterised by low levels of inventory. In fact, for service companies' current liabilities often exceed current assets. To illustrate this point, consider Getinge, a leading manufacturer of medical devices, and ISS, one of the world's largest commercial providers of facility services.

Current ratio	Year 1	Year 2
Getinge	2.11	2.13
ISS	1.00	0.96

Getinge's current ratio is twice as high as ISS's, which indicates that Getinge has a significantly lower short-term liquidity risk than ISS. This difference is, however, driven by differences in the business model of the two types of businesses. A capital intensive business with delivery of physical goods, like Getinge, naturally has a relatively higher current ratio compared to less capital intensive firms like ISS, which delivers services. The example illustrates that it is important to adjust for differences in the operational structure before interpreting the current ratio.

With this in mind, the current ratio for Rörvik Timber (end of year balances) is calculated as:

Current ratio (SEKm)	Year 1	Year 2	Year 3	Year 4	Year 5	Year 6
Total short-term assets	469	425	646	796	1,181	846
Total short-term liabilities	211	367	596.1	635.9	802.4	980
Current ratio	2.22	1.16	1.08	1.25	1.47	0.86

As shown, Rörvik Timber experiences a decline in the current ratio. In year 1 the current ratio is a comfortable 2.22. Five years later the current ratio dropped to 0.86 indicating that current liabilities exceed current assets. As Rörvik Timber is a manufacturing company, you would expect a significantly higher current ratio. The decrease in the current ratio over time along with the level of the current ratio in year 6 signals high short-term liquidity risks. More interestingly, the most significant drop in the current ratio is at the time when the annual report for year 2 is released, which is four years before Rörvik Timber's suspension of payments. Therefore, despite some of the shortcomings outlined above, the current ratio signals a potential liquidity problem four years before Rörvik Timber suspended its payments.

Cash flow from operations to short-term debt ratio

The **cash flow from operations (CFO) to short-term debt (current liabilities) ratio** is another financial ratio used to measure the short-term liquidity risk:

$$\text{CFO to short-term debt ratio} = \frac{\text{Cash flow from operations}}{\text{Current liabilities}}$$

The CFO to short-term debt ratio deviates from the current ratio by using the actual cash flows generated from operations rather than current and potential cash flow resources (current assets). By replacing current assets with cash flow from operations, the convertibility-to-cash problem of current assets is avoided. Furthermore, cash flow from operations seems to be a better indicator of the cash available to serve current liabilities on an ongoing basis than current assets. The following tabulation shows the CFO to short-term debt ratio for Rörvik Timber (end of year balances) from year 1 to year 6.

CFO to short-term debt ratio	Year 1	Year 2	Year 3	Year 4	Year 5	Year 6
Cash flow from operations	10	61	76	14	−112	47
Current liabilities	211	367	596	636	802	980
CFO to short-term debt ratio	5%	17%	13%	2%	−14%	5%

In most of the years, the cash flow from operations ratio is 5% or lower. A CFO to short-term debt ratio of only 5% seems low. This indicates that Rörvik can only pay 5% of its current liabilities from its operating cash flows on an annual basis; i.e. it takes 20 years to repay current liabilities. However, as with some of the other ratios the CFO to short-term debt ratio is difficult to interpret in the absence of a proper benchmark.

Cash burn rate

The **cash burn rate** is one of the most conservative financial ratios used to measure short-term liquidity risk and is typically only used on companies with negative earnings. The ratio measures how long a company is able to fund projected costs without any further cash contribution from shareholders or creditors. The ratio is defined as:

$$\text{Cash burn rate} = \frac{\text{Cash and cash equivalents} + \text{securities} + \text{receivables}}{\text{EBIT}}$$

The cash burn rate is typically used in businesses which do not yet have a proper level of earnings. Start-up companies, biotech companies and similar types of businesses are characterised by significant investments (cash outlays) and little or no earnings. This implies that operating profit (EBIT) often equals operating costs for these types of companies. In Table 7.3 the cash burn rate for four biotech companies have been calculated.

The cash burn rate is calculated in months. This shows how many months the biotech companies can continue operations assuming the current performance and without additional funding from shareholders or debt-holders. The table shows that Angel Biotechnology has 'easy converted to cash assets' (cash) for three months of operations in year 2. In comparison, Genmab has cash for 27 months of operations in year 2.

The usefulness of the ratio depends on the ability to estimate future costs as well as revenues. In the above example we used EBIT from the last fiscal year. It may prove to be a poor proxy for future cash needs. For example, Genmab doubled its expenses from year 1 to year 2, which significantly worsened the cash burn rate in year 2.

Measuring long-term liquidity risk

There are a variety of ratios that measure a firm's long-term liquidity risk. We introduce some of the most frequently applied ratios. Financial ratios measuring the long-term liquidity possess the same strengths and weaknesses as the financial ratios measuring the short-term liquidity risk. For example, all of them rely on historical accounting data and therefore are backward looking.

Financial leverage

An indicator of the long-term liquidity risk is **financial leverage** which can be measured in different ways:

$$\text{Financial leverage} = \frac{\text{Total liabilities}}{\text{Equity}}$$

A variation of financial leverage is the **solvency ratio**:

$$\text{Solvency ratio} = \frac{\text{Equity}}{\text{Total liabilities} + \text{equity}}$$

The financial leverage and the solvency ratio provide identical information about the long-term liquidity risk. Generally, a high financial leverage and a low solvency ratio indicate high long-term liquidity risk. In determining the financial leverage and the solvency ratio, it is important that all financial obligations are recognised in the balance sheet including leases and other contractual obligations, which are 'off balance'. The same is true for equity. All values should be included when determining equity. In this context, it is important to determine whether the ratios should be based on book values or market values. If market values are available it is generally recommended that they are used. Market values are closer to the realisable value.

Table 7.3 Cash burn rate for selected biotech companies

	Genmab (DK) DKK (000)		Medarex (US) USD (000)		4SC (GER) Euros (000)		Angel Biotech. (UK) GPB		Neurosearch (DK) DKK (000)	
	Year 1	Year 2	Year 1	Year 2	Year 1	Year 2	Year 1	Year 2	Year 1	Year 2
Accounts receivable	217,139	161,461	29,013	21,793	131	580	126,687	199,392	17,741	18,515
Other financial assets	3,561,690	1,691,999	311,437	281,186	6,858	14,687	–	–	127,711	218,790
Cash and cash equivalents	131,753	70,013	37,335	72,482	10,335	7,346	42,034	73,233	727,527	237,125
Easy converted to cash assets, total	3,910,582	1,923,473	377,785	375,461	17,324	22,613	168,721	272,625	872,979	474,430
EBIT	−437,133	−869,998	−195,884	−186,955	−8,303	−12,695	−1,208,399	−1,057,548	−253,455	−366,000
Cash burn rate (no. of months)	107	27	23	24	25	21	2	3	41	16

Table 7.4 **William Demant Holding's financial leverage and solvency ratio**

William Demant Holding (DKKm)	Year 1	Year 2
Equity, market value	28,063	12,718
Equity, book value	435	541
Liabilities, total	3,726	3,926
Financial leverage, market values	**0.1**	**0.3**
Financial leverage, book values	8.6	7.3
Solvency ratio, market values	**0.9**	**0.8**
Solvency ratio, book values	0.1	0.1

To illustrate this point in Table 7.4 we have calculated the financial leverage and solvency ratio based on both book values and market values for one of the leading hearing aid manufacturers William Demant Holding.

The reported financial ratios based on book values and market values, respectively, provide a different picture of William Demant Holding's long-term liquidity risk. While the financial leverage and solvency ratio based on book values indicate that the long-term liquidity risk is high for William Demant Holding the same ratios based on market values provide opposite signals; i.e. that the long-term liquidity risk is low. These opposite signals are driven by the difference in market value and book value of equity. For example, in year 2 the market value of equity exceeds book value of equity by a multiple of 23.5. If book values are used to evaluate the liquidity risk of William Demant Holding, it is very likely that incorrect conclusions are drawn.

Given these considerations, Rörvik Timber's financial leverage and solvency ratio based on book values and market values are shown in Table 7.5.

Table 7.5 **Rörvik Timber's financial leverage and solvency ratio (end of year balances)**

Rörvik Timber (SEKm)	Year 1	Year 2	Year 3	Year 4	Year 5	Year 6
Equity, market values	151	143	261	610	769	140
Equity, book values	201	205	243	314	466	215
Liabilities, total	567	544	759	875	1,309	1,386
Shareholders' equity and total liabilities	768	749	1,002	1,189	1,775	1,601
Financial leverage, market values	3.75	3.81	2.91	1.43	1.70	9.90
Financial leverage, book values	2.82	2.66	3.12	2.78	2.81	6.45
Solvency ratio, market values	0.20	0.19	0.26	0.51	0.43	0.09
Solvency ratio, book values	0.26	0.27	0.24	0.26	0.26	0.13

Ideally both ratios should be compared to an industry benchmark. Given this caveat the financial leverage based on book value appears to be moderate to high and the solvency ratio appears accordingly to be moderate to low in the first five years. For example, the financial leverage based on book values fluctuates in between 2.7 and 3.1. In year 6 the financial leverage increases dramatically. The financial leverage gets close to 10. This clearly indicates that the long-term liquidity risk of Rörvik Timber is high. The example requires a few additional comments. First, in the case of Rörvik Timber, analysts would not be better off using market values. In fact, if they apply market values, financial leverage decreases from 3.75 in year 1 to 1.70 in year 5 indicating a decreasing liquidity risk at the company. This indicates the deficiencies of using market values. If the market does not capture the fundamental value of the company it may provide misleading signals. Second, as noted previously it is difficult to interpret both financial leverage and the solvency ratio in the absence of a proper benchmark. Finally, neither financial leverage nor the solvency ratio provide any clear signal of a dramatic change in the long-term liquidity risk until the suspension of payments takes place.

Interest coverage ratio

The interest coverage ratio is an alternative financial ratio measuring the long-term liquidity risk:

$$\text{Interest coverage ratio} = \frac{\text{Operating profit (EBIT)}}{\text{Net financial expenses}}$$

The **interest coverage ratio** measures a company's ability to meet its net financial expenses. More specifically, the ratio shows how many times operating profit covers net financial expenses. The higher the ratio, the lower the long-term liquidity risk. Since EBIT is not a cash flow measure some analysts prefer to replace EBIT with cash flow from operations:

$$\text{Interest coverage ratio (cash)} = \frac{\text{Cash flow from operations}}{\text{Net financial expenses}}$$

There are different rules of thumb for what characterises an appropriate level of the interest coverage ratio. However, due to different levels of the interest coverage ratio across industries there is no common practice.

Table 7.6 illustrates Rörvik Timber's interest coverage ratio covering a six-year period. The interest coverage ratio based on EBIT improves gradually from year 1 to year 5, which indicates a decrease in the long-term liquidity risk. In year 6 the interest coverage ratio is negative which supports a high long-term liquidity risk. It is significant to note that the interest coverage ratio based on cash flow from operations is negative in year 5. In the example of Rörvik Timber an interest coverage ratio based on cash flows therefore provides more timely information about the liquidity risk than an interest coverage ratio based on EBIT.

Table 7.6 **Rörvik Timber's interest coverage ratio**

Rörvik Timber (SEKm)	Year 1	Year 2	Year 3	Year 4	Year 5	Year 6
Operating profit/loss	26.2	11.7	73.2	107.8	267.7	−233.1
Cash flow from operations	10.1	61.3	75.5	14.0	−112.1	47.4
Net financial expenses	16.0	13.4	14.4	16.6	30.9	60.2
Interest coverage ratio	1.6	0.9	5.1	6.5	8.7	−3.9
Interest coverage ratio (cash)	0.6	4.6	5.2	0.8	−3.6	0.8

Cash flow from operations to debt ratio

The cash flow from operations to debt ratio is another financial ratio measuring the long-term liquidity risk. It is defined as follows:

$$\text{CFO to debt ratio} = \frac{\text{Cash flow from operations}}{\text{Total liabilities}}$$

The **CFO to debt ratio** measures the extent to which current cash flow from operations are sufficient to repay liabilities. A high CFO to debt ratio signals a low long-term liquidity risk, as the company has sufficient cash to repay its liabilities. In comparison to the CFO to short-term liabilities ratio, CFO to liabilities ratio also includes all non-current liabilities.

Capital expenditure ratio

The **capital expenditure ratio** is yet another ratio, which intends to measure the long-term liquidity risk. It is defined as follows:

$$\text{Capital expenditure ratio} = \frac{\text{Cash flow from operations}}{\text{Capital expenditure}}$$

The ratio shows the proportion of capital expenditure a company is able to fund through its operations. A ratio greater than 1.0 indicates that cash flows from operations are sufficient to support capital expenditures. Since capital expenditures vary across a company's lifecycle the ratio will naturally vary accordingly. For that purpose, you may choose to include reinvestment as a proxy for capital expenditure:

$$\text{Capital expenditure ratio (reinvest)} = \frac{\text{Cash flow from operations}}{\text{Reinvestments}}$$

A capital expenditure ratio based on reinvestments removes the impact of growth in investments and show to what extent a company is able to finance reinvestments from internally generated funds. In other words, a capital expenditure ratio based on reinvestments provides evidence on the sustainability of the business model. If the capital expenditure ratio based on reinvestments in general is below 1.0 this is a sign that the company does not have a sustainable business model. Often companies do not disclose the level of reinvestments. In these instances, depreciation may serve as proxy for reinvestments.

Rörvik Timber's CFO to debt ratio and the capital expenditure ratio are reported in Table 7.7. If we ignore year 1, the CFO to debt ratio is decreasing over time and

Table 7.7 Rörvik Timber's CFO to debt ratio and capital expenditure ratio (end-of-year balances)

Rörvik Timber	Year 1	Year 2	Year 3	Year 4	Year 5	Year 6	Average
Cash flows from operating activities	10.1	61.3	75.5	14.0	−112.1	47.4	
Liabilities, total	566.8	544.2	759.0	874.8	1,308.8	1,385.9	
CFO to debt ratio	0.02	0.11	0.10	0.02	−0.09	0.03	0.02
Net investments in non-current assets	61.9	17.9	37.0	46.7	88.3	74.5	
Depreciations (reinvestments)	35.0	35.0	36.0	40.5	48.1	59.6	
Capital expenditure ratio	0.16	3.42	2.04	0.30	−1.27	0.64	0.29
Capital expenditure ratio (reinvest)	0.29	1.75	2.10	0.35	−2.33	0.80	0.38

is disturbingly close to zero. The average CFO to debt ratio is only 0.02.[1] Therefore, based on the cash flow generation from operations in the years 1–6, it would take Rörvik Timber 50 years to repay its debt. The capital expenditure ratio is also decreasing over time and more importantly, Rörvik Timber has problems financing its capital expenditure through its internally generated funds. The capital expenditure ratio based on reinvestments is on average 0.38,[2] indicating that Rörvik Timber is only able to finance 38% of its reinvestments from cash flows from operations. This indicates that Rörvik Timber's business model is not sustainable. Both the CFO to debt ratio and the capital expenditure ratio indicate a high liquidity risk in Rörvik Timber.

In Table 7.8 the different financial ratios measuring Rörvik Timber's short- and long-term liquidity risk are summarised. If the financial ratios serve their purpose they should be able to predict the suspension of payments well before year 7. In the last column in Table 7.8, we indicate which annual report the financial ratio may signal a potential liquidity problem. If the level of financial ratio is critically low or if the financial ratio is developing in the wrong direction it signals liquidity problems. As we have noted several times, it is difficult to evaluate whether the level of a financial ratio is at a critical level without a proper benchmark. Therefore, the above interpretation is highly subjective. Given this caveat it appears that financial ratios measuring the short-term liquidity risk are timelier than financial ratios measuring the long-term liquidity risk. Furthermore, four financial ratios signal potential liquidity problems several years prior to the suspension of payments. However, financial leverage and the interest coverage ratio do not provide any indication of liquidity problems before Rörvik Timber suspends its payments. This indicates that these financial ratios are not timely indicators of liquidity risk; at least in the case of Rörvik Timber. In summary, the example highlights the importance of using more than just one financial ratio when analysing the liquidity risk of a company.

Table 7.8 A summary of the financial ratios measuring the liquidity risk of Rörvik Timber

Ratio	Year 1	Year 2	Year 3	Year 4	Year 5	Year 6	Year of signal
			Short-term liquidity risk				
Liquidity cycle (days)	75	59	50	61	94	54	Year 5
Current ratio	2.22	1.16	1.08	1.25	1.47	0.86	Year 2
CFO to short-term debt ratio	5%	17%	13%	2%	−14%	5%	Year 1/4
			Long-term liquidity risk				
Financial leverage, market values	3.8	3.8	2.9	1.4	1.7	9.9	Year 6
Financial leverage, book values	2.8	2.7	3.1	2.8	2.8	6.5	Year 6
Interest coverage ratio	1.6	0.9	5.1	6.5	8.7	−3.9	Year 6
Interest coverage ratio (cash)	0.6	4.6	5.2	0.8	−3.6	0.8	Year 4
CFO to debt ratio	0.02	0.11	0.10	0.02	−0.09	0.03	Year 1/4
Capital expenditure ratio (reinvest)	0.3	1.8	2.1	0.3	−2.3	0.8	Year 1/4

Figure 7.1 offers an example of how to merge the two types of liquidity risk. Scenarios that deserve attention are when companies are facing either short-term liquidity risk, long-term liquidity risk or both. If a company is primarily facing short-term liquidity

	Long-term liquidity risk		
		Low (High solvency)	High (Low solvency)
Short-term liquidity risk	Low	OK	Restructure the company in time or suspension of payment is likely
	High	OK, but fix short-term problems	Suspension of payment is likely in the future

Figure 7.1 Overall assessment of the short- and long-term liquidity risk

problems it should take necessary steps to overcome these problems. Lack of funding until the launch of a new collection is an example of a short-term liquidity problem. A convincing action plan to overcome short-term funding problems will most likely convince shareholders and lenders to provide the necessary funding. Long-term liquidity problems are often more challenging. Examples include the expiration of a patent or increased competition on core markets, which deteriorates profit. Timely and convincing restructuring plans need to be developed and implemented in time to meet the problem of sufficient funding in the long run. If the necessary steps are not taken in time, the company is facing the risk of bankruptcy. Companies tackling both short- and long-term liquidity risk are likely bankruptcy candidates.

If companies are using measures, similar to the ones discussed in this chapter, to evaluate the probability that a customer (or supplier) suspends its payment and the likely economic consequence of a suspension of payments, a risk map may prove useful. Figure 7.2 provides an example of a risk map.

	Probability of suspension of payments		
		Low	Medium	High
Financial consequences	Low	Customer A	Customer C	
	Medium			
	High	Customer B		Customer D

Figure 7.2 Risk map of customers

There is only a low probability that customer A suspends its payments. Even in cases where it suspends its payment the financial consequences are low. Customer B is also attractive in the sense that the probability that it suspends its payment is low. However, in case it suspends its payments the financial consequences may be severe. Customer D is the least attractive customer on the risk map. There is a high probability that it suspends its payment. Furthermore, the financial consequences are high in the event of a suspension of payments.

Shortcomings of financial ratios measuring the short- and long-term liquidity risk

As noted previously, financial ratios measuring liquidity risk are:

- Based on historical accounting information and, as a result, backward-looking
- Only describing parts of a company's financial position
- Less useful in the absence of an appropriate benchmark
- Less useful if they are not used together.

Furthermore, since the financial ratios rely on accounting data it is important that differences in accounting quality across time and across companies are adjusted for. For example, reported EBIT may be affected by a gain or a loss that is transitory in nature. Reported EBIT is therefore not sustainable in the future and adjustments need to be made accordingly. In Chapter 13 we discuss the concept of accounting quality in further detail.

For these reasons we generally suggest that the analysis is supplemented with a comprehensive analysis that uncovers all important aspects of a company's financial position. In addition to the financial analysis outlined in this chapter, it should include a strategic analysis which encompasses an assessment of the industry attractiveness and the competitive edge of the company being analysed relative to its peers. Ideally, the financial analysis and the strategic analysis should be merged into a quantitative assessment of the future cash flow potential of the company; i.e. a forecast of the short- and long-term cash flow. In Chapters 8 and 11 we discuss these issues in greater detail. In Chapter 8 we examine various forecasting techniques and in Chapter 11 we elaborate further on how to assess the credit risk of a company using both financial ratios, rating models and forecasting of cash flows.

Conclusions

This chapter focuses on estimation of the short- and long-term liquidity risk. The essential points to remember include:

- Knowledge of the company's liquidity is important, as lack of liquidity may lead to loss of business opportunities and, in a worst case, suspension of payments.
- Financial ratios offer the advantage of being easy to calculate. This implies that many companies can be analysed with only modest effort. Financial ratios are therefore a cost-efficient way to rank businesses based on their liquidity risk. This also explains why rating agencies rely on financial ratios when evaluating companies' credit risk. Rating models are explained in greater detail in Chapter 11.
- Despite the appealing nature of financial ratios they should be used with caution. Financial ratios are usually based on historical figures and often describe only parts of a company's result and financial position. Since the financial ratios rely on

accounting data the concept of accounting quality needs to be taken into account before calculating and interpreting financial ratios measuring the short- and long-term liquidity risk. Furthermore, in the absence of a proper benchmark the usefulness of financial ratios decreases.

- A combination of a qualitative and a quantitative assessment leading to reliable forecast of the short- and long-term cash flow potential is expected to offer the best estimate for the short- and long-term liquidity risk. While Chapter 8 discusses forecasting in further detail, Chapter 11 addresses different ways to estimate the credit risk. You may find it useful to re-visit this chapter when reading Chapter 11 on credit risk.

Review questions

- Why is it important to monitor the short- and long-term liquidity closely?
- Provide examples of financial ratios measuring the short-term liquidity.
- Provide examples of financial ratios measuring the long-term liquidity.
- What are the potential shortcomings of financial ratios?
- How can these shortcomings be addressed?

APPENDIX 7.1

Rörvik Timber's financial statements

Income statement (SEKm)	Year 1	Year 2	Year 3	Year 4	Year 5	Year 6
Net turnover	1,306.9	1,434.0	1,879.1	2,113.0	2,641.8	2,390.4
Cost of goods sold	−1,245.3	−1,350.3	−1,712.1	−1,925.4	−2,273.6	−2,488.7
Gross profit/loss	61.6	83.7	167.0	187.6	368.2	−98.3
Selling expenses		−28.0	−39.6	−42.8	−51.6	−51.8
Administrative expenses		−44.1	−50.1	−54.4	−56.0	−65.8
Other operating income		7.0	8.5	28.1	20.8	71.0
Other operating expenses	0.0	−6.9	−12.6	−10.7	−13.7	−88.2
Depreciations and write-downs of fixed assets	−35.4					
Operating profit/loss	26.2	11.7	73.2	107.8	267.7	−233.1 ▶

Income statement (SEKm)	Year 1	Year 2	Year 3	Year 4	Year 5	Year 6
Profit/loss from interests in group companies	1.4	3.0	1.0	0.0	0.0	0.0
Interest income and similar income	0.7	0.4	0.9	0.4	0.0	0.0
Interest expenses and similar expenses	−16.7	−13.8	−15.3	−17.0	−30.9	−60.2
Profit/loss after financial income and expense	11.6	1.3	59.8	91.2	236.8	−293.3
Transfers to/from untaxed reserves	0.0	0.0	0.0	0.0	0.0	0.0
Profit/loss before tax	11.6	1.3	59.8	91.2	236.8	−293.3
Taxes	−4.0	1.0	−17.2	−26.0	−67.4	82.1
Net profit/loss	7.6	2.3	42.6	65.2	169.4	−211.2

(The terminology as in Rörvik Timber's annual report is adopted)

Assets (SEKm)	Year 1	Year 2	Year 3	Year 4	Year 5	Year 6
Long-term assets						
Intangible assets						
Goodwill	4.7	4.7	30.4	42.7	125.7	140.5
Other intangible assets						5.4
Total intangible assets	4.7	4.7	30.4	42.7	125.7	145.9
Tangible assets						
Buildings and land	93.4	99.6	109.8	113.0	149.8	160.1
Plant and machinery	167.4	191.6	191.9	210.3	259.4	382.1
Equipment, tools and installations	7.1	7.1	13.0	14.8	19.9	27.4
New plant in progress	19.4	6.3	10.7	12.4	37.8	16.8
Total tangible assets	287.3	304.6	325.4	350.5	466.9	586.4
Financial assets						
Interests in associated companies	4.3	6.4	–	–	–	–
Other long-term securities	2.4	0.1	–	–	–	–
Deferred tax receivables	–	0.8	0.5	–	–	21.7
Other long-term receivables	–	7.2	0.4	–	0.6	1.2
Total financial assets	6.7	14.5	0.9	–	0.6	22.9
Total long-term assets	298.7	323.8	356.7	393.2	593.2	755.2

▶

(continued)

Assets (SEKm)	Year 1	Year 2	Year 3	Year 4	Year 5	Year 6
Short-term assets						
Stocks on hand and related items						
Stocks on hand	296.1	268.7	379.0	396.2	742.4	478.8
Total stocks on hand and related items	296.1	268.7	379.0	396.2	742.4	478.8
Short–term receivables						
Accounts receivable from customers	111.3	107.0	170.0	272.3	279.1	314.1
Tax receivables	3.6	2.6	3.7	4.2	–	1.1
Other receivables	24.2	17.7	31.2	79.5	108.4	3.8
Prepaid expenses and deferred income	24.2	24.7	40.4	42.4	50.8	47.2
Total short-term receivables	163.3	152.0	245.3	398.4	438.3	366.2
Cash on hand and bank deposites	9.7	4.5	21.4	1.3	0.7	0.5
Total short-term assets	469.1	425.2	645.7	795.9	1,181.4	845.5
Total assets	767.8	749.0	1,002.4	1,189.1	1,774.6	1,600.7

Shareholders equity and liabilities (SEKm)	Year 1	Year 2	Year 3	Year 4	Year 5	Year 6
Shareholder equity						
Share capital	138.6	138.6	138.6	138.6	138.6	138.6
Other accrued restricted reserves/ statutory reserves	101.9	94.4	94.4	94.4	94.4	94.4
Other reserves		1.5	−2.5	3.2	−0.8	−0.8
Retained profits	−47.1	−32.0	−29.7	12.9	64.2	193.8
Net profit/loss for the year	7.6	2.3	42.6	65.2	169.4	−211.2
Total shareholder equity	201.0	204.8	243.4	314.3	465.8	214.8
Long-term liabilities						
Deferred tax liabilities	29.5	28.5	40.2	50.8	71.3	–
Bank overdraft	220.5					
Other liabilities and credit institutions	97.6	111.5	91.3	150.0	364.0	249.0
Financial leasing agreements	8.2	37.2	28.9	38.1	61.1	146.1
Other liabilities – long-term	–	–	2.5	–	10.0	10.8
Total long-term liabilities	355.8	177.2	162.9	238.9	506.4	405.9

▶

Shareholders equity and liabilities (SEKm)	Year 1	Year 2	Year 3	Year 4	Year 5	Year 6
Short-term liabilities						
Bank overdrafts/credit line		178.1	211.1	186.1	289.3	346.2
Accounts payable	126.7	128.5	236.9	295.9	317.6	321.8
Taxes due	0.3	0.7	5.3	–	36.7	43.9
Other obligations to credit institutions	20.1	0.8	18.8	10.0	14.0	144.1
Other liabilities–short-term	9.4	10.9	14.6	56.3	68.1	12.3
Accrued expenses and prepaid income	54.5	48.0	109.4	87.6	76.7	111.7
Total short-term liabilities	211.0	367.0	596.1	635.9	802.4	980.0
Total shareholders equity and liabilities	767.8	749.0	1,002.4	1,189.1	1,774.6	1,600.7

Invested capital (assets)	Year 1	Year 2	Year 3	Year 4	Year 5	Year 6
Goodwill	5	5	30	43	126	141
Other intangible assets	0	0	0	0	0	5
Buildings and land	93	100	110	113	150	160
Plant and machinery	167	192	192	210	259	382
Equipment, tools and installations	7	7	13	15	20	27
New plant in progress	19	6	11	12	38	17
Interests in associated companies	4	6	0	0	0	0
Deferred tax receivables	0	1	1	0	0	22
Stocks on hand	296	269	379	396	742	479
Accounts receivable from customers	111	107	170	272	279	314
Tax receivables	4	3	4	4	0	1
Other receivables	24	18	31	80	108	4
Prepaid expenses and deferred income	24	25	40	42	51	47
Assets, operating	756	737	981	1,188	1,773	1,599

Non-interest bearing debt						
Deferred tax liabilities	30	29	40	51	71	0
Accounts payable	127	129	237	296	318	322
Taxes due	0	1	5	0	37	44
Other liabilities – short-term	9	11	15	56	68	12
Accrued expenses and prepaid income	55	48	109	88	77	112
Non-interest-bearing debt, total	220	217	406	491	570	490
Invested capital (net operating assets)	535	521	574	697	1,203	1,109

(continued)

Invested capital (liabilities)	Year 1	Year 2	Year 3	Year 4	Year 5	Year 6
Equity						
Share capital	139	139	139	139	139	139
Other accrued restricted reserves/statutory reserves	102	94	94	94	94	94
Other reserves	0	2	−3	3	−1	−1
Retained profits	−47	−32	−30	13	64	194
Net profit/loss for the year	8	2	43	65	169	−211
Equity, total	201	205	243	314	466	215
Net interest-bearing debt						
Other long-term securities	2	0	0	0	0	0
Other long-term receivables	0	7	0	0	1	1
Cash on hand and bank deposites	10	5	21	1	1	1
Other liabilities – long-term	0	0	3	0	10	11
Bank overdraft	221	0	0	0	0	0
Other liabilities and credit institutions	98	112	91	150	364	249
Financial leasing agreements	8	37	29	38	61	146
Bank overdrafts/credit line	0	178	211	186	289	346
Other obligations to credit institutions	20	1	19	10	14	144
Net interest-bearing debt	334	316	331	383	737	895
Invested capital (equity and NIBD)	535	521	574	697	1,203	1,109

Notes

1 The average CFO to debt ratio is calculated as:

$$\frac{\sum_{Year\,1}^{Year\,6} CFO}{\sum_{Year\,1}^{Year\,6} Liabilities,\ total}$$

2 The average capital expenditure ratio is calculated as:

$$\frac{\sum_{Year\,1}^{Year\,6} CFO}{\sum_{Year\,1}^{Year\,6} Capital\ expenditure}$$

PART 3

Decision making

Introduction to Part 3

The previous chapters described the information available in the annual reports and how to measure a firm's historical profitability, growth and liquidity risk. Chapters 8 to 12 apply the accounting information and the historical analysis in different decision contexts.

Chapter 8 describes how to build pro forma statements that articulate; that is they relate to each other in a certain way. It identifies key strategic and financial value drivers and provides guidance on how to develop your own value driver map. Furthermore, the steps involved in developing reliable estimates are addressed and different techniques are introduced to evaluate the achievability of forecasts.

Chapter 9 provides an overview of firm valuation techniques. Present value models such as the discounted cash flow model (DCF model) and the economic value added model (EVA model) are presented and the chapter illustrates under which conditions the different present value approaches yield identical value estimates. Popular multiples including the P/E multiple and the EV/EBIT multiple are presented and the theoretical link to present value approaches is established. Finally, the liquidation approach is introduced and the distinction between an orderly liquidation and a distress liquidation is discussed.

Chapter 10 highlights why the cost of capital plays a central role in many decision contexts including valuation and compensation. Weighted average cost of capital (WACC) is defined and the chapter elaborates on how to estimate the components of WACC. The estimation of a firm's capital structure and its required rate of return on equity and debt are discussed.

Chapter 11 focuses on credit analysis and discusses the importance of estimating exposure at default, probability of default, and probability of recovery in case of default. It explains the difference between the fundamental analysis approach and the statistical approach in credit analysis. The chapter illustrates how to conduct a credit analysis based on fundamental analysis. An introduction to ratings from credit agencies is provided and the distinction between an investment grade and a speculative grade are shown. Finally, the chapter gives a short introduction to some of the statistical approaches available for credit analysis.

Chapter 12 addresses a number of analytical issues when designing an accounting-based bonus plan for executives. The chapter discusses the choice of performance measure, the pay to performance relation and the choice of performance standard. Furthermore, accounting issues such as the treatment of transitory items and changes in accounting policies in bonus contracts are addressed.

CHAPTER 8

Forecasting

Learning outcomes

After reading this chapter you should be able to:

- **Identify key strategic and financial value drivers**
- **Design your own value driver map**
- **Prepare pro forma financial statements that articulate**
- **Develop reliable forecasts based on a strategic as well as a financial statement analysis**
- **Evaluate whether forecasts are realistic**
- **Understand the challenges of forecasting**

Forecasting

So far we have focused on accounting data and the measurement of historical profitability, growth and risk. In this chapter the lens changes from a historical view to a forward-looking view and demonstrates how to develop a company's pro forma income statement, balance sheet and cash flow statement. The development of **pro forma statements** is at the heart of financial statement analysis. Investors typically prepare pro forma statements with the purpose of valuing a business. They may also analyse a firm's future cash position in order to evaluate the need for infusion of capital. Lenders usually prepare pro forma statements with the purpose of evaluating a customer's (business's) ability to service its debt. In addition, they may explore the future business potential. As a final example, management prepares pro forma statements for planning purposes and to provide performance targets.

We will build on the foundation laid out in Chapters 4 and 5 and separate operating activities from financing activities, when forecasting future earnings and cash flows. As noted in Chapter 4 operations (including investment in operations) is the primary driving force behind a firm's value creation and, therefore, important to monitor and measure. Financing, on the other hand, conveys information on how operations are funded and provide useful information about a firm's financial risks.

In this chapter we make a distinction between the technical and the estimation-related aspects of forecasting. By technical aspects we refer to the design of the value driver setup and to the fact that pro forma statements must articulate; i.e. that the bookkeeping is performed properly. By estimation related aspects we refer to the quality of the sources and analyses supporting the assumptions and estimates underlying the pro forma statements. It is important to emphasise that the approach adopted in this chapter rests on the assumption that the analyst is an 'outsider' and therefore has access to publicly available information only. If internal information is available, a more refined forecasting approach can be developed.

In this chapter we refer to the term 'value driver'. We make a distinction between strategic and financial value drivers. A **strategic value driver** is a strategic or an operational initiative that can be undertaken by a company with the purpose of improving value. Examples of strategic drivers are: development of new products, entrance to new markets and outsourcing of production or back-office activities. Strategic drivers are industry and company specific. A strategic driver is sometimes referred to as an executional driver. A **financial value driver** is a financial ratio or number that mirrors the company's underlying performance and is closely related to value creation. Examples of financial value drivers are growth, margins and investment ratios. The linkage between strategic and financial value drivers is illustrated here.

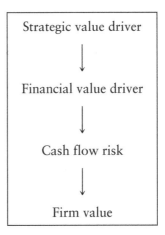

The linkage between strategic and financial value drivers suggests that it is the strategic and operating performance of a company that affects the financial value drivers. This implies that financial value drivers do not create value per se. However, if a financial value driver is positively affected by an operational initiative, such as cost cutting, it affects cash flows and value positively.

The design of pro forma statements

There are many ways to design a forecasting system that ensures that the underlying bookkeeping is performed properly; i.e. that debit and credit balance. Some prefer a 'line-item' approach where each accounting item is forecast without reference to the expected level of activity. Others prefer a **sales-driven forecasting approach** reflecting that different accounting items such as operating expenses and investments are driven by the expected level of activity (i.e. sales growth). In this chapter we favour a sales driven approach as we believe it ensures a better link between the level of activity in a company and the related expenses and investments than a line-item approach.

In Table 8.1 we have designed a template in accordance with the sales-driven approach. As the purpose of the template is to illustrate the design of pro forma statements, which articulate, it is kept relatively simple. The template relies on eight value drivers only and the level of aggregation is consequently high. For example,

Table 8.1 The value driver structure for creating simple pro forma statements

Step			Value drivers
	Income statement		
1	Revenue	I	Revenue growth
2	Operating expenses (excl. depreciation)		(1 – 3)
3	= **Earnings before interest, taxes, depreciation and amortisation (EBITDA)**	II	EBITDA-margin: $\left(\dfrac{\text{EBITDA}}{\text{Revenue}}\right)$
4	Depreciation and amortisation	III	Depreciation as a percentage of intangible and tangible assets **(11)**
5	= **Operating income before tax (EBIT)**		(3 – 4)
6	Tax on EBIT	IV	Tax rate
7	= **Net operating profit after tax (NOPAT)**		(5 – 6)
8	Net financial expenses before tax	V	Net borrowing rate × NIBD **(18)**
9	Tax shield		(IV) × (8)
10	= **Net income**		(7 – 8 + 9)
	Balance sheet		
	Assets		
11	Intangible and tangible assets	VI	Intangible and tangible assets as a percentage of revenue
12	Net working capital + Inventory + Receivables – Accounts payable – Other operating liabilities	VII	Net working capital as a percentage of revenue
13	**Invested capital (net operating assets)**		(11 + 12)
	Liabilities		
14	Equity, beginning of period		
15	+ Net income		(10)
16	– Dividends		(28)
17	**Equity, end of period**		(14 + 15 – 16)
18	Net interest-bearing debt (NIBD)	VIII	Net interest-bearing debt as a percentage of invested capital **(13)**
19	**Invested capital (Equity + NIBD)**		(17 + 18)
	Cash flow statement		
20	NOPAT		(7)
21	+ Depreciation and amortisation		(4)
22	– Δ Net working capital		(Δ12)
23	– Net investments (non-current assets)		(Δ11 + 4)
24	= **Free cash flow to the firm (FCFF)**		
25	New net financial liabilities		(Δ18)
26	Net financial expenses after tax		(8 – 9)
27	= **Free cash flow to equity holders (FCFE)**		(24 +/–25 – 26)
28	– Dividends		All FCFE is paid as dividends (–27)
29	= **Cash surplus**		(27 – 28) = 0

the template does not distinguish between different types of operating expenses; only total operating expenses are forecast. Later in this chapter we discuss how you might expand the template to comprehend more value drivers and thereby also more accounting variables. The first column in Table 8.1 explains the number of steps that need to be taken before you have prepared a pro forma income statement, balance sheet and cash flow statement. The second column explains the accounting items that are forecast. The third column highlights the eight financial value drivers that need to be forecast and finally the fourth column explains how each accounting item is calculated. The basic idea of the template is that if you follow all 29 steps, the result will be a set of comprehensive pro forma income statements, balance sheets and cash flow statements which articulate. In that regard it is just like following the recipe in a cookery book – except that the outcome has to be digested in a different way!

This section demonstrates how the template can be used to prepare pro forma statements. By relying on a simple numerical example as outlined in Table 8.2, we make a distinction between the *historical period*, *the explicit forecasting period* and *the terminal period*. The historical period is used as a foundation for our forecasts and provides insights about the trends and levels of the eight financial value drivers listed in Table 8.1. The explicit forecasting period reflects the period where financial value drivers are not assumed to be constant; i.e. it is possible to change the level and direction of each of the eight financial value drivers. The terminal period reflects a 'steady state' environment and assumes that everything remains constant; i.e. it is not possible to change the level or direction of any of the financial value drivers subsequent to the first year of the terminal period. Accordingly, every forecast item grows by the same constant in the terminal period.

As seen in the upper half of Table 8.2 the eight financial value drivers remain constant during the last four years. Assuming the business environment remains stable in the future, we extrapolate the historical performance into the explicit forecasting period. Therefore, the value drivers in the explicit forecasting period exactly mirror the realised value drivers. In the terminal period we assume that the growth rate drops to 2% reflecting the expected long-term growth in the economy as a whole. Other value drivers remain unchanged in the terminal period. Based on these forecast assumptions we have developed a pro forma income statement, balance sheet and cash flow statement that articulate as shown in Table 8.2.

In Table 8.3 we show how the projected financial data in Table 8.2 have been calculated (allowing for rounding errors). We follow the same steps as in Table 8.1. For example, step 1 in Table 8.3 is calculated as last year's revenue $\times$ 1 + the growth rate ($121.6 \times (1 + 0.05) = 127.6$). While most accounting items in Table 8.3 are self-explanatory we elaborate on the estimation of investments in intangible and tangible assets and net financial expenses. Investments in intangible and tangible assets are calculated as the difference between intangible and tangible assets at the end and at the beginning of the period plus depreciation and amortisation during that period. Depreciation and amortisation are added back since they do not have any cash impact.

Intangible and tangible assets, end of period
+ Depreciation and amortisation
– Intangible and tangible assets, beginning of period
= Investments in intangible and tangible assets

Table 8.2 An example of a pro forma income statement, balance sheet and cash flow statement

Forecast assumptions	Historical period					Explicit forecasting period (forecast horizon)					Terminal period	
	-4	-3	-2	-1	0	1	2	3	4	5	6	7
Revenue growth		5%	5%	5%	5%	5%	5%	5%	5%	5%	2%	2%
EBITDA/revenue		30%	30%	30%	30%	30%	30%	30%	30%	30%	30%	30%
Depreciation/intangible and tangible assets		20%	20%	20%	20%	20%	20%	20%	20%	20%	20%	20%
Interest rate		8%	8%	8%	8%	8%	8%	8%	8%	8%	8%	8%
Tax rate		25%	25%	25%	25%	25%	25%	25%	25%	25%	25%	25%
Intangible and tangible assets/revenue		60%	60%	60%	60%	60%	60%	60%	60%	60%	60%	60%
Net working capital/revenue		40%	40%	40%	40%	40%	40%	40%	40%	40%	40%	40%
Net interest bearing debt/invested capital		50%	50%	50%	50%	50%	50%	50%	50%	50%	50%	50%

Income statement	-4	-3	-2	-1	0	1	2	3	4	5	6	7
Revenue	100.0	105.0	110.3	115.8	121.6	127.6	134.0	140.7	147.7	155.1	158.2	161.4
Operating expenses	-70.0	-73.5	-77.2	-81.0	-85.1	-89.3	-93.8	-98.5	-103.4	-108.6	-110.8	-113.0
EBITDA	**30.0**	**31.5**	**33.1**	**34.7**	**36.5**	**38.3**	**40.2**	**42.2**	**44.3**	**46.5**	**47.5**	**48.4**
Depreciation and amortisation	-12.0	-12.6	-13.2	-13.9	-14.6	-15.3	-16.1	-16.9	-17.7	-18.6	-19.0	-19.4
EBIT	**18.0**	**18.9**	**19.8**	**20.8**	**21.9**	**23.0**	**24.1**	**25.3**	**26.6**	**27.9**	**28.5**	**29.1**
Tax on EBIT	-4.5	-4.7	-5.0	-5.2	-5.5	-5.7	-6.0	-6.3	-6.6	-7.0	-7.1	-7.3
NOPAT	**13.5**	**14.2**	**14.9**	**15.6**	**16.4**	**17.2**	**18.1**	**19.0**	**19.9**	**20.9**	**21.4**	**21.8**
Net financial expenses, beginning of year NIBD	-3.8	-4.0	-4.2	-4.4	-4.6	-4.9	-5.1	-5.4	-5.6	-5.9	-6.2	-6.3
Tax shield	1.0	1.0	1.1	1.1	1.2	1.2	1.3	1.3	1.4	1.5	1.6	1.6
Net earnings	**10.7**	**11.2**	**11.7**	**12.3**	**12.9**	**13.6**	**14.3**	**15.0**	**15.7**	**16.5**	**16.7**	**17.0**

Balance sheet	-4	-3	-2	-1	0	1	2	3	4	5	6	7
Intangible and tangible assets	60.0	63.0	66.2	69.5	72.9	76.6	80.4	84.4	88.6	93.1	94.9	96.8
Net working capital	40.0	42.0	44.1	46.3	48.6	51.1	53.6	56.3	59.1	62.1	63.3	64.6
Invested capital (net operating assets)	**100.0**	**105.0**	**110.3**	**115.8**	**121.6**	**127.6**	**134.0**	**140.7**	**147.7**	**155.1**	**158.2**	**161.4**

Table 1

Equity, begin	50.0	50.0	52.5	55.1	57.9	60.8	63.8	67.0	70.4	73.9	77.6	79.1
Net earnings		11.2	11.7	12.3	12.9	13.6	14.3	15.0	15.7	16.5	16.7	17.0
Dividends		−8.7	−9.1	−9.6	−10.0	−10.5	−11.1	−11.6	−12.2	−12.8	−15.2	−15.5
Equity, end	50.0	52.5	55.1	57.9	60.8	63.8	67.0	70.4	73.9	77.6	79.1	80.7
Net interest-bearing debt (NIBD)	50.0	52.5	55.1	57.9	60.8	63.8	67.0	70.4	73.9	77.6	79.1	80.7
Invested capital (equity and NIBD)	**100.0**	**105.0**	**110.3**	**115.8**	**121.6**	**127.6**	**134.0**	**140.7**	**147.7**	**155.1**	**158.2**	**161.4**

Cash flow statement

NOPAT	14.2	14.9	15.6	16.4	17.2	18.1	19.0	19.9	20.9	21.4	21.8
Depreciation and amortisation	12.6	13.2	13.9	14.6	15.3	16.1	16.9	17.7	18.6	19.0	19.4
Net working capital	−2.0	−2.1	−2.2	−2.3	−2.4	−2.6	−2.7	−2.8	−3.0	−1.2	−1.3
Investments, intangible and tangible assets	−15.6	−16.4	−17.2	−18.1	−19.0	−19.9	−20.9	−22.0	−23.0	−20.8	−21.3
Free cash flow to the firm (FCFF)	**9.2**	**9.6**	**10.1**	**10.6**	**11.2**	**11.7**	**12.3**	**12.9**	**13.6**	**18.3**	**18.6**
Net interest-bearing debt (NIBD)	2.5	2.6	2.8	2.9	3.0	3.2	3.4	3.5	3.7	1.6	1.6
Net financial expenses, beginning of year debt	−4.0	−4.2	−4.4	−4.6	−4.9	−5.1	−5.4	−5.6	−5.9	−6.2	−6.3
Tax shield	1.0	1.1	1.1	1.2	1.2	1.3	1.3	1.4	1.5	1.6	1.6
Free cash flow to equity (FCFE)	**8.7**	**9.1**	**9.6**	**10.0**	**10.5**	**11.1**	**11.6**	**12.2**	**12.8**	**15.2**	**15.5**
Dividends	−8.7	−9.1	−9.6	−10.0	−10.5	−11.1	−11.6	−12.2	−12.8	−15.2	−15.5
Cash surplus	**0.0**	**0.0**	**0.0**	**0.0**	**0.0**	**0.0**	**0.0**	**0.0**	**0.0**	**0.0**	**0.0**

Please note that rounding errors may occur.

Table 8.3 An elaboration of the first forecasting year in Table 8.2 (rounding errors may occur)

Step		Value drivers	Calculations (year 1)
	Income statement		
1	Revenue	I	$121.6 \times (1 + 5\%) = 127.6$
2	Operating expenses (excl. depreciation)		$127.6 - 38.3 = 89.3$
3	**= Earnings before interest, taxes, depreciation and amortisation (EBITDA)**	II	$127.6 \times 30\% = 38.3$
4	Depreciation and amortisation	III	$76.6 \times 20\% = 15.3$
5	**Operating income before tax (EBIT)**		$38.3 - 15.3 = 23.0$
6	Tax on EBIT	IV	$23.0 \times 25\% = 5.7$
7	**= Net operating profit after tax (NOPAT)**		$23.0 - 5.7 = 17.2$
8	Net financial expenses before tax	V	$8\% \times 60.8$ (beginning of year NIBD) $= 4.9$
9	Tax shield		$4.9 \times 25\% = 1.2$
10	**= Net income**		$17.2 - 5.1 + 1.3 = 13.6$
	Balance sheet		
	Assets		
11	Intangible and tangible assets	VI	$127.6 \times 60\% = 76.6$
12	Net working capital – Inventory – Accounts receivable – Accounts payable – Other operating liabilities	VII	$127.6 \times 40\% = 51.1$
13	**Invested capital (net operating assets)**		$76.6 + 51.1 = 127.6$
	Liabilities		
14	Equity, beginning of period		60.8
15	Net income		13.6
16	Dividends		-10.5
17	= Equity, end of period		63.8
18	Net interest-bearing debt (NIBD)	VIII	$127.6 \times 50\% = 63.8$
19	**Invested capital (Equity + NIBD)**		$63.8 + 63.8 = 127.6$
	Cash flow statement		
20	NOPAT		17.2
21	+ Depreciation and amortisation		15.3
22	Net working capital		$48.6 - 51.1 = -2.4$
23	Net investments (fixed assets)		$72.9 - 76.6 - 15.3 = -19.0$
24	**= Free cash flow to the firm (FCFF)**		$17.2 + 15.3 - 2.4 - 19.0 = 11.2$
25	New net financial obligation		$63.8 - 60.8 = 3.0$
26	Net financial expenses after tax		$-4.9 + 1.2 = -3.7$
27	**= Free cash flow to equity holders (FCFE)**		$11.2 + 3.0 - 3.7 = 10.5$
28	– Dividends		-10.5
29	**= Cash surplus**		$10.5 - 10.5 = 0.0$

Table 8.4 Calculation of investments in intangible and tangible assets (rounding errors may occur)

Investments, intangible and tangible assets	Forecast year						
	1	2	3	4	5	6	7
Intangible and tangible assets, end of period	76.6	80.4	84.4	88.6	93.1	94.9	96.8
Depreciation	15.3	16.1	16.9	17.7	18.6	19.0	19.4
Intangible and tangible assets, beginning of period	−72.9	−76.6	−80.4	−84.4	−88.6	−93.1	−94.9
Investments, intangible and tangible assets	**19.0**	**19.9**	**20.9**	**22.0**	**23.0**	**20.8**	**21.3**

In Table 8.4 we show how investments in intangible and tangible assets are calculated for each forecast year. Net financial expenses are measured as the net borrowing rate multiplied by net interest-bearing debt at the beginning of the year. Since we intend to apply the example for valuation purposes in the next chapter it is useful to apply the net interest-bearing debt at the beginning of the year when calculating net financial expenses.

The template outlined in Table 8.1 – and exemplified in Tables 8.2, 8.3 and 8.4 – is a powerful tool to obtain an understanding of how to develop pro forma financial statements which articulate. For example, it stresses the importance of forecasting all accounting items, as this is the only way to ensure that the pro forma statements articulate. The template also highlights the financial value drivers that need to be forecast and illustrate the internal coherence of the different statements. It demonstrates that it is possible to develop a pro forma income statement, balance sheet and cash flow statement based on only a few financial value drivers.

It is important to note that the template rests on a number of assumptions that may not necessarily reflect the underlying economics of a company. For example, we assume that all cash surpluses are paid out as dividends. This may be a poor description of a company's de facto dividend policy. It may therefore be necessary to modify the template accordingly. In the next section we address some of the modifications that you may consider when refining the template.

Designing a template for forecasting

When you design your own template for forecasting purposes there are many issues that need to be taken into account. Some of these issues are discussed in this section. Specifically we raise and discuss the following questions:

- Do the financial value drivers in the template reflect the underlying economics of a company?
- Are all relevant value drivers included?
- Is the level of aggregation of the financial value drivers appropriate?

Do financial value drivers in the template reflect the underlying economics of a company?

Even though each financial value driver in the template has been carefully designed to reflect the underlying economics of a company there may be circumstances where a value driver needs to be modified. The following three examples illustrate this issue.

First, the template assumes a linear relationship between intangible and tangible assets and revenue. While this is a fair description for firms that gradually invest in such assets according to the level of activity, it may also be a poor description if investments are more discrete in nature and mainly done years apart. For example, airports only invest in a new terminal maybe every tenth or twentieth year. Therefore, airports serve as a prime example of an industry where investments are only carried out with large time intervals. This idea is illustrated in Figure 8.1.

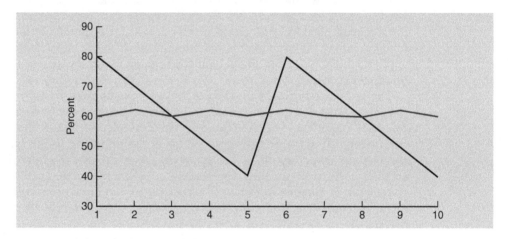

Figure 8.1 Intangible and tangible assets as a percentage of revenue

The coloured line reflects a company that gradually invests in intangible and tangible assets according to the level of activity whereas the black line mirrors a company that invests every fifth year. The illustration highlights the lack of stability in the investment driver (value driver VI in the template) when investments take place years apart. If a company's investment plans are known or if the investments reflect the latter case described above it may be more useful to change the investment driver to simply reflect the expected level of investments each year.

Second, in the template net financial expenses are calculated as the net borrowing rate $\times$ the net interest-bearing debt (NIBD) by the end of each forecast year while in the example net financial expenses are based on net interest-bearing debt at the beginning of each forecast year. Assuming a steady growth in net interest-bearing debt during each forecast year it appears more appropriate to apply the average net interest-bearing debt as deflator. This is, however, easy to integrate in the template by simply calculating net financial expenses as follows:

Net financial expenses = Net borrowing rate $\times$ average NIBD

Third, in the template dividends are a function of the cash surplus earned during each forecast year; i.e. the cash not consumed in operations, investments and financing. However, some companies operate with a target pay-out ratio. In those cases it may be more appropriate to estimate dividends as a function of the pay-out ratio and net earnings:

$$\text{Dividends} = \text{Net earnings} \times \text{payout ratio}$$

In case dividends are no longer a residual of the cash surplus, and thereby violate the final step in the template, it is necessary to modify the template accordingly. It may therefore be useful to consider net interest-bearing debt as a final step ('plug') in the template that ensures an articulation of the pro forma statements. Net interest-bearing debt is then estimated as follows:

$$\text{Net interest-bearing debt, end of period}$$
$$= \text{Net interest-bearing debt, beginning of period} + \text{cash surplus}$$

Are all value drivers in the template included?

There may be aspects of a company's economy that are not properly addressed in the template for reasons of simplicity. For example, the template assumes that all taxes are paid as earnings are generated (e.g. all taxes on earnings generated in year 1 are paid in year 1). This is a heroic assumption since companies are mostly able to defer taxes into future periods due to an attractive tax driven depreciation scheme. Therefore, for those companies it is important to add deferred tax liability as an additional value driver in the template, as net cash inflows will otherwise be underestimated. Assuming deferred tax liabilities are a function of the activity in a company the deferred tax driver can either be defined as:

$$\frac{\text{Deferred tax liability}}{\text{Revenue}}$$

or

$$\frac{\text{Deferred tax liability}}{\text{Intangible and tangible assets}}$$

A more exact estimation of deferred tax liability requires information about the future taxable income. We ask you to refer to Chapter 14 if you want further information on how deferred tax liabilities are calculated.

Is the level of aggregation in the template appropriate?

As noted previously the template is based on a high level of aggregation. For example, operating expenses are estimated as the residual of the EBITDA margin (e.g. if the EBITDA margin is estimated at 5%, operating expenses amount to 95% of revenues). This implies that the template does not distinguish between the different types of (operating) expenses and therefore does not allow you to forecast each type of expenses separately. In cases where more detailed information about the cost structure is available, it may be useful to apply a more refined approach allowing each operating expense to be forecast separately. The following tabulation provides an example of an alternative value driver setup for operating expenses for companies reporting expenses by function.

Cost of goods sold	=	Cost of goods sold as a percentage of revenue
Sales and distribution costs	=	Sales and distribution costs as a percentage of revenue
Administration cost	=	Administration as a percentage of revenue
R&D expenses	=	R&D as a percentage of revenue
Special items, net	=	Special items as a percentage of revenue

In this modified value driver setup the EBITDA margin becomes a residual; i.e. a result of revenue minus operating expenses. Obviously, the proposed value driver setup for operating expenses should be modified for companies reporting expenses by nature.

Net working capital as a percentage of revenue serves as another example of a high level of aggregation. Net working capital can be decomposed into the following variables:

- Inventory
- Accounts receivable
- Other operating receivables
- Accounts payable
- Other operating liabilities.

It is even possible to decompose those variables further. For example, other operating liabilities can be decomposed into tax payable, VAT, salaries due to employees, etc. Often it makes sense to apply a more refined approach when predicting net working capital. Companies take initiatives to strengthen different components of net working capital and this must be reflected in the pro forma statements. An example of a more refined approach is the one outlined below.

Inventory	=	Inventory as a percentage of revenue
Accounts receivable	=	Accounts receivable as a percentage of revenue
Other receivables	=	Other receivables as a percentage of revenue
Accounts payable	=	Accounts payable as a percentage of revenue
Other operating liabilities	=	Other operating liabilities as a percentage of revenue

In this modified value driver setup net working capital is a function of inventory, accounts receivable, other receivables, accounts payable and other operating liabilities and is expressed as a percentage of revenue.

Figure 8.2 illustrates how the eight financial value drivers listed in the template in Table 8.1 can be further refined to accommodate these observations. It shows that it

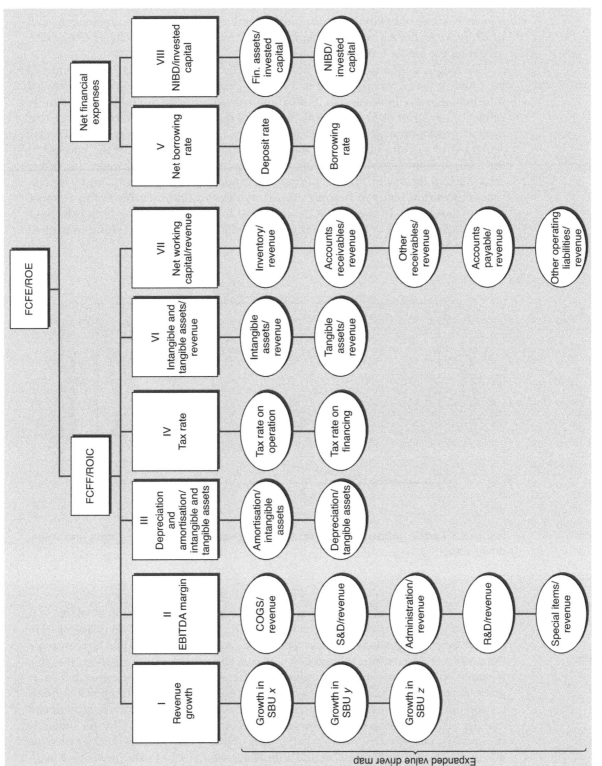

Figure 8.2 Expanded value driver map

is possible to expand the financial **value driver map** considerably allowing the analyst a greater degree of flexibility. The number of value drivers has been expanded from 8 to 23. In Appendix 8.1 we apply elements of the more refined value driver setup when preparing pro forma statements for Carlsberg.

The design of the value drivers and thereby the level of aggregation is influenced by a number of factors that need to be taken into account. For example, if detailed information is available such as internal information it seems useful to apply a more refined value driver approach. If the purpose of the analysis is short-term forecasting such as predicting next year's earnings, a more refined value driver approach also seems useful as more information tends to be available. However, if the purpose of the analysis is long-term forecasting, it is likely that a more aggregated value driver setup such as the one in Table 8.1 is more appropriate. This is mainly due to the fact that information tends to become cruder and less accurate the further in advance forecasts are made. In these cases analysts tend to focus on the long-term behaviour of key financial value drivers such as growth and EBITDA margins. This is illustrated in Figure 8.3.

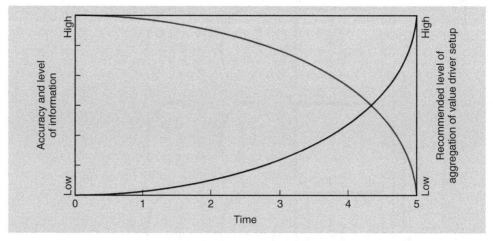

Figure 8.3 Factors influencing the level of aggregation of accounting data and value driver setup

The coloured line reflects the level and the accuracy of information available at a given point in time and the black line illustrates the recommended level of aggregation of value driver setup relative to time. The figure suggests that as analysts forecast more than just a few years into the forecast horizon, the quality of information available typically do not justify a refined value driver setup in line with the expanded value driver map in Figure 8.2. In these cases analysts are usually better off applying industry specific levels and trends on aggregated financial value drivers such as growth and margins. These financial value drivers tend to revert towards a mean for the industry. In summary, analysts are probably better off working with a more refined set of value drivers for short-term forecasting and a more aggregated set of value drivers for long-term forecasting.

The estimation of financial value drivers

So far we have focused on designing a financial value driver map that describes fundamental aspects of the underlying economics of a company and developing pro forma statements that articulate. While it is relatively simple to design a value driver map and develop pro forma statements that articulate it is more time consuming and challenging to develop estimates for each financial value driver. It requires that each estimate in the pro forma statements is supported by useful sources and carefully conducted analyses. The GIGO principle also applies in this context, i.e. garbage in garbage out. It is therefore essential that the analyst can 'see' into the future with a high degree of visibility. In the following sections we discuss how a **strategic analysis** as well as a financial statement analysis help the analyst in generating better forecasts.

Strategic analysis

The strategic literature provides guidance on the structure and types of analyses that analysts can follow to cover important aspects of a company's cash flow potential and risk. In this section we suggest a top-down approach that aims at understanding:

- The nature of the company's business environment
- Macro factors influencing the company's cash flow potential and risks
- Industry factors influencing the company's cash flow potential and risks
- Company specific factors influencing the cash flow generation and risks
- Value chain analysis
- A company's Strength, Weakness, Opportunities and Threats.

In the following we describe each of these steps involved in a top-down approach.

The nature of a company's business environment

It may be useful to take an initial view of the stability of the company's business environment and uncover the complexity and dynamics of the industry. This helps the analyst to decide on the appropriate level of analysis.

Dynamics and complexity refer to the stability of the market and simplicity of the product or services being delivered to customers, respectively. The perception is that if the market is stable or even static and the products are simple, the analyst only needs to conduct the analysis on a historical basis as a means of forecasting future outcomes. On the other hand, if the market is dynamic and/or if the product(s) or service(s) are complex, it makes less sense to rely purely on historical information. The competition may rapidly change or new products or services may be introduced which change the competitive landscape. In these cases it is important to obtain a fundamental understanding about the underlying drivers of the market and the next generation of products or services. These thoughts are illustrated in Figure 8.4.

The first step of the strategic analysis sets the scope of the analysis. If the market is stable and the product or service is fairly simple, the analysts will most likely make a relatively plain analysis relying to a large extent on past performance. On the other hand, if the market is not stable or if the product or service tends to become more complicated over time, the analyst will tend to make a more thorough analysis dealing with the uncertainties of the market and the products or services being offered. Historical data will no longer satisfy the analyst. The analyst will search for information that provides insights about the market and the next generation of

187

		Product: Simple	Product: Complex
Market	Stable	Simple analysis Simple forecasting	Thorough analysis Scenario forecasting
	Dynamic	Thorough analysis Scenario forecasting	Thorough analysis Scenario forecasting

Figure 8.4 The dynamic of the market and the complexity of the product

products or services being offered. Furthermore, the forecasting is most likely based on scenarios.

Macro factors influencing the company's cash flow potential and risk

The primary objective of the macro analysis is to detect macro factors that may affect a company's cash flow potential and risk. In Table 8.5 a number of macro factors are listed. The model is also known as the **PEST** model indicating the impact of political, economic, social and technical factors on cash flow and risk. It is important to stress that the list of macro factors is not exhaustive.

Table 8.5 PEST analysis of environmental influences

Political/legal	**Economic factors**
• Monopolies legislation • Environmental protection laws • Taxation policy • Foreign trade regulations • Employment law • Government stability	• Business cycles • GNP trends • Interest rates • Money supply • Inflation • Unemployment • Disposable income • Energy availability and cost
Sociocultural factors	**Technological**
• Population demographics • Income distribution • Social mobility • Lifestyle changes • Attitudes to work and leisure • Consumerism • Levels of education	• Government spending on research • Government and industry focus of technological effort • New discoveries/development • Speed of technology transfer • Rates of obsolescence

Legislation and environmental protection laws are examples of political factors affecting the condition under which companies operate. Business cycles and employment rates are economic factors affecting the demand of companies' products and services. Similarly, sociocultural factors such as population demographics and lifestyle changes affect the underlying demand for companies' products and services. Finally, technological factors such as government spending on research and the speed of new technology have an impact on companies' opportunities to offer products and services timely to the market.

Macro factors affect industries and companies differently and it is therefore important that analysts understand which macro factors are likely to affect a company's cash flows and risks and which of those factors that are currently the most important ones and which are potentially more important in the future.

Industry factors influencing the company's cash flow potential and risks

The attractiveness of an industry is ultimately a result of the possibility of earning acceptable returns, i.e. returns equal to or above the cost of capital. There are different drivers that affect the attractiveness of an industry, but in general it seems well accepted that more competition reduces the chances of obtaining abnormal returns, i.e. returns that exceed the cost of capital. In order to understand the competition in an industry the 'five forces' approach serves as a useful checklist. The **five forces analysis** approach illustrated in Figure 8.5 highlights different forces affecting the competition in an industry and the possibility to earn attractive returns. In the following section, we briefly describe each of the five forces.

An analysis of *potential entrants* provides the analyst with an understanding of the threats of new players in the industry. New entrants generally bring new capacity and a desire to gain market shares which ultimately affect returns negatively. Typical barriers to entry (which protect the returns in an industry) include:

- Economies of scale
- Product differentiation
- Capital requirements

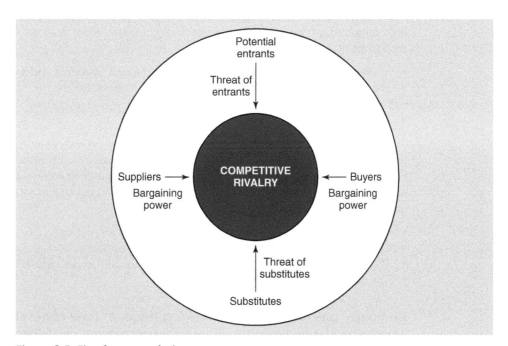

Figure 8.5 Five forces analysis

- Switching costs
- Access to distribution channels
- Government policy.

An analysis of the *rivalry* among existing competitors provides the analyst with an understanding of the level of competition. If competition is tough it will tend to affect returns negatively. Competition or rivalry occurs because one or more competitors either feel the pressure or see the opportunity to improve the position on the market. Competition can go from sparse or gentle to intense or warlike. The level and type of competition is a result of a number of interacting structural factors. In general, competition tends to get intense if the industry is characterised by:

- Slow industry growth
- Numerous competitors
- Customers that perceive the product as commodities
- Overcapacity
- High fixed cost
- High exit barriers.

An analysis of the potential pressure from *substituting products* provides the analyst with an understanding of the potential risk of substituting products on the market. Substitutes limit the potential returns of an industry as high returns in an industry will make substitutes more attractive. The possible risk of substituting products vary across industries, but substituting products deserve more attention if they:

- Have the potential to improve the price-performance relative to current products in the industry
- Are produced by industries earning high returns.

An analysis of the *bargaining power of buyers* provides the analyst with an understanding of the relative strength between buyers and the industry. If buyers possess a high bargaining power it typically limits the potential returns in an industry. Buyers tend to be powerful if:

- A large portion of sales in an industry is purchased by a given buyer
- The products purchased from the industry are commodities
- The switching costs are low
- They experience low returns.

An analysis of the *bargaining power of suppliers* provides the analysts with an understanding of the relative strength of suppliers relative to the industry. If suppliers have the bargaining power over the participants in an industry they can squeeze profitability of the industry by raising the prices or lowering the quality of the products or services being offered. Suppliers are powerful if:

- They are more concentrated than the industry
- The industry is not an important outlet for the suppliers
- The products or services being offered are important to the industry
- The industry faces high switching costs.

Company specific factors influencing the cash flow generation and risks

The macro and industry analyses describe the opportunities and threats that a company experiences. The external analyses ideally provide the analysts with an understanding of the market potential; i.e. the market size, market growth and the opportunity to earn attractive returns. It is not clear, however, what share of the market that the company will gain. Furthermore, a sense of achievable margins or returns cannot be obtained without an analysis of the company's competences relative to its peers. An analysis of a company's competitive advantage is therefore crucial.

When assessing a company's competitive advantage it is useful to consider its available resources and the uniqueness of those resources. The analyst wants to assess the nature of the resource base, the strength of those resources, and the extent to which the resources are unique and difficult to imitate. A company's resources can be divided into the following types:

- Physical resources (e.g. location, quality and utilisation of property, plant and equipment)
- Human resources (e.g. adaptability, skills)
- Financial resources (e.g. financial leverage, ability to generate profit)
- Intangibles (e.g. brand names, image, relationship with key players in the industry).

Not all resources are equally important and analysts should therefore focus on understanding the strength and uniqueness of the most critical resources. A benchmarking of the most important resources with peers is a powerful way of examining the strength and uniqueness of key resources.

Value chain analysis

A **value chain analysis** is a means of describing the activities within and around a company and relating them to an assessment of the competitive strength of the company relative to its peers. Figure 8.6 provides an example of a value chain analysis.

The value chain describes both the primary and supporting activities of a company. The identification and understanding of the primary activities are crucial when determining the competitive advantage of a company, i.e. the possibility of obtaining attractive market shares and margins. An understanding of how efficient a company

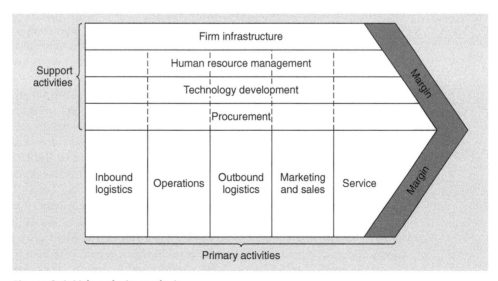

Figure 8.6 **Value chain analysis**

	Production	S&D	Administration	R&D	Depreciation	
	COGS/ revenue	S&D/ revenue	Administration/ revenue	R&D/ revenue	Depreciation/ revenue	Operating expenses/ revenue
Company x	40%	20%	5%	5%	15%	85%
Company y	45%	22%	6%	4%	17%	94%
Difference	+5%	+2%	+1%	−1%	+2%	+9%

Figure 8.7 **An adapted value chain analysis**

is in managing its support activities and how well they support the primary activities is equally important. A value chain analysis combined with a benchmarking analysis provides the analyst with an efficient tool to evaluate the competitive advantage of a company. The following example illustrates how analysts may apply an adapted value chain analysis combined with benchmarking purely based on external information.

The adapted value chain analysis (see Figure 8.7) informs the analyst about the cost efficiency of peers in the industry. In the figure, company x is more cost efficient in each function except for R&D. The operating expenses make up 85% of revenue in company x and 94% in company y. The analysis also reveals that cost of goods sold and sales and distribution (S&D) are the most important functions to monitor for the analysts as they make up the majority of operating expenses. Finally, company y spends less of its revenue on R&D compared to company x, which may affect future revenue negatively. Based on the adapted value chain analysis it seems safe to conclude that company x is in a position to gain higher market shares and better margins than company y.

A company's Strengths, Weaknesses, Opportunities and Threats (SWOT)

The last aspect of a strategic analysis is the identification of key issues (strategic drivers) based on the external and internal analyses. It is only at this stage of the analysis that a sensible assessment can be made of the opportunities and threats and strengths and weaknesses. External analyses such as the PEST analysis and Porter's Five Forces lead to a better understanding of a company's opportunities and threats and ultimately the attractiveness of the industry. Internal analyses of a company's resources and competences lead to a better understanding of its strengths and weaknesses and thereby its competitive advantage relative to its peers. The critical factors identified in the external and internal analyses can be summarised in a **SWOT** matrix. Table 8.6 provides an example of a SWOT matrix which summarises the strengths, weaknesses, opportunities and threats.

Figure 8.8 is an attractiveness matrix which is a different way of summarising the findings from the external and internal analyses. It positions the company based on the industry attractiveness and its competitive advantage relative to its peers. The company's and its competitors' current position in the matrix is visualised by the circle. The size of the circle is an indicator of the current market share and the arrow indicates the company's expected future position in the attractiveness map. For example, company

Table 8.6 SWOT matrix

External factors

Opportunities	Threats
• Market size	• Cyclicality
• Market growth rate	• Inflation
• Barriers to entry	• Regulation
• Bargaining power of suppliers	• Workforce availability
• Bargaining power of buyers	• Environmental issues
• Subsidies	• Substitutes

Internal factors

Strengths	Weaknesses
• Management	• Distribution
• Financial resources	• Administration
• R&D	• Image
• Production	• Brands
• Profitability	• Social responsibility

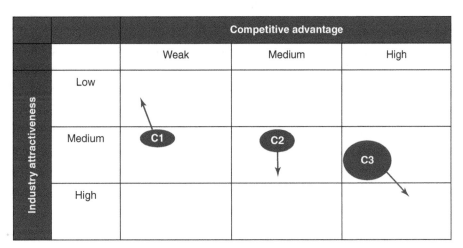

Figure 8.8 Attractiveness matrix

3 (C3) has currently the biggest market share and appears more competitive than its peers C1 and C2. Furthermore, the analysis indicates that C3 will be more competitive than C1 and C2 in the future. This suggests that C3 is likely to experience higher growth rates and margins in the future than C1 and C2 – information that is indeed useful when projecting these value drivers.

It is important that the strategic analysis leads to a better understanding of the key strategic value drivers; i.e. the strategic and operational factors influencing the financial value drivers. Furthermore, it should give the analyst a first-class sense of the growth and margin potential of the industry and company being specifically analysed.

Financial statement analysis

The financial statement analysis offers the analyst insights about the historical levels and trends in key financial value drivers. It is therefore a useful foundation when developing reliable projections of a company's earnings capacity, investment requirements and financing needs. In this section we discuss briefly the different steps involved in developing reliable historical levels and trends on each financial value driver. It draws on the material covered in previous chapters.

Since the objective is a time series analysis, the analyst needs to address the following issues before calculating and interpreting financial value drivers for a specific company.

- Are accounting policies the same over time?
- Are reported earnings affected by special items?
- Has the company introduced new products or entered new market(s) with a different risk profile?
- Has the company acquired or divested businesses, which have changed the levels and trends in key financial value drivers?

The purpose of a time series analysis is to identify and analyse the levels and trends in the underlying performance of a company. It is, therefore, important to eliminate any noise in the signals from the time series analysis. In Chapters 13–15 we discuss each of the above issues in further detail.

The next step is to calculate the financial value drivers. The historical financial value drivers provide useful information to the analyst about the level and trend in each driver. If a long time series is available the analyst obtains information about the behaviour of the financial drivers in periods of both recovery and recession. Furthermore, the historical analysis gives the analyst an understanding of the average level and the maximum and minimum value of each financial value driver. This idea is represented in Figure 8.9.

In the example the EBITDA margin fluctuates between 4% and 6% during the past eight years and the average EBITDA margin is close to 5%. This information provides

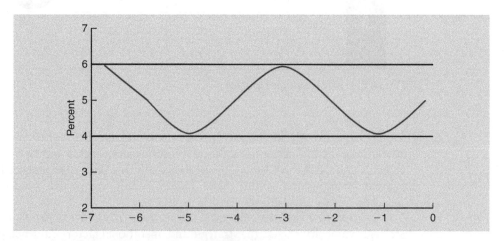

Figure 8.9 Time series behaviour of EBITDA-margin

the analyst with much greater comfort when forecasting the future EBITDA margin. Assuming a stable competitive environment, it seems reasonable to expect an EBITDA margin within a band of 4% to 6% in the explicit forecasting period and an EBITDA margin close to 5% in the terminal period. The estimation and analysis of the historical financial value drivers therefore provide the analyst with an interval within which the drivers typically fluctuate.

In summary, the strategic analysis identifies key strategic value drivers. Furthermore, it provides insights about the growth and margin potential. The financial statement analysis informs us about the historical levels and trends in key financial value drivers. If the information that can be extracted from the strategic and financial statement analysis is combined it serves as a powerful means to generate reliable estimates of each financial value driver. The value driver map in Figure 8.2 has been modified to accommodate these observations and is shown in Figure 8.10. It summarises the results from the strategic analysis and financial statement analysis. In the modified value driver map we have included numbers for illustrative purposes. For example, growth fluctuates between 2% and 6% and is decreasing over time. Furthermore, growth is primarily organically driven. The strategic analysis shows what initiatives the company has taken to support future growth. These pieces of information together with an understanding of the market attractiveness form an analyst's expectation about future growth.

An evaluation of the estimates supporting the pro forma statements

It is important that the required performance to support the estimates underlying the pro forma statements is achievable. A crucial step in the forecasting process is therefore an evaluation of the estimates and the pro forma statements. In this section we briefly discuss different methods to evaluate the quality of the estimates underlying pro forma statements.

The first method compares expected performance with current and past performance. As noted in Chapter 5, ROIC is the overall profitability measure of a firm's operations and it is therefore recommended to apply ROIC for this purpose. The basic idea of the approach is illustrated in Figure 8.11. In this example, past performance (ROIC) fluctuates around 8–10%. Assuming a stable competitive environment, it seems reasonable to assume a ROIC within the same interval in the forecasting period. As a result, a long-term ROIC around 9% seems achievable. The scenario is therefore dubbed 'realistic' in the figure. In the optimistic scenario we assume a long-term ROIC of 14% which is well above past performance. If you are to believe this scenario the analyst must provide compelling evidence such as a successful launch of a new product or a successful entrance into a new and more profitable market. Even if the analyst is able to provide compelling evidence you may still not be convinced. As you may recall from Chapter 6, ROIC tends to revert towards a long-term mean which is the opposite of the time series behaviour of the optimistic scenario.

A complementary approach is to evaluate the quality of the analytical work and the supporting evidence. If the key assumptions are not supported by compelling evidence and superior analyses the estimates appear less reliable. On the other hand, if key assumptions are supported by hard evidence and proper analyses we tend to have

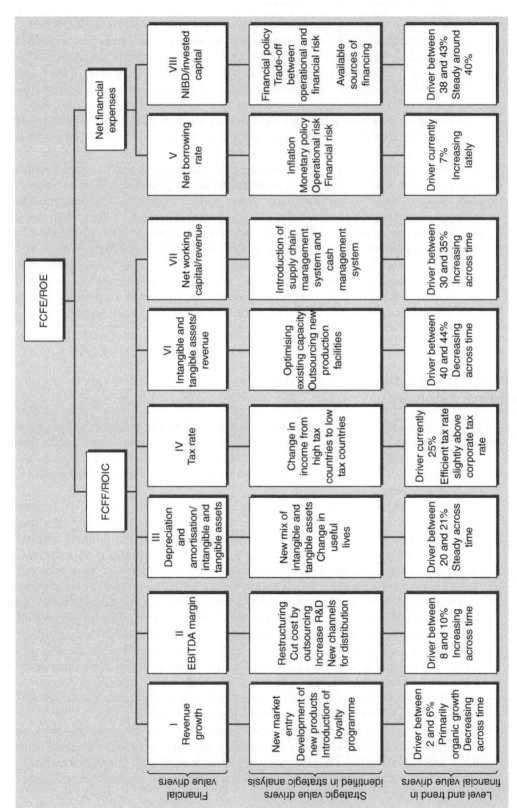

Figure 8.10 Modified value driver map reflecting financial and strategic value drivers

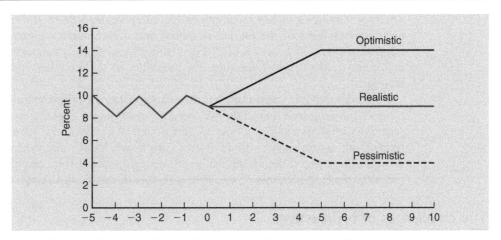

Figure 8.11 ROIC as a tool to evaluate the quality of the pro forma statement

greater faith in the estimates and pro forma statements. These ideas are captured in the **evidence-relevance model** illustrated in Figure 8.12.

The evidence-relevance model gives an easy overview of the supporting evidence of the different assumptions. For example, Figure 8.12(a) is a case where key assumptions (highest relevance) are supported by strong (the highest level of) evidence and

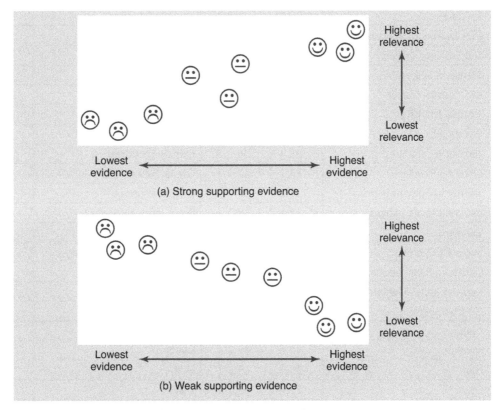

Figure 8.12 Examples of the evidence-relevance model

analyses. Examples of key assumptions include revenue growth and EBITDA margin and an assessment of the market potential and a company's competitive advantage relative to peers. In Figure 8.12(b) key assumptions are only supported by weak evidence and analyses which question the reliability of the estimates and the pro forma statements.

As a final step it is important that the analyst obtains an understanding of the sensitivity of the projected financials. We therefore recommend that the analyst conducts a sensitivity analysis exploring how an adjustment of key financial value drivers affects financial measures such as the FCF (free cash flow), ROIC, and the interest coverage ratio. In this context the identification of strategic value drivers can also be used as a means to develop scenarios. This topic is further discussed in Chapters 9 and 11.

The challenges of forecasting

To illustrate the challenges of forecasting Table 8.7 shows analysts' estimates of Carlsberg's and Heineken's EPS one and two years ahead. The basic idea of the example is to demonstrate that even among well-educated analysts, who have access to

Table 8.7 Analysts' two-year forecast of Carlsberg's (DKK) and Heineken's (euro) EPS

Carlsberg	+1	+2	Heineken	+1	+2
Davy Stockbrokers	29.9		Evolution Securities	2.5	2.8
Jyske Bank	28.3	33.2	Deutsche Bank Research	2.5	2.9
Credit Suisse	30.8	34.2	Société Générale	2.7	2.9
ESN-Danske Markets Equities	34.9	43.5	ING Wholesale Banking	2.4	2.9
SEB Enskilda Research	27.7	32.1	Petercam	2.5	2.6
Bernstein Research	35.2	40.2	Davy Stockbrokers	2.4	
ABG Sundal Collier	30.1	36.5	Bernstein Research	2.7	3.0
Nordea Markets	27.4	33.1	Rabo Securities	2.5	2.9
Swedbank	29.6	34.3	KBC Securities	2.4	2.7
Evolution Securities	28.4	35.2	Natixis Securities	2.7	3.2
Natixis Securities	33.7	42.1	Credit Suisse	2.1	2.3
Nomura Equity Research	31.2	35.8	Oddo Securities	2.4	2.7
ING Wholesale Banking	32.8	39.2	Fortis Bank Nederland	2.4	2.7
Carnegie	33.1		Kepler Capital Markets	2.4	2.7
Société Générale	31.9	37.8	Nomura Equity Research	2.3	2.6
Deutsche Bank Research	30.6	34.3	CA Cheuvreux	2.3	
Kepler Capital Markets	28.7	33.7	Keijser Securities	2.2	
CA Cheuvreux	28.7	31.1	ESN-SNS Securities	2.7	2.9
Mean	30.7	36.0	Mean	2.4	2.8
Median	30.6	35.2	Median	2.4	2.8
High	35.2	43.5	High	2.7	3.2
Low	27.4	32.1	Low	2.1	2.3
Std. dev.	2.4	3.6	Std. dev.	0.2	0.2

the same pieces of information, and who are capable of performing the same type of analyses there is a disagreement about the earnings potential of a given company.

As seen from Table 8.7 there is a disagreement among analysts about the earnings potential of both breweries. For example, next year's (+1) EPS for Carlsberg fluctuates between DKK 27.4 and DKK 35.2 and for Heineken it fluctuates between €2.1 and €2.7. Furthermore, the analysts' forecast dispersion increase as the forecast horizon expands. For example, the standard deviation and the distance between the lowest and highest estimate of Carlsberg's EPS widens as analysts expand the forecast horizon from one to two years. The estimates of Heineken's EPS provide similar tendencies.

The example illustrates the challenges of forecasting and stresses the importance of providing supporting evidence behind each estimate. It is therefore crucial to devote the necessary time and effort in developing estimates that are supported by useful sources and excellent analyses. Extrapolations of past performance or simply pure guesswork are not attractive alternatives. In these cases the underlying value drivers are not properly understood and will most likely lead to greater biases in the estimates underlying the pro forma statements.

Conclusions

This chapter focuses on forecasting. The most important points to keep in mind are:

- Identification of key strategic and financial value drivers is crucial when developing reliable estimates.
- The pro forma income statement, balance sheet and cash flow statement must always articulate.
- It is important that the chosen value driver map reflects the underlying economics of the company being analysed. Analysts are probably better off working with a more refined set of value drivers for short-term forecasting and a more aggregated set of value drivers for long-term forecasting.
- A strategic analysis provides the analyst with useful information about an industry's attractiveness and the company's competitive advantage relative to its peers. Furthermore, it identifies key strategic value drivers that have significant impact on the financials. Financial statement analysis provides the analyst with useful information about the levels and trends in key financial value drivers. Together, the strategic analysis and the financial statement analysis serve as efficient means to generate reliable estimates.
- It is crucial that the estimates supporting the pro forma statements appear achievable. A comparison of expected performance with current and past performance is one way to evaluate the estimates. The evidence-relevance model is another way of examining the estimates. The evidence-relevance model evaluates the quality of the analytical work and supporting evidence on relevant factors influencing cash flows and risk.
- The developed pro forma statements reflect just one out of many outcomes. It is therefore important that the analyst obtain an understanding of the sensitivity of the financials. Sensitivity analyses should always be a part of forecasting.
- Forecasting is not an easy task. We demonstrate that even among well-educated analysts that have access to the same pieces of information there are disagreements about the earnings potential for the same company. It stresses the importance of

collecting the most useful information and conducting the necessary analyses to develop reliable estimates. In short, the analyst must be dedicated to deliver the best possible estimates.

Review questions

- What does it mean that pro forma statements articulate?
- How do you ensure that pro forma statements articulate?
- Describe the eight value drivers in the value driver map.
- Describe factors affecting the eight value drivers.
- Which elements are contained in a strategic analysis?
- What is the structure of a financial statement analysis?
- Do you prefer an aggregated value driver setup or a more refined one when developing pro forma statements?
- How do you judge if estimates appear achievable?

APPENDIX 8.1

Carlsberg case

In this appendix we demonstrate the forecasting of Carlsberg's income statement, balance sheet and cash flow statement. With some modifications we rely on the value driver map discussed in Figure 8.2.

The income statement, balance sheet and cash flow statements are therefore in most cases derived from revenue forecasts. Furthermore, the pro forma statements clearly distinguish between operating and financing activities. This implies that the chosen reporting format mirrors the analytical format outlined in Chapters 4 and 5.

In the following section the estimation of each forecast assumption is discussed. An overview of the historical and forecast value drivers is provided in Table 8.8.

Revenue

Revenue is a function of the underlying market growth and Carlsberg's ability to deliver competitive products relative to peers. Carlsberg divides its markets into three areas: Northern and Western Europe, Eastern Europe and Asia. While the Northern and Western European markets are mature and experience growth rates close to 0% at best, the other two markets are characterised as growth markets. Carlsberg has grown on average 10% in the last five years of which half is driven by organic growth. In most recent years Carlsberg's organic growth has improved due to the

Table 8.8 Carlsberg: forecast assumptions

	Historical value drivers					Forecast value drivers			
	Year 4	Year 5	Year 6	Year 7	Year 8	Year E1	Year E2	Year E3	Year E4
Financial value drivers									
Growth drivers									
Organic growth	−2.0%	3.0%	6.4%	10.0%	8.0%				
Revenue growth	5.0%	4.3%	7.5%	7.8%	27.4%	5.0%	5.0%	4.0%	3.0%
Cost drivers (margins)									
Cost of sales as a percentage of revenue	45.4%	45.3%	44.9%	46.5%	48.0%	47.0%	46.5%	46.0%	45.0%
Sales and distribution costs as a percentage of revenue	33.3%	33.2%	32.4%	30.5%	28.0%	28.0%	28.0%	28.0%	28.0%
Administration as a percentage of revenue	7.2%	7.3%	7.1%	6.6%	6.3%	6.3%	6.3%	6.3%	6.3%
Other income and expenses as a percentage of revenue	1.7%	1.1%	0.6%	1.1%	1.2%	1.1%	1.1%	1.1%	1.1%
Income before tax from associates as a percentage of revenue	0.8%	0.8%	0.3%	0.3%	0.2%	0.2%	0.2%	0.2%	0.2%
EBITDA margin (excluding special items)	*16.6%*	*16.2%*	*16.6%*	*17.8%*	*19.1%*	*19.8%*	*20.3%*	*20.8%*	*21.8%*
Special items	−1.6%	−1.0%	0.1%	−0.7%	−2.2%	−1.1%	−1.1%	−1.1%	−1.1%
EBITDA margin (including special items)	*15.0%*	*15.2%*	*16.7%*	*17.0%*	*16.9%*	*18.7%*	*19.2%*	*19.7%*	*20.7%*
Depreciation as a percentage of PPE	12.5%	12.5%	14.4%	12.5%	11.1%	12.0%	12.0%	12.0%	12.0%
EBIT margin	*8.0%*	*8.5%*	*9.5%*	*10.9%*	*10.6%*	*12.3%*	*12.8%*	*13.3%*	*14.4%*
Tax rate	23.1%	27.5%	28.3%	28.6%	−11.2%	25.0%	25.0%	25.0%	25.0%
NOPAT margin	*5.7%*	*6.0%*	*6.8%*	*7.8%*	*9.7%*	*9.2%*	*9.6%*	*10.0%*	*10.8%*
Investment drivers									
Intangible assets as a percentage of revenue	53.7%	54.3%	51.8%	47.4%	141.3%				
Property, plant and equipment as a percentage of revenue	56.3%	53.5%	49.6%	49.4%	56.8%	55.0%	55.0%	55.0%	54.0%
Other non-current assets	10.8%	8.8%	6.2%	6.3%	8.6%	8.0%	8.0%	8.0%	8.0%
Non-current assets as a percentage of revenue	*120.8%*	*116.6%*	*107.6%*	*103.1%*	*206.7%*	*63.0%*	*63.0%*	*63.0%*	*62.0%*
Net working capital decomposed into:									
Inventories as a percentage of revenue	7.9%	7.5%	7.8%	8.5%	8.9%	8.9%	8.8%	8.7%	8.5%

▶

Table 8.8 (*continued*)

	Historical value drivers					Forecast value drivers			
	Year 4	Year 5	Year 6	Year 7	Year 8	Year E1	Year E2	Year E3	Year E4
Trade receivables as a percentage of revenue	17.3%	15.7%	14.9%	14.2%	10.6%	11.0%	11.0%	11.0%	11.0%
Other current assets as a percentage of revenue	5.7%	9.8%	5.2%	5.5%	7.6%	7.0%	7.0%	7.0%	7.0%
Deferred tax liabilities as a percentage of revenue	6.4%	6.2%	5.9%	4.9%	16.4%	16.0%	16.0%	16.0%	16.0%
Trade payables as a percentage of revenue	11.2%	11.9%	12.5%	13.0%	13.3%	13.0%	13.0%	13.0%	13.0%
Other liabilities as a percentage of revenue	17.9%	17.9%	15.6%	15.3%	17.8%	17.5%	17.5%	17.5%	17.5%
Net working capital as a percentage of revenue	*−4.6%*	*−2.9%*	*−6.1%*	*−5.0%*	*−20.4%*	*−19.6%*	*−19.7%*	*−19.8%*	*−20.0%*
Financing drivers									
NIBD as a percentage of invested capital excl. Intangibles	111.9%	105.2%	111.2%	105.6%	188.6%	180.0%	175.0%	170.0%	170.0%
Net financial expenses as a percentage of NIBD	10.6%	4.9%	3.6%	5.3%	14.4%	7.0%	7.0%	7.0%	7.0%

acquisition of Russian breweries. We expect that Carlsberg is able to grow 5% annually the next two years and will have reached its long-term growth rate of 3% in year E5. It may look conservative based on the last three years' organic growth. However, the important Russian market is currently under pressure due to higher duties on beers and the Northern and Western European markets show no sign of growth. The estimates ignore the impact of acquisitions. As a first step, we generally recommend that you develop pro forma statements without the impact of acquisitions. It gives you a much clearer view of a company's profitability and financial sustainability. For example, a company that grows organically in line with the economy should be able to generate sufficient cash flow to repay debt. As a second step, you can add acquisitions to explore their impact on a company's profitability and financial sustainability.

Operating expenses

Carlsberg has continuously improved the relation between operating expenses and revenue (EBITDA margin) since year 4. This is mainly driven by the excellence programmes initiated during the last five to eight years, but also influenced by the synergies obtained from acquisitions. Carlsberg has not yet reached its full potential and expects to improve the operating expense to revenue relation (i.e. its profit margin) gradually during the next five years. Specifically, we expect that Carlsberg is able to improve its cost of sales to revenue relation from 48% to 45% during the next five years. Other cost drivers remain unchanged from the last fiscal year.

Income from associates

After the acquisitions of the Russian breweries the ratio 'income from associates as a percentage of revenue' has dropped to 0.2%. We conjecture that associates will grow with the same speed as Carlsberg's main activities and estimate the income from associates to be 0.2% of revenue going forward.

Special items, net

Special items are typically transitory in nature. However, since year 4 special items make up −1.1% of revenue on average. It indicates that special items are recurring. We therefore predict that special items remain at the same level as the historical average; i.e. −1.1% of revenue.

Depreciation

Intangible assets consist almost entirely of goodwill and trademarks; items which are tested for impairment. Since year 4 the management of Carlsberg has assessed that the value of those assets can be maintained for an indefinite period. We predict that Carlsberg can maintain its track-record and do therefore not incorporate any impairment losses on goodwill and trademarks in the forecast period.

Depreciation on property, plant and equipment (PPE) has fluctuated between 8% and 14%. We assume that depreciation remains constant as a percentage of PPE and predict 12% in line with the depreciation rate in most recent years.

Borrowing rate

We estimate a borrowing rate of 7%. It reflects the impact that the acquisition programme has had on Carlsberg's credit rating, but also the expansion in the credit spreads in the light of the financial crisis.

Tax rate

With the exception of year 8 Carlsberg's efficient tax rate has been close to the marginal tax rate. Since the corporate tax rate has been reduced to 25% in Denmark, we tax Carlsberg's income with 25%, while we acknowledge that actual cash taxes are somewhat lower due to deferred taxes. We apply the same tax rate on operating income and (net) financial expenses.

Non-current assets

As noted above we only include organic growth in our estimates. This implies that we only forecast PPE and other non-current assets. Intangible assets are assumed constant in the forecasting period. Before the acquisition of the Russian breweries Carlsberg had steadily improved the relation between PPE and revenue from 56% to 49%. After the acquisition the relationship between PPE and revenue increased to 57%. Based on past experience and statements from the management, we expect that Carlsberg gradually improves the relation between PPE and revenue to 54% in year E5. Other non-current assets are expected to make up 8% of revenue.

Net working capital

After the acquisition of the Russian brewery the relation between the different components of net working capital and revenue changed dramatically. Our estimates for net working capital reflect the new structure, and we believe that Carlsberg is able to maintain approximately the same level of efficiency in the forecast horizon as in year 8.

Net interest-bearing debt

Net interest-bearing debt is measured as a percentage of invested capital excluding intangible assets. As noted above we assume that intangible assets remain constant in the forecasting period. It does therefore not make much sense to measure net interest-bearing debt against a constant (i.e. intangible assets). Furthermore, excluding intangible assets from invested capital makes the valuation much easier in Chapter 9.

Carlsberg has announced that it will reduce its net interest-bearing debt relative to invested capital (excluding intangible assets). We expect that Carlsberg in the long run will finance 170% of invested capital (excluding intangible assets) by net interest-bearing debt.

Dividends

Dividends are estimated as the residual of the excess cash. Thus, cash which is not consumed in operations, investments or financing is assumed paid out as dividends to the shareholders. Although dividends are normally paid out after the general assembly, i.e. three to five months after the fiscal year end, we assume that dividends have a cash impact at the fiscal year-end. The year 8 accounts have been modified accordingly. This implies that the dividend in year 8 is assumed to be paid to shareholders at the fiscal year-end reducing shareholders equity and increasing net interest bearing debt by DKK 534 million.

Tables 8.9, 8.10 and 8.11 show the resulting pro forma income statements, balance sheets and cash flow statements for Carlsberg.

An evaluation of the estimates supporting the pro forma statements

In Table 8.12 we assess whether the estimates appear achievable. The key ratio in our assessment is ROIC. The ratio is measured before-tax to avoid the influence of different corporate tax rates across time. The significant investments in the Russian breweries affect ROIC negatively in the short run. However, in line with management we believe that Carlsberg is able to re-establish the profitability at the level prior to the acquisition. Our predictions indicate that Carlsberg's long run ROIC is just above 9%. Overall, the ratios indicate that the estimates underlying the pro forma statements appear achievable. However, the estimates do not leave much room for slack. The improvement in ROIC is primarily driven by a significantly higher EBIT margin and any mismanagement will affect Carlsberg's profitability negatively and thereby make the estimates less achievable.

Table 8.9 Carlsberg: pro forma income statement

Income statement (DKKm)	Historical Year 8	Forecast Year E1	Year E2	Year E3	Year E4	Year E5
Net revenue	59,944	62,941	66,088	68,732	70,794	72,918
Cost of sales	−28,756	−29,582	−30,731	−31,617	−31,857	−32,813
Gross profit	31,188	33,359	35,357	37,115	38,937	40,105
Sales and distribution costs	−16,814	−17,655	−18,537	−19,279	−19,857	−20,453
Administrative expenses	−3,765	−3,953	−4,151	−4,317	−4,446	−4,580
Net other operating income	728	692	727	756	779	802
Share of profit before tax, associates	108	126	132	137	142	146
Operating profit before special items	11,445	12,569	13,528	14,413	15,553	16,020
Net special items	−1,309	−683	−717	−746	−768	−791
EBITDA	10,136	11,886	12,811	13,667	14,785	15,228
Depreciation and amortisation	−3,771	−4,154	−4,362	−4,536	−4,587	−4,725
EBIT	6,365	7,732	8,449	9,131	10,197	10,503
Tax on EBIT	−567	−1,933	−2,112	−2,283	−2,549	−2,626
NOPAT	5,798	5,799	6,337	6,848	7,648	7,877
Net financial expenses before tax	−3,456	−3,603	−3,442	−3,505	−3,533	−3,538
Tax on net financial expenses	864	901	860	876	883	885
Net financial expenses	−2,592	−2,703	−2,581	−2,629	−2,650	−2,654
Group profit after tax	3,206	3,096	3,755	4,219	4,998	5,224

Table 8.10 Carlsberg: pro forma balance sheet

	Historical	Forecast				
Invested capital (DKKm)	Year 8	Year E1	Year E2	Year E3	Year E4	Year E5
Non-current assets						
Intangible assets	84,678	84,678	84,678	84,678	84,678	84,678
Property, plant and equipment	34,043	34,618	36,349	37,802	38,229	39,375
Other non-current assets	5,185	5,035	5,287	5,499	5,663	5,833
Total non-current assets	**123,906**	**124,331**	**126,314**	**127,979**	**128,570**	**129,887**
Current assets						
Inventories	5,317	5,602	5,816	5,980	6,017	6,198
Trade receivables	6,369	6,924	7,270	7,560	7,787	8,021
Other current assets	4,568	4,406	4,626	4,811	4,956	5,104
Total current assets	**16,254**	**16,931**	**17,712**	**18,351**	**18,760**	**19,323**
Non-interest-bearing debt						
Deferred tax liabilities	9,803	10,071	10,574	10,997	11,327	11,667
Trade payables	7,993	8,182	8,591	8,935	9,203	9,479
Other operating liabilities	10,669	11,015	11,565	12,028	12,389	12,761
Total non-interest-bearing debt	**28,465**	**29,268**	**30,731**	**31,960**	**32,919**	**33,907**
Invested capital (net operating assets)	**111,695**	**111,994**	**113,294**	**114,370**	**114,411**	**115,303**

	Historical	Forecast				
Invested capital (DKKm)	Year 8	Year E1	Year E2	Year E3	Year E4	Year E5
Equity						
Total equity begin		60,217	62,825	63,216	63,894	63,865
Group profit after tax		3,096	3,755	4,219	4,998	5,224
Dividends/issues of new shares	534	−488	−3,364	−3,541	−5,027	−5,848
Total equity end	**60,217**	**62,825**	**63,216**	**63,894**	**63,865**	**63,240**
Net interest-bearing debt (NIBD)	50,944					
Dividend adjustment	534					
Net interest-bearing debt (NIBD)	**51,478**	**49,170**	**50,078**	**50,477**	**50,547**	**52,063**
Invested capital	**111,695**	**111,994**	**113,294**	**114,370**	**114,411**	**115,303**

Table 8.11 Carlsberg: pro forma cash flow statement

	Forecast				
Cash flow statement (DKKm)	Year E1	Year E2	Year E3	Year E4	Year E5
NOPAT	5,799	6,337	6,848	7,648	7,877
Depreciation and amortisation	4,154	4,362	4,536	4,587	4,725
Changes in inventories	−285	−214	−164	−38	−181
Changes in trade receivables	−555	−346	−291	−227	−234
Changes in other current assets	162	−220	−185	−144	−149
Changes in deferred tax liabilities	268	504	423	330	340
Changes in trade payables	189	409	344	268	276
Changes in other operating liabilities	346	551	463	361	372
Cash flow from operations	**10,078**	**11,381**	**11,974**	**12,785**	**13,027**
Investments, non-current assets	−4,579	−6,344	−6,202	−5,179	−6,042
Free cash flow to the firm	**5,499**	**5,037**	**5,772**	**7,607**	**6,985**
Net financial expenses after tax	−2,703	−2,581	−2,629	−2,650	−2,654
Changes in NIBD	−2,308	909	398	70	1,516
Free cash flow to equity holders	**488**	**3,364**	**3,541**	**5,027**	**5,848**
Dividends/issues of new shares	−488	−3,364	−3,541	−5,027	−5,848
Cash surplus	**0**	**0**	**0**	**0**	**0**

Table 8.12 Carlsberg: assessment of forecast assumptions

	Historical					Forecast				
Budget evaluation	Year 4	Year 5	Year 6	Year 7	Year 8	Year E1	Year E2	Year E3	Year E4	Year E5
Growth, organic	−2.0%	3.0%	6.4%	10.0%	8.0%	5.0%	5.0%	4.0%	3.0%	3.0%
ROIC before tax	8.1%	7.5%	9.2%	11.4%	8.2%	6.9%	7.5%	8.0%	8.9%	9.1%
EBIT margin	7.9%	8.4%	9.5%	10.9%	10.6%	12.3%	12.8%	13.3%	14.4%	14.4%
Turnover ratio, invested capital	1.02	0.89	0.97	1.05	0.77	0.56	0.59	0.60	0.62	0.63

Valuation

After reading this chapter you should be able to:

- Make a distinction between the different approaches available for valuation
- Conduct a valuation based on the present value approach
- Understand the theoretical equivalence of the different present value models
- Conduct a valuation based on multiples
- Understand the prerequisites for using multiples
- Conduct a valuation based on the liquidation approach
- Understand when a liquidation approach appears more suitable for valuation than the present value approach and multiples

Valuation

The value of any asset (or liability for that matter) is calculated as the future income generated by the asset discounted to present value with a discount factor which takes into consideration the time value of money and risk associated with the income generated by the asset.

To value an asset the following factors need to be known:

Future income – typically cash flows – and a proper discount rate

For fixed income streams such as bonds this is fairly straight forward, if the bonds are held to maturity. However, for most assets future income is only known with perfect hindsight. Also, the discount factor must be estimated and as with all estimates this requires judgement. This is why so many finance textbooks have been devoted to calculating risk (and the discount factor). In this chapter, we discuss and present how a company can be valued using various valuation models. The techniques may seem quite complicated at first. However, keep in mind that valuing a firm is essentially no different from valuing any asset: we need to forecast the future income stream and estimate a discount rate.

Valuation of companies is carried out in a variety of different contexts. Below we have listed examples of areas where valuation techniques are used:

- Merger and acquisitions
  - Generational successions
  - Hostile takeovers
  - Spin-offs
- Initial public offerings (IPOs)
- Stock issues

- Stock analyses
- Tax purposes (transactions between closely related parties)
- Management tools (value-based management)
- Compensation (stock options)
- Privatisations
- Fairness opinions
- Impairment tests.

Valuation is typically associated with topics such as merger and acquisitions and stock analyses. However, as the list indicates the different valuation techniques are applied in many other circumstances. Examples include value-based management, impairment tests and fairness opinions. In this chapter, we address commonly used valuation models. This implies that special **valuation approaches** are not the focus of this chapter. For example, in some countries tax authorities have developed their own valuation techniques to examine the possibility that a transaction between closely related parties reflects market values. Such techniques are not discussed.

We have made a distinction between technical and economical aspects of valuation. By technical aspects we refer to the basic understanding of the different valuation approaches including what drives value and how those approaches are related. By economical aspects we refer to the quality of input (forecast assumptions). In this chapter, we have emphasised the technical aspects of valuation, as the economical aspect of valuation has been covered in the previous chapter on forecasting.

Moreover, an understanding of the technical issues of valuation is essential for several reasons. First, it is important that the analyst understands the basic concepts of the most frequently applied valuation approaches and the level of computational skills needed. Second, it is equally important that the analysts understand to what extent valuation models are theoretical equivalent and therefore (ought to) yield identical value estimates. This piece of information is useful when selecting between different valuation approaches. Furthermore, by using two or more equivalent valuation approaches, the analyst ensures that valuation is unbiased in the sense that it does not contain any technical errors. Third, it is important that the analysts understand how the different valuation approaches can be used in interaction. By using different valuation approaches the analyst can stress test the value estimate from different valuation perspectives.

The valuation approaches discussed in this chapter measures either **enterprise value (EV)** or **market value of shareholders' equity**. Enterprise value is the expected market value of a company's invested capital; i.e. the market value of its operations. Enterprise value therefore includes both the estimated market value of equity and the estimated market value of net interest-bearing debt, as reflected in Figure 9.1.

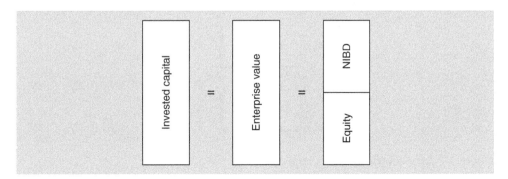

Figure 9.1 The distinction between enterprise value and shareholders' equity

Net interest-bearing debt (NIBD) is the difference between enterprise value and shareholders' equity.

Approaches to valuation

The number of different valuation approaches can be quite overwhelming, however, they can generally be classified into four groups as shown in Figure 9.2. The first group of valuation approaches is based on discounting future income streams or cash flows. We refer to these models as present value approaches. The type of income stream that is discounted varies across the different present value approaches but most commonly dividends, free cash flows and excess returns are discounted.

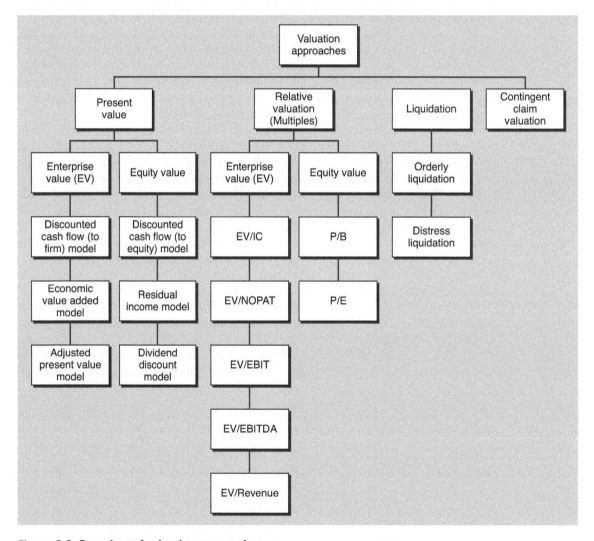

Figure 9.2 **Overview of valuation approaches**

The **relative valuation** approach, often referred to as **multiples,** is the second group of valuation approaches. Using these techniques, the value of a company can be estimated by applying the price of a comparable company relative to a variety of accounting items such as revenue, EBITDA, EBIT, net income, cash flow or book value of equity.

The **liquidation** approach is the third category of valuation approaches. Here the value of a company's equity is estimated by measuring the net proceeds that a company can obtain if it liquidates all its assets and settle all its liabilities.

Contingent claim valuation models – also referred to as real option models – is the fourth category of valuation approaches and applies option pricing models to measure the value of companies that share option characteristics.

Several surveys have found that practitioners favour the present value approach and multiples when valuing a company. Figure 9.3 reports the results of a survey (Petersen et al. 2006) which examines how analysts' value privately held companies. The present value approach and multiples are adopted in almost all cases. Financial analysts use the liquidation approach in less than 20% of the cases and the real option approach is hardly ever used.

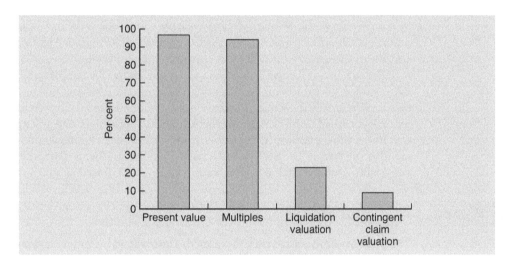

Figure 9.3 Frequency by which practitioners apply a valuation approach

The four different approaches address valuation from different perspectives and it is important that the analyst understands the merits and demerits of each approach when choosing a valuation model. In this chapter, we discuss the present value approaches, multiples and the liquidation approach in further detail. Although the real option approach has appealing characteristics it is rarely ever used by practitioners. The complexity of the valuation approach and challenges of providing reliable estimates explain the limited use.

UNIVERSITY OF WINCHESTER
LIBRARY

The attributes of an ideal valuation approach

In this section, we describe four attributes that characterise an ideal valuation approach, to develop a set of criteria that can be used to differentiate between the various valuation approaches:

- Value attributes:
  - Precision (unbiased estimates)
  - Realistic assumptions
- User attributes
  - User friendly
  - Understandable output.

First, the precision of the valuation approach is obviously important. Assuming a forecast with perfect hindsight, the valuation approach must yield an unbiased estimate. For example, the dividend discount model is assumed to be a theoretically consistent valuation approach and therefore yield unbiased value estimates. Second, the valuation must be based on realistic assumptions; i.e. assumptions that are well founded, for instance with reference to past performance. The second attribute is very much related to the first attribute. If an analyst is not able to comply with the underlying assumptions of a valuation approach, the value estimate will be biased. The first two attributes address the accuracy of a valuation approach and are referred to as 'value attributes'.

Third, a valuation approach should be user friendly. This implies that it is characterised by a low level of complexity, easy access to input data and not time consuming to use. Finally, ideally the value estimate can be communicated in laymen terms. For example, it is regarded as informative if the valuation approach is able to explain any deviation in the value estimate from the book value of equity. The third and fourth attributes are also referred to as 'user characteristics'. In the following part, the four attributes are used to evaluate each of the valuation approaches described in subsequent sections.

Present value approaches

The present value approaches estimate the intrinsic value of a company based on analysts' projections of the cash flows of a company and the discount factor that reflects risk in the cash flow and the time value of money. A basic premise of present value approaches is that they are all derived from the dividend discount model. Therefore, as we demonstrate in this section, the different present value approaches are theoretically equivalent. This implies that if they are based on the same input they shall yield identical value estimates. In Appendix 9.1, we apply the different present value approaches on Carlsberg. To illustrate how to estimate the value of a company using different present value approaches, we apply the pro forma statements which were prepared in the previous chapter. Table 9.1 provides a summary of the key figures from the pro forma statements.

Due to the nature of the various present value approaches, we require different measures of cost of capital also defined as discount rates. More specifically, we need input to estimate the following cost of capital expressions:

- Required rate of return on assets (r_a)
- Required rate of return on net interest-bearing debt (NIBD) (r_d)

Table 9.1 **Summary of key financial data**

Summary of key data	Last fiscal year	Explicit forecasting period (forecast horizon)					Terminal period	
	0	1	2	3	4	5	6	7
Revenue growth	5.0%	5.0%	5.0%	5.0%	5.0%	5.0%	2.0%	2.0%
NOPAT	16.4	17.2	18.1	19.0	19.9	20.9	21.4	21.8
Net financial expenses	−4.6	−4.9	−5.1	−5.4	−5.6	−5.9	−6.2	−6.3
Tax shield	1.2	1.2	1.3	1.3	1.4	1.5	1.6	1.6
Net earnings	12.9	13.6	14.3	15.0	15.7	16.5	16.7	17.0
Invested capital (net operating assets)	121.6	127.6	134.0	140.7	147.7	155.1	158.2	161.4
Equity, end	60.8	63.8	67.0	70.4	73.9	77.6	79.1	80.7
Free cash flow to the firm (FCFF)	10.6	11.2	11.7	12.3	12.9	13.6	18.3	18.6
Free cash flow to equity (FCFE)	10.0	10.5	11.1	11.6	12.2	12.8	15.2	15.5
Dividends	10.0	10.5	11.1	11.6	12.2	12.8	15.2	15.5

Table 9.2 **Different measures on cost of capital**

Cost of capital	Forecast horizon				Terminal period		
	1	2	3	4	5	6	7
Debt/equity	0.333	0.339	0.345	0.352	0.359	0.359	0.359
Required rate of return on assets (r_a)	8.750%	8.750%	8.750%	8.750%	8.750%	8.750%	8.750%
Required rate of return on debt, after tax (r_d)	6.0%	6.0%	6.0%	6.0%	6.0%	6.0%	6.0%
Required rate of return on equity (r_e)	8.996%	9.000%	9.004%	9.009%	9.014%	9.019%	9.019%
WACC	8.256%	8.250%	8.243%	8.237%	8.229%	8.221%	8.221%

- Required rate of return on equity (r_e)
- Weighted average cost of capital (WACC).

In Table 9.2 we therefore report estimates for the different measures on cost of capital that allow us to show that the various present value approaches yield identical value estimates based on the pro forma statements summarised in Table 9.1.

We allow the required rate of return on equity and WACC to fluctuate with any changes in the capital structure. This is a prerequisite ensuring that the different present value approaches yield identical values. In Chapter 10 we provide additional information on how the different measures of cost of capital are estimated and how they relate to each other.

The dividend discount approach

Although the dividend discount model is not the most popular of the present value approaches, it serves as the basis for the other present value approaches. This explains why the dividend discount model is the first approach discussed in this chapter.

According to the dividend discount model the value of a company is the present value of all future dividends. In case of an infinite dividend stream and a constant discount factor (r_e) the dividend discount model is specified as:

$$\text{Market value of equity}_0 = \sum_{t=1}^{\infty} \frac{\text{Dividend}_t}{(1 + r_e)^t}$$

where
r_e = Required rate of return on equity

According to the dividend discount model only future dividends and the required rate of return on equity affect the market value of a company. This implies that firm value is positively affected by higher future dividends and a lower required rate of return on equity. Since projection of dividends to infinity is almost impossible, and indeed time consuming, a two-stage dividend discount model is often preferred.

$$\text{Market value of equity}_0 = \sum_{t=1}^{n} \frac{\text{Dividend}_t}{(1 + r_e)^t} + \frac{\text{Dividend}_{n+1}}{(r_e - g)} \times \frac{1}{(1 + r_e)^n}$$

where
n = Number of periods with extraordinary growth rates (forecast horizon)
g = The long-term stable growth rate (terminal period)

The two-stage dividend discount model divides the projections of dividends into two periods: an explicit forecast period (forecast horizon) where growth in dividends deviates from the long-term growth rate and a terminal period where growth in dividends is assumed constant.

The basic idea of the two-stage dividend discount model is that the growth rate of a company will eventually approach the long-term growth rate of the economy in which the company operates. Since companies are not at the same stage in their lifecycle, the forecast horizon deviates between companies. For high growth companies the forecast horizon is typically longer than for more mature companies with growth rates close to the long-term growth rate. The assumption that growth remains constant to infinity in the terminal period may seem heroic. However, it is a pragmatic solution to a tedious and time-consuming projection of dividends to infinity. While it is acknowledged that hardly any company will grow at a constant rate to infinity the underlying assumption is that the growth rate fluctuates around a long-term mean. The specification applied to calculate the terminal value is also referred to as the Gordon's growth model. There are a few issues that need to be addressed when calculating the terminal value. First, since the terminal value usually accounts for 60–80% of the entire value of a company it is crucial that careful attention is dedicated to the estimation of each of the parameters entering into the calculation. Therefore, careful considerations must be made when estimating the parameters in the terminal value formula; the entry value of dividends, the required rate of return on equity and the expected long-term growth rate of dividends. Second, it is crucial that the forecasting horizon is sufficiently long to ensure that the growth rate in the terminal period reflects the long-term growth rate of the industry in which the company operates.

In Table 9.3 we have illustrated how to estimate the value of a company using the dividend discount model by relying on the summary of key financial data reported in Table 9.1 and the required rate of return on equity in Table 9.2.

Table 9.3 Dividend discount model

Dividend discount model (rounding errors may occur)	1	2	3	4	5	6	7
Dividends	10.54	11.07	11.63	12.21	12.82	15.16	15.46
Required rate of return on equity (r_e)	8.996%	9.000%	9.004%	9.009%	9.014%	9.019%	9.019%
Discount factor	0.917	0.842	0.772	0.708	0.650	0.596	
Present value of dividends	9.7	9.3	9.0	8.6	8.3	9.0	
Present value of dividends in forecast horizon	54.0						
Present value of dividends in terminal period	131.3						
Estimated market value of equity	185.2						

The present value of dividends in the forecast horizon amounts to 54.0. The terminal value is 131.3 and is calculated as:

$$131.3 = \frac{15.46}{0.09019 - 0.02} \times 0.596$$

In the example the terminal value makes up approximately 71% of the estimated market value of equity which underlines the importance of the terminal value term.

Under normal circumstances the numbers would be reported with only one decimal place. However, by allowing more than just one decimal place it is easier to replicate the estimated market value of 185.2. Furthermore, as mentioned above the cost of capital is not assumed constant across time, which reflects that the capital structure based on market values is not constant in the forecast horizon. Finally, the terminal value calculation (Gordon's growth model) rests on a steady-state assumption; i.e. that all items in the pro forma statements grow at the same rate. Due to the nature of the value driver setup we must forecast two years into the terminal period to ensure that we comply with the steady state assumption. This implies that the present value of dividends in the forecast horizon include six years and that dividends in year 7 serves as entry value in the calculation of the terminal value.

Except for forecast assumptions that are prerequisites for any present value approach the dividend discount model does not rely on any other assumptions. Consequently, it yields unbiased value estimates (assuming forecasts with perfect hindsight). Therefore, based on the value attributes the dividend discount model is attractive. While the dividend discount model is technically a relatively simple valuation approach it requires inputs that are usually based on many different sources and which are time consuming to generate. Furthermore, laymen often consider the book value of equity as the likely value of equity. In cases where the estimated market value of equity deviates from the book value of equity the dividend discount model does not offer any intuitive explanation for this discrepancy. Consequently, while the dividend discount model yields an unbiased value estimate it does not necessarily have attractive user attributes. Finally, while the value of a firm is calculated as the present value of all future dividends, dividends are merely distribution of value created and do not reveal anything about *how* value is created (i.e. dividends tell nothing about a firm's underlying operations except for the signalling effect). This is what is called the dividend conundrum.

The discounted cash flow approach

The discounted cash flow model is undoubtedly the most popular of the present value approaches. It is widely adopted by practitioners and entire textbooks are based on this valuation approach. The discounted cash flow model can be specified in two ways. One approach is used to estimate the enterprise value of a company and another approach estimates the equity value of a company. In the following section we discuss both approaches.

The enterprise value approach

According to the discounted cash flow model the value of a company is determined by the present value of future free cash flows. In case of an infinite cash flow stream the discounted cash flow model can be specified as:

$$\text{Enterprise value}_0 = \sum_{t=1}^{\infty} \frac{\text{FCFF}_t}{(1 + \text{WACC})^t}$$

where
FCFF_t = Free cash flow to the firm in time period t.
WACC = Weighted average cost of capital

According to the discounted cash flow model only the free cash flows to the firm and WACC affect the market value of a company. This implies that firm value is positively affected by higher free cash flows and a lower WACC.

The discounted cash flow model can also be specified as a two-stage model:

$$\text{Enterprise value}_0 = \sum_{t=1}^{n} \frac{\text{FCFF}_t}{(1 + \text{WACC})^t} + \frac{\text{FCFF}_{n+1}}{\text{WACC} - g} \times \frac{1}{(1 + \text{WACC})^n}$$

As you can see from the above specifications, the discounted cash flow model shares many of the same characteristics as the dividend discount model. However, the discounted cash flow model as specified above estimates enterprise value as opposed to market value of equity. It is therefore necessary to deduct the market value of net interest-bearing debt from the enterprise value to obtain an estimated market value of equity.

Based on the data reported in Tables 9.1 and 9.2, respectively, we show how to calculate the value of a company using the discounted cash flow model in Table 9.4. The present value of FCFF in the forecast horizon amounts to 59.9. The terminal value is 186.2 and is calculated as:

$$186.2 = \frac{18.62}{0.08221 - 0.02} \times 0.622$$

The 18.62 is the free cash flow in year 7 (as shown in Table 9.4), which is expected to grow by 2% ($g = 2\%$) in perpetuity. WACC is 8.221% from year 7 and in perpetuity. Finally, 0.622 is the result of:

$$\frac{1}{(1 + \text{WACC})^n} = \frac{1}{(1 + 0.08221)^6}$$

Table 9.4 Discounted cash flow model – an enterprise value approach

Discounted cash flow model (allowing for rounding errors)	1	2	3	4	5	6	7
Free cash flow to the firm (FCFF)	11.2	11.7	12.3	12.9	13.6	18.3	18.6
WACC		8.256%	8.250%	8.243%	8.237%	8.229%	8.221%	8.221%
Discount factor		0.924	0.853	0.788	0.728	0.673	0.622	
Present value, FCFF		10.3	10.0	9.7	9.4	9.1	11.4	
Present value of FCFF in forecast horizon	59.9
Present value of FCFF in terminal period	186.2
Estimated enterprise value	246.0
Net interest-bearing debt	−60.8
Estimated market value of equity	185.2

This part of the equation is used to discount the value of the free cash flow in the terminal period to present value. It should be noted that the number of years used for discounting is six and not seven. The reason for this is that the expression

$$\frac{18.62}{0.08221 - 0.02}$$

is an annuity in perpetuity, which already discounts back the cash flow by one period (this can be shown mathematically).

In this example the terminal value accounts for approximately 76% of the estimated enterprise value, which once again underlines the importance of the parameters supporting the terminal value. As you can see from the numerical examples both the dividend discount model and the discounted cash flow model yield identical value estimates.

The equity value approach

The discounted cash flow model from an equity perspective is specified as:

$$\text{Market value of equity}_0 = \sum_{t=1}^{\infty} \frac{\text{FCFE}_t}{(1 + r_e)^t}$$

where
FCFE_t = Free cash flow to the equity in time period t
r_e = Investors required rate of return

As you may recall from the previous chapter the only difference between FCFF and FCFE is the transactions with debt holders. Since FCFE accounts for transactions with debt holders the discounted cash flow model based on FCFE yields a value estimate of the equity. As shown above, the discounted cash flow model which relies on FCFF yields a value estimate of both equity and net interest-bearing debt, i.e. enterprise value.

The approach can also be specified as a two-stage model:

$$\text{Market value of equity}_0 = \sum_{t=1}^{n} \frac{\text{FCFE}_t}{(1 + r_e)^t} + \frac{\text{FCFE}_{n+1}}{r_e - g} \times \frac{1}{(1 + r_e)^n}$$

Table 9.5 Discounted cash flow model – an equity approach

Discounted cash flow model (allowing for rounding errors)	1	2	3	4	5	6	7
Free cash flow to equity (FCFE)	10.5	11.1	11.6	12.2	12.8	15.2	15.5
Required rate of return on equity (r_e)	8.996%	9.000%	9.004%	9.009%	9.014%	9.019%	9.019%
Discount factor		0.917	0.842	0.772	0.708	0.650	0.596
Present value, FCFE		9.7	9.3	9.0	8.6	8.3	9.0
Present value of FCFE in forecast horizon	54.0						
Present value of FCFE in terminal period	131.3						
Estimated market value of equity	185.2						

Using the data from Tables 9.1 and 9.2 we have shown how to calculate the value of a company using the discounted cash flow model from an equity perspective (Table 9.5). As you may have noticed the numbers are exactly the same as in the dividend discount model. This is due to the fact that FCFE is assumed to be paid out as dividends in the pro forma statements developed in the previous chapter. The value estimate is accordingly identical to the value estimates of the dividend discount model.

Assumptions

Both cash flow models rest on the assumption that cash surpluses are paid out as dividends or reinvested in projects with a net present value equal to zero (i.e. returns earned on investments equal the cost of capital). In the previous chapter on forecasting we defined cash surplus as the net cash flow after taking into account cash flows from operations, investments and financing. The following example illustrates the implications of deviation from the assumption. It is based on the following data:

- An investment project with an expected lifetime of one year
- No initial cash outlay
- The investment project is 100% equity financed $\Rightarrow$ FCFF = FCFE
- The investment generates a FCFF of 1,000 by the end of the first forecast year
- The FCFF of 1,000 is paid out as dividends with 500 in the first forecast year and the remaining amount in the second forecast year
- Cash surplus after the first forecast year is 500
- Cost of capital is 10%.

Relying on these assumptions the value of the investment project is 909.1 based on the discounted cash flow model (DCF):

$$DCF = 909.1 = \frac{1,000}{1.1}$$

Assuming that the cash surplus of 500 after the first forecast year is reinvested at a rate equal to the cost of capital of 10%, the dividend discount model (DDM) yields a value estimate identical to the discounted cash flow model:

$$DDM = 909.1 = \frac{500}{1.1} + \frac{550}{(1.1)^2}$$

thus the investment should be carried out if it costs less than 909.1.

The cash flow in year 2 is 550 since the cash surplus of 500 earns a return of 10%. Now assume that the cash surplus is invested in a project that only returns 5% but where the cost of capital is still 10%. In this case, the dividend discount model yields a value estimate of 888.4, which deviates from the value estimate based on the discounted cash flow model:

$$DDM = 888.4 = \frac{500}{1.1} + \frac{500 \times (1 + 0.05)}{(1.1)^2}$$

The above illustrates that if cash surplus is reinvested at a rate (in the example 5%) different from the cost of capital (in the example 10%) the discounted cash flow model yields a biased value estimate. In the example, the discounted cash flow model overestimates the value of the project as cash surplus is reinvested at a rate below the cost of capital.

The pro forma statements prepared in the previous chapter and summarised in Table 9.1 assumes that cash surplus is paid out as dividends. This feature ensures that the cash flow projections are in compliance with the assumption underlying the discounted cash flow models. This also explains why both cash flow models in the above examples yield a value estimate identical to the dividend discount model.

In summary, if the analyst complies with the underlying assumption the discounted cash flow models yield an unbiased value estimate. Since there is a strong pressure on management to pay out excess cash as dividends (or buy back shares) in most companies, it seems fair to argue that it is a realistic assumption that cash surplus earns a return equal to cost of capital; i.e. an assumption that most companies comply with. Therefore, based on the value attributes the discounted cash flow model appears as an attractive valuation approach.

Although both discounted cash flow models are technically relatively simple valuation approaches they require inputs that are time consuming to generate. Furthermore, the discounted cash flow models do not provide any intuitive explanation to laymen why the value estimate deviates from the book value of equity. In conclusion, the discounted cash flow models provide unbiased value estimates. However, the valuation approach is time consuming to use and does not necessarily generate a value estimate that is easy to communicate to laymen.

Excess return approach

Excess return approaches such as the **Economic Value Added (EVA) model** and the **Residual Income (RI) model** have gained increasing attention in recent years. Both the EVA model and the RI model rely on accrual accounting data as opposed to the dividend discount model and the discounted cash flow models that rely on cash flow data. Despite this difference they are theoretically equivalent valuation approaches. The excess return approach can be specified in two ways. The EVA model estimates the enterprise value of a company, while the RI model estimates the equity value of a company. In the following section we discuss both approaches.

The EVA model

According to the EVA model the value of a company is determined by the initial invested capital (book value of equity plus net interest-bearing debt) plus the present value of all future EVAs. In the case of an expected infinite lifetime the EVA model can be specified as:

$$\text{Enterprise value}_0 = \text{Invested capital}_0 + \sum_{t=1}^{\infty} \frac{\text{EVA}_t}{(1 + \text{WACC})^t}$$

where

$$\text{EVA}_t = \text{Economic Value Added (NOPAT}_t - \text{WACC} \times \text{invested capital}_{t-1})$$

The EVA model uses the invested capital from the last fiscal year ($t = 0$) as a starting point for valuation. It then adds the present value of all future EVAs, which yields the enterprise value of a company. Based on the EVA model firm value is therefore positively affected by higher future EVAs and a lower WACC.

The EVA model can also be specified as a two-stage model:

$$\text{Enterprise value}_0 = \text{Invested capital}_0 + \sum_{t=1}^{n} \frac{\text{EVA}_t}{(1 + \text{WACC})^t} + \frac{\text{EVA}_{n+1}}{\text{WACC} - g} \times \frac{1}{(1 + \text{WACC})^n}$$

The two-stage EVA model consists of three terms: the invested capital from the last fiscal year, the present value of EVAs in the forecast horizon and the present value of EVAs in the terminal period. When using the EVA model it is necessary to subtract the market value of net interest-bearing debt from the enterprise value to obtain an estimated market value of equity.

Based on the numerical example in Tables 9.1 and 9.2 we show how to calculate the value of a company using the EVA model (Table 9.6).

Table 9.6 The Economic Value Added model

Economic Value Added model (allowing for rounding errors)	1	2	3	4	5	6	7
NOPAT	17.2	18.1	19.0	19.9	20.9	21.4	21.8
Invested capital, beginning of period	121.6	127.6	134.0	140.7	147.7	155.1	158.2
WACC		8.256%	8.250%	8.243%	8.237%	8.229%	8.221%	8.221%
Cost of capital		10.0	10.5	11.0	11.6	12.2	12.8	13.0
EVA		7.2	7.6	7.9	8.4	8.8	8.6	8.8
Discount factor		0.924	0.853	0.788	0.728	0.673	0.622	
Present value of EVA		6.6	6.5	6.3	6.1	5.9	5.4	
Invested capital, beginning of period	121.6							
Present value of EVA in forecast horizon	36.7							
Present value of EVA in terminal period	87.8							
Estimated enterprise value	246.0							
Net interest-bearing debt	−60.8							
Estimated market value of equity	185.2							

Invested capital from the last fiscal year is 121.6. The present value of EVAs in the forecast horizon is 36.7 and the present value of EVAs in the terminal period is 87.8 and is calculated as:

$$\text{EVA} = 87.8 = \frac{8.78}{0.08221 - 0.02} \times 0.622 \qquad \text{(allow for rounding errors)}$$

In the example the terminal value makes up 36% of the estimated enterprise value which is less than the terminal value in the cash flow models. This difference is due to the fact that the EVA model uses invested capital as a starting point. Only excess returns are added to invested capital. In the extreme case where future excess returns equal zero the terminal value makes up 0% of the enterprise value. Excess returns equal zero if ROIC = WACC. In other words, book value of equity equals market value of equity if, and only if, the return on invested capital equals the weighted average cost of capital.

This brings us to one of the interesting features of the EVA model. It explicitly shows when a company is traded below or above its book value of invested capital. The estimated market value of a company is above the book value of invested capital when the present value of expected EVAs is positive and below when the present value of expected EVAs is negative. Only in the scenario where return on invested capital equals the cost of capital is the market value equal to the book value of invested capital.

Finally, as illustrated in the numerical example the EVA model yields a value estimate identical to the dividend discount model and the discounted cash flow models, which underlines the equivalence of the different **present value models**.

The residual income (RI) model
The RI model measures firm value from an equity perspective and is defined as:

$$\text{Market value of equity}_0 = \text{Book value of equity}_0 + \sum_{t=1}^{\infty} \frac{RI_t}{(1 + r_e)^t}$$

where
RI_t = Residual income $[(\text{return on equity}_t - r_e) \times \text{book value of equity}_{t-1}]$ in time period t

The transactions with debt holders make up the difference between the EVA model and the RI model. While the EVA model measures value from both an equity and debt perspective (enterprise value) the RI model measures value from an equity perspective only.

The RI model can also be specified as a two-stage model:

$$\text{Market value of equity}_0 = \text{Book value of equity}_0 + \sum_{t=1}^{n} \frac{RI_t}{(1 + r_e)^t} + \frac{RI_{n+1}}{r_e - g} \times \frac{1}{(1 + r_e)^n}$$

Relying on the data in Tables 9.1 and 9.2 we show how to calculate the value of a company using the RI model (Table 9.7).

The estimated market value of equity based on the RI model consists of three terms: the book value of equity from last fiscal year (60.8), the present value of RI in the forecast horizon (40.4) and the present value of RI in the terminal period (84.1). The terminal value is calculated as:

$$84.1 = \frac{9.91}{(0.09019 - 0.02)} \times 0.5960$$

Table 9.7 The Residual Income model

Residual Income model (allowing for rounding errors)	1	2	3	4	5	6	7
Net earnings	13.6	14.3	15.0	15.7	16.5	16.7	17.0
Equity, beginning of period	60.8	63.8	67.0	70.4	73.9	77.6	79.1
Required rate of return on equity (r_e)	8.996%	9.000%	9.004%	9.009%	9.014%	9.019%	9.019%
Cost of capital	5.5	5.7	6.0	6.3	6.7	7.0	7.1
Residual income	8.1	8.5	8.9	9.4	9.9	9.7	9.9
Discount factor	0.917	0.842	0.772	0.708	0.650	0.596	
Present value of residual income	7.4	7.2	6.9	6.6	6.4	5.8	
Equity, beginning of period	60.8						
Present value of RI in forecast horizon	40.4						
Present value of RI in terminal period	84.1						
Estimated market value of equity	185.2						

The RI model shows that the estimated market value of equity is above the book value of equity only in the scenario where the present value of expected RIs is positive; i.e. future returns on equity exceed the cost of equity capital. The estimated market value of equity is below the book value of equity in a scenario where the present value of expected RIs is negative. The expected market value of equity is exactly equal to the book value of equity when the present value of expected RIs is zero.

Assumption

Both the EVA model and the RI model rest on the clean-surplus assumption; i.e. that all revenues, expenses, gains and losses in the forecast period are recognised in the income statement. This implies that neither revenues nor expenses are allowed to bypass the income statement in the pro forma statements. The following two examples illustrate the implications of violating the clean-surplus assumption.

Example 9.1 **Assumption fulfilled**

- A company expects an infinite annual income of 100
- Pay-out ratio is 100%; i.e. dividends is equal to 100
- Year 1 is the first year in the forecast period
- The book value of equity by the end of year 0 is 1,000
- The company is 100% equity financed which implies that EVA is equal to RI
- The company's cost of capital is 10%.

On the basis of these assumptions the value of the company is 1,000 based on both the dividend discount model and the excess return approach.

$$\text{Dividend discount model: } 1,000 = \frac{100}{0.1}$$

$$\text{Excess return approach: } 1,000 = 1,000 + \frac{(100 - 0.1 \times 1,000)}{0.1}$$

| Example 9.2 | **Assumption violated** |

In this example, the company recognises expenses of 500, which in the first example was recognised as expense in the income statement, directly on equity in the first forecast year. This is obviously a violation of the clean-surplus assumption and implies that the expected income in year 1 is 600 (100 + 500). Other assumptions remain unchanged from the first example. Since dividends are still 100 in each forecast year the value based on the dividend discount model is 1,000. However, the value based on the excess return approach changes as a consequence of the violation of the clean surplus assumption.

$$\frac{EVA}{RI}: 1{,}454.5 = 1{,}000 + \frac{600 - (0.1 \times 1{,}000)}{1.1} + \frac{100 - (0.1 \times 1{,}000)}{0.1} \times \frac{1}{1.1}$$

The estimated market value is 1,454.5 or 454.5 more than the properly estimated value. This corresponds exactly to the present value of the 500 that bypasses the income statement. The excess return approach therefore yields biased value estimates when revenues or expenses bypass the income statement. ■

In summary, if an analyst complies with the clean-surplus assumption the EVA and the RI models yield unbiased value estimates. Since clean-surplus behaviour is natural when preparing pro forma statements, i.e. recognising all revenues and expenses in the income statement, the assumption appears realistic.[1] Therefore, based on the value attributes the EVA and RI models are attractive valuation approaches.

The EVA and RI models rely on the same set of data as the dividend discount model and the discounted cash flow models. They are therefore just as time consuming to use as the cash driven valuation approaches. However, both the EVA and the RI model generate value estimates that appear easier to understand. When using the EVA or RI model it becomes obvious that the estimated market value exceeds the book value of equity only when returns exceed cost of capital. We believe that this is an attractive feature, as it makes the value estimate easier to understand.

Adjusted present value approach

The **adjusted present value approach** (APV) is a variant of the enterprise-value-based DCF model, as it accounts for the tax shield on net interest-bearing debt separately. It calculates the value of the company as the sum of the present value of FCFF and the tax shields of interests on net interest-bearing debt, respectively. Since the value of the tax shield of interests is valued separately the discount factor excludes the impact of the tax shield. This implies that WACC, which include the impact of the tax shield on interests, is replaced by the required rate of return on assets (r_a).

$$\text{Enterprise value}_0 = \sum_{t=1}^{\infty} \frac{FCFF_t}{(1 + r_a)^t} + \frac{TS_t}{(1 + r_a)^t}$$

where
TS_t = Tax shield on net interest-bearing debt in time period t
r_a = Required rate of return on assets

The first term of the APV approach expresses the value of a company without the value of the tax shields from debt; i.e. the value of a company's operations. The second term of the APV approach adds the present value of the tax benefits from net interest-bearing debt.

The APV approach can also be specified as a two-stage model:

$$\text{Enterprise value}_0 = \sum_{t=1}^{n} \frac{FCFF_t}{(1+r_a)^t} + \frac{FCFF_{n+1}}{r_a - g} \times \frac{1}{(1+r_a)^n} + \sum_{t=1}^{n} \frac{TS_t}{(1+r_a)^t} + \frac{TS_{n+1}}{(r_a - g)} \times \frac{1}{(1+r_a)^n}$$

As you can see from the above specifications, the two-stage APV approach shares the same characteristics as other discounted cash flow models. However, the impact of the tax shield on firm value is valued separately.

We illustrate how to apply the APV approach (Table 9.8) in calculating the value of a company using the data from Tables 9.1 and 9.2.

Table 9.8 The adjusted present value approach

Adjusted present value (allowing for rounding errors)	1	2	3	4	5	6	7
Free cash flow to the firm (FCFF)	11.2	11.7	12.3	12.9	13.6	18.3	18.6
Tax shield on net interest-bearing debt	1.2	1.3	1.3	1.4	1.5	1.6	1.6
Required return on assets (r_a)	8.75%	8.75%	8.75%	8.75%	8.75%	8.75%	8.75%
Discount factor	0.920	0.846	0.778	0.715	0.657	0.605	
Present value of FCFF	10.3	9.9	9.6	9.2	8.9	11.0	
Present value of tax shield	1.1	1.1	1.0	1.0	1.0	0.9	

Present value of FCFF in forecast horizon	58.9
Present value of FCFF in terminal period	166.8
Estimated market value of operations (A)	225.7
Present value of tax shield in forecast horizon	6.2
Present value of tax shield in terminal period	14.2
Estimated market value of tax shield (B)	20.3
Estimated enterprise value (A + B)	246.0
Net interest-bearing debt	−60.8
Estimated market value of equity	185.2

The value estimate consists of four terms. The first term measures the present value of FCFF in the forecast horizon and yields 58.9. The second term measures the present value of FCFF in the terminal period and yields 166.8 and is measured as:

$$166.8 = \frac{18.62}{(0.0875 - 0.02)} \times 0.605$$

The sum of the first two terms yields the value of the operations and is equal to 225.7. The third term measures the present value of the tax shield in the forecast horizon and the final term measures the value of the tax shield in the terminal period:

$$14.2 = \frac{1.58}{(0.0875 - 0.02)} \times 0.605$$

The sum of the third and fourth terms equals 20.3 (6.2 + 14.2) and measures the present value of the tax benefit from net interest-bearing debt. The value estimate based on the APV approach shows that the tax benefit from borrowing amounts to 8% (20.3/246.0) of the estimated enterprise value.

In summary, the APV approach is a variation of the discounted cash flow approach where the value of the tax shield is measured separately. This may be considered an attractive feature as it allows the analyst to discount the tax shield at a rate different from the rate used on operations. Some may argue that the risk on the tax shield is lower than the risk on operations. Except for this difference, the APV approach shares the same characteristics as the discounted cash flow model and rests on the assumption that cash surplus is paid out as dividends or reinvested in projects that yield a net present value of zero.

An evaluation of the present value approaches

The different present value approaches are deduced from the dividend discount model and yield identical value estimates. This implies that when they are used on real business cases they should yield identical values. There are a few premises that the analysts must meet (and understand) to ensure that the present value approaches yield identical value estimates. They are:

- The valuations must be based on the same set of pro forma statements, which must articulate.
- The analyst complies with the underlying assumption(s) of each present value approach.
- The cost of capital reflects the projected capital structure.
- Each variable in the pro forma statements in the terminal period grows at the same (constant) rate ensuring the steady-state assumption. Due to the nature of the value driver setup and the way some of the present value approaches are defined, it is typically necessary to forecast more than just one year into the terminal period before each variable grows at the same rate. In our example from Chapter 8 we forecast two years into the terminal period which ensures that we comply with the steady-state assumption.
- The implementation of a valuation approach in a spreadsheet is free of errors. This implies that the spreadsheet does not contain any errors such as wrong signs (for instance it would be wrong if an increase in inventories would have a positive effect on the free cash flow) or incorrect cell references.

Unless the analysts deviate from any of these premises they would be indifferent when choosing between the various present value approaches as they all yield identical value estimates as just demonstrated.

There may, however, be user attributes that make an analyst prefer one model over the other. For example, some analysts may find it a useful that the value approach is explicit in explaining why a value estimate deviates from the book value of equity. In such cases an excess return model is superior. Other analysts may find it useful that the valuation approach measures the impact of the tax shield on firm value separately. In such cases an APV model is superior.

The relative valuation approach (multiples)

Valuation based on multiples is often popular among practitioners. One explanation for the popularity is the apparently low level of complexity and the speed by which a valuation can be performed. However, a thorough valuation based on multiples is both quite complicated and time consuming. In this section we discuss some of the most frequently applied multiples, but also introduce multiples that are only rarely used. We also show that multiples can be deduced from the present value approach. This implies that multiples ideally yield value estimates that are equivalent with the present value approaches. In reality, however, this only happens by chance. One explanation is that short-cuts are made when multiples are applied. Another explanation is that the analyst's forecast may deviate from the general market expectations.

In this section we demonstrate how multiples can be used for valuation purposes and highlight some of the crucial assumptions underlying multiples. In Appendix 9.1, we show how multiples can be used to value Carlsberg.

How are multiples applied for valuation purposes?

A valuation based on multiples relies on the relative pricing of peers' earnings. The following examples illustrate different ways that multiples can be used for valuation purposes.

Example 9.3 **Applying multiples from peers**

An analyst values a publicly traded company. Based on the current market price the enterprise value is 120 and the expected EBIT next year is 10. The company is therefore traded at an EV/EBIT multiple of 12. In order to evaluate the current market value, the analyst finds five companies from within the same industry that are also publicly traded. Their EV/EBIT multiples are reported as follows:

	EV/EBIT
Peer 1	7.0
Peer 2	12.0
Peer 3	8.0
Peer 4	9.0
Peer 5	6.0
Mean	8.4
Median	8.0

The mean and the median EV/EBIT is 8.4 and 8.0, respectively, which is well below 12. The comparison informs the analyst that the company being valued is on average approximately 50% more expensive than peers in the industry. This indicates that the company is either currently overvalued relative to its peers or has better prospects. ■

Example 9.4 **Stress test of valuation**

The analyst decides to make a valuation based on the discounted cash flow approach. Based on the analyst's own projections of future cash flows she obtains an enterprise value of

100, which corresponds to an EV/EBIT multiple of 10. She now wants to stress test her cash flow based valuation and compares the EV/EBIT multiple of 10 with peers relative valuation (median EV/EBIT = 8). That comparison shows that the company is on average 25% more valuable than its peers. Therefore, either the projections on which the cash flow valuation is based are too optimistic, indicating that the company is overvalued, or the company has better prospects than the peers and therefore traded at a higher EV/EBIT multiple. ■

Example 9.5 — **Valuing privately held firms**

A privately held firm wants to be listed on a stock exchange. The company expects to earn an EBIT of 50 next year. To derive an estimated market value, when the firm becomes listed on the stock exchange, management applies multiples from peers. Based on the EV/EBIT multiples from peers listed in Example 9.3 the following value estimates are calculated.

	EV/EBIT (peers)	Estimated EBIT	Expected enterprise value
Mean	8.4	50	420
Median	8.0	50	400
Low	6.0	50	300
High	12.0	50	600

Based on mean and median values of peers the EV/EBIT value is between 400 (8 × 50) and 420 (8.4 × 50). On the other hand, if the privately held company is priced according to the lowest EV/EBIT among the peers the value is 300 (6 × 50) and if priced according to the highest EV/EBIT the value is 600 (12 × 50). ■

These three examples illustrate different ways that multiples can be used. In Example 9.3, multiples of peers are compared. Example 9.4 illustrates how to apply multiples to stress test a valuation based on another approach. Finally, Example 9.5 illustrates how to apply multiples in valuing privately held companies.

In the above examples the EV/EBIT multiple has been applied. In reality, however, there are a wide range of multiples available. Figure 9.2 lists some of the most popular multiples applied by analysts. The multiples are divided into two groups. One set of multiples estimates the enterprise value of the company and includes multiples such as EV/EBITDA and EV/EBIT. Another set of multiples estimates the value of the equity and includes multiples such as P/E and M/B.

A valuation based on multiples critically relies on the assumption that companies which are compared are truly comparable; i.e. share the same economic characteristics and outlook. Furthermore, the accounting numbers must be based on the same quality; i.e. based on the same set of accounting policies and excludes the impact of transitory items. In the following section, we address each of these issues.

What drives multiples?

In this section we look at how multiples relate to the present value approach, to obtain a deeper understanding on the fundamental value drivers that influence multiples. This information is useful when selecting comparable companies for valuation purposes and in Box 9.1 we derive a range of multiples from the present value approaches.

| Box 9.1 | The equivalence between the present value approach and multiples |

The relative valuation approach can be divided into one set of multiples used to estimate the enterprise value and another set of multiples aimed at estimating the market value of equity. Below we deduce a range of multiples from the discounted cash flow model in order to estimate enterprise value (EV). Subsequently, we infer equity-based multiples from the dividend discount model.

Enterprise-value-based multiples

Assuming a constant growth rate the discounted cash flow can be expressed as:

$$EV = \frac{FCFF}{WACC - g}$$

By replacing FCFF with NOPAT × (1 − reinvestment rate) we obtain the following expression:

$$EV = \frac{NOPAT \times (1 - \text{reinvestment rate})}{WACC - g}$$

where reinvestment rate is the share of NOPAT that is reinvested in the business and is equal to:

(change in net working capital + change in non-current assets) / NOPAT.

Substituting NOPAT with ROIC × invested capital and dividing the equation with invested capital yields an EV/IC multiple:

$$\frac{EV}{IC} = \frac{ROIC \times (1 - \text{reinvestment rate})}{WACC - g} \Rightarrow \frac{EV}{IC} = \frac{ROIC - g}{WACC - g} \qquad \left(\frac{EV}{IC}\right)$$

where IC is invested capital.

By multiplying the denominator in

$$\left(\frac{EV}{IC}\right)$$

with ROIC we get an expression for the EV/NOPAT multiple:

$$\frac{EV}{NOPAT} = \frac{ROIC - g}{WACC - g} \times \frac{1}{ROIC} \qquad \left(\frac{EV}{NOPAT}\right)$$

Substituting NOPAT with EBIT × (1 − t) and multiplying the equation with (1 − t) results in the well-known EV/EBIT multiple:

$$\frac{EV}{EBIT} = \frac{ROIC - g}{WACC - g} \times \frac{1}{ROIC} \times (1 - t) \qquad \left(\frac{EV}{EBIT}\right)$$

where t equals the corporate tax rate.

If we replace EBIT with EBITDA × (1 − depreciation rate) and multiply the equation with (1 − depreciation rate) we obtain an expression for the EV/EBITDA multiple:

$$\frac{EV}{EBITDA} = \frac{ROIC - g}{WACC - g} \times \frac{1}{ROIC} \times (1 - t) \times (1 - \text{depreciation rate}) \qquad \left(\frac{EV}{EBITDA}\right)$$

where the depreciation rate is defined as:

$$\frac{\text{Depreciation}}{EBITDA}$$

Finally, substituting EBITDA with revenue × EBITDA margin and multiplying the equation with the EBITDA-margin yields the EV/Revenue multiple:

$$\frac{EV}{Revenue} = \frac{ROIC - g}{WACC - g} \times \frac{1}{ROIC} \times (1 - t)$$

$$\times (1 - depreciation\ rate) \times EBITDA\ margin \qquad \frac{EV}{Revenue}$$

Equity-based multiples

Assuming a constant growth rate the dividend discount model can be expressed as:

$$MVE = \frac{Dividend}{r_e - g}$$

where MVE equals the market value of equity.

Replacing dividends with net earnings × payout ratio:

$$MVE = \frac{Net\ earnings \times payout\ ratio}{r_e - g}$$

and substituting net earnings with ROE × BVE we get:

$$MVE = \frac{ROE \times BVE \times payout\ ratio}{r - g}$$

where BVE is the book value of equity. Replacing the payout ratio with (1 − RR) and dividing the equation with BVE yields an expression for the M/B multiple:

$$\frac{MVE}{BVE} = \frac{ROE \times (1 - RR)}{r_e - g} \Rightarrow \frac{MVE}{BVE} = \frac{ROE - g}{r_e - g} \qquad \left(\frac{M}{B}\right)$$

where BVE is the book value of equity and RR is the retention rate; i.e. the share of net earnings that is ploughed back into the business.

By multiplying the denominator in

$$\frac{MVE}{BVE}\ \left(also\ defined\ as\ \frac{M}{B}\right)$$

with ROE we obtain an expression for the P/E multiple:

$$\frac{MVE}{E} = \frac{ROE - g}{r_e - g} \times \frac{1}{ROE} \qquad \left(\frac{P}{E}\right)$$

Based on the expressions derived in Box 9.1 we find that different factors affect multiples and these factors are summarised in Table 9.9. It is useful as it informs the analyst about the underlying requirements when using different multiples. For example, a valuation based on equity-based multiples requires that the companies that are compared have identical expected growth rates, cost of capital and profitability. Furthermore, the analyst faces additional requirements if some of the enterprise value based multiples are used. A valuation based on the EV/EBIT multiple requires that the expected tax rate is identical across companies which are compared. This assumption may be challenged if cross-country multiples are applied. A valuation that relies on the EV/EBITDA multiple requires in addition that the expected depreciation rate remains identical across companies that are compared. Although the capital intensity tends to be similar within an industry there may still be differences due to variations

Table 9.9 Factors influencing the multiples

Equity-based multiples						
P/E	ROE	r_e	g			
M/B	ROE	r_e	g			
Enterprise-value-based multiples						
EV/NOPAT	ROIC	WACC	g			
EV/EBIT	ROIC	WACC	g	Tax rate		
EV/EBITDA	ROIC	WACC	g	Tax rate	Depreciation rate	
EV/Revenue	ROIC	WACC	g	Tax rate	Depreciation rate	EBITDA margin
EV/IC	ROIC	WACC	g			

in the adopted strategies. One company may in-source its production while another may outsource its production. This difference will affect the depreciation rate and will make a comparison more difficult. Finally, a valuation that uses the EV/Revenue multiple requires an identical expected EBITDA margin across the companies being compared.

The multiples derived in Box 9.1 can also be used to explain why some companies are traded at a multiple below peers, while others are traded at a multiple above peers. In the following example we demonstrate what characterises companies traded at a low and a high P/E and M/B, respectively.

Example 9.6

The illustrations in this example are based on companies that share many of the same characteristics. They have the same cost of capital (10%) and the expected growth rate is either 2% (*g*1) or 4% (*g*2). The only difference is the expected profitability, where expected ROE varies from 5% for Company A to 15% for Company C.

	Company A	Company B	Company C
ROE	5%	10%	15%
r_e	10%	10%	10%
*g*1	2%	2%	2%
*g*2	4%	4%	4%

Based on the derived M/B multiple

$$\frac{ROE - g}{r_e - g}$$

the following M/B values can be calculated for the three companies.

M/B multiple	*g*1 = 2%	*g*2 = 4%
Company A	$\dfrac{5\% - 2\%}{10\% - 2\%} = 0.38$	$\dfrac{5\% - 4\%}{10\% - 4\%} = 0.17$
Company B	$\dfrac{10\% - 2\%}{10\% - 2\%} = 1.00$	$\dfrac{10\% - 4\%}{10\% - 4\%} = 1.00$
Company C	$\dfrac{15\% - 2\%}{10\% - 2\%} = 1.63$	$\dfrac{15\% - 4\%}{10\% - 4\%} = 1.83$

Company A is earning a return below its cost of capital and is consequently traded below its book value of equity. Company B is earning a return at its cost of capital and is traded at its book value of equity. Finally, Company C is earning a return above its cost of capital and is therefore traded above its book value of equity. The example illustrates that the relation between return on equity and the cost of capital is the deciding factor for the M/B multiple. The following generic rule applies for the M/B multiple.

$$\text{ROE} < r_e \Rightarrow \text{M/B} < 1$$
$$\text{ROE} = r_e \Rightarrow \text{M/B} = 1$$
$$\text{ROE} > r_e \Rightarrow \text{M/B} > 1$$

Example 9.6 also illustrates that growth is only interesting if it earns a return above the cost of capital. In the scenario where ROE is below the cost of capital the M/B drops from 0.38 to 0.17 when the expected growth rate increases from 2% to 4%. On the other hand, in the scenario where ROE exceeds cost of capital the M/B goes from 1.63 to 1.83 when the expected growth rate increases from 2% to 4%.

If we apply the derived **P/E multiple**

$$\frac{P}{E} = \frac{\text{ROE} - g}{r_e - g} \times \frac{1}{\text{ROE}}$$

on the assumptions in this example, we obtain the following P/E multiples for the three companies.

M/B multiple	g1 = 2%	g2 = 4%
Company A	$\dfrac{5\% - 2\%}{10\% - 2\%} \times \dfrac{1}{5\%} = 7.5$	$\dfrac{5\% - 4\%}{10\% - 4\%} \times \dfrac{1}{5\%} = 3.3$
Company B	$\dfrac{10\% - 2\%}{10\% - 2\%} \times \dfrac{1}{10\%} = 10.0$	$\dfrac{10\% - 4\%}{10\% - 4\%} \times \dfrac{1}{10\%} = 10.0$
Company C	$\dfrac{15\% - 2\%}{10\% - 2\%} \times \dfrac{1}{15\%} = 10.8$	$\dfrac{15\% - 4\%}{10\% - 4\%} \times \dfrac{1}{15\%} = 12.2$

Company B earns a return similar to the cost of capital and obtains a P/E of 10. This corresponds to the reciprocal value of cost of capital (1/cost of capital) and is also referred to as the normalised P/E ratio. Company A earns a return below its cost of capital and is traded below its normalised P/E. Company C, on the other hand, earns a return above its cost of capital and is traded above its normalised P/E.

Example 9.6 also illustrates that growth adds to value only when a firm earns a return above its cost of capital. Only company C earns a return above its cost of capital and experiences an increasing P/E multiple as growth increases. This questions the general perception that growth in EPS leads to a higher P/E multiple. A prerequisite is that growth in EPS is profitable; i.e. that a company earns a return above the cost of capital. ∎

Example 9.5 **(continued)**

In Example 9.5 above we estimated the value of a privately held company based on multiples from its peers. The estimated value ranged from 300 to 600 depending on the peer chosen. This is obviously a wide range that needs to be narrowed further. A comparison of the fundamental value drivers of the privately held company with its peers would help to reduce the wide value range. Assuming that the company's fundamental value drivers mirror those of peers 3 and 4 it seems reasonable to apply the EV/EBIT multiples from these peers. As the EV/EBIT multiples from peers 3 and 4 are traded in the range of 8 to 9 it yields an enterprise value between 400 and 450 (assuming an expected EBIT of 50 as in the example). ∎

Accounting differences

In Chapters 13, 14 and 15 we show how different accounting principles lead to different financial statements. A valuation based on multiples is also a comparison of accounting numbers between related companies. This implies that accounting numbers from the companies being compared must be based on the same set of accounting principles. Otherwise noise is introduced in the valuation. Today, many countries are adopting IFRS. This implies that the accounting principles are increasingly harmonised across countries, which reduces the problem. However, IFRS are typically adopted by listed companies whereas privately held companies tend to use local GAAP. Since local GAAP in many countries are not identical to IFRS, it makes valuation of privately held companies more challenging. In addition, the vast majority of all companies are non-listed. Even within IFRS there is some degree of flexibility. For example, IFRS increasingly relies on accounting standards that involve the management's judgement; especially as fair value is increasingly used as a measurement basis. This implies that a comparison of two sets of accounting numbers (financial statements) that are both based on IFRS needs to be scrutinised for any differences before they are used for valuation purposes.

As discussed in Chapters 13, 14 and 15 items such as gains and losses from divestment of assets and restructuring charges are typically transitory in nature. We therefore recommend that they are excluded from the accounting numbers used for valuation purposes. By excluding the impact of transitory items the valuation is purely based on recurrent (permanent) items which reflect the earnings potential much better than non-recurrent items. In reality, a transitory item is primarily a problem if realised accounting numbers are used as opposed to projected accounting numbers that tend to be based on recurrent items.

Example 9.5 (continued)

The privately held company being valued complies with local GAAP. It deviates from IFRS which the peers have adopted. A comparison of the two sets of accounting practices reveals the following two major differences.

1 Goodwill is recognised and amortised over 10 years according to local GAAP, whereas goodwill is tested for impairment, at least on an annual basis, according to IFRS. The privately held company has amortised goodwill of 20 in the first forecast year. The impairment tests conducted by the peers have not revealed any need for recognising impairment losses of goodwill.

2 According to local GAAP the fair value of the warrants at grant date is recognised directly on an equity account over the vesting period. According to IFRS the fair value of the warrants at grant date is recognised as an expense in the income statement over the vesting period. The privately held company has recognised 5 directly on equity in the first forecast year.

In order to compare the two sets of accounting numbers we adjust the accounting numbers of the privately held company so that they are in compliance with IFRS.

EBIT according to local GAAP	50
Amortisation of goodwill, added back	+20
Fair value of warrants at grant date	−5
EBIT according to IFRS	65

Assuming no need for impairment of goodwill we add back the amortisation of goodwill of 20 and expense, 5, from the warrant programme which yield an adjusted EBIT of 65 and a modified value estimate of 520–585 using an EV/EBIT multiple between 8 and 9. The example shows that any bias in the EBIT estimate due to accounting differences is multiplied by the EV/EBIT multiple. It is therefore crucial that any accounting differences are adjusted for when accounting numbers are used for valuation purposes. In the example, the impact of the accounting differences on expected EBIT is 15 (65 − 50) and the difference in value estimate (noise) is between 120 and 135 due to the multiplier effect from the EV/EBIT multiple (8–9). ∎

Additional considerations

There are a few additional considerations that need to be addressed when valuing companies using multiples. These include:

- Normalisation of earnings
- The use of current versus expected earnings
- The measurement of averages
- Impact of trading a majority share.

Normalisation of earnings

In privately held firms there are cases where earnings are biased and therefore do not reflect the 'true' earnings of the company. This is typically the case where the owner serves as the CEO and receives a salary that deviates from the market norm or when the company is paying for services that are not returning any benefits. An example includes pocket money to spouses paid by the company. It is, however, important that the earnings used for valuation is adjusted for such issues; i.e. normalised. By normalising earnings the valuation reflects the true value potential of the company and is not influenced by an atypical salary to the owner or the private consumption of the owner.

The use of current versus expected earnings

Analysts are typically confronted with the choice of using current earnings, trailing earnings (earnings accumulated over the last four quarters) or expected earnings as denominator in the multiple. Since current earnings and trailing earnings inform about past performance, which is not necessarily a good indicator of future performance, we recommend the use of expected earnings. This recommendation is also supported by research. For example, Liu et al. (2002) find that multiples based on expected earnings yield more accurate value estimates than multiples based on current earnings.

The measurement of averages

When the sample of potential comparable companies has been limited to companies with similar characteristics an average of the multiples of these companies is often calculated. This begs the question whether the average should be based on the mean, the value weighted mean, the harmonic mean or the median. The difference between the measures is shown in Example 9.7.

Example 9.7

	Value weight	Multiple
Peer 1	0.10	55.0
Peer 2	0.20	10.0
Peer 3	0.30	9.0
Peer 4	0.15	20.0
Peer 5	0.15	14.0
Peer 6	0.10	8.0
Mean		19.3
Median		12.0
Value-weighted mean		16.1
Harmonic mean		12.6

The mean is a simple average of the multiples of the six peers. The median constitutes the middle value of the ordered set of multiples. The value-weighted mean uses the relative market value of each peer when measuring the mean. Finally, the harmonic mean is calculated as:

$$\text{Harmonic mean} = \frac{n}{\sum_{i=1}^{n} \frac{1}{\text{multiple}_i}} = \frac{6}{\frac{1}{55} + \frac{1}{10} + \frac{1}{9} + \frac{1}{20} + \frac{1}{14} + \frac{1}{8}} = 12.6$$

Where n is the number of peers. Both the median and the harmonic mean avoid the impact of extreme multiples. In the example, Peer 1 is traded at a multiple of 55 which dominates the simple mean estimate. Excluding that observation results in a mean of 12.2 which is close to both the median and harmonic mean. Research generally supports the use of harmonic means. For example, Baker and Ruback (1999) find that the harmonic mean generates more accurate value estimates than multiples based on mean, median, and a value-weighted mean. ■

Impact of trading a majority share on firm value

An investor is typically willing to pay a premium for a controlling interest in a company. This is due to the fact that a controlling interest allows the investor to make changes in the operating activities and thereby improve firm value. As multiples obtained from listed companies are based on trading of minority shares it is necessary to adjust the value estimate in cases where a controlling interest is traded. The control premium fluctuates but the historical average is approximately 30% and it is therefore essential to adjust the value estimates accordingly.

An evaluation of the relative valuation approach

A valuation based on multiples appears technically simple and easy to perform. However, a valuation based on multiples relies on a number of restrictive assumptions that complicate the valuation and makes it time consuming. Unless the analyst complies with these assumptions the relative valuation approach yields a biased value estimate. When applied in practice there is a tendency that all assumptions are not necessarily fulfilled (for instance it's time consuming to adjust for differences in accounting policies) which lead to biased value estimates. Despite this shortcoming multiples also have appealing features. Most of all, the approach relies on market prices which contain value relevant information (assuming an efficient market). A multiple expressing the price to earnings ratio reflects the opinions of investors and how much they are willing to pay for earnings in a company or an industry and offer, therefore, useful complementary information to the present value approach, which to a large degree relies on the analyst's own expectations (forecasts).

The liquidation approach

The liquidation value is the estimated amount that a company could be sold for if all assets were sold and liabilities settled (paid off). The liquidation value represents the value of the alternative uses of assets. In a healthy industry with attractive growth rates and healthy returns, a company's liquidation value is typically less than its value as a going concern. In an industry with negative outlooks and poor returns, a company's liquidation value may exceed its value as a going concern. There are two types of liquidation values, depending on the time available for the liquidation process:

* *The orderly liquidation value* assumes an orderly sale process. It assumes that the owners have the time necessary to sell each asset in its appropriate season and through channels that yield the highest price achievable.
* *The distress liquidation value* assumes that an orderly sale process is not an option and that the sale of assets has to be 'pushed through the system' due to time constraints.

Due to the nature of the sale process the orderly liquidation value exceeds the distress liquidation value. Depending on the type of assets and the sale process chosen, the difference between the two values can be substantial. An estimation of the liquidation value typically follows these steps:

	Book value of equity
$+/-$	The difference between the liquidation value and book value of assets
$+/-$	The difference between the liquidation value and book value of liabilities
$+/-$	The liquidation value of off-balance sheet items
$-$	Fees to lawyers, auditors, etc.
$=$	Liquidation value

Book value of equity serves as a starting point for the estimation of the liquidation value. The next step is to adjust the value of recognised assets, so that they reflect the liquidation value. The adjustment of the book value of assets depends on a range of factors including:

* The measurement basis used
* Alternative uses of assets

- The level of maintenance
- The number of potential buyers
- The time available for the sales process.

The third step is to adjust the value of recognised liabilities, so that they reflect the liquidation value. The adjustment of the book value of liabilities depends on a range of factors including:

- The measurement basis used
- Terms of the liabilities
- Time available for the sales process
- The possibility to make arrangements with lenders.

The fourth step is to include the liquidation value of off-balance sheet items; i.e. items not recognised on the balance sheet. They may include law suits, disputes, leasing, guarantees for loans and capital commitment agreed to be made at a later date than the balance sheet date. Finally, the liquidation value is adjusted for fees to advisers involved in the liquidation process such as lawyers and auditors.

| Example 9.8 | The owners of the Dyeing Corporation want to sell its business and due to the bleak outlook of the industry they have decided to estimate the value of its business based on the liquidation approach. The book value of equity is 100.

Experts believe that the liquidation value of the assets is 30 below the book value of those assets. Further, an assessment of liabilities recognised in the balance sheet indicates that the book value underestimates the liquidation value by 15. The company is also involved in a lawsuit where a competitor is sued for 50 for violating one of the company's patents. The lawyer expects that there is 40% probability that the court will rule in favour of Dyeing Corporation. As the company has not recognised the potential benefits from the law suit on the balance sheet the liquidation value is positively affected by 20 (40% of 50). The estimated fees to advisers including lawyers and other experts are 10. The liquidation value, which yields 65, is summarised in the following tabulation.

Book value of equity	100
The difference between the liquidation value and book value of assets	−30
The difference between the liquidation value and book value of liabilities	−15
The liquidation value of off-balance sheet items (lawsuit)	+20
Fees to lawyers, auditors, etc.	−10
Liquidation value	65

An evaluation of the liquidation approach

The liquidation approach is fundamentally different from the present value approach and multiples. It values a company as if it were to go out of business. The liquidation approach yields an unbiased value estimate only in cases where the present value approach and multiples yield estimates below the liquidation value. This implies that the approach is best suited when the going concern of a business is questioned and when alternative uses of the assets would yield a higher return. From a user perspective the liquidation approach has some appealing features. It is relatively easy to apply and the value estimate is easy to communicate to laymen. Furthermore, as owners would not accept a price below the liquidation value the approach informs about the minimum value of a business. Analysts may therefore use the approach to establish the minimum value of a business.

Conclusions

There are four approaches available for valuation:

- The present value approach
- The relative valuation approach
- The liquidation approach
- The contingent claim approach.

The present value models are derived from the dividend discount model. This implies that they yield identical value estimates. Therefore, from a valuation perspective analysts should be indifferent when choosing between the various present approaches. There may, however, be user attributes that make a present value model more appealing than others. For example, an excess return approach such as the EVA model is informative about when a company is traded above and below its book value of equity. We argue that this is an attractive feature as it makes communication of value estimates to laymen easier.

A valuation based on multiples appears technically simple and easy to perform. However, a valuation based on multiples relies on a number of restrictive assumptions that complicate the valuation and makes it time consuming. This implies that the approach only yields unbiased value estimates under very restrictive assumptions. Despite this shortcoming multiples should be seen as a complementary valuation approach to the present value approach. For example, multiples rely on market prices that reflect the opinions of many investors as opposed to the present value approach which mainly relies on the analyst's own expectations. Multiples therefore serve as a useful method to stress test value estimates based on the present value approach.

The liquidation approach values a company as if it were to go out of business. The liquidation approach is therefore best suited when the going concern of a business is questioned and when alternative uses of assets would yield a higher return.

Review questions

- Which approaches can be used for valuing a firm?
- What are the attributes of an ideal valuation approach?
- What is the theoretically correct model for valuing firms?
- Why do present value models yield identical values?
- What are multiples?
- What are major assumptions which must be fulfilled in order to apply multiples?
- What is the rationale behind using the liquidation model?

APPENDIX 9.1

Carlsberg case

In this appendix we value Carlsberg based on the present value approach and multiples. The valuation relies on projections of Carlsberg's financials prepared in Appendix 8.1. A summary of the key financial figures are listed in Table 9.10.

Table 9.10 A summary of Carlsberg's key financial figures

Summary of key financial figures (DKKm)	Year E1	Year E2	Forecast Year E3	Year E4	Terminal period Year E5
Revenue growth	5.0%	5.0%	4.0%	3.0%	3.0%
NOPAT	5,799	6,337	6,848	7,648	7,877
Invested capital excluding intangibles, beginning of the year	27,017	27,316	28,616	29,692	29,733
Free cash flow to the firm (FCFF)	5,499	5,037	5,772	7,607	6,985
Tax shield on net interest-bearing debt	901	860	876	883	885
Dividends	488	3,364	3,541	5,027	5,848

In Table 9.11 we report estimates for the different measures on Carlsberg's cost of capital that give us the opportunity to show the value estimates based on different present value approaches. We allow the different cost of capital measures to fluctuate with any changes in the capital structure. As noted previously this is a prerequisite ensuring that the different present value approaches yield identical values. In Appendix 10.1 we provide additional information on how the different measures on cost of capital have been estimated.

Table 9.11 Different measures on Carlsberg's cost of capital

Estimation of cost of capital	Year E1	Year E2	Forecast Year E3	Year E4	Terminal period Year E5
Debt/equity	0.525	0.509	0.489	0.473	0.473
Required rate of return on assets (r_a)	8.00%	8.00%	8.00%	8.00%	8.00%
Required rate of return on debt, after tax (r_d)	5.25%	5.25%	5.25%	5.25%	5.25%
Required rate of return on equity (r_e)	8.59%	8.52%	8.51%	8.49%	8.47%
WACC	7.35%	7.40%	7.41%	7.42%	7.44%

Based on the estimates summarised in Tables 9.10 and 9.11, respectively, we calculate the value of Carlsberg and we apply four of the present value models discussed previously in Tables 9.12, 9.13, 9.14 and 9.15.

Table 9.12 **An estimated market value of Carlsberg based on the dividend discount model**

Dividend discount model (DKKm)		Forecast horizon			Terminal period
	Year E1	Year E2	Year E3	Year E4	Year E5
Dividends	488	3,364	3,541	5,027	5,848
Discount factor	0.921	0.849	0.782	0.721	
Present value of dividends	450	2,855	2,769	3,623	
Present value of dividends in forecast horizon	9,697				
Present value of dividends in terminal period	77,019				
Expected market value of group equity	86,716				
Estimated market value of minority interests	7,532				
Expected market value of equity	79,185				

Table 9.13 **An estimated market value of Carlsberg based on the discounted cash flow model**

Discounted cash flow model (DKKm)		Forecast horizon			Terminal period
	Year E1	Year E2	Year E3	Year E4	Year E5
Free cash flow to the firm (FCFF)	5,499	5,037	5,772	7,607	6,985
Discount factor	0.932	0.867	0.808	0.752	
Present value of FCFF	5,123	4,369	4,661	5,718	
Value of FCFF in forecast horizon	19,871				
Value of FCFF in terminal period	118,323				
Estimated enterprise value	138,194				
Net interest-bearing debt	51,478				
Expected market value of group equity	86,716				
Estimated market to book	1.44				
Book value of minority interests	5,230				
Estimated market value of minority interests	7,532				
Expected market value of equity	79,185				

Table 9.14 **An estimated market value of Carlsberg based on the economic value added model**

Economic value added model (DKKm)		Forecast horizon			Terminal period
	Year E1	Year E2	Year E3	Year E4	Year E5
NOPAT	5,799	6,337	6,848	7,648	7,877
Invested capital, beginning of period, excluding intangibles	27,017	27,316	28,616	29,692	29,733
WACC	7.35%	7.40%	7.41%	7.42%	7.44%

Table 9.14 (*continued*)

Economic value added model (DKKm)	Forecast horizon				Terminal period
	Year E1	Year E2	Year E3	Year E4	Year E5
Cost of capital	1,985	2,021	2,120	2,205	2,212
EVA	3,814	4,316	4,728	5,443	5,666
Discount factor	0.932	0.867	0.808	0.752	
Present value of EVA	3,553	3,744	3,818	4,092	
Invested capital, beginning of period, excluding intangibles	27,017				
Value of EVA in forecast horizon	15,206				
Value of EVA in terminal period	95,971				
Estimated enterprise value	138,194				
Net interest-bearing debt	51,478				
Expected market value of group equity	86,716				
Estimated market to book	1.44				
Book value of minority interests	5,230				
Estimated market value of minority interests	7,532				
Expected market value of equity	79,185				

Table 9.15 **An estimated market value of Carlsberg based on the adjusted present value model**

Adjusted present value model (DKKm)	Forecast horizon				Terminal period
	Year E1	Year E2	Year E3	Year E4	Year E5
Free cash flow to the firm (FCFF)	5,499	5,037	5,772	7,607	6,985
Tax shield on net interest-bearing debt	901	860	876	883	885
Required rate of return on assets (r_a)	8.00%	8.00%	8.00%	8.00%	
Discount factor	0.926	0.857	0.794	0.735	
Present value of FCFF	5,092	4,318	4,582	5,591	
Present value of tax shield	834	738	696	649	
Present value of FCFF in forecast horizon	19,584				
Present value of FCFF in terminal period	102,690				
Estimated market value of operations (A)	122,274				
Present value of tax shield in forecast horizon	2,917				
Present value of tax shield in terminal period	13,004				
Estimated market value of tax shield (B)	15,920				
Estimated enterprise value (A + B)	138,194				
Net interest-bearing debt	51,478				
Expected market value of group equity	86,716				
Estimated market value of minority interests	7,532				
Expected market value of equity	79,185				

The different present value models yield an identical value estimate of Carlsberg. In the following section, we will briefly discuss some of the premises that each value estimate is based on. First, invested capital used in the EVA model excludes the impact of intangibles. By excluding intangibles, which is assumed constant in the pro forma statements, we ensure that the EVA is growing at a constant rate in the terminal period. Second, we assume that the book value of net interest-bearing debt is a good proxy for the market value of net interest-bearing debt. Finally, we estimate the market value of minority interests by using the group's estimated market to book of 1.44:

Estimated market value of minority interests: $7,532 = 1.44 \times 5,230$

The estimated value of Carlsberg's equity is DKK 79,185 million, which is well above the current market value of DKK 57,394 million. In order to examine the robustness of that value estimate we conduct:

- A sensitivity analysis and
- A multiple valuation.

Sensitivity analysis

A valuation should always be accompanied by a sensitivity analysis that examines the valuation consequences of changing some of the key value drivers. Ideally, the sensitivity analysis is inspired by the fundamental analysis that is the foundation of the pro forma statements. In Table 9.16 we explore the valuation consequences of changing the growth rate and the EBITDA margin by $+/-1.0$ percentage-point.

Table 9.16 Sensitivity analysis – impact of the value estimate of Carlsberg

		Growth rate				
		−1.0%	−0.5%	0.0%	0.5%	1.0%
EBITDA margin	−1.0%	53,650	61,228	70,326	81,449	95,357
	−0.5%	57,305	65,236	74,755	86,394	100,946
	0.0%	60,961	69,243	79,185	91,339	106,536
	0.5%	64,617	73,250	83,614	96,284	112,126
	1.0%	68,272	77,257	88,043	101,229	117,716

The sensitivity analysis reveals that the value estimate is sensitive to changes in the growth rate as well as the EBITDA margin. For example, by changing the growth rate as well as the EBITDA margin by $+1$ percentage-point annually in the pro forma statements the value estimate improves from DKK 79,185 million to DKK 117,716 million. It demonstrates that a value estimate based on the present value approach is indeed sensitive to changes in key value drivers and underlines the importance of devoting the time necessary to prepare realistic pro forma statements.

Multiple valuation

As peers for the multiple valuation we have chosen Heineken, SabMiller and AB Inbew (Table 9.17). They are all global players such as Carlsberg and based on market shares they are, together with Carlsberg, some of the biggest breweries in the world.

Table 9.17 provides a summary of key financial numbers which are used to calculate a range of multiples. Transitory (non-recurring) items are removed from the financials

Table 9.17 A summary of the peers' key financial figures including market values

Key figures (million)	Carlsberg DKK	Heineken euro	AB InBew euro	SabMiller US$
Revenue	59,944	14,319	16,102	21,410
EBITDA excluding transitory items	11,438	2,242	5,333	4,598
EBIT excluding transitory items	7,667	1,036	4,022	3,560
NOPAT	6,808	604	3,318	2,391
Net earnings excluding transitory items and minority interests (E)	3,793	190	2,433	2,098
Expected net earnings (E$_{+1}$)	4,434	1,096	3,374	2,772
Invested capital (IC)	111,695	14,135	60,382	27,455
Book value of equity	55,521	4,471	16,126	17,545
Market cap (equity)	57,394	16,084	32,059	83,632
NIBD	50,944	9,383	42,827	9,211
Minority interests in equity	5,230	281	1,429	699
Enterprise value (EV)	113,568	25,748	76,315	93,542

and, thus, earnings measures only consist of recurrent (permanent) items. We calculate multiples based on both Carlsberg's current market value and the value estimate of 79,185 obtained from the present value models. The estimated multiples are shown in Table 9.18.

Table 9.18 Multiples and fundamental value drivers of the four breweries

Multiples	Carlsberg Current market value	Carlsberg Present value estimate	Heineken	AB InBew	SabMiller	Harmonic mean (excl. Carlsberg)
EV/NOPAT	16.7	20.2	42.6	23.0	39.1	32.4
EV/EBIT	14.8	18.0	24.9	19.0	26.3	22.9
EV/EBITDA	9.9	12.0	11.5	14.3	20.3	14.6
EV/Revenue	1.9	2.3	1.8	4.7	4.4	3.0
EV/IC	1.0	1.2	1.8	1.3	3.4	1.8
P/E	15.1	20.9	84.5	13.2	39.9	26.6
P/E$_{+1}$	12.9	17.9	14.7	9.5	30.2	14.5
M/B	1.0	1.4	3.6	2.0	4.8	3.0
ROE after tax	6.8%		4.3%	15.1%	12.0%	7.8%
ROIC after tax	6.1%		4.3%	5.5%	8.7%	5.7%
Expected growth in EPS next five years	14.8%		10.0%	18.0%	13.5%	13.1%
Beta (risk)	1.29		0.84	0.82	0.97	0.87
Efficient tax rate	11.2%		41.7%	17.5%	32.8%	26.9%
Depreciation rate	33.0%		53.8%	24.6%	22.6%	29.0%
EBITDA margin	19.1		15.7%	33.1%	21.5%	21.3%

A comparison of multiples that are based on the current market value reveals that Carlsberg is traded at a discount relative to most of its peers. For example, Carlsberg's EV/EBIT multiple is 35% below the harmonic mean of the three peers. If we apply the value estimate of 79,185 from the present value approach as numerator in the multiples, Carlsberg is traded at a discount relative to its peers only if realised accounting numbers are used. However, as noted previously multiples based on forward looking information yield on average more accurate value estimates. A comparison of the P/E_{+1} multiple indicates that Carlsberg is traded at a premium of 23% relative to its peers. This indicates that the present value estimate of 79,185 may be too optimistic.

As noted before, a valuation based on multiples requires that the companies, which are compared, have identical expected growth rates, cost of capital and profitability. In Table 9.18 a comparison of different measures for profitability, growth and risk are provided. A comparison of ROIC and ROE indicates that Carlsberg's profitability is similar to its peers. For example, Carlsberg's ROIC is almost identical with the harmonic mean of its peers. Further, analysts' consensus forecast of Carlsberg's expected growth rate for the next five years is also similar to the peers' expected growth rate. While Carlsberg's expected growth rate is 14.8% the peers expected growth rate is 13.1%. Carlsberg's β is 1.29 and well-above average β of the peers. This indicates that Carlsberg's risk exceeds the risk of the peers and supports that Carlsberg ought to be traded at a discount relative to its peers.

Even though all four breweries comply with IFRS there may still be accounting differences, which make a valuation based on multiples less applicable. In Table 9.19 we therefore compare some of the critical estimates used in the annual report of the four breweries.

A comparison of the accounting estimates applied shows that they are reasonably similar across the different breweries. In a few cases where differences occur they can be ascribed to the category of 'natural differences'. For example, Carlsberg's discount

Table 9.19 A comparison of critical accounting estimates

GAAP	Carlsberg IFRS	Heineken IFRS	AB InBew IFRS	SabMiller IFRS
Amortisation and depreciation	Useful lives (years):			
Strategic brands		40–50		
Other brands	Max 20	15–25	3–18	10–40
Customer related intangibles	Max 20	5–30	3–18	10–15
Buildings	20–40	30–40	20–33	20–50
PPE	5–15	5–30	5–15	2–30
Returnable packaging	3–10		5–10	1–10
IT	3–5		3–5	
Impairment tests	Pre-tax risk free rate	Post-tax WACC:		
Western Europe	3.9–13.3%	7.6%	na	7–12.6%
Eastern Europe incl. Russia	7.9–16.1%	9.6–14.1%	na	7–12.6%
The Americas		8.2–13.1%	na	7.1–13.7%
Africa and Middle East		7.6%	na	10.7–20.4%
Asia	4.5–10.9%		na	10.7–20.4%

Table 9.19 (*continued*)

GAAP	Carlsberg IFRS	Heineken IFRS	AB InBew IFRS	SabMiller IFRS
Impairment tests		Growth rates:		
Western Europe	1.5%	2.1%	na	1.5–2.0%
Eastern Europe incl. Russia	2.5%	2.9%	na	1.5–2.0%
The Americas		1.7–7.3%	na	1.5%
Africa and Middle East		3.1–7.4%	na	3.0–4.0%
Asia	1–5%		na	3.0–4.0%
Defined benefit plan (weighted average):				
Discount rate	4.6%	5.6–6.7%	4.9%	4.8–6.5%
Expected return on plan assets	4.6%	5.7–5.9%	4.2%	n.a.
Future salary increases	2.6%	3.0–4.0%	3.1%	2.5–3.5%
Future retirement benefit increases	1.6%	1.5–2.8%	1.8%	2.5–4.0%
Operating leasing (million)				
One-year leases	774	66	72	69
Total future lease payments	2,651	378	1,132	294
One-year leases as percentage of EBITDA	6.8%	2.9%	1.4%	1.5%
Total leases as percentage of invested capital	0.7%	0.5%	0.1%	0.3%

factor used for impairment is in general lower than its peers. However, according to IAS 36 Carlsberg adjusts for risk in the cash flow and therefore apply a risk-free rate as a discount factor as opposed to the three peers that adjust for risk in the discount factor.

Table 9.19 also shows that operating leasing plays a more important role as a source of financing in Carlsberg than is the case in the three other breweries. Since operating leasing affects EBIT and EBITDA more negatively than financial leasing (or buying the assets) it seems reasonable to argue that Carlsberg's EBIT and EBITDA are slightly undervalued relative to its peers. In summary, a comparison of the accounting practice of the four breweries does not reveal a 'smoking gun'; i.e. differences that affect the multiple valuation materially.

Summary

The present value approach yields a value estimate of DKK 79,185 million which is approximately 38% above Carlsberg's current market value. The multiple valuations show that Carlsberg estimated market value is between its current value of DKK 57,394 million and the present value estimate of DKK 79,185 million.

Note

1 Items which are recognised as directly on equity (comprehensive income) are hardly ever forecast. A case in point: A currency translation difference in subsidiaries is an example of a comprehensive income item. The best bet on the currency rate in the future is the rate of today (random walk). Thus, it is hard to imagine that firms forecast such currency translation differences.

References

Baker, M. and R. Ruback (1999) 'Estimating Industry Multiples', Working paper, Harvard University, Cambridge, MA.

Liu, J., D. Nissim and J. Thomas (2002) 'Equity valuation using multiples', *Journal of Accounting Research*, No. 1, March, 135–72.

Petersen, C., T. Plenborg and F. Schøler (2006) 'Issues in valuation of privately-held firms', *Journal of Private Equity*, Winter, 1–16.

CHAPTER 10

Cost of capital

After reading this chapter you should be able to:

- Understand why the cost of capital is useful for analytical purposes including performance measurement, valuation and credit analysis
- Measure the weighted average cost of capital (WACC)
- Measure the required rate of return on equity
- Identify appropriate proxies for the risk-free rate
- Apply different techniques for measuring equity risk including the systematic risk and risk premium
- Understand that although advanced techniques are available in estimating the cost of capital it still involves a great deal of judgement

Cost of capital

Cost of capital is a central concept in financial analysis and is applied in many different contexts. In Chapter 5 we used the cost of capital as a benchmark when calculating economic valued added (EVA); i.e. value is added when returns exceed the cost of capital. In Chapter 9 we applied the cost of capital as a discount factor when calculating the present value of future cash flows. In Chapter 11 we touch upon the cost of capital from a lender's perspective and finally, in Chapter 12 we apply the cost of capital as a performance standard (benchmark) when designing an accounting-based bonus plan.

To be successful, a company must accept risk. Successful organisations take calculated risks to achieve their objectives. For example, a biotech company spends considerable resources on research and development projects hoping to develop effective (profitable) products. Shipping companies make large investments in vessels believing that there will be a demand for transportation of cargo across countries and continents. Companies design and market clothing trusting that there will be demand for their collections. Risk is therefore inevitable in running a business.

Since a company's stakeholders are risk averse, they want to be compensated for bearing risks. Banks and equity investors, for example, expect to be compensated for providing funds to risky projects. Consequently, stakeholders need to translate the underlying risk of an investment project into a cost of capital measure. The estimation of cost of capital, however, is challenging at best. Furthermore, lenders and shareholders do not necessarily agree on a common standard for measuring cost of capital. Each stakeholder is left to themselves in measuring cost of capital. This creates considerable uncertainty surrounding the estimation of cost of capital.

It is important that analysts are aware of the different methods of measuring cost of capital and apply a suitable one in their analysis. In Chapter 9 we applied the following measures of cost of capital when valuing a company:

- Required rate of return on assets (r_a)
- Required rate of return on equity (r_e)
- Weighted average cost of capital (WACC).

When analysts apply the adjusted present value (APV) model they use the required rate of return on assets to discount the free cash flow to the firm (FCFF) and the tax shield. Further, in order to use the DCF model and the EVA model analysts use **WACC** to discount the free cash flow to the firm (FCFF) and EVA, respectively. And when analysts apply the dividend discount model and the residual income model they use the required rate of return on equity as the discount factor.

Since the required rate of return on equity (r_e) and assets (r_a) are either directly or indirectly embedded in WACC, we focus on explaining and estimating the components of WACC in the next section. In Appendix 10.1 we estimate WACC for Carlsberg.

Weighted average cost of capital (WACC)

WACC is a weighted average of the required rate of return (cost of capital) for each type of investor. The following formula for WACC includes equity and net interest-bearing debt:

$$\text{WACC} = \frac{\text{NIBD}}{(\text{NIBD} + \text{E})} \times r_d \times (1 - t) + \frac{\text{E}}{(\text{NIBD} + \text{E})} \times r_e$$

where
NIBD = (Market value of) net interest-bearing debt
  E = (Market value of) equity
 r_d = Required rate of return on NIBD
 r_e = Required rate of return on equity
  t = Corporate tax rate

It is possible to extend WACC to include other forms of financing, for example, minority interests and hybrid forms of financing such as convertible bonds. This is done simply by adding additional sources of financing, and their respective weights, in the WACC expression. The components of WACC are discussed in the remaining part of this chapter. We focus on methodologies which can be used to estimate the **capital structure** (the proportion of debt and equity) and the required rate of return on equity. We will only briefly address the estimation of the required rate of return on debt, as it is discussed in further detail in Chapter 11.

Capital structure

Market values reflect the true opportunity costs of investors (equity) or lenders (debt). Consequently, the capital structure must be based on market values. This causes a problem since most companies, as mentioned earlier, are privately held. For privately held firms, it is therefore necessary to estimate the market value of equity and net interest-bearing debt. Only rarely do companies disclose their long-term capital structure; i.e. their target capital structure. In fact, we would argue that only a modest number of companies have a clear policy for their target capital structure. This implies that analysts must rely on alternative techniques in estimating a firm's capital structure, so it is based on market values (and not book values, which are of course known).

One option would be to apply the capital structure of comparable traded companies. However, this means finding companies that are truly comparable, which may prove difficult in countries where only a modest number of companies are listed. One way to address this problem is to expand the sample size by building on companies listed on other major stock markets. This increases the chances of finding comparable companies. The analyst should, however, be aware of any institutional differences which may affect the debt to equity ratio in a given country. The capital structure for selected industries is shown in Table 10.1. The data are based on publicly traded European companies.

Suppose you want to calculate WACC for a company within the air transportation industry. Based on the average from the industry the proportion of net interest-bearing debt and equity are 32.5% and 67.5%, as highlighted in Table 10.1.

Another method used to estimate the capital structure based on *market values* is to infer it using an iteration procedure. This method is typically used in connection with valuation and requires that comprehensive forecasts have been prepared. Based on the forecasts, iterations are made until the estimated value of equity mirrors the value of equity used in the calculation of the capital structure in the WACC expression. In Chapter 9, we applied the iteration procedure to ensure that the capital structure in

Table 10.1 Proportion of debt and equity among selected industries

Industry	Number of firms	E/(NIBD + E)	NIBD/(NIBD + E)
Investment Co. (Foreign)	15	100.00%	0.00%
Investment Co.	18	99.46%	0.54%
Insurance (Prop/Cas.)	87	98.80%	1.20%
Educational Services	39	98.66%	1.34%
Internet	266	98.20%	1.80%
Shoe	20	97.44%	2.56%
Entertainment Tech	38	97.29%	2.71%
Utility (Foreign)	6	97.00%	3.00%
E-Commerce	56	96.74%	3.26%
Computer Software/Svcs	376	96.68%	3.32%
Heavy Construction	12	96.53%	3.47%
Semiconductor	138	95.67%	4.33%
Telecom. Equipment	124	94.78%	5.22%
Computers/Peripherals	144	94.55%	5.45%
Bank (Canadian)	8	94.42%	5.58%
Reinsurance	11	93.94%	6.06%
Metals & Mining (Div.)	78	93.84%	6.16%
Precious Metals	84	93.29%	6.71%

▶

Table 10.1 (*continued*)

Industry	Number of firms	E/(NIBD + E)	NIBD/(NIBD + E)
Human Resources	35	93.01%	6.99%
Tobacco	11	92.99%	7.01%
Drug	368	92.77%	7.23%
Petroleum (Integrated)	26	92.62%	7.38%
Medical Supplies	274	92.56%	7.44%
Insurance (Life)	40	92.27%	7.73%
Semiconductor Equip	16	91.82%	8.18%
Biotechnology	103	91.66%	8.34%
Pharmacy Services	19	91.08%	8.92%
Information Services	38	90.86%	9.14%
Metal Fabricating	37	90.77%	9.23%
Precision Instrument	103	90.58%	9.42%
Steel (General)	26	90.08%	9.92%
Oilfield Svcs/Equip.	113	89.88%	10.12%
Beverage	44	89.70%	10.30%
Market	**7,364**	**79.93%**	**20.07%**
Air Transport	49	67.50%	32.50%
Food Wholesalers	19	67.43%	32.57%
Trucking	32	67.21%	32.79%
Newspaper	18	66.65%	33.35%
Maritime	52	66.36%	33.64%
Water Utility	16	66.25%	33.75%
Packaging & Container	35	65.58%	34.42%
Cable TV	23	62.56%	37.44%
Electric Utility (West)	17	62.38%	37.62%
Natural Gas Utility	26	60.12%	39.88%
Electric Util. (Central)	25	57.90%	42.10%
Electrical Equipment	86	55.29%	44.71%
Property Management	12	53.43%	46.57%
Auto & Truck	28	50.46%	49.54%
Securities Brokerage	31	44.81%	55.19%
Homebuilding	36	43.70%	56.30%
Financial Svcs. (Div.)	294	34.07%	65.93%

Source: Damodoran

the projected balance sheet mirrored the capital structure used in calculating WACC. When forecasts are available the iteration method is relatively easy to use and has the advantage that data from comparable companies are not needed. Generally, we suggest that analysts rely on the capital structure of comparable companies as well as the iteration method. The two methods provide useful information about the capital structure and by relying on both methods potential measurement errors may be reduced.

Estimation of owners' required rate of return

Most financial textbooks suggest using the Capital Asset Pricing Model (CAPM) when estimating the investors' required rate of return. According to CAPM the investors' required rate of return is defined as:

$$r_e = r_f + \beta_e \times (r_m - r_f)$$

where
r_e = Investors' required rate of return
r_f = Risk-free interest rate
β_e = Systematic risk on equity (levered beta)
r_m = Return on market portfolio

The basic idea of CAPM is that by holding a sufficiently broad portfolio of shares, investors will only pay for the risk that cannot be diversified away. It is only the **systematic risk** (β) which is priced.

The equation for the required rate of return (r_e) is also labelled the security market line (SML) and is a relative pricing model showing the equilibrium between the risk premium of a company and the risk premium of the market portfolio. The return on the market portfolio is ideally based on the return on all types of assets; but is usually based on stock returns for companies listed on a stock exchange.

The risk premium is based on the market portfolio's risk premium (the difference between r_m and r_f). β indicates the relative risk of a company in relation to the market portfolio. The risk premium is adjusted up or down depending on the systematic risk (β_e) in a company. The method is graphically illustrated in Figure 10.1.

In the following section, we discuss different methods that can be used in estimating the **risk-free interest rate**, the systematic risk (β) and the risk premium.

Estimation of the risk-free interest rate (r_f)

The risk-free interest rate expresses how much an investor can earn without incurring any risk. Theoretically, the best estimate of the risk-free rate would be the expected return on a zero-β portfolio. Due to the cost and problems in constructing a zero-β portfolio this method has proven not to be useful in practice. Instead a government bond is usually used as proxy for the risk-free rate. The underlying assumption is that a government bond is risk free. The use of the yield curve from a government bond as proxy for the risk interest rate may be a reasonable proxy in most cases. However, there are examples where the government bond has proven to be risky and it should therefore be used with care.

Each projected cash flow should ideally be discounted using a government bond with a similar duration. This implies that an expected short-term rate that is expected to apply in each future period (forward rate) should be applied. However, this is tedious and would require a recalculation of the cost of capital in each forecast year. Furthermore, most valuations are based on the two-stage present value approach

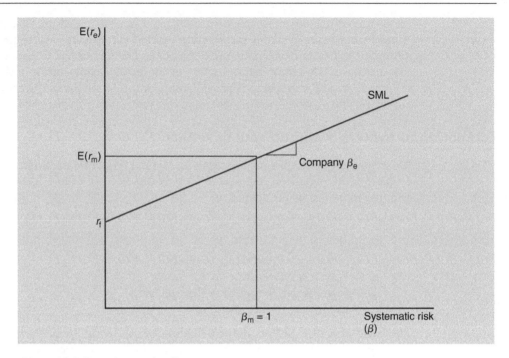

Figure 10.1 Security market line

where all parameters in the terminal period are assumed to be constant. In spite of this, as shown in Figure 10.2 the UK yield is not stable at any point in time. This leaves the analyst with the question which yield to apply in the terminal period. For these reasons most analysts apply a single yield to maturity from a government bond that best matches the cash flows being valued or analysed. Although there are different government bonds to choose from, we prefer a zero-coupon government bond.

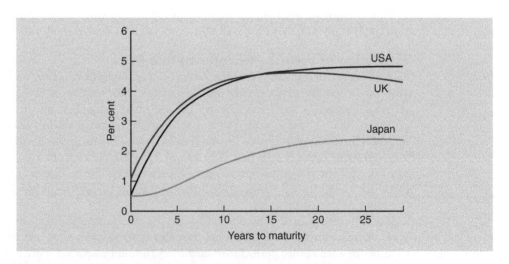

Figure 10.2 Yields on different zero-coupon government bonds
Source: DataStream

They are also known as stripped bonds or strips. This is motivated by the fact that the maturity is better established than alternative bonds and reinvestment risk is avoided. For valuation purposes, where the time horizon is often infinite a zero-coupon rate based on a 10-year or 30-year government bond is applied.[1] While the 30-year government bond often matches the underlying cash flow better, it may also suffer from illiquidity which affects the yields. To handle issues such as inflation, it is important that the government bond is denominated in the same currency as the underlying cash flows. This implies that local government bonds should be applied.

In Figure 10.2 we report the yield to maturity on zero-coupon government bonds from the UK, the USA and Japan versus their years to maturity. This curve is also referred to as the yield curve or term structure of interest rates. As of February 2010, the 10-year UK and US government bonds yield close to 4.2%. On the other hand, the 10-year Japanese bond yields approximately 1.6%, which is considerably lower than the UK and the US bonds. The difference is explained by an expectation of a rising exchange rate of Japanese yen vis-à-vis the US dollar (USD) and the British pound (GBP).

Estimation and interpretation of systematic risk (β_e)

A key lesson from looking at Figure 10.1 is that the **owners' required rate of return** increases if systematic risk increases. This seems intuitively right. The higher the systematic risk, the more investors require in compensation for investing in a company. These considerations are combined as follows:

$\beta_e = 0$ Risk-free investment
$\beta_e < 1$ Equity investment with less systematic risk than the market portfolio
$\beta_e = 1$ Equity investment with the same systematic risk as the market portfolio
$\beta_e > 1$ Equity investments with greater systematic risk than the market portfolio

Usually, estimation of β_e is based on historical stock returns. Basically, all value-relevant information is reflected in stock returns. Any fluctuations in stock returns will reflect the uncertainty of the investors. Specifically, β_e measures the co-variation between the company-specific returns and the market portfolio's stock returns. Figures 10.3, 10.4 and 10.5 illustrate the co-variation between company specific stock returns and market portfolio returns.

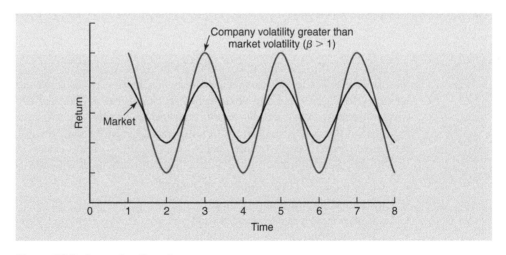

Figure 10.3 β greater than 1

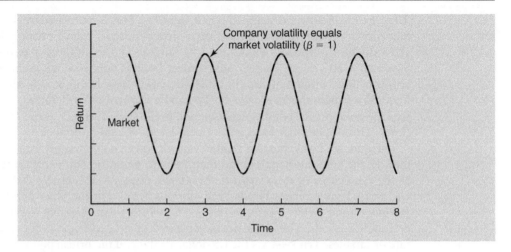

Figure 10.4 β equal to 1

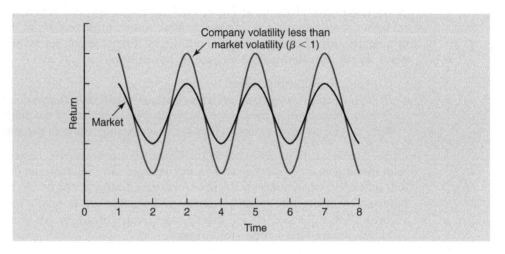

Figure 10.5 β less than 1

Figure 10.3 illustrates that the volatility in stock returns for the company is greater than the volatility in the market portfolio. Estimation of β_e is greater than 1 in this scenario. In Figure 10.4 the volatility of stock returns is identical for both the company and the market portfolio (equity market). β_e in this scenario equals 1. Finally, in Figure 10.5 the volatility of the company's equity is lower than the volatility of equity returns of the market portfolio. Therefore, β_e in this scenario is lower than 1.

The above approximation of β suffers from a number of weaknesses including:

- Lack of liquidity in the company's shares
- Lack of stability in β across time
- Lack of ex-ante price observations
- Lack of observations (privately held firms).

Lack of liquidity in a company's shares leads to an (apparent) relatively stable development of stock returns and, hence, a low volatility. This implies a low β estimate that does not necessarily reflect the underlying risk of the company. Therefore, companies that are not traded frequently will often suffer from these deficiencies; indicating that the β estimate may not reflect the underlying risk of the company.

Furthermore, β is often not stable across time. While a change in β may reflect a change in the underlying risk of the company, it may also reflect measurement problems. For example, the interval between each observation (daily, weekly or monthly returns) that is used to estimate the systematic risk, and the period used (12 months, 3 years, 5 years), have proven to affect the β estimate and sometimes quite considerably.

An estimation of the systematic risk requires a long time series of historical observations. This may be problematic for most companies. Observations for companies with only a short track record are limited. For privately held companies it is obviously a problem and the method is, therefore, not directly applicable to the majority of companies, since they are privately held. In most countries the number of companies listed on a stock exchange is less than 1%. In other words about 99% of all companies do not meet the data requirements of CAPM. Later in this chapter this issue is discussed in more depth.

As with other input data to valuation, CAPM ideally warrants the use of ex-ante stock prices (i.e. future stock prices). These are obviously not available, which is why historical stock prices are used in most cases. However, it is doubtful whether such an extrapolation from historical data is meaningful. The underlying assumption is that the risk of a company remains stable over time. This is hardly the case for all companies. Companies that change their strategy or acquire a new business may face a different risk profile over time.

Table 10.2, obtained from Fernandez (2009a), illustrates the uncertainty of β estimates. The example shows β estimates of Coca-Cola, Disney and Wal-Mart stores

Table 10.2 Beta estimates of three companies according to most used websites and databases

Databases	Coca-Cola	Walt Disney	Wal Mart stores
Bloomberg	0.79	1.06	0.58
Cnbc	0.60	1.00	0.30
Damodaran	0.61	0.88	0.19
Datastream	0.31	0.72	0.13
Ft.Com	0.80	1.06	0.57
Google Finance	0.60	1.03	0.26
Hoovers	0.60	1.00	0.20
Infomercados	0.33	1.39	0.31
Msn Moneycentral	0.54	1.03	0.16
Quote	0.54	1.13	0.19
Reuters	0.53	1.01	0.17
Smartmoney	0.61	1.03	0.26
Thomson Banker	0.55	1.09	0.38
Value Line	0.55	1.00	0.60
Vernimmen website	–	1.08	0.71
Yahoo Finance	0.63	0.99	0.28
Max	0.80	1.39	0.71
Min	0.31	0.72	0.13

Source: Fernandez 2009a

based on the most used websites and databases and illustrates a large dispersion in the beta estimates:

- The β estimates of Coca-Cola range from 0.31 to 0.80
- The β estimates of Disney range from 0.72 to 1.39
- The β estimates of Wal-Mart stores range from 0.13 to 0.71.

The lack of homogeneity in β estimates reflect the different ways that can be used to measure β. But it is also a symptom of measurement problems, and analysts will need to overcome these in order to provide a solid estimate of systematic risk. Typically analysts will use the average of different estimates in the hope that measurement errors cancel each other out. However, often they will also rely on alternative methods when estimating systematic risk. Two such methods are discussed in further detail in the next section.

Alternative methods of measuring the systematic risk (β_e)

This section discusses two methods used in addressing both the potential measurement problems of β and the lack of (price) observations (i.e. for privately held companies). First, we describe the use of β_e from comparable companies and subsequently, we discuss the estimation of β_e based on a company's fundamental risk factors.

Estimation of β_e from comparable companies

One way to get beyond the lack of liquidity or lack of observations is to use β estimates from comparable companies. Assuming an efficient capital market and adequate liquidity in the comparable companies' shares, many of the above estimation problems of β could be avoided.

The method includes the following steps:

1 Identify comparable listed companies (peer groups) with sufficient liquidity (trading) of shares.
2 Estimate β for each of the comparable companies.
3 Calculate the unlevered β (β asset) for each of the comparable companies (adjustments for financial risks).
4 Calculate the average of unlevered βs for comparable firms.
5 Calculate β for the target company by levering unlevered β from comparable companies.

Often there will be differences in financial leverage between the comparable companies and the company to be assessed. It is necessary that adjustments are made for those differences. This is done in steps 3 and 5 above. By calculating an unlevered β, the effect of financial leverage on β is removed. The following β relation may be used for this purpose:

$$\beta_a = \frac{\beta_e + \beta_d \times \dfrac{\text{NIBD}}{\text{E}}}{\left(1 + \dfrac{\text{NIBD}}{\text{E}}\right)}$$

where

β_a = Systematic risk on assets; i.e. operating risk (unlevered β)
β_d = Systematic risk on debt
NIBD/E = Target firm's capital structure based on market values
(net interest-bearing debt to equity ratio)

The unlevered β, also defined as β asset, measures the operating risk in the industry. To estimate the systematic risk, we must lever the unlevered β using the company's capital structure. This is done through the following β relation:

$$\beta_e = \beta_a + (\beta_a - \beta_d) \times \frac{\text{NIBD}}{\text{E}}$$

The levered β is a function of operating risk (unlevered β) and **financial risk** (capital structure of the target company). In Chapter 5, we provide estimates of the unlevered β for different industries. For instance, the average unlevered β for companies in the beverage industry is 0.81. Assuming a β debt of 0.6 and a financial leverage of 1 (i.e. net interest-bearing debt equals equity) result in the following systematic risk for Carlsberg:

$$\beta_e = 0.81 + (0.81 - 0.60) \times \frac{1.0}{1.0} = 1.02$$

In this example, Carlsberg's systematic risk is close to the market average of 1, indicating that Carlsberg has a risk profile similar to the average company on the stock market.

Determining the systematic risk based on comparable companies is not unproblematic. In addition to the general estimation problems with β as described above, a crucial requirement for the application of the method is that companies which are included in the analysis have the same risk profile. In this respect, it is not always a sufficient condition that the companies belong to the same industry. The adaptation of different business models may lead to different operating risks. For example, one company may use a large number of subcontractors, which may lead to a more flexible cost structure, while another company may in-source all major components, which may lead to a less flexible cost structure. Obviously, a more flexible cost structure, all things being equal, leads to lower operating risks.

Estimation of β_e from fundamental factors

An alternative method for estimation of β_e is to build on the fundamental characteristics of a firm's risk profile. Analysts will often have the insights needed for using this method, as they should possess detailed knowledge of the company. A creditor builds up a relationship with its customer (company) over a long time period and obtains valuable knowledge about the company. Equity analysts usually analyse the same companies over longer time periods and build a unique knowledge about the companies they cover in their analysis. Even in cases where the creditor or equity analyst has no prior knowledge of the analysed company, they will, through a thorough analysis, accumulate facts that could be useful in a comprehensive risk assessment.

There are many ways to structure a risk assessment based on fundamental factors. Above it was shown that β_e is a function of operating and financial risks:

$$\underbrace{\beta_e = \beta_a}_{\substack{\text{Operating} \\ \text{risk}}} + \underbrace{(\beta_a - \beta_d) \times \frac{\text{NIBD}}{\text{E}}}_{\substack{\text{Financial} \\ \text{risk}}}$$

The first part, β_a, measures operating risk, while the second part, $(\beta_a - \beta_d) \times \text{NIBD/E}$, measures financial risk. It is therefore relevant to consider the factors affecting operating and financial risks. A distinction is further made between the firm's ability to affect and control risk. Generally, we believe that risks, which the company can influence or control, are more 'attractive' than risks which the company cannot influence or control.

The boundary between what can be influenced or controlled varies across firms. Political and socio-economic conditions are examples of areas where the company has little or no influence and control. The company's reputation, competition and regulation are areas where the company has some degree of influence but no control. Finally, operating aspects such as internal control systems and the choice of cost structures are areas where the company has considerable influence as well as control.

Below we discuss risk factors related to a company's operating and financing activities, and we assess the extent to which a company has the ability to affect or control the various risk indicators.

Operating risk

When assessing operating risk, the focus is on factors affecting the volatility in operating earnings, and we now discuss the following three categories of risk factor:

- External risks
- Strategic risks
- Operational risks.

Each of the risk indicators are briefly discussed in the following section.

External risks

External risks are conditions outside a company that can affect a firm's operating earnings. Examples of external risks are the evolution of commodity prices, GDP growth, political stability and commercial law. Typically, companies have little or no ability to influence or control those risks. Within the same industry, companies are affected roughly equally by these risk factors. Rising commodity prices naturally affect everyone in the industry, and it is possible for a firm to hedge risk in the short term only by using financial instruments (derivatives). For example, when the price of aviation fuel increases, it significantly affects the airlines' earnings, since fuel is a major expense for airlines. To the extent that airlines cannot transfer rising commodity prices to higher ticket prices, operating profits could be affected substantially.

Growth in GDP and business cycles in general hit earnings differently. Cyclical companies such as producers of luxury goods are particularly dependent on the purchasing power of their customers because their products on the functional level can be easily replaced by substantially cheaper products. Conversely, pharmaceutical companies are typically independent of the stage in the business cycle. Their products are protected by patents and for many customers (patients) and the products are necessities for survival or for improving quality of life. Overall, operating earnings are less stable for cyclical companies and operating risks correspondingly higher.

Strategic risks

Assessment of strategic risks typically involves industry issues. Examples of indicators of a company's strategic risks are:

- Intense competition in the industry
- Relative competitive advantages
- Reliance on one or a few suppliers
- Reliance on one or a few customers
- The risk of technological innovations from competing companies
- Ability to adjust prices to rising commodity prices.

An improvement in these indicators of operating risk will generally lead to more stable earnings. Therefore, a reduction of dependence on only a few customers or suppliers will, other things being equal, stabilise earnings and consequently reduce operating risk. Similarly, an improved ability to adjust prices to rising commodity prices reduces operating risk.

Operational risks

In assessing the operating risks focus is on company-specific factors that may affect the stability of operating earnings. **Operational risks** will vary between companies and a significant risk factor for one type of business can be an insignificant factor for another company. Examples of indicators of a company's operating risks are:

- The firm's lifecycle
- Choice of cost structure
- Success in research and development
- Product quality and innovation
- Brand name awareness
- Quality/usefulness of information systems
- Utilisation of production facilities and equipment (efficiency)
- Quality of management/staff
- Quality of internal control systems.

Generally, an improvement of the operating factors reduces operating risk. For example, the longer a company has existed, the greater the sustainability of the business model. This position will affect investors and creditors in assessing operating risk. This is illustrated in Figure 10.6, which shows that risk is decreasing during the firm's lifecycle. Until the company reaches the maturity phase, the risk gradually decreases as a result of greater faith in the business model. This is rewarded by investors and creditors as they require a lower rate of return.

Similarly, better information technology leads to better and more timely information, which should improve decision making and reduce the risk of making inappropriate decisions. Furthermore, a more flexible cost structure will, other things being equal, reduce operating risk.

In summary, a company has various possibilities to control and influence external, strategic and operating risks. Generally, the company's management has to deal with all three types of operating risk factors. Managers are expected to adapt the organisation

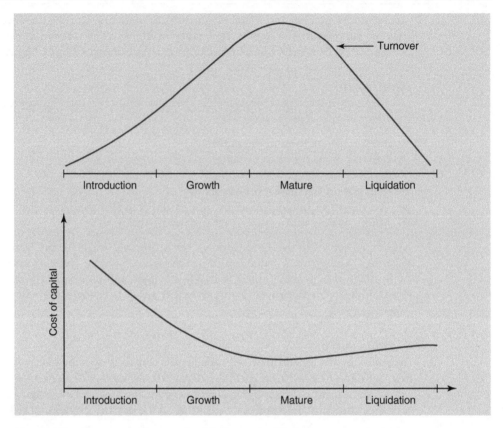

Figure 10.6 A company's cost of capital over its lifecycle

to the current economic situation and exploit market opportunities. In assessing operating risks analysts must cope with risks in the market, in which the firm competes, and evaluate how skilled the executives are in managing the various types of operating risk. Table 10.3 gives an example of how the operating risk can be assessed.

Financial risk

Analysis of financial risk aims at assessing the effect of debt on financial risk. Since equity investors receive their claims after debt holders, they require a higher rate of return than debt holders. This implies that financial leverage affects equity investors' perception of risk. Loan characteristics may also affect the financial risk of a company. We now briefly elaborate on the impact of financial leverage and loan characteristics on financial risk.

Financial leverage

Financial leverage measures the size of net interest-bearing debt relative to equity. If a company is financed entirely with equity, there will not be any financial risks. However, most companies use debt as a financing source. Also shown previously, debt affects the systematic risk on equity (β_e) through the following β relation:

$$\beta_e = \beta_a + (\beta_a - \beta_d) \times \frac{\text{NIBD}}{\text{E}}$$

Table 10.3 Overall assessment of operating risks

Types of operating risk	Low, medium or high risk	The firm's ability to manage operating risks
External risk		**Reasonable**
Market conditions	Medium	Is affected by the business cycle
Legislation	High	The firm tries to affect public opinion by debating, advertisements etc.
Strategic risk		**Not sufficient**
Rivalry among competitors	High	Management has not been able to overcome the negative growth
Suppliers power	Low	
Customers power	High	Considerable customer concentration with related downward pressure on prices
Market growth	High	High risk of lower and more instable operating earnings
Substitute products	High	
Operational risk		**Not sufficient**
Exploiting production facilities	High	Management has not adapted production capacity to the negative growth
Quality of management	High	High level of fixed costs
Choice of cost structure	High	

Total assessment of operating risk: high
The firm's market and earnings are under severe pressure

Management seems to handle external risks in a sensible manner, but there is insufficient attention to the strategic and operational risk indicators

The β relation is exemplified in Table 10.4 and is based on the following assumptions:

$$\text{Risk-free interest rate} = 5\%$$
$$\text{Risk premium} = 5\%$$
$$\beta_a = 0.8$$
$$\beta_d = 0.0$$
$$\text{Corporate tax rate} = 30\%$$

By allowing financial leverage to vary the relation between systematic risk and the owners' required rate of return is as shown in Table 10.4. The systematic risk and the owners' required rate of return increase linearly with financial leverage. Investors are expected to be compensated for higher financial leverage.

Table 10.4 Relation between financial leverage and owners' required rate of return

NIBD to EV (Equity + NIBD)	0%	50%	67%	75%	80%	83%
Financial leverage (NIBD/equity)	0	1.0	2.0	3.0	4.0	5.0
Systematic risk (β_e)	0.8	1.6	2.4	3.2	4.0	4.8
Owners' required rate of return	9%	13%	17%	21%	25%	29%

Loan characteristics

By using debt a company has a number of options, all of which affect financial risk. Specifically, analysts should assess the following aspects of a firm's loan portfolio:

- Fixed or variable interest rates
- Short- or long-term loans (duration)
- Repayment profile
- Local currency or foreign currency.

A fixed-rate loan guarantees a known payment profile. There is no risk on the payments (interest expense) on these types of loans. However, the value of a fixed-rate loan changes if interest rates change (balance sheet risk). The opposite is true for loans with variable interest rates. For these types of loans there is a significant earnings risk as the payments and related interest expenses change with variations in the interest rates. This leads to more volatile earnings. In contrast, there is no risk on the market and book value of the loans (balance sheet risk).

Fixed-rate loans may be short or long term. The duration of the loan affects the interest rate. Typically, the yield curve has a positive slope indicating that the interest rate increases with the term of maturity. The higher interest rate compensates for the duration of risk and is, therefore, a premium paid by companies to lock the interest rate for a longer time period. Companies that choose loans with short maturities typically obtain a lower interest rate, but assume at the same time a refinancing risk, since refinancing may be at a higher interest rate.

It is possible to borrow in foreign currencies. Loans in foreign currencies are typically chosen to hedge cash inflows from the same foreign currency, but can also be selected for more speculative reasons. In Figure 10.2 we showed the yield structures on government bonds issued in the USA, UK and Japan. The interest rate on a Japanese government bond is lower than similar bonds in the USA and the UK. The difference in interest rates embraces different expectations about the trend in these currencies. Therefore, there is an implicit expectation of a rising exchange rate of Japanese yen compared to US dollars and British pounds. Companies borrowing in Japanese yen achieve a lower interest rate, but at the expense of assuming currency risks.

Generally, businesses that use short-term loans with variable interest rates in foreign currencies are prone to considerable financial risks. However, in assessing the financial risk of a firm the analysis should take the specific circumstances into account. For instance, a foreign currency loan intended to hedge future revenues in the same currency is a financial transaction, which intends to reduce a firm's total risk in a sensible and affordable manner.

It is important to note that financial risk cannot be assessed independently of operating risk. Companies may purposely choose a high level of financial risk because they have the necessary financial flexibility. But if the financial risk is derived from economic problems (low operating earnings), this kind of risk has a negative impact on the future room to manoeuvre and, ultimately, the survival of a company.

Companies have significant opportunities to influence and control financial risk. For financially viable firms, the use of debt may reflect a desire to grow and enhance profitability. Companies that are financially troubled, however, use debt to ensure its survival. In such cases the company has fewer opportunities to influence and control financial risk.

An overall assessment of the financial risk may be carried out as illustrated in Table 10.5.

Table 10.5 Overall assessments of the financial risks

Types of financial risk	Assessment of risk level	The company's ability to handle financial risks
Financial leverage	High	**Reasonable → Insufficient**
		Its choice of high financial leverage is historically conditioned. As the operating earnings are under pressure, the high financial leverage should be monitored closely. Managers do not seem to be aware of this
Loan characteristics:		**Reasonable → Insufficient**
1 Variable interest rate	High	As a result of the increased pressure on operating earnings, it is assessed as being
2 Short term to maturity	High	risky to use variable rates with short maturity
3 Primarily in euro (foreign currency)	Low	Most of its revenue billed in euros

Total assessment: high financial risk

Overall risk assessment (β_e)

Generally, companies try to balance operating and financial risks. Companies with high operating risks typically try to minimise financial risks. Empirical evidence seems to support this. Based on publicly traded companies the link between operating risk (β_a) and financial risk (debt to equity ratio) can be shown as in Figure 10.7.

As is evident from the figure, there is a negative correlation between the estimates of operating risk (β asset) and financial risks (financial leverage). For instance, it is clear that companies with high operating risks have a low level of debt.

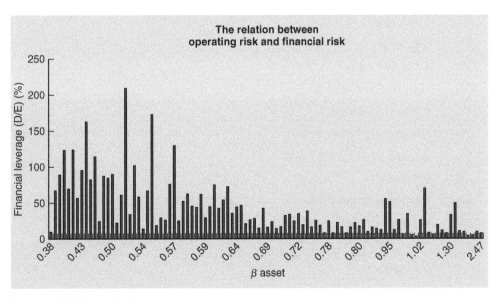

Figure 10.7 Financial leverage and operating risk

Table 10.6 Conversion of a qualitative assessment of risk to an estimate of β_e

Operating risk	Financial risk	Total risk	β equity (β_e)
Low	Low	Very low	0.40–0.60
Low	Neutral	Low	0.60–0.85
Low	High	Neutral	0.85–1.15
Neutral	Low	Low	0.60–0.85
Neutral	Neutral	Neutral	0.85–1.15
Neutral	High	High	1.15–1.40
High	Low	Neutral	0.85–1.15
High	Neutral	High	1.15–1.40
High	High	Very high	1.40 →

Table 10.6 is an example of how the qualitative assessment of the operating and financial risk can be converted to a β estimate. A qualitative assessment of operating and financial risks can be summarised in many different ways and the method outlined here is just one of several techniques that can be used. For example, Fernandez (2009a) provides an alternative method, which he names the 'MASCOFLAPEC' method (based on the first letter of each risk indicator) as shown in Table 10.7.

Table 10.7 The 'MASCOFLAPEC' method for assessing systematic risk

Weight		Low 1	Average 2	Substantial 3	High 4	Very high 5	Weighted risk
10%	**M** Management	1					0.10
25%	**A** Assets: business/industry/ products					5	1.25
3%	**S** Strategy				4		0.12
15%	**C** Country risk				4		0.60
10%	**O** Operational leverage				4		0.40
15%	**F** Financial leverage		2				0.30
5%	**L** Liquidity of investment					5	0.25
5%	**A** Access to sources of funds			3			0.15
2%	**P** Partners				4		0.08
5%	**E** Exposure to other risks		2				0.10
5%	**C** Cash flow stability			3			0.15
100%							3.50
	β equity =	3.5	$\times$	0.5	=	**1.75**	

Source: Fernandez 2009a

As can be seen from Table 10.7, many of the same risk indicators are included in the qualitative risk assessment. In the example, the weighted risk of 3.5 is multiplied by 0.5 to obtain an estimate for β equity. The adjustment factor of 0.5 is based on calibration, but is ultimately subjectively determined. In summary, the qualitative methods simply add to common sense and in combination with CAPM may prove to be a powerful method in estimating systematic risk.

We would like to note, however, that the estimation of risk based on qualitative factors is not unproblematic. First, there is no consensus on what affects operating and financial risk. Second, estimation of the overall risk is associated with a high degree of subjectivity. Two analysts may therefore estimate the risk differently despite identical information. Finally, the method does not distinguish between the systematic (non-diversified) and unsystematic (diversified) risk. By applying the method analysts may unintentionally blend systematic and unsystematic risk. Consequently, a qualitative assessment of risk based on the company's fundamental risks factors does also suffer from measurement problems.

Estimation of market portfolio risk premium

The market portfolio's risk premium is the difference between market returns and returns from risk-free investments. There are typically two ways in which the risk premium can be determined:

- Ex-post approach
- Ex-ante approach.

The ex-post approach examines the difference between the historical returns on the stock market and the historical returns on risk-free investments (usually approximated by the yield on a treasury bond) 50 to 100 years back in time. The assumption behind the method is that the market portfolio's historical risk premium is a reasonable indicator of the *future* market portfolio's risk premium. It could be argued that an assumption is unlikely to hold. Jorion and Goetzmann (2000) provide an example of the ex-post method. They find that the market risk premium in the USA is (approximately) 4.3%.

The ex-ante method attempts, on the basis of analysts' consensus earnings forecast, to infer the market portfolio's implicit risk premium. Claus and Thomas (2001) provide an example of the ex-ante method and find a market risk premium of around 3% in the USA.

Table 10.8 lists examples of market risk premiums used by 884 professors in different countries. As the table shows, there is no consensus about the magnitude of the risk premium. In the European countries the average risk premium is 5.3%. In the USA the risk premium is 6.3% and in other countries the risk premium is 7.9%. Furthermore, the risk premium varies considerably within each region. The risk premium is in most cases justified by references to books or articles. Only 22 professors calculate their own risk premium. Table 10.9 reveals the five most popular references used to justify the risk premium.

The diversity in the market portfolio's risk premium, detailed in Table 10.8 reflects different risk perceptions of the different markets but also masks significant methodological estimation problems. First, estimating the market portfolio risk premium depends on the time period used. For example, Jorion and Goetzmann (2000, p. 8) point out that the risk premium is sensitive to survivorship bias. They point out that

Table 10.8 Market risk premium used by 884 professors

	Average	USA 6.3%	Europe 5.3%	UK 5.5%	Canada 5.4%	Australia 5.9%	Other 7.9%	Total
	St. dev.	2.2%	1.5%	1.9%	1.3%	1.4%	3.9%	
	Maximum	19.0%	10.0%	10.0%	8.0%	7.5%	27.0%	
Market risk premium used in 2008	Q3	7.2%	6.0%	7.0%	6.0%	7.0%	10.0%	
	Median	6.0%	5.0%	5.0%	5.1%	6.0%	7.0%	
	Q1	5.0%	4.1%	4.0%	5.0%	6.0%	5.5%	
	Minimum	0.8%	1.0%	3.0%	2.0%	2.0%	2.0%	
	Number	487	224	54	29	23	67	884
The risk premium is justified by:								
I do not justify the number		93	53	20	6	2	21	195
Reference to books or articles		151	138	28	14	11	27	369
Historic data		87	14	3	6	8	9	127
Own research/calculations		8	7	3	3	0	1	22
Do not answer		14	11	0	0	2	8	35

Source: Fernandez 2009b

Table 10.9 References to justify the market risk premium used

References	USA	Europe	UK	Canada	Australia	Other	Total
Ibbotson	53	9	3	2	1	3	71
Dimson, Marsh and Staunton	11	23	9	1	4	1	49
Damodaran	15	21	0	2	1	3	42
Brealey and Myers	16	12	2	0	1	4	35
Fernandez	3	18	1	0	0	0	22

Source: Fernandez 2009b

both Sweden and the United States were only mildly affected by the Second World War. By comparison, Japan was hit hard. The average risk premium on the market portfolio was −0.34% in Japan during the period 1921–1944. In the post-war period (from 1949–1996) the market portfolio risk premium in Japan was 5.5%. Furthermore, there is the issue whether to use arithmetic or geometric averages. For example, Copeland et al. (2000) finds that the size of market portfolio risk premium varies considerably depending on whether the risk premium is estimated based on the arithmetic or geometric mean. They find that the geometric mean is, as expected, lower than the arithmetic mean.

In summary, it can be concluded that there is uncertainty about which method(s) to use when determining the risk premium. In addition, there is uncertainty about the true level of the risk premium.

CAPM and liquidity

Liquidity refers to the costs and problems associated with converting stocks or assets for cash. A marketable ownership is considered attractive since it conveys the ability quickly to convert assets (shares) to cash, with minimum transaction costs and with a high degree of certainty of realising the expected net proceeds. Equity traders have long recognised the importance of liquidity in stocks and empirical studies seem to support that investors demand a discount for investing in stocks with limited or no liquidity. For example, Petersen et al. (2006) find that investors adjust the required rate of return to account for the lack of liquidity. Investors attach a liquidity premium of up to 3–5 percentage points. The required rate of return on equity which includes a liquidity premium is calculated as:

$$r_e = r_f + \beta_e \times (r_m - r_f) + \text{liquidity premium}$$

Therefore, the liquidity premium is simply added to the required rate of return on equity.

Estimation of the interest rate on debt

In the following section, we will briefly discuss how to estimate the interest rate on debt. In general terms the cost of debt after tax is calculated as:

$$r_d = (r_f + r_s) \times (1 - t)$$

where
r_d = Required rate of return on net interest-bearing debt (NIBD)
r_f = Risk-free interest rate
r_s = Credit spread (risk premium on debt)
t = Corporate tax rate

The required rate of return on NIBD consists of three variables: the risk-free rate, the credit spread, which is equivalent to the risk premium on debt, and the corporate tax rate. Since the risk-free rate has already been discussed, and the different techniques in estimating the credit spread will be discussed in further detail in Chapter 11, we will only elaborate on the corporate tax rate.

Corporation tax

An estimation of the borrowing rate after tax requires knowledge of the corporate tax rate. To the extent that operating profits exceed borrowing costs, the corporate tax rate shall be applied. For companies with operations abroad, it is necessary to examine the local corporate tax rates, and the proportion of total borrowing costs that relate to loans in foreign subsidiaries. For groups with a number of subsidiaries this information can be difficult to obtain. Based on the view that the effective corporate tax rate is a weighted average of the group's different corporate tax rates, it may be argued that the effective corporate tax rate should be used. The use of the effective tax rate, however, rests on a large number of assumptions, which may be difficult to fulfil in practice. For example, the use of the effective corporate tax rate assumes that the company's borrowing costs are distributed in the same way as the firm's operating earnings. Moreover, the effective corporate tax rate is affected by different tax depreciation schemes for different types of assets. For these reasons we generally favour the use of the corporate tax when estimating the tax shield.

Table 10.10 **Calculation of the WACC with and without corporate tax (tax shield)**

Debt ratio	0%	50%	67%	75%	80%	83%
Financial leverage (debt/equity)	0	1	2	3	4	5
Systematic risk (β_e)	0.8	1.6	2.4	3.2	4	4.8
Owners required rate of return	9%	13%	17%	21%	25%	29%
WACC (without corporate tax)	**9.0%**	**9.0%**	**9.0%**	**9.0%**	**9.0%**	**9.0%**
WACC (with corporate tax)	9.0%	8.3%	8.0%	7.9%	7.8%	7.8%

Following the example given in Table 10.4, WACC may be calculated as shown in Table 10.10. As the table shows, WACC is constant at 9% when excluding tax. This implies that when the tax advantage of debt is ignored WACC becomes a function of the risk-free rate and operating risk (β_a). When the tax benefits of debt are introduced (tax shield), WACC is, however, reduced if the debt proportion increases. In Table 10.10 WACC changes from 9% to 7.8% at a debt ratio of 83%. This decrease is often less in practice. First, the example does not take investor taxes into account. The finance literature shows that it will only be possible to use the tax shield fully when investors are taxed similarly on returns from debt and equity capital, respectively. Second, the example does not consider the risk of bankruptcy. Therefore, it is expected that lending rates will gradually increase with financial leverage. This will reduce the advantage of using debt.

Conclusions

This chapter focuses on estimation of the components of WACC. The key points to remember include:

- Cost of capital is fundamental in financial analysis and is used in areas such as performance measurement, valuation, credit analysis and executive compensation.
- An estimation of WACC requires knowledge of the company's long-term capital structure and lenders' and owners' required rate of return.
- The capital structure is based on market values. The capital structure of comparable companies and the iteration method can be used when market values are not observable.
- The risk-free rate is usually based on a zero-coupon government bond.
- Owners' required rate of return is typically estimated based on the Capital Asset Pricing Model (CAPM).
- The market premium varies across countries.
- Estimates from comparable companies and from a qualitative assessment of the company's operating and financial risk factors may prove useful when estimating the systematic risk.

We would like to emphasise that estimation of cost of capital is a challenging task. While it may be tempting to rely purely on the quantitative methodologies outlined in this chapter, we highly recommend that qualitative factors are included as well when estimating the different components of cost of capital.

Review questions

- Why is cost of capital a useful concept in financial statement analysis?
- What is meant by the capital structure?
- What is the interpretation of a company with a β of 2.0?
- Which fundamental factors should be considered when measuring β?
- How is WACC measured?
- How is the required rate of return on equity measured?
- What are appropriate proxies for the risk-free interest rate?
- How can the market risk premium be measured?

APPENDIX 10.1

Carlsberg case

In Appendix 9.1 we valued Carlsberg by applying different present value approaches. As part of the valuation different cost of capital expressions were used:

Valuation model applying required rate of return on equity
Dividend discount model

Valuation models applying WACC
Discounted cash flow (to firm) model
Economic value added model

Valuation model applying required rate of return on assets
Adjusted present value model

In the following section, we discuss the estimation of the required rate of return on assets, the required rate of return on equity and WACC, respectively.

Required rate of return on assets

The required rate of return on assets is defined as follows:

$$r_a = r_f + \beta_a \times (r_m - r_f)$$

Since the cash flow is measured in DKK we apply the yield on a Danish government bond as proxy for the risk-free rate. A 10-year zero-coupon Danish government bond yields 4%. (Ideally, we should apply the yield curve. However, with the purpose of keeping things simple we apply the yield on a 10-year zero-coupon government bond.)

Because the unlevered β is not directly observable we unlever the levered β (systematic risk on equity) applying the following β relation

$$\beta_a = \frac{\beta_e + \beta_d \times \dfrac{\text{NIBD}}{\text{E}}}{1 + \dfrac{\text{NIBD}}{\text{E}}}$$

Based on the systematic risk on equity and debt and the capital structure from peers we are able to calculate the unlevered β for the industry. We rely on estimates from peers to reduce the impact of measurement errors (Table 10.11).

Table 10.11 β estimates and capital structure

	β_e	β_d	D/E	β_a
Heineken	0.84	0.50	0.58	0.72
AB InBew	0.82	0.70	0.34	0.79
SabMiller	0.97	0.40	0.11	0.91
Mean	0.88	0.53	0.34	0.81

Source: Damodaran

These β estimates of debt are based on a subjective assessment of the credit risk of each of the peers. We elaborate further on credit risk in Chapter 11. The mean value of the unlevered β is approximately 0.8.

In Table 10.8 we list different risk premiums used across different countries. We apply a risk premium of 5% which is close to the average risk premium used in Europe. Based on these estimates we calculate the required rate of return on assets for Carlsberg as 8% (4% + 0.8 × 5% = 8%).

Required rate of return on equity

The required rate of return on equity is defined as follows:

$$r_e = r_f + \beta_e \times (r_m - r_f)$$

Since estimates are available for the risk-free rate and the risk premium we only need an estimate for the systematic risk on equity.

By leveraging the unlevered β (0.8) we obtain an estimate of the systematic risk on equity. We apply the following β relation to obtain an estimate for the systematic risk on equity:

$$\beta_e = \beta_a + (\beta_a - \beta_d) \times \frac{\text{NIBD}}{\text{E}}$$

Using the iteration procedure we obtain the following capital structure by the beginning of the first forecast year (see Appendix 9.1):

$$\frac{\text{NIBD}}{\text{E}} = \frac{51{,}478}{86{,}716}$$

Please note that we apply the beginning of year capital structure when leveraging the unlevered β. As proxy for β debt we apply 0.6. This estimate is based on a credit rating of Carlsberg and is further discussed in Chapter 11. This yields the following estimate for the levered β for Carlsberg:

$$\beta_e = 0.8 + (0.8 - 0.6) \times \frac{51{,}478}{86{,}716} = 0.92$$

Further, the required rate of return on equity is 8.6% (reported as 8.59% in Table 10.12):

$$r_e = 4\% + 0.92 \times 5\% = 8.6\%$$

Table 10.12 Carlsberg's cost of capital

Estimation of cost of capital		Forecast horizon				Terminal period
	Year 6	Year E1	Year E2	Year E3	Year E4	Year E5
Tax rate		25.00%	25.00%	25.00%	25.00%	25.00%
β asset		0.80	0.80	0.80	0.80	0.80
β debt		0.60	0.60	0.60	0.60	0.60
β equity		0.92	0.90	0.90	0.90	0.89
Estimated market value of equity	86,716	93,680	98,301	103,125	106,853	110,059
Net interest-bearing debt (NIBD)	51,478	49,170	50,078	50,477	50,547	52,063
Debt/equity (NIBD/E)	0.59	0.52	0.51	0.49	0.47	0.47
Risk-free rate (default free bond 10 year)		4.00%	4.00%	4.00%	4.00%	4.00%
Risk premium		5.00%	5.00%	5.00%	5.00%	5.00%
Required rate of return on assets (r_a)		8.00%	8.00%	8.00%	8.00%	8.00%
Required rate of return on debt, before tax (r_d)		7.00%	7.00%	7.00%	7.00%	7.00%
Required rate of return on debt, after tax		5.25%	5.25%	5.25%	5.25%	5.25%
Required rate of return on equity (r_e)		8.59%	8.52%	8.51%	8.49%	8.47%
WACC		7.35%	7.40%	7.41%	7.42%	7.44%

WACC

WACC is defined as follows:

$$\text{WACC} = \frac{\text{NIBD}}{\text{NIBD} + \text{E}} \times r_d \times (1 - t) + \frac{\text{E}}{\text{NIBD} + \text{E}} \times r_e$$

Assuming a tax rate of 25% and a required rate of return on debt of 7% (4% + 0.6 × 5% = 7%) Carlsberg's WACC in the first forecast year is 7.35%:

$$\text{WACC} = \frac{51,478}{51,478 + 86,716} \times 7\% \times (1 - 0.25) + \frac{86,716}{51,478 + 86,716} \times 8.59\%$$

$$= 7.35\%$$

In Table 10.12 we report the expected annual cost of capital for Carlsberg. Using the iteration procedure we allow the capital structure to vary across time. This implies that a new estimate for the systematic risk on equity, required rate of return on equity and WACC are provided each year. As shown in this example, the systematic risk on equity, the required rate of return on equity and WACC vary only modestly due to changes in the capital structure. This also indicates that the use of a variable WACC only makes sense when the changes in the capital structure are material over time.

Note

1 The 10-year is a geometric weighted average estimate of the expected short-term rates (forward rates).

References

Claus, J. and J. Thomas (2001) 'Equity premia as low as three percent? Evidence from analysts' earnings forecasts for domestic and international stock markets', *The Journal of Finance*, October.

Copeland, T., T. Koller and J. Murrin (2000) *Valuation: Measuring and managing the value of companies*, John Wiley & Sons.

Fernandez, P. (2009a) 'Betas used by professors: a survey with 2,500 answers', Working Paper, IESE Business School, May.

Fernandez, P. (2009b) 'Market risk premium used in 2008 by professors: a survey with 1,400 answers', Working Paper, IESE Business School, April.

Jorion, P. and W. N. Goetzmann (2000) 'A century of global stock markets', Working Paper 7565, National Bureau of Economic Research.

Petersen, C., T. Plenborg and F. Schiøler (2006) 'Issues in valuation of privately held firms', *Journal of Private Equity*, Winter.

CHAPTER 11

Credit analysis

Learning outcomes

After reading this chapter you should be able to:

- Make a distinction between the different approaches available for credit analysis
- Recognise that credit analysis is an art and not a science
- Estimate the expected loss if a firm goes bankrupt
- Understand the difference between exposure at default, probability of default, and probability of recovery in case of default
- Conduct a credit analysis based on the fundamental analysis approach (expert-based approach)
- Understand ratings from credit agencies and the distinction between an investment grade and a speculative grade, respectively
- Calculate the value at risk based on the fundamental credit analysis approach
- Recognise the key differences between the fundamental credit analysis approach and the statistical models in credit analysis

Corporate credit analysis

Credit analysis provides the answer to this question, by assessing a company's ability to pay its financial obligations in a timely manner. It examines the probability that a company may default, and the potential loss in the event of default.

Most lending institutions are involved in credit analysis, whether banks or institutional investors such as insurance companies and pension funds. Banks extend loans to companies and use credit analysis to make distinctions between financially healthy companies and companies which are likely to default. Institutional investors use credit analysis to find out whether debt securities are sound investments. Credit analysis is, however, not limited to banks and institutional investors. Companies assess the credit quality of their customers. Customers assess the credit quality of their suppliers to ensure that they will provide warranty services, replacement parts and product updates. Auditors examine whether a company is a going concern. Competitors examine the consequences of the potential financial distress of the key competitor.

Credit analysis is an art, not a science. This means that credit decisions are highly subjective in nature. However, it does not mean that there is not a framework that can be useful in making credit decisions. At least two frameworks are available for credit analyses. **Fundamental credit analysis**, also referred to as an expert-based approach, is a framework, where the analyst carefully scrutinises the target firm by asking insightful questions and leaves no stones unturned. **Statistical models** serve as another framework for credit analysis. The underlying assumption of these models is that statistically meaningful behaviour in the financial ratios can be identified allowing the analysts to predict the probability of a default. In this chapter, we emphasise the fundamental credit analysis approach. We will also briefly elaborate on the statistical models for credit analysis at the end of the chapter.

Credit analysis aims at estimating the **expected loss** in the event of a default. The expected loss is defined as follows:

$$\text{Expected loss} = \text{exposure at default} \times \text{probability of default}$$
$$\times (1 - \text{probability of recovery})$$

Exposure at default expresses the potential loss in case of a default and is equal to the maximum loss that a creditor may experience. The probability of default is an estimate of the likelihood that a company may default. The probability of recovery measures the degree to which a company is able to meet its obligation in the event of defaulting. The following example illustrates the concept of expected loss.

Example 11.1 Assume that a company owes 1,000. Therefore, the exposure at default is 1,000. The probability of default is 25% and the probability of recovery is 100%. In this example the expected loss, which the lender may experience, is zero as the probability of recovery is 100%.

$$\text{Expected loss} = 1,000 \times 25\% \times (1 - 100\%) = 0 \qquad \blacksquare$$

In order to estimate the expected loss, it is necessary to provide estimates for the following variables:

1 Exposure at default
2 Probability of default
3 Probability of recovery.

The credit analysis must cover each of these issues. While the estimation of a company's exposure at default is relatively straightforward, it is much more challenging to provide estimates of the probability of default and recovery. In this chapter, we present an outline of the different steps involved in credit analysis using the fundamental credit analysis approach. While not all credit analyses follow the same process, the steps are representative of typical approaches. Moreover, it provides a useful insight into estimating the expected loss.

The fundamental credit analysis approach

Fundamental credit analysis is essentially a systematic and comprehensive analysis of a company's ability to repay its liabilities (debt) on time and in full. It typically includes the following eight steps:

Assessing the exposure at default
1 An understanding of the intended use of the loan
2 An understanding of the type of financing (loan).

Estimating probability of default
3 A strategic analysis of the firm
4 An analysis of the firm's accounting quality
5 An assessment of the firm's financial health based on financial ratios
6 A simulation of future cash flows to evaluate the firm's ability to service debt.

Estimating probability of recovery
7 Available security and collaterals and its liquidation value in case of financial default.

Estimating the expected loss
8 Summarising the results of the credit analysis (credit rating).

A thorough credit analysis should include not only the analysed firm but also related persons or firms. A related person is someone who has either control or joint control over the analysed firm, has significant influence over the analysed firm or is a member of the key management personnel of the analysed firm. A related firm is basically a firm which is a member of the same group as the analysed firm. IAS 24 requires firms to make related party disclosures to ensure that an entity's financial statements contain the disclosures necessary to draw attention to the possibility that its financial position and profit or loss may have been affected by the existence of related parties and by transactions and outstanding balances with such parties. For example, an owner's financial problems may affect an otherwise financially healthy company. The owner may use the ownership as a pledge for private loans and in cases, where the owner is not able to meet his or her obligations on private loans, the bank may force a realisation of the collateral; i.e. the ownership of the company. This typically has negative implications for the company, thereby affecting its creditworthiness.

Similar concerns should be raised for firms belonging to the same group. Financial problems in a parent company may affect a subsidiary negatively. The subsidiary may be forced to pay extraordinary high dividends to the parent, which has a negative impact on the subsidiary's ability to invest in the future. The subsidiary may also guarantee for some of the parent's obligations. In either case it affects the creditworthiness of the company negatively. It is therefore important that the credit analysis carefully considers those parties as well when assessing the credit risk of a firm.

We now elaborate on each of the eight steps outlined above.

Step 1: An understanding of the intended use of the loan

It is essential in a proper credit analysis that the analyst understands the intended use of the loan. The analyst needs to know the size of the loan, and what it will be used for, to help determine the type of loan required. A retailer, which expands its business, needs short-term financing such as an open line of credit or a working capital loan to finance inventory and receivables. A real estate investor, on the other hand, needs long-term financing such as a mortgage loan and other similar committed facilities to finance property investments.

An understanding of the intended use of the loan provides the analyst with a deeper knowledge of the inherent risk of the entire loan arrangement. For example, the risk involved in an open line credit offered to a mature and financially healthy company is much less than the risk in an open line credit offered to a company with no track-record and poor financial performance.

The size of the loan must also be established, as it gives the analyst an insight about the business potential and information about the potential risk.

Step 2: An understanding of the type of financing (loan)

The type of financing offered is typically a function of the intended use and the financial health of the borrower. In the following section, we describe different types of loans available to firms. It is important to stress that the list is not exhaustive. In fact, today it is possible to design essentially any type of loan requested by a borrower.

Loan

Corporate loans are typically extended by banks and take two forms, bilateral and syndications. A bilateral loan is the most simple and is usually found in small and medium-sized companies, where banks are willing to take a large counterparty exposure. In syndicated loans, borrowers typically select one or more banks to act as arrangers, with one member of the group typically being appointed as the agent bank. The agent coordinates all negotiations, payments and administration between the parties during the life of the transaction. Other banks are invited to participate in the loan.

It is essential to differentiate between uncommitted and committed facilities. An uncommitted facility allows the lender to renege a commitment at any time. A committed facility, on the other hand, commits the lender to engage its capital during the entire lending period. It is well-known that loans can take many forms. Below we list some of the common types of loans:

- Open line credit – a credit facility that permits the borrower to receive cash up to some specified maximum for a specified term, typically one year. A fee is charged on the unused credit facility.
- Revolving line of credit – a credit facility that may be used if credit is needed beyond the short run. A fee is charged for the unused credit facility.
- Working capital loan – a credit facility used to finance inventory and receivables.
- Mortgage loan – a credit facility used to finance real estate. It is typically long term.
- Lease financing.

Bond

Corporate bonds, also referred to as notes, are debt obligations issued by the borrower directly into the public fixed income markets. Their tenure can extend up to 30 years and there are even some perpetual fixed-income instruments. A company issuing **bonds** typically selects a lead underwriter, who arranges the placement of the bonds with investors. As bonds are placed with retail investors in the public markets, the requirements for disclosure are more demanding than for loans.

Medium-term notes

Medium-term notes, also referred to as MTNs, are a flexible form of financing available to borrowers with high credit quality. Firms with high credit quality register MTN programmes with dealers acting as agents, who distribute the programmes in the markets.

They share many of the same characteristics as bonds, but the difference is the fact that dealers have no underwriting obligations and distribute MTNs on best effort basis.

Private placement

Private placements are an issue of debt that is placed primarily with insurance companies. Their term is typically of longer duration and up to 30 years. Documentation and disclosure are negotiated with the parties involved. Companies may see private placement as a way of diversifying their sources of financing, but may also be seen as the only financing available in case of financial problems.

Convertible debt and other hybrid instrument

Convertible debt is a debt instrument that can be exchanged for a specified number of shares within a specified date and at an agreed price (strike price). Since convertible debt contains an equity element, it is contractually subordinated to most other types of debt. Companies may rely on convertible bonds as a source of financing if the alternative is issuance of new stocks. For many years the finance community has devoted considerable resources to the development of new and more innovative hybrid instruments. Today there is a wide range of hybrid instruments available and they can essentially be designed to match the needs of any company. This includes the option to convert debt to equity, different degrees of maturity and flexible payment of interests including the option to defer interest payments in case of cash shortage.

Steps 1 and 2 provide the analyst with an understanding of the exposure at default, and will help answer the following questions:

- Who is the borrower?
- What is the intended use of the proceeds?
- What is the debt amount requested?
- What is the currency?
- What are the price and the coupon?
- What is the maturity?
- What are the interest payment dates?
- What is the rank of debt obligations?

Step 3: A strategic analysis of the firm

The purpose of the strategic analysis is to identify and assess credit risk; i.e. factors that have a potential to affect cash flows negatively and eventually impair a company's ability to meet its obligations. In Chapter 8 on forecasting we discussed how the strategic literature provides guidance on the structure and types of analyses, which analysts can follow to cover important aspects of a company's cash flow potential and risk. In Chapter 10 on the cost of capital we discussed risk factors related to a company's operating and financing activities, and assessed to what extent a company has the ability to influence and control various risk indicators.

The strategic analyses discussed in both chapters are overlapping and are useful in identifying and assessing factors, which have a potential to affect the future cash flow generation negatively, and thereby increase the risk that a company will not be able to meet its future obligations. As with any type of analyses the strategic analysis is no better than the data available and the analysis performed. It is therefore crucial that

UNIVERSITY OF WINCHESTER LIBRARY

the analyst devotes the necessary time and resources in collecting useful information and performing the analysis.

Step 4: An analysis of a firm's accounting quality

The objective is to examine whether reported accounting numbers are influenced or even manipulated by management with the purpose of portraying the company as being financially healthier than the underlying economics justify. In Chapter 13, we discuss the concept of accounting quality and the steps involved in examining the accounting quality of a firm. Building on the foundation laid out in Chapter 13 we provide a checklist on accounting issues which can be used to evaluate the accounting quality of a company as part of a credit assessment. The checklist is as follows:

- Which GAAP is used?
- Is the audit opinion clean?
- Has there been a recent change in external auditors?
- Has the company faced any recent regulatory actions, including restatements and amended filings?
- Have there been any recent changes in measurement method, estimates or reclassifications among accounts?
- Do the accounting policies appear realistic as compared to peers?
- Has there been a change in the accounting period?
- Are the reported earnings numbers primarily driven by recurrent or non-recurrent items?
- Are there accounting items which are not yet recognised (off-balance sheet items), but which have a potential to affect the cash flow?
- Does the annual report contain any 'red flags'?

An analysis of the accounting quality should give the analyst comfort in the reported accounting numbers. However, if the analysis of the accounting quality reveals any inconsistencies it will, on the other hand, question the quality of the reported accounting numbers. The analyst should therefore adjust the accounting numbers along the guidelines given in Chapters 14 and 15. If it is not possible to make adjustments, for instance because the necessary information is not available and applying assumptions and estimates would make accounting numbers too unreliable, the analyst should interpret the accounting numbers with care.

Step 5: An assessment of a firm's financial health based on financial ratios

Companies assessing the credit risk of their suppliers or customers usually use accounting numbers from financial reports (e.g. the annual report). They rely on financial ratios similar to the ones discussed in Chapters 5–7. In Chapter 5 we describe financial ratios measuring the profitability of a company, Chapter 6 outlines financial ratios measuring growth, and finally Chapter 7 discusses financial ratios measuring the short-term and long-term liquidity risk. Each of these financial ratios describes important aspects of a firm's financial health.

Banks and other financial institutions often rely on credit rating models similar to the ones adopted by credit agencies like Standard & Poor's and Moody's. Credit rating models use selected financial ratios in the ranking of companies based on their credit risk. The financial ratios are selected based on statistical tests and those tests' ability to rank companies according to their credit risk. Table 11.1 lists financial ratios

Table 11.1 Credit rating of industrials

Adjusted key industrial financial ratios

US industrial long-term debt

Three years median	High			Rating			Low
	AAA	AA	A	BBB	BB	B	CCC
EBIT Interest cover (×)	**21.4**	10.1	6.1	3.7	2.1	0.8	0.1
EBITDA interest cover (×)	26.5	12.9	9.1	5.8	3.4	1.8	1.3
Free operating cash flow/total debt (%)	84.2	25.2	15.0	8.5	2.6	−3.2	−12.9
FFO/total debt (%)	128.8	55.4	43.2	30.8	18.8	7.8	1.6
Return on capital (%)	**34.9**	21.7	19.4	13.6	11.6	6.6	1.0
Operating income/revenue (%)	27.0	22.1	18.6	15.4	15.9	11.9	11.9
Long-term debt/capital (%)	13.3	28.2	33.9	42.5	57.2	69.7	68.8
Total debt/capital (%)	22.9	37.7	42.5	48.2	62.6	74.8	87.7
Number of companies	8	29	136	218	273	281	22

for industrials and, as reported in the table, a number of key financial ratios, which describe different aspects of a company's profitability and risk, are used. Return on capital (return on invested capital) and operating income as a percentage of revenue (profit margin) are profitability ratios, while the other ratios focus on a company's risk factors. The ranking shows what is required for industrial firms to achieve a given rating. For example, operating income (EBIT) must be at least 21.4 times interest expenses or return on invested capital (return on capital) must be greater than 34.9% to achieve the best possible rating (AAA). It is important to emphasise that the thresholds vary between industries and may change over time and among industries. The key ratios in Table 11.1 apply to US industrial firms only.

An explanation of the different ratings is provided in Table 11.2. Credit ratings from 'AAA' to 'BBB−' correspond to an investment grade. Ratings below 'BBB−' are equivalent to a speculative grade (also known as high yield or junk bonds). Obviously, credit ratings have to be industry-specific as the financial structure varies across industries. As we noted in Chapter 5, companies, which for example offer standard commodities, often operate in areas characterised by significant competition. Within these industries, there is an upper limit to the profit margin. To be able to attract capital for such entities, they need to generate high turnover rates (e.g. inventory turnover). The industry-specific ratings take such issues into consideration.

Moody is another well-respected rating agency whose credit rating model is illustrated in Table 11.3. Moody's uses slightly more (and different) financial ratios than the rating in Table 11.1. For example, whereas this requires an EBIT of 21.4 × interest expenses to achieve the highest possible rating, Moody's requires EBITA (where 'A' is amortisation of intangible assets) to be at least 17.0 × interest

Table 11.2 Explanation of the different ratings

	'AAA'	Extremely strong capacity to meet financial commitments. Highest rating
	'AA'	Very strong capacity to meet financial commitments
	'A'	Strong capacity to meet financial commitments, but somewhat susceptible to adverse economic conditions and changes in circumstances.
↑ Investment grade	'BBB'	Adequate capacity to meet financial commitments, but more subject to adverse economic conditions
	'BBB–'	Considered lowest investment grade by market participants
Speculative grade ↓	'BB+'	Considered highest speculative grade by market participants
	'BB'	Less vulnerable in the near-term but faces major ongoing uncertainties to adverse business, financial and economic conditions
	'B'	More vulnerable to adverse business, financial and economic conditions but currently has the capacity to meet financial commitments
	'CCC'	Currently vulnerable and dependent on favourable business, financial and economic conditions to meet financial commitments
	'CC'	Currently highly vulnerable
	'C'	A bankruptcy petition has been filed or similar action taken, but payments of financial commitments are continued
	'D'	Payment default on financial commitments

Ratings from 'AA' to 'CCC' may be modified by the addition of a plus (+) or minus (−) sign to show relative standing within the major rating categories

Table 11.3 Ratings for non-financial corporations

Credit rating	Aaa	Aa	A	Baa	Ba	B	Caa−C
EBITA/Average AT	15.3%	15.6%	12.5%	10.1%	9.6%	7.3%	2.0%
Operating margin	14.9%	17.0%	13.8%	12.6%	12.2%	8.5%	1.6%
EBITA margin	14.8%	17.5%	15.2%	13.9%	13.4%	9.4%	2.4%
EBITA/IntExp	17.0	13.7	8.2	5.1	3.4	1.5	0.3
(FFO + IntExp)/IntExp	15.5	15.5	9.6	6.6	4.7	2.6	1.5
Debt/EBITDA	0.9	1.0	1.7	2.4	3.3	5.0	6.3
Debt/BookCap	22.7%	32.5%	39.1%	44.8%	53.5%	70.2%	92.5%
FFO/Debt	117.3%	68.4%	43.8%	29.2%	21.8%	12.0%	4.3%
RCF/NetDebt	96.3%	38.4%	38.7%	27.7%	20.0%	11.7%	4.6%
CAPEX/DepExp	1.6	1.4	1.3	1.2	1.2	1.1	0.9
Rev Vol	5.6	4.4	5.5	7.2	10.7	9.2	11.1

Source: Moody's Financial Metrics™

expenses. Therefore, Moody's uses operating earnings before amortisation expenses (a non-cash item) in calculating the interest coverage ratio.

Tables 11.1 and 11.3 apply a slightly different notation for the various ratings. Moody's ratings between 'Aaa' and 'Baa' are equivalent to an 'investment grade', while ratings below Baa are labelled 'speculative grade'. However, note that the financial ratios applied in both ratings cover essentially the same aspects of a company's profitability and risk.

In the following example, we use Rörvik Timber to exemplify the rating of industrials given in Table 11.1. As you may recall from Chapter 7, Rörvik Timber suspended its payments in year 7.

Example 11.2 In Table 11.4 a credit rating is provided for Rörvik Timber covering years 1–6. In each year the performance of a selected financial ratio is translated into a credit rating. For example,

Table 11.4 Credit rating of Rörvik Timber based on a rating (threshold) of industrials

Credit rating (year 6)	AAA	AA	A	BBB	BB	B	CCC	<CCC
EBIT interest cover (×)								X
EBITDA interest cover (×)								X
FOCF/Total debt (%)							X	
FFO/Total debt (%)								X
Return on capital (%)								X
Operating income/Revenue (%)								X
Long-term debt/Capital (%)		X						
Total debt/Capital (%)				X				

Credit rating (year 5)	AAA	AA	A	BBB	BB	B	CCC	<CCC
EBIT interest cover (×)			X					
EBITDA interest cover (×)			X					
FOCF/Total debt (%)								X
FFO/Total debt (%)					X			
Return on capital (%)			X					
Operating income/Revenue (%)								X
Long-term debt/Capital (%)		X						
Total debt/Capital (%)		X						

Credit rating (year 4)	AAA	AA	A	BBB	BB	B	CCC	<CCC
EBIT interest cover (×)			X					
EBITDA interest cover (×)				X				
FOCF/Total debt (%)							X	

▶

Table 11.4 (*continued*)

Credit rating (year 4)	AAA	AA	A	BBB	BB	B	CCC	<CCC
FFO/Total debt (%)					X			
Return on capital (%)					X			
Operating income/Revenue (%)								X
Long-term debt/Capital (%)		X						
Total debt/Capital (%)		X						

Credit rating (year 3)	AAA	AA	A	BBB	BB	B	CCC	<CCC
EBIT interest cover (×)				X				
EBITDA interest cover (×)					X			
FOCF/Total debt (%)					X			
FFO/Total debt (%)						X		
Return on capital (%)						X		
Operating income/Revenue (%)								X
Long-term debt/Capital (%)		X						
Total debt/Capital (%)		X						

Credit rating (year 2)	AAA	AA	A	BBB	BB	B	CCC	<CCC
EBIT interest cover (×)						X		
EBITDA interest cover (×)								X
FOCF/Total debt (%)				X				
FFO/Total debt (%)								X
Return on capital (%)							X	
Operating income/Revenue (%)								X
Long-term debt/Capital (%)			X					
Total debt/Capital (%)				X				

Credit rating (year 1)	AAA	AA	A	BBB	BB	B	CCC	<CCC
EBIT interest cover (×)						X		
EBITDA interest cover (×)					X			
FOCF/Total debt (%)								X
FFO/Total debt (%)						X		
Return on capital (%)							X	
Operating income/Revenue (%)								X
Long-term debt/Capital (%)				X				
Total debt/Capital (%)			X					

in year 1 the EBIT interest cover of Rörvik Timber translates into a 'B' rating. In some cases, the level of a financial ratio is so poor that it does not even meet a 'CCC' rating. An example is the operating income/revenue ratio in year 1. These cases are classified as '<CCC'.

The credit rating of Rörvik Timber reveals a gradual improvement in the credit risk until year 5. In fact, many of the financial ratios of Rörvik Timber in year 5 correspond to an 'A' rating or better. However, in year 6 the picture changes completely. Five out of eight financial ratios lead to a rating worse than 'CCC', which indicates that Rörvik Timber has severe financial problems. The example illustrates that financial ratios may be useful in assessing the credit risk of a company. However, it also shows that financial ratios are not necessarily timely indicators of credit risk as in the case of Rörvik Timber. As noted above, Rörvik Timber suspended its payments in the spring of year 7, which corresponds with the release of the annual report for year 6. ∎

Step 6: A simulation of future cash flows to evaluate the firm's ability to service debt

One of the problems of credit rating models and financial ratios in general is that they are backward-looking and do not incorporate information about the future cash flow potential. It is therefore useful to project cash flows. The concept of forecasting, which is presented in Chapter 8, is a useful foundation for the projections of cash flows. As noted previously it is important that the analyst can 'see' into the future with a high degree of visibility. The strategic analysis as well as the financial statement analysis literature offer 'lenses' that analysts can use to make more reliable forecasts of each financial value driver.

Based on likely scenarios identified in the strategic analysis it is possible to evaluate the probability that a company can meet its future obligations. The simulation of future cash flows can be based on different levels of sophistication. The simplest approach is probably a simulation of cash flows based on a 'worst case', a 'base case' and a 'best case' scenario. Each of these simulations is used to evaluate whether a firm's cash flow is sufficient to service debt (i.e. paying instalments and interests on the loan). Let's illustrate the method in the next three examples using Rörvik Timber.

Example 11.3 Worst case scenario

Rörvik Timber's performance in year 6 was bad. As a worst case scenario we predict that Rörvik Timber is not able to improve its performance from year 6. Furthermore, we assume zero growth in all future years. The forecast assumptions and the derived cash flows are shown in Table 11.5. The cash flow from operating activities and the cash flow from investing activities are negative in every single year in the forecast period. This implies that there is no cash available to service the debt (payment of interest expenses and repayment of debt). In fact, in years E1–E5 shareholders need to provide SEK 1,109 million in additional capital to support operations.

Table 11.5 Worst case scenario: projections of Rörvik Timber's cash flows

	Average		Forecast assumptions				
	Years 1–6	Year 6	Year E1	Year E2	Year E3	Year E4	Year E5
Revenue growth	12.8%	−9.5%	0.0%	0.0%	0.0%	0.0%	0.0%
EBITDA margin	4.2%	−7.2%	−7.2%	−7.2%	−7.2%	−7.2%	−7.2%
Interest rate			8.0%	8.0%	8.0%	8.0%	8.0%
Tax rate, efficient	11.9%	28.0%	28.0%	28.0%	28.0%	28.0%	28.0%
Depreciation as a percentage of intangible and tangible assets	10.0%	8.2%	8.2%	8.2%	8.2%	8.2%	8.2%
Intangible and tangible assets as a percentage of revenue	22.4%	30.6%	30.6%	30.6%	30.6%	30.6%	30.6%
Deferred tax receivable		21.7	0.0%	0.0%	0.0%	0.0%	0.0%
Inventories as a percentage of revenue	21.4%	20.0%	20.0%	20.0%	20.0%	20.0%	20.0%
Receivables as a percentage of revenue	14.5%	15.3%	15.3%	15.3%	15.3%	15.3%	15.3%
Operating liabilities as a percentage of revenue	17.9%	20.5%	20.5%	20.5%	20.5%	20.5%	20.5%
Interest-bearing debt as a percentage of invested capital	62.9%	80.6%	80.6%	80.6%	80.6%	80.6%	80.6%

	Years 1–6		Year E1	Year E2	Year E3	Year E4	Year E5
Cash flow from operating activities			−107.9	−107.9	−107.9	−107.9	−107.9
Cash flow from investing activities			−60.0	−60.0	−60.0	−60.0	−60.0
Cash flow from financing activities			−68.0	−50.5	−50.5	−50.5	−50.5
Cash flow infusion (+) or dividends (−)			235.9	218.4	218.4	218.4	218.4
ROIC	4.7%		−15.3%	−15.4%	−15.4%	−15.4%	−15.4%

■

Example 11.4 **Base case scenario**

In the base case scenario we assume that Rörvik Timber is able to recover its EBITDA margin to 4.2% corresponding to the average operating performance in years 1–6. Furthermore, we assume that intangible and tangible assets, as a percentage of revenue, gradually approach the average level from years 1–6 of 22%. The adjustment of these forecast assumptions results in the estimates shown in Table 11.6.

ROIC improves to 4.8% in year E5, which is close to the average ROIC of 4.7% in the past six years. Due to the expected improvement in the EBITDA margin and the assumed

Table 11.6 Base case scenario: projections of Rörvik Timber's cash flow

	Average		Forecast assumptions				
	Years 1–6	Year 6	Year E1	Year E2	Year E3	Year E4	Year E5
Revenue growth	12.8%	−9.5%	0.0%	0.0%	0.0%	0.0%	0.0%
EBITDA margin	4.2%	−7.2%	4.2%	4.2%	4.2%	4.2%	4.2%
Interest rate			8.0%	8.0%	8.0%	8.0%	8.0%
Tax rate, efficient	11.9%	28.0%	28.0%	28.0%	28.0%	28.0%	28.0%
Depreciation as a percentage of intangible and tangible assets	10.0%	8.2%	8.2%	8.2%	8.2%	8.2%	8.2%
Intangible and tangible assets as a percentage of revenue	22.4%	30.6%	28.0%	26.0%	24.0%	22.0%	22.0%
Deferred tax receivable		21.7	0.0%	0.0%	0.0%	0.0%	0.0%
Inventories as a percentage of revenue	21.4%	20.0%	20.0%	20.0%	20.0%	20.0%	20.0%
Receivables as a percentage of revenue	14.5%	15.3%	15.3%	15.3%	15.3%	15.3%	15.3%
Operating liabilities as a percentage of revenue	17.9%	20.5%	20.5%	20.5%	20.5%	20.5%	20.5%
Interest-bearing debt as a percentage of invested capital	62.9%	80.6%	80.6%	80.6%	80.6%	80.6%	80.6%

	Years 1–6	Year E1	Year E2	Year E3	Year E4	Year E5
Cash flow from operating activities		88.5	87.4	86.3	85.2	85.2
Cash flow from investing activities		8.1	−3.1	0.8	4.7	−43.1
Cash flow from financing activities		−115.9	−83.9	−81.7	−79.5	−40.9
Cash flow infusion (+) or dividends (−)		19.2	−0.4	−5.4	−10.4	−1.2
ROIC	4.7%	3.2%	3.6%	4.1%	4.7%	4.8%

improvement in the utilisation of intangible and tangible assets, the projected cash flows in years E2–E5 are just sufficient to meet financial obligations. ∎

<Example 11.5> **Best case scenario**

The best case scenario rests on the assumption of an annual growth rate of 5%, the EBITDA margin improves to 6%, and intangible and tangible assets as a percentage of revenue improves gradually to 22% in year E5 (Table 11.7).

Table 11.7 Best case scenario: projections of Rörvik Timber's cash flow

	Average		Forecast assumptions				
	Years 1–6	Year 6	Year E1	Year E2	Year E3	Year E4	Year E5
Revenue growth	12.8%	−9.5%	5.0%	5.0%	5.0%	5.0%	5.0%
EBITDA margin	4.2%	−7.2%	6.0%	6.0%	6.0%	6.0%	6.0%
Interest rate			8.0%	8.0%	8.0%	8.0%	8.0%
Tax rate, efficient	11.9%	28.0%	28.0%	28.0%	28.0%	28.0%	28.0%
Depreciation as a percentage of intangible and tangible assets	10.0%	8.2%	8.2%	8.2%	8.2%	8.2%	8.2%
Intangible and tangible assets as a percentage of revenue	22.4%	30.6%	28.0%	26.0%	24.0%	22.0%	22.0%
Deferred tax receivable		21.7	0.0%	0.0%	0.0%	0.0%	0.0%
Inventories as a percentage of revenue	21.4%	20.0%	20.0%	20.0%	20.0%	20.0%	20.0%
Receivables as a percentage of revenue	14.5%	15.3%	15.3%	15.3%	15.3%	15.3%	15.3%
Operating liabilities as a percentage of revenue	17.9%	20.5%	20.5%	20.5%	20.5%	20.5%	20.5%
Interest-bearing debt as a percentage of invested capital	62.9%	80.6%	80.6%	80.6%	80.6%	80.6%	80.6%

	Years 1–6	Year E1	Year E2	Year E3	Year E4	Year E5
Cash flow from operating activities		106.8	110.9	115.2	119.6	125.6
Cash flow from investing activities		−28.1	−38.6	−33.3	−27.5	−87.0
Cash flow from financing activities		−77.0	−49.2	−51.2	−53.3	−9.1
Cash flow infusion (+) or dividends (−)		−1.8	−23.2	−30.7	−38.9	−29.6
ROIC	4.7%	6.1%	6.8%	7.5%	8.2%	8.4%

In the best case scenario ROIC improves to 8.4%, which is well above the historical average of 4.7%. Cash flow in each forecast year is sufficient to meet the financial obligations. In fact, in the best case scenario Rörvik Timber is able to pay dividends to its shareholders. ■

Ideally, probabilities are attached to each scenario, which gives the analyst a better impression of the likelihood of a default. Figure 11.1 provides an example of an outcome of such a simulation process. It provides an excellent overview of the likelihood that a company defaults based on the probabilities of each scenario. In the examples, the three scenarios result in a default. This is equivalent to a 4% (1% + 1% + 2%) chance that the company defaults.

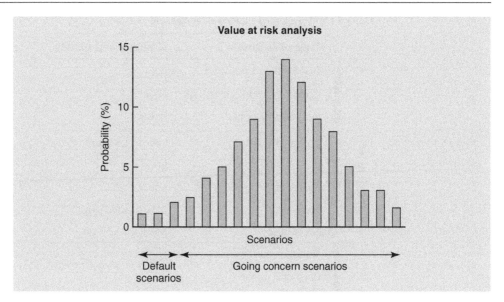

Figure 11.1 An illustration of the probability of default based on simulations

There are more advanced simulation methods available than the relatively simple approach outlined above. They include among others Monte Carlo simulations, which are stochastic techniques relying on random numbers and probability statistics to determine the probability of corporate default. Before considering adopting the more advanced simulation approaches it is, however, important that solid pro forma statements that articulate have been developed and likely outcomes identified.

Steps 3–6 provide the analyst with an understanding of the probability of a corporate default. Some of the questions that Steps 3–6 should be able to answer include:

- Which of the identified strategic factors are most likely to affect the cash flows in the future?
- Are the financial statements of high quality?
- Do the financial ratios indicate any financial problems?
- Do simulations of cash flows indicate any financial problems?
- What is the probability of corporate default?

Step 7: Available security and collaterals and its liquidation value in case of financial default

Unless loans are short term and the borrower exposes the lender to minimal default risk, security or collateral is usually required. Creditors often secure their loans by requiring a pledge in the asset on which the borrowing is based. The pledge ensures that if the borrower defaults, the lender can realise the asset (collateral) to satisfy its claims against the borrower. The challenge from a lender's perspective is to ensure that the collateral is of such quality that it ensures a full recovery in case a default is likely. In Table 11.8, we describe different types of collateral and their respective liquidity and quality. Liquidity refers to how easy it is to convert an asset to cash. Quality refers to how well the book values reflect the liquidation value of assets.

Table 11.8 **Types and quality of collaterals**

Type of asset		Type of collateral	Liquidity and quality
	Intangible	Goodwill and brands	Low
		Contracts and concessions	Low
		Patents and rights	Low
	Tangible	Property	Low to medium
		Plant	Low
		Equipment	Low
		Inventory	Low to medium
		Receivables	Medium to high
	Financial	Traded securities	High
		Cash and bank accounts	High

The most liquid assets like cash and traded securities are typically the assets where the book values and liquidation values are also most aligned. For the least liquid assets, like intangible assets, there is a greater uncertainty as to whether book values reflect liquidation values. Many of the thoughts outlined in Chapter 9 on the calculation of the liquidation value can be used to examine the quality of assets (collateral). This includes issues such as the measurement basis, alternative uses of the assets, the level of maintenance, the number of potential buyers, and the time available for the liquidation process.

There are other ways to obtain security than having a pledge in an asset. For example, a guarantee from the parent company or a subsidiary is another way of obtaining the same type of security. Obviously, the quality of such securities depends on the parent company's or subsidiary's ability to meet potential obligations. Recovery rate averages in case of a corporate default are reported in Table 11.9.

The table reveals that secured debt yields the highest recovery rates. For example, the recovery rate for secured bank debt is 74.1% and only 2.5% for junior subordinated bonds. The statistics also reveal that the recovery rate is on average below 100% for all types of debt. These numbers indicate that the book value of an asset is not necessarily a good proxy for the liquidation value.

Some of the questions that Step 7 should be able to answer include:

- What is the collateral?
- What is the liquidity of the collateral?
- What is the quality of the collateral?
- What is the recovery prospect?

Step 7 provides the analyst with an estimate of the recovery prospects in case of a corporate default.

Table 11.9 Ultimate recovery rate averages from S&Ps, reported in Ganguin and Bilardello (2004)

Instrument type	Average ultimate recovery (%)	Standard deviation	Observations
Secured bank debt	**74.1**	32.4	331
Senior secured bonds	45.8	36.5	42
Senior unsecured bonds	36.8	35.1	198
Senior subordinated bonds	21.3	30.8	116
Subordinated bonds	15.0	24.7	55
Junior subordinated bonds	**2.5**	4.1	4

Step 8: Summarising the results of the credit analysis (credit rating)

Steps 1–7 provide the analyst with an understanding of the exposure at default, the probability of default and an estimate of the recovery prospects. Each step in the credit analysis process therefore provides valuable information to the analyst. Assuming that the analyst is able to obtain reliable estimates of the exposure at default, the probability of default and the probability of recovery, it is possible to estimate the expected loss. For example, assume that the analysis of Rörvik Timber shows that the exposure at default is SEK 100 million. The expected probability of default is between 40% and 50% and the probability of recovery is between 70% and 80% in case of a corporate default. On the basis of these estimates the expected loss on Rörvik Timber is between SEK 8 million and SEK 15 million:

$$\text{Expected loss} = \text{SEK } 100 \text{ million} \times 40\% \times (1 - 80\%) = \text{SEK } 8 \text{ million}$$

$$\text{Expected loss} = \text{SEK } 100 \text{ million} \times 50\% \times (1 - 70\%) = \text{SEK } 15 \text{ million}$$

Banks and credit agencies typically summarise their analyses in a credit rating. Table 11.10 provides an example of such a credit rating and summarises the results of the different steps involved in the credit analysis including the strategic analysis, the financial ratio analysis, the simulation of future cash flows, and the value of the collateral. A weight is assigned to each of these four factors. The weights can be established subjectively, but in most cases they are based on statistical analyses. In the example, the financial ratio analysis is assigned a weight of 20% of the final **credit score** reflecting that it is primarily based on historical information. Simulation of cash flows based on different scenarios is assigned a higher weight of 30%, as it reflects an ex-ante perspective. It is interesting to observe that the indicated rating in the example is 'BBB' while the actual rating is 'A'. The difference reflects an expected improvement in some of the four factors within the next 12 months, which justifies a better rating than current performance supports.

In Table 11.11 we provide an example of a summary of Moody's rating of Carlsberg. The credit rating consists of four factors. The strategic factors are assigned a weight of 45% (22.5% + 22.5%) and the financial factors are assigned a weight of 55% (19% + 36%). Carlsberg's indicative rating is 'Ba', which is equivalent to

Table 11.10 Summary of a credit rating (example)

Industry/company name	AAA	AA	A	BBB	BB	B	CCC
Factor 1: Strategic analysis (20%)							
(a) External risk			x				
(b) Strategic risk				x			
(c) Operation risk					x		
(d) Financial risk			x				
Factor 2: Financial ratio analysis (20%)							
(a) EBIT interest cover (×)		x					
(b) EBITDA interest cover			x				
(c) Free operating cash flow/total debt (%)					x		
(d) FFO/total debt (%)				x			
(e) Return on capital (%)			x				
(f) Operating income/revenue (%)			x				
(g) Long-term debt/capital (%)			x				
(h) Total debt/capital (%)				x			
Factor 3: Simulation (30%)							
(a) Scenario 1			x				
(b) Scenario 2				x			
(c) Scenario 3					x		
Factor 4: Recovery (30%)							
(a) Orderly liquidation value			x				
(b) Distress liquidation value				x			
Rating:							
(a) Indicated rating from methodology				x			
(b) Actual rating assigned			x				

a speculative grade. However, the actual rating is 'Baa', which is equivalent to the lowest rating within investment grades. According to Moody's they expect Carlsberg to meet the following credit metrics by the end of the year and to maintain them: RCF[1] to Net Debt above 18% and the Debt to EBITDA ratio below 3.5. Currently, Carlsberg RCF to Debt is 11.3% and Debt to EBITDA ratio is 4.8. This implies that if Carlsberg cannot meet these thresholds at year end they will most likely receive a speculative grade ('Ba1').

Table 11.11 Moody's credit rating of Carlsberg

Alcoholic beverage industry	Aaa	Aa	A	Baa	Ba	B	Caa
Factor 1: Scale and diversification (22.5%)							
(a) Global net sales		US$11.8					
(b) Diversification by market					x		
(c) Product/brand diversification			x				
Factor 2: Franchise strength and growth potential (22.5%)							
(a) Efficiency of distribution infrastructure				x			
(b) Quality of brand portfolio and market position			x				
(c) Innovation and organic revenue growth				x			
Factor 3: Profitability and efficiency (19%)							
(a) Efficiency/potential for cost reduction			x				
(b) Profitability (EBITA margin)				13.70%			
(c) Return on avg. assets (EBITA/avg. assets)						8.7%	
Factor 4: Financial policy and credit metrics (36%)							
(a) Financial policy				x			
(b) FFO/net debt						13.20%	
(c) Debt/EBITDA						4.8	
(d) RCF/net debt						11.30%	
(e) EBIT/interest expense						2.4	
(f) Free cash flow/debt							1.40%
Rating:							
(a) Indicated rating from methodology					Ba1		
(b) Actual rating assigned				Baa3			

Source: Carlsberg's website.

In Table 11.12 we report the cumulative default rates across different classes of risk. The analysis shows that there is a clear correlation between ratings and default rates. For example, none of the companies (0.00%), which have obtained an 'AAA' credit rating, defaulted in the first year after the rating. On the other hand, 30.95% of the companies assigned a 'CCC' rating defaulted after the first year of a credit rating. The statistics reported in Table 11.12 reveal that the probability of default increases rapidly in the early years of a credit rating. In summary, the default rates reported justify that credit analysis in line with the eight steps matters.

Table 11.12 Cumulative default rates (%) by year after credit rating has been assigned

	Year 1	Year 2	Year 3	Year 4	Year 5	Year 6	Year 7	Year 8	Year 9	Year 10	Year 11	Year 12	Year 13	Year 14	Year 15
AAA	0.00	0.00	0.03	0.07	0.11	0.20	0.30	0.47	0.54	0.61	0.61	0.61	0.61	0.75	0.92
AA	0.01	0.03	0.08	0.17	0.28	0.42	0.61	0.77	0.90	1.06	1.20	1.37	1.51	1.63	1.77
A	0.05	0.15	0.30	0.48	0.71	0.94	1.19	1.46	1.78	2.10	2.37	2.60	2.84	3.08	3.460
BBB	0.36	0.96	1.61	2.58	3.53	4.49	5.33	6.10	6.77	7.60	8.48	9.34	10.22	11.28	12.44
BB	1.47	4.49	8.18	11.69	14.77	17.99	50.43	22.63	24.85	26.61	28.47	29.76	30.99	31.70	32.56
B	6.72	14.99	22.19	27.83	31.99	35.37	38.56	41.25	42.90	44.59	45.84	46.92	47.71	48.68	49.57
CCC	30.95	40.35	46.43	51.25	56.77	58.74	59.46	59.85	61.57	62.92	63.41	63.41	63.41	64.25	64.25

Source: Ganguin and Bilardello, 2004.

Pricing credit risk

In this section we briefly discuss how credit risk translates into risk premiums. In general, the pricing of a loan is affected by the lender's cost of administering and servicing the loan and a premium for the exposure to default risk. (Factors like the lender's cost of borrowed funds and a return on the equity necessary to support the lending operation also affect the risk premium.)

In Table 11.13 we report the spreads (risk premiums) measured over a two-year period across different credit ratings. The spread covers a premium for the exposure to default risk and the administration and service cost. As shown in the table the spreads increase as the credit rating worsens. For example, an 'AAA' rating results in a spread between 0.6% and 1.9% whereas a 'B' rating results in a spread between 2.6% and 13.1%. So if US Treasury 10-year bonds had an interest rate of 3.38% firms with a 'B' grade had to pay up to 3.38% + 13.1% = 16.48%. It supports that lenders and investors require a compensation for higher credit risk.

The large deviation of spreads within a rating reflects the uncertainty on the credit markets due to the financial turmoil in 2008 and 2009. For example, the spread of a 'B'-rated obligation has fluctuated between 3.2% and 13.1%. It is, however, also an indication that spreads do not remain constant over time.

Table 11.13 US industrial ratings and 10-year spread

Adjusted key industrial financial ratios

US industrial long-term debt

Three years median	AAA	AA	A	BBB	BB	B	CCC
EBIT interest cover (x)	21.4	10.1	6.1	3.7	2.1	0.8	0.1
EBITDA interest cover (x)	26.5	12.9	9.1	5.8	3.4	1.8	1.3
Free operating cash flow/total debt (%)	84.2	25.2	15.0	8.5	2.6	−3.2	−12.9
FFO/total debt (%)	128.8	55.4	43.2	30.8	18.8	7.8	1.6
Return on capital (%)	34.9	21.7	19.4	13.6	11.6	6.6	1.0
Operating income/revenue (%)	27.0	22.1	18.6	15.4	15.9	11.9	11.9
Long-term debt/capital (%)	13.3	28.2	33.9	42.5	57.2	69.7	68.8
Total debt/capital (%)	22.9	37.7	42.5	48.2	62.6	74.8	87.7
Number of companies	8	29	136	218	273	281	22

US industrial 10-year spread (two-year high/low) to US Treasury, 10 year

US Treasury, 10 year	AAA	AA	A	BBB	BB	B
3.38%	**1.9**	2.4	3.6	4.7	11.2	**13.1**
3.38%	**0.6**	0.7	0.8	1.3	2.6	**3.2**

Source: Bloomberg

Carlsberg obtained a 'Baa3' rating based on Moody's terminology, which is equivalent to the lowest rating within investment grades. This corresponds to a 'BBB' rating according to the terminology in Table 11.1. The expected 10-year spread on a 'BBB' rated obligation has fluctuated between 1.3% and 4.7% within the last two years with an average of 3% ((1.3% + 4.7%)/2).

Prediction of corporate default using statistical models

This chapter has so far discussed the various steps involved in a fundamental credit analysis approach, where analysts carefully scrutinise important aspects of a firm's financial health. As noted in the introduction statistical models serve as another framework for credit analysis. In this section we will briefly discuss some of the arguments in favour of the statistical models and provide a few examples. For a deeper insight into the statistical models on credit risk, which are also dubbed bankruptcy models, you should consult the relevant literature (see References, page 298).

The prediction of bankruptcies is a complicated process that involves hard work and analytical skills as outlined in Steps 1–8 above. We believe that the prediction of a corporate default based on statistical models cannot substitute for hard work and analytical skills. However, the statistical models are useful in selecting financial ratios for the analysis of corporate defaults. An example of this is the financial ratios used in rating models. Furthermore, the statistical approach may be preferred in cases where the fundamental analysis approach is too costly. Using statistical methods enables lenders to analyse a large number of firms quickly.

The underlying assumption of the statistical models is that meaningful behaviours in financial ratios can be identified allowing the analysts to calculate the probability of a corporate default. In the following section, we describe three different types of statistical models used to predict bankruptcy.

Univariate analysis

Out of 30 financial ratios Beaver (1966) finds six that are useful in predicting the bankruptcy of a firm. The development of these six financial ratios during a five-year period prior to bankruptcy is reported in Figure 11.2. In each graph the average ratio for bankrupt firms is compared with those of comparable firms that did not go bankrupt. Bankrupt firms are depicted with a full drawn line. As shown in the figure the performance of bankrupt firms is poor relative to non-bankrupt firms. For example, the financial ratios are persistently lower for bankrupt firms than for non-bankrupt firms. Furthermore, the financial ratios worsen as the bankruptcy date gets closer. The levels and development of the financial ratios support that they contain useful information in the prediction of a corporate default.

The bankruptcy studies make a distinction between two types of error. A type 1 error classifies a firm as not likely to default when it actually does default. A type 2 error classifies a firm as likely to default when it does not default. Both types of errors are associated with costs to the lender. A type 1 error is costly as the lender risks losing the total debt outstanding. A type 2 error is costly as the lender loses profitable customers and businesses to other lenders.

Type 1 and type 2 errors in Beaver's study are reported in Table 11.14. Five years prior to the bankruptcy there is a 43% (29/(29+33)) chance of a type 1 error; i.e.

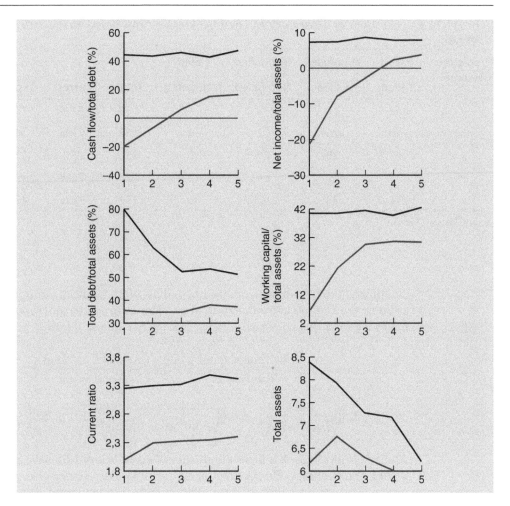

Figure 11.2 Comparison of mean values of six selected financial ratios for bankruptcy firms and non-bankruptcy firms five years prior to bankruptcy
Source: Beaver (1966).

that the lender classifies a firm as not likely to default when it actually defaults. This is not much better than flipping a coin. However, as the bankruptcy date gets closer, type 1 errors are reduced to 22% (17/(17 + 62)). Type 2 errors fluctuate between 3% (2/(2 + 64)) and 8% (6/(6 + 69)).

Multiple discriminant analysis

Multiple discriminant analysis is a statistical technique used to classify an observation into one of several *a priori* groupings – in this case bankruptcy versus non-bankruptcy groups. A multiple discriminant analysis attempts to derive a linear combination of financial ratios which best distinguish between the bankruptcy and non-bankruptcy firms. Based on a sample of firms that went bankrupt in the past and a random sample of firms that did not, the analysis determines a set of discriminant coefficients. These coefficients are then multiplied on selected financial ratios to obtain a so-called Z-score.

Table 11.14 Classifications of bankruptcy and non-bankruptcy firms based on the cash flow to total debt ratio

Predicted outcome	Failed	Non-failed	Non-failed	Failed				
	Failed	Failed	Non-failed	Non-failed	Total	Correct	Type 1	Type 2
1	62	17	75	4	158	87%	22%	5%
2	50	26	71	6	153	79%	34%	8%
3	47	28	69	6	150	77%	37%	8%
4	33	29	64	2	128	76%	47%	3%
5	31	23	60	3	117	78%	43%	5%

Source: Beaver (1966)

Altman (1968) find that from the original list of 22 financial ratios, five are selected as doing the best job in combination of predicting corporate bankruptcy. Altman estimates the following coefficients on each of the five financial ratios:

$$\text{Z-score} = 1.2\left(\frac{\text{Working capital}}{\text{Total assets}}\right) + 1.4\left(\frac{\text{Retained earnings}}{\text{Total assets}}\right)$$

$$+ 3.3\left(\frac{\text{EBIT}}{\text{Total assets}}\right) + 0.6\left(\frac{\text{Market value of equity}}{\text{Book value of liabilities}}\right) + 1.0\left(\frac{\text{Sales}}{\text{Total assets}}\right)$$

Altman (1968) finds that firms obtaining a Z-score below 1.81 have a high probability of going bankrupt. On the other hand, firms with a Z-score above 2.99 have a low probability of going bankrupt. Firms with a Z-score in between 1.81 and 2.99 are in a grey area, and therefore need to be analysed further.

The Z-score classifies 95% of the observations correctly one year prior to the bankruptcy. There is a 6% chance of a type 1 error and a 3% chance of a type 2 error one year prior the bankruptcy, which supports that the model is doing fairly well. The model has subsequently been further improved (Altman 1983).

Logit analysis

Logit regression is an alternative method to the multiple discriminant analysis. It has the advantage of estimating probabilities of bankruptcy. Ohlson (1980) is one of the first attempts using the logit approach. The logit model defines the probability of bankruptcy as follows:

$$\text{Probability of bankruptcy} = \frac{1}{1 + e^{-y}}$$

where

e equals 2.718282

Ohlson's model that predicts bankruptcy within one year defines y as follows:

$$y = -1.32 - 0.407(\text{Size}) + 6.03\left(\frac{\text{Total liabilities}}{\text{Total assets}}\right)$$

$$- 1.43\left(\frac{\text{Current assets} - \text{current liabilities}}{\text{Total assets}}\right) + 0.076\left(\frac{\text{Current liabilities}}{\text{Current assets}}\right)$$

$$- 2.37\left(\frac{\text{Net income}}{\text{Total assets}}\right) - 1.33\left(\frac{\text{Funds from operations}}{\text{Total liabilities}}\right) + 0.285\,(\text{Dummy1})$$

$$- 1.72\,(\text{Dummy2}) - 0.521\left(\frac{\text{Change in net income}}{|\text{Net income}_t| + |\text{Net income}_{t-1}|}\right)$$

where dummy1 is 1 if net income was negative for the last two years and zero otherwise and dummy2 is 1 if total liabilities exceeded total assets and zero otherwise.

The cut-off which minimises the sum of errors is 3.8%. This implies that for values below 3.8% there is a low probability of bankruptcy and for values above 3.8% there is an increased probability of bankruptcy. At the cut-off rate of 3.8%, there is 17.4% chance of a type 1 error and 12.5% chance of a type 2 error.

In Table 11.15 we report the probability of bankruptcy of Rörvik Timber using both Altman's Z-score model and Ohlson's logit model. The Z-score is above the critical level of 2.99 in years 3–5 indicating a low probability of bankruptcy. In year 6, the Z-score is below the critical threshold of 1.81 indicating a high probability of bankruptcy. This supports that the Z-score approach is able to differentiate between high and low probabilities of bankruptcy. However, in the example of Rörvik Timber the signal of a high probability of bankruptcy is not available until the company actually suspends its payments. In that regard, the Z-score model suffers from the same deficiencies as the financial ratios used to measure the short- and long-term liquidity risk in Chapter 7; the signal(s) come too late.

The probability of bankruptcy is well above the cut-off point of 3.5% in the entire period using the Ohlson's logit model, which is an indication of a high probability of bankruptcy. One explanation for the high probability of bankruptcy in the entire period is due to the size variable. In Ohlson's model size plays an important role. Large companies have a lower probability of bankruptcy than smaller companies. Since Rörvik Timber is a relatively small company compared to its US counterparts it biases the probabilities of bankruptcy upwards.

In summary, bankruptcy models as discussed in this section are useful approaches in measuring bankruptcy risk where other methods such as the fundamental credit analysis approach appears too costly. They are also useful in selecting financial ratios for the analysis of bankruptcy. However, they also suffer from deficiencies, for example:

- As demonstrated, financial ratios ought to be compared with peers from the same industry. This implies that coefficients must be estimated at industry levels.
- The studies reported in this section were produced quite a while ago and assuming that the coefficients are not stable across time, it is necessary to generate a new set of coefficients on a regular basis.
- The cut-off score that best distinguishes bankrupt from non-bankrupt firms is based on judgements. Thus, two persons may arrive at different conclusions even if they

Table 11.15 Application of the Z-score model and the logit model to Rörvik Timber

Altman's Z-score model	Year 2	Year 3	Year 4	Year 5	Year 6
Working capital/total assets	0.68	0.77	0.80	0.80	0.63
Retained earnings/total assets	0.00	0.06	0.06	0.12	−0.18
EBIT/total assets	0.05	0.24	0.30	0.50	−0.48
Market value of equity/book value of liabilities	0.16	0.21	0.42	0.35	0.06
Sales/total assets	1.91	1.87	1.78	1.49	1.49
Z-score	2.81	3.15	3.36	3.26	1.52
Probability of bankruptcy	Medium	Low	Low	Low	High

Ohlsson's logit model	Year 2	Year 3	Year 4	Year 5	Year 6
Size (natural logarithm)	−1.17	−1.22	−1.25	−1.32	−1.30
Total liabilities/total assets	4.38	4.57	4.44	4.45	5.22
(Current assets − current liabilities)/total assets	−0.11	−0.07	−0.19	−0.31	0.12
Current liabilities/current assets	0.09	0.08	0.10	0.11	0.07
Net income/total assets	−0.01	−0.10	−0.13	−0.23	0.31
Funds from operations/total liabilities	−0.21	−0.18	−0.03	0.16	−0.06
Dummy1	0.00	0.00	0.00	0.00	2.85
Dummy2	0.00	0.00	0.00	0.00	0.00
Change in net income /($|$Net income$_t| + |$Net income$_{t-1}|$)	0.28	−0.47	−0.11	−0.23	4.74
Intercept	−1.32	−1.32	−1.32	−1.32	−1.32
Value of y	1.93	1.29	1.50	1.31	10.63
Probability of bankruptcy	87%	78%	82%	79%	100%

rely on the same dataset. Further, the cut-score may not be stable across time and may need to be re-calibrated.

- The bankruptcy models purely rely on historical information and do not include forward-looking information. Further, the bankruptcy models do not include qualitative information that inform about the financial health of a company. This is a problem in cases where the qualitative information is not included in the financial ratios. This may involve information about a licence or a patent that is about to expire and which will affect the cash flow negatively.

- Each statistical approach relies on setup assumptions that appear more or less realistic. In cases, where some of these assumptions are violated it may question the validity of the model.

Conclusions

This chapter focuses on corporate credit analysis. The most important points to remember are:

- The expected loss is estimated as exposure at default $\times$ probability of default $\times$ (1 − probability of recovery).
- The fundamental credit analysis approach presents the building blocks that help in analysing a company's ability to pay instalments and interests on its debt in a timely manner. It also includes estimation of the recovery prospects. You should be in a position to identify all essential risks related to a particular company and to measure them through strategic analyses, ratio analysis including benchmarking with peers and through financial forecasts including simulation of different scenarios.
- The prediction of a corporate default involves hard work, analytical skills and a great deal of judgement. It is therefore important to emphasise that corporate credit analysis is an art and not an exact science.
- Credit agencies have created scoring systems to rank credit risk along a continuum, with grades ranging from almost no risk to high risk (firm unable to service its debt). By assigning ratings on a predetermined scale, analysts can benchmark the credit quality across companies from different industries. A particular rating also provides an indication of the premium that would be required for a particular risk, assuming that the market is efficient. The higher risk, the higher the reward will be.
- The statistical models are useful in selecting financial ratios for the analysis of corporate defaults. Further, the statistical approach may be preferred in cases where the fundamental analysis approach appears too costly.

Review questions

- What are the different approaches available for credit analysis?
- How can the potential loss if a firm goes bankrupt be estimated?
- What is meant by exposure at default, probability of default, and probability of recovery in case of default?
- What types of loans are available for companies?
- What are the steps in the fundamental analysis approach (expert-based approach)?
- How do credit agencies rate debt?
- What are the advantages and disadvantages of a fundamental credit analysis approach?
- What are the advantages and disadvantages of using statistical models in credit analysis?
- Why is credit analysis an art and not an exact science?

Note

1 According to Moody's RCF equals funds from operations (cash flow from operations) less preferred dividends less common dividends less minority dividends.

References

Altman, E.I. (1968) 'Financial ratios, discriminant analysis and the prediction of corporate bankruptcy', *Journal of Finance*, September.

Altman, E.I. (1983) *Corporate Financial Distress*, John Wiley & Sons.

Beaver, W. (1966) 'Financial ratios as predictors of failure', *Journal of Accounting Research*, Supplemental, Empirical research in accounting: Selected studies.

Ganguin, B. and J. Bilardello (2004) *Fundamentals of Corporate Credit Analysis*, McGraw-Hill.

Ohlson, J. (1980) 'Financial ratios and the probabilistic prediction of bankruptcy', *Journal of Accounting Research*, Spring.

CHAPTER 12

Accounting-based bonus plans for executives

Learning outcomes

After reading this chapter you should be able to:

- List major issues in designing bonus plans
- Discuss choice of performance measure(s), accounting issues, link between performance and bonus, and bonus threshold
- Discuss accounting issues in designing bonus contracts
- Understand how bonus contracts should incorporate transitory items
- Understand how bonus contracts must take into consideration changes in accounting policies
- Identify the most appropriate measure of performance
- Discuss the most appropriate target level of performance
- Recognise how rewards should be linked to performance

Introduction to executive compensation

Modern corporations are run by managers who typically own only a small fraction of the company's shares. This leads to the well-known agency problem: how do investors (principal) ensure that managers (agent) strive to create shareholder value? Basically, two approaches may come into play. First, the principal may monitor the agent closely. Second, the principal may offer the incentive of compensation. This chapter discusses the second approach or more specifically:

What constitutes an appropriate accounting-based **bonus plan**?

Executive compensation, including bonus plans, has been a topic of considerable controversy in academia and business communities for a number of years. Many find that exorbitant bonuses are unfair. However, the fundamental idea behind bonus plans (executive compensation) is quite straightforward. Bonus plans should align the interests of management (agent) and the owners (principal) and ensure that management act in accordance with a firm's strategy in order to maximise long-term *value creation*.

Bonus plans come in different formats and may be linked to stock market performance, non-financial performance measures or financial performance measures, as depicted in Figure 12.1.

Compensation may be linked to a firm's performance on the stock market. Management may be rewarded options or warrants, which are directly related to the stock price or a cash bonus if the stock price increases to a predefined level as determined

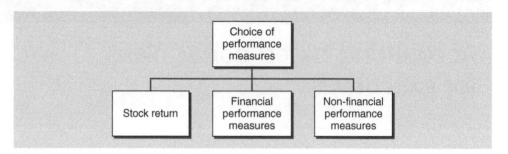

Figure 12.1 Performance measures used in bonus plans

by the bonus contract. Linking rewards to the stock price provides a direct link between management's effort and value creation.

Financial performance measures include numerous absolute earnings measures such as sales, gross profit, EBIT, EBITDA, NOPAT and net earnings as well as relative performance measures such as return on invested capital (ROIC), return on equity (ROE), economic value added (EVA) or similar metrics. Financial performance measures also include various measures of cash flows including the free cash flow and cash flow return on investment (CFROI).

Finally, non-financial performance measures include a variety of measures including, but not limited to, customer satisfaction, employee satisfaction, product and service quality, productivity, process improvements, innovation, leadership and a host of other non-financial measures. Bonus contracts may include several of these non-financial performance measures. In addition, such performance measures are often used in combination with financial performance measures.

As our book examines how accounting is used for decision-making purposes, the focus in this chapter is on bonus contracts based on accounting-based performance measures (i.e. financial performance measures). We discuss specific issues that are relevant in designing and understanding accounting-based bonus plans. For those who are interested in bonuses based on stock prices and non-financial performance measures, there is a rich literature on these topics. Also, while executive compensation is often based on stock options and warrants, such bonus contracts require that market data (i.e. stock prices and stock returns) are available. The majority of firms in most, if not all countries, are non-listed, so such market data are simply not available. Furthermore, stock prices do not provide a good line of sight below top management levels; that is middle management and other employees have little or no control over the bottom line in the income statement and, therefore, the associated cash flows, which ultimately determine firm value and stock prices.

Since managers are often compensated with a base salary and a bonus, firms have to offer a competitive package that offers these components. The bonus should offer managers sufficient compensation to work long hours, take calculated risks and make the necessary unpleasant decisions in order to maximise shareholder value. Stated differently, in order to attract, retain and motivate talented people firms must pay a total remuneration package, which will retain management even during times with poor performance due to market and industry factors. If, for example, performance is poor due to a financial crisis, but management is doing better than expected (say, compared to peers), the firm should try to retain management. Consequently, without a proper compensation package there is a risk that managers choose to leave the firm.

An appropriate bonus plan provides sufficient compensation to retain managers, who achieve above-average relative performance.

This chapter continues as follows: in the next section, we discuss the features of a well-designed bonus plan, followed by a section, which describes and discusses the components of a bonus plan in more detail. An important element in this section is an analysis of the merits and demerits of various accounting metrics used in bonus plans. Finally, a section is devoted to describing various EVA bonus plans; such plans have some desirable characteristics as discussed in this chapter.

Characteristics of an effective bonus plan

As a starting point it should be noted that a one-size-fits-all bonus plan does not exist. Nonetheless, bearing in mind that bonus plans aim at attracting and retaining management, the remuneration board (and managers) should take the following issues into consideration in designing a bonus contract of high quality:

- Congruence (criterion 1)
- Controllability (criterion 2)
- Simplicity (criterion 3)
- Accounting issues (criterion 4).

These criteria are discussed below.

Congruence

A crucial part of a bonus plan is to align the interests of management (agent) and owners (principal). Management should only be awarded a bonus to the extent that they act in the interest of the owners. As a result, the degree of alignment between the objective of the shareholders and the objective of the managers, that is **congruence**, is a major issue to clarify in a compensation system. Accounting-based performance measures used in bonus plans should support corporate strategy in order to maximise shareholder value and, therefore, reflect (true) economic income. Ideally, bonus should reflect value created by management. Value created during a financial year is measured as the difference between firm value at year end and firm value at the beginning of the year plus dividends paid to shareholders. For example, if the stock price is 100 at 1 January, year 1 and 120 at 31 December, year 1 management has been able to create 20 in value.[1] This is naturally under the condition that investors have not paid in additional share capital or received dividends during year 1.

However, unless a firm is listed on a stock exchange, firm value is not known at any date. To determine firm value and calculate value created during a financial year would require that the present value of *all* future cash flows are estimated every year at year end. Naturally, forecasting the amount, timing and risk of such cash flows is at best a difficult task, as we saw in Chapter 8. In addition, reporting poor performance (i.e. a decrease in firm value during a financial year), so that no bonus should be awarded, could be avoided simply by being a bit more optimistic in making the cash flow forecasts. Due to the difficulties in estimating cash flows, various accounting-based performance metrics are used as a proxy for value creation. In accounting language the above implies that a congruent performance measure shall account for earnings, investments (e.g. future cash flows include investments in non-current assets and working capital), account for risk (the cost of capital), and represent unbiased accounting (e.g. cash flows eliminate potential accounting noise for example by adding back depreciation). If so the performance measure(s) becomes a reliable and accurate signal of value creation.

However, unbiased accounting may be difficult to obtain. First, accounting regulation may introduce biases in the reported accounting measures. An example includes the use of FIFO versus average costs when measuring the value of inventory. Second, bonuses based on various earnings measures give management an incentive to change accounting policies and estimates in order to increase bonuses. For instance, management may be tempted to write-off large amounts on assets in periods where they will not be able to meet bonus targets anyway. In that case expenses are charged to current year's income, while making it easier to reach targets in future periods.

Since value is created throughout the lifetime of a company, congruence also demands that managers undertake actions which emphasise the long run. For instance, managers should invest in research and development projects (with a positive net present value) even though the effect on earnings and EVA is negative when the investments are initially made. In practice, obtaining congruence is far more difficult than it sounds as discussed throughout this chapter.

Congruence is paramount in any bonus contract. The other characteristics of a well-designed bonus plan are to no avail, if the bonus plan does not support investors' interest. For instance, a performance measure may be controllable and simple, but if it is not congruent with value creation, such a measure is of little or no use.

Controllability

An important premise in any bonus plan is that there is a strict link between management's efforts and the performance measure bonus is based on. In other words, management should be rewarded only to the extent that they have an impact on firm performance. However, a variety of events cannot be 'controlled' by management. Controllability ensures that managers will not become unmotivated having their pay tied to things beyond their control. Terror, earth quakes, tax rates, interest rates, political inference etc. are just a few examples of events that may affect a firm's performance. A case in point is interest rates that are dependent upon a number of macroeconomic factors beyond management's control. Or consider the corporate tax rate which may change and have changed considerably over time in most countries. How can this be controlled in a bonus contract? Who decides which events are uncontrollable by management? Is it possible at all to separate the (economic) effects from such events? These open questions indicate that the effects of 'uncontrollable events' on bonus should be decided by the compensation committee on a case by case basis.

By eliminating random factors beyond managers' control, managers' actions are measured based on what they can control. Random factors may be removed by adjusting the performance measure(s). However, this may be at the expense of simplicity and introduce adverse effects.

Simplicity

Simplicity suggests that measures, which are simple as well as easy to understand, manage and communicate, should be incorporated into a bonus contract.

Measures actually used by firms, as for instance EBIT and net earnings, are simple and easily understood measures. Such targets are easily tracked. Simple targets may reinforce managers' focus and can be used by compensation committees and investors to monitor managers' actions and to identify their contribution to the success or failure of the firm. Simplicity, therefore, has the potential to limit managers' discretion and reduce the pay to performance gap.

However, overemphasising simplicity may misalign the interests of agent and principal. For instance, simple performance measures like operating profit (EBIT) have several flaws. Growth in EBIT, or similar accounting-based metrics, are not in itself a guarantee of value creation. Also, such measures have a short-term focus and disregard the long-term effects.

Accounting issues

Since reported figures may be a noisy measure of the true underlying performance due to earnings management and/or the inclusion of 'special items', 'transitory items' and the like, it may be argued that reported figures should be properly adjusted to better reflect the 'true' performance. Therefore, in spite of the fact that the calculation of the financial performance measures (e.g. EBIT, ROIC) is fairly simple, such performance measures raise a number of questions on which the decision makers have to take a stance. For instance, should management be awarded or punished as a consequence of:

(a) Transitory or special accounting items such as gains and losses from the sale of fixed assets?
(b) Changes in accounting policies?
(c) Changes in accounting estimates?

Bonus plans that explicitly address the consequences of unusual items and changes in accounting policies and estimates on earnings are considered to be of higher quality than other contracts.

(a) Transitory accounting items

One dollar of earnings is valued differently by shareholders. Earnings generated from the core business (permanent earnings) are regarded as more valuable than earnings based on transitory items (i.e. the impact of changes in accounting principles and unusual accounting items recognised as part of earnings). Examples of elements, which are often labelled 'special items', 'transitory items' or the like, include gains and losses from disposal of assets, restructuring charges, discontinued activities, etc. The treatment of those items raises at least two questions in relation to compensation:

1 Should transitory items affect compensation?
2 Who decides what is considered a transitory item?

These issues are discussed below.

1 Should transitory items be included in performance measures?

If management are paid a cash bonus based on operating measures (e.g. EBIT), it might be argued that 'special items' should be included at least to the extent they are related to core operations. The problem is that it may have a positive NPV (net present value), but a negative effect on this year's performance measure. For example,

303

restructuring or reorganising a firm to better meet the challenge of changing market conditions is clearly an ongoing part of running a business. However, as the following examples illustrate, there is a need to consider these items on a case by case basis.

Example 12.1 **Transitory item should be included in the performance measure**

A group has sold its packaging division after an attractive offer from a competitor. The accounting profit amounts to €250 million. The board (and management) find that they have made an excellent deal, as they believe that they will never be able to get a satisfactory return (that is at least equal to the WACC) on the proceeds from the disposal of the packaging division. The board estimates that the transaction has improved the value of the firm by €100 million. The question is whether the €250 million should be recognised in the accounting measure that bonus is based on. There is no doubt that the accounting profit of €250 million is a transitory item. At the same time investors' real profit is less than €250 million (€100 million). However, management has created value for the investors by selling off the packaging division. Thus, the accounting-based performance measure used in a bonus contract should reflect the profit from disposing of the packaging division. Alternatively, management might be awarded a separate bonus for divestment of the packaging division. ∎

Example 12.2 **Transitory item should not be included in the performance measure**

There are, however, also transitory accounting items that should not be included in the performance measure. A paint producer has just closed down a production line and accordingly experienced a loss of €25 million due to restructuring costs. However, as the expected cost savings are €15 million per year for the next 10 years the total effect is a positive NPV of €67 million (assuming a WACC of 10%). If management does not close down the production line, the owners will forego a profit of €67 million.

The issue here is also a horizon problem – management should act as to secure long-term profitability of the firm. This can be obtained by measuring EBIT exclusive of transitory items that have an effect on future years' performance. Another way to mitigate the horizon problem would be to award management a separate bonus based on the expected profit from closing down the production line. Finally, the horizon problem may be overcome by using multi-period performance measures. ∎

---

2 Who decides if an item is transitory?

A further complication is the question of who eventually decides whether an item is 'transitory' or 'permanent' – the bonus committee or management. A solution to this problem may be to list every transitory item in the bonus contract. However, it seems a daunting task to imagine every possible transaction or event that might be characterised as 'transitory'. Deciding what constitutes a transitory item on a case by case basis is an alternative solution. This solution is also problematic for a number of reasons. For example, it's bureaucratic, and against the principle of simplicity, since it (potentially) leaves the bonus committee and management with an ongoing discussion of which items are *truly* transitory. Therefore, it is difficult to provide a general recommendation on transitory items.

(b) How should changes in accounting policies affect bonuses?

Changes in accounting policies may take place for several reasons. The question is how such changes should be accounted for in bonus contracts. We address two types of changes: mandatory changes and voluntary changes.

Financial statement information shall contain relevant and reliable information and give a 'true-and-fair-view' of a firm's earnings and financial position. This leaves room for management's discretion. *Voluntary changes* in accounting practices (e.g. change in its income recognition policy from the point of sale to the percentage of completion method) may have a significant effect on the reported numbers. Ideally, voluntary changes should only affect bonuses if it improves accounting earnings as a measure of 'true' performance. If the changes distort the measurement of the 'true' underlying performance of the firm, the changes should not affect bonus. At the least, the bonus contract should include clauses that describe how voluntary changes should be accounted for. Since earnings management can be used to increase the validity of earnings measures (by using proprietary information) or manipulate earnings (e.g. paint a rosy picture of the firm), it is not a simple task to control for voluntary changes in a bonus contract.

A prominent example of *mandatory changes* in accounting policies is that all listed companies within the EU must comply with the international financial reporting standards (IAS/IFRS) as of 1 January 2005. Changing from local regulation (e.g. UK GAAP) to international standards had, in many cases, a significant effect on reported earnings. For instance, as a result of the change from amortising goodwill over its useful lifetime to an impairment test only approach companies with significant amounts recognised as goodwill experienced a substantial increase in reported earnings. A bonus plan should include clauses that determine whether and how the bonus should be affected by mandatory changes. For instance, the contract may determine that the bonus plan shall be recalibrated in case of changes in accounting policies.

(c) How should changes in accounting estimates affect bonuses?

Accounting estimates may be changed for a variety of reasons. A few examples are:

- The estimated lifetime of depreciable assets change due to the emergence of new technology
- The write-down of accounts receivables becomes much larger due to a financial crisis.

Should the bonus contract be renegotiated or recalibrated if accounting estimates change? A bonus contract may have a clause that states whether changes in accounting estimates have a material effect on the performance measure, then the contract shall be re-negotiated. This raises the obvious question. When is a change material? If a contract has various clauses which call for recalibration or renegotiation, it may be at the expense of simplicity. If, as a result of the change, the performance measure becomes more in line with value creation, it could be argued that no recalibration of the contract is needed. This raises the obvious question of how the bonus should be affected in the period, where the estimates have been changed.

In summary, a well-designed bonus plan should make managers work in the best interest of the owners. Bonuses should reflect managerial effort and performance, while being simple to understand and communicate to the involved parties. A well-designed bonus plan should also help retain managerial talent at a fair cost and preferably applicable to various market conditions and stages in a firm's lifecycle. Naturally, no single measure of performance satisfies all four criteria. But this provides a useful framework for understanding and designing bonus contracts and points to the fact that it is essential to strike the right balance between the different characteristics, as they may not be in agreement with each other.

These overall guidelines for designing a bonus contract are considered further, as part of the discussion on the components of a bonus plan.

Components of a bonus plan

Executive bonus plans can be categorised in terms of three basic components: (1) choice of **performance measure**(s), (2) choice of **performance standards** and (3) choice of **performance structure** (see, for example, Murphy (2001)).

1 Choice of performance measure(s)
   (a) Does it support the firm's strategy?
   (b) How can it be avoided that management focus solely on short-term performance?
   (c) Should a bonus plan be based on one or multiple performance measures?
2 Choice of performance standards
   (a) Should performance be based on internal or external standards?
   (b) Should bonuses be based on reported earnings, budgets or some other measures, when internal standards are used?
   (c) What are proper benchmarks for external standards?
   (d) What are the pros and cons of internal and external standards?
   (e) How and when should the performance standard be calibrated?
3 Choice of pay to performance structure
   (a) Should bonus be linearly tied to performance without an upper/lower limit?
   (b) Should bonus be non-linear with a minimum (floor) and a maximum (cap)?
   (c) Should bonus be paid as a lump sum?

Essentially, this means that compensation committees at each level of organisational responsibility should address these basic issues:

- What is the most appropriate measure of performance?
- What is the most appropriate benchmark of performance?
- How should bonus be linked to performance?

These issues are discussed in separate sections below. We believe that bonus committees and executives should consider these issues carefully when writing bonus contracts. The issues listed above are often case specific, which makes it difficult to make general recommendations. It is, however, our intention to pinpoint major problems that parties involved in designing bonus contracts may use as a checklist when writing bonus contracts.

Example 12.3 **A bonus plan**

To illustrate the above issues, consider this simplified example of a fictitious bonus plan. The board of directors wishes to implement a bonus plan for the newly appointed CEO. The firm is in a turnaround position and has experienced huge losses in the past. The board of directors has a strong focus on improving operating performance. How could a bonus contract be designed, which takes into consideration that the CEO should pay particular attention to operations? Here is a simple suggestion.

Performance measure

Since the CEO should focus on improving operations, the board of directors decides that EBIT is a proper accounting-based performance measure. By linking bonus to EBIT, the CEO will presumably focus on improving operating performance and pay less attention to how operating activities have been financed.

Performance standard

Once EBIT has been chosen as the performance measure, a proper benchmark or threshold must be decided. The strong focus on improving operating performance made the board of directors choose projected EBIT (an internal standard) as the benchmark.

Performance structure

The board of directors decide that a lump sum of €0.8 million is paid in case that realised EBIT is in excess of projected EBIT.

Accounting issues

The bonus contract states that in case of material changes in accounting policies or accounting estimates, EBIT shall be adjusted. ∎

Is this a well-designed accounting-based bonus plan? Think about this for a few minutes before reading on. We will get back to the example after a discussion on choice of performance measures, performance standards, performance structure and accounting issues.

Choice of performance measures

Choice of performance measures are critical since it has been empirically shown that 'you get what you measure and reward', that is, managers take actions consistent with incentives from those performance measures. Therefore, the performance measure should be tightly correlated to firm value. The right performance measure should influence management decisions and create incentives to pursue the right decisions. Performance measures may be absolute measures ranging from the top line to the bottom line in the income statement and a number of in-between measures such as gross profit, EBIT, EBITDA and EBT. Alternatively, performance measures may be relative measures including such metrics as ROIC, ROE, EVA or benchmarking against a peer group.

Ideally, in an annual bonus plan the performance measure should reflect value created during the year. This would require that the firm's value is estimated at the beginning of the year and at year end. The difference between the two would be value created during the period. Obviously, comparing an ex-post single-period performance measure such as EBIT, ROIC, EVA etc. with a (forward looking) **multi-period performance measure** such as shareholder value added (SVA) is not very useful. EBIT (etc.) and SVA serve two very distinct and different purposes. While EBIT, and similar measures, are short-term performance measures measuring last year's performance, SVA is multi-period performance measure measuring the long-term earnings capacity of a company.

The distinction between EBIT etc. (labelled performance measure in the figure) and SVA is highlighted in Figure 12.2.

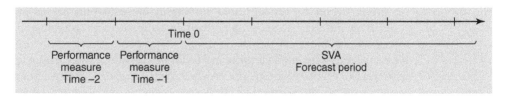

Figure 12.2 Single-period versus multi-period performance measures

The single-period accrual-based performance measure(s) are (partly) backward-looking and measure value creation for short-term intervals. This is in contrast to the cash-flow-based SVA concept, which is both forward looking, takes growth and risk into consideration and measures value creation throughout a firm's lifetime. Therefore, the cash-flow-based SVA concept will emerge as a superior performance measure of earnings capacity in the long term compared to the accrual-based EBIT etc.

The choice of accounting-based performance measures raises some concerns. Accounting-based performance measures provide management with incentives to focus on short-term performance, which in the compensation literature is defined as the 'horizon problem'. Value creation, however, is a long-term phenomenon. Looking at a single year reveals little about the long-term cash-generating ability of a business. Lengthening the performance measurement horizon reduces short-term bias. The horizon issue is especially problematic if management is close to retirement or plan to quit. Management, close to retiring or leaving office, may focus on short-term earnings by, for example, postponing investments in R&D and marketing and avoiding restructuring plans that affect current-year's earnings negatively, but has a positive effect on earnings in future years. As a result, by initiating restructuring, executives may be punished (accounting earnings are lower) even though restructuring is (presumably) sound from an economic point of view.

A related issue is whether one or several measures should be used. Performance measures are frequently incomplete or imperfect representations of the economic consequences of the manager's action. Therefore, the choice of performance measure is not obvious. To avoid that management focuses on short-term profit, one periodic performance measures (e.g. net earnings) might be replaced by a multiple periodic (financial) measure. The use of a **bonus bank** where bonuses are allocated over a number of years may also mitigate the horizon problem. Finally, the bonus contract may include several non-financial measures.

Feltham and Xie (1994) recommend the use of only one performance measure if, and only if, the performance measure is perfectly congruent and noiseless. In other cases, more than one performance measure is recommended. They suggest that increasing the number of performance measures may, first, lead to a rise in the set of workable actions, which may increase the likelihood that a more preferred action will be implemented and, second, may reduce the risk imposed on the agent to make a particular action. Essentially, a multi-dimensional performance measure system may represent a more accurate definition of the organisation's goals.

On the other hand, it is recommended to use only one or a few simple measures in a bonus plan. Using simple targets makes it easier for management to stay focused, for investors or compensation committees to monitor managers' actions, and to identify a manager's success in creating value. Simplicity, therefore, has the potential to limit management discretion and reduce the pay to performance gap. In contrast, complex measures or standards may make managers misallocate effort across tasks or over-complicate the decision-making process. Complexity, therefore, may dilute manager's incentives, encourage management discretion, and widen the pay-to-performance gap.

As many different accounting performance measures are used in compensation contracts, we will move on to discuss the pros and cons of commonly used **absolute performance measures** such as turnover, EBIT, net earnings and earnings per share (EPS). In addition, we also examine the pros and cons of **relative performance measures** such as return on invested capital (ROIC) and economic value added (EVA).

Absolute performance measures

Measures based on accounting numbers have some helpful characteristics that make them useable in bonus plans and explain their prominent role in performance evaluation and compensation. First, management should strive to increase earnings since firm value depends on future earnings (eventually turned into cash flows) (criterion 1). Second, earnings are generally controlled by management. All actions undertaken or initiated by management affect earnings and top management is responsible for 'the bottom line' (criterion 2). Third, earnings are simple measures already reported by firms. Accounting data are easy to communicate and widely understood. By simply studying interim reports or internal reports managers are consistently updated on how their day-to-day actions affect profitability. Fourth, accounting data are verifiable and subject to a variety of internal (internal audit) and external controls (external auditing). Finally, they integrate the results of all organisational activities into a single logical measure.

However, absolute performance measures also have some disadvantages. It is important to note at least four fundamental problems with accounting-based measures of performance. First, earnings are single-period measures whereas economic value is driven by the cash flows generated over the lifetime of the firm or asset. Second, even over a single period earnings correspond poorly to cash flows, since they omit investments in working capital and non-current assets. By ignoring capital investments, earnings do not include total cost required to produce earnings and therefore is not a proper measure of value creation. Third, earnings do not account for risk. As a result, reported earnings of similar size may be of different quality due to differences in risk. Finally, accounting-based performance measures can easily be manipulated (earnings management), questioning their effectiveness as objective measures of management performance.

Net turnover

If growth is desired, for instance because a firm wants to penetrate new markets, turnover might be a relevant performance measure (i.e. management is rewarded based on growth in turnover). The advantage of this measure is that it is unaffected by classification of costs and capitalisation versus expensing of certain forward looking expenses. It might even be argued that turnover is unaffected by accounting policies, so that earnings management is not an issue. On the other hand, it could be argued that accounting policies do matter. Approximately 40% of all accounting restatements in the USA concern revenue recognition. Furthermore, turnover does not account for costs, invested capital and risk. For instance, by acquiring a new company turnover will increase 'automatically', when the two companies merge.

EBIT

EBIT is a highly relevant performance measure, as it measures the outcome of a firm's core business (before tax) regardless of how the company has financed its activities. However, it raises several issues including (but not limited to):

- Should R&D and other forward-looking costs (e.g. marketing costs) be expensed or capitalised?
- How should transitory items be accounted for?
- How should changes in accounting estimates affect compensation?

It is paramount for biotech and high tech firms to invest in R&D to become commercially successful. For those firms recognising investments in R&D as expenses as incurred may make it difficult for management to achieve their bonuses especially for new firms, if they are based on earnings measures such as EBIT.

A further complication is the fact that EBIT only partially accounts for investments (e.g. depreciation and amortisation are expensed). For instance, EBIT growth may be obtained simply by raising additional share capital or increasing interest-bearing debt and investing the proceeds in assets with a return below its cost of capital even though this destroys value (negative NPV).

Net earnings

Net earnings as a performance measure has the advantage that it captures all income and expenses no matter how these items are classified in the income statement. (It should be noted though that some items (also labelled dirty surplus items) bypass the income statement but are included in comprehensive income.) Nonetheless, it raises the same concerns as listed under EBIT. In addition, the effects of capital structure and taxes come into play. A firm may often have a policy of maintaining a certain capital structure leaving little discretion to management. On the other hand, if the capital structure is changed by issuing new capital and repaying interest-bearing debt, earnings increase (cost of capital to the owners is not shown as an expense in the income statement). Should this improvement in earnings affect bonus? If not, how should it be accounted for in the bonus contract?

The corporate tax rate has declined considerably over time in most countries, which has had a positive effect on net earnings. Management has no control over the development in corporate tax rates questioning the wisdom of measuring performance on an after-tax basis.

Earnings per share (EPS)

A popular measure of performance is EPS. This number is also reported consistently in the business press. At first glance it looks like an excellent measure of performance. Naturally, shareholders prefer to earn as much as possible for each share invested in a company. If earnings per share increase, this should increase shareholder value.

However, EPS does not take into account risk, investments and time value of money. In addition, EPS depends on applied accounting policies and does not consider the opportunity cost of capital: if maximisation of EPS is the objective, then every investment pays, as long as it generates a return above the lending rate. In fact, in Chapter 6 we demonstrate that firms may be able to grow EPS, while firm value does not increase.

Relative performance measures

Relative performance measures make it possible to link bonus more directly to value creation. EVA is a prime example. As illustrated in Chapter 9 on valuation, firm value (enterprise value) can be expressed as invested capital plus the net present value of all future EVAs. Therefore, EVA is directly linked to value (criterion 1). Other relative measures include return on invested capital (ROIC) and return on equity (ROE).

Relative performance measures have the advantage of being self-correcting. For example, an extension of the amortisation period for intangible assets results in a higher EBIT (lower amortisation costs) but also in higher invested capital. Accordingly, both the numerator and denominator increase. As another example, consider that leases are reclassified as finance leases: part of the lease payment becomes financial expenses, so EBIT improves compared to treating leases as operating leases. However, invested capital also increases as a lease asset is recognised. In EVA calculations [(ROIC − WAAC) × Invested capital] there are therefore two effects which tend to level each other out. EBIT (or NOPAT) increases (the numerator in ROIC calculations), but so does invested capital (the denominator in ROIC calculations). The exact impact on ROIC, and EVA, depends on the terms in the lease contract such as the duration of the contract, the lifetime of the leased assets and the implicit discount factor.

Using peer performance as a relative performance measure has the further advantage that it protects management from common risk. For example, during a recession firms within a given industry are all hurt the same way. For instance, firms selling consumer durables (cyclical firms) are all likely to experience a huge decline in demands for their products. By benchmarking against competitors, management may still be able to earn a bonus even if performance is 'bad' (but 'good' compared to the industry). This should help in retaining management even in bad times. Also, a bonus plan based on benchmarking against peers is likely to be robust to various market conditions in the sense that common risk factors are controlled for (criterion 2). No calibration of the bonus plan is necessary, since all firms in a peer group face common risk and rewards (whether an upswing or downturn), so these factors are 'filtered-out'.

However, a comparison with a peer group requires that firms are comparable on accounting policies and risk. If they are not adjustments need to be made. As discussed extensively above such adjustments may not be easy to make and must most likely be based on a number of assumptions. Thus the criterion of simplicity (criterion 3) is hardly fulfilled.

More importantly, relative performance measures are single-period measures of performance, and have the same inherent problems as other performance measures that do not consider the long-term effects of management's actions.

ROIC and ROE

Financial ratios such as ROIC and ROE have the advantage that they are easily understood. In comparison to absolute performance measures, they have an additional useful feature: they account for investments (invested capital and shareholders' equity, respectively), but these ratios are still single-period measures and fail to account for risk, which is the cost of capital. By ignoring the cost of capital, accounting measures fail to give an indication of the company's ability to create value. To take risk into account ROIC and ROE may be measured net of cost of capital, which is equivalent to measure EVA.

On the downside, in itself, ROIC and ROE are not reliable signals of value creation. First, returns are single-period earnings measures based on historical book values. Second, these ratios do not account for risk (cost of capital). The level of ROIC and ROE must be compared to the proper cost of capital before it can be determined if value has been created. Third, even if these factors are considered, the problem is that ROIC and ROE measures investors return on *book value* of assets and equity, respectively, while investors want a fair return on their investments measured at *market values*. Obviously, book values and market values may differ significantly. For instance, in a law firm the most valuable assets are the employees of the firm. The value of employees is not recognised in the balance sheet. This makes it fairly easy for law firms to obtain high returns on *book value* of assets, without necessarily earning a nice return on the market value of the firm's true assets. Finally, accounting returns are prone to accounting distortion just like absolute performance measures. It is also problematic that managers may choose not to initiate investments, which have positive net present value, but reduces ROIC or ROE in the short term. Example 12.4 illustrates this point.

Example 12.4 A firm's ROIC is currently 15%, while WACC is assumed to be 10%. These figures tell us that the firm's EVA is positive, so that managers create value. Invested capital amounts to 1,000. Management faces a new business opportunity. They can invest 500 with an expected return of 60; that is ROIC is 12% on the project. Should such a project be undertaken?

Assume that the risk of the project is on par with the risk of the company's existing projects; that is WACC is 10%. Evidently, since ROIC = 12% > WACC = 10%, value is created. What happens to ROIC?

As demonstrated in Table 12.1, investment in the new project has a negative effect on ROIC. The combined ROIC becomes $2/3 \times 15\% + 1/3 \times 12\% = 14\%$, a decrease of exactly 1%. In conclusion, if managers are rewarded based on the level of or improvement in ROIC or similar measures, they may choose to reject projects with positive NPV. ∎

Table 12.1 **The effect on ROIC when adding projects**

	Existing project	New project	Combined projects
Invested capital	1,000	500	1,500
Return	150	60	210
ROIC	15%	2%	14%

EVA (Economic Value Added)

In its pure form, EVA seems to be the ideal performance measure. Economic profit (economic value added) is not obtained until all capital providers have been compensated. Therefore, unlike accounting measures of earnings, EVA measures economic profit by reducing profit with the cost of debt *and* cost of equity. The popularity of EVA as a performance measure is probably due to the alleged advantages of EVA compared to other accounting-based performance measures (e.g. EBIT). Advantages of EVA include:

- Consistent with value creation
- Motivates management to invest in projects with rates of return above the cost of capital
- Cost of capital becomes visible for management
- Objective measurability ex-post
- General applicability (firm level, divisional level etc.)
- Simple to communicate.

EVA is claimed to be the best surrogate for or the predictor of future share price performance; an increase in EVA should therefore result in an increase in firm value. As illustrated in Chapter 9 on valuation, firm value equals invested capital plus the present value of future EVAs. Therefore maximising EVAs is equivalent to the maximisation of discounted cash flows and firm value. That is EVA is directly linked to value creation. However, unlike DCF, which is inherently an ex-ante measure, EVA can be used as an ex-post measure. This should lead to goal congruence between equity holders and managers.

Even though EVA from a theoretical point of view has its merits as a measure of a firm's value creation (economic profit), it's not a perfect measure. First, it needs to be recognised that EVA remains a historic income measure and does not anticipate future earnings or losses. Second, EVA is prone to accounting distortion. In fact, the EVA literature recommends a host of accounting adjustments (more than 150!) before calculating EVA. For instance, EVA adjustments include capitalisation of certain expenses (marketing costs and research and development costs), adding back of amortised goodwill, and adding deferred tax liabilities to equity. At best it is a daunting task to make an assortment of adjustments so that EVA becomes an economic meaningful performance indicator.

To avoid this tedious task of adjustments, bonus may, alternatively, be based on the change in EVA from year to year. In this case, a low (high) initial invested capital due to, say, conservative (aggressive) accounting initially produces high (low) EVA figures. A positive change in EVA, consequently, requires an even higher future level of EVA, whether or not current EVA is low (aggressive accounting policies) or high (conservative accounting policies). If you reward management for improving EVA, it really doesn't matter what value you assign to the assets. This implies that rewarding growth in EVA is not prone to accounting distortion.

Second, EVA does not take the *horizon problem* (single- *vs* multiple-period performance measures) into consideration in the sense that it only considers the effects of transactions on the current year's financial statements and cannot accurately reflect the impact of decisions that may have implications over several periods. Restructuring costs, for example, have a negative effect on the current year's EVA (unless these costs are capitalised in which case the effect is less) even though future periods' EVA may improve, so that initiating restructuring costs has a positive effect on firm value (the project's NPV is positive). In fact, findings in extant EVA literature question whether EVA is a better measure of value creation than (various) earnings figures. For instance, Biddle et al. (1996) find that on average EVA does not dominate earnings as a performance measure in explaining stock price developments.

Furthermore, it can easily be shown that capital investment decisions that have a positive net present value (NPV) and which should add value to the firm do not necessarily yield positive accounting profits, return on investments or EVA in every period of the project's life. The only way to ensure such an outcome would be to value the assets (investment) at net present value of their expected cash flows. Although this is acceptable in economic decision-making terms, it is not feasible from the viewpoint of reporting performance, and as such measures would be overly subjective. For example, a manager could improve reported performance merely by making slightly optimistic estimates of the outcome of future events. Second, when multiple periods are considered, historical earnings only represent the true growth in value of a business if the assets it possesses are valued in terms of future expectations rather than historical costs. That is, GAAPs would have to be cast aside and assets valued at the NPV of their future cash flows. At the very least, such an approach requires a great deal of subjective judgement on the part of managers, and is therefore open to significant manipulation.

In summary, accounting-based performance measures have the characteristics shown in Table 12.2. Based on the table, the conclusion is fairly clear. Metrics such as EVA and residual income, which aim at measuring economic profit, appear superior to other accounting-based measures of performance.

Table 12.2 Characteristics of accounting-based performance measures

Criterion function	Earnings measures (e.g. EBIT, net earnings)	Return measures (e.g. ROIC, ROE)	Economic profit (e.g. EVA, RI)
Congruence			
Ability to account for invested capital	Low	High	High
Ability to account for risk	Low	Low	High
		Risk may be accounted for by comparing ROIC and ROE to cost of capital, but this is equivalent to measuring economic profit (EVA, RI)	EVA takes the cost of debt and the cost of equity into consideration
Reliable signal of value creation	Low	Low	Medium
			EVA is a signal of value creation, but projects with positive NPVs may have negative EVAs in some years
Controllability	Medium	Medium	Medium
	Management has control over everything that enters the bottom line but outside factors are not controlled for (e.g. a recession)	Management has control over everything that enters the bottom line but outside factors are not controlled for (e.g. a recession)	Management has control over everything that enters the bottom line but outside factors are not controlled for (e.g. a recession)
Simplicity	High	High	Medium to low
	Easy to understand and measure	Easy to understand and measure	Generally easy to understand, but adjustments and calculation of cost of capital complicates the calculation of economic profit
	Already reported by the firm	Typically reported by the firm	Requires a substantial communication effort
No. of accounting issues	High	High	High/Low
	Prone to earnings management	Prone to earnings management	If absolute EVA is used, accounting policies matter a great deal
	Accounting for special items is problematic	Accounting for special items is problematic	If change in EVA is used, accounting policies and estimates matter to a lesses extent

Choice of performance standards

After the performance measure(s) has been established, a threshold to gauge performance against must be set. Murphy (2001) argues that bonuses in practice are based on performance measured relative to a performance standard; i.e. a benchmark.

Arguably, a high level of, say, turnover or EBIT does not in itself suggest that value is created neither in the short term nor in the long term. For performance measures to be useful there must be a standard of comparison, for example past performance or performance of comparable firms or industries (peer-groups). Performance standards typically correspond to 'expected performance' or, more precisely, the level of performance required for a bonus to be earned, the so-called 'target bonus'.

Benchmarking may be based on two types of standards:

- Internal standards
- External standards.

These two types of standards are discussed below.

Internal standards

'Internally determined' standards are directly affected by management actions in the current or prior year. Internal standards are standards where the performance measure is compared to an internal performance measure. 'Budget standards' include bonus plans based on performance measured against the firm's projected performance. 'Prior-year standards' is another example and include plans based on an improvement in realised sales, operating earnings, net earnings, earnings per share (EPS) etc. from last year. A third example of an internal standard is a comparison of realised earnings with the cost of capital. For instance, EBIT (return on invested capital, ROIC) may be compared to the weighted average cost of capital (WACC). Alternatively, net earnings (return on equity, ROE) may be compared to investors' cost of capital. Furthermore, 'discretionary standards' include plans where the performance targets are set subjectively by the board of directors following a review of the company's business plan, prior-year performance, projected performance, and a subjective evaluation of the difficulty in achieving projected performance. Finally, 'timeless standards' include plans measuring performance relative to a fixed standard (such as an 8% return on assets, where the '8%' is constant across years, or moves in a predetermined way independent of actual performance, say, it must increase by 0.1% per year). This leaves the following five internal standards:

- Budget standards
- Prior-year standards
- Realised earnings versus cost of capital
- Discretionary standards
- Timeless standards.

A short discussion of these standards merits and demerits follow below.

Budget standards

Comparing performance to an approved budget seems to be a proper performance standard. For instance, if market penetration is high on the agenda, turnover may be the relevant performance measure. A measure for turnover could be the approved budget effectively linking bonus to growth in turnover. Likewise, EBIT or other earnings measures could be linked to budget.

There are many downsides of using budgets. First, if market conditions change dramatically it may be difficult for management to reach budget target(s). Second, performance standards cause problems whenever managers, whose performance are measured relative to the standard, have an influence over the standard-setting process as with budgets. This may encourage them to bias the budget downwards to make it easier to beat the budget. Third, if management realise that budget cannot be reached, they may engage in earnings management. If management performs well below budget next year's budget may reflect past year's actual performance (which is poor due to earnings management) making it easier for management to fulfil the budget next year. Similarly, standards based on budgeted performance lead to earnings management, since managers know that good current performance will be penalised in the next period through an increased performance standard. This may make managers avoid actions this year that might have an undesirable effect on next year's budget. Finally, using budgets as a standard almost inevitably lead to discussions about performance targets. This makes the budget process unnecessarily bureaucratic.

Prior-year standards

From a pure criterion of costs (cost–benefit analysis) associated with measuring performance, standards based on past performance should be preferred since historical performance data are easily available.

Past performance may, however, be a poor standard to gauge performance against. Evidently, during an economic upturn past performance is easier to 'beat', while during downturns it is hard or impossible for management to improve past performance. A further pitfall of using prior years' performance as a benchmark is that management may engage in earnings management. For example, if management realises that the past year's performance cannot be beaten, they may be tempted to take a 'big bath'. They do not receive a bonus anyway, but they increase the likelihood of obtaining a bonus next year. This is due to the fact that this year's performance is going to be poor (as a result of the 'big bath'), but also due to the fact that future expenses have been recognised this year (another consequence of the 'big bath').

Realised earnings versus cost of capital

Essentially, these measures quantify value creation by calculating EVA. For example, net earnings (return on equity, ROE) may be compared to investors' cost of capital (required rate of return, r_e). If ROE $> r_e$, residual income is positive. Alternatively, ROIC may be compared to WACC; if ROIC exceeds WACC, EVA is positive. Therefore, using cost of capital as a benchmark introduces the same issues (benefits and pitfalls) as using EVA or other measures of economic income.

A major problem in using cost of capital as a benchmark is that it has to be calculated. Investors' cost of capital (investors' required rate of return) is not known, and this is also why investors' cost of capital is not recognised in the income statement. Cost of capital must therefore be estimated. As discussed in Chapter 10 on cost of capital, calculating cost of capital hinges on a number of assumptions and estimates. Also, ideally, cost of capital should be calculated for each new project, if these projects have a risk profile which is material different from the risk profile of a firm's remaining businesses. A related issue is how cost of capital shall reflect changes in interest rates or other economic conditions. For example, should WACC or investors' required rate of return be adjusted to accommodate for changes in interest rates? Finally, using cost of capital as a benchmark may trigger discussions among business units or divisions. Management of such units would probably argue that they have a low cost of capital.

Discretionary standards

'Discretionary standards' have a great advantage. They are flexible and can be altered to reflect various business and market conditions. During a financial crisis the performance target may be substantially lower than under a boom. If the board wants to pursue a higher market share, albeit at the expense of lower current earnings, they may reward management based on sales growth. The problem with discretionary standards is that they are very subjective and may not be transparent for management; i.e. it is difficult for management to identify the performance criteria.

Timeless standards

Timeless standards are not as easily influenced by the participants in the bonus plan, which is a valid argument for using such standards.

However, even these standards are influenced to some degree, such as when the timeless standards are initially set or the external peer group initially defined. Furthermore, timeless standards may be disconnected to the real world due to changes in a firm's risk profile or the level of interest rates.

External standards

External standards are standards that are defined in relation to elements outside the firm and include benchmarking against competitors. 'Peer group' standards include performance measured relative to other companies in the industry or market; often a self-selected group of peer companies. Such performance measures include, but are not limited to, sales, operating earnings, net earnings, ROIC, ROE or EVA. A benefit of this comparison is that macroeconomic factors are 'evened out'. If ROIC, for example, is at an all time high due to an economic upturn, competitors are also likely to perform exceptionally well, effectively limiting the size of bonus. Murphy (2001) finds support for the use of external standards. He finds that income smoothing is prevalent in companies using internal standards (e.g. budget and last year's result), but not in companies using external standards. This suggests that bonus plans based on external standards better capture the value contribution of management.

Even though external standards have its merits, the use of such standards raises some concerns. For instance, which firms can be regarded as truly comparable firms? Since management (or bonus committees) has some discretion in picking the peer group, there is a risk that firms which perform well below the industry norm are chosen. Furthermore, using external standards hardly makes performance contracts simple (criterion 3) and it may be costly to measure performance. The reason why contracts based on benchmarking against peers are not simple is the fact that these peers shall have the same risk profile and comparable accounting policies. If not, adjustments need to be made. In addition, comparable firms are also likely to recognise income and expenses, which should be regarded as transitory (and therefore excluded before making the comparison). Who decides which items to classify as transitory? Taking care of such items requires that peer group financials are properly adjusted making the bonus contract costly and complicated. If the use of external standards becomes too complicated, there is a risk that the incentive from the bonus plan vanishes. Ultimately, it may result in a bonus plan that does not motivate the management.

In summary, internal and external standards have the characteristics shown in Table 12.3. Based on the table it is difficult to recommend the use of one of the types of standards at the expense of the other. Controllability seems to favour the use of external standards, but they are not as simple to understand and communicate as internal standards. Furthermore, differences in what is regarded as transitory items and accounting practices need to be adjusted for.

Table 12.3 Characteristics of internal and external standards

	Internal standards	External standards
Congruence	Medium	Medium
	Cost of capital is theoretically the right benchmark	Beating competitors signals better performance than in the industry
	Estimation problems in calculating cost of capital	Beating competitors does not ensure value creation
	Beating budget or last year's earnings does not guarantee value creation	
Controllability	Medium	High
	Management is responsible for and controls everything that enters into the budget or last year's performance	Common non-controllable factors are accounted for (e.g. interest rates, growth, inflation etc.)
	Whether budget or last year's performance is used certain market factors are outside management control	
Simplicity	High	Low
	Budget or last year's earnings are measures that are easy to understand and communicate	The choice of peer group is problematic. For example, what if the firm is a conglomerate?
No. of accounting issues	Medium	High
	Management may bias budget	Peer group financials may have to be adjusted to account for differences in transitory items and accounting practices
	Prone to earnings management	

Choice of pay to performance structure

An open question in designing bonus contracts is how bonus should be tied to performance. For instance, should a bonus be linear in the sense that there is no upper or lower limit to the size of the bonus or should it be non-linear with a cap and a floor, so that bonuses are restricted to fall within a certain interval? The following represents pay-to-performance structure contracts:

1 Linearity between performance and bonus.
2 Non-linearity with a minimum and a maximum bonus.
3 A lump sum bonus.

These issues are discussed below.

Linearity between performance and bonus

At first glance, linearity seems to be the proper way to link bonus to performance. The better the performance (in whatever way it's measured), the higher the awarded compensation. In fact, extant literature suggests that the pay-to-performance structure should be linear since it mitigates the incentive to manage the performance measure. Figure 12.3 illustrates a simple pay-off profile. Based on this figure there is no upper limit to the bonus that management may be rewarded. But the plan also

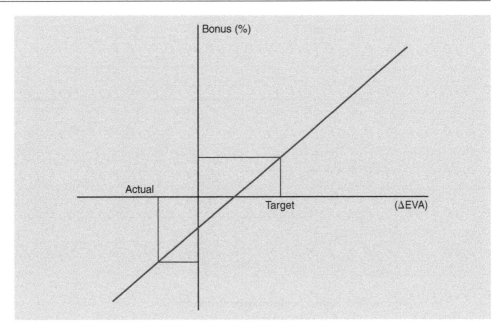

Figure 12.3 **A simple pay-off profile**

dictates that if performance falls well short of target performance (negative bonus), management may have to pay back their salaries in part or in full. For example, in Figure 12.3 the actual bonus would be negative. It is highly unlikely that anyone would enter such a contract.

In addition, compensation committees must consider issues such as: Is it reasonable that compensation may be exorbitant if performance is excellent due to a bull market? What if the performance is excellent, but the main competitors are performing even better? What if the company has negative earnings? Does this imply that bonus should be negative? In this case should the negative bonus be off-set against future positive bonuses (bonus bank)? If so would it be at the expense of increased retention risk?

Non-linearity

Another possibility is to limit the bonus to a certain range (floor and cap), so that it is capped. In between the minimum and maximum bonus, the correlation between performance and bonus is linear (but could in principle be concave, convex or any other form). The advantage of such a method is that it regulates a non-perfect bonus contract (criteria 1, 2 and 4), while it should still be possible to pay a competitive salary, if the bonus contract is properly calibrated. For instance, during a boom performance may be excellent due to an extraordinary high demand for the firm's products. By capping the bonus it does not become exorbitant due to factors outside management's control. Also, these thresholds (floor and cap) do help to avoid certain undesirable behaviours (exploitation of the system in the short term) but also encourage others (smoothing of performance from one year to the next), as described shortly.

To illustrate a non-linear pay-to-performance structure, consider Figure 12.4. Under a typical plan, no bonus is paid until a threshold performance (usually expressed as a percentage of the performance standard) is achieved, and a 'minimum bonus' (usually

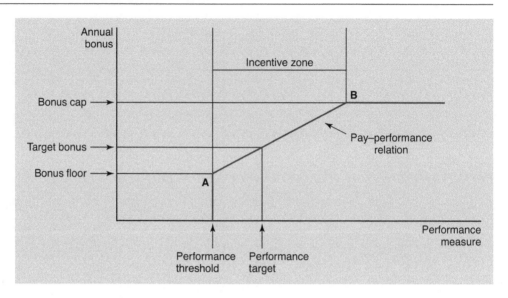

Figure 12.4 Pay-to-performance structure

expressed as a percentage of the target bonus) is paid at the threshold performance. Target bonuses are paid for achieving the performance standard, and there is typically a 'cap' on bonuses paid (again expressed as a percentage or multiple of the target bonus). The range between the threshold (floor) and cap is labelled the 'incentive zone', indicating the range of performance achievement where marginal improvement in performance corresponds to marginal improvement in bonuses. In summary, a typical bonus plan with a cap and a floor has these elements:

1 A target bonus plan for achieving target financial performance, for example projected operating profit.
2 A threshold level of performance that must be attained before any bonus is earned (floor).
3 A cap on the bonus payout.

Since bonuses are based on cumulative annual performance (e.g. EBIT, budget realisation), and since managers can revise their daily effort and investment decisions based on assessments of year-to-date performance, the non-linearities in the typical bonus plan cause predictable incentive problems. Non-linear bonus plans provide the executives with an incentive to manage earnings. In particular, if year-to-date performance suggests that annual performance will exceed that required to achieve the bonus cap, as depicted by 'B' in Figure 12.4, managers will withhold effort and will attempt to 'inventory' earnings for use in a subsequent year (Healy 1985).

If, on the other hand, year-to-date performance suggests that performance will be far below the floor, depicted by 'A' in Figure 12.4, management may be tempted to take a 'big bath' (e.g. make too large provisions for restructuring, depreciate and amortise assets too quickly etc. in order to improve future profitability). Since managers have no incentive to work hard they may even plan to reduce the performance further, in order to lower the budget standard (or any other benchmark used in the bonus plan) in the following year. Research documents that floors and caps on bonus contracts provide incentives to shift reported earnings between periods (Healy 1985).

Finally, when expected performance is moderately below the incentive zone, the discontinuity in bonus payments at threshold yields strong incentives to achieve the performance threshold (through counterproductive earnings manipulation as well as through hard work), because the pay–performance slope at the threshold is effectively infinite.

Lump sum

Alternatively, bonus may be paid out as a lump sum, if management are able to perform as stipulated in the bonus contract. It is critical in this respect that if executives during the year find it hard to reach their target, they may not be motivated to work in the best interest of the company's owners. When it becomes obvious that the year-to-date performance suggests that annual performance will exceed that required to achieve the maximum bonus, managers may withhold effort and try to store earnings for use in subsequent years, for example by delaying sales efforts, incurring restructuring expenses that could have waited until next year, investing heavily in R&D projects at year end or recognising impairment losses by using conservative estimates. Lump sum bonuses thus have the same problems as non-linear bonus plans.

In summary, the pay-to-performance structure has the characteristics outlined in Table 12.4. Does the summary in the table suggest that a bonus contract should be capped (non-linear) or uncapped (linear)? Congruence favours linearity since management should keep up the good work even if performance is above target and there is little risk of earnings management since there is no need to keep performance within a band (cap and floor). Simplicity and accounting issues also seem to point to the use of linearity in the bonus contract. Controllability issues seem to favour a non-linear bonus plan. Furthermore, imperfect bonus plans suggest that bonus should be capped.

Table 12.4 Characteristics of the pay-to-performance structure

	Linearity	Non-linearity (cap/floor)
Congruence	High	Medium
	High management effort as bonus is not capped	Regulates an imperfect contract
	Little risk of earnings management as bonus is not capped even if performance is extremely high	Low management effort if performance is above/below threshold
	Poor performance is penalised	Risk of gaming/earnings management
	Does not have a 'mechanism' that reduces the impact of imperfect bonus plans	Poor performance is not penalised
Controllability	Medium	Medium/high
	Bonus may be too high (low) due to uncontrollable events	Regulates a non-perfect contract
Simplicity	High	Low
	Direct link between performance and bonus	Setting floor/cap is tedious and prone to distortion
No. of accounting issues	Medium/Low	High
	No earnings management	Risk of earnings management
	Risk that transitory items are not effectively eliminated making bonus too high/low	

EVA-based bonus contract – a feasible solution to accounting-based performance measures

Before discussing EVA as a performance measure let us revisit Example 12.3 (p. 306). While the contract outlined in the beginning of the chapter may seem reasonable it opens a number of issues including:

- EBIT does not take invested capital or risk into consideration.
- The CEO may be able to bias target performance (projected EBIT).
- The CEO is rewarded and punished for factors outside his or her control (business conditions, inflation, etc.).
- The CEO may engage in earnings management if there is a risk that realised earnings become far in excess of or far below forecast EBIT.
- The contract does not consider the effects of special items or changes in accounting policies and estimates.

In summary, it is not as good a bonus contract as initially believed. It is easy to understand and communicate but has several shortcomings including a lack of alignment of the interests of management and owners.

As discussed above EVA-based bonus plans, while not perfect, are commonly used and probably a reasonable bet if accounting-based performance measures are to be used in bonus plans. EVA bonus plans come in many flavours. We do not intend to illustrate all of them, but concentrate on two of the popular ones named the xy plan and the modern bonus plan, respectively.

The xy plan

In the xy plan bonus consists of two components. A bonus calculated as a percentage of the change in EVA during a financial year (x component), no matter whether the bonus becomes negative or positive, and an additional bonus calculated as a percentage of actual EVA, but only if EVA is positive (y component). We have illustrated the xy plan by using a simple example.

Example 12.4 An illustration of an xy plan

Bonus = x% × change in EVA + y% × EVA

x = A percentage change in EVA, no matter whether the change is positive or negative

y = A percentage of EVA, if EVA is positive, and 0% if EVA is negative

Assume that x is 10% and y is 5%. Bonus over a 5-year period may be calculated as shown in Table 12.5. If managers improve EVA, there is an immediate reward (bonus) coming from the first term. This is the case even if EVA is negative. Therefore, even during bad times or following a recession, management may be awarded a bonus if they can improve profitability (a positive change in EVA) even if EVA has still not become positive. EVA improvement goals give incentives to restructure the company without discouraging the manager. They represent the achievable improvements.

Table 12.5 *xy* bonus plan

	Year 1	Year 2	Year 3	Year 4	Year 5
EVA last year	10.0	12.0	15.0	10.0	−10.0
EVA this year	12.0	15.0	10.0	−10.0	31.0
Change in EVA	2.0	3.0	−0.5	−20.0	41.0
x: 10% × ΔEVA	0.2	0.3	−0.5	−2.0	4.1
y: 5% × EVA	0.6	0.8	0.5	0.0	1.6
Total bonus	0.8	1.1	0.0	−2.0	5.7

The second term ensures that management is compensated for sustaining EVA. For instance, in year 2 the reward from *y* becomes 0.75 (rounded to 0.8 in Table 12.5) due to the *level* of EVA. The above contract rewards both the level of and development in EVA over time. Of course, if EVA falls, there is also an immediate and sustained penalty, as the bonus becomes negative. It is unlikely that management in that case is willing to forgo (or pay back) base salary. To overcome this problem a bonus bank may be used as discussed below.

As long as EVA is negative *y* is zero. In this case, *x* should make managers concentrate all their effort on improving business performance, since they can only obtain their bonus based on a positive change in EVA and not on the level of EVA. In practice, *x* and *y* are set in accordance with the fundamentals of the business and the target levels of compensation for the participating managers. ∎

The implementation of bonus contracts may require the use of a 'bonus bank' (deferred compensation as further illustrated below) to take account of 'negative bonuses' and to create long-term incentives (extending managerial horizon). Banking strikes the optimal balance between short-term and long-term goals of the firm. For instance, in year 4 (see Table 12.5) total bonus would be negative (−2.0) without a bonus bank. This would mean that managers had to repay bonuses (or salaries) earned in the past. Not a very feasible solution in practice.

A bonus bank separates the calculation of the bonus from its actual payment. The basic idea is that bonuses are not being paid in full unless a satisfactory performance is obtained in subsequent years. While bonuses are calculated for each period (typically a year), the bonus bank levels the bonus out in accordance with the time frame used in the bonus bank (e.g. every year, one-third of the accumulated bonuses will be paid if the bank functions on a three-year basis). Table 12.6 illustrates this mechanism.

Table 12.6 An example of a bonus bank

	Year 1	Year 2	Year 3	Year 4	Year 5	Total
Bank beginning of period	100.0	80.0	80.0	60.0	60.0	100.0
Bonus earned	20.0	40.0	10.0	30.0	0.0	100.0
Available for payout	120.0	120.0	90.0	90.0	60.0	200.0
Payout (ratio one-third)	40.0	40.0	30.0	30.0	20.0	160.0
Bank end of period	80.0	80.0	60.0	60.0	40.0	40.0

Before any bonus is paid out, the bonus must pass through a bank account that starts with an opening balance, which in this case is 100. The initial credit in the bank corresponds to a fictitious amount granted to management and subsequently to accumulated funds not yet paid. Without an opening balance, a negative bonus in year 1 would mean that the bank was underfunded. This opening balance may arise in three different ways. First, it may just be part of the formula that determines the bonus, but is unfunded (i.e. no money is deposited in the bank account). Second, it may be contributed by managers who participate in the bonus plan and put at risk, essentially meaning that they could lose the 100 just as investors can lose their entire investment. Finally, the firm may loan the 100 to the managers' bank account subject to amortisation over, say, 5 years. Then in each of the first 5 years of the bonus plan, 20 of the bonus amount that would otherwise be paid are retained to pay off the loan of 100. By the end of year 5, 100 of equity will have accumulated in the bank account to replace the debt. This is basically equivalent to a leveraged buyout.

In each year, the bonus available for payout is calculated as the opening balance plus the bonus earned during the year. In the illustrative plan in Table 12.6 one-third is paid out and the remaining is banked forward. For example, in year 1 the total amount available for payout was 120 consisting of 100 (the opening balance) plus 20 (bonus earned during the year). With a payout ratio of one-third, managers are paid 40 leaving 80 in the bank account. This procedure continues in the following year and so on. The idea behind the bonus bank is multi-stringed:

- Smoothing of bonus payments (less fluctuation in strongly volatile industries)
- Bonus is based on long-term value creation since profits out of a project are not paid out immediately and can be offset by negative profits in later periods
- Good performance is rewarded
- Bad performance is penalised.

The banking of the bonus helps to align the interests between agent and principal in the long term. Suppose that management may perform according to target ('target year'), overperform ('good year') or underperform ('bad year'). These three scenarios are illustrated in Table 12.7.

Table 12.7 **Bonus bank: different scenarios**

	Target year	Good year	Bad year
Bank beginning of period	100.0	100.0	100.0
Bonus earned	25.0	100.0	−50.0
Available for payout	125.0	200.0	50.0
Bonus paid (ratio one-third)	41.7	66.7	16.7
Bank end of period	83.3	133.3	33.3

As is evident, bonus paid and the balance on the bank account is vastly different depending upon the performance. For example, in a bad year bonus is still being paid, since the bank balance before payout is still positive, but lower due to the negative bonus earned. This is equivalent to shareholders experiencing capital losses. Furthermore, actual bonus paid (16.7) is much lower than under a 'normal year' (target year). Again, a comparison to shareholders' returns in a bad year can be made. The lower bonus payout mimics a cut in dividends.

Good calibration of a bonus system is obviously a determining factor. Successive mediocre performance results can stem from a recession affecting all firms in an industry, so that managers running the firm are not to blame. That is why such contracts often include discretionary exit clauses, to prevent the relevant managers from leaving. Managers who leave the firm on their own will not necessarily be paid the accumulated amounts in their bank account. Broadly speaking a bonus bank is similar to having some accumulated stocks in the company and receiving some dividends related to performance.

The modern EVA bonus plan

More recently the *xy* **bonus plan** has been modified, leaving the following **modern EVA bonus plan** (or so it is called in the literature). According to the plan, bonus consists of a target bonus paid if a predetermined target is obtained plus an additional bonus for improvement in EVA in excess of an expected increase in EVA:

$$\text{Bonus} = \text{Target bonus} + y\% \times (\Delta\text{EVA} - \text{EI})$$

where

$$\text{Target bonus} = \text{Bonus for achieving expected EVA improvement}$$
$$\text{EI} = \text{Expected EVA improvement}$$
$$\Delta\text{EVA} - \text{EI} = \text{Excess EVA improvement}$$

In this plan, the performance measure is excess EVA improvement. There are several reasons for the popularity of this plan. For instance, EVA improvement is a measure that applies to all companies, not just companies with positive EVA. Also, EVA improvements provide a more direct link to excess returns, the ultimate measure of wealth creation. Whenever a company's market value includes the value of future growth (and not just the value of current operations), EVA improvements are necessary for a firm's investors to earn a cost-of-capital return. The bonus earned is the sum of a target bonus plus a fixed percentage of EVA improvement, which can be positive or negative.

A target bonus is necessary to make the bonus plan consistent with the labour market practice of paying a substantial bonus for normal or expected performance, thus limiting retention risk. The bonus earned can be negative and is uncapped on both the upside and downside. In addition, the bonus earned is credited to a bonus bank, and the bonus bank balance, rather than the current year bonus earned, determines the bonus paid. Typically, the payout rule for the bonus bank is 100% of the bonus bank balance (if positive), up to the amount of the target bonus, plus one-third of the bank balance in excess of the target bonus. When the bonus bank balance is negative, no bonus is paid. Table 12.8 illustrates how it works.

In years 1 and 2 management has been able to obtain at least 'expected EVA improvement' and are therefore rewarded their target bonus plus a bonus of 2% of excess EVA improvement. In year 2 management has exactly performed according to target (an expected EVA improvement of 50) and hence receive their target bonus of 2.0, but no bonus for excess EVA improvement. Without a bonus bank, management should repay 2.0 in year 3 and 1.0 in year 4. This is one of the reasons why a

Table 12.8 **Modern bonus plan**

	Year 1	Year 2	Year 3	Year 4	Year 5	Total
EVA last year	−250.0	−150.0	−100.0	−150.0	−150.0	−250.0
EVA this year	−150.0	−100.0	−150.0	−150.0	0.0	0.0
EVA improvement (ΔEVA)	100.0	50.0	−50.0	0.0	150.0	250.0
Expected EVA improvement (EI)	50.0	50.0	50.0	50.0	50.0	250.0
Excess EVA improvement ΔEVA − EI	50.0	0.0	−100.0	−50.0	100.0	0.0
Target bonus (A)	2.0	2.0	0.0	0.0	2.0	6.0
2% of (ΔEVA − EI) (B)	1.0	0.0	−2.0	−1.0	2.0	0.0
Total bonus (A) + (B)	3.0	2.0	−2.0	−1.0	4.0	6.0

bonus bank enjoys popularity. It's hardly likely that management would accept to be charged for a negative bonus. In fact, they would probably leave office before year-end. Depending upon the contract, this might end up as a battle in court.

Total bonus over the 5-year period amounts to 6.0 and consists of target bonus of 6 (target is achieved in three out of five years) and a bonus of 0, as EVA has improved by 250 over the 5-year period, which exactly offsets expected improvements of 250. However, in year 3 and year 4, EVA improvement is less than expected, so that the 'y component' becomes negative, which means that management must pay in some way or another. Here the bonus bank comes into play. If bonuses calculated in Table 12.8 are being 'banked', the bonus bank may look as shown in Table 12.9, which highlights a number of issues in bonus banks:

- Should the bonus bank have a starting balance to avoid its depletion in year 1?
- What happens if the bonus bank becomes negative?
- Should the balance in bonus bank be paid out to managers who leave?

These issues should be carefully considered if a bonus bank is introduced in a bonus contract.

Table 12.9 **Bonus bank**

	Year 1	Year 2	Year 3	Year 4	Year 5	Total
Bank beginning of period	0.0	0.7	0.4	−1.6	−2.6	0.0
Target bonus	2.0	2.0	0.0	0.0	2.0	6.0
Bonus for excess EVA improvement	1.0	0.0	−2.0	−1.0	2.0	0.0
Available for payout	3.0	2.7	−1.6	−2.6	1.4	6.0
Payout[1]	2.3	2.2	0.0	0.0	1.4	6.0
Bank end of period	0.7	0.4	−1.6	−2.6	0.0	0.0

[1]Payout is calculated as target bonus + one-third of remaining bank balance

Conclusions

When designing bonus contracts the parties involved should pay close attention to the choice of performance measure(s), performance standard and performance structure. In choosing performance measure, standard and structure, the compensation committee and managers should consider the following issues:

- Does the contract align the interest of management and investors (congruence)?
- Can management control the performance measure that bonus is based on (controllability)?
- Is the bonus contract easy to understand and communicate (simplicity)?
- What are the accounting issues that need to be considered in a bonus contract?

While we discuss design issues in preparing bonus contracts, we do not provide clear-cut answers as how to control for all these issues. In fact, we raise a number of questions that bonus committees as a minimum should consider when writing bonus contracts. We hope that a thorough discussion of those issues *prior* to writing bonus contracts may prevent intense interpretations once the contract has been issued. It all adds up to establishing a bonus contract that aligns the interest of management and owners.

Review questions

- Which performance measures can be used in bonus plans?
- What characterises an effective bonus plan?
- What are the components of a bonus plan?
- What are absolute performance measures?
- What are relative performance measures?
- How should transitory items be treated in a bonus plan?
- How should changes in accounting policies or estimates be treated in a bonus plan?
- What are the pros and cons of accounting-based performance measures such as EBIT, EBITDA, net earnings etc.
- Is economic value added (EVA) a perfect performance measure?
- What are internal performance standards?
- What are external performance standards?
- What are the issues in linearity between performance and bonuses?
- What is a bonus bank?

Note

1 It should be pointed out that during a boom, value creation may have taken place even if management did a poor job. That is value is not necessarily created by excellent management.

References

Biddle, G., R.M. Bown and J.S. Wallace (1996) 'Evidence on the relative and incremental information content of EVA, residual income, earnings and operating cash flow', Working paper, University of Washington, Seattle, WA.

Feltham, G.A. and J. Xie (1994) 'Performance measure congruity and diversity in multi-task principal/agent relations', *Accounting Review*, 69.

Healy, P. (1985) 'The effect of bonus schemes on accounting decisions', *Journal of Accounting and Economics*, 7, 85–107.

Murphy, K. (2001) 'Performance standards in executive contracts', *Journal of Accounting and Economics*, 30, 245–78.

PART 4

Assessment of accounting data

Introduction to Part 4

In this book, we have not so far challenged the quality of accounting. Accounting data has been used uncritically to calculate financial ratios, and ultimately shed light on a firm's growth, profitability and risk.

In the following three chapters, the focus is directed towards the quality of accounting data. As will become evident during these chapters, definition, recognition, measurement and classification of accounting items are associated with a number of accounting policy choices, estimates and judgements that open up for possible manipulation of reported accounting numbers. Even in those cases where management does not intend to manage reported accounting numbers, noise in financial data may be inevitable. This will be the case if, for instance, a firm must change accounting policies due to new or revised reporting regulations. This makes it difficult to separate the consequences of changes in applied accounting policies and real changes in a firm's underlying operations, which is problematic in making time-series analyses or benchmarking against competitors. The point to remember is: The annual report should *not* be used uncritical in calculating financial ratios etc.

In order to assess accounting quality the following issues should be kept in mind:

1 Several different accounting regimes (including IFRS and US GAAP) exist.
2 Even within a given accounting regime (e.g. IFRS) some flexibility is inherent.
3 The number of estimates to be made by management has increased due to the extended use of fair value as a measurement basis.

A short discussion of these issues is provided below.

Different accounting regimes

Generally, a proper financial statement analysis requires that a firm uses the same accounting policies over time (time-series analysis) or that firms which are compared have identical accounting policies (cross-sectional analysis). This may not always be the case. For instance, if a firm in the UK is compared to a US firm, these two firms prepare financial statements based on IFRS and US GAAP, respectively.

In addition, the discretion that management may exert varies considerably within different accounting regimes. The conjecture is that the two major accounting regimes – IFRS and US GAAP – are fundamentally different. It is acknowledged that there is an ongoing convergence project, which aims at aligning IFRS with US GAAP. US GAAP is believed to be rule-based, while IFRS standards are principle based. The key point to remember is that, as an analyst, you must be aware of the fact that management exercises judgements and makes a number of estimates in preparing financial statements. As a consequence, managers may behave either opportunistically (use earnings management to manipulate earnings) or provide highly relevant data by reporting financial data, which takes into account management's proprietary knowledge about the company as an insider.

Flexibility within accounting regimes

Even within the same accounting regime, firms may not be comparable. Listed firms in the EU, for example, must comply with IFRS, while non-listed firms generally have to comply with domestic accounting regulation (e.g. UK GAAP). For example, this makes a comparison between two UK-based firms problematic since the financial statements for the two firms may be based on different accounting regulation.

Increasing number of estimates made by management

In preparing financial statements, management need to make a number of estimates. Typical examples include estimation of the useful life of depreciable assets and uncollectable receivables. In recent years, fair value measurement has become more prevalent. This requires further estimates to be made. A prime example is impairment tests. Management needs to estimate future cash flows and the cost of capital to calculate if, say machinery, is impaired (i.e. the carrying amount of machinery is greater than its value in use). As is well known (see Chapters 8–10), estimating cash flows and cost of capital is a daunting task.

While this book is not about accounting regulation per se, accounting quality plays a major role in any financial statement analysis. Assessing accounting quality is at the heart of financial analysis and will be discussed fully in this part of the book.

Chapter 13 defines the concept of accounting quality. The purpose of the chapter is to provide insight into issues which should be examined in order to assess the quality of accounting numbers. In Chapters 14 and 15 financial statements are discussed in order to identify possible sources of noise in annual reports due to accounting flexibility. The chapters include a lengthy discussion and analysis of analytical issues related to definition, recognition, measurement and classification of accounting items and discuss potential economic consequences of inherent accounting flexibility in financial statements.

CHAPTER 13

Accounting quality

After reading this chapter you should be able to:

- Define and understand the concept of accounting quality
- Identify the steps involved in examining the accounting quality
- Understand the motives for accounting manipulation
- Assess the quality of applied accounting policies
- Discuss the importance of separating transitory from permanent items
- Evaluate the quality of information in the annual report
- Identify red flags
- Discuss and analyse the economic consequences of differences in applied accounting policies

Accounting quality

What do firms such as Enron, Tyco, Qwest International, Xerox, Waste Management HIH, World Com and Parmalet have in common?

They are all being accused of manipulating financial statements to make themselves look healthier than they really are. **Accounting quality** in these firms is viewed by analysts as poor, and in many cases management has been sued for manipulating reported accounting numbers.

In this book reported accounting numbers have so far been used *as reported*. However, as the statement above indicates, it is important to examine the quality of reported accounting numbers. Accounting quality is a central concept in financial statement analysis. In practice, reported accounting numbers, which are used in calculating financial ratios, should be adjusted to make them comparable over time or across firms. This ensures that changes in financial ratios reflect changes in a firm's underlying operations and financial position and not changes or differences in accounting policies. A number of issues may cause noise in accounting numbers:

- Application of accounting policies
- Accounting estimates
- Classification of accounting items
- Accounting items or events which are regarded as permanent versus transitory.

This chapter defines good accounting quality and elaborates on the reasons why firms over time and across firms may not be comparable. Chapters 14 and 15 focus on analytical issues and economic consequences of reported financial data in order to identify items that are likely to become sources of noise in carrying out financial statement analysis.

Definition of good accounting quality

There is no universal definition of good accounting quality in the literature or among practitioners. Naser (1993, p. 59) speaks about the concept accounting quality by defining creative accounting as:

> *The process of manipulating accounting figures by taking advantage of the loopholes in accounting rules and the choices of measurement and disclosure practices in them to transform financial statements from what they should be, to what preparers would prefer to see reported, and the process by which transactions are structured so as to produce the required accounting results rather than reporting transactions in a neutral and consistent way.*

This definition of creative accounting suggests that *good accounting quality* is characterised by financial statements that provide an objective (neutral) picture of a firm's financial position and is free of manipulation.

Among analysts, earnings quality is sometimes used as an indicator of the quality of financial statements. For example, Penman (2010) defines earnings quality in this way:

> *Quality of earnings is the degree to which current earnings serves as an indicator of future earnings.*

In Penman's definition of earnings quality, permanent (recurring) accounting items are characterised as having high quality. Transitory items (e.g. one-time items or 'special items' which are not permanent accounting items) are considered of lower quality.

Compared to Penman's narrow definition, this book has a broader perspective on accounting quality. In our view, the analyst must keep in mind the *purpose* of the analysis and the *decision model* applied before assessing accounting quality. As illustrated in previous chapters, different stakeholders use a variety of decision models and will therefore also require different types of accounting information and data. To demonstrate our viewpoint, consider an analyst who wants to value a firm based on a present value model (e.g. the EVA model). In that case, an analysis of historical earnings is used as input to forecasting the level and trend of future earnings. The analysts will therefore regard accounting quality as the extent to which past earnings is a good indicator of future earnings (Penman's definition). In addition, the analyst might find helpful information by studying management's review and discussion. For instance, how does management see the future? Has management been able to perform as predicted in their outlook? Even though such information is not necessarily quantitative, they may supplement financial data when assessing a firm's prospects.

Now look at accounting from a lender's perspective. Lenders are interested in assessing the liquidity and solvency of a firm. Lenders need to examine whether the firm has debt or potential debt, which is not recognised in the balance sheet, and which requires future cash outflows. To examine whether a firm has such debt, lenders need to look at a firm's accounting policies and read the notes carefully. Or consider a worst case scenario, a liquidation of the firm. In this case good accounting quality would be if all assets and liabilities were recognised in the balance sheet at liquidation value since the firm's ability to repay debt would depend upon the net proceeds from selling the assets and settling the liabilities. Again, lenders need to read the section on accounting policies carefully to find out how assets and liabilities are measured (valued).

Executive compensation may be linked to various accounting-based performance measures. Since some items may be transitory in nature and outside management's control, performance measures used in bonus contracts should probably exclude such items. In respect to executive compensation good accounting quality is characterised by financial statements, which clearly distinguish between permanent and transitory accounting items.

In summary, an assessment of accounting quality requires a thorough investigation of financial statements, applied accounting policies and notes, management's discussion and supplementary reports. It is rarely sufficient just to examine the financial statements. The above considerations are illustrated in Figure 13.1. Based on the above discussion, our book defines accounting quality as follows:

Good accounting quality is defined as the financial reporting that provides the input which best supports the decision models used.

An annual report that provides accounting information which enables users to make rational economic decisions is regarded as having high quality.

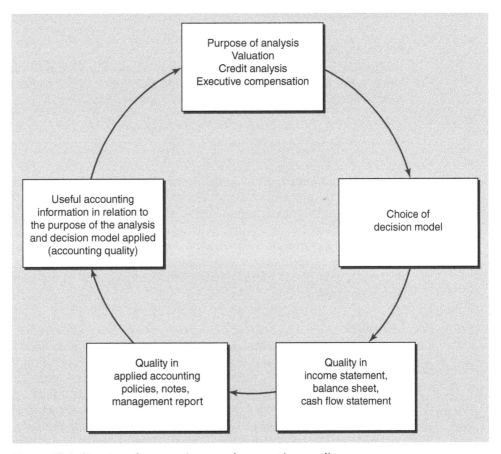

Figure 13.1 Structure for assessing good accounting quality

The purpose of financial statement analysis and good accounting quality

As illustrated in the previous section, the purpose of financial statement analysis will affect the type of accounting information that users demand. In fact, the assessment of accounting quality cannot be made without knowing the type of accounting user. In this section, good accounting quality is discussed based on three different accounting users: *equity focused accounting users* such as financial analysts, corporate finance employees and investors, *debt capital focused accounting users* including lenders, suppliers and customers and *compensation focused accounting users* such as the board of directors, compensation committees and consultants.

Equity oriented stakeholders

Equity focused stakeholders need to estimate firm value. In Chapter 9, we discussed the following valuation methods (decision models):

- Present value method
- Multiples
- Liquidation method.

These decision models are discussed below.

Present value method

The present value method includes an array of models. One such model is the economic value added (EVA) model. Under the assumption of a constant required rate of return (WACC), firm value at time zero is expressed as:

$$\text{Enterprise value}_0 = \text{Invested capital}_0 + \sum_{t=1}^{\infty} \frac{(\text{ROIC}_t - \text{WACC}) \times \text{Invested capital}_{t-1}}{(1 + \text{WACC})^t}$$

As is evident from the EVA model, future profitability (return on invested capital, ROIC) must be forecast in order to estimate firm value. The analysts rely on historical accounting numbers to determine the level and possible trends in future profitability. Hence, good accounting quality is characterised by reported earnings that clearly distinguish between transitory (need not to be forecast) and permanent accounting items and are based on identical accounting policies over time. If accounting policies change over time, changes in a firm's performance may simply reflect changes in a firm's accounting policies.

Multiples

To value a firm using multiples, a comparison is made between firms within the same industry. Based on this comparison, it must be decided whether a firm should be valued at the average multiple for the industry or a higher or lower multiple. In Chapter 9, we saw how the value of the firm is estimated by multiplying a firm's earnings such as EBIT or net earnings with a proper earnings capitalisation factor. However, before using multiples a number of issues must be assessed. First, applied accounting policies must be comparable for the firms that are compared. In addition, earnings in the comparable firms must be of the same 'quality'. It does not make sense from an analytical point of view to compare a firm, whose earnings are primarily based on permanent sources of income, with earnings which are mostly transitory in nature. Good accounting quality is, consequently, characterised by accounting policies that are identical across firms and reported earnings that make it possible for analysts to separate transitory from permanent accounting items.

Liquidation method

As discussed in Chapter 9, the liquidation method aims at estimating the realisable value of assets and liabilities of a firm. In this context good accounting quality is characterised by the recognition of all accounting items in the balance sheet and measuring those items at the break-up value (liquidation value). As noted in Chapter 9, net assets are unlikely to be measured at liquidation value as financial statements are prepared under the assumption of 'going concern' unless otherwise stated.

Debt capital oriented stakeholders

Lenders, such as financial institutions, apply different decision models as described in Chapter 11. The following three types of decision models are now discussed:

- Forecasting method
- Credit rating method
- Liquidation method.

Forecasting method

The forecasting method requires that the future economic development of a firm is projected in order to evaluate its ability to repay debt or its need for borrowing in the future (potential business opportunities seen from the lenders point of view), and identifying the call for further collaterals. Good accounting quality for debt capital providers is, therefore, characterised by financial statements that clearly separate permanent earnings from transitory earnings, which are based on identical accounting policies over time, and thereby more effectively signal the valuation creation and financial position of the firm being evaluated.

Credit rating method

As shown in Chapter 11, the credit rating method is based on a number of financial ratios. Those ratios each describe different aspects of a firm's profitability and risk. The credit rating model is relatively more static than the forecasting method in assessing credit risk. This puts heavy constraints on the underlying data (financial statements). A requirement of the underlying data is that the current financial ratios are a fair representation of the future level of those financial ratios. Good accounting quality is therefore characterised by financial statements that contain sufficient information for creditor to assess the 'stability' in the financial ratios. Furthermore, since credit rating models compare companies, the accounting policies should be identical across companies which are being compared.

Liquidation method

Lenders may use the liquidation method to examine a firm's ability to repay debt in case it suspends its payments. As for equity stakeholders, good accounting quality for loan providers is characterised by financial statements that recognise all asset and liabilities (also the ones not previously recognised such as operating lease contracts and law suits) at a value close to the liquidation value.

Compensation oriented stakeholders

Executive compensation may be based on financial performance measures as illustrated in Chapter 12. Earnings measures such as EBITDA, EBIT, EBT or net earnings (E) are among the most popular earnings measures in determining executives' performance-related bonuses. If a firm's objective is to maximise investors' welfare, the selected earnings measure should reflect this. Thus, there should be a strong link between the selected earnings measure and firm value.

Empirical evidence indicates that earnings measures used in bonus contracts do not seem to distinguish clearly between permanent and transitory accounting items. In respect to accounting-based bonus plans there are reasons to include certain transitory accounting items in measuring performance. For example, in Chapter 12, we argued that a loss due to under-insurance should be included in the performance measure used in calculating bonus. The following example considers Royal Unibrew.

Example 13.1 On 28 December, year 1, Royal Unibrew issues the following announcement:

> Royal Unibrew has decided to try to sell the Group's English Brewery Robert Cain & Co. Ltd . . . In relation to the decision to divest Robert Cain & Co. Ltd impairment of assets, provisions and the like of approx. €6–7 million are expected to be recognised in the income statement for year 1. . . On a yearly basis the disposal of Robert Cain & Co. Ltd is expected to improve Royal Unibrew's core earnings (EBIT) by approx. €3 million.

As shown in the announcement, Royal Unibrew will report a loss of €6–7 million in year 1. On the other hand, EBIT will increase by approximately €3 million in subsequent years. Even though the divestment of Robert Cain & Co. Ltd seems reasonable from an economic point of view, management will be penalised in year 1, if their bonus is based on a single-period earnings measure such as EBIT or net earnings. ■

In summary, good accounting quality clarifies those issues allowing the analyst or compensation committee to make informed decisions.

As illustrated by the three stakeholder groups, accounting users have different objectives and use different decision models (depending on the purpose of the analysis), which affect the conception of good accounting quality. This issue is discussed in greater detail in Chapters 14 and 15.

Assessment of accounting quality

A general analysis of accounting quality is a time consuming task as many areas must be explored. Below, we present a list of issues which accounting users should examine in order to assess accounting quality:

- Motives for accounting manipulation
- The quality of applied accounting policies
- Permanent (recurring) versus transitory (non-recurring) accounting items

- The level of information in the financial statements
- Identification of 'red flags'.

The list is not exhaustive, but covers substantial issues which analysts should consider carefully. Each of the issues is discussed in greater detail below.

Motives for accounting manipulation

To identify whether accounting manipulation is an issue, the analysts should be aware of the specific motives management may have to exploit the flexibility in accounting regulation. Flexibility in accounting regulation can be exploited more or less aggressively and in some cases management may be tempted to circumvent current accounting rules. Motives management may have to promote explicit interests include the following.

Blurring of poor management. Management may choose accounting policies that enhance job security. This may happen by selecting accounting policies that do not provide a true and fair view of a firm's profitability and financial position. Management which has been under pressure for an extended period of time may especially be tempted to exploit the flexibility in accounting regulation to promote their own interests. Management has a number of possibilities to 'beautify' the financial position of a firm. Management might for instance reduce forward looking expenses such as research and development costs and marketing expenses or change accounting estimates for non-current assets (i.e. change the expected lifetime of depreciable assets) and hereby extend the accounting lifetime of those assets, which reduces accounting depreciations. In all cases it has a positive effect on current earnings.

Performance related pay. A related area is management compensation. As shown in Chapter 12, a variety of accounting-based performance measures are used in bonus contracts. This type of compensation promotes management's motives to apply accounting policies, and estimates, in order to maximise its own welfare. Management may be tempted, for example, to recognise impairment losses in periods where performance is so poor that management will not achieve a bonus anyway. In such cases, current earnings include future costs. Management has thereby made it easier to reach future bonus targets.

Debt-covenants. In debt financing, the contract between borrower and lender often include the so-called debt-covenants. A debt covenant is an agreement that the borrower has to deliver a minimum performance on certain financial ratios such as the interest coverage ratio and financial leverage. In the event that the borrower's performance results in a breach of the covenants, the lender may require a renegotiation of the terms or call the debt. This may prove costly for the firm and they may therefore be tempted to choose accounting policies, and estimates, which reduce the likelihood of violation of the covenants. Gramlich et al. (2001) find that American firms reclassify debt on the balance sheet to avoid breaching debt-covenants. For example, they find that short-term debt is reclassified as long-term debt so as to improve the acid test ratio or similar measures of short-term risk.

Political (regulation) considerations. Firms that are prone to supervision from various public authorities have motives to manage reported accounting numbers in a desired direction. Firms, which have a dominating market position, will often be closely monitored by public authorities. For example, most countries have a dominating player in the telecom market. In Germany, Deutsche Telekom has a dominating position and, in Spain, Telefónica, S.A. has a dominating position. As a consequence,

UNIVERSITY OF WINCHESTER
LIBRARY

various public authorities oversee different aspects of the firms' finances, including their price policies and reported earnings. In case these analyses indicate that the telecom firms use their dominant positions on the telecom market to earn excess profit, authorities may intervene and regulate in favour of their competitors. Therefore, firms with a dominating market position may have an incentive to hide the economic advantages by applying accounting policies, and estimates, in their favour.

Competitive issues. Certain competitive considerations may also affect a firm's reporting practice. Firms may choose not to reveal profitable areas by not disclosing segment information or choose accounting policies, which affect accounting numbers in a desired direction.

Capital market issues. Firms that consider raising capital on a stock exchange or are about to be acquired have a special interest in appearing as profitable and financially sound as possible. Gramlich and Sørensen (2004) examine 58 firms one year subsequent to their initial public offerings. They find that the firms in general use accounting policies that either improve income or reduce expenses in order to align with expected earnings.

The above examples show that there are various motives for accounting manipulation. It is therefore important to assess the quality of the financial statements, as we shall now show.

The quality of applied accounting policies

In assessing applied accounting principles several issues should be examined in order to assess the quality of the reported accounting numbers. As stated in Chapter 14, management has some discretion in choosing accounting policies. In addition, management needs to make a number of estimates. For example, estimating the useful lifetime of non-current assets often involve a great deal of judgement. Even if there is a relatively detailed regulation, management can by their actions affect the income statement, the balance sheet and the cash flow statement in a number of ways. For instance, management may postpone or advance planned investments in areas such as marketing and research and development. In the following section, the impact of applied accounting policies on reported accounting measures is examined. We have separated this issue into the following two topics:

1 Are the firm's financial statements based on conservative or liberal accounting policies?
2 Does management use accounting policies to promote their own interests?

1 Conservative versus liberal accounting policies

Often a distinction is made between **conservative and liberal accounting policies**. Conservative accounting policies are characterised by the prudent measurement of assets. Expensing development costs as incurred is evidence of conservative accounting policies, while capitalisation of development costs is an indication of relatively more liberal accounting policies. Even though accounting regulation allows fewer choices for recognition and measurement of accounting items, international accounting regulation leaves room for alternatives. Conservative accounting policies are by many believed to be synonymous with good accounting quality. The idea is that for lenders and equity investors, conservative accounting policies are a safeguard against losses on loans and investments, respectively.

The use of liberal versus conservative accounting policies may have a large effect on invested capital and financial ratios including return on invested capital. Obviously, this may have economic consequences as financial ratios are used in decision models and in various contracts (e.g. debt-covenants and bonus contracts). Thereby, applied accounting policies may affect firm value or a firm's borrowing capacity. This is not appropriate as it is the underlying performance, ultimately expressed as cash flows, which should affect the value or loan capacity of a firm; not the choice of accounting policies. Example 13.2 illustrates the possible economic consequences of choosing conservative accounting policies or estimates versus liberal accounting policies or estimates. This should help answering the question: are conservative accounting policies of higher quality than liberal accounting policies? While the example focuses on different estimates (judgements), the example could just as well have focused on different accounting policies *per se* such as capitalisation of development costs versus expensing such costs as incurred or the choice of FIFO versus average costs for inventory accounting.

Example 13.2 | ## Conservative versus liberal accounting policies

Two firms within the same industry produce the exact same products. Historically, both firms have had an EBITDA of 131,680 each year and yearly investments of 100,000. Risks have also been on a par for the two firms with a required rate of return of 10%. The only difference between the two firms is that they estimate the lifetime of depreciable assets differently. One firm depreciates non-current assets over two years (a conservative accounting estimate), while the same assets are depreciated over a four-year period in the other firm (a liberal accounting estimate). Both firms are 100% equity financed and they depreciate by the full rate in year 1, year 2 etc. On the basis of these assumptions the following numbers and ratios can be calculated as shown in Table 13.1.

Table 13.1 Conservative versus liberal accounting policies

Accounting practice	Conservative	Liberal
EBITDA	131,680	131,680
Depreciation and amortisation	−100,000	−100,000
EBIT	31,680	31,680
Non-current assets beginning of period	50,000	150,000
Investment per year	100,000	100,000
Depreciation per year	−100,000	−100,000
Non-current assets end of period	50,000	150,000
Free cash flow	31,680	31,680
Return on invested capital (ROIC)	63.4%	21.1%
Required rate of return	10%	10%

In this example, it is assumed that 'steady state' has been reached, which signals all accounting numbers, financial ratios and cash flows are exactly the same in all future periods. As illustrated, EBIT is identical for the two firms but non-current assets are measured differently

341

due to differences in depreciation policies. For the conservative firm non-current assets are calculated as follows:

Investment	Book value Year 1	Book value Year 2	Book value Year 3	Book value Year 4	Book value Year 5	Total book value
Year 1	50,000	0	0	0	0	50,000
Year 2	0	50,000	0	0	0	50,000
Year 3	0	0	50,000	0	0	50,000
Year 4	0	0	0	50,000	0	50,000
Year 5	0	0	0	0	50,000	50,000

For example, in year 3 book value of non-current assets becomes 50,000 and relates to the investment made in year 3 only. The reason is that investments made in year 1 was fully depreciated by the end of year 2, while the investment made in year 2 was fully depreciated by the end of year 3 (by 50% in year 2 + 50% in year 3). Note that book value at the end of each year becomes constant at 50,000. Depreciation also becomes constant at 100,000. In year 3, the depreciation expense consists of 50,000 in depreciation of investments made in year 2 plus 50,000 in depreciation of investments made in year 3. In year 4, depreciation is calculated as 50,000 related to the investment in year 3 plus 50,000 related to the investment made in year 4 and so on for the subsequent years.

For the liberal firm non-current assets are calculated as follows:

Investment	Book value Year 1	Book value Year 2	Book value Year 3	Book value Year 4	Book value Year 5	Total book value
Year 1	75,000	0	0	0	0	75,000
Year 2	50,000	75,000	0	0	0	125,000
Year 3	25,000	50,000	75,000	0	0	150,000
Year 4	0	25,000	50,000	75,000	0	150,000
Year 5	0	0	25,000	50,000	75,000	150,000

Note that for the liberal firm non-current assets become constant at 150,000 consisting of assets with a value of 25,000, 50,000 and 75,000, respectively. Every year from year 3 this will be the case, since book value will be the sum of assets not yet fully depreciated. Furthermore, depreciation becomes a constant 100,000 from year 4. This is due to the fact that in year 4 four assets (investments) are depreciated by 25,000 each, namely the assets acquired in years 1, 2, 3 and 4. By the beginning of year 5, the investment made in year 1 is fully depreciated (by 25% in years 1, 2, 3 and 4), but another investment of 100,000 is made. This investment is depreciated by 25,000. Thus depreciation in year 5 again becomes 100,000; 25,000 related to each investment made in years 2, 3, 4 and 5.

Contrary to what many may have believed, ROIC is substantially higher at 63.4% for the firm applying conservative accounting policies versus 21.1% for the firm with liberal accounting policies. This is due to the fact that earnings are the same for the conservative firm and liberal firm (in the 'steady-state' phase), while the conservative firm has less invested capital.

As cash flow is unaffected by differences in applied accounting policies or estimates, the free cash flow is identical for both firms. In the following section the potential economic consequences of differences in accounting estimates are illustrated.

Valuation

In this section, both firms are valued based on the EVA model. It is assumed that both firms' financials and applied accounting policies remain identical across time. Invested capital, ROIC and risk, as shown in Table 13.1, are consequently used as estimates of the future economic development in the two firms. Based on these assumptions and the EVA model, value for the two firms can be calculated as:[1]

$$\text{Conservative accounting policies} = 50,000 + \frac{(63.4\% - 10\%) \times 50,000}{10\%} = 316,800$$

$$\text{Liberal accounting policies} = 150,000 + \frac{(21.1\% - 10\%) \times 150,000}{10\%} = 316,800$$

As demonstrated, the value of the two firms is identical even though they report vastly different accounting numbers. The firm, which applies conservative accounting policies, reports invested capital of 50,000. In comparison, invested capital amounts to 150,000 in the firm that uses liberal accounting policies. In spite of different starting points for valuation, the higher return on invested capital in the firm with conservative accounting policies compensates exactly for the firm's lower invested capital. The result should not come as a surprise. The two firms generate identical free cash flows and assuming identical risks across the two firms, they should have identical values.

An alternative valuation model is the discounted cash flow model (DCF model), which should yield the same value for the two firms, since the cash flows are identical. In the DCF model future cash flows are converted to present value by discounting the cash flows by an appropriate discount factor. In our example, the free cash flows amount to 31,680 (in perpetuity) and the proper discount factor is 10%. Since cash flows are constant, the present value of future free cash flows is calculated as an annuity in perpetuity:

$$\text{DCF model:} \frac{31,680}{10\%} = 316,800$$

Since the conservative and liberal firms have the same cash flows, they are both valued at 316,800; just as they were if the EVA model was used as illustrated above.

In summary, accounting policies do not affect firm value if present value models are applied. Therefore, if present value models are used it cannot be concluded that financials based on conservative accounting policies (or estimates) are of higher quality than financials based on liberal accounting policies.

Now suppose that valuation is based on the multiple price to book (P/B). (Price to book is defined as the market value of equity divided by book value of equity.) The firm with liberal accounting policies wishes to be listed on a stock exchange. To estimate firm value it is compared with the firm applying conservative accounting policies, which is already listed on a major stock exchange. Assume that this listed (conservative) firm is traded at a P/B ratio = 316,800/50,000 = 6.3. That is, the market value of equity (P) is more than six times the book value of equity.

The value of the firm, applying liberal accounting policies, can accordingly be calculated as $6.3 \times 150,000 = 945,000$, which is three times the price of the firm applying conservative accounting policies. The difference in value is due to differences in accounting policies between the two firms. As a consequence of differences in the accounting policies, equity is recognised at a value that is three times as large in the firm that uses liberal accounting policies.

As a result of using multiples for valuation purposes, estimated firm value is sensitive to applied accounting policies. This example further illustrates that financial statements based on conservative accounting policies are not necessarily of higher quality than financial statements based on liberal accounting policies if multiples are used. Rather, good accounting quality is characterised by identical accounting policies across firms (peers) used as benchmarks.

Finally, the consequences of conservative and liberal accounting policies on firm value are illustrated assuming the liquidation method is used. The assumptions and data are as before. Total assets and equity for the two firms amount to:

Accounting policies	Conservative	Liberal
Assets	50,000	150,000
Equity	50,000	150,000

It is evident that assets are valued differently due to different accounting policies for non-current assets. In a worst case scenario, the liquidation value determines the value of the firm, and ultimately whether investors and bankers have lost their investments in the firm. Neither conservative accounting policies nor liberal accounting policies are likely to provide an unbiased estimate of the value of individual assets or liabilities. Liberal accounting policies signal a liquidation value, which is significantly higher than the one based on conservative accounting policies. This may give the lenders the impression that the liquidation value (worst case scenario) is much higher than will be the case if liquidation of the firm does take place.

Credit rating

Taken at face value, the balance sheet numbers (book value of equity is three times as high for the liberal firm) further suggest that the firm which uses conservative accounting policies has less collateral to put up and therefore is a more risky investment opportunity (other things being equal) than the firm using liberal accounting policies. On the other hand, credit risk will (presumably) be lower, if lenders base their loan commitments on a conservative valuation of non-current assets. It is questionable, however, if conservative accounting policies are of higher quality (seen from a lender's or a creditor's point of view) than liberal accounting policies. The effect of conservative accounting policies may well be a loss of profitable business opportunities; that is a lender may decline to provide further funding due to the apparently low value of assets.

The credit rating system is also affected by applied accounting policies. In this example, ROIC is substantially different for the two firms:

Accounting policies	Conservative	Liberal
Return on invested capital	63.4%	21.1%

ROIC is three times higher for the firm applying conservative accounting policies. If ROIC is considered in isolation, the firm applying conservative accounting policies would achieve an AAA rating on the rating system shown in Table 11.1. In comparison the firm that chooses liberal accounting policies would obtain only an A rating. The difference in rating, considering ROIC only, triggers a higher borrowing rate (cost of capital) for the firm with liberal accounting policies.

The above exemplifies that the choice of a decision model influences the requirement for types of accounting information. The example, in addition, illustrates that accounting policies (conservative/liberal accounting policies) affect decision models differently. For instance, equity-based decision models such as the EVA model are immune to applied accounting policies, while decision models such as multiples and the liquidation method are affected by accounting policies including the use of conservative versus liberal accounting practice. Firms applying conservative accounting policies are often regarded as being prudent when measuring profitability, growth and risks, implying that lenders risks are reduced. However, as the example indicates, reported financial statements based on conservative accounting policies are not necessarily of higher quality than financial statements applying liberal accounting policies. ∎

2 Use of accounting policies to promote special interests

As indicated above, there are a number of reasons why management uses accounting policies to promote particular interests. Schipper (1989, p. 92) proposes a representative academic definition of earnings manipulation that she refers to as 'earnings management':

> A purposeful intervention in the external financial reporting process, with the intent of obtaining some private gain.

It is therefore important to uncover potential management motives and to examine the accounting policies carefully.

'Big Bath' accounting is the process where corporations write-off or write-down certain assets from their balance sheets or recognise large chunks of restructuring costs. The write-off removes or reduces the carrying value of asset and results in lower net income. The objective is to 'take one big bath' in a single year so future years will show improved earnings numbers. This technique is often employed in a year when sales are down as a result of external factors, when the company would report a loss in any event or after a change in top management. Corporations will often wait until a bad year to employ this 'big bath' technique to 'clean up' the balance sheet. Although the process is discouraged by auditors, it is still used.

The following is a typical example of 'big bath' accounting.

Example 13.3 A listed company sacks their CEO and shortly after his successor is appointed. A few months after taking office the new CEO recognises an impairment loss on development projects of approximately €12 million, which is almost a 50% write-off. Assuming an amortisation period of 10 years, future earnings will increase by €1.2 million per year in the coming 10-year period.

In this scenario, the newly appointed CEO is likely to report higher future earnings as the likelihood of having to report an impairment loss is heavily reduced (development projects are written-off by 50%). ∎

Permanent versus transitory accounting items (earnings persistence)

Financial statement analysis often includes forecasting future earnings. In predicting future accounting numbers, past financial statements provide valuable information that can be used to establish the level and trends in future accounting numbers. An examination of historical financial statements also helps the analysts to distinguish between permanent and transitory accounting items.

Accounting users may find guidance in accounting regulation and reporting practices. For instance, transitory accounting items are often classified and disclosed separately from recurring accounting items. The following provides a list of a number accounting items, which may be transitory in nature:

- Special items
- Discontinued operations
- Restructuring costs
- Changes in accounting estimates
- Changes in accounting policies
- Gains and losses that are not part of core business
- Impairment losses on non-current assets.

In the following section, these accounting items are discussed and exemplified.

Special items

IFRS no longer permit firms to classify items in the income statement as extraordinary items. This is in contrast to US GAAP, where extraordinary items are permitted but restricted to infrequent, unusual and rare items that affect profit and loss. In light of this it raises an important issue: how shall IFRS firms classify and disclose items, which used to be reported as extraordinary items? The answer to this question is that firms choose to label items that are irregular as 'special items', 'exceptional items' or the like.

Some events are clearly irregular and caused by events outside firms' control. Such events include:

- Expropriation
- Hurricanes, flooding and other natural disasters.

Under US GAAP such items are classified as extraordinary items, while IFRS firms are left with the choice of including them as a separate line item in the income statement and make the necessary disclosure.

There is also a number of accounting items, which may be classified as special items by firms, but which are normally part of ordinary activities. These items include, but are not limited to:

- Write-down of inventories
- Write-down of accounts receivable
- Impairment of non-current assets
- Reversal of impairment losses and provisions
- Restructuring costs
- Disposal of non-current assets
- Law suits (litigations)
- Corrections of errors related to prior years.

Arguably, the above list represents typical events that are within the scope of a firm's normal operating activities. For example, that a firm divests assets or business units or has to recognise an impairment loss on non-current assets, inventory or accounts receivable is part of the risk inherent in running a business. Nonetheless, disclosing the above items separately may be useful for financial statement users; at least if they are material. This makes it possible for users to make their own stance on 'special items'; that is how to treat such items in an analysis.

Example 13.4 Bayer Group

To illustrate special items, consider the Bayer Group (see Table 13.2). Bayer is a global enterprise with core competencies in the fields of healthcare, nutrition and high-tech materials.

Table 13.2 Bayer Group annual report – five-year financial summary

Bayer Group	Year 5	Year 6	Year 7	Year 8	Year 9
	€ million	€ million	€ million	€ million	€ million
Sales	24,701	28,956	32,385	32,918	31,168
Sales outside Germany	84.4%	84.4%	85.1%	85.4%	86.7%
EBIT	2,514	2,762	3,154	3,544	**3,006**
EBIT before special items	3,047	3,479	4,287	4,342	**3,772**
EBITDA	4,122	4,675	5,866	6,266	5,815
EBITDA before special items	4,602	5,584	6,777	6,931	6,472
Income before income taxes	1,912	1,980	2,234	2,356	1,870
Income after taxes	1,595	1,695	4,716	1,724	1,359

Based on the above, the effect of special items can be calculated. For example, in year 9 special items amount to €3,772 million − €3,006 million = €766 million or approximately 25% of EBIT. Bayer Group's special items are summarised in Table 13.3.

Bayer Group reconciles special items as shown in Table 13.4.

Table 13.3 Bayer Group annual report – five-year financial summary

	Year 5	Year 6	Year 7	Year 8	Year 9
	€ million	€ million	€ million	€ million	€ million
Special items, EBIT	533	717	1,133	798	**766**
Special items, as a percentage of EBIT	21%	26%	36%	23%	**25%**
Special items, EBITDA	480	909	911	665	657
Special items, as a percentage of EBITDA	12%	19%	16%	11%	11%

Table 13.4 Bayer Group Annual report – reconciliation of special items

	EBIT Year 8	EBIT Year 9	EBITDA Year 8	EBITDA Year 9
	€ million	€ million	€ million	€ million
After special items	**3,544**	**3,006**	**6,266**	**5,815**
HealthCare	**583**	**372**	**465**	**320**
Schering PPA effects	208	0	208	0
Schering integration costs	157	87	111	79
of which gain from divestitures	−69	−114	−6	−114
Write-downs	98	32	26	0
Restructuring	0	47	0	35
Litigations	106	180	106	180
Additional funding for the pension assurance association	0	26	0	26
Other	14	0	14	0
CropScience	**166**	**219**	**153**	**197**
Restructuring	166	177	153	155
Litigations	0	35	0	35
Additional funding for the pension assurance association	0	7	0	7
MaterialScience	**49**	**140**	**47**	**105**
Restructuring	49	130	47	95
Additional funding for the pension assurance association	0	10	0	10
Reconciliation	**0**	**35**	**0**	**35**
Litigations	0	10	0	10
Additional funding for the pension assurance association	0	25	0	25
Total special items	**798**	**766**	**665**	**657**
Before special items	**4,342**	**3,772**	**6,931**	**6,472**

Further, Bayer Group explains:

Although EBIT before special items and EBITDA before special items are not defined in the international Financial Reporting Standards, they represent key performance indicators for the Bayer Group. The special items comprise effects that are non-recurring or do not regularly recur or attain similar magnitudes. EBITDA is the EBIT as reported in the income statement plus amortisation and write-downs of intangible assets and depreciation and write-downs of property, plant and equipment.

As the reconciliation reveals Bayer Group's special items include restructuring costs and litigation expenses. Arguably, such expenses are part of a firm's operating business. Restructuring is necessary for a firm to stay competitive. The risk of being sued (litigations) is something that many firms, if not all firms, experience. Therefore, though Bayer Group classifies restructuring and litigation as special items, analysts must carefully consider if they need to be included in forecasting earnings. It is noteworthy that special items are recognised every single year, are always negative (expenses) and are roughly between €500 million and €1,100 million. This indicates that special items are recurring and should be included in forecasting earnings. While these items may be hard to predict, a fair bet would be to use the average figure for the past three to five years. For Bayer Group this would mean that projected operating expenses should include special items of around €800 million per year.

Likewise, if managers are rewarded a bonus based on financial performance it raises the question if they should be punished (or rewarded) for special items. A closer look at Bayer Group's annual report exposes that the board of management are entitled to bonuses as follows:

The short-term incentive award for management is calculated according to the Group's EBITDA margin before special items and the weighted average target attainment of the HealthCare, CropScience and MaterialScience subgroups. The Supervisory Board can adjust this award according to individual performance. The target attainment of the subgroups is measured chiefly in terms of their EBITDA before special items. A qualitative appraisal in relation to the market and competitors is also taken into account.

Source: Bayer annual report, combined management report

As illustrated, Bayer Group has decided that management compensation should be based on a performance measure excluding special items. It is an open question whether this is a wise decision. Again, it is worth noting that special items are consistently negative. ■

Discontinued operations

For most, if not all, firms the organisation must be adjusted continuously by selling-off (unprofitable) business units or acquiring new businesses. This fact complicates an analyst's work in several ways. First, it introduces noise in a time-series analysis, as changes in the underlying profitability may be caused by changes in the underlying risk. A change in the risk profile has an effect on cost of capital and ultimately firm value and loan terms. This will be the case if, for instance, a business unit with a different risk profile than the remaining business units is divested. Second, it complicates the analyst's work in connection with forecasting. The analysts make forecasts based on the remaining part of the business. This requires that it is possible to adjust accounting numbers back in time in order to use them as a base for forecasting. This kind of information is seldom available.

According to IFRS 5: 'Non-current Assets Held for Sale and Discontinued Operations', a firm has to disclose a variety of information about discontinuing operations. The data that has to be revealed include:

> *On the face of the income statement a single amount comprising the sum of the post-tax profit or loss of the discontinued operation and the post-tax gain or loss recognised on the measurement to fair value less costs to sell or on the disposal of the assets (or disposal group).*
>
> *An analysis of the amount above must be presented either on the face of the income statement or in the notes. This analysis must include revenue, expenses, pre-tax profit or loss and related income taxes in a section distinct from continuing operations and prior periods are re-presented so that the disclosures relate to all operations classified as discontinued by the latest balance sheet date.*
>
> *The net cash flows attributable to the operating, investing, and financing activities of a discontinued operation must be presented separately on the face of the cash flow statement or disclosed in the notes and is required for prior periods.*

In addition, comparative figures in the financial statements must be restated. In reality, firms often adjust accounting numbers from the previous financial year only. As a longer time-series than two years is necessary in order to identify the level and trends in key financial ratios, the analysts will face the dilemma that reported accounting numbers for past years include the effects of continuing as well as discontinuing operations making past numbers less useful for forecasting purposes. Analysts must judge to what extent this creates noise in the analysis. Subsequently, analysts must consider the impact discontinued operations has on accounting numbers that have not been adjusted. If qualified estimates on historical growth, profitability and risk for the continuing operations are impossible, the analysts must settle for accounting numbers for the past two years.

Example 13.5 **Wolseley**

Wolseley is a specialist trade distributor of plumbing and heating products to professional contractors and a leading supplier of building materials to the professional market with approximately 47,000 employees and 4,400 branches worldwide. Wolseley is quite informative about discontinued operations. For example, note 9 to their annual report for year 5 provides the information displayed in Table 13.5.

In addition, Wolseley discloses separately the results of continuing from the results discontinuing operations in its five-year summary, which prevent noise in a time-series analysis (see Table 13.6). As seen in Table 13.6, Wolseley has separated out discontinued operations for the current year plus the past four years. Wolseley presents detail in excess of what is required by IAS. In doing so, Wolseley provides analysts with the necessary information to examine past performance as a benchmark for future performance. Naturally, the five-year summary is not as detailed as a normal income statement, so analysts may still need to make informed estimates and judgements.

Table 13.5 Wolseley, annual report

9. Discontinued operations

On 6 May, the Group completed the sale of Stock Building Supply Holdings LLC which comprised the majority of its US Building Materials segment. In accordance with IFRS 5, 'Non-current assets held for sale and discontinued operations', this business has been classified as discontinued and prior periods have been restated on a consistent basis.

(a) The results of the discontinued operations, which have been included in the consolidated income statement, are as follows:

	Year 5 Before exceptional items £m	Year 5 Exceptional items £m	Year 5 Total £m	Year 4 Before exceptional items £m	Year 4 Exceptional items £m	Year 4 Total £m
Revenue	1,140	–	**1,140**	1,735	–	**1,735**
Cost of sales	−896	–	**−896**	−1,330	–	**−1,330**
Gross profit	244	–	**244**	405	–	**405**
Operating expenses:						
amortisation of acquired intangibles	−12	–	**−12**	−30	–	**−30**
impairment of acquired intangibles	−288	–	**−288**	−114	–	**−114**
other	−361	−156	**−517**	−509	−6	**−515**
Operating expenses: total	−661	−156	**−817**	−653	−6	**−659**
Operating loss before tax	−417	−156	**−573**	−248	−6	**−254**
Tax credit	152	61	**213**	84	2	**86**
Loss on disposal of stock	–	−159	**−159**	–	–	**–**
Tax credit on loss on disposal of stock	–	78	**78**	–	–	**–**
Loss from discontinued operations	−265	−176	**−441**	−164	−4	**−168**

Table 13.6 Wolseley annual report – five-year summary

Five-year summary	Year 5 £m	Year 4 (restated) £m	Year 3 (restated) £m	Year 2 (restated) £m	Year 1 (restated) £m
Revenue from continuing operations					
UK and Ireland	2,699	3,203	3,171	2,690	2,351
France	2,144	2,116	1,872	1,725	1,644
Nordic	2,113	2,290	1,670	–	–
Central and Eastern Europe	965	908	846	735	642
Europe	7,921	8,517	7,559	5,150	4,637
US plumbing and heating	5,820	5,613	5,685	5,396	3,858
Canada	700	684	619	646	512
North America	6,520	6,297	6,304	6,042	4,370
	14,441	14,814	13,863	11,192	9,007
Trading profit from continuing operations					
UK and Ireland	55	176	211	201	183
France	32	103	101	91	98
Nordic	96	159	102	–	–
Central and Eastern Europe	–	–	32	31	30
Europe central costs	−4	−10	−13	−7	−4
Europe	179	428	433	316	307
US plumbing and heating	317	397	411	378	260
Canada	32	39	42	44	36
North America plumbing and heating	349	436	453	422	296
North America loan services	−24	−19	−5	−3	−2
North America central costs	−8	−8	−10	−11	−1
North America	317	409	438	408	293
Group central costs	−49	−50	−43	−37	−25
	447	787	828	687	575
Amortisation of acquired intangibles	−105	−105	−88	−24	−4
Impairment of acquired intangibles	−490	−57	–	–	–
Exceptional items	−458	−70	–	–	–
Operating (loss)/profit from continuing operations	−606	555	740	663	571
Net interest payable	−145	−156	−119	−65	−37
Share of after tax loss of associate	−15	–	–	–	–
(Loss)/profit on ordinary activities before tax from continuing operations	−766	399	621	598	534
Tax credit/(charge)	34	−157	−159	−214	−144
(Loss)/profit on ordinary activities after tax from continuing operations	−732	242	462	384	390
(Loss)/profit from discontinued operations	−441	−168	12	153	89
(Loss)/profit attributable to equity shareholders	−1,173	74	474	537	479
Ordinary dividends	–	−74	−211	−186	−155

Restructuring costs

Restructuring costs are an accounting item that frequently appears in the income statement. Firms need to adapt their existing business to prevailing market conditions or integrate newly acquired activities or firms. In these cases, firms must recognise expenses such as salaries to employees who are dismissed, costs related to termination of lease contracts, etc. Restructuring costs reflect planned actions and provisions that are made to cover those costs. The accounting item is consequently based on management estimates and judgements. The analysts must carefully consider and monitor the accounting item, as it may be used to smooth earnings across time or write-off large amounts (earnings management) so future earnings improve.

Smoothing earnings can be accomplished by, for instance, making provisions in excess of what is actually needed. This provides a firm with the opportunity to reverse (recognise as a reduction of future costs) the provision in subsequent years. Thereby a firm's earnings appear more stable than the underlying operations seem to dictate. Restructuring costs often occur in connection with a change in top management. Management taking office makes use of the opportunity to 'take a big bath' and makes significant provisions for that purpose. If provisions prove to be too large, they are reversed and recognised as income in future years making future earnings higher. Even if provisions made for restructuring are not too large, future earnings are likely to increase. For example, restructuring may include job cuts (lower future personnel expenses) or write-down of assets (lower future depreciation expenses).

In Example 13.6, the Swedish telecom company Ericsson is used to illustrate restructuring charges.

Example 13.6 **Ericsson**

Total announced job cuts are now about 6,500, generating huge restructuring charges with the intention of bringing equally huge cost savings. The Swedish telecom giant said that sales had dropped owing to cuts in investment by mobile phone operators in a number of markets, including in developing nations in central Europe, the Middle East and Africa. In a sign of the impact of the economic crisis on the telecom industry, Ericsson's net profit plunged by 92% to 314 million Swedish Kronor (€30.7 million, $43.4 million) between October and December. That was in contrast to a net profit of 3.89 billion Swedish Kronor in the same period last year, the company said in a statement. The profit margin was much lower than expected as analysts polled by Dow Jones Newswires had forecast a net profit of 3.23 billion Swedish Kronor. Restructuring costs nearly doubled to 4.3 billion Swedish Kronor in the fourth quarter, compared to 2.3 billion Swedish Kronor in the same period last year, and for the full year the charges totalled 11.3 billion Swedish Kronor, the company said. The company estimates that its restructuring programme will cost up to 14 billion Swedish Kronor and bring annual savings of between 15 billion and 16 billion Swedish Kronor.

'When the initial (restructuring) programme was announced, it was anticipated that the actions would result in a reduction of the number of employees by some 5,000, of which about 1,000 in Sweden', Ericsson said.

'The 5,000 has been exceeded and is estimated to reach approximately 6,500', the company said in the statement. Ericsson has also suffered from the difficulties at its two joint ventures, Sony Ericsson and ST-Ericsson, which together chalked up charges of 1.46 billion Swedish Kronor. Sales fell by 13% to 58.3 billion Swedish Kronor in the fourth quarter in the wake of the global economic crisis and growing competition from telecom equipment industry with the rise of China's Huawei. Ericsson said the anticipated decline in sales of older GSM networks had accelerated owing to the economic crisis, but was not yet offset by the growth in mobile broadband and investments in next-generation IP networks.

'During the second half of the year Networks' sales were impacted by reduced operator spending in a number of markets', chief executive Hans Vestberg said in a statement. 'During the year, operators in a number of developing markets, especially central Europe, Middle East and Africa, became increasingly cautious with investments', he said. 'Meanwhile, other markets including China, India and the US continued to show good development with major network buildouts', Vestberg said. Ericsson shares opened 2.6% lower at 70.05 Swedish Kronor at the Stockholm stock exchange after the company announced its results.

Source: http://swedishwire.com/

■

Management may be tempted to 'clean up' in the so-called forward-looking expenses, and as a consequence real future costs are recognised this year. Therefore, it is more likely that future earnings improve. As the provisions for restructuring cover planned initiatives and are based on estimates, the analyst should be particularly on the alert.

Changes in accounting estimates

A number of items in the financial statements are based on estimates and judgements, which require that management in reporting financial data expresses the most likely economic outcome of future events based on the information available at the date the annual report is endorsed. IAS 8 provides a number of examples on accounting estimates:

- The size of expected losses on receivables
- The size of net realisable value for inventories
- The expected lifetime and thereby depreciation period for intangible and tangible non-current assets
- Depreciation methods (e.g. straight-line depreciation)
- Measurement of deferred tax assets
- The size of warranty provisions on sold goods
- The size of pension provisions.

Accounting estimates are likely to be one of the sources that make the most 'noise' in the annual accounts. This is mainly due to the fact that management has some discretion in determining the size of expected losses on receivables or the expected lifetime of an asset. The above list provides just a few examples of accounting items that require management to make estimates. In reality, most accounting items require estimates to be made. For example, the use of percentage-of-completion method as the recognition criteria for income is to some extent based on accounting estimates (e.g. calculating the percentage of completion). An accounting user should be careful in assessing accounting items that require substantial judgements (accounting estimates). Unfortunately, in many instances, it may be difficult to track changes in accounting estimates.

A change in an accounting estimate is an adjustment of the carrying amount of an asset or a liability. Changes in accounting estimates result from new information related to internal or external factors. The effect of changes in accounting estimates are identified retrospectively by recognising the impact in the income statement as follows:

- In the period of the change, if the change affects that period only; or
- In the period of the change and future periods, if the change affects both.

A firm shall disclose the nature and amount of changes in accounting estimates that has an effect in the current period or is expected to have an effect in future periods. However, if the amount of the effect in future periods is not disclosed because estimating it is impracticable, an entity shall disclose that fact.

Source: IAS 8, paras 39, 40

The following three examples (JJB Sports plc, ThyssenKrupp AG and Woodside) illustrate the analytical problems associated with changes in accounting estimates.

Example 13.7 **JJB Sports plc**

JJB Sports plc, a leading UK sports retailer, improved operating earnings by £7.6 million (according to their annual report) by reducing depreciation expenses, resulting from a review of the useful economic lives. The details are provided in JJB Sports Annual Report note 5:

> Following an impairment review on the value of goodwill in the Balance sheet a further review was carried out on the useful economic lives of property, plant and equipment. It was found that many items of property, plant and equipment had useful economic lives that more closely matched the length of the short-term lease of the property in which they were constructed rather than the 10-year economic life which had formed the basis of the depreciation charge in previous accounting periods. The useful economic lives of these items of property, plant and equipment have been restated with effect from 31 January and the rates have been changed as follows:
>
> The annual rate of depreciation for freehold land and buildings has been reduced from 2.5 per cent to 2.0 per cent.
>
> The annual rate of depreciation for the costs of mezzanine floors within the Distribution Centre, together with other costs associated with the structure of the distribution centre and head office buildings, has been reduced from 10.0 per cent to 2.0 per cent. Both the distribution centre and head office are freehold.
>
> The annual rate of depreciation on certain categories of costs within the health clubs, retail stores, head office and distribution centre have been reduced from 10.0 per cent to 4.0 per cent (or a percentage relative to the period of the lease of which the assets are situated, if lower than 25 years). These categories of costs include electrical, air conditioning, plumbing and mechanical assets and the construction costs relating to swimming pools.

Source: JJB Sports Annual Report

An explanation for the change in the useful lives was given in JJB's Interim report for a 26-week period. The chairman and chief executive argue that:

> While undertaking the impairment review on the value of goodwill in the balance sheet for the introduction of IFRS, the Board also considered the carrying value of property, plant and equipment. The review found that many items of property, plant and equipment within our operating units, have useful economic lives that more closely match the length of the short-term lease of the property in which they are constructed, rather than the 10-year economic life which had formed the basis of the depreciation charge in previous accounting periods. The useful economic lives of these items of property, plant and equipment have been restated with effect from 31 January and the consequent effect

upon the income statement for the 26 weeks to 31 July is to reduce the charge for depreciation by £4.3 million.

Source: JJB Sports Interim Report

JJB Sports operating profit fell sharply from approximately £62 million in year 5 to £34 million in year 6. The drop in profit would have been even higher, if JJB Sports had not extended the useful lifetime of its depreciable assets (see Table 13.7).

Table 13.7 **JJB Sports operating profit**

Consolidated income statement for the 52 weeks to 29 January	52 weeks to 29 January	53 weeks to 30 January
	Year 6	Year 5 (restated)
	£000	£000
Continuing operations		
Revenue	745,238	773,339
Cost of sales	−393,075	−402,082
Gross profit	352,163	371,257
Other operating income	3,177	3,079
Distribution expenses	−21,722	−19,272
Administration expenses	−30,705	−31,637
Selling expenses	−268,564	−261,321
Operating profit	34,349	62,106

Whether the extended lifetime of the assets can be justified is hard to tell. However, the explanation that the transition to IFRS had led to rethinking the useful lifetime seems questionable. Depreciable assets should be depreciated over their useful lives, whether IFRS or local GAAP is applied.

The improved profitability (higher operating earnings) may have economic consequences. For instance, JJB Sports may receive a better credit rating, and, therefore, obtain better financing terms, since solvency ratios improves due to the higher assets base. Also, if management obtains bonuses based on earnings, they may have a motive to manage earnings (e.g. utilise accounting policies and estimates which increase earnings). In fact, JJB do have bonus schemes:

Performance related bonus

The Executive Directors are entitled to a performance related bonus scheme to which members of the Associate Director Board of JJB are also entitled. This bonus takes the form of an annual payment, calculated as a percentage of basic salary, based upon the annual pre-tax profits of the Group but dependent upon profit targets being achieved.

Source: JJB Sports Annual Report

Naturally, even though management have bonus schemes or may obtain cheaper funding it does not mean that they manipulate earnings. However, it is important to emphasise that as an analyst, you should be on the alert that if a firm makes changes in accounting estimates then reported earnings may not be taken at face value.

Example 13.8 ThyssenKrupp AG

A company with negative taxable income may carry this loss forward and offset it against future taxable income. Therefore, tax loss carry-forwards represents an asset (i.e. it is recognised as a deferred tax asset), as future income taxes will become smaller. A firm may not be able to fully recover the tax loss carry-forwards. In this case, the asset related to tax loss carry-forwards should not be recognised in full.

To illustrate tax loss carry-forwards, have a closer look at ThyssenKrupp AG. In their annual report they note:

> For deferred tax assets, a valuation allowance of euro 60 (last year: 20) million was established for tax loss carry-forwards. In general, deferred tax assets are recognised to the extent it is considered more likely than not that such benefits will be realised in future years. Management believes that, based on a number of factors, the available evidence creates sufficient uncertainty regarding the ability to realise tax loss carry-forwards. In determining this valuation allowance, all positive and negative factors, also including prospective results were taken into consideration in determining whether sufficient income would be generated to realise deferred tax assets. ∎

Just by reading ThyssenKrupp's criteria for recognising tax assets, including tax loss carry-forwards, it is evident that a great deal of judgement must be exercised by management. The value of the deferred tax asset and the related valuation allowance depends on *prospective results*.

Example 13.9 Woodside

Woodside is Australia's largest publicly traded oil and gas exploration and production company. In its annual report 'Summary of significant accounting policies', the firm states:

> Changes in accounting estimates
> During the year, the Group re-evaluated its estimate of the costs to restore operating facilities, taking into account changes in the method of restoration. The change in estimate associated with the change in the method of restoration resulted in a decrease to the provision for restoration of $779 million and a decrease in the related assets of $779 million. ∎

A decrease in assets improves future profitability, as total depreciation expenses are reduced by $779 million. For an analyst, it is difficult to judge whether the change is warranted or due to earnings management. Restoration of operating facilities far into the future requires a great deal of judgement concerning the timing of the restoration and the costs of restoring the facilities.

Changes in accounting policies

Changes in accounting policies (sometimes labelled accounting principles) may be mandatory or voluntary. For example, all listed groups in the EU had to apply international financial reporting standards as of 1 January 2005 (mandatory change). In

357

these cases, when the applied accounting policies are adjusted to comply with new regulation, firms are taken to act in good faith. Changes in applied accounting policies, however, create comparison problems in a time-series analysis.

IAS 8 requires that the accumulated changes in applied accounting policies by the beginning of the year are recognised directly in equity and that comparatives must be restated to reflect the new practice. As an illustration of the effects of transition to IFRS consider SABMiller, one of the world's leading breweries. In their annual report ending 31 March, they report reconciliation of profit as shown in Table 13.8.

Table 13.8 SABMiller's annual report, note 30

Reconciliation of profit for the year ended 31 March

	UK GAAP US$m	UK to IFRS US$m	IFRS US$m
Revenue	12,901	–	12,901
Net operating expenses	−11,152	798	−10,354
Operating profit	1,749	798	2,547
Operating profit before exceptional items	1,705	427	2,132
Exceptional items	44	371	415
Exceptional items recognised after operating profit	366	−366	–
Net finance costs	−167	24	−143
Interest payable and similar charges	−263	24	239
Interest receivable	96	–	96
Share of post-tax results of associates	246	−98	148
Profit before taxation	2,194	358	2,552
Taxation	−850	27	−823
Profit after taxation	1,344	385	1,729

As can be seen from SABMiller's financial statements, the firm's operating profit increases from US$1,749 million to US$2,547 million after the transition from UK CAAP to IFRS, an increase of US$798 million or 46%. Net earnings increase by US$385 million (from US$1,344 million to US$1,729 million), which is an increase of approximately 26%. The major reason for this significant increase in earnings can be attributed to goodwill. Note (a) to SABMiller's note 30 explains:

Notes to the reconciliations

(a) Goodwill

Under UK GAAP, goodwill was amortised over its estimated useful life (the group typically applied a 20-year life to goodwill, with the exception of goodwill in Amalgamated Beverage Industries (ABI) which has an indefinite life and was subject to annual impairment reviews). Under IFRS, the amortisation of goodwill is no longer permitted and goodwill is reviewed for impairment on an annual basis.

As a result the amortisation charge of US$366 million was reversed and, as a consequence of this change, the profit attributable to minority interests also increased by US$22 million.

As explained in the note, the effects of avoiding amortisation of goodwill amounts to an increase in operating profit of US$366 million. This leaves analysts on their own to restate accounting numbers for past periods, as if goodwill had never been amortised. Naturally, financial statements from prior years are not based on IFRS. These annual reports have been published in the past in compliance with UK GAAP, and the only way analysts can restate accounting numbers to reflect IFRS standards is to do it manually. For example, to adjust for the effects of changes in accounting policies for goodwill in the above SABMiller example, analysts are required to try to carry out impairment tests for each of the comparable years. In other words, they must restate historical accounting numbers for goodwill as if impairment tests had been carried out in the past. This is not likely to improve the information content of the comparable figures. Simply restating accounting numbers as if goodwill had not been amortised historically seems more appropriate. Hereby, the accounting policies become reasonably identical in the analysed period. Unfortunately, turning to the financial review does not provide much help. The comparative figures in the five-year financial review are simply not restated, as shown in Table 13.9.

The above examples illustrate areas that are influenced by the applied accounting policies. There are other areas that should be included as well, for instance, the extent to which applied accounting policies ensure recognition of all accounting items, including debt in the balance sheet. This is important in a credit assessment.

Analysts need to be aware of changes in accounting principles. Firms must disclose whether they change accounting principles, so analysts should always look out for this information, and assess the accounting consequences of such a change. For example, changing accounting principles introduces noise in a time-series analysis. Is an improvement in profitability due to an improvement in the underlying true performance of a firm or is it due to changes in accounting principles? This is difficult to tell if accounting principles change over time. In valuing firms, multiples like the EV/EBIT ratio are often used. If SABMiller is valued at, say, 10 times EBIT, the lack of goodwill amortisation of US$366 million would improve estimated firm value by US$3,660 million (10 × US$366 million). Credit analysts should also consider the effects of changes in accounting principles. Non-amortisation of goodwill strengthens the balance sheet and allows the firm to look healthier (higher solvency). However, in a worst case scenario (i.e. liquidation of the firm), the value of goodwill is zero.

Gains and losses that are not part of core business

A gain or loss from disposal of a non-current asset is measured as the difference between the sales price (less costs to sell) and the book value on the date of disposal. Gains or losses are recognised as part of operations. In reality, such gains and losses are often included as part of depreciation expenses, as they basically express that prior years depreciation expenses have been either too high (a gain on disposal is recognised) or too low (a loss on disposal is recognised).

A gain or loss from disposal of non-current assets is transitory of nature, since it is not possible to generate future income from the disposed assets. It is therefore important to distinguish gains and losses from operating income and expenses; especially if large parts of a firm's assets are sold.

Table 13.9 SABMiller's annual report: Five-year financial review

Five-year financial review for the years ended 31 March

The information included in the five-year summary for the years ended 31 March year 2 to 31 March year 4 is as published under UK GAAP and has not been restated to IFRS. The main adjustments in changing to IFRS are as explained in note 31. Also as explained in note 31, IAS32 and IAS39, which deal with financial instruments, are being applied from 1 April year 5 and consequently the figures for the year ended 31 March year 5 do not reflect the impact of those standards.

	IFRS Year 6 US$m	IFRS Year 5 US$m	UK GAAP Year 5 US$m	UK GAAP Year 4 US$m	UK GAAP Year 3 US$m	UK GAAP Year 2 US$m
Income statements						
Revenue (including associates' share)	17,081	14,543	14,543	12,645	8,984	4,364
Revenue (excluding associates' share)	15,307	12,901	12,901	11,366	8,167	3,717
Operating profit	2,575	2,547	2,104	1,383	803	619
Net finance costs	−299	−143	−143	−152	−142	−83
Share of associates' post-tax results	177	148	159	115	79	49
Taxation	−779	−823	−776	−534	−319	−187
Minority interests	−234	−208	−203	−167	−125	−105
Profit for the year	1,440	1,521	1,141	645	296	293
Adjusted earnings	**1,497**	**1,224**	**1,251**	**925**	**581**	**350**
Balance sheets						
Non-current assets	23,951	12,869	12,287	11,483	10,431	4,758
Current assets	2,825	2,778	2,941	2,316	1,819	933
Total assets	**26,776**	**15,647**	**15,228**	**13,799**	**12,250**	**5,691**
Derivative financial instruments	−178	–	–	–	–	–
Borrowings	−7,582	−3,340	−3,339	−3,707	−3,523	−1,535
Other liabilities and provisions	5,417	−3,552	−3,586	−3,108	−2,377	−1,102
Total liabilities	**−13,177**	**−6,892**	**−6,925**	**−6,815**	**−5,900**	**−2,637**
Net assets	13,599	8,755	8,303	6,984	6,350	3,054
Total shareholders' equity	13,045	8,077	7,665	6,165	5,572	2,309
Minority interests in equity	554	678	638	819	778	745
Total equity	**13,599**	**8,755**	**8,303**	**6,984**	**6,350**	**3,054**

Example 13.10 **FLSmidth**

FLSmidth is a global engineering group employing approximately 10,500 people in 42 countries worldwide. During an extended period of time, the firm has reduced its number of business units. Gains and losses of disposal of business units and other non-current assets comprise a substantial contribution to FLSmidth's (reported) earnings. In Table 13.10 the contribution from disposal of assets (business units) for FLSmidth is provided. For comparison purposes, earnings both excluding and including gains and losses from disposal of non-current assets are reported.

Table 13.10 FLSmidth – earnings effects of gains and losses on disposal of non-current asset

FLSmidth	Year 1	Year 2	Year 3	Year 4	Year 5	Year 6	Year 7	Average
Gains/losses from disposal	99	115	1,357	108	121	−517	714	285
Earnings before tax excluded gains/losses	1,019	1,032	1,399	621	−133	−830	−3,264	−22
Earnings before tax	1,118	1,147	2,756	729	−12	−1,347	−2,550	263

As expected, the contribution from gains and losses varies considerably over time. Furthermore, average earnings during the seven year period were a deficit of 22 million, if gains and losses from disposal of non-current assets were excluded. This clearly indicates that FLSmidth on average only reports positive earnings numbers due to gains from disposal of assets. From an analytical point of view reported earnings appears to be of low quality as it almost entirely consists of gains and losses from disposal of non-current items; i.e. items that are transitory items in nature. ■

Impairment losses on non-current assets

According to IAS 16 and IAS 36 non-current assets must be written-down if net realisable value is lower than book value; that is if assets are impaired. Assets may be impaired for a variety of reasons including:

• Damage of the asset
• Technical obsolescence
• Discontinuation of production
• Reduced profitability for the produced products.

A write-off of a non-current asset reduces future depreciation and amortisation expenses making it easier for management to improve profitability in future periods. Alternatively, a write-off may be regarded as an adjustment to previous year's amortisation and depreciation expenses. In this case, management has either misjudged the true lifetime of depreciable and amortisable assets or has engaged in earnings management. Most firms need to write down assets from time to time. The analytical problem arises when a firm decides to write off large amounts. The following example illustrates this.

Example 13.11 World Com

World Com, a former American phone company recognised a write-off of goodwill and other assets of approximately US$80 billion in March 2003. From an analytical point of view, it is fair to assume that the impairment is not due to a sudden value destruction of the assets; the sheer magnitude of the impairment loss makes this hard to believe. Prior years reported earnings are obviously overvalued and accounting quality appears to be low. The problem in World Com's is that the impairment loss is arguably recognised too late. In fact, shortly after the impairment loss is reported, World Com is declared bankrupt. Analysts need to get access to information or signals, which have a material impact on the assessment of growth, profitability and risk, as soon as possible. In the case of World Com, the signal came too late.

The above assessment of transitory accounting items illustrates that many types of such items are likely to be found in annual reports. Bradshaw and Sloan (2002) found in an American study that the so-called 'special items' (transitory items) are increasing over time. The results of this study are shown in Figure 13.2. ■

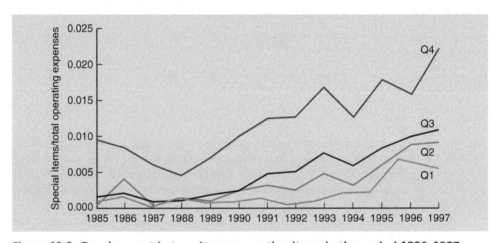

Figure 13.2 **Development in transitory accounting items in the period 1985–1997**

As is evident, transitory accounting items have the greatest impact in the fourth quarter, which indicates that management uses these accounting items in order to manage earnings. In this way, management may for instance be able to report earnings that are on a par with analysts' earnings forecasts.

Generally, accounting users should be wary of accounting items classified as transitory. The critical accounting user needs to examine the extent to which accounting items are truly transitory. The analyst might ask the obvious question: is it the case that transitory accounting items are likely to be recurring in nature and mainly include items that reduce earnings (i.e. items are expenses or losses)? Could it not be that items and events that are labelled transitory vary across time and firms?

It has been confirmed by a number of studies that transitory items in many cases are truly permanent, though it may be acknowledged that such items fluctuate substantially over time making them hard to forecast. Doyle et al. (2003), for instance, find that accounting items, which are classified as transitory items, in reality are often permanent. Even more interestingly, analysts seem to ignore this issue. Doyle et al. demonstrate that analysts, who exclude (in earnings) the so-called transitory items, tend to overrate a firm's future cash flow potential.

In case the analysed firm is characterised by a high number of transitory accounting items, these items should be carefully considered in, for instance, forecasting. The task is not an easy one, as the amount and the events recognised as transitory accounting items may vary greatly over time. Analysts may try to circumvent the problem by averaging special items, which are considered permanent by analysts. For example, Bayer Group has reported special items (regarded by analysts as being permanent) amounting to €533 million, €717 million, €1,133 million, €798 million and €766 million, respectively during the past five years. Analysts may wish to forecast such items using the average amount of €789 million. By not separating permanent from transitory accounting items in forecasting, accounting users commit an (unintentional) error and may consequently miscalculate the future cash flow potential of the analysed firm.

The level of information in financial statements

An important issue in assessing accounting quality is to evaluate whether the level of information is satisfactory. The level of information can be assessed along at least two dimensions: (1) The availability of information and (2) the quality of information. The availability of information refers to whether the analysts have sufficient data to make potential adjustments. As discussed, analysts need to separate transitory from permanent accounting items. It is therefore important that firms provide the data that are needed to make a qualified distinction between these types of accounting items. As illustrated above, Bayer Group discloses special items separately, which makes it possible for analysts to make their own judgements.

The other dimension is the quality of the data that firms provide. To be useful, information should be reliable and relevant. It may prove difficult to measure the quality of the reported data. The following examples illustrate how analysts might assess the reliability of information provided by management in financial reports. In order to measure management's credibility, outlook (e.g. earnings forecasts) may be compared to realised results. This comparison is made for Hartmann and DSV Group for the past years.

Example 13.12 **Hartmann**

Hartmann is among the three largest manufacturers of moulded-fibre egg packaging in the world and also manufactures moulded-fibre industrial packaging. Hartmann has adjusted earnings forecasts downward seven times in five years and during this period of time, the firm overestimated EBIT by approximately DKK 30 million per year. It is on average an overestimation of EBIT by approximately 40%. See Table 13.11.

Table 13.11 Stock exchange announcements from Hartmann – downward adjustments by Hartmann

Year 1	Year 2	Year 3	Year 3	Year 4	Year 4	Year 5
Downward adjustment of EBIT from 101 DKKm to 80–85 DKKm	Downward adjustment of EBIT from 49 DKKm to 25–35 DKKm	Downward adjustment of EBIT from 105 DKKm to 70 DKKm	Downward adjustment of EBIT from 70 DKKm to 60 DKKm	Downward adjustment of EBIT from 80–90 DKKm to 70 DKKm	Downward adjustment of EBIT from 70 DKKm to 40 DKKm	Downward adjustment of EBIT from −15 DKKm to −65 DKKm

■

Example 13.13 **DSV**

For another example, consider the DSV Group. The DSV Group offers end-to-end transport and logistics solutions worldwide. Table 13.12 compares management's outlook in the annual report with realised earnings. Even though the budget deviations vary over time, the total budget discrepancy is only DKK 11 million or approximately DKK 2 million per year. It is a budget discrepancy of less than 1% compared to Hartmann's budget discrepancy of 40%.

Table 13.12 Budgeted and realised earnings before tax for DSV Group

DSV Group (DDK million)	Year 1	Year 2	Year 3	Year 4	Year 5	Year 6	Total
Budgeted earnings before tax	111	137	182	310	539	539	1.818
Realised earnings before tax	117	144	195	315	507	529	1.807
Budget difference	6	7	13	5	−32	−10	−11

The above comparison clearly indicates that information provided by the DSV Group is of higher quality than data provided by Hartmann; at least as far as earnings forecasts are concerned.

Example 13.14 **Danisco**

Danisco is a leading manufacturer of ingredients. Below Danisco's financial target for its most important division, Ingredients and Sweetener, is shown in Figure 13.3. As the graph illustrates, Danisco has a target ROIC of 15%. By comparing the financial target of a ROIC of 15% with realised returns for the period year 1 to year 5, a substantial difference is apparent. Danisco did not hit its target during the analysed five-year period. ROIC fluctuates around 9–10% in the period; far from the target of 15%. Thus, Danisco's own financial target seems to be too ambitious. Analysts most likely overestimate the potential in the division Ingredients and Sweetener if a ROIC of 15% is used as a starting point for forecasting.

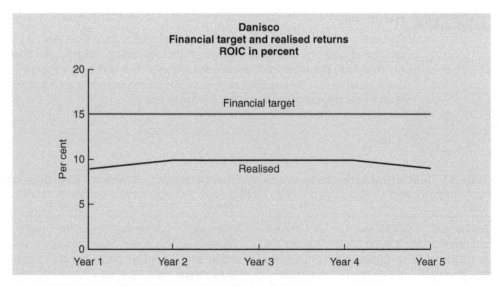

Figure 13.3 Comparison of realised and target ROIC

Another important indicator of quality of data in the annual report is the auditors' report. These reports may contain valuable information as illustrated in Example 13.15.

Example 13.15 ## Valence Technology

Valence Technology, which is listed on NASDAQ, is an international leader in the development, manufacturing and supply of lithium phosphate energy storage solutions. The firm received an audit opinion containing a 'going concern' qualification, as illustrated in the following quotation from the report.

REPORT OF INDEPENDENT REGISTERED PUBLIC ACCOUNTING FIRM

To the Board of Directors and Shareholders of Valence Technology, Inc. and Subsidiaries Austin, Texas.

We have audited the accompanying consolidated statements of operations and comprehensive loss, stockholders' deficit, and cash flows of Valence Technology, Inc. and subsidiaries (the 'Company') for the year ended March 31, Year 6. These financial statements are the responsibility of the Company's management. Our responsibility is to express an opinion on these financial statements based on our audit.

We conducted our audit in accordance with the standards of the Public Company Accounting Oversight Board (United States). Those standards require that we plan and perform the audit to obtain reasonable assurance about whether the financial statements are free of material misstatement. An audit includes examining, on a test basis, evidence supporting the amounts and disclosures in the financial statements. An audit also includes assessing the accounting principles used and significant estimates made by management, as well as evaluating the overall financial statement presentation. We believe that our audit provides a reasonable basis for our opinion.

In our opinion, such consolidated financial statements present fairly, in all material respects, the results of operations, comprehensive loss, and cash flows of the Company for the years ended March 31, Year 6 in conformity with accounting principles generally accepted in the United States of America.

As discussed in Note 3 to the consolidated financial statements the Company adopted SFAS 123R during the year ended March 31, Year 7.

The accompanying consolidated financial statements have been prepared assuming that the Company will continue as a going concern. As discussed in Note 2 to the consolidated financial statements, the Company's recurring losses from operations, negative cash flows from operations and net stockholders' capital deficiency raise substantial doubt about its ability to continue as a going concern. Management's plans concerning these matters are also described in Note 2. The consolidated financial statements do not include any adjustments that might result from the outcome of this uncertainty.

We also have audited, in accordance with the standards of the Public Company Accounting Oversight Board (United States), the Company's internal control over financial reporting as of March 31, Year 8, based on criteria established in Internal Control – Integrated Framework issued by the Committee of Sponsoring Organizations of the Treadwayomission

(COSO) and our report dated June 16, Year 8 expressed an adverse opinion on the effectiveness of the Company's internal control over financial reporting.

PMB HELIN DONOVAN, LLP

Austin, Texas

June 16, Year 8

The Auditors' report states that Valence's financial statements present fairly the results of operations, comprehensive loss and cash flow. However, they also state:

As discussed in Note 2 to the consolidated financial statements, the Company's recurring losses from operations, negative cash flows from operations and net stockholders' capital deficiency raise substantial doubt about its ability to continue as a going concern. Management's plans concerning these matters are also described in Note 2. The consolidated financial statements do not include any adjustments that might result from the outcome of this uncertainty. ∎

The auditors therefore question Valence's ability to continue its businesses as a going concern. Analysts should thoroughly consider the reported accounting numbers. For instance, if it is questionable whether the company is able to continue as a going concern, lenders may have to call the debt. In that case, what matters is the liquidation value of Valence's assets and liabilities, whose values are generally not reflected in the annual report except for items marked-to-market (fair value) such as cash and securities.

Often, information in the financial statements is not sufficient to make the adjustments that are necessary to obtain identical accounting policies over time or across of firms. The analyst may therefore consider to what extent it affects financial ratios. If valuable information is left out of the annual report, the analyst should be sceptical. Reported earnings are assessed to be of lower quality, if important pieces of information related to earnings are not disclosed.

Identification of 'red flags'

Analysts may identify various issues and problems in carrying out financial statement analysis. Such issues are often named 'red flags'. In the previous sections, a large number of factors used in assessing accounting quality have been discussed. All those factors are considered in identifying red flags. In addition, certain conditions relating to the firm's financial position may indicate a red flag (the list is not exhaustive):

- The quality of a firm's business model
- Unsatisfactory development in accounting numbers and financial ratios
- The firm's ability to convert accounting income to cash flows.

Quality of a firm's business model

When assessing the quality of a firm's business model, it is crucial that operations have proved its sustainability. Often, it is suggested that a historical financial statement analysis should cover a five-year period. In assessing the quality of the firm's business model, it is often a good idea to examine operating earnings over an even longer period of time. This requires that the underlying business model is fairly identical throughout the analysed period.

Example 13.16 | **Andersen & Martini**

Since the mid-1980s Andersen & Martini has been listed on the Copenhagen Stock Exchange. The firm sells automobiles. As illustrated in Figure 13.4, Andersen & Martini has had operating earnings circling around zero. Average operating earnings (EBIT) over the period is close to a deficit of DKK 1 million. In comparison, net earnings before tax average DKK 7 million annually. This implies that Andersen & Martini has had average annual earnings of approximately DKK 8 million from activities that are outside the scope of its core business. There is hardly any doubt that Andersen & Martini's business model is not sustainable in the long run and unless analysts observe significant strategic changes, the firm's long-term survival may be questioned. It should be noted that earnings not related to Andersen & Martini's core business basically consisted of interest earned on the firm's securities (bonds). ∎

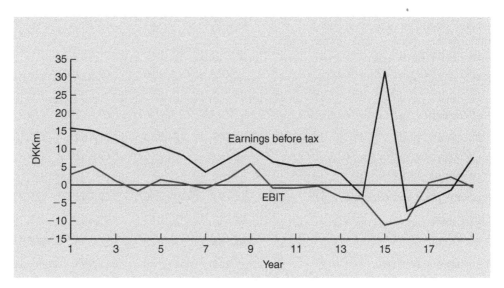

Figure 13.4 Assessment of Andersen & Martin's business model

Unsatisfactory development in accounting numbers and financial ratios

An unsatisfactory level and trend in accounting numbers and financial ratios often expose problems related to a firm's economic position – within vital areas of profitability, risk or growth. Table 13.13 highlights key figures for the past five years for Oki Electric Industry, a company listed on the Tokyo Stock Exchange. A quick look at Oki's financials reveals the following.

During the past five years, sales decreased by approximately 21% (from Yen 688,542 million to Yen 545,680 million). Total assets fell by even more (almost 35%), indicating that Oki improved asset turnover. However, gross profit deteriorated by 27%. Net earnings show the same negative trend except for a substantial improvement in year 8, but net income in year 8 was barely positive. Not surprisingly, Oki reports poor financial ratios. For instance, return on equity changed from 8.6% (11,174/130,040)

367

Table 13.13 Oki Electric Industry – five-year summary (from annual report)

Five-year summary

Oki Electric Industry Co., Ltd and consolidated subsidiaries

Years ended March 31

	Millions of yen				
	Year 9	Year 8	Year 7	Year 6	Year 5
For the year:					
Net sales	545,680	719,677	718,767	680,526	688,542
Cost of sales	410,658	554,343	560,817	514,483	504,340
Gross profit	135,021	165,334	157,949	166,043	184,202
Operating income (loss)	410	6,200	(5,410)	10,593	27,220
Other income (expenses), net	−36,810	−1,337	−10,720	−133	−8,920
Income (loss) before income taxes, minority interests and equity in earnings (losses) of affiliates	−36,400	4,863	−16,130	10,460	18,299
Net income (loss)	−45,011	567	−36,446	5,058	11,174
At year end:					
Total current assets	275,247	374,334	405,161	379,135	374,278
Total investments and long-term receivables	34,423	33,653	58,025	71,052	61,492
Property, plant and equipment, net	61,170	125,788	129,696	125,223	126,470
Other assets	26,121	37,043	35,515	43,244	44,996
Total assets	396,963	570,819	628,398	618,655	607,237
Total current liabilities	205,965	311,180	318,996	295,865	313,828
Total long-term liabilities	132,313	158,262	193,428	182,770	163,369
Total net assets	58,683	101,376	115,973	140,019	130,040
Common stock	76,940	76,940	76,940	67,882	67,877

in year 5 to –77% (–45,011/58,683) in year 9. The debt-to-equity ratio increased from 3.7 (477,197/130,040) in year 5 to 5.8 (338,278/58,683) in year 9. In conclusion, Oki's growth and profitability deteriorated substantially over the five-year period. At the same time, financial risk increased.

The stock market did not appreciate the development in Oki. During the period the stock price fell sharply from approximately 500 to under 100 – a decrease of more than 80%.

In case the analysis indicates the occurrence of red flags, it will most likely affect the value of the firm negatively. Lenders will likewise seek compensation for the greater risk by charging a higher price (interest rate).

The firm's ability to convert accounting earnings to cash flows

Accounting-based earnings measures are indicators of how much cash that has been created in a given period. However, in some cases, accounting-based earnings may not materialise in cash flows. Creative bookkeeping and accounting manipulation may cause a discrepancy between accounting-based earnings and cash flows. Even though cash flows and earnings in the long run should be of the same magnitude, there are some natural exceptions. Firms, which grow substantially, often need to make huge investments (in working capital and non-current assets) and therefore report negative cash flows. However, over the lifetime of a firm accumulated accounting earnings and accumulated cash flows ought to match. If earnings and cash flows do not correlate in the long run, analysts should be critical of the validity of reported earnings. Ultimately, the analyst may find that accounting-based performance measures (e.g. EBIT) are inappropriate in assessing a firm's future earnings potential.

To assess a firm's ability to convert earnings to cash flows, the cash conversion rate is a useful tool:

$$\text{Cash conversion rate} = \frac{\text{FCFE}}{\text{Net earnings}} \times 100$$

where

FCFE = The free cash flow to equity, where investments in non-current assets equal reinvestments (reinvestments = depreciation + amortisation expenses)

The cash conversion rate eliminates the effect of acquired growth and expresses, in per cent, the part of net earnings, which is converted to cash. As reinvestments are typically not reported by companies, analysts have to apply proxies for reinvestments. One possibility is to use depreciation and amortisation as a proxy for reinvestments. To illustrate the idea the cash conversion rate for ISS, one of the largest facility services companies in the world, is shown in Table 13.14.

Table 13.14 **Cash conversion rate for ISS**

(All amounts in DKKm)	Year 1	Year 2	Year 3	Year 4	Year 5
FCF	460	795	874	1,058	1,739
Net earnings	487	622	830	898	1,115
Cash conversion rate	94%	128%	105%	118%	156%

The level as well as the trend in the cash conversion rate is positive in ISS. With the exception of year 1 the cash conversion rate is in excess of 100%, which indicates good cash management. DKK 1 million in core earnings (before goodwill amortisation) is converted to cash in excess of DKK 1 million. An immediate interpretation is that accounting earnings are of high quality.

Sloan (1996) shows in an American study that the closer the association between cash flows and accounting-based earnings, the better accounting-based earnings are in signalling next year's earnings. In addition, Sloan demonstrates that investors to some extent ignore that certain firms use accruals to affect reported accounting earnings. It seems as though investors overvalue next year's earnings in firms that use accruals to improve reported earnings (earnings management). By avoiding these types of firms and buying shares in firms, where there is a close link between cash flows and accounting earnings excessive returns may be obtained. Sloan's research supports that accounting earnings, at some point in time, must be converted to cash flows. If this does not happen, the value of reported accounting earnings is of limited relevance, i.e. of low quality.

Total assessment of accounting quality

The analysts should make a total assessment of accounting quality. This assessment may be used to make the necessary precautions before calculating financial ratios. A total evaluation of accounting quality may also be used to rank firms against one another. A firm that achieves the best rating will, other things being equal, be a more attractive investment opportunity or a likely candidate for offering credit facilities. In Table 13.15 we demonstrate how a simple rating of accounting quality may be carried out.

Table 13.15 **Total assessment of accounting quality**

Assessment of the following statements:	True				False
	1	2	3	4	5
Analysis of accounting quality has generally shown:					
Few motives for accounting manipulation	X				
A high degree of quality in accounting policies		X			
A high degree of recurring accounting items	X				
A high level of information in the annual report		X			
Few 'red flags' in the financial statements		X			
Total appraisal	1, 6				

As seen in the table, a low value is synonymous with a high level of accounting quality, while a high value signifies low accounting quality. The analysts may make the same assessment of firms they cover. As an example, consider the assessment of the accounting quality of four firms within the same industry shown in Table 13.16.

Table 13.16 **Example on rating of the accounting quality of four firms within the same industry**

Firm 3	1.6
Firm 1	2.4
Firm 2	2.8
Firm 4	4.0

'Firm 3' is characterised by financial statements of substantially higher quality than 'firm 4'. In case both firms report identical accounting figures and financial ratios, greater credibility is assigned to the accounting numbers and financial ratios reported by 'firm 3'. This will most likely result in a more efficient pricing of the firm's shares reducing investors required rate of return. On the other hand, a firm that manipulates accounting figures may also cheat in other areas. In this case, the pricing on the firm's shares is affected negatively reflecting that investors require a higher rate of return.

The above analysis is based on the five areas that are all part of assessing accounting quality in this book. There is nothing preventing an analyst in choosing other areas than those discussed in this book. The crucial point is that accounting quality is examined carefully. Furthermore, each of the five areas is weighted equally. The analysts may choose to assign a different weight to each area. For example, by assessing earnings quality the extent of recurring earnings may be considered more important than the general level of information in the annual report.

Conclusions

When assessing a firm's accounting quality the analysts will hardly ever obtain a consistent and neutral assessment of a firm's growth, profitability and risk. It's difficult to see through every accounting entry and often reported (financial) data are insufficient in respect of assessing accounting quality of the analysed firm. Additionally, making adjustments to the financial statements requires that the analysts make a number of estimates and judgements. This also implies that the results of the analysts' efforts in assessing accounting quality are indicative only. The fathers of fundamental analysis, Graham and Dodd (1934, p. 352), express it as follows: 'It must always be remembered that the truth which the analyst uncovers is first of all not the *whole* truth and, secondly, not the *immutable* truth. The result of his study is only a *more nearly correct version of the past.*'

Detailed insight into the analysed firm, including its accounting policies, is needed. Furthermore, there is a need to compare accounting policies across comparable firms in order to determine industry norms. There might be a need for further clarification of various accounting items, which often requires that management is contacted. Experience indicates that listed firms often respond to such requests, while non-listed firms do not find that they are obliged to do so.

Most importantly, you must remember that uncritical use of accounting information may cause losses for the lender, investor and other users of financial statements. Due care must be taken in carrying out financial statement analysis.

Review questions

- What is meant by accounting quality?
- Why might management be interested in managing or manipulating earnings?
- What are the steps in examining accounting quality?
- How is the quality of accounting policies assessed?

- Why should analysts care about transitory items?

- How can the analysts evaluate the quality of information in the annual report?

- What are 'red flags'?

- What are the economic consequences of differences in applied accounting policies?

Note

1 Assuming 'steady-state' in financial ratios in all future periods, the EVA model can be shown as:

$$\text{Enterprise value} = \text{Invested capital} + \frac{(\text{ROIC} - \text{WACC}) \times \text{invested capital}}{\text{WACC}}$$

The second term is an annuity in perpetuity.

References

Bradshaw, M.T. and R.G. Sloan (2002) 'GAAP versus the street: An empirical assessment of two alternative definitions of earnings', *Journal of Accounting Research*, No. 1: 41–66.

Doyle, J.T., R.J. Lundholm and M.T. Soliman (2003) 'The predictive value of expenses excluded from pro forma earnings', *Review of Accounting Studies*, No. 8: 145–74.

Graham, B. and D. Dodd (1934) *Security Analysis*, McGraw-Hill.

Gramlich, J., M.L. McAnally and J. Thomas (2001) 'Balance sheet management: The case of short-term obligations reclassified as long term debt', *Journal of Accounting Research*, No. 2: 283–95.

Gramlich, J. and O. Sørensen (2004) 'Voluntary management earnings forecasts and discretionary accruals: Evidence from Danish IPOs', *European Accounting Review*, vol. 13, 2: 235–59.

Naser, K.H.M. (1993) *Creative Financial Accounting: Its Nature and Use*, Prentice Hall.

Penman, S. (2010) *Financial Statement Analysis and Security Valuation*, 4th edn, McGraw-Hill.

Schipper, K. (1989) 'Commentary on earnings management', *Accounting Horizons*, 3: 91–102.

Sloan, R.G. (1996) 'Do stock prices fully reflect information in accruals and cash flows about future earnings?', *The Accounting Review*, No. 3: 289–315.

CHAPTER 14

Accounting flexibility in the income statement

Learning outcomes

After reading this chapter you should be able to:

- Discuss and understand a firm's accounting policies
- Understand how changes in a firm's accounting policies affect the financial statements
- Understand the potential impact of accounting flexibility on revenue recognition, non-recurring and special items and non-capitalisation of expenses
- Map economic consequences due to accounting flexibility
- Comprehend management's potential discretion on reported accounting numbers and chosen disclosure policy
- Make adjustments to financial statements so they can be used as input to decision models

Accounting flexibility in the income statement

So far we have taken reported financial data at face value. For instance, in reformulating the financial statements for analytical purposes, we discussed how to separate operating from financing items. However, we did not make any adjustments to firms' reported numbers. Why might accounting numbers need to be adjusted as part of the analysis? Consider the following statement.

> Financial data and various financial ratios serve as input to decision models (e.g. the DCF model). Based on the decision model, the analyst makes his or her recommendations and a decision is made (e.g. whether to buy or sell shares). This process is depicted as follows:
>
> ---
> Financial data and financial ratios → Decision models → Economic decisions
> ---

It is noteworthy that reported financial data is based on (1) a firm's accounting policies (flexibility in choosing between alternative accounting methods) and (2) a number of subjective estimates (management discretion). As a result, reported financial data, used for decision purposes, may vary greatly depending upon *who* is preparing the financial statements. For example, imagine that 10 CFOs (or auditors) were asked to prepare financial statements for an IT firm, which produces hardware and develops and sells software and business solutions. Would they report the same accounting numbers? Highly unlikely. Just consider a few issues:

If the firm sells computer equipment with two years of 'free' support and software updates how much should be recognised as revenue each year? Should inventory be accounted for using the FIFO method or some other method? Should R&D be expensed as incurred or capitalised? What is the expected lifetime of the firm's property, plant and equipment? How much of accounts receivable is uncollectable? Is goodwill impaired and needs to be written down? And so on.

Answers to such questions depend upon the accounting policies used by the firm and estimates and underlying assumptions made by the preparer of the financial statements (e.g. expected useful lifetime for intangible and tangible assets). Furthermore, even in those cases where management does not intend to affect reported accounting figures in a desired direction, biased accounting information (noise) may be inevitable. This will be the case if, for instance, a firm must change accounting policies due to new or revised reporting regulation. An example is the mandatory use of IFRS for all listed groups in the EU from 2005. If these groups do not adjust the historical accounting numbers retrospectively, it is at best difficult to separate the consequences of changes in applied accounting policies and real changes in a firm's underlying operations. This is problematic in a time-series analysis or when benchmarking against competitors. Therefore, financial statements are likely to contain measurement errors even if the CFOs have the best intentions to portray the true underlying performance of the firm. To produce unbiased financial data would require perfect foresight, which nobody has. In conclusion, since recorded data depend upon accounting policy choices and estimates, reported financial data depend upon *who* is preparing the financial statements.

In this and the following chapter, we go behind reported numbers to assess **accounting flexibility** and how it may distort the analysis. If not properly accounted for, the distortion may have (severe) economic consequences. An overview of the two chapters is provided below:

Chapter 14: Accounting flexibility in the income statement	Chapter 15: Accounting flexibility in the balance sheet
Changes in accounting policies	Inventory accounting
Revenue recognition criteria	Intangible and tangible assets
Non-recurring and special items	Lease accounting
Non-capitalisation of expenses	Provisions
	Deferred tax liabilities

It should be pointed out that other accounting issues can be found in practice. However, a thorough understanding of the issues listed above should help analysts to assess other accounting items, and evaluate how firms' accounting policies and estimates for those items affect various decision models. It should be noted that items listed above do not always cause 'noise' in the analysis. For instance, if a firm is valued based on discounting its projected cash flows, depreciation and amortisation expenses (related to the item 'Intangible and tangible assets' above) should not matter.[1]

In the next section we make a short introduction to **accounting regulation** in an attempt to highlight major characteristics across accounting regimes followed by a description of accounting flexibility. Finally, we discuss potential economic consequences of the inherent flexibility in reporting financial statements.

Accounting regulation and flexibility

Firms must provide financial information that can be used by a variety of users for decision-making purposes. To be useful, financial data should be relevant, reliable and comparable. Annual accounts are generally audited (depending on local accounting regulation) by independent auditors. Nonetheless, reported financial data would depend upon not only accounting policy choices and estimates but also the accounting regulation which the firm must comply with.

Accounting regulation around the world differs (see Figure 14.1); as a consequence, reported numbers (financial statements) depend upon the accounting regulation a firm must comply with. A prime, and often used, example is Daimler Benz. In 1994, Daimler Benz reported profits of approximately US$ 100 million according to what is believed to be conservative German accounting rules. In comparison, under US GAAP, Daimler Benz reported a US$ 1 billion loss.[2] Even within the same country, firms may have to apply different accounting standards. For instance, in the EU listed groups must comply with IFRS, but non-listed firms follow local GAAP.[3]

Accounting regimes	
IFRS	Local GAAP
Mandatory for EU listed firms and a host of other countries outside of the EU	(e.g. US GAAP, German GAAP etc.)
Less strict rules for SMEs	The government in a country decides
(small and medium-sized enterprises)	if IFRS may be used for SMEs

Figure 14.1 **Differences in accounting regimes**

Accounting regulators, whether IASB, FASB or other local accounting regimes, face some serious challenges as they should develop accounting standards which:

- Are the same over time, across industries and across accounting regimes
- Are strict and detailed, with little flexibility, to avoid earnings management, *but*
- Are also flexible enough to provide management the opportunity to report financial data which incorporates their propriety information about the company.

Uniform accounting standards attempt to mitigate managements' ability to record similar economic transactions in a dissimilar way over time or across companies. Even if standards become universal, measurement issues are still not eliminated. The uses of fair value as a measurement attribute and impairment tests involve a great deal of judgement, which may hinder comparability across firms. Even the most rigid and strict rules do not, and probably should not, prevent management using judgements and estimates in preparing financial statements. A simple example can be used to illustrate this point.

Example 14.1 Accounting regulation around the world requires firms to amortise intangible assets over their useful lives, unless those intangibles have an indefinite lifetime.[4] However, regulation is not so strict as to determine the useful lifetime of such assets. It would make no sense to make a standard which requires all intangible assets to be amortised over a predetermined period of time, say, five years. The actual lifetime of those assets hinges on numerous assumptions, which may vary greatly across industries and time. For instance, if a firm that produces different kinds of drugs capitalises development expenses, the amortisation period for these expenses should match the period the drugs are being sold on the market. This period would often be difficult to estimate (maybe unless the firm has a patent on the drugs), as cheaper or better drugs may come to the market and leave a prior blockbuster almost worthless. ∎

It should be noted that there is an ongoing convergence project that aims at aligning IFRS with US GAAP. In addition, over time more countries have selected to apply IFRS. Therefore, in the long run a set of universal acceptable accounting standards may occur.[5] However, these standards are likely to be mandatory for listed firms only. Since the majority of firms in every country are non-listed there may still be major differences between accounting regulation for listed versus non-listed firms.

Even if only one set of accounting standards is considered, major differences in reported numbers are likely to occur for identical firms. This is due to the fact that management needs to make estimates, judgements (assumptions) and predictions (forecast) as underlying premises for producing financial statements. For example, management need to make impairment tests. This requires forecasts (predictions) of the assets' future net cash inflows. If the assets cannot generate sufficient cash inflows (i.e. if book value exceeds the present value of the future cash flows),[6] then the assets are impaired and an impairment loss must be recognised as an expense. Changing the forecasts and/or the discount rate slightly may mean that an impairment loss that should have been recognised is avoided or vice versa. This implies that a firm may not recognise an impairment loss, which they should have recognised. Why management may wish to 'colour' the financial statements has been discussed in Chapter 13.

Accounting flexibility also includes lack of regulation. Naturally, regulation cannot foresee every business transaction, which needs to be recorded today or sometimes in the distant future. As a result, this accounting regulation has little to say or may be silent on how to account for various complex transactions. The IAS T/B considers this in IAS 8:

In the absence of a Standard or an Interpretation that specifically applies to a transaction, other event or condition, management must use its judgement in developing and applying an accounting policy that results in information that is relevant and reliable, IAS 8.10. In making that judgement, management must refer to, and consider the applicability of, the following sources in descending order:

- *The requirements and guidance in IASB standards and interpretations dealing with similar and related issues.*
- *The definitions, recognition criteria and measurement concepts for assets, liabilities, income and expenses in the Framework. [IAS 8.11]*

Source: www.iasplus.com

It is ultimately left to research and practice to examine whether accounting standards that have strict rules are preferable in the sense that they provide the best data for decision making. On the one hand, having strict rules makes it more difficult for managers to manage earnings, for instance, in an attempt to meet bonus targets or analysts' forecasts. On the other hand, management has a detailed understanding of their company's business model and factors that affect profitability, growth and risk. Therefore, requiring strict rules with little discretion may mean that management is not able to report numbers which takes into consideration the proprietary information that they hold.

Conceptual framework

Standard setters such as IASB and FASB have developed a **conceptual framework** and a number of standards, which prescribe how firms deal with the definition, recognition and measurement of the elements of financial statements, how elements are presented (classification) and which information needs to be disclosed. These issues are discussed below.

Definition of elements
For example:

- Which transactions to recognise?
- Which items qualify as assets and which as expenses?
- Which items qualify as revenue and which as liabilities or equity?

Recognition criteria
For example:

- When should items be recognised?
- What conditions must be met for items to be recognised?

Measurement issues
For example:

- Which measurement attributes should be assigned to accounting items at initial recognition?
- How should items be valued at future dates?

Classification issues
For example:

- How should items be classified in the financial statements?
- How detailed should items be classified?

Disclosure issues
For example:

- What other kind of information is needed?
- How much voluntary information is provided?

The following simple examples are used to illustrate why definition, recognition, measurement, classification and disclosure issues should be considered in any financial statement analysis.

Example 14.2 | Definition of assets

According to IFRS, assets are defined as resources under an entity's control, as a result of a past event and from which the firm is likely to obtain future economic benefits. The following two examples illustrate how the definition of assets has an impact on the financial data:

- If a firm launches a huge marketing campaign it is likely to increase future sales (future economic benefits), but marketing costs are not capitalised. This implies that a proper match between revenue and costs is impossible due to the definition of assets.
- Human capital is the most valuable resource for many firms. A law firm may have acquired an office building, office furniture, cars and information technology. All such assets are easily replaceable and recognised as assets. However, the most important resources, the employees of the law firm, are not recognised as assets, since employees do not meet the definition of an asset. They are not under the firm's control, but are generally free to leave with fairly short notice. This will have an impact on reported invested capital and thereby also on financial ratios such as ROIC and profit margin. ∎

Example 14.3 | Recognition of development costs – assets or expenses

To qualify as an asset, three conditions must be met. Assets are resources (1) controlled by an entity, (2) as a result of a past event, and (3) future economic benefits from these resources are expected to flow to the entity. Furthermore, to be recognised in the balance sheet, assets must pass the recognition criteria, which is that the value (costs) of asset(s) can be measured reliable.

In some industries, for example the biotech industry, firms are highly dependent upon successful R&D projects. It is not unusual in such industries that R&D amounts to 20% to 25% of revenue (turnover). IAS 38 on intangible assets states:

- Charge all research costs to the income statement.
- Development costs shall be capitalised only after technical and commercial feasibility of the asset for sale or use have been established. This means that the entity must intend and be able to complete the intangible asset and be able to demonstrate how the asset will generate future economic benefits.

Furthermore, if an entity cannot distinguish the research phase of an internal project (used to create an intangible asset) from the development phase, the entity treats the costs for the entire project as if it was incurred in the research phase only (i.e. all costs are expensed as incurred).

This raises two fundamental issues from an analytical point of view:

1 How much of a firm's R&D activities should be related to the development phase?
2 Should development costs be expensed or capitalised (recognised as assets)?

Naturally, it has a significant effect on reported numbers to which extent costs related to R&D activities are considered to be development costs, and if these costs are expensed as incurred or capitalised. Knowing that historically perhaps only one out of 10 R&D projects becomes commercially successful, you could ask: should a firm capitalise only one out of every

10 projects (and, if so, which one?) or should it capitalise 10% of all development costs, as a firm would presumably not carry out any new R&D projects without believing that some of them will eventually become successful? ∎

Example 14.4 Measurement – turnover

A firm specialises in selling unsold hotel rooms on the Internet. The firm charges 5% of the price as a fee for providing this service. If a customer buys five nights for, say, €1,000, the agent receives a fee of €50, while the hotel gets the remaining €950. Should the agent recognise revenue of €1,000 and costs of €950 or only the fee of €50 as revenue?

Some firms sell products with an extended warranty period. Kia Motors, for instance, sells cars in many countries with a seven-year warranty. The obvious question to ask is: how much of the revenue from selling cars should be deferred to future periods to match the costs associated with repairing cars under the warranty? Or, alternatively, how much should Kia recognise as provisions for the extended warranty obligations the firm faces? ∎

Example 14.5 Subsequent measurement of assets

A firm buys highly specialised equipment to be used in its chemical production process. At year end, this equipment must be recognised as assets, but at what value? Possible **measurement** attributes include:

- Historical costs less depreciation, amortisation and impairment losses
- Amortised costs
- Replaceable value
- Liquidation value
- Fair value
- Value in use
- Insured value
- Tax-based value
- Etc.

Some would argue that assets should be measured at their 'true' value. But what is the 'true' value? Naturally, there is no unequivocal answer to this question. For instance, if the analyst wants to make a valuation of assets based on a present value approach, the present value of future earnings (cash flows) from using the equipment (along with other assets) would be the relevant value. However, if the firm is financially troubled, valuation may be based on the liquidation model (worst case scenario). In this case, the liquidation value would be the preferred measurement attribute. ∎

Example 14.6 Classification

Accounting items may be classified in different ways. For instance, restructuring costs may be included in production costs (and, therefore, part of a firm's core operations, i.e. included in EBIT), while other firms choose to highlight restructuring and similar costs in a separate line item by labelling them 'special items', 'abnormal items', 'unusual items', 'extraordinary items'[7] or the like.

Analysts need to be able to single out transitory items. For example, in forecasting future earnings (and cash flows) transitory items should be disregarded. They therefore prefer that restructuring and similar costs are classified as a separate line item in the income statement. ∎

| Example 14.7 | Disclosure |

In order for users of financial statements to get a deeper understanding of the reported numbers, firms must disclose a wide range of information in the notes to the financial statements. The Framework for the Preparation and Presentation of Financial Statements (Framework) paragraph F.21 notes that:

> The financial statements also contain notes, supplementary data and other information that
>
> (a) Explain items in the balance sheet and income statement
> (b) Disclose the risks and uncertainties affecting the entity
> (c) Explain any resources and obligations not recognised in the balance sheet.

This may sound as though disclosure is a safe bet. By reading the notes, the analyst should be well-informed about numbers entered into the financial statements. While it is true that you, as an analyst, should read the notes and other supplementary material in the annual report carefully, disclosure still poses some challenges.

First, it is up to management to decide how much information they want to reveal. As shown above, notes and other supplemental information should *explain or disclose* accounting items and risk factors affecting a firm. Expressions such as explain and disclose are somewhat vague leaving much discretion to management.

Second, as an analyst, you will often need to separate out non-recurring items. Such information may be found on the face of the income statement as items marked, for example, 'special items' or 'unusual items'. However, non-recurring items may not be shown as separate line items leaving the analyst to be looking elsewhere; i.e. in the notes and supplementary information.

Finally, the amount of time you devote to reading the notes and other supplemental information depends on the purpose of your analysis and the decision model that you use; be sure to apply a cost–benefit analysis before getting carried away reading everything in the annual report. ∎

Accounting flexibility in the income statement

Before carrying out financial statement analysis, an analyst should reflect upon the quality of the data available. As discussed throughout this book, the quality of data cannot be defined without reference to the purpose of the analysis and the decision model applied. At the general level, analysts should be aware that biased accounting numbers are more likely to occur under the following circumstances:

- When transactions span a long time horizon (e.g. construction contracts)
- When transactions are complex (e.g. derivatives)
- When accounting standards lack clarity and are complex (e.g. IFRS 3)
- When a great deal of judgement is needed in applying the standard (e.g. impairment tests)
- When management may choose between different accounting methods (e.g. inventory accounting based on FIFO versus average costs).

Analysts need to consider if data are biased, which may make it necessary to adjust reported financial data as part of the analysis. As a starting point, the analyst might get an indication of the quality of the financial data by considering the business model, the industry in which the firm operates and the accounting policies applied in the annual report. Knowing the firm's accounting policies, business model and the industry help the analyst to identify whether accounting data are likely to create noise. For example, if the firm operates within the retail industry accounting flexibility and measurement errors should not be big issues. Sales and cash receipts take place simultaneously and most expenses are directly related to sales. Measurement problems basically relate to non-current assets and inventory. On the other hand, firms in construction industries (e.g. shipyards) are prone to measurement errors. The earnings process takes place as production progresses, and analysts have hardly any chance to assess whether the estimated percentage of completion, and, therefore, revenue, is unbiased.

In the following sections and in Chapter 15, we focus on how accounting flexibility affects financial statements and discuss potential economic consequences. When assessing analytical issues an analyst should ask questions such as:

- What characterises the industry?
- What major accounting method choices are made by management?
- Are accounting policies the same as for other firms within the industry?
- Have accounting policies changed over time?
- What are the major estimation issues?
- What are the key limitations in the information provided in the financial statements, notes and supplementary reports?

The answers to such questions help the analyst to decide whether adjustments need to be made to the data at hand. A thorough knowledge of the business and insight into accounting flexibility is definitely warranted before the analyst carries out his or her analysis.

Changes in accounting policies and estimates

Since the trend and levels of past earnings serve as indicators for future earnings, analysts should be aware of changes in a firm's accounting policies, as they are likely to introduce noise in a time-series analysis. Changes in accounting policies can happen for two main reasons:

1 Voluntary changes. Management find that a change is needed for financial statements better to reflect the underlying performance and financial position of the firm.
2 Mandatory changes. Firms are required to adopt new accounting standards or may have to comply with a new accounting regime.

An analyst should try to dig further into *why* a firm changes its accounting policies and assesses the effects on financial statements. While the comparable figures in the financial statements have been changed, for instance, in reporting 2005 financial data according to IFRS, the comparable figures for 2004 must be based on IFRS as well, key figures in the financial summary are often not restated. Certainly, if analysts look at annual reports from before 2004 they are still based on local GAAP. Consider accounting for goodwill. Prior to applying IFRS most countries required goodwill to be amortised over its useful lifetime. IFRS does not allow amortisation of goodwill, but goodwill shall be tested for impairment at least annually or whenever there is an indication that goodwill is impaired.

Table 14.1 Amortisation *vs* non-amortisation of goodwill

	Year 1	Year 2	Year 3	Year 4	Year E1	Year E2
Revenue	200,000	200,000	200,000	200,000	200,000	200,000
EBITDA	60,000	60,000	60,000	60,000	60,000	60,000
Goodwill amortisation	20,000	20,000	0	0	0	0
Goodwill impairment	0	0	0	0	?	?
EBIT	**40,000**	**40,000**	**60,000**	**60,000**	?	?
EBIT margin	20%	20%	30%	30%	?	?
Invested capital	100,000	80,000	80,000	80,000	80,000	80,000
ROIC	NA	44.4%	75.0%	75.0%	?	?

Table 14.1 illustrates the effects for a firm switching to IFRS in year 4.[8] Suppose that the firm used to amortise goodwill over a five-year period, but ceases to amortise goodwill in year 4. The firm restates the numbers for year 3. That is, goodwill amortisation is added back, as if no goodwill amortisation took place in year 3. By the end of year 4, the analyst wants to value the firm. The analyst uses the EBIT margin as an important value driver. Apparently, the EBIT margin improves from 20% in years 1 and 2 to 30% in years 3 and 4. Should the analyst forecast the EBIT margin at 20% or 30% or some other figure? Well, why not 30%? As illustrated in the Table 14.1, by the question mark, the firm may have to recognise an impairment loss on goodwill in the forecast period (since goodwill is no longer amortised), but it has no cash flow consequences, so 30% should be a safe bet? Probably not – Goodwill represents future abnormal earnings. According to economic theory, abnormal earnings cease to exist in the long run. Assume that the firm was right in amortising goodwill over a five-year period. As a result, to keep revenue and EBIT at a high level (maintain abnormal profit), the firm needs to invest in goodwill on a continuous basis. In the example, goodwill has no value (produces no future cash flows) after five years (by the end of year E1). Therefore, if the analyst fails to recognise this, he or she does not take into account that investments in goodwill are necessary in the future; just as the firm needs to reinvest in tangible assets. In conclusion, in the Table 14.1 example, a future EBIT margin of 20% is probably a fair or reasonable estimate.

Revenue recognition criteria

Management has a strong focus on revenue (sometimes labelled turnover or sales), the top line in the income statement, and so should analysts. The performance of a firm is critically dependent upon its ability to generate future sales. In fact, most other value drivers are affected by the sales growth as discussed extensively in the chapter on forecasting. Also, it has been documented that approximately 40% of accounting restatements in the USA are related to improper recognition of revenues. Finally, accounting regulation contains little guidance as how to account for income (revenue and gains).[9]

In this section, we discuss accounting for revenue arising from the sale of goods, rendering of services and construction contracts. The major issues in revenue recognition relate to when revenue shall be recognised (timing of recognition) and to a lesser extent by which amount revenue shall be recognised (measurement). Recognition and measurement are discussed in subsequent sections, but first we turn to a short discussion of the definition of revenue.

Definition of revenue

IAS 18 'Revenue' defines revenue as follows:

> *Revenue is the gross inflow of economic benefits during the period arising in the course of the ordinary activities of an entity when those inflows result in increases in equity, other than increases relating to contributions from equity participants.*

This definition means that inflows of economic benefits are only recognised as revenue to the extent that they result in an increase in equity. As a consequence, revenue shall be net of sales taxes, goods and service taxes, duties and value added taxes. Such taxes do not represent an increase in equity. They are just collected on behalf of third parties and have to be paid eventually in cash by the company. Similarly, discounts, rebates etc. should be subtracted from revenue, as they do not represent economic benefits. This is also why revenue is labelled net revenue or net turnover by some companies. From an analytical point of view, compliance with the definition should not pose any serious challenges. Nonetheless, analysts should read the note on accounting policies related to revenue to make sure that firms comply with the definition. For instance, in bad times, management could be tempted to include gains on sales of securities or property, plant and equipment as part of revenue in order to boost the top line in the income statement.

Timing of recognition

The time at which revenue shall be recognised is often a complex issue. As illustrated in Figure 14.2, revenue can be recognised at different points in time ranging from the date of an order from a customer and until warranty expires. The question is: at what point of time should revenue be recognised?

When should revenue be recognised?					
Order	Production	Sales/invoice	Payments from customers	Expiration of right of return	Expiration of time warranty

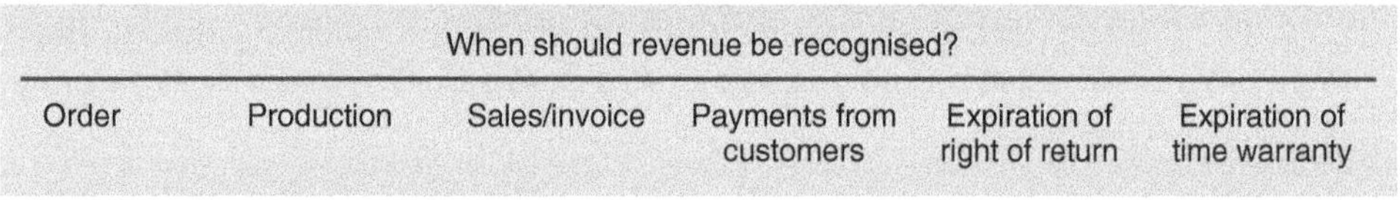

Figure 14.2 Recognition of revenue

It could be argued that revenue should be recognised, when a firm receives an order. At this time the stock price is likely to go up (if the stock market believes that it's a profitable order). Since the stock price increases, recognising revenue at this time seems to provide *relevant* information to investors. However, accounting regulation (whether IFRS or US GAAP) does not permit recognition at the date of an order; the conditions that need to be fulfilled are simply not met.

At the other extreme, recognition could be delayed until warranty expires. Here there is simply no more uncertainty attached to the transaction. Revenue can be measured *reliably* albeit at the expense of *relevance*. However, only under very rare circumstances would a firm postpone revenue recognition until warranty expires.

For a vast number of companies the timing of when sales are recognised should not be problematic. Retail stores, for instance, buy goods from its vendors and store it (no pre-orders and no production process). When customers make their purchases, they pick up the goods in the store, pay at the cash register and get a receipt. Sales, invoicing and payment take place simultaneously, and if there are no warranty or other after-market promises (e.g. right of returns), recognition of sales for retail stores should not pose a problem from an analytical point of view. For other types of firm, the time from when a customer places an order and to when warranty expires may span several years; in such cases the analyst should be particularly careful in interpreting firms' performance.

When revenue shall in fact be recognised, and by which amount, depends on several factors. First, pricing contingencies (e.g. extended warranty) may affect the timing of recognition. Second, if transactions include multiple elements or deliveries, revenues should be allocated to the different components. This requires a thorough knowledge of the business model and the industry to which the firm belongs. Finally, a distinction should be made between sales of goods and rendering of services and construction contracts, since services and construction contracts may span multiple periods and revenue is recognised according to a separate standard: IAS 11 'Construction Contracts'.

In summary, recognition of revenues is fact and industry dependent and analysts need to possess knowledge of the analysed firm's sales policies and industry characteristics. Below, we extend the discussion of timing issues further by dividing it into three parts:

1 Pricing contingencies
2 Multiple elements and deliveries
3 Rendering of services and construction contracts.

Pricing contingencies

For revenue to qualify for recognition, IAS 18 set forth a number of criteria that must be met (IAS 18.14). One of the criteria is that 'the entity has transferred to the buyer the significant risks and rewards of ownership of the goods'. In practice, enterprises may retain significant risks in a number of cases. In those cases, the firm shall defer revenue or recognise a provision, for example because the firm offers its customers:

• A price guarantee
• The right to return goods
• Extended warranty
• Extended credit terms.

The analyst needs to take into account how firms recognise such pricing contingencies. Management may try to boost revenue by offering unusual terms, by, say extending warranty to cover a five-year period. This requires that firms either defer revenue or make provisions for the potential future costs of repairs covered by the warranty. Unless the extended warranty is priced separately, management has a great deal of discretion in recognising and measuring deferred revenue and warranty provisions.

Price and return agreements

A firm may offer its customers a price guarantee for instance by paying the difference if customers are able to find the firm's products at lower prices in other stores or to return products within a period with a full cash refund. In such cases, a firm should recognise a liability, which reflects such agreements. A simplified example illustrates how return agreements are accounted for. Suppose that on average 5% of all goods sold are returned to firms that have return policies, which allow customers to return products within two weeks. Furthermore, assume that all customers pay in cash. If firm A recognises that customers do return products, while firm B does not take this into account in their financial statements, the two firms would report as follows (the data reflects sales from year 1 only):

	Firm A		Firm B	
	Year 1	Year 2	Year 1	Year 2
Revenue	100	0	100	0
Cost of returned goods	5	0	0	5
Net revenue	**95**	**0**	**100**	**−5**
Provision for returned goods	5	−5	0	0
Cash	100	−5	100	−5

By not recognising that customers return products, firm B overstates earnings by 5 in year 1 (no expense related to returned goods is recognised), but understates it in year 2 by the same 5 *if we look at one transaction only*. If sales are fairly constant, accounting policies for price and return agreements make little difference. Assume in the above example that sales in year 2 amount to 100. Firm A would again recognise sales, net of warranty expenses of, 95. Firm B would also recognise sales net of warranty costs of 95 – namely the sales of 100 in year 2 less the returned products from year 1 of 5.

Accounting regulation requires firms to recognise a provision for goods (likely) to be returned as does firm A in the simplified example. No revenue is deferred as the costs incurred or to be incurred in respect of the transaction can be measured reliably. The costs yet to be incurred (returned goods) can be measured reliably, for example, based on experiences from prior years. However, if there is a significant amount of unpredictable returns of goods, revenue should be deferred. Of course, the amount that has to be deferred needs to be estimated by management again leaving leeway for management discretion.

Extended warranty

If a firm sells products with extended warranties, part of revenues might have to be deferred since the sales price includes the pricing of the extended warranty, and it is questionable if revenue related to warranty has been earned.

Assume that a firm sells for 100 in year 1. They offer an extended three-year warranty on their products. The firm estimates that 6% of the total sales price relates to warranty. Costs of goods sold (COGS) excluding estimated warranty expenses amount to 54. How should revenue be recognised?

Alternative 1	Year 1	Year 2	Year 3	Year 4	Total
Revenue	94	2	2	2	100
COGS	−54				−54
Warranty expenses		−2	−2	−2	−6
Gross profit	**40**	**0**	**0**	**0**	**40**
Alternative 2					
Revenue	100	0	0	0	100
COGS	−54				−54
Warranty expenses	−6	0	0	0	−6
Gross profit	**40**	**0**	**0**	**0**	**40**
Provisions (liability)	6	4	2	0	NA

Note: It is assumed that sales take place at year end. Thus, no revenue related to warranty is recognised in year 1.

Alternative 1 better reflects the 'true' earnings process, as revenue related to warranty is deferred and recognised during the warranty period. In alternative 2, revenue is overstated in year 1 since the entire proceeds from sales are recognised.

Both alternatives provide management with opportunities to manage earnings. How much income they defer or how much they recognise as a provision to cover future repairs depends upon their best estimate of the price customers would have paid for the extended warranty and the amount of future warranty expenses, respectively. If they overestimate (underestimate) future warranty expenses, gross profit in year 1 would be too low (high) and future gross profit too high. Both ways of accounting for warranty expenses are probably within the boundaries of generally accepted accounting principles (GAAP).

Multiple elements or deliveries

Often, a sales transaction may involve several elements or deliveries. In such cases, the sales transaction should be separated into its different components, which permits management great flexibility as of how much revenue to relate to each component. Examples of special areas where revenue recognition issues are complex and deserve some attention include:

1 Vouchers
2 Subscriptions to publications
3 Advertising revenues
4 Installation fees
5 Up-front fees
6 Software and hardware.

The list is not exhaustive.

Vouchers are used extensively in the retail sector. For example, if a 'two for the price of one' product promotion is offered; the question is whether it is appropriate to recognise the revenue from the sale of both products with the free element being recorded as a cost? It could be argued that vouchers should be treated like discounts or rebates as a reduction in revenue. However, IAS 18 is not explicit on this point.

Subscriptions to publications (newspapers, magazines etc.) are not actually earned until the newspapers or magazines are published. Cash received prior to issuing the publications shall be classified as deferred income (unearned income) and classified as a liability.

The issue in recognising *advertising revenue* is to establish when revenue has been earned. Is it earned when the advertising is complete (e.g. ready for publication or TV)? Normal practice is to recognise the revenue as the production process proceeds or when the advertising is made public.

The treatment of *installation fees* depends upon whether the installation fees are significant. For instance, sellers of hi-fi equipment and TV sets may offer to install TVs in their customers' homes at no extra costs. If such installation is not a significant part of the total revenue, then the firm should merely include the fees in the sales price of the TVs. Therefore the time of the revenue recognition will be that for the sale of goods, which is normally at the time of delivery.

For *up-front fees*, the critical event will still be the provision of the service/goods. Membership fees in a golf club or fitness centre are examples of up-front fees. If the revenue has not been earned then up-front fees are, in essence, deferred income. Arguably, the membership fees should be allocated to the period over which the members are expected to stay members.

Technology firms often enter contracts with several elements. Each of these elements should be valued, and recognised as revenue, separately. *Software* contracts often contain both installation of the software on computers and additional services like online support, software upgrades for a period of time and inhouse training in how to using the software. The initial part of the contract (that relates to the software) can be recognised immediately, but the other components shall be recognised as the services are rendered. Unless the contract specifies how much the customer pays for the software and additional services respectively, management has discretion in how to allocate the revenue to each component of the contract.

Likewise sales of *hardware* may include several components; for instance, installation of software, online-support, and onsite repairs. Each component accounts for part of the revenue agreed upon in the contract. This leaves much room for management to allocate revenue to each component as they see fit, unless the contract clearly specifies the price for each element.

Rendering of services and construction contracts

Architects, auditors, lawyers and consulting firms, who offer services, and construction companies, who offer products, use IAS 11 'Construction Contracts' for revenue recognition purposes. According to IAS 11, revenues are recognised as the orders are produced (or services rendered), since production of, say a ship or an office building, constitute the firm's earnings process. Revenue is recognised based on the percentage of completion method. The following example illustrates how construction contracts are accounted for.

Example 14.8 **Construction contracts**

A large cruise ship is ordered by a firm offering cruises in the Mediterranean Sea. Assume that the following information is provided:

- The agreed price is €800 million (excluding VAT)
- The costs of building the ship are estimated to €600 million (excluding VAT)
- The shipyard expects to complete 25% of the ship every year (years 1–4)
- The buyer approves the ship at the date of delivery.

How is this transaction recorded in the shipyard's account, if the percentage of completion method is used?

	Year 1	Year 2	Year 3	Year 4	Total
Realised accumulated completion	25%	50%	75%	100%	
Revenue	200	200	200	200	800
Costs	150	150	150	150	600
Profit	**50**	**50**	**50**	**50**	**200**

Not surprisingly, revenue and earnings are recognised as building the ship progresses. In year 1, 25% of the ship has been built. Since the price of the ship is 800, 25% × 800 = 200 is recognised as revenue, and 50 (25% × 200) is recognised as profit. How does the shipyard (or the auditors) know the percentage of completion? There are several ways of estimating completion. They can inspect the ship to get an idea of the progress. More often they use costs as a measure. In the above example, if the shipyard has spent 150 in year 1, it indicates that 25% (150/600) of the ship has been built.

In year 3, the shipyard realises that the cost of building the ship is going to skyrocket from 600 to 900. Expenses for years 1 and 2 were 150 annually. For year 3 and 4 the shipyard forecasts expenses of 300 annually. How shall this additional information be recorded?

Percentage of completion	Year 1	Year 2	Year 3	Year 4	Total
Forecast	25%	50%	75%	100%	
Revised	16.7%	33.3%	75.0%	100.0%	
Revenue	200	200	200	200	800
Costs	150	150	400	200	900
Profit	**50**	**50**	**−200**	**0**	**−100**

The shipyard now faces a loss of 100 (800 − 900). Since the firm already recognised a profit of 100 (50 in both year 1 and year 2), the firm must recognise a loss of 200 in year 3 according to generally accepted accounting principles. ■

Example 14.8 illustrates that reporting revenues and earnings based on the percentage of completion is like selling rubber by the metre. Once again, analysts should be on the alert if the firm they analyse uses IAS 11 on construction contracts.

Measurement

From an analytical perspective, measurement of revenue (the amount to be recognised as revenue) includes a variety of issues, which should be considered. For instance:

- How much revenue should be recognised if the firm acts as an agent?
- How shall barter transactions be accounted for?
- How shall revenues from sales abroad (receipts in foreign currencies) be accounted for?

These issues are discussed below.

Agents

Some agents specialise in selling unsold tickets (e.g. flights and hotel rooms) on the internet. Assume that a travel agent receives a commission fee of 5% for selling otherwise unsold tickets to overseas flights. Essentially, the travel agent could recognise revenue in one of two ways:

	Alternative 1	Alternative 2
Revenue	200	–
Commissions, revenue	–	10
Cost of airline tickets	−190	0
Profit	**10**	**10**

Agents should only recognise the commission fees as revenue, as they represent increases in equity. Also, if the agent is unable to sell those tickets they just go unsold and the agent bears no risk. Practically speaking the agent has no inventory and therefore no risk. Consequently, If the agent sells tickets totalling 200, the agent ought to recognise revenue of 10 (5% × 200). The agent may be tempted to recognise sales of 200 and expenses of 190 to boost the top-line (earnings are unaffected). Analysts should be aware of such tricks, by carefully reading the note on applied accounting policies.

Barter transaction

During the 'dot com' era many internet companies had negative earnings, but investors believed there was still potential for incredible growth rates and future earnings. These companies were often engaged in barter transactions (i.e. exchange services or goods). For instance, two firms (A and B) may agree upon making links to each other's internet sites. They agree that such advertising should be priced at 100. Here is how many firms recorded such a transaction:

	Firm A	Firm B
Revenue	100	100
Marketing expenses	−100	−100
EBIT	**0**	**0**

The operating profit from making such transactions was zero for both companies. If the firms agreed upon a new and similar barter transaction next year, but now at a price of 120, it would seem like those firms were enjoying huge growth rates. According to current IFRS, firms may not account for barter transactions as just described.

Sales abroad

Currency fluctuations related to *sales abroad* may affect revenue considerably. Novo Nordisk states in its annual report for year 8, that:

> . . . *One obvious example of the impact that currency developments had on Novo Nordisk in year 8 was the impact on sales growth. In year 8, Novo Nordisk*

achieved sales growth of 12% when adjusted for the impact of currencies. However, in reported terms sales growth was 9% due to negative exchange rate impact compared to the Danish kroner of approximately 3%, or more than DKK 1 billion.

Such currency fluctuations make sales forecasting (or forecasting expenses if goods are purchased in foreign countries) difficult. It does require that the analyst is able to separate the effect of the number of items sold from the effects of exchange rates changes. For analytical purposes (e.g. forecasting), an analysis of the historical growth rates should reflect that the real growth rate in year 8 was 9%. The analyst has to look carefully in the annual report for the currency effects on revenue growth, as growth rates are an important value driver in any firm.

Detection of aggressive revenue recognition policies

Sales are the bread and butter of any firm. Boosting revenues lead to higher earnings. Therefore, it is hardly surprising that accounting restatements are often related to sales. How can analysts detect if a firm's revenue recognition policies are too aggressive? There are several signs, which may be an indication of such improper (or creative) accounting policies. For example:

- Does the firm properly disclose its revenue recognition policies?
- Has the firm changed its revenue recognition policies lately?
- Are the firm's revenue recognition policies comparable to its main competitors?
- Does accounts receivable increase more than sales?
- Is there evidence of significant related party revenues?
- How do measures such as revenue per employee, revenue per euro of invested capital, revenue per euro of property, plant and equipment or similar metrics compare with the industry?
- Is there a strong link between sales (or operating earnings) and cash flows from sales (or operating cash flows) over time?

It is important to point out that these are only indicators. A decrease in accounts receivable turnover, for example, may be due to the fact that the firm purposely extended its credit terms to customers in an attempt to increase sales.

Non-recurring and special items

As discussed extensively in Chapter 13, analysts need to be able to separate transitory (or non-recurring) items from permanent (or recurring items). There is no universal definition of such items. Examples of non-recurring items that are often labelled 'special items', 'unusual items' and the like (indicating they are non-recurring) include:

- Prior-period adjustments
- Net operating loss carry forwards
- Restructuring charges
- Gains or losses on the sale of assets
- Effects of a strike or of an extended period in which critical raw materials are unavailable
- Effects of abnormal price fluctuations
- Write-offs and other expenses related to acquisitions
- Uncollectable accounts receivable in excess of what is normal (in the industry)

- Gains or losses from settling lawsuits
- Other non-recurring items.

Analysts should be aware of the classification of such items. If they are truly non-recurring they should be disregarded in forecasting future earnings. However, they may have to be regarded as part of core earnings. For instance, firms may spend considerable amounts on restructuring on a continuous basis in order to stay competitive. In this case, restructuring costs should probably be included in forecasting future expenses. A separate issue to consider is by what amount such expenses should be forecast. A workable solution would be to average the restructuring costs over, say, the past five years and use this average for forecasting purposes. Forecasting the amount may be the truly difficult issue, as restructuring charges usually fluctuate substantially over time. Again, in assessing special items the analyst should read any information about such items in the annual report with great interest. An understanding of the industry should also help the analyst. For example, firms within the fashion industry may have to recognise large write-downs on inventory, since collections may fail from time to time making them unsaleable. If firms classify such write downs as special items, the analyst should carefully consider how to include them in their analysis.

Non-capitalisation of expenses

A major issue in financial reporting is the extent to which certain costs should be recognised as expenses or capitalised and recognised as assets subject to depreciation (or amortisation) and impairment tests. Below, we discuss capitalisation versus expensing of costs (i.e. whether certain expenses warrant recognition in the balance sheet). A discussion of recognition seems warranted as there is often a fine line between recognising versus not recognising certain items in the balance sheet. Depending on how such expenses are accounted for, the effects on reported data and financial ratios may be quite large.

Many intangible resources (assets) are expensed. A number of studies find that such resources represent assets and therefore ought to be capitalised. However, the measurement of assets (and liabilities) often requires the estimation of future amounts. GAAP requires that these assets can be measured with some minimum level of reliability. If this is not possible, such assets are not recognised but expensed as incurred. Consequently, most internally generated intangibles, including assets such as brands, master heads, publishing titles, customer lists, goodwill and items similar in substance, must be expensed immediately. Likewise, marketing expenses and other forward looking costs are expensed as incurred.

An exception to this rule is research and development expenses (R&D). Research costs cannot be capitalised, but development costs shall be capitalised if some strict conditions are met. For instance, technical and commercial feasibility of the intangible asset for sale or use must be established. In reality, this means that the entity must intend to and be able to complete the intangible asset and demonstrate how the asset will generate future economic benefits.

This raises two fundamental questions: (1) when does a firm enter the development phase of R&D projects and (2) in the development stage, when is there sufficient evidence to support capitalisation of development costs? Consider the following example, which shows the effects of capitalisation versus expensing of R&D projects.

Example 14.9 **Expensing versus capitalisation**

A firm has the option to capitalise development costs. How would capitalisation of such costs affect reported numbers and financial ratios? Assume the following pieces of information:

Price per project – annual investments in R&D projects at the beginning of the year	100
Return per year per project at year end (cash flow)	30
Useful lifetime of each project	5 years
Internal rate of return per project (IRR)	15.2%

Note: In the following examples full depreciation in the year of the investment is assumed.

If the firm recognises R&D costs as incurred, it would report the following numbers in the income statement (extract):

Income statement (extract)	Year 1	Year 2	Year 3	Year 4	Year 5	Year 6
EBITDA (excluding development costs)	30	60	90	120	150	150
R&D costs	−100	−100	−100	−100	−100	−100
EBIT	**−70**	**−40**	**−10**	**20**	**50**	**50**

Income statement – development costs expensed as incurred

From year 5 EBIT becomes constant. Each year, a new project, which costs 100 and earns 30 per year for five years, is added, while an 'old' project expires. For instance, in year 5 the project undertaken in year 1 has expired and provides no returns in subsequent years.

Had the firm chosen to capitalise development expenses, the development assets would be calculated as follows:

Capitalisation of development costs					
Financial year	Investment	Acc. inv.	Depreciation	Acc. deprec.	Book value
Year 1	100	100	20	20	80
Year 2	100	200	40	60	140
Year 3	100	300	60	120	180
Year 4	100	400	80	200	200
Year 5	100	500	100	300	200
Year 6	100	600	100	400	200
Year 7	100	700	100	500	200
Year 8	100	800	100	600	200
Year 9	100	900	100	700	200
Year 10	100	1,000	100	800	200

From year 5 book value becomes constant at 200. Every year a new investment of 100 is capitalised (adding 100 to book value), but at the same time 100 is recognised as a depreciation (amortisation) expense, namely five projects amortised by 20 each.

If the firm capitalises development costs as just illustrated, it would, therefore, report the following numbers in the income statement (extract):

Income statement (extract)	Year 1	Year 2	Year 3	Year 4	Year 5	Year 6
EBITDA	30	60	90	120	150	150
Amortisation of R&D assets	−20	−40	−60	−80	−100	−100
EBIT	**10**	**20**	**30**	**40**	**50**	**50**

As is evident from Example 14.9, when the firm reaches steady state, reported EBIT would be the same whether the firm expenses or capitalises development costs. However, there are major differences between the two reporting practices for development costs. First, consider EBITDA, which is used for instance in valuing firms based on the EV/EBITDA multiple. The firm would report these EBITDA numbers, depending on its accounting policies for development costs:

Income statement (extract)	Year 1	Year 2	Year 3	Year 4	Year 5	Year 6
EBITDA, R&D costs capitalised	30	60	90	120	150	150
EBITDA, R&D costs expensed as incurred	−70	−40	−10	20	50	50

If R&D costs are expensed as incurred, EBITDA would be 100 less compared to an accounting policy of capitalising R&D expenses. This is due to the simple fact that the entire investment (100) is subtracted from EBITDA. However, EBITDA (or EBITA) is not affected if R&D costs are capitalised subject to amortisation.

Second, the balance sheet would look different:

Balance sheet, assets (extract)	Year 1	Year 2	Year 3	Year 4	Year 5	Year 6
R&D costs expensed	0	0	0	0	0	0
R&D costs capitalised	80	140	180	200	200	200

By expensing R&D costs, no related assets are recognised in the balance sheet, so total assets would be higher for firms that capitalise R&D expenses or other forward looking costs.

Several conclusions can be drawn based on the above simplified example. First, in early years, firms that are conservative (and expense R&D costs as incurred) would report lower earnings, since the entire investments are expensed immediately. Second, in later years, reported earnings would be approximately[10] the same whether R&D costs are expensed as incurred or capitalised (subject to amortisation). Third, since assets related to R&D activities are not recognised if R&D costs are expensed, ROIC would be higher than if the firm had capitalised such costs (see Figure 14.3). Fourth, subtotals such as EBITDA and EBIT are affected differently. Finally, non-recognition of R&D assets would result in a lower solvency (e.g. debt-to-equity ratio).

The effect of capitalising versus expensing R&D costs on ROIC is shown in Figure 14.3. The assumptions are the same as in the example above, except that the firm in addition has other assets of 200, which earn a return of 10% per year. Without other assets, the firm would have a ROIC of infinity, if all R&D costs were expensed as incurred.

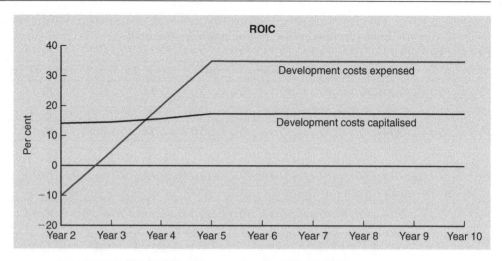

Figure 14.3 ROIC based on expensing versus capitalising R&D

If all costs are expensed as incurred, ROIC is clearly downward biased in early periods, but upward biased in later periods. On the other hand, if all expenses are capitalised and depreciated over the expected useful lifetime of five years, ROIC is fairly constant over time, as it should be considering the underlying assumptions.

Notice IFRS allows development costs to be capitalised. Research costs must be expensed as incurred. Analysts, however, are free to make any adjustments they seem fit (like capitalising all R&D expenses) to get the necessary quality in the data they use as input to their decision models.

In a time-series analysis failing to capitalise R&D outlays would make an interpretation of ROIC difficult. If R&D are expensed as incurred, while the returns (cash flows) from such projects keep coming several years after (five years in the example), income and expenses are not properly matched. As illustrated in Figure 14.3 the huge increase in ROIC over time should not be interpreted as an improvement in profitability. On the other hand, if R&D expenses are capitalised the analyst is faced with estimation issues related to determining the useful life of such assets and the recognition of impairment losses. Again, this illustrates that financial ratios should be interpreted with care.

Accounting flexibility and economic consequences

It should not come as a surprise that reported accounting numbers have economic consequences; after all, financial statements are intended to help users make (economic) decisions. Also, firms typically enter into various contracts, which are based on accounting data. Prominent examples are debt covenants and accounting-based bonus plans.

We will now move on to examine the following issue:

> What are the potential economic consequences of reported accounting data, which to a large extent depends on accounting policies and management's subjective estimates and assumptions?

As a starting point, consider the following illustrative examples:

Example 14.10 Assume that two comparable firms, within the same industry, estimate the useful lives of tangible assets differently. Firm A depreciates these assets over a 10-year period, while firm B, like most other firms in the industry, depreciates similar assets over a five-year period. What are the accounting issues an analyst following firm A should consider?

Well, if the analyst wants to value firm A based on a cash flow model (e.g. DCF model), he or she needs not be concerned. Depreciation has no cash flow effects.[11] However, if the analyst wants to use multiples, say, EV/EBIT, to value firm A and uses firm B (and other firms within the same industry) as a benchmark, he or she needs to make adjustments to the financial statements to make the firms truly comparable. ∎

Example 14.11 Or look at credit analysis. Naturally, differences in accounting estimates (in this case the depreciation scheme) will affect financial ratios, and, thus, ultimately the cost of debt, if the credit analyst (e.g. loan officer) applies rating models such as the one provided in Table 11.1; that is unless the analyst makes the necessary adjustments. In a worst case scenario, the loan officer may consider calling in the loan with liquidation of the firm as a result. In this case, the bank needs to know the fair value of all the firm's assets and liabilities to assess whether the firm is able to repay the bank loan. Thereafter, for the loan officer, good accounting quality would be the extent to which reported assets and liabilities reflect the fair value (sales price) and settlement amounts of those items. Naturally, with a depreciation scheme for firm A, which is quite different from other firms in the industry, book value of tangible assets in firm A may be far from fair value. In this case accounting quality is low. ∎

Example 14.12 Finally, consider bonus plans. Assume that bonuses are rewarded by benchmarking firm A's operating performance (e.g. EBIT) against competitors performance. Management in firm A may obtain higher operating earnings, and receive a bonus due to the fact that they apply aggressive accounting policies by simply extending the estimated lifetime of depreciable assets. ∎

In the following three sections, we discuss accounting policies and flexibility in reporting financial data and how they have an impact on:

- Firm value
- Credit rating
- Accounting-based bonus plans.

Put more bluntly: what are the economic consequences of a firm's flexibility in reporting financial data, which critically depends upon management's application of GAAP? For each of the three purposes (firm valuation, credit rating and accounting-based bonus plans) we keep the decision model in mind. As discussed throughout this book, we cannot assess accounting quality, carry out financial statement analysis and make informed decisions without knowing the purpose of the analysis and the method or model we wish to apply. If the financial data reported by firms are inadequate for our analysis, we may have to make the proper adjustments. In this respect, an important point needs to be made: *before carrying out the analysis, an analyst should carefully consider materiality and the cost of making the analysis versus the likely benefits.* Uncritically making a variety of adjustments, without taking due care of the costs (time spend) of the analysis and benefits, should be avoided by all means.

Accounting issues in valuation

As stated in Chapter 9, the value of an asset or a firm is the present value of the net cash flows generated by the asset/firm. Therefore, any present value model implicitly requires an estimate of future cash flows. In the discounted cash flow approach (and similar present value approaches), cash flows are calculated based on the projection of the income statement (accrual-based earnings) and the balance sheet. Multiples, as the name implies, are used to estimate firm value by multiplying an accounting-based measure of performance (e.g. EBIT, EBITDA) by a proper capitalisation factor; the basic justification is that accounting earnings eventually convert to cash flows. Finally, using the liquidation approach, the value of the firm is simply the net proceeds (cash) from selling the assets and settling the liabilities recognised in the firm's balance sheet and off-balance. In conclusion, all valuation models hinge on accounting data, as cash flows are derived from current or projected accounting numbers. Eventually, noise in financial data may have an impact on estimated firm value if the analyst (or potential investor) does not recognise this.

Present value approach

It stands to reason that management may be tempted to adopt accounting policies, which allow the outlook of the firm to look rosier, since higher future returns increase value based on cash flows.[12] However, at the outset DCF, EVA and similar *present value approaches* depend on future (economic) income – so past accounting policies should not matter? Take the EVA model; it relies on the underlying assumption of 'clean surplus'.[13] If this requirement is met past accounting numbers do not matter as shown in Chapters 9 and 13. If a firm is conservative (aggressive) in applying accounting policies, and, therefore, reports low values on its investments (overstates asset values), this is simply reflected in future EVAs. For a firm with conservative accounting policies future EVAs would account for substantially more enterprise value as opposed to a firm applying aggressive accounting policies for financial reporting purposes. Cash flow models (e.g. the DCF model) rely on *future* cash flows – so, apparently, accounting policies should not matter in this case either.

However, since good accounting quality is characterised by the extent to which past earnings is a good indicator of future earnings and clearly distinguishes between recurring (permanent) and non-recurring (transitory) items, measurement errors in accounting data might provide biased estimates of future earnings. In general, estimation errors increase for transactions spanning multiple periods and with the complexity of the transactions; so the estimated firm value may be affected by accounting policy choices. In applying present value approaches, an analyst needs to consider a variety of issues including:

1 Revenue recognition
2 Non-recurring and special items.

These issues are discussed below.

1 Revenue recognition

As discussed extensively in Chapter 8 on forecasting, growth in revenue represents the most important value driver. This is intuitively easy to understand. An extra dollar of revenue increases performance measures like EBITDA, EBIT and EBT by up to one dollar. More importantly, as we demonstrated in Chapter 8, costs are typically directly linked to revenue (forecasting profit margins like EBIT or EBITDA margins), and so are investments.

Not surprisingly, an analyst should therefore consider a firm's revenue recognition policies and related notes carefully as part of valuing a firm. Analysts should be aware of techniques used to boosting revenues or otherwise reporting biased sales. Bias in reported revenues can happen for a variety of reasons.

While the list is not exhaustive, the following are examples of transactions and special cases an analyst should be looking for:

- Barter transactions (grossing up revenue)
- Sale and lease back transactions
- Channel stuffing
- Multiple deliveries
- Extended warranty
- Seller financing
- Construction contracts
- Bill and hold arrangements
- Consignment sales
- Selling to affiliates.

Revenue recognition is considered conservative if a firm does not recognise revenue until all risks have passed to the buyer. For example, if a firm offers extended warranty, the full revenue would not be recognised until warranty expires. Revenue recognition policies may also be aggressive if revenue is recognised although risk remains. For example, recognising revenue immediately for a service contract spanning several years would be aggressive accounting, and likely outside the boundaries of IFRS. Analysts should assess whether a firm seems overly aggressive or conservative in revenue recognition. There are several ways of detecting aggressive revenue recognition policies including:

- Comparing revenue recognition policies with industry norms
- Looking for the trend in accounts receivable turnover (number of days)
- Examining if the firm change its revenue recognition policies.

Revenue recognition policies that depart from industry norms may be a sign of aggressive (or conservative for that matter) recognition policies. The analyst should look into such matters by examining why the firm deviates, and ask whether the firm provides compelling reasons for its accounting policies in its annual report?

Another way to detect aggressive accounting policies would be to calculate various financial ratios. Obviously, looking at the trend in accounts receivable turnover could give an indication of a firm's accounting policies. A decrease in the turnover ratio might be a sign of aggressive accounting policies. Maybe the firm provides cheap financing to customers who are not creditworthy? Or maybe revenues for multiple deliveries are recognised too soon? This would increase accounts receivable, since customers would not have to pay until some future date.

If not explicitly stated in the notes, revenue recognition policies are unchanged from last year. Firms in financial distress especially may be tempted to change revenue recognition policies to look more profitable. If a firm changes its accounting policies, the analyst should consider the effects and the rationale behind such changes. If analysts do not consider changes in revenue recognition policies they may be misled by the reported growth rate. Therefore, estimated firm value may be biased.

UNIVERSITY OF WINCHESTER
LIBRARY

Example 14.13 **Sales in foreign currencies**

Assume that a UK firm has a significant proportion of its sales made in dollars (USD), while all other transactions are denoted in British pounds (GBP). It does not use any hedging instruments. The UK firm assumes that annual growth in the coming three to five years is going to be around 10% (measured in dollars).

In January year 9 an analyst wishes to value the UK firm by projecting future sales (and earnings) based on past sales. Assume that sales in the US market during year 8 amounted to GBP 10 million. Furthermore, suppose that the average USD/GBP ratio was 1.8 for sales transactions in year 8 and that the USD/GBP ratio by the end of year 8 is 1.5.

The analyst believes that the firm's sales forecasts are realistic, but is unaware of and have not considered the development in the exchange rate between US dollars and British pounds. Based on the belief that sales in the USA will grow by 10% in year 9, the analyst makes the following sales forecast for year 9 in GBP:

Projected sales for year 9 in the US market:

Sales in year 8 in GBP × (1 + growth rate) = GBP 10 million × 1.10 = GBP 11.0 million

Is this a realistic sales projection? Assuming that valuation is carried out shortly after the end of the last financial year (year 8) and the dollar remains at a level of approximately USD/GBP = 1.5 throughout year 9, it is evident that estimated sales in GBP will be strongly downward biased. The estimated value of the company will therefore, other things being equal, also be downward biased. The error in the budget is that sales forecast in the USA (sales in USD) are effectively converted to GBP based on the average USD/GBP exchange rate for all transactions taking place in year 8 and not on the current much higher exchange rate. It is generally assumed that foreign exchange markets are efficient, particularly for highly liquid currencies. Presuming that the current USD/GPB exchange rate of 1.5 is a better indicator of the year 9 exchange rate than the average rate of 1.8 in year 8, the forecast sales in the USA for first budget year (year 9) is

USD 11 million × 1.8/1.5 = GBP 13.2 million (rounded)

This is a significantly higher amount than the projected sales of GBP 11.0 million, which did not consider the effects of exchange rate changes. Ideally, for firms with large sales in foreign currencies, information about the average exchange rate and net position would be valuable.

2 Non-recurring and special items (transitory items)

Generally, transitory items should be disregarded in forecasting future earnings. This begs the question: what characterises such non-recurring items? Firms applying IFRS are no longer permitted to classify items as extraordinary items. As an alternative, many firms recognise a variety of items in the income statement labelling them 'special items', 'unusual items' etc., probably in an attempt to convince investors and lenders that such items should be disregarded in assessing the firm's performance. From an analytical point of view, the problem is that special items contain a vast number of different transactions and neither IFRS nor US GAAP define special items or specify how they should be classified. It is entirely up to the management's discretion to decide which items and events to include as special items.

If non-recurring or special items are merely prior years' expenses (note that special items are mainly costs) recognised too late or future expenses recognised too early, then the practice of ignoring non-recurring items and focusing on recurring operating income results in noise in the assessment of a firm's earnings potential. For forecasting purposes these items may, therefore, have to be included. Furthermore, a variety of different charges, which really are recurring, may be labelled special items. As exemplified by Carlsberg (see Table 14.2) such special items tend to occur every single year.[14] For exemplification purposes, consider termination and restructuring charges. Restructuring has become a 'catch-all' for expenses that firms wish analysts should disregard in assessing

Table 14.2 Carlsberg annual report

NOTE 7   Special items

(DKK million)	Year 9	Year 8
Gain on sale of Braunschweig Brauerei and fighter brand activities, Carlsberg Deutschland (2008: impairment of brewery)	49	−135
Impairment of finite brands	−37	−
Impairment (year 8) and restructuring of Leeds Brewery, Carlsberg UK	−67	−197
Loss on disposal of Türk Tuborg	−	−232
Relocation costs, termination benefits and impairment of non-current assets in connection with new production structure in Denmark	−40	−19
Termination benefits and impairment of non-current assets in connection with new production structure at Sinebrychoff, Finland	−20	−30
Provision for onerous procurement contracts	−175	−245
Termination benefits etc. in connection with operational excellence programmes	−31	−150
Termination benefits in connection with restructuring of sales force etc., Carlsberg UK	−34	−
Termination benefits etc., Carlsberg Italia	−56	−93
Termination benefits etc. in connection with restructuring, Brasseries Kronenbourg, France	−95	−291
Termination benefits in connection with restructuring, Carlsberg Deutschland	−72	−
Restructuring, Ringnes, Norway	−	−26
Other restructuring costs etc., other entities	−100	−154
Integration costs related to acquisition of part of the activities in S&N	−17	−69
Special items, net	**−695**	**−1,641**
If special items had been recognised in operating profit before special items, they would have been included in the following items:		
Cost of sales	−353	−919
Sales and distribution expenses	−157	−114
Administrative expenses	−179	−226
Other operating income	94	27
Other operating expenses	−100	−409
	−695	−1,641
Impairment of goodwill	−	−
Special items, net	**−695**	**−1,641**

Special items constitute significant items that cannot be attributed directly to the group's ordinary operating activities and are significant over time.

core operations and risk. The term has a positive undertone implying that the firms have taken due care of their poor operations or businesses and therefore have a bright future. Disregarding restructuring charges may create too rosy a picture of past performance and should be considered carefully in forecasting future earnings.

Arguably, restructuring charges in a broad sense are part of core operations, as every firm needs to adjust its businesses to changing market conditions. Labelling costs associated with tuning the company to make it stay competitive should not prevent an analyst from including such costs in forecasting future earnings. Restructuring charges and other special items, however, may fluctuate substantially over time making such costs difficult to forecast. For forecasting purposes, analysts might estimate such future expenses by, for instance, calculating the average of restructuring charges recognised during the past five years. Notice once again that financial statement analysis is not an exact science. There is no way of knowing the amount of future special items; all analysts can do is to forecast earnings based on available information and realistic assumptions.

Multiples

Valuation based on *multiples* is also prone to accounting distortion. Again, as an analyst, you must consider the data needed for your analysis. In other words, what constitutes high accounting quality if multiples are used? As discussed in Chapter 9, the use of multiples requires that firms are truly comparable in the sense they have the same accounting policies, growth opportunities, profitability and risk. A variety of multiples are used to estimate firm value – both enterprise value and market value of equity – including:

- Enterprise value-based multiples
  - EV/Revenue
  - EV/EBIT
  - EV/EBITDA
  - EV/NOPAT
  - EV/IC
- Equity-based multiples
  - P/E
  - M/B

The different multiples and their merits and demerits are discussed in Chapter 9 on valuation. In the following sections, we discuss the economic consequences of accounting method choices and accounting judgements (assumptions) in valuing firms based on several of the above multiples.

EV/Revenue multiples

Some would argue that EV/Revenue is the best multiple in the sense that it is basically unaffected by accounting policies, since accounting method choices and estimates for inventory, depreciation policies, deferred taxes etc. can be disregarded. However, the multiple also disregards all costs. Therefore, if firms have different cost structures or differ in respect to their income–expense relation, the EV/Sales multiple may result in biased firm value estimates. Due to the heavy reliance on revenue, analysts should be aware of accounting policies for revenue recognition. It's a good idea that you read the section on accounting policies for revenues carefully. Sales multiples may be a bad valuation multiple because:

- Firms in the industry use different accounting method choices for revenue, for example in regard to extended warranty, multiple deliveries and service or construction contracts.
- Firms may engage in barter transactions and recognise exchanging goods or services as revenue.
- Firms may have intercompany sales and boost earnings by selling products or services within a group.
- Sales may be boosted by selling at a price below or near costs.
- Discounts, duties, rebates, value added tax, sales tax etc. are recognised as costs rather than a reduction in revenue.
- Revenues are recognised prematurely using channel stuffing or other questionable methods.
- Revenues are positively affected by a favourable exchange rate, which is non-lasting.

Suffice it to say that sales multiples should be used with extreme care.

EV/EBITDA, EV/EBIT and EV/NOPAT multiples

Other analysts favour multiples such as EV/EBITDA and EV/EBIT. For example, the popularity of using EBITDA is that it is presumably a proxy for the cash flow. A prerequisite for applying multiples is that the firm being valued applies accounting policies and uses estimates which are comparable to its competitors. Accounting policies may vary across firms for a variety of items, and if differences in accounting policies and estimates have a material effect on reported financial data, the analyst needs to make adjustments to make data across firms truly comparable. Common accounting issues in applying multiples in the income statement, which may require adjustments to reported figures to be made, include:

Accounting item	Issue
Non-recurring and special items	Are special items recognised as part of operating income or classified after EBIT?
Non-capitalisation of expenses (investments)	Are costs which truly represent assets expensed as incurred?
	When do firms capitalise capital expenditures?
	What kind of costs are capitalised?

We discuss these issues below. The important point to remember is: if firms uses different accounting method choices or estimates *and* these differences are material, then adjustments need to be made before applying multiples.

Non-recurring and special items

Naturally, items that a firm labels 'special items' need to be scrutinised by the analyst. Should such items be part of EBIT (or EBITDA, or whichever operating performance measure that is used)? Ideally, EBIT should represent future permanent earnings as the main source of free cash flows. The analyst must examine the annual report carefully to single out items that are truly non-recurring as such items should be excluded from EBIT.

Non-capitalisation of expenses

Unsurprisingly, it is quite likely that valuation based on multiples also requires adjustments to financial statements by capitalising development costs or other forward looking expenses to make firms comparable on accounting policies. Even though high-tech firms, biotech companies etc. are dependent upon successful research projects, they may have different accounting policies regarding capitalisation of development costs.

If development costs are capitalised by some firms but not by other firms in the peer group, adjustments need to be made. This is especially important if EBITDA multiples are used. For firms that capitalise development costs subject to amortisation and impairment losses, amortisation expenses and impairment losses are recognised after EBITDA, while development costs which are expensed as incurred become part of EBITDA.

Even if EBIT is used there might be significant differences in reported EBIT between capitalising versus non-capitalising firms. Consider two identical firms that differ only in so far as the way they recognise development costs. For the past three years, the firms have spent the following amounts on a single development project, which starts producing cash inflows from year 3, as illustrated in Table 14.3.

Table 14.3 **Capitalising versus expensing development costs**

	Year 1	Year 2	Year 3
Development expenses	20	25	30
Income statement (excerpt)			
Capitalising firm			
EBITDA before development costs	30	40	50
Development costs	0	0	0
EBITDA	**30**	**40**	**50**
Amortisation of development costs	0	0	15
Depreciation expenses	5	6	7
EBIT	**25**	**34**	**28**
Expensing firm			
EBITDA before development costs	30	40	50
Development costs	20	25	30
EBITDA	**10**	**15**	**20**
Amortisation of development costs	0	0	0
Depreciation expenses	5	6	7
EBIT	**5**	**9**	**13**

It is assumed that the *capitalising firm* amortises development projects using straight-line depreciation and an estimated lifetime of five years. Therefore, in year 3, the amortisation expense becomes $[(20 + 25 + 30)/5] = 15$. In years 1 and 2 the development expenses have been capitalised with no amortisation since the project was still being developed. For the *expensing firm*, development costs are expensed as incurred. Since development expenses are fairly high in the example (as is often the case with high-tech companies in the biotech industry), EBIT is materially lower for the expensing firm. However, at some future point of time, capitalising firms 'catch-up', as those firms need to amortise their development projects over their useful lifetime. In fact, over the entire lifetime of a development project total expenses recognised by expensing firms and capitalising firms must match.

The same is not true for EBITDA. Since the capitalising firm will classify development projects after EBITDA (as opposed to expensing firms which expense development projects as incurred) they will always report a higher EBITDA. For instance, in year 3 EBITDA is 150% ((50 − 20)/20) higher for the capitalising firm than for the expensing firm.

To adjust for differences, an analyst may need to adjust capitalisation to non-capitalisation or vice-versa depending on whether the peer group uses the one or the other accounting method. This is done as shown in Tables 14.4 and 14.5.

Table 14.4 Adjustment from capitalising to expensing development costs

Income statement (excerpt)	Year 1	Year 2	Year 3
Costs of development projects	20	25	30
Capitalising to expensing			
EBITDA as reported	30	40	50
Deduct development costs	20	25	30
EBITDA	**10**	**15**	**20**
Amortisation of development costs	0	0	15
Add back amortisation of development costs	0	0	−15
Depreciation expenses	5	6	7
EBIT	**5**	**9**	**13**

Table 14.5 Adjustment from expensing to capitalising development costs

Expensing to capitalising	Year 1	Year 2	Year 3
EBITDA before development costs	30	40	50
Development costs	20	25	30
Add back development costs	−20	−25	−30
EBITDA	**30**	**40**	**50**
Amortisation of development costs	0	0	15
Depreciation expenses	5	6	7
EBIT	**25**	**34**	**28**

In practice, the exercise is likely to be a bit more difficult. For example, in adjusting from expensing to capitalisation, the analyst needs to make highly subjective assumptions: how much of the total development expenses should be capitalised? What is the estimated lifetime of the project? When should amortisation begin, that is when is the project completed? Should amortisation be on a straight-line basis or should some other method be applied? Answers to such questions are most likely found by monitoring peers' adopted accounting policies and estimates.

P/E and M/B multiples

P/E and M/B both aim at estimating market value of equity based on net earnings and book value of equity, respectively. Some argue that the P/E multiple is preferable as classification of income and expenses do not matter. Earnings, the bottom line, capture it all regardless of how items have been classified. Likewise, classification of assets and liabilities should not matter, as book value of equity is simply the difference between total assets and total liabilities. However, when applying the P/E and M/B multiples analysts face many of the same accounting issues as discussed above. In addition, the only difference between enterprise-based multiples (like EV/EBIT) and equity-based multiples like P/E is the effect of financial leverage. Two firms, which are identical on all parameters (accounting policies, growth and profitability) *except* for financial leverage (i.e. the capital structure), shall be priced at a different multiple.

Consider the M/B ratio. The denominator in this ratio is book value of equity. Since book value of equity captures the difference between total assets and total liabilities, recognition criteria for (every group of) assets and (every group of) liabilities have an effect on the market-to-book ratio. Evidently, if a firm capitalises development costs, while competitors do not, applying the M/B ratio would bias the capitalising firm's value upward (book value of equity would be higher due to the capitalisation of expenses).

Accounting issues in credit analysis

Financial institutions (banks, mortgage institutions etc.) employ models (credit rating models and forecasting including value at risk analyses) to rank potential and existing customers according to risk. Lenders will charge interest on loans according to their risk. But higher interest rates are not the only method used by lenders to compensate for risk. Protective debt covenants are written into loan agreements that allow the lender some controls of actions undertaken by the borrower. Such covenants may for instance:

- Allow for monitoring the debt by requiring audits and monthly reports.
- Decide when the lender can call the loan; i.e. when financial ratios are below a threshold (e.g. if the interest coverage ratio is below a predefined target).
- Limit the borrower's ability to weaken its balance sheet (e.g. by requiring a debt–equity ratio below 3.0).
- Restrict the ability to pay out dividends or carry out investments above a certain threshold.

Generally speaking, according to such contracts debt becomes cheaper if a firm is able to improve profitability (e.g. EBIT and ROIC) and/or reduce risk (e.g. an increase in the interest coverage ratio or a decrease in the debt-to-equity ratio).

In the following sections, we discuss the economic consequences of differences in accounting policies and estimates depending on the credit rating model applied. How does regulatory flexibility and management discretion (as described in Chapter 13) affect the various credit rating models, and what are the potential economic consequences? From a lender's point of view, the economic consequences can be severe if flexibility in accounting is not uncovered because management may be tempted to exploit accounting flexibility to obtain debt financing, if the firm is in need of cash.

The lender may say 'no' when in fact they should say 'yes' (loss of business opportunities). This is often labelled a type 2 error. However, it is more likely that lenders may grant loans they should not have granted (labelled a type 1 error).

Credit rating models and financial ratios

Violation of debt covenants may have severe economic consequences for a firm including increases in interest rates paid on loans, calls for repayment of debt or a requirement that the firm put up (additional) collaterals. In a worst case scenario, the firm may not be able to comply with its debt covenants and may have to close down due to lack of liquidity. It is evident that management, to avoid default on debt, may be tempted to exploit loopholes in accounting regulation and/or make estimates and assumptions which improve financial ratios, so that lenders cannot call the debt. For example, if management is able to reclassify finance leases as operating leases, debt is kept off-balance making the balance sheet look healthier.

Lenders should basically consider any and all accounting policy choices and estimates, since everything that has an impact on accounting numbers has an impact on financial ratios. Below, we discuss one of these issues, namely accounting policy changes and accounting changes.

Accounting policy choices and accounting changes

Financial ratios used for credit rating purposes are clearly affected by a firm's accounting policies. For example, as discussed in Chapter 15, we find that ROIC is overstated for mature firms, if development costs are expensed as incurred, while risk measures such as the debt–equity ratio would be downward biased due to the lack of recognising R&D assets.

Accounting changes may be voluntary or mandatory. In covenants, the bank needs to specify that GAAP is to be consistently applied. If not, a change in financials included in covenants may be attributed to a change in a firm's profitability and risk or to accounting changes, whether mandatory or voluntary. Naturally, debt covenant violations from accounting changes would hurt a firm. Likewise, lower interest rates on borrowing due to apparently improved profitability and risk would be unfair, if it is based on accounting changes and not real changes in the underlying risk and performance of a firm.

To ensure that accounting policies do not have economic consequences in the sense that it affects interest rates or lenders opportunity to recall debt, accounting method choices should be the same within an industry. This is recognised by large rating agencies such as Standard & Poor's and Moody's. For instance, Standard & Poor's includes deferred tax in permanent capital (invested capital) in the calculation of ROI (return on capital) (Standard & Poor's 'Formulas for Key Ratios' Corporate Ratings Criteria and Standard & Poor's 2003 'Corporate Ratings Criteria').

Forecasting (value-at-risk analysis)

Lenders should make a careful assessment of budgets prepared by a firm's management. To assess the quality of budgets, lenders may use budget control in line with the recommendations in Chapter 8. For instance, how is ROIC in future periods compared to ROIC historically? Also, historical financial data may be noisy measures of future earnings and cash flows if accounting policies and estimates have changed over time. Budgets prepared for negotiating financing with lenders do not have to follow IFRS, US GAAP or whichever accounting regime the firm complies with. As a consequence, lenders need to make sure that the budget is based on the same set of accounting policies and estimates as in the past. If not lenders should examine, why accounting policies or estimates have changed and how it affects growth, profitability and risk. Since value-at-risk analysis requires forecasting future cash flows, the issues raised in the discussion of *present value approaches* also apply to issues that should be considered in any value-at-risk analysis.

Liquidation models

Good accounting quality in using the liquidation model for credit rating purposes (worst case scenario) has the following characteristics:

- All assets and liabilities are measured at fair value, which they are generally not if a firm is perceived as a going concern.
- All items which represent inflow or outflow of economic benefits in a liquidation should be recognised as assets and liabilities in the financial statements.

The liquidation model represents firm value in a worst case scenario. If a firm is not able to service its debt, the lender may call the debt. As discussed in Chapter 9 on valuation, the proceeds the investor (or in this case the lender) will eventually receive depend on how quickly the firm needs to sell the assets and settle the liabilities. A forced liquidation will most likely result in lower net proceeds. In any event, what do the financial statements tell us about the potential break-up value of a firm? Reverting back to Chapter 13 on accounting quality, remember that good accounting quality is the extent to which *all* assets and liabilities are recognised in the balance sheet and measured at fair value (which is hardly ever the case). The *liquidation method* is thoroughly discussed in Chapter 15 where accounting flexibility in the balance sheet is examined.

Accounting issues in executive compensation

Bonuses based on financial performance measures also have some inherent problems to be considered by the analyst. Typically, cash bonuses are based on one or more of several different performance measures such as revenue, EBIT, EBITDA, ROIC, EVA, and other similar metrics. Consider a cash bonus based on reported EBIT. Management can simply enhance the chance of getting a bonus merely by extending the estimated lifetime of depreciable assets, and, therefore, charge the income statement, and EBIT, with a lower depreciation expense.

In this section, the focus is on how accounting flexibility may affect bonuses. Since accounting-based bonuses are directly linked to accounting measures of performance, measurement errors (bias) and flexibility in choosing between alternative accounting policies (e.g. FIFO versus average costs) have economic consequences. We now discuss two types of accounting-based performance measures:

1 Absolute performance measures (e.g. revenue, EBIT, EBITDA, EBT)
2 Relative performance measures (e.g. ROIC, EVA).

Absolute performance measures (financial measures)

The use of revenue EBIT, EBITDA or similar metrics as a performance measure in bonus plans has the advantage that management compensation is tied to a firm's operating performance. Furthermore, EBITDA has the alleged advantage that management cannot increase bonuses for example by simply changing the estimated lifetime of depreciable assets. Nonetheless, certain accounting issues should be considered.

Revenue

To the extent that bonus compensation is based on growth in net sales it can be debated whether directors should be rewarded (punished) for a favourable (unfavourable) development of the exchange rate.

A remuneration committee should consider whether executives deserve credit for growth due to positive changes in the price of foreign currencies. An argument for including exchange rate differences (gains or losses) in performance measures used in bonus plans might be that management has focused on the adverse effects on exchange rate risk, and therefore takes the necessary steps to avoid losses, for instance, by using financial instruments or (if possible) to make sales and purchases in the same currency. On the other hand, in reality, it is at best difficult to make a perfect hedge. This would require perfect prediction of future transactions (e.g. sales) in foreign currencies.

Other analytical issues raised previously on revenue should also be considered. These include, among other things, barter transactions, channel stuffing, multiple deliveries, extended warranty, construction contracts and consignment sales.

Non-capitalisation of expenses

In certain industries, such as biotech and high-tech industries, huge investments in research and development projects are essential for firms' survival in the long run. If such investments are expensed as incurred, it would be difficult for managers to obtain a bonus in relatively young firms when bonuses are based on realised operating earnings.

For mature companies, EBIT is largely unaffected by whether development projects are capitalised and amortised or expensed as incurred. As invested capital is lower for firms that expense development costs as incurred, management in companies where bonuses are based on financial ratios, e.g. return on invested capital, have a greater opportunity to obtain a bonus when development projects are expensed.

Relative performance measures (e.g. ROIC, EVA)

Relative performance measures have the inherent advantage that potential accounting distortion due to the flexibility in reporting financial statements are 'self-correcting'. For example, the mandatory change in accounting for goodwill for firms which switched to IFRS had two effects, which tend to level each other out. On the one hand, operating earnings (and net earnings) increased (the numerator in ROIC calculations), but so did invested capital (the denominator), as goodwill is no longer amortised.

Nonetheless, changes in accounting policies and non-capitalisation of expenses may have economic consequences and should be considered in a bonus contract. For instance, for start-up firms huge investments in R&D penalise earnings. Even though invested capital also becomes lower, the total effect will most likely be a lower ROIC and EVA compared to if the firm had capitalised such costs. Furthermore, the horizon problem (i.e. expenses or investments and the related income appear in different financial years) comes into play, since R&D is expensed as incurred while the potential return on R&D investments are recognised in subsequent years.

Conclusions

In assessing a firm's growth, profitability and risk, the analysts may not obtain a complete and objective assessment of a firm's performance by taking the financial statements at face value. The way a firm defines, recognises, measures, classifies and discloses accounting items affects the reported accounting numbers. Therefore, analysts must be critical of reported financial data and may have to make adjustments to those numbers before carrying out the analysis.

Essentially, measurement issues are at the heart of financial statement analysis. The combination of different estimates and assumptions combined with different measurement bases is the reason why financial statements may look quite different across time or across firms; even if the underlying transactions are the same.

It's difficult to see through every accounting entry and often the (financial) data are insufficient in respect to assessing earnings quality of the analysed firm. Furthermore, in making adjustments to reported financial data requires that the analyst makes a number of estimates and assumptions. To make such adjustments is a craft that requires expertise and hard work.

Some of the lessons to be learned are:

- Applied accounting policies should be carefully studied
- Changes in accounting policies or estimates may have severe economic consequences
- Growth in revenue is an important value driver and analysts should consider carefully the effects of aggressive, conservative or unusual accounting policies for revenue
- A huge variety of items and events may be recognised as special items. Analysts should carefully consider the treatment of such items in their analysis.

Most importantly, remember that uncritical use of accounting information may cause losses for the lender, investor and other users of financial statements. Therefore, due care must be taken in carrying out financial statement analysis.

Review questions

- What is regulatory flexibility?
- What is meant by management discretion?
- List examples of accounting items where some flexibility in choices of accounting methods is allowed due to regulatory flexibility.
- List examples of accounting items which require that management uses its discretion.
- Why do a firm's accounting policies matter?
- Discuss some of the analytical issues when analysing a company's revenue?

APPENDIX 14.1

PricewaterhouseCoopers has a number of publications comparing local GAAP with IFRS including:

- Comparison of IFRS and Australian FRS 2005
- Comparison of IFRS, US GAAP and Belgian GAAP 2006
- Comparison of IFRS and Hong Kong FRS 2008
- Comparison of IFRS, US GAAP and Indian GAAP 2009
- Comparison of IFRS, Indonesian GAAP and US GAAP 2005
- Comparison of IFRS, US GAAP and Italian GAAP 2008
- Comparison of IFRS and US GAAP for investment companies
- Comparison of IFRS, US GAAP and JP GAAP 2009
- Comparison of IFRS, US GAAP and JP GAAP 2008
- Comparison of IFRS and Korean GAAP 2008
- Comparison of IFRS and Luxembourg GAAP 2004
- Comparison of IFRS and Malaysian FRS
- Comparison of IFRS and Malaysian PERS
- Comparison of IFRS, US GAAP and Mexican GAAP 2009
- Comparison of IFRS and UK GAAP 2007
- Comparison of IFRS and US GAAP 2009
- Slovak Accounting Act No 431/2002 (New), Accounting Act No 563/1991 (Old) and IAS

Source: www.pwc.com

APPENDIX 14.2

Estimates within the boundaries of GAAP:

- Changing depreciation methods
- Changing the useful lives used for depreciation purposes
- Changing estimates of salvage value used for depreciation purposes
- Determining the allowance required for uncollectable accounts or loans receivable
- Determining the allowance required for warranty expenses
- Deciding on the valuation allowance required for deferred tax assets
- Determining the presence of impaired assets and any necessary loss accrual
- Estimating the stage of completion for percentage-of-completion contracts
- Estimating the likelihood of realisation of contract claims
- Estimating write-downs required for certain investments
- Estimating the amount of restructuring accruals
- Judging the need for and amount of inventory write-downs
- Estimating environmental obligation accruals
- Making or changing pension accrual assumptions
- Determining the portion of the price of a purchase transaction to be assigned to acquired in-process research and development
- Determining or changing the amortisation periods for intangibles

- Deciding the extent to which various costs such as landfill development, direct-response advertising, and software development should be capitalised
- Deciding the proper hedge-classification of financial derivative
- Determining whether an investment permits the exercise of significant influence over the investee company
- Deciding whether a decline in the market value of an investment is other than temporary

Source: Mulford and Comiskey, 2002 (p. 65)

Notes

1 However, depreciation might matter depending upon the value driver setup. For instance, in a firm using liberal accounting policies, investments may be too low (e.g. forecasts do not recognise that investments need to be made if non-current assets are not fully depreciated).

2 It may seem counter-intuitive that Daimler Benz reported a profit in a conservative accounting regime. What should be kept in mind, however, is that conservative accounting principles 'allow' for making reserves in good times and use these reserves to inflate earnings in bad times.

3 IFRS have even rules for SME (small and medium-sized) enterprises. It depends on accounting regulation in each country whether or not non-listed firms shall or may comply with IFRS.

4 In this case intangible assets must be tested for impairment at least on an annual basis.

5 As seen in Appendix 14.1, there are still differences to be settled. PwC and other major accounting firms have devoted considerable resources in explaining differences between GAAP regimes.

6 Impairment losses need not be recognised even if book value exceeds net present value of the future cash flow generated by the asset(s). This is the case if the market price of the asset(s) exceeds book value. However, for tangible (depreciable) assets market values are often not available.

7 It should be noted that IFRS does not permit classification of items in the income statement as 'extraordinary items'. Nonetheless, firms may wish to classify transactions in a separate line item, if the firms believe those transactions require special attention; for instance if they are non-recurring events.

8 Naturally, there might be a number of other items that are affected when firms comply with another set of standards (i.e. IFRS). In Table 14.1 only the effects of the change in accounting for goodwill is shown.

9 It should be noted that IAS/IFRS standards in addition to IAS 18 contain a number of standards which relate to specific types of income. Those standards include IAS 11 'Construction Contracts', IAS 17 'Leases', IAS 28 'Investments in Associates', IAS 39 'Financial Instruments', IAS 41 'Agriculture' and IFRS 6 'Exploration for and Evaluation of Mineral Resources'. For most firms, however, the relevant standard for recognition of income is IAS 18.

10 In practice, firms would grow investments at times and have negative growth at other times (e.g. due to a financial crisis). In these cases reported earnings would only be approximately the same.

11 While it is generally the case that depreciation has no effect on earnings capitalisation models like the DCF-model, this is not always true. It depends upon the value driver setup. For instance, a too long (short) depreciation period may have as a consequence the fact that investments in the forecast period become too low (high).

12 Unless the potential investor/buyer is able to see through the window dressing.

13 Clean surplus means that all income and expense items are recognised as part of earnings.

14 It should be noted that Carlsberg also reported special items in prior years (i.e. special items are recognised every year).

Reference

Mulford and Comiskey (2002) *The Financial Numbers Game: Detecting Creative Accounting Practices*, Wiley.

CHAPTER 15

Accounting flexibility in the balance sheet

Learning outcomes

After reading this chapter you should be able to:

- Understand how a firm's accounting policies regarding asset and liability recognition affect the financial statements
- Understand the potential impact of management discretion on reported accounting numbers
- Discuss potential economic consequences of firms' accounting choices and estimates regarding inventory accounting, intangible and tangible assets, lease accounting and deferred tax liabilities
- Make adjustments to financial statements so they can be used as inputs to decision models

Accounting flexibility in the balance sheet

In this second part on accounting flexibility we discuss analytical issues related to assets and liability recognition and the related income and expenses. As in the previous chapter, we have provided numerous examples on why accounting flexibility may have severe economic consequences.

Assets, liabilities and related expenses

Inventory accounting

Inventory is an accounting item that is treated differently in different jurisdictions. Despite the convergence project aimed at aligning US GAAP with IFRS, regulation on inventory accounting differs. IFRS allows valuing inventory using either the flow assumption[1] FIFO (First in First Out) or weighted average costs, but, unlike in the USA, LIFO (Last in First Out) is prohibited. The consequences for gross profit and inventory of the three different accounting methods for inventory are shown in Table 15.1. The example rests on the assumptions made in the table, where details about inventory are provided for a firm experiencing increases in costs over time (Firm A), and a firm (Firm B) with costs of inventories decreasing over time. The effect on earnings and assets of using FIFO, LIFO and average cost, respectively for the two firms are shown in Table 15.2.

Table 15.1 Accounting for inventory (example)

	Firm A: Retail store			Firm B: Computer chips		
	No. of units	Price per unit	Costs/ Sales	No. of units	Price per unit	Costs/ Sales
Beginning inventory	10	5	50	20	14	280
Purchase 1	10	7	70	20	12	240
Purchase 2	10	7	70	20	10	200
Purchase 3	10	9	90	20	8	160
Total available	**40**	**7**	**280**	**80**	**11**	**880**
Sold	−20			−20		
Ending inventory	**20**			**60**		
Revenue	20	12	240	20	15	300

Note: It is assumed that beginning inventory is the same regardless of whether the firm uses FIFO, LIFO or average cost. In practice beginning inventory would be different depending upon the cost assumption. However, this has no bearing on the conclusions.

Table 15.2 Accounting for inventory (example, continued)

	Firm A	Firm B
FIFO		
Sales	240	300
Cost of goods sold	−120	−280
Gross profit	**120**	**20**
Closing inventory	160	600
LIFO		
Sales	240	300
Cost of goods sold	−160	−160
Gross profit	**80**	**140**
Closing inventory	120	720
Average cost		
Sales	240	300
Cost of goods sold	−140	−220
Gross profit	**100**	**80**
Closing inventory	140	660

Table 15.3 **Unbiased accounting for inventory**

	Firm A	Firm B
Cost of goods sold (COGS)	180	160
Gross profit	60	140
Inventory	180	480

How would the numbers in Table 15.2 have looked if they were to represent fair values? Table 15.3 shows us. For firm A the fair value of inventory would be 20 units of 9 apiece = 180, since current costs are 9 for each unit. Incidentally, fair value of costs of goods sold (COGS) would also be 180, since 20 units have been sold. For firm B the unbiased numbers would be 160 for COGS (20 units of 8 apiece) and 480 for inventory (60 units of 8 apiece).

A closer look at Table 15.2 shows that neither FIFO, LIFO nor average cost represents unbiased values. For example, if gross profit should represent the profit of buying and selling goods at current prices, firm A would have sales of 240 (as reported), but cost of goods sold would be 180 (20 units of 9). Therefore, gross profit of 120 (FIFO) is upward biased by 60. Closing inventory (160) on the other hand is downward biased, as inventory at current prices would amount to 180.

Under LIFO gross profit amounts to an unbiased 140 for firm B. However, LIFO is not allowed according to IFRS (but is used in the USA). Furthermore, the only reason why gross profit is unbiased is the fact that the number of units sold (20) matches the latest purchase. Therefore, COGS represents the cost of the most recent purchase. Finally, if closing inventory should be measured at fair value, it must reflect current prices. For firm B, this would mean that inventory needs to be valued at 480 (60 units at 8 apiece).

A further issue to be considered is that IFRS and US GAAP require inventory to be written down to net realisable value.[2] This is required, for instance, if the cost of inventory is not recoverable due to damage, slow moving items or simply downward pressure on prices. In such cases, the use of LIFO or average cost may depress earnings substantially. For instance, as illustrated in Table 15.2 closing inventory for firm B amounts to 720 under LIFO, while current cost is much lower at 480. In all likelihood firm B needs to take a hit on earnings by writing down inventory to its net realisable value.

In conclusion, inventory cost accounting is an example of an accounting method choice that results in either a fair indicator of the performance of a firm (gross profit), or a good measure of the fair value of inventory or vice versa.

Finally, it should be noted that the choice of accounting method for inventory may have direct economic consequences. In some countries, taxable income is (partly) based on accounting numbers. The USA is a case in point. If US firms use LIFO and prices are rising, gross profit and hence earnings and taxable income would be lower than if FIFO was used.

Intangible and tangible assets

Depreciation and amortisation
Depreciation and amortisation methods are another example of flexibility in accounting method choices. Firms must depreciate their tangible and intangible assets in

a systematic manner over the useful lifetime of those assets. Neither IFRS nor US GAAP require a specific method. Firms may use the straight-line method (constant charge over the useful life unless the asset's residual value changes), the diminishing balance method (decreasing charge over time), the units of production method (charge based on the expected use or output) or similar methods that most closely reflect the expected pattern of consumption of the future economic benefits embodied in the asset.

Under IFRS, firms may use the revaluation model as an alternative to the cost model for property, plant and equipment (PPE). The revaluation model requires a firm to value PPE at fair value at the date of the revaluation less any subsequent accumulated depreciation and accumulated impairment losses. Intangible assets are generally accounted for using the cost model (intangibles measured at cost less any accumulated amortisation and any accumulated impairment losses). However, the revaluation model is also applicable to intangible assets, but only if fair value can be determined by reference to an active market. In reality, the use of the revaluation model for intangible assets is likely to be limited. An example of an intangible asset traded on an active market is carbon dioxide (CO_2). US GAAP, on the other hand, generally requires that non-financial assets are measured at historical costs (less depreciation/amortisation and impairment losses). Therefore, major differences in valuing non-financial assets may exist between firms complying with IFRS (cost versus revaluation model) as well as between IFRS firms and firms using US GAAP.

Management has a great deal of flexibility in accounting for non-financial, non-current assets (tangible and intangible assets). First, management needs to estimate how long such assets are productive, as they must be depreciated over their useful lifetime.[3] Second, those assets must pass impairment tests. If the recoverable amount is less than its carrying amount, an impairment loss should be recognised in the income statement. Estimating the recoverable amount involves a great deal of judgement. Finally, if firms choose to use the revaluation model, judgement must be exercised to estimate fair value.

Ideally, the depreciation/amortisation method of tangible and intangible assets should reflect the flow of future benefits generated by those assets. However, implementing this method would require that future benefits could be forecast with certainty. So accounting regulation sacrifices relevance for reliability by requiring firms to follow a predetermined amortisation schedule[4] with the most common method being straight-line depreciation/amortisation.

A firm faces several issues in their choice of depreciation method:

1 What is the cost of the asset?
2 What is the estimated useful life of the asset (which can be quite different from its physical life and technological life)?
3 What is the expected salvage value by the end of the asset's useful life?
4 What is the pattern of benefits derived from the asset likely to be?

While determining the cost of the asset is usually quite straightforward, indirect production costs leave room for judgements on the part of management. Estimating the useful life and salvage value is more complicated and depends on a number of factors including type of assets and usage.

Nonetheless, management must exercise their best estimate in calculating the annual depreciation charge. The pattern of benefits has a bearing on the depreciation method applied. If an asset's productivity is declining over time, it indicates that depreciation charges should be high in early years, but lower in subsequent years. In reality, a number of depreciation methods may be used including the straight-line method, reducing balance method, sum of the year's digits method and output or usage method. IAS simply states the depreciable amount (cost less residual value) must be allocated on a systematic basis over the asset's useful life, and the depreciation method used should reflect the pattern in which the asset's economic benefits are consumed by the entity. While these different methods have different implications, Example 15.1 discusses the impact of the highly uncertain and subjective estimate of the useful lifetime on financial statements. The arguments raised in the example could easily be adapted to differences in depreciation methods for non-current assets.

Since accounting data and financial ratios are used in a variety of contexts and contracts, financial statements' ability to reflect the true underlying performance and risk of a company is paramount. For instance, if financial ratios are severely biased, a firm risk paying too much interest on its debt or if accounting data paint too rosy a picture of risk and performance, a bank may provide funds to a firm at rates that are too low (i.e. not profitable for the bank).

While a great number of financial ratios and other measures of performance are used for valuation purposes, in credit rating models and in bonus plans, return on invested capital (ROIC) is maybe the most important one, as it reflects the total return on a firm's operations. Therefore, to illustrate the effects on various assumptions about the lifetime of depreciable and amortisable assets, our focus is on ROIC. For ROIC to be an unbiased estimate of the underlying performance of a firm, it should be a fair proxy of the internal rate of return (IRR).[5]

To illustrate the consequences of different estimates of and judgements about the useful lifetime of depreciable (or amortisable) assets, various earnings measures and financial ratios are calculated based on unbiased, conservative (depreciating too quickly) and aggressive estimates (depreciating too slowly) of the useful life of depreciable assets. In all cases, straight-line depreciation is used. Example 15.1 rests on the major assumptions listed at its start.

Example 15.1	The consequences of depreciation, revaluation and impairment policies
Price per project – annual investments in depreciable assets at the beginning of the year	100,000
Return per year per project at year end (EBITDA)	18,744
Useful lifetime of each project	8 years
Internal rate of return per project	10%

Note: In the following examples full depreciation in the year of the investment is assumed (e.g. 12.5% in year 1, if lifetime is assumed to be 8 years).

The internal rate of return is calculated as:

$$100,000 = \sum_{t=1}^{8} \frac{18,744}{(1 + IRR)^t} \rightarrow IRR = 10\%$$

First, consider that the firm depreciates its investments over an eight-year period, so the depreciation period perfectly matches the actual lifetime of each project (investment). If the firm uses straight-line depreciation, it would report the financials[6] shown in Table 15.4. From year 8 ROIC becomes constant and close to the internal rate of return of 10%, while in the early years ROIC is somewhat low compared to the internal rate of return of 10%. This ought to be expected, as ROIC is the accounting-based measure of IRR, and unbiased accounting should reflect the true underlying performance of a firm. As stated above, it is assumed that the investments are depreciated by a full year in the year of the investment.[7]

Table 15.4 **Financial data and ratios based on depreciation over the actual lifetime of projects**

Depreciation schedule: 8-year, straight-line

Year	EBITDA	Depreciation	EBIT	Book value at beginning of period	ROIC
1	18,744	12,500	6,244	100,000	6.2%
2	37,489	25,000	12,489	187,500	6.7%
3	56,233	37,500	18,733	262,500	7.1%
4	74,978	50,000	24,978	325,000	7.7%
5	93,722	62,500	31,222	375,000	8.3%
6	112,467	75,000	37,467	412,500	9.1%
7	131,211	87,500	43,711	437,500	10.0%
8	**149,955**	**100,000**	**49,955**	**450,000**	**11.1%**
9	149,955	100,000	49,955	450,000	11.1%
10	149,955	100,000	49,955	450,000	11.1%
15	149,955	100,000	49,955	450,000	11.1%
20	149,955	100,000	49,955	450,000	11.1%

In year 8 and all future years, EBITDA becomes $8 \times 18,744 = 149,955$ (allowing for rounding errors), since one project expires and is replaced by a new one. Depreciation becomes constant $8 \times 12,500 = 100,000$ as eight projects are depreciated by 12,500 each. Finally, the carrying value of the projects amounts to 450,000 as there are eight projects with a (yet) non-depreciated value as shown in Table 15.5.

Unbiased accounting requires perfect foresight. The problem is that in real life we do not have this information. That is why the useful lifetime may be estimated differently by different firms. In addition, even if management had absolute knowledge of the lifetime of assets, they may still want to apply aggressive or conservative estimates to increase their performance-based bonuses or otherwise obtain a favourable outcome of their reporting. What happens if the firm applies a conservative estimate of the useful lifetime believing that a four-year period reflects the economic lifetime of each project? In this case the accounting

Table 15.5 **Calculation of book value**

Project	Book value at beginning of the year
1: Depreciated by 7 times 12.5%. Remaining value 12.5%	12,500
2: Depreciated by 6 times 12.5%. Remaining value 25.0%	25,000
3: Depreciated by 5 times 12.5%. Remaining value 37.5%	37,500
4: Depreciated by 4 times 12.5%. Remaining value 50.0%	50,000
5: Depreciated by 3 times 12.5%. Remaining value 62.5%	62,500
6: Depreciated by 2 times 12.5%. Remaining value 75.0%	75,000
7: Depreciated by 1 times 12.5%. Remaining value 87.5%	87,500
8: Investment made at the beginning of the year	100,000
Total	**450,000**

Table 15.6 **Financial data and ratios based on conservative accounting**

Depreciation schedule: 4-year, straight-line

Year	EBITDA	Depreciation	EBIT	Book value at beginning of period	ROIC
1	18,744	25,000	−6,256	100,000	−6.3%
2	37,489	50,000	−12,511	175,000	−7.1%
3	56,233	75,000	−18,767	225,000	−8.3%
4	74,978	100,000	−25,022	250,000	−10.0%
5	93,722	100,000	−6,278	250,000	−2.5%
6	112,467	100,000	12,467	250,000	5.0%
7	131,211	100,000	31,211	250,000	12.5%
8	**149,955**	**100,000**	**49,955**	**250,000**	**20.0%**
9	149,955	100,000	49,955	250,000	20.0%
10	149,955	100,000	49,955	250,000	20.0%
15	149,955	100,000	49,955	250,000	20.0%
20	149,955	100,000	49,955	250,000	20.0%

figures and related financial ratios become as shown in Table 15.6. As before, notice that EBITDA becomes constant after eight years. Perhaps more surprisingly, depreciation also becomes constant at 100,000. This is because four projects are depreciated by 25,000 (25% p.a.) each. But in contrast to the previous example, depreciation is constant from year 4, not year 8. Invested capital also comes into steady-state in year 4. Invested capital of 250,000 consists of the value of projects not fully depreciated (four projects with remaining values of 25,000, 50,000, 75,000 and 100,000 respectively). ROIC is clearly understated in early years, but overstated in later years (20.0% compared to IRR of 10%). Again, the actual ROIC depends on the depreciation schedule (including whether depreciation is made in full in year 1) and method (here assumed to be straight-line).

Finally, Table 15.7 illustrates the consequences of a depreciation period of 12 years, which is far longer than the true lifetime of each project of eight years. Not surprisingly, ROIC is much higher than for conservative and unbiased accounting, in the early years and even significantly higher than IRR especially in year 8. Depreciation charges are clearly too low, and even though invested capital is too high, the end result is a higher ROIC (the denominator dominates the numerator). However, from year 11 ROIC is downward biased. EBIT and invested capital have become constant, but invested capital consists of assets, which should have been fully depreciated.

Table 15.7 Financial data and ratios based on aggressive accounting

Depreciation schedule: 12-year, straight-line

Year	EBITDA	Depreciation	EBIT	Book value at beginning of period	ROIC
1	18,744	8,333	10,411	100,000	10.4%
2	37,489	16,667	20,822	191,667	10.9%
3	56,233	25,000	31,233	275,000	11.4%
4	74,978	33,333	41,644	350,000	11.9%
5	93,722	41,667	52,056	416,667	12.5%
6	112,467	50,000	62,467	475,000	13.2%
7	131,211	58,333	72,878	525,000	13.9%
8	149,955	66,667	83,289	566,667	14.7%
9	149,955	75,000	74,955	600,000	12.5%
10	149,955	83,333	66,622	625,000	10.7%
12	**149,955**	**100,000**	**49,955**	**650,000**	**7.7%**
20	149,955	100,000	49,955	650,000	7.7%

■

Based on the above examples it can be concluded that the relation between ROIC and IRR is as follows:

- For firms which have been in business for a few years only, ROIC is significantly lower than IRR, unless the depreciation policy is liberal (aggressive).
- For mature firms the relation between ROIC and IRR depends upon the depreciation policy:
  - Unbiased depreciation policies: ROIC is a fair proxy for IRR
  - Conservative accounting policies: ROIC overstates IRR
  - Aggressive accounting policies: ROIC understates IRR.

As a result of measurement errors from depreciating/amortising too quickly, book values (invested capital) become undervalued – therefore, ROIC and other measures of performance are upward biased. One consequence of this is the so-called 'old plant trap'. Firms with old plant, property and equipment, which have been (almost) entirely depreciated, will have low carrying values and relatively high rates of accounting returns (e.g. ROIC and ROE). But when these assets are replaced by new ones, book values will increase substantially, causing accounting rates of return to decrease. The old plant trap is sprung when investors mistake the high accounting rates of return for firms with old plants for high economic rates of return. The interpretation of ROIC should be taken with care, as it is heavily influenced by a firm's accounting policies.

Naturally, a number of other financial ratios are affected as well. The economic consequences of accounting policies may be severe, depending on the extent to which these ratios are used in credit rating, bonus contracts or valuation based on multiples.

Impairment losses

Even though most tangible and intangible assets are depreciated[8] additional expenses shall be recognised if those assets are impaired. An impairment loss is expensed when the carrying amount (book value) of an asset exceeds its recoverable amount. The recoverable amount is the higher of an asset's fair value less costs to sell (sometimes called net selling price) and its value in use. According to IAS 36.6 value in use is the present value of the future cash flows expected to be derived from the asset. In other words, if the selling price of an asset is not known (which is presumably the case for most (specialised) assets used in production), a firm shall use valuation techniques for measuring value in use. Measuring value in use is therefore highly subjective.

According to US GAAP, the carrying amount is compared with the undiscounted cash flows. If the carrying amount is lower than the undiscounted cash flows, no impairment loss is recognised. Therefore, the analysts need to be aware that impairment losses are more likely to occur for firms using IFRS standards (cash flows are discounted) compared to firms using US GAAP.

The consequences of impairment losses on selected earnings measures and financial ratios are depicted in Table 15.8, which builds on the assumptions in Table 15.4.

Due to the impairment losses, invested capital is reduced by 80,000 in year 9. For the remaining four years of the assets' lifetime, depreciation is lower by 20,000 (80,000/4 = 20,000) annually due to a lower investment base. As a result, ROIC is negative in year 9, where the impairment loss is recognised, but high in subsequent years. ROIC is positively affected by both an increase in the numerator (adjusted EBIT) and a decrease in the denominator (adjusted invested capital). Naturally, the impairment loss could reflect a general economic recession or simply a bad business climate within the industry. In such cases, the impairment loss reflects (correctly) that future cash flows are expected to be lower than originally forecast. Alternatively, the impairment loss might be an example of management playing the earnings management game ('big bath' accounting). By taking a big hit on earnings in year 9 with a huge impairment charge (maybe it's a bad year anyway) future earnings increase.

It is difficult for analysts to determine if impairment tests and the related (potential) recognition of impairment losses provide an unbiased estimate of assets (net of impairment write-offs) and earnings or if management uses the judgements and estimates inherent in carrying out impairment tests to manage earnings. Unless fair value can be established with reference to an active market or a bid for the asset, impairment tests

Table 15.8 Financial data and ratios after recognition of impairment losses

	Year 8	Year 9	Year 10	Year 11	Year 12	Year 13	Year 14
EBITDA	149,955	149,955	149,955	149,955	149,955	149,955	149,955
Depreciation and amortisation	−100,000	−100,000	−100,000	−100,000	−100,000	−100,000	−100,000
EBIT (unadjusted)	**49,955**	**49,955**	**49,955**	**49,955**	**49,955**	**49,955**	**49,955**
Impairment losses	0	−80,000	0	0	0	0	0
Adjustments to depreciation	0	0	20,000	20,000	20,000	20,000	0
EBIT (adjusted)	**49,955**	**−30,045**	**69,955**	**69,955**	**69,955**	**69,955**	**49,955**
Invested capital	450,000	450,000	450,000	450,000	450,000	450,000	450,000
Impairments	0	−80,000	−60,000	−40,000	−20,000	0	0
Invested capital, adjusted	**450,000**	**470,000**	**490,000**	**410,000**	**430,000**	**450,000**	**450,000**
ROIC (unadjusted)	**11.1%**	**11.1%**	**11.1%**	**11.1%**	**11.1%**	**11.1%**	**11.1%**
ROIC, adjusted	**NA**	**−6.7%**	**18.9%**	**17.9%**	**17.1%**	**16.3%**	**11.1%**

require that the value in use is calculated. To calculate value in use, management needs to forecast future economic benefits (cash flows) and apply a proper discount rate. This leaves much room for management to manage earnings. Analysts are left with two choices, in order to assess whether earnings management is taking place. They may dig up information in the annual report about the assumptions underlying the impairment tests, and they may find inspiration in assessing the realism in the tests by comparison with assumptions made by competitors.

Revaluation

A firm's property, plant and equipment may be *revalued* if fair value can be measured reliably. For instance, the fair value (market value) of an office building can be determined by independent realtors. If two professional realtors end up with an estimate of the value of the office building of 105,000 and 115,000 respectively, the firm may choose to revalue the office building from its current book value of, say, 100,000 to the average value of the realtors' estimate (105,000 + 115,000)/2 = 110,000. Since the revaluation reserve of 10,000 is credited to equity and not recognised as income, it becomes a comprehensive income item; unless the firm is in the investment property business. In that case IAS 40 applies, and gains or losses arising from changes in the fair value of investment property must be included in net profit or loss.

Using the above example and assuming that investments are depreciated over its useful lifetime (as illustrated in Table 15.4), we exemplify the effects of a revaluation in year 9 (accounting items have reached steady-state). The example is analogous to the impairment loss example: instead of an impairment loss of 80,000 a revaluation of 80,000 (on depreciable assets) is recognised (see Table 15.9).

Here we assume that the revalued assets have an estimated remaining (average) lifetime of four years. Operating profit (EBIT) does not increase as a consequence of the

Table 15.9 **Financial data and ratios after revaluation**

	Year 8	Year 9	Year 10	Year 11	Year 12	Year 13	Year 14
EBITDA	149,955	149,955	149,955	149,955	149,955	149,955	149,955
Depreciation and amortisation	−100,000	−100,000	−100,000	−100,000	−100,000	−100,000	−100,000
EBIT (unadjusted)	**49,955**	**49,955**	**49,955**	**49,955**	**49,955**	**49,955**	**49,955**
Depreciation on revaluations	0	0	−20,000	−20,000	−20,000	−20,000	0
EBIT (adjusted)	**49,955**	**49,955**	**29,955**	**29,955**	**29,955**	**29,955**	**49,955**
Invested capital	450,000	450,000	450,000	450,000	450,000	450,000	450,000
Revaluations	0	80,000	60,000	40,000	20,000	0	0
Invested capital, adjusted	**450,000**	**530,000**	**510,000**	**490,000**	**470,000**	**450,000**	**450,000**
ROIC	11.1%	11.1%	11.1%	11.1%	11.1%	11.1%	11.1%
ROIC, adjusted	**NA**	**11.1%**	**5.7%**	**5.9%**	**6.1%**	**6.4%**	**11.1%**

revalued amount. On the contrary, depreciation expenses related to property increase proportionally to the increase in the gross value of the depreciable assets. As a result ROIC is downward biased (until the revalued amount has been fully depreciated). In addition, revaluation shall be made with sufficient regularity to ensure that book value does not differ materially from fair value at the balance sheet date. A further increase in the market value of the assets will, therefore, require even higher depreciation charges in the future. While ROIC is downward biased, the balance sheet better reflects fair value. Risk measures such as the debt–equity ratio improves. Again, how analysts relate to revaluation depends on the purpose of their analysis and the decision model they intend to use.

Accounting for leases

Leases may be accounted for using two vastly distinct methods. If lease contracts are classified as operating leases, lease obligations are not recognised in the balance sheet (and nor are lease assets), but the contract is disclosed as a contingent liability. On the other hand, finance leases (or capital leases as they are called in the USA), the alternative to operating leases, are recognised as lease assets with an offsetting lease liability.

Lease is a prime example of assets and liabilities that may or may not be recognised depending upon the contract as discussed previously. Consider that firm A enters a lease contract with the following characteristics:

Lease payment per year (constant)	22,961
Lease period	6 years
Internal rate of return (discount rate)	10%
Salvage value after year 6	Zero

Firm A recognises leases as operating leases. In this case, the yearly lease payment is recognised as an expense in measuring EBIT. However, had firm A recognised the contract as a finance lease (capital lease), the firm would have to capitalise the lease payments and recognise leased assets and corresponding lease liabilities in the balance sheet. To do so the value of the leased assets and corresponding lease liability must be calculated at the inception of the lease contract. According to generally accepted accounting principles (GAAP), the lease assets should be recognised as the present value of the future minimum lease payments as set forth in the lease contract. In the above example, the leased assets, and the lease obligation, is measured as:

$$\text{NPV} = \frac{22{,}961}{(1+0.1)^1} + \frac{22{,}961}{(1+0.1)^2} + \frac{22{,}961}{(1+0.1)^3} + \frac{22{,}961}{(1+0.1)^4} + \frac{22{,}961}{(1+0.1)^5} + \frac{22{,}961}{(1+0.1)^6} = 100{,}000$$

The effect on the financial statements would be as shown in Tables 15.10 and 15.13. The leased assets and lease obligations are quite simply recorded as if the assets had been purchased on account. The assets are depreciated over their useful lifetime on (in this example) a straight-line basis. Every year depreciation expenses of 16,667 are recognised in the income statement, while the leased assets are gradually being depreciated to zero by the end of year 6 (salvage value is considered to be zero). Notice that the depreciation expense is unrelated to the yearly lease payment of 22,961.

Table 15.10 Reported lease assets after converting to finance leases

	Book value at beginning of period	Depreciation	Book value at end of period
Year 1	100,000	16,667	83,333
Year 2	83,333	16,667	66,667
Year 3	66,667	16,667	50,000
Year 4	50,000	16,667	33,333
Year 5	33,333	16,667	16,667
Year 6	16,667	16,667	0
Total		100,000	

The lease payments are related to the lease obligations. If the firm had bought the leased assets on account, outstanding debt would be recorded as shown in Table 15.11. For instance, the lease payment in year 1 would consist of an interest expense of 10,000 (10% × 100,000), while the remaining 12,961 (22,961 – 10,000) would be an instalment (amortisation of the lease obligation). After six years, the lease obligation has been repaid in full as reflected in Table 15.11. If the value of the leased assets and the lease obligation do not add up to zero by the end of year 6, the calculations are flawed. Therefore, analysts can control their calculations if they convert operating leases to finance leases for analytical purposes.

Assume that firm A has a constant EBITDA of 32,000 over time and net financial expenses (excluding interest on lease obligations) of 3,000. The income statement

Table 15.11 Reported lease obligations after converting to finance leases

	Lease obligation beginning of period	Interest expense	Payment	Amortisation	Lease obligation end of period
Year 1	100,000	10,000	22,961	12,961	87,039
Year 2	87,039	8,704	22,961	14,257	72.782
Year 3	72,782	7,278	22,961	15,682	57,100
Year 4	57,100	5,710	22,961	17,251	39,849
Year 5	39,849	3,985	22,961	18,976	20,873
Year 5	20,873	2,087	22,961	20,873	0
Total		37,764	137,764	100,000	

Table 15.12 Income statements with leases classified as operating leases

Operating lease	Year 1	Year 2	Year 3	Year 4	Year 5	Year 6	Total
Income statement (excerpt)							
Turnover	82,000	82,000	82,000	82,000	82,000	82,000	492,000
Operating expenses excluding leases	50,000	50,000	50,000	50,000	50,000	50,000	300,000
Lease payments	22,961	22,961	22,961	22,961	22,961	22,961	137,764
EBIT	**9,039**	**9,039**	**9,039**	**9,039**	**9,039**	**9,039**	**54,236**
Financial expenses, net (excluding interest on lease debt)	3,000	3,000	3,000	3,000	3,000	3,000	18,000
Interest on lease debt	0	0	0	0	0	0	0
Earnings before tax	**6,039**	**6,039**	**6,039**	**6,039**	**6,039**	**6,039**	**36,236**

would be quite different depending on how leases are accounted for as illustrated in Table 15.12 (classification as operating leases) and Table 15.13 (leases classified as finance leases).

If leases are classified as operating leases, the entire payment would be recognised as an operating expense. No balance sheet entries should be made (except for the cash payments which reduces a firm's cash balance or bank deposit), and no financial expenses would be recognised.

On the other hand, in a finance lease the lease contract affects both sides in the balance sheet as lease assets and lease obligations, respectively. The effect on income would be twofold: an increase in the depreciation expense (depreciation of lease assets) and an increase in financial expenses (interest on leasing debt).

Table 15.13 Income statements after converting to finance leases

Finance lease	Year 1	Year 2	Year 3	Year 4	Year 5	Year 6	Total
Income statement (excerpt)							
Turnover	82,000	82,000	82,000	82,000	82,000	82,000	492,000
Operating expenses excluding leases	50,000	50,000	50,000	50,000	50,000	50,000	300,000
Depreciation on leased assets	16,667	16,667	16,667	16,667	16,667	16,667	100,000
EBIT	15,333	15,333	15,333	15,333	15,333	15,333	92,000
Financial expenses, net (excluding interest on lease debt)	3,000	3,000	3,000	3,000	3,000	3,000	18,000
Interest on lease debt	10,000	8,704	7,278	5,710	3,985	2,087	37,764
Earnings before tax	**2,333**	**3,629**	**5,355**	**6,623**	**8,348**	**10,246**	**36,236**

In year 1 the effect on EBIT after reclassifying the lease contracts would be:

Reported EBIT	9,039
+ Add back lease payment (leases recognised as operating leases)	+22,961
− Subtract depreciation on leased assets	−16,667
Adjusted EBIT	**15,333**

Unsurprisingly, the total effect on earnings before taxes (EBT) over time of recognising leases as finance as opposed to operating leases is zero. The total expense recognised is equivalent to the total payments made; no more, no less. However, the effect on EBITDA, EBIT, net financial expenses and earnings before taxes (EBT) *within* each financial year varies between the two ways leases may be accounted for. For instance, in years 1 and 6, the expense related to the lease contract is as shown in Table 15.14.

It should be noted that a new standard on accounting for leases is currently being considered. IASB is running a project on leases to ensure that the assets and liabilities arising from lease contracts are recognised in the statement of financial position. However, at the moment leases may still be accounted for as operating leases.

Table 15.14 Income effects of operating versus finance leases

	Operating leases		Finance leases	
	Year 1	Year 6	Year 1	Year 6
EBIT	−22,961	−22,961	−16,667	−16,667
Financial expenses	0	0	− 10,000	− 2,087
EBT	**−22,961**	**−22,961**	**−26,667**	**−18,754**

Provisions

An important issue in reporting financials is whether all liabilities are recognised in the financial statements or kept off balance. It must often be judged whether a certain item or event requires recognition as a liability, disclosure as a contingent liability or should be disregarded (i.e. no information provided in the annual report at all).

A liability is a current obligation of an entity arising from past events, the settlement of which is expected to result in outflow from the entity of resources embodying economic benefits. Most liabilities pose no problems from an analytical point of view, as they contain little uncertainty. Many liabilities have fixed payment dates and amounts set by a contract. Borrowing arrangements (e.g. bank loans) and accounts payable fall into this category. An amortisation schedule specifies the timing and amount of interests and principal payments.

At the other extreme some liabilities may be highly uncertain. A frequently used example is unsettled lawsuits. Such liabilities are (mostly) recognised as contingent liabilities. In between the two extremes are liabilities where the firm must estimate the timing and/or the amount of payment. Restructuring charges and deferred tax liabilities are prominent examples.

These differences in uncertainty are reflected in accounting regulation, which have three separate categories of liabilities: liabilities, provisions and contingent liabilities. As noted above, a liability is a present obligation of an entity arising from past events, the settlement of which is expected to result in outflow from the entity of resources embodying economic benefits. Provisions are liabilities of uncertain timing or amount. Finally, contingent liabilities are defined as obligations that arise from past events and whose existence will be confirmed by occurrence or non-occurrence of one or more future events not wholly within the control of the entity. A contingent liability is also defined as a present obligation that arises from past events but is not recognised because it is not probable that an outflow of resources embodying economic benefits will be required to settle the obligation or the amount of the obligation cannot be measured with sufficient reliability.

Provisions may be hard to separate from contingent liabilities, as illustrated below:

Provisions	Contingent liabilities
A present obligation from past events	A present obligation from past events existence of which depends on future events and/or
A probably outflow of economic benefits	Outflow of economic benefits is not probable and/or
An evaluation of timing and amount	A reliable estimate of outflow cannot be made

A liability is recognised as a provision if there is a *probable* outflow of economic benefits. Naturally, this requires judgement on the part of management that is responsible for producing the annual report. If the outflow of economic benefits is not probable or cannot be estimated *reliably*, the liability is no longer a provision but a contingent liability. Finally, if the possibility of an outflow of resources is *remote* no liability is recognised or disclosed. As is apparent there might often be a thin line between provisions and contingent liabilities. From an analytical point of view, however, it may have a huge impact on earnings and financial ratios how liabilities are incorporated in the financial statement.

Type of obligation	Financial statement treatment
Liabilities	Recognised as current and non-current liabilities, respectively
Provisions	Recognised as a separate item under current and non-current liabilities, respectively
Contingent liabilities	Disclosed. Not recognised in the balance sheet
Remote possibility of outflow of economic benefits	No information provided in the annual report

An analyst should be aware of these subtle differences between different types of liabilities. Contingent liabilities like pending lawsuits and operating lease contracts may represent potential large future outflows of cash. This underlines the point that an analyst should read the annual report and notes carefully, and remember what he or she already knows about the business and industry.

Provisions shall be measured at fair value if discounting is material. Provisions may be quite large and of a different nature. In year 8 the E.ON Group – one of the world's largest investor-owned power and gas companies – reported the provisions shown in the excerpt from its annual report in Table 15.15.

Table 15.15 E.ON Group Miscellaneous Provisions (Annual Report, note 25)

(25) Miscellaneous Provisions

The following table lists the miscellaneous provisions as of the dates indicated:

€ in millions	31 December, Year 8		31 December, Year 7	
	Current	Non-current	Current	Non-current
Non-contractual obligations for nuclear waste management	127	9,138	133	10,022
Contractual obligations for nuclear waste management	161	3,931	300	3,335
Personnel obligations	633	716	593	690
Other asset retirement obligations	290	1,193	301	943
Supplier-related obligations	309	320	451	290
Customer-related obligations	458	141	296	80
Environmental remediation and similar obligations	45	557	32	456
Other	2,237	3,202	1,886	2,257
Total	**4,260**	**19,198**	**3,992**	**18,073**

As E.ON's miscellaneous provisions amounted to €23,458 million (19,198 + 4,260) and reported equity was €38,427 million, provisions must be considered material. Furthermore, note 9 in the annual report discloses that 'Other interest expense includes the accretion of provisions for asset retirement obligations in the amount of €759 million'. This amount reflects the discounting of provisions. Since another year has passed the present value of the provisions increases (in the E.ON example by €759 million).

Provisions are prone to distortion since a great deal of subjectivity is involved: what are the costs associated with settling the provision (amount)? when shall the provision be settled (settlement date)? and what rate of interest (discount factor) should be applied in order to determine the present value of the provision? Even though it has become harder to use provisions as a tool for income smoothing or earnings management,[9] provisions still involve a great deal of judgement. To illustrate the impact of provisions on financial statements, the following example demonstrates how different assumptions and estimates concerning provisions affect financial statements.

Example 15.2 | **Provisions**

A firm has recognised large provisions, due to a major restructuring of its operations. Part of these restructuring costs is related to an environmental clean-up (land contamination) in year 4. The assumptions behind this provision are as follows:

Financial year	Year 1
Nominal provision	13,310
Settlement date (end of year)	Year 4
Discount rate (before tax)	10%

Recognition of this provision in the income statement and the balance sheet is as follows:

	Year 1	Year 2	Year 3	Year 4	Total
Operating expenses	10,000	0	0	0	10,000
Financial expenses	0	1,000	1,100	1,210	3,310
Total expenses	**10,000**	**1,000**	**1,100**	**1,210**	**13,310**
Provisions	10,000	11,000	12,100	0	
Cash	0	0	0	−13,310	−13,310

∎

In Example 15.2, the recognised provision by the end of year 1 is calculated as $13,310/(1 + 0.10)^3 = 10,000$. The difference between the nominal provision to be paid by the end of year 4 (13,310) and the operating expense recognised in year 1 (10,000) is recognised as financial expenses in years 2, 3 and 4. These expenses simply reflect the changes in the present value of the provision as the settlement date gets closer.

Since provisions are subject to a number of estimates and assumptions, an analyst should be aware of the consequences of changing the underlying assumptions. The effect of changing (1) the nominal provision, (2) the settlement date and (3) the discount rate are discussed next.

1 Change in nominal provision

Assume that by the end of year 2, the firm's best estimate of the provision changes from 13,310 to 16,638 at the settlement date in year 4.

	Year 1	Year 2	Year 3	Year 4	Total
Operating expenses (change in nominal provision)	0	2,750	0	0	12,750
Financial expenses		1,000	1,375	1,513	3,888
Total expenses	**10,000**	**3,750**	**1,375**	**1,513**	**16,638**
Provisions	10,000	13,750	15,125	0	
Cash (settlement of provision)	0	0	0	−16,638	−16,638

The change in the estimated provision of 16,638 − 13,310 = 3,328 has an effect on operating expenses in year 2, as they increase by $3,328/(1 + 0.10)^2 = 2,750$ (allowing for rounding errors). The total change in provisions in year 2 is hereafter 3,750 calculated as operating expenses of 2,750 plus financial expenses of 10% of 10,000 = 1,000.

2 Settlement date (date provision has to be paid for)

The present value of the nominal provision increases every year as the settlement date gets closer. The change in the present value of the provision is recognised as a financial expense. If the estimate of when the provision shall be settled changes, a financial expense or financial income must be recognised in the income statement.

In year 2 the firm changes its estimate of the settlement date for the provision, as it finds that production may be extended by a year before land contamination is needed. The consequences for the financial statements become:

	Year 1	Year 2	Year 3	Year 4	Year 5	Total
Operating expenses	10,000	0	0	0	0	10,000
Financial expenses	0	1,000	1,000	1,100	1,210	4,310
Financial income (change in settlement date)	0	1,000	0	0	0	1,000
Total expenses	**10,000**	**0**	**1,000**	**1,100**	**1,210**	**13,310**
Provisions	10,000	10,000	11,000	12,100		
Cash	0	0	0	0	−13,310	−13,310

As seen in this example, income/expenses due to a change in the settlement date are recognised as financial income and expenses. The provision is unchanged in year 2. This is explained by two opposite effects. Financial expenses increase by $10\% \times 10,000 = 1,000$, as the settlement date has become one year closer. At the same time financial income of 1,000 is recognised, as the settlement date has been postponed by a year. This financial income is calculated as: $13,310/(1 + 0.10)^2 - 13,310/(1 + 0.10)^3 = 11,000 - 10,000 = 1,000$.

3 Discount factor

Recognition of provisions at fair value requires discounting of the nominal amount to be paid in the future. Discounting shall take the time value of money and risk into consideration. Fair value is measured as the amount a firm would have to pay in order to settle the recorded provision at the financial year end.

Changes in the discount factor, for example, due to changes in the general interest level or inflation has an impact on the present value of the provision. The difference between the capitalised value of the provision before and after the change in the discount rate shall be recognised in the income statement as a financial item.

Assume that the discount factor is being reassessed by the firm and is now estimated to be 15% due to higher perceived risk. The consequences are:

Discount rate: 15%	Year 1	Year 2	Year 3	Year 4	Total
Operating expenses	8,752	0	0	0	8,752
Financial expenses		1,313	1,510	1,736	4,558
Total expenses	**8,752**	**1,313**	**1,510**	**1,736**	**13,310**
Provisions	8,752	10,064	11,574	0	
Cash				−13,310	−13,310

Financial expenses increases to 1,313 in year 2 and are calculated as $8,752 \times 15\%$. In total financial expenses amount to 4,558 compared to 3,310 if a discount rate of 10% was used. Unsurprisingly, the example highlights that as a consequence of an increase in the discount rate, financial expenses are at a higher level in each period. It should be pointed out that higher interest rates are likely to reflect an increase in inflation, which may affect the nominal provision upward.

Assuming that no provisions have been recognised prior to year 1, the example illustrates that the discount factor has a huge impact on allocation of the provision between operations (EBIT) and net financial expenses. The above examples are summarised in Table 15.16.

In summary, the total effect on net earnings (before tax) is the same in the two examples, namely accumulated expenses of 13,310. With a discount rate of 10% operating expenses are considerably higher than if a 15% discount rate was used, while financial expenses (interests) are correspondingly lower. The choice of discount factor consequently has a great impact on reported operating earnings (EBIT, EBITDA and NOPAT etc.) and financial expenses.

Table 15.16 **Accounting treatment of provisions if assumptions change**

Assumptions	Changes in assumptions	Effects on the income statement and balance sheet	
		Income statement	Balance sheet
Amount (Nominal provision)	Increases	Operating expense increases (Increase in depreciation charge[2]) Interest expenses increase	Provision increases (Related assets increase[2])
	Decreases	Operating expenses decrease (Decrease in depreciation charge[2]) Interest expenses decrease	Provision decreases (Related assets decrease[2])
Settlement date	Later	Interest expenses, net decrease	Provision decreases (Related assets decrease[2])
	Sooner	Interest expenses, net increase	Provision increases (Related assets increase[2])
Discount rate	Higher	Operating expenses decreases[1] (Decrease in depreciation charge[2]) Interest expenses increase	Provision decreases (Related assets decrease[2])
	Lower	Operating expenses increases[1] (Increase in depreciation charge[2]) Interest expenses decrease	Provision increases (Related assets increase[2])

Notes

[1] Operating expenses are only affected at initial recognition.

[2] For certain provisions the off-setting (debit) entry is an addition to assets, which affects the depreciation expense. Likewise, if provisions decrease (debit-entry), assets decrease (credit-entry) with a lower depreciation charge as a consequence. For example, provisions related to restoration of a site (e.g. removing oil rig and cleaning-up) would be capitalised and added to the cost of the assets (subject to depreciation).

Deferred tax liabilities

Another provision which should be carefully considered by the analyst is **deferred tax liabilities**. Deferred tax liabilities arise due to differences between taxable income and accounting earnings. Accounting earnings are calculated based on IFRS, US GAAP or local GAAP, while taxable income is the result of applying tax regulations. For most countries accounting profit and taxable income are based on entirely different sets of rules. Example 15.3 shows how deferred tax liabilities are calculated (see Table 15.17) and recognised in the financial statements.

Example 15.3 Calculation of deferred tax liabilities

Assumptions:	
Investment in equipment	100
Estimated useful lifetime, years	10
Salvage value	0
Accounting depreciation, straight-line	10% per year
Depreciation, taxable income, straight-line	25% per year
Corporate tax rate (flat rate)	30%

■

Table 15.17 Calculation of deferred tax liabilities

	Carrying value	Tax base	Difference	Balance sheet (accumulated deferred tax liability)	Income statement (change in deferred tax liability)
Year 1	90	75	15	30% × 15 = 4.5	Tax expense: 4.5
Year 2	80	50	30	30% × 30 = 9.0	Tax expense: 4.5
Year 3	70	25	45	30% × 45 = 13.5	Tax expense: 4.5
Year 4	**60**	**0**	**60**	**30% × 60 = 18.0**	**Tax expense: 4.5**
Year 5	50	0	50	30% × 50 = 15.0	Tax income: 3.0
Year 6	40	0	40	30% × 40 = 12.0	Tax income: 3.0
Year 7	30	0	30	30% × 30 = 9.0	Tax income: 3.0
Year 8	20	0	20	30% × 20 = 6.0	Tax income: 3.0
Year 9	10	0	10	30% × 10 = 3.0	Tax income: 3.0
Year 10	0	0	0	30% × 0 = 0.0	Tax income: 3.0
Total effect by the end of year 10				0	0

This example is simplified as only one asset is included. In addition, the tax rate is considered constant over time. Firms typically make investments on a continuous basis, and corporate tax rates have changed significantly over time. Nonetheless, Example 15.3 helps to illustrate a major analytical issue: are deferred tax liabilities true liabilities, and if not, what are they? The example indicates that deferred tax liabilities are overstated. For instance, by the end of year 4 a total deferred tax expense of 18 has been recognised with an off-setting liability of 18. These expenses have not yet been paid (that is why they are called deferred). Since these tax liabilities are paid at a future date (maybe far into the future or never) if firms make new investments, it would be obvious to discount them to present value.

Table 15.18 Calculation of deferred tax liabilities (*continued*)

	Carrying value (book value)	Tax base	Difference	Balance sheet (accumulated deferred tax liability)	Income statement (change in deferred tax liability)
Year 1	**90**	**75**	**15**	**30% × 15 = 4.5**	Tax expense: 4.5
Year 2					
Investment 1	80	50	30		
Investment 2	90	75	15		
Total year 2	**170**	**125**	**45**	**30% × 45 = 13.5**	Tax expense: 9.0
Year 3					
Investment 1	70	25	45		
Investment 2	80	50	30		
Investment 3	90	75	15		
Total year 3	**240**	**150**	**90**	**30% × 90 = 27.0**	Tax expense: 13.5
Year 4					
Investment 1	60	0	60		
Investment 2	70	25	45		
Investment 3	80	50	30		
Investment 4	90	75	15		
Total year 4	**300**	**150**	**150**	**30% × 150 = 45.0**	Tax expense: 18.0
Year 5					
Investment 1	50	0	50		
Investment 2	60	0	60		
Investment 3	70	25	45		
Investment 4	80	50	30		
Investment 5	90	75	15		
Total year 5	**350**	**150**	**200**	**30% × 200 = 60.0**	Tax expense: 15.0
Year 6					
Investment 1	40	0	40		
Investment 2	50	0	50		
Investment 3	60	0	60		
Investment 4	70	25	45		
Investment 5	80	50	30		
Investment 6	90	75	15		
Total year 6	**390**	**150**	**240**	**30% × 240 = 72.0**	Tax expense: 12.0
Total year 7	**420**	**150**	**270**	**30% × 270 = 81.0**	Tax expense: 9.0
Total year 8	**440**	**150**	**290**	**30% × 290 = 87.0**	Tax expense: 6.0
Total year 9	**450**	**150**	**300**	**30% × 300 = 90.0**	Tax expense: 3.0
Total year 10	**450**	**150**	**300**	**30% × 300 = 90.0**	Tax expense: 0.0

Why are deferred tax liabilities regarded as a provision? Provisions are characterised by uncertainty regarding the timing or amount used to settle the liability. The actual amount paid to settle deferred tax liabilities, sometimes in the future, depends upon the corporate tax rate at that point in time, which may be different from the tax rate as of today (uncertainty related to the amount), *and* the settlement date depends upon a firm's future investments (creates uncertainty regarding the timing). To illustrate this point, look at Table 15.18, which is an extension of Table 15.17. Now assume that the firm invests 100 in equipment in all future years. Often firms grow by a factor which reflects inflation and real growth. An investment of 100 every year is therefore a conservative estimate.

Table 15.18 demonstrates that if a firm invests a constant amount annually, deferred tax liabilities may never have to be paid. In the example the deferred tax liability increases steadily over time until year 9. From year 9 and forward the deferred tax liability stabilises at 90. The firm has recognised a total tax expense of 90 (change in deferred tax liability) over time. This expense, however, has never been paid and will not be paid in the foreseeable future, if the firm stays in business. Even if the deferred tax liability is going to be settled eventually, for instance, when or if the firm closes down, the present value of this liability may be negligible, implying that no deferred tax expense should be recognised. IAS 12 does not allow firms to discount deferred tax liabilities. For analytical purposes there might be good reasons for doing so or disregarding deferred tax liabilities all together. This is why Stewart (1991), and others who use similar metrics, suggest treating deferred tax liabilities as quasi equity (i.e. the deferred tax liability does not represent outflow of economic benefits).

Accounting flexibility and economic consequences

In the following section, we focus on how the accounting for inventory, intangible and tangible assets, leases, provisions, deferred liabilities and pensions may distort the financial data that are used by different decision models in different decision contexts.

Accounting issues in valuation

Present value approaches

We will now discuss how inventory accounting, intangible and tangible assets and deferred tax liabilities may influence the value obtained from using present value approaches.

Inventory accounting

Inventory accounting policies may have direct economic consequences. In the USA for instance, firms that use LIFO in the annual report must also apply LIFO for tax purposes. If costs of inventory are increasing, LIFO would reduce a firm's earnings compared to FIFO, since cost of goods sold is based on the most recent acquisitions. As a result, tax payable would be lower for firms using LIFO.

Even without this direct connection between inventory accounting and cash flows (lower taxes), the accounting choice for inventory accounting may have an effect on estimated firm value. It depends on the actual value driver setup used for forecasting, if, and to what extent, accounting policies affect the estimated value of a firm. Suppose that a firm uses the EBIT margin and asset turnover ratio as two important value drivers since the product of the two equals ROIC. The consequences of using FIFO versus average costs are illustrated in Tables 15.19 and 15.20 and built on Table 15.1.

Table 15.19 **FIFO versus average costs**

	No. of units	Price per unit	Costs/sales
Beginning inventory	10	5	50
Purchase 1	10	7	70
Purchase 2	10	7	70
Purchase 3	10	9	90
Total available	40	7	280
Sold	−20		
Ending inventory	20		
Revenue	20	12	240

Note: It is assumed that beginning inventory is the same regardless of whether the firm uses FIFO or average costs

If firm A uses FIFO ending inventory becomes 160 (10 units at 7 + 10 units at 9) and cost of goods sold (COGS) becomes 280 − 160 = 120. COGS are calculated as: Beginning inventory + purchases − ending inventory = 50 + 230 − 160 = 120. If average costs are used, ending inventory becomes 140 calculated as 20 units at an average price of 7, and COGS amounts to 280 − 140 = 140.

Furthermore, assume that the income statement and balance sheet (excerpt) would be as shown in Table 15.20, depending on whether the firm uses FIFO or average costs.

As can be seen in Table 15.20, the financial ratios indicate that the profitability is apparently higher, and the risk apparently lower if firm A uses FIFO. The reason is that under FIFO, gross profit is higher since cost of goods sold are based on past (lower) inventory costs. Moreover, risk is lower as inventory is carried at recent costs, which is higher than past costs (since prices are increasing). It should be noted that ROIC does not necessarily increase if FIFO is applied, as both the numerator (EBIT) and denominator (invested capital) increases. Had inventory costs decreased over time, profit margin and risk measures would have improved if average costs were used for inventory accounting.

When valuing a firm, analysts should be aware that the choice of inventory accounting does affect important value drivers (e.g. EBIT margins and asset turnover) and potentially the estimated firm value.

Intangible and tangible assets

Even though depreciation, amortisation and impairment losses have no cash flow consequences, they may still have an impact on firm value. First, impairment losses are a signal of expected poor future performance or indicate that depreciation and amortisation expenses in the past have been insufficient. The exception is impairment losses on goodwill and intangible assets with indefinite lifetimes. These assets are not

Table 15.20 **Income statement and balance sheet**

Income statement (excerpt)	Firm A FIFO	Firm A Average costs
Sales	240	240
Cost of goods sold	–120	–140
Gross profit	120	100
Other operating costs including depreciation	–60	–60
EBIT	60	40
Net financial expenses	–20	–20
Earnings before taxes (EBT)	40	20
Corporate tax	–16	–8
Net earnings	24	12
Balance sheet (excerpt)		
Non-current assets (operating assets)	120	120
Inventory	160	140
Other current assets (operating assets)	20	20
Total assets	300	280
Equity	124	112
Non-current liabilities, interest-bearing	100	100
Current liabilities, non-interest-bearing	76	68
Total equity and liabilities	300	280
Revenue	240	240
Invested capital	224	212
EBIT margin	25%	17%
Asset turnover	1.07	1.13
ROIC (before tax)	26.8%	18.9%
Solvency, debt–equity ratio	1.4	1.5

Note: It is assumed that invested capital is constant over time.

amortised but subject to impairment tests at least annually. Therefore, it cannot be stated that past amortisation expenses have been insufficient for such assets. More interestingly, despite that, asset impairments more likely reflect a flawed business model, recognising impairment losses today results in increased earnings and financial ratios like ROIC, in future periods. If an asset impairment is recorded every time management makes a bad investment, it stands to reason that net income excluding

435

impairment losses will always look better, since income excludes the effects of all the bad investments.

Second, when impairment losses are recognised, firms may report them as 'restructuring charges' or use a similar classification to correct overvalued assets. If analysts disregard impairment losses for valuation purposes believing they are non-recurring, and, therefore, need not be forecast, they risk getting forecasts and value estimates that are too optimistic. This is because impairment losses may represent an adjustment of insufficient depreciation of assets, so the impairment charges simply correct a systematic overstatement of past earnings. In such cases, analysts should be aware of how the earnings trend may be distorted.

Companies continually replace plant and equipment in line with the emergence of new technology or physical wear and tear. Lack of specification (notes) on gains and losses on the sale or scrapping of these assets is problematic for at least two reasons:

1 Should such gains and losses be regarded as recurring or non-recurring items?
2 Do such gains and losses reflect that the firm's depreciation policies are overly aggressive or overly conservative?

Gains and losses resulting from disposing of assets are often considered non-recurring and the inclusion of such gains or losses in reported income lowers the quality of earnings, as they make noise in forecasting future earnings. However, if such gains and losses occur frequently, it is difficult to argue that they should be considered as non-recurring.

Consistently reporting gains (losses) indicate that a firm is applying conservative (aggressive) accounting policies for depreciable and amortisable assets. To assess if gains (losses) are due to overly conservative (aggressive) accounting policies and estimates, a firm's accounting policies and estimates may be compared with the ones reported by other firms within the same industry. For forecasting purposes, analysts might level gains/losses out by forecasting them as the average of past gains/losses over a period of time. The analyst may have to look carefully in the annual report for information on such items. Past gains/losses may be recognised as part of the depreciation expense or otherwise be unspecified (e.g. because they are part of 'special items' or other income/expenses without further specification), in which case it may be difficult to assess the level of such items. If a firm's accounting policies and estimates are overly conservative (aggressive), maybe management is overly conservative (aggressive) on other accounting items as well. As discussed in Chapter 13, it cannot be concluded that conservative accounting policies provide higher accounting quality.

Deferred tax liabilities

Taxes play an important role when valuing a company. Depending on the jurisdiction, corporate tax rates may vary substantially. Taxes are an expense, which must be treated like other expenses in valuing a company. Tax recognised in the income statement consists of tax payable plus the change in deferred tax during the fiscal year, that is part of taxes not yet payable.

Without access to income tax returns, the analyst may attempt to assess the impact of taxes on future earnings by a closer examination of the following elements:

- Accounting versus tax depreciation rates
- The company's projected growth (investment)
- Permanent differences
- Non-recognised tax assets.

Essentially, the larger the difference between accounting depreciation and tax depreciation and the higher future investments (growth), the greater the accumulated deferred tax liabilities. If an increase in deferred tax liabilities in the forecasting period is not taken into consideration, the estimated tax payable (cash outflow) will be too high and accordingly, the estimated firm value will be downward biased.

Permanent differences are income and expenses, which enter the income statement but are not included in taxable income or vice versa. In contrast temporary differences, such as differences in accounting depreciation and depreciation for tax purposes, reverses over time. For example, in many tax jurisdictions fines and expenses resulting from violations of law may be expensed in the income statement, but they are not tax deductible. Permanent differences should be analysed. Are they fairly constant over time or do they fluctuate substantially? In general, there is not much an analyst can do about such differences. To fully incorporate them would also mean that the analyst is up-to-date with current tax legislation. Nonetheless, if permanent differences have a large impact on the tax rate, say, the corporate tax rate is 20%, while the effective tax rate fluctuates around 25%, analysts might forecast the tax rate at 25% and thereby reduce the estimated cash flow too much. We examine this in greater detail below.

Analysts should also consider non-recognised tax assets. Firms operating at a loss may have large tax deficits, which can be offset against future taxable income.[10] If it is not likely that the firm is going to have positive earnings and taxable income in the future, these tax deficits do not represent future cash flows (tax savings). If, however, the analysts anticipate that the firm is going to be profitable, the tax deficits from prior years, not yet recognised, represent true economic benefits (future tax savings) and should be included in the forecast cash flows. For example, if a firm has €100 million in accumulated tax deficits, and the corporate tax rate is 25%, the analyst may add €25 million to the estimated firm value; or some smaller amount, which takes into effect that the tax deficits may be utilised over more than one period (i.e. taxable income in the first forecast year is not sufficient to recover the entire tax deficits), so that the unrecognised tax asset needs to be discounted to reflect present value.

It should be evident from the previous paragraphs that an assessment of future tax rates is an extremely complex issue, and the tax rates must be evaluated in the context of the analysed company. Even if the analyst has great knowledge of the company, he or she still doesn't have access to the firm's income tax returns.

Nonetheless, when valuing a firm, forecast earnings must be net of corporate tax. This raises the question of what the forecast tax rate should be. At least three tax rates are likely candidates:

1 The effective tax rate from the past
2 The firm's marginal tax rate in the jurisdiction to which it belongs
3 Tax payable (i.e. deferred tax is disregarded).

If the firm's effective tax rate in the past is fairly constant it could be used as a proxy for forecasting future tax rates.

A number of factors explain why the effective tax rate may differ substantially from the marginal corporate tax rate. These factors include permanent differences between accounting income and taxable income, tax-losses carry forwards, write-offs of deferred tax assets, limitations in how tax losses may be utilised across jurisdictions, and adjustments to tax paid in prior year(s). Since such factors are hard to forecast, it could be argued that the corporate tax rate (i.e. the firm's marginal tax rate) should be used in forecasting earnings.

Finally, since only cash flows matter, forecast tax expenses for valuation purposes should only consist of taxes to be paid; i.e. deferred tax liabilities should be disregarded. This would require that the analyst has access to the firm's income tax returns, which they do not unless they are insiders. Therefore, analysts have no other alternative than assuming that forecast taxes are paid as recognised in the forecast income statement. This does not take into account the fact that forecast tax comprises both tax payable and deferred tax liabilities, but it is probably the most pragmatic solution. As a general rule this would lead to an estimated firm value that is downward biased; tax expenses recognised are higher than tax payable. For high growth firms the difference between tax payable and taxes recognised in the income statement may be substantial. For these firms, we therefore recommend the estimation of deferred tax liabilities.

Multiples

EV/EBITDA, EV/EBIT and EV/NOPAT multiples
As noted in Chapter 9 and in the previous chapter, a prerequisite for applying multiples is that the firm being valued apply accounting policies and uses estimates which are comparable to its competitors. Accounting policies may vary across firms for a variety of items, and if differences in accounting policies and estimates have a material effect on reported financial data, the analyst needs to make adjustments to make data across firms truly comparable. Common accounting issues, which may require adjustments to be made to reported figures, are listed in Table 15.21.

Inventory accounting
As inventory costs are rising (falling), firms using FIFO appear to be more profitable (less profitable) than firm's using either LIFO or average costs. EBIT, EBITDA

Table 15.21 **Accounting issues in applying multiples**

Accounting item	Issue
Inventory accounting	Do the firms use the same cost assumptions (e.g. FIFO, LIFO or average costs)?
Depreciation, amortisation and impairment	Do the firms assume the same lifetime for depreciable and amortisable assets?
	Do they apply the same depreciation and amortisation method?
	Are the assumptions underlying impairment tests comparable across firms?
Leases	Are leases contracts recognised as operating or financial leases?
Provisions	Are provisions discounted?
	Are discounts factors comparable across firms?

and other measures of profitability are higher (lower) for FIFO firms for the simple fact that cost of goods sold are based on past, lower costs of inventory (more recent, higher costs of inventory).

Fortunately, US firms using LIFO must disclose a LIFO reserve account. The LIFO reserve is the difference between the carrying amount of inventory using LIFO and the amount (current or replacement cost) that would have been reported had the firm used FIFO. LIFO inventory contain older costs, which may have little relationship to current costs. In fact, if costs are increasing rapidly, inventory based on LIFO (inventory are measured at past, lower costs) may be significantly lower than current costs. In Example 15.4, we illustrate how a LIFO reserve can be used to translate EBIT based on LIFO to EBIT based on FIFO.

| Example 15.4 | **LIFO versus FIFO**

Assume that a US firm, which uses LIFO, recognises the following book value of inventory and discloses the following LIFO reserve in the footnotes for the past four years:

	Year 0	Year 1	Year 2	Year 3
Inventory at LIFO	30	35	37	40
LIFO reserve	10	7	12	20

This illustrates that had the firm used FIFO the carrying value (book value) of inventory would have been higher. For instance, book value of inventory would have been 40 (30 + 10) in Year 0.

Suppose the firm's reported operating income for the years 1–3 is as shown in Table 15.22. If comparable firms – which comply with IFRS – use FIFO, how should the US firm's EBIT be adjusted to take care of accounting differences?[11] This is illustrated in Table 15.23. By referring to the footnotes tabulation at the beginning of Example 15.4, it is possible to calculate the change in the LIFO reserve. For instance, in year 3 the LIFO reserve increases from 12 at year end 2 to 20 at year end 3, an increase of 8. Since ending inventory in year 3 would be higher by 8 if FIFO is used, cost of goods sold (COGS) would be 8 lower. This is because COGS = Beginning inventory + Purchases – Ending inventory.

EBIT as if the firm had used FIFO would, therefore, become as shown in Table 15.24. Especially, in year 3 the difference between LIFO and FIFO is significant. The difference is $[(8 \times 100)/30] = 26.7\%$. If comparable firms applying FIFO are valued at 10 times EBIT,

Table 15.22 Income statement, inventory accounting using LIFO

Income statement (excerpt)	Year 1	Year 2	Year 3
Sales	240	280	220
Cost of goods sold	–140	–170	–150
Gross profit	100	110	70
Other operating costs incl. depreciation	–60	–50	–40
EBIT	**40**	**60**	**30**

Table 15.23 **Adjustment from LIFO to FIFO**

	Year 1	Year 2	Year 3
Inventories carried at LIFO	35	37	40
LIFO reserve	7	12	20
Inventories adjusted to FIFO	**42**	**49**	**60**
Cost of goods sold at LIFO	140	170	150
Change in LIFO reserve	3	–5	–8
Cost of goods sold at FIFO	**143**	**165**	**142**

Table 15.24 **Income statement, inventory accounting using FIFO as opposed to LIFO**

Income statement (excerpt)	Year 1	Year 2	Year 3	Total
Sales	240	280	220	740
Cost of goods sold	–143	–165	–142	–450
Gross profit	**97**	**115**	**78**	**290**
Other operating costs including depreciation	–60	–50	–40	–150
EBIT using FIFO	**37**	**65**	**38**	**140**
EBIT using LIFO	40	60	30	130
Difference in EBIT	**–3**	**5**	**8**	**10**

failing to adjust for differences in inventory accounting would affect estimated firm value by 10×8 based on the most recent EBIT. That is the owners of the US firm would obtain a price which is 80 below what it should have been if the necessary adjustments are not made. Table 15.24 also illustrates that the total increase in EBIT by applying FIFO amounts to 10; the difference between the LIFO reserve in year 0 (10) and year 3 (20), as shown in the tabulation at the beginning of Example 15.4.

If the firm that needs to be valued and the comparable firms all comply with IFRS, and they use different cost assumptions for inventory accounting (FIFO for some firms and average costs for other firms), the analyst has no way of knowing the effect on EBIT since no reserve has to be disclosed for firms using average costs. This complicates the task for the analyst, as he or she may try to assess the magnitude on EBIT on different inventory cost assumptions by looking at how prices (costs) have developed within the industry. If costs are relatively stable over time, it is probably not necessary to make adjustments. However, in some industries, costs may change dramatically over time. For example, prices on computer chips and related high-tech components have deteriorated substantially over time. In such cases, adjustments may have to be made before applying the multiple. ■

Depreciation, amortisation and impairment

Adjusting for differences in accounting policies is sometimes more problematic than it sounds. To illustrate this, take a closer look at the following example. Firm A is being valued. The average (mean) EV/EBIT for three comparable firms (firms B, C and D) is assumed to be 10. This means that if there were no differences in accounting policies between the firms A, B, C and D, firm A's enterprise value would be 10 times EBIT. (Chapter 9 also discusses whether the multiple should be based on the median, the mean, the value weighted mean or the harmonic mean. It should be noted that the difference between these measures can be quite substantial.) Assume that an analysis of the firms indicates that the firms' accounting policies and estimates are comparable except for depreciation schedules as shown in Table 15.25.

Table 15.25 Accounting policies for peer companies

Accounting item	Firm A	Firm B	Firm C	Firm D
Depreciation period for machinery and equipment, number of years	3–5	2–10	5–10	5–8

As can be seen in Table 15.25, the depreciation period is stated as an interval for all firms. This is normal practice as firms employ a number of assets with different useful lifetimes. However, this raises the fundamental question as to whether firm A, B, C and D depreciates similar assets over dissimilar periods of time. If so it will be necessary to making adjustments before applying the multiple.

At least two reasons might explain why the firms use different depreciation periods. First, management in the four firms may have different perceptions about the useful lifetime of similar assets (even though based on experience they probably should be able to get a fair estimate of the lifetime). Second, the differences may reflect differences in the firm's asset bases. For instance, firms B and C (with longer expected lifetimes of their assets) may have a larger part of tangible assets with a fairly long useful lifetime.

It is problematic whether the differences shown in Table 15.25 reflect the fact that some firms are overly conservative in their estimates (i.e. depreciating and amortising assets too quickly) or overly aggressive (i.e. depreciating too slowly). The diligent analysts may try to take care of the problem in various ways. For instance, if the firms have recognised large impairment losses in the past, this may be an indication that assets are depreciated too slowly. Likewise, gains on the disposal of machinery and equipment may indicate that a firm depreciates too quickly. Even if such signals are not obtainable, the analyst might include in his or her report that the value estimate based on the EV/EBIT multiple may contain noise. Furthermore, including a sensitivity analysis would give the analyst an indication of the magnitude on value of differences in accounting estimates. Finally, an analyst could estimate the average age of the assets and the average depreciable lives as follows:

$$\text{Average age of assets} = \frac{\text{Accumulated depreciation}}{\text{Depreciation expense}}$$

$$\text{Average depreciable life} = \frac{\text{Gross investment in tangible assets}}{\text{Depreciation expense}}$$

Table 15.26 Reported depreciation

	Investment	Depreciation expense	Accumulated depreciation	Book value
Year 1	200	20	20	180
Year 2	0	20	40	160
Year 3	0	20	60	140
Year 4	0	20	80	120

Assume that a firm states an interval for depreciation. In addition to this, the firm reports the following (excerpt) as shown in Table 15.26. In this case the assets average age and depreciable life are calculated as follows:

$$\text{Average age of assets} = \frac{\text{Accumulated depreciation}}{\text{Depreciation expense}} = \frac{80}{20} = 4 \text{ years}$$

$$\text{Average depreciable life} = \frac{\text{Gross investment in tangible assets}}{\text{Depreciation expense}} = \frac{200}{20} = 10 \text{ years}$$

As illustrated, the average age of the assets is four years and the average depreciable life is 10 years. The firm will need to depreciate the investment of 200 for another six years.

If the average age of the assets or the average depreciable life in firm A differs substantially from those of the comparable firms, adjustments may need to be made before applying the multiples. For example, a low average depreciable life of the assets in firm A may indicate that assets are depreciated too quickly. Therefore, before applying a multiple like the EV/EBIT, EBIT for firm A may have to be adjusted upward to reflect that recorded depreciation expenses are too high. In practice, such fine distinctions are hardly ever made. In any event, before carrying out the analysis, an analyst should carefully consider materiality and the cost of making the analysis versus the likely benefits.

Leases

Leases pose another problem as described in Chapter 14. The total expenses recognised under operating leases and finance (capital) leases are the same over time but different amounts are charged within a year and classified differently in the income statement. Dependent on the nature of the leased assets, operating lease expenses may be recognised as part of production costs (e.g. lease of machinery and equipment), sales and distribution costs (e.g. lease of car fleet to sales representatives) or administrative expenses (e.g. lease of office equipment or executive cars to the CEO and CFO).

Assume that a firm has the opportunity to buy assets at a price of 100,000 with an estimated lifetime of six years. The firm can borrow at 10%. Alternatively, the firm may lease the assets paying 22,961 annually for six years. Referring to the example on leases outlined earlier in this chapter (see page 424), we have calculated the amounts outlined in Table 15.27.

Table 15.27 **Operating vs finance leases**

	Operating leases		Finance leases	
	Year 1	Year 6	Year 1	Year 6
Production costs and/or Sales and distribution costs and/or Administration costs	–22,961	–22,961	16,667	–16,667
EBIT	–22,961	–22,961	–16,667	–16,667
Financial expenses	0	0	–10,000	–2,087
Earnings before tax (EBT)	–22,961	–22,961	–26,667	–18,754

In the case of finance leases the costs of 16,667 is the depreciation of the assets (machinery, equipment etc.). With an EV/EBIT multiple of 10 the effect on the estimated value by reclassifying leases from operating leases to financial leases would be an increase in value of $62,940[10 \times (22,961 - 16,667)]$.

Provisions

Management has great discretion in the recognition of provisions. The absolute amount of the provision, the time to settlement and the discount rate used to measure provisions at fair value (present value) may all have a significant effect on the total expense recognised in the income statement and how the expense is divided between operating expenses and financial expenses. If multiples such as EV/EBITDA and EV/EBIT are used, the analyst must consider the assumptions and estimates made by management carefully. Consider two identical firms, which both recognise a provision of 133.1 to be paid in three full years from now. Firm A uses a discount factor of 10%, while firm B discounts the provision to present value by using a discount rate of 5%. Example 15.5 illustrates how the two firms would report operating earnings.

Example 15.5 **How different assumptions on provisions affect the income statement**

First, the provision recognised in year 1 is the present value of the estimated amount to be paid by the end of year 4. If the discount factor is 10% (5%), this amount is calculated as

$$\frac{133.1}{1.1^3} = 100\,(133.1/1.05^3 = 114.98)$$

as illustrated in Table 15.28.

Table 15.28 **Discounting of provisions – book value of provisions**

Discounting of provisions, NPV at year end	Year 1	Year 2	Year 3	Year 4
Firm A: Discount factor 10%	100.0	110.0	121.0	133.1
Firm A: Discount factor 5%	115.0	120.7	126.8	133.1

Table 15.29 **Effects of discounting provisions by 10%**

Firm A	Year 1	Year 2	Year 3	Year 4	Total
EBIT excluding provisions	200.0	200.0	200.0	200.0	800.0
Provisions (an operating expense)	100.0	0.0	0.0	0.0	100.0
EBIT	**100.0**	**200.0**	**200.0**	**200.0**	**700.0**
Financial expenses	0.0	10.0	11.0	12.1	33.1
Earnings before taxes, EBT	**100.0**	**190.0**	**189.0**	**187.9**	**666.9**

Table 15.30 **Effects of discounting provisions by 5%**

Firm B	Year 1	Year 2	Year 3	Year 4	Total
EBIT excluding provisions	200.0	200.0	200.0	200.0	800.0
Provisions (an operating expense)	115.0	0.0	0.0	0.0	115.0
EBIT	**85.0**	**200.0**	**200.0**	**200.0**	**685.0**
Financial expenses	0.0	5.7	6.0	6.3	18.1
Earnings before taxes, EBT	**85.0**	**194.3**	**194.0**	**193.7**	**666.9**

Second, the financial expenses for firm A would be 10 in year 2 (110 – 100 = 10) and for firm B financial expenses would amount to 5.7 in year 2 (120.7 – 115 = 5.7) and so on for the coming years. Therefore, reported income for the two firms is as shown in Tables 15.29 and 15.30.

Note that total earnings before taxes would be the same for the two firms. This shouldn't come as a surprise. Naturally, the total expense that is recognised is exactly 133.1, which is what the two firms will have to pay to settle the liability. However, the two firms differ in respect to how much they recognise provision as operating expenses (firm A: 100; firm B: 115) and financial expenses (firm A: 33.1; firm B: 18.1). If firm value is based on an EBIT(DA) multiple, firm A appears more valuable in year 1. That is unless the analyst looks through the accounting differences and makes the necessary adjustments. ∎

Accounting issues in credit analysis

Credit rating models and financial ratios

Violation of debt covenants may have severe economic consequences for a firm including higher costs of borrowing, calls for repayment of debt or a requirement that the firm put up collaterals. In a worst case scenario, the firm may not be able to comply with its debt covenants and may have to close down due to lack of liquidity. It is evident that management, to avoid default on debt, may be tempted to exploit loopholes in accounting regulation and/or make estimates and assumptions that improve financial ratios, so that lenders cannot call the debt. For example, if management is able to reclassify finance leases as operating leases, debt is kept off-balance making the balance sheet look healthier.

Lenders should basically consider any and all accounting policy choices and estimates, since everything that has an impact on accounting numbers has an impact on financial ratios. We now discuss a few of these issues.

- Intangible and tangible assets (depreciation and revaluation)
- Leases.

Depreciation and revaluation

Revaluations improve a company's solvency ratio. To the extent that debt covenants contain a solvency ratio, revaluation could mean that a firm obtains less strict loan terms. The same is true in connection with mortgage lending, where cost of borrowing depends on the collaterals. A higher valuation makes the loan more secure, which means that borrowing costs will be lower. It should be pointed out that mortgage lenders usually make their own assessments, and revaluations in the financial statements do not directly affect the loan terms.

Revaluations lead to a decrease in return on invested capital (ROIC). Invested capital (the denominator) increases by the revalued amounts (net of depreciation), while operating income decreases (the numerator), since it's the revalued assets which are depreciated. Whether the overall result of the revaluation – improved solvency but a deterioration of profitability – leads to lower borrowing costs cannot be answered with certainty as borrowing costs ultimately depends upon numerous financial ratios.

Leases

Operating leasing is an example of off balance sheet financing, since large liabilities (finance lease obligations) are not recognised in the balance sheet. As a result, solvency ratios show that financial risk is less for firms classifying leases as operating leases.

A company's borrowing costs (interest rates, fees, commissions etc.) depend on the risk the lender (e.g. a bank) assumes in providing a loan. Standard & Poor's rates companies in categories AAA–CCC (a total of seven categories), where class AAA is the best rating, meaning it includes companies which are very creditworthy. For example, S&P requires that total debt is less than 5% of total capital for industrial firms to deserve an AAA classification.

Standard & Poor's financial ratios are adjusted to take into account that management may have an interest in classifying leases as operating leases. Standard & Poor's states in their 'Credit Stats: Adjusted Key U.S. Industrial Financial Ratios' that financial ratios shall be adjusted, so that operating leases are capitalised; i.e. recognised as finance leases.

Liquidation models

The liquidation model represents firm value in a worst case scenario. If a firm is not able to service its debt, the lender may call the debt. As discussed in Chapter 9 on valuation, the proceeds the investor (or in this case the lender) will eventually receive depend upon how quickly the firm needs to sell the assets and settle the liabilities.

Table 15.31 Measurement attributes for common assets according to IFRS

Type of assets	Measurement basis	Comments
Intangible assets	Cost less accumulated amortisation and impairment losses; *alternatively* fair value (in rare cases)	Measurement to fair value requires an active market for intangibles. Goodwill cannot be sold as a separate asset and is worth zero if a firm is liquidated
Tangible assets	Cost less accumulated depreciation and impairment losses (cost model); *alternatively* fair value (revaluation model)	Historical cost less depreciation is a mechanic way of allocating cost (depreciation) to matching income generated by the assets. Unless the alternative method of revaluation is used, book value of tangible assets is only by chance a good proxy of fair value
Financial assets held to maturity	Amortised costs	If interest rates fluctuate substantially, fair value may be far from book value (amortised costs)
Financial assets held for trading	Fair value	These assets often have quoted market prices
Leases (finance)	Fair value (present value of future lease payments) less depreciation	See comments on tangible assets
Inventories	Costs	A firm may use several methods including FIFO and average costs. If FIFO is used, book value of inventory could be materially different from fair value
Accounts receivable	Amortised costs	Book value may not be a good indicator of fair value if insufficient allowance for uncollectability has been made
Contingent assets	Not recognised	Law suits, contingent tax assets etc. May have a potential value

A forced liquidation will most likely result in lower net proceeds. In any event, what do the financial statements tell us about the potential break-up value of a firm?

Consider the measurement of common assets and liabilities as provided in Tables 15.31 and 15.32. Whether book values of assets and liabilities are good indicators of the fair value depends primarily on the type of assets and liabilities recognised in the balance sheet, the firm's accounting policy choices, including its recognition policies for assets and liabilities, and management's estimates and judgements.

While it is not possible to illustrate every combination of accounting policies, Example 15.6 should give the analyst a thorough understanding of how accounting policies and judgements by management are related to the liquidation value of the firm.

Table 15.32 **Measurement attributes for common liabilities according to IFRS**

Type of liability	Measurement basis	Comments
Financial liabilities held to maturity	Amortised costs	If interest rates fluctuate substantially, fair value may be far from book value (amortised costs)
Financial liabilities held for trading	Fair value	These liabilities often have quoted market prices
Finance leases	Fair value less repayment of lease obligations	If a firm is liquidated, lease obligations still have to be paid regardless of whether the leased assets can be used
Provisions	Expenditure required to settle liability. Present value if time value of money is material	Actual cash outflows to settle provisions may be high compared to book value since provisions are discounted*
Deferred tax	Tax rate enacted by the end of the reporting period. Discounting is not allowed	If a firm sells its assets for less than book value, deferred tax liabilities are overstated
Accounts payable	Amortised costs	If accounts payable fall due within a few months, book value should represent fair value
Contingent liabilities	Not recognised, but disclosed in the notes	Operating leases. Payments on lease contracts still have to be made, even if the firm discontinues its operations. Law suits. Often kept off-balance to avoid admitting 'guilt'

* For instance a firm may have to pay for cleaning-up (removing plants, removing chemicals in the ground), when the firm closes down. These costs shall be recognised today, even if the firm anticipates paying them in the far future, and are discounted to reflect the present value of the provision.

Example 15.6 **The impact of accounting policies and management judgements on the liquidation value**

Consider firm A and its latest balance sheet in condensed form in Table 15.33. Furthermore, assume that the firm pays a flat tax rate of 40% on all income.[12] Finally, from the notes in the annual report, you will realise that the deferred tax liabilities are related to tangible and intangible assets only.

If you are a credit analyst (maybe a loan officer in a major bank) and consider calling the loan because of violation of debt covenants, for instance, because the interest coverage ratios exceeded the threshold set forth in the contract, then:

> Do you believe that firm A is able to recover its debt in case of a suspension of payments?

Take a short break to consider the question . . .

In order to answer such a question, you need to understand the alternative uses of firm A's assets (and liabilities). For instance, they might be valuable for other firms in the industry.

Table 15.33 **Balance sheet for firm A**

Accounting item	Book values
Tangible assets	500
Intangible assets	100
Financial assets	220
Inventories	120
Accounts receivable	230
Other assets	40
Financial liabilities, bank loans	−600
Deferred tax liabilities	−200
Other liabilities	−40
Book value of equity	**370**

Note: The firm pays a flat corporate tax rate of 40%

Since our focus is on accounting issues, we consider accounting issues related to estimating break-up value (liquidation value) of the firm:

- What accounting method choices has firm A applied?
- Does the firm use conservative or aggressive accounting policies?
- What are the measurement basis for assets and liabilities?
- Does the firm have assets and liabilities, which are not recognised in the balance sheet?

You can assess a firm's accounting choices in several ways. First, you might compare its accounting policies with the ones from other firms within the same industry. To do so, you need to read the notes on accounting policies carefully and evaluate whether firm A's accounting policies are materially different from industry practice.

Second, an analysis of gains (losses) reported by firm A in the past gives an indication of whether the firm uses conservative or aggressive accounting policies. If firm A has reported gains (losses) on disposal of non-current assets in the past (selling machinery, office equipment, company cars etc.), it suggests that management has been conservative (liberal) in applying depreciation and amortisation policies. Third, the note on accounting policies provide you the answers regarding how assets and liabilities are measured (e.g. historical costs or fair value). Finally, studying the annual report and industry characteristics should help you find out if there are any indications that firm A may have unrecognised assets and liabilities such as deferred tax assets, in process R&D, unsettled law suits, operating leases and erroneous contracts. While information about operating leases can be found in the notes (they are disclosed as contingent liabilities) other non-recognised items may not be disclosed in the annual report. For instance, certain industries are known for having numerous pending lawsuits. If firm A operates in, say, the biotech industry it is likely to have pending lawsuits, as companies in such industries go to great lengths in protecting their patents. The potential compensation (future economic benefits) from these lawsuits is not likely to be recognised as assets and may not even be disclosed due to the great uncertainty about the outcome (if disclosed they are regarded as contingent assets).

Now assume that the estimated market value of the tangible assets for firm A would be 100 (compared to book value of 500), while intangible assets would have a market value of zero (compared to book value of 100). Market values are far below book values. This could be the case, for example, because tangible assets consist of specialised items, with little or no alternative use, and intangible assets of goodwill, which is a non-separable asset.

Furthermore, suppose that all assets, except tangible and intangible assets, on average could be sold at book value, while book value of financial liabilities and other liabilities are stated at fair value (i.e. these liabilities could be settled by paying book value). Would company A be able to repay its loans? If we look at the information already provided, the answer is apparently 'No'.

The market value of net assets is minus 130, as illustrated in Table 15.34, which indicates that the lender would have to recognise a potential loss on the bank loan of 130 (unless the bank has collaterals). The loss may be even larger as legal fees also need to be considered or the loss could turn out to be lower if it is 'shared' with other liabilities. However, as argued below, an analyst must consider all facts and possess great knowledge about how financial statements are produced. The bank is actually likely to be paid in full. The reason for this is that as tangible assets are sold at less than book value, the related deferred tax liability would change as shown in Table 15.35.

Table 15.34 Market value of assets for firm A

Accounting item	Estimated proceeds from liquidation
Book value of equity	370
Loss on tangible assets, depreciable (500 – 100)	–400
Loss on intangible assets, depreciable (100 – 0)	–100
Difference between market value and book value for all other assets and liabilities	0
Total market value of net assets	**–130**

Table 15.35 Fair value of tax liability for firm A

	Book value of depreciable assets	Tax rate (flat)	Book value of deferred tax liability	Calculate tax base of tangible assets, Y	Solve for Y (tax value/ tax base)	Fair value of tax liability
Firm A	600	40%	200	$(600 - Y) \times 0.4 = 200$	$Y = 100$	(Sales price – tax value) $\times$ $t = (100 - 100) \times$ 40% = 0

The deferred tax liability (book value is 200) is calculated as the difference between book values and tax values multiplied by the corporate tax rate. Since the tax rate is 40% and the deferred tax liability is 200, the difference between the book value of tangible assets and its tax value must be 500 (200/0.4). Therefore, by selling assets booked at 600 for only 100, the fair value of the tax liability becomes 0 as compared to the book value of 200. Another way of making this calculation is to acknowledge that tangible assets sell for 500 less than book value. As a result, the gain for tax purposes is 500 less. Accordingly, firm A can settle its tax

Table 15.36 **Estimated net proceeds for firm A**

Accounting item	Estimated market values
Tangible assets	100
Intangible assets	0
Financial assets	220
Inventories	120
Accounts receivable	230
Other assets	40
Other liabilities	−40
Deferred tax liabilities	0
Estimated proceeds to pay off bank loans	670
Financial liabilities, bank loans	−600
Estimated net proceeds after repaying all debt	**70**

liability by paying 0, that is 200 (500 × 40%) *less* than book value (book value of deferred tax liability is 200). In conclusion, the firm can settle its tax liability without paying the tax authorities, even though the book value was 200.

Now you realise – see Table 15.36 – that firm A should be able to repay the debt. This is the opposite answer we came to before! In fact, 70 is left in cash to pay consultants, legal fees etc. ∎

In conclusion, a thorough estimation of liquidation values of assets and liabilities requires knowledge about how accounting items are measured in the balance sheet. Financial assets and liabilities in general pose no problems, but most other assets, which are not measured at fair value, do. It could be argued that a lender should not care about the book value of assets and liabilities. What matters is the proceeds that can be obtained from selling the firm's assets and settling the liabilities. However, the analysts (in this case a lender) need to estimate the likely net cash inflow from liquidating the firm, before he or she calls the debt. If the proceeds are estimated to be low, the lender may wish to continue providing finance hoping for better times.

Accounting issues in executive compensation

Bonuses based on financial performance measures also have some inherent problems to be considered by the analyst. Typically, cash bonuses are based on one or more of several different performance measures such as revenue, EBIT, EBITDA, ROIC, EVA, and other similar metrics. Consider a cash bonus based on reported EBIT. Management can simply enhance the chance of getting a bonus merely by extending the estimated lifetime of depreciable assets, and, thus, charge the income statement, and EBIT, with a lower depreciation expense.

In this section, focus is on how accounting flexibility may affect bonuses. Since accounting-based bonuses are directly linked to accounting measures of performance, measurement errors (bias) and flexibility in choosing between alternative accounting policies (e.g. FIFO versus average costs) have economic consequences. We examine two types of accounting-based performance measures:

1 Absolute performance measures (e.g. revenue, EBIT, EBITDA, EBT)
2 Relative performance measures (e.g. ROIC, EVA)

These are discussed below.

Absolute performance measures

The use of EBIT, EBITDA or similar metrics as a performance measure in bonus plans has the advantage that management compensation is tied to a firm's operating performance. Furthermore, EBITDA has the alleged advantage that management cannot increase bonuses, for example, by simply changing the estimated lifetime of depreciable assets. Nonetheless, certain accounting issues should be considered.

Intangible and tangible assets (depreciation and amortisation)
The role of depreciation and amortisation in bonus contracts depends on how bonus contracts are designed. By now it should be clear that conservative or liberal accounting affects earnings levels, invested capital and financial ratios.

A need for recognising impairment of goodwill is apparently profound if new management takes office. The new management team could hardly be blamed, they would argue, that goodwill has to be written down due to events happening before they were in charge. In such a case though, their bonuses would probably not be affected.

If the company permanently amortises too quickly (too slowly), gains (losses) on sale of assets will frequently occur. Liberal (conservative) accounting policies improve (reduce) the bottom line. Managers who achieve bonuses based on an absolute performance measure may therefore be interested in pursuing liberal accounting policies. Managers who are rewarded bonuses based on a relative performance measure may on the other hand, be more interested in pursuing conservative accounting policies. For example, a company that has a fairly constant level of investment, achieves a higher ROIC, once it has reached steady-state, since a shorter amortisation period reduces invested capital.

Leases
Accounting policies for leases will be important in the context of bonus compensation. The choice of classifying leases as either operating or financial leases has an impact on operating earnings, net financial expenses, interest-bearing debt, invested capital and financial ratios. Since we concentrate here on absolute performance measures, the question is, how accounting policies for leases affect various earnings measures.

By reporting leases as financial leases (capital leases), part of the lease expense is recognised as a financial expense that is after operating earnings. This provides management with incentives to capitalise leases, if their bonuses are based on EBIT, EBITDA, NOPAT or similar measures of operating earnings. Lease accounting has a large effect on EBITDA and EBIT. If a firm uses operating leases, the entire lease payment is charged against EBIT or EBITDA. However, if leases are recognised as finance leases, part of the expenses are recognised as financial expenses that are not included in EBIT or EBITDA. As a result, bonuses based on operating performance measures such as EBIT, are higher if leases are recognised as financial leases.

451

UNIVERSITY OF WINCHESTER

Relative performance measures

Provisions

Even though it has become more difficult for management to use 'big bath' accounting, recognising provisions is still prone to earnings management. Management may be tempted to recognise large restructuring costs. For example:

- Restructuring costs are often perceived to be non-recurring, and management might argue such expenses should be disregarded in performance measures used in bonus plans.
- Future earnings are likely to improve since future costs are recognised today. For instance, restructuring costs may include impairment losses, and as a result future depreciation expenses become lower.

Discounting of provisions is particularly problematic, in relation to the distinction between operating and financing items. By discounting provisions, part of provisions becomes interest expenses. The larger the discount factor, the larger the portion of provisions is regarded as financial expenses. For the sake of consistency in the data, a compensation committee can choose from two options for including provisions in bonus plans (EVA).

1 Reclassifying the interest element of provisions in the income statement as operating expenses, or
2 Reclassify provisions (in the balance sheet) as interest bearing (and include the interest part as financial expenses in the income statement).

Deferred taxes

In the context of performance measurement, deferred taxes are often considered as an equity component ('quasi' equity). For example, deferred taxes are generally added to equity in EVA calculations. Copeland et al. (2000) includes deferred tax in invested capital. They justify it by arguing that investors expect a firm to earn a return on all capital invested in the firm, and deferred tax liabilities are available in the sense they are not paid and may never have to be paid as demonstrated in this chapter. This also implies that taxes on earnings should only include tax payable and not the deferred tax liabilities.

As illustrated in Chapter 14, deferred tax liabilities may be deferred far into the future or may never have to be paid. Therefore, arguably, deferred tax liabilities should be regarded as an equity component. Here is how the adjustments need to be made.

Example 15.7 **Converting tax liabilities to equity in EVA calculations**

Table 15.37 illustrates a standard analytical income statement and balance sheet (excerpt). Return On Invested Capital is calculated as

$$\frac{\text{NOPAT}}{\text{Invested capital}} \times 100$$

In the example, NOPAT = EBIT − tax on EBIT. Invested capital is the average capital.

Table 15.37 **Condensed analytical financial statements**

	Year 0	Year 1	Year 2	Year 3
Operating earnings, EBIT		100	103	111
Net financial expenses		−15	−13	−11
Earnings before taxes, EBT		**85**	**90**	**100**
Taxes		−34	−36	−40
Net earnings, E		**51**	**54**	**60**
EBIT		100	103	111
Taxes on EBIT		−40	−41	−44
NOPAT		**60**	**62**	**67**
Operating assets	510	546	572	618
Operating liabilities excluding deferred taxes	−100	−100	−100	−100
Deferred taxes	−20	−25	−17	−23
Invested capital	**390**	**421**	**455**	**495**
Equity	230	281	335	395
Net interest-bearing debt	160	140	120	100
Invested capital	**390**	**421**	**455**	**495**
Return on invested capital		**14.8%**	**14.1%**	**14.0%**

Therefore, for year 1, ROIC becomes:

$$\text{Effective tax rate: } \frac{\text{Taxes}}{\text{EBT}} \times 100 = \frac{34}{85} \times 100 = 40\%$$

and

$$\text{NOPAT} = \text{EBIT} - 40\% \text{ effective tax rate} = 100 - 40 = 60$$

The average invested capital in year 1 amounts to $(390 + 421)/2 = 405.5$ so ROIC becomes

$$\frac{60}{405.5} \times 100 = 14.8\%$$

Now if deferred taxes are regarded as an equity component, the calculations of ROIC would change as shown in Table 15.38.

In year 0, equity and invested capital increase by 20 since deferred tax liabilities are regarded as equity. In years 1, 2 and 3, tax in the income statement is net of the deferred tax component (that is the change in the differed tax liability) and equity changes by an

Table 15.38 Calculation of ROIC, deferred tax regarded as equity

	Year 0	Year 1	Year 2	Year 3
Operating earnings, EBIT		100	103	111
Net financial expenses		−15	−13	−11
Earnings before taxes, EBT		**85**	**90**	**100**
Tax payable		−34	−36	−40
Add back change in deferred taxes		5	−8	6
Net earnings, E		**56**	**46**	**66**
EBIT		100	103	111
Taxes on EBIT		−40	−41	−44
Add back change in deferred taxes		5	−8	6
NOPAT		**65**	**54**	**73**
Operating assets	510	546	572	618
Operating liabilities excluding deferred taxes	−100	−100	−100	−100
Deferred taxes	0	0	0	0
Invested capital	**410**	**446**	**472**	**518**
Equity	250	306	352	418
Net interest-bearing debt	160	140	120	100
Invested capital	**410**	**446**	**472**	**518**
Return On Invested Capital		**15.2%**	**11.7%**	**14.7%**

equal amount. For instance, in year 1, the deferred tax liability increases by 5 from 20 to 25. Therefore, to reverse the effects, tax on EBIT is reduced by 5 and equity increases by 5. This is, obviously, under the assumption that deferred taxes are related to operations only. It is often the case that deferred taxes are related to differences in accounting depreciation and depreciation for tax purposes (i.e. operations).

Assume that WACC is 12%. In this case, EVA would be positive for all years (ROIC > 12%) before adjusting for deferred tax. If deferred tax is regarded as equity, EVA would be slightly negative in year 2 since ROIC is 11.7% as shown in Table 15.38. ■

Conclusions

This chapter highlights potential economic consequences of a firm's accounting choices and management discretion in producing financial statements. As illustrated, accounting policies and accounting flexibility may have a large impact on financial data and ratios. Since accounting data are used as input to numerous decision models, firm valuation, credit analysis and bonuses are affected by a firm's (management's) accounting policies and estimates.

Some of the lessons to be learned are:

- Applied accounting policies and estimates should be carefully studied
- Changes in accounting policies or estimates may have severe economic consequences
- Inventory accounting methods have direct cash flow consequences, if the method used for accounting purposes is applied for tax purposes as well
- Depreciation and amortisation policies may have economic consequences even though a firm's underlying cash flows are unaffected
- Impairment losses have no cash flow consequences but may reflect a flawed business model or aggressive amortisation policies
- Lease contracts may be recognised as operating leases or finance leases. The effect on operating earnings, debt and financial ratios differs substantially between the two methods
- Deferred taxes are problematic, but should be considered as they are likely to affect valuation, bonuses and credit rating.

Any financial statement analysis should include a careful examination of a firm's major accounting policies and management's estimates and assumptions.

Review questions

- List examples of accounting items where some flexibility in accounting methods choices are allowed due to regulatory flexibility.

- List examples of accounting items, which requires management uses its discretion.

- Give examples of accounting items, which are based on management's estimates.

- How does revaluation affect a firm's ROIC and other financial ratios?

- What is the distinction between a liability, a provision and a contingent liability?

- Discuss why deferred tax liabilities may be considered as 'quasi equity'.

- What is the effect of a change in the discount rate used in measuring provisions?

APPENDIX 15.1

Overview of the purposes of financial statement analysis

Purpose of analysis	Decision model or method	Examples of accounting issues ('noise')
Valuation (estimating enterprise value or market value of equity)	Present value approach (DDM model, DCF model, EVA model and APV model)	Changes in accounting method choices (e.g. from FIFO to average cost)
		Changes in accounting estimates
		Non-disclosed transitory items
		Aggressive versus conservative accounting policies

▶

(continued)

	Multiples	Differences in accounting policies across firms
		Different definitions of transitory items (special items, abnormal items etc.) across firms
	Liquidation model	Overvalued assets due to insufficient recognition of impairment losses
		Non-recognised assets and liabilities (e.g. pending lawsuits, operating leases)
Credit analysis	Forecasting and value-at-risk	Changes in accounting method choices (e.g. from FIFO to average cost)
		Changes in accounting estimates
		Non-disclosed transitory items
		Aggressive versus conservative accounting policies
	Financial ratios (rating model)	Changes in accounting method choices (e.g. from FIFO to average cost)
		Changes in accounting estimates
		Non-disclosed transitory items
		Aggressive versus conservative accounting policies
	Liquidation model	Overvalued assets due to insufficient recognition of impairment losses
		Non-recognised assets and liabilities (e.g. pending lawsuits, operating leases
Bonus contracts	Choice of performance measures (relative and absolute performance measures)	Restructuring charges, development costs and other forward looking costs (expensed today but with a positive NPV)
		Changes in accounting estimates
		Non-disclosed transitory items
		Aggressive versus conservative accounting policies

Notes

1 If it isn't possible to register the physical flow of inventories, a firm needs to make an assumption about which goods are being sold. FIFO (LIFO) assumes that the goods bought first (last) are the first (last) being sold. So, FIFO (LIFO) value ending inventory at current prices (historical prices).

2 According to US GAAP inventory is carried at the lower of cost and market with market generally meaning replacement cost. This is slightly different than IFRS since net realisable value is the market price *less* cost necessary for completion and sales cost (e.g. marketing expenses).

3 Intangible assets are, strictly speaking, amortised. In the following the term depreciation is used to embrace both depreciation and amortisation.

4 However, IFRS standards allow some assets to be revalued at fair value as an alternative to recognising those assets at historical costs less depreciation and impairment losses.

5 IRR is the internal rate of return. It is measured as the return (in percentage), which makes the net present value of the investment and all future cash flows equal to zero.

6 Depreciating over the useful lifetime is not exactly the same as unbiased accounting. Unbiased accounting would mean that IRR = ROIC for all periods. For this to happen, the firm had to use a progressive depreciation scheme.

7 In reality, investments are depreciated depending on the actual date these investments are made. From an analytical point of view, the best bet would be to depreciate by only half of the deprecation rate (e.g. if the useful lifetime of the assets is 10 years, depreciation in year 1 would be 5%).

8 An exception is intangible assets with an indefinite lifetime (e.g. goodwill). Such assets are not amortised but subject to impairment tests annually and whenever there is an indication that the intangible asset may be impaired.

9 For instance, a firm cannot recognise a provision on the grounds it wants to be prudent (conservative). Accounting for restructuring costs illustrates this point. According to GAAP a provision for restructuring shall only be recognised after a detailed formal plan is adopted and has been promulgated. A board decision is not sufficient.

10 In some jurisdictions, tax losses can even be carried back and offset against past (positive) taxable income.

11 In the example it is assumed that no other material differences between US GAAP and IFRS exist in arriving at EBIT.

12 Corporate tax rates differ substantially across countries and over time. Moreover, it may or it may not be flat depending on the jurisdiction. Finally, some countries use accelerated depreciation, while other countries require other methods for depreciation of tangible and intangible assets for tax purposes. Suffice is to say that large differences exist between different tax jurisdictions. However, the point made in the example can equally well be made for firms in countries with corporate taxes which are not flat rate.

References

Copeland, T., T. Koller and J. Murrin (2000) *Valuation: Measuring and Managing the Value of Companies*, 3rd edn, John Wiley & Sons.

Stewart, G. B. (1991) *The Quest for Value*, Harper Business.

Glossary

Chapter 1

Accounting standards Definitive statements of best practice issued by a body having suitable authority.

Book value The value at which an asset or liability is carried at on a balance sheet.

Compensation analyst Uses a company's financial statements to determine performance-based management compensation.

Contingency models A group of valuation models that calculate the value of a company by applying option pricing models.

Credit analyst Assesses a company's ability to repay its obligations (liabilities), with goals pertaining to the amount and terms of credit to be extended to the firm.

Credit rating Estimates the creditworthiness of an individual, company or even a country.

Current assets Cash and other assets expected to be converted to cash, sold or consumed either in a year or in the operating cycle (whichever is longer).

Current liabilities Liabilities which are due within 12 months after the reporting date.

Equity Defined as the book value of total assets minus book value of total liabilities.

Equity analyst Values the residual return in the company after all claims have been satisfied.

Fair value The amount at which an asset or liability can be exchanged in an arm's-length transaction between a willing buyer and a willing seller.

FASB Financial Accounting Standard Board, USA. It is a non-governmental body, which the US SEC has charged with establishing and

maintaining generally accepted accounting standards for professional accountants.

Forecasting The process of making statements (in financial terms) about events whose actual outcomes have not yet been observed.

GAAP Generally Accepted Accounting Principles.

IASB International Accounting Standards Board, an independent body that sets accounting standards (IFRS) accepted as a basis for accounting in many countries.

IFRS International Financial Reporting Standards.

Intangible assets Defined as identifiable non-monetary assets that cannot be seen, touched or physically measured and that are identifiable as a separate asset.

Interest-bearing debt A liability that carries an interest.

Inventories The raw materials, work-in-process goods and completely finished goods that are considered to be the portion of a business's assets that are ready or will be ready for sale.

Investors' required rate of return The return an investor expects from investing in a company. It is also referred to as the investors' hurdle rate or opportunity cost.

Liquidation models A group of valuation models used to calculate the value of a company by measuring the net proceeds that a company can obtain if it liquidates all its assets and settle all its liabilities.

Liquidation value The net proceeds that a company can obtain if it liquidates all its assets and settle all its liabilities.

458

Non-current assets   Assets which are not settled within 12 months after the reporting date.

Non-current liabilities   Liabilities which are not settled within 12 months after the reporting date.

Operating liabilities   Liabilities that are non-interest bearing such as accounts payable.

Present value models   A group of valuation models used to calculate the value of a company by discounting future cash flows.

Provisions   A liability where the amount to be settled and/or timing are uncertain.

Receivables   Money owed to a company by its clients and shown in its accounts as an asset.

Relative valuation models   A group of valuation models used to estimate the value of a company by applying the price of a comparable company relative to a variety of accounting items such as revenue, EBITDA, EBIT or net income.

Securities   Generally a fungible, negotiable financial instrument representing financial value. Securities are broadly categorised into debt securities and equity securities.

Standard & Poor's   A credit rating agency.

Tangible assets   Tangible assets are those that have a physical substance and can be touched, such as buildings, real estate, vehicles, production facilities and equipment.

Value at risk (VaR)   The expected mark-to-market loss on a portfolio at a given probability (assuming normal markets and no trading in the portfolio). If a portfolio of assets has a one-day 95% VaR of $1 million, a loss of $1 million or more on this portfolio is expected on 1 day in 20.

Chapter 2

Assets   The rights or other access to future economic benefits controlled by an entity as a result of past transactions or events.

Balance sheet   A summary of a company's financial position at a specific point in time.

Cash flow from financing activities   Measures the cash impact from transactions with debt holders and shareholders.

Cash flow from investing activities   Measures the cash impact from investment in non-current assets.

Cash flow from operating activities   Measures the cash generated in the operations.

Cash flow statement   Reports a company's cash receipts, cash payments, and the net change in the company's cash resulting from the company's operating, investing and financing activities.

Classification   Refers to how accounting items are classified in the financial statements.

Double-entry bookkeeping   Based on the principle of duality, which means that every economic event that is recorded has two aspects which offset or balance each other (labelled debit and credit entries).

Expenses   Decrease in economic benefits during the accounting period in the form of outflows or depletion of assets or occurrence of liabilities that result in decrease in equity, other than those relating to distributions to equity participants.

Financial statements   Documents such as income statements and balance sheets presenting accounting information which are expected to be useful for a variety of decision purposes.

Function of expense method   Operating expenses are classified according to the function to which they belong such as production, sales and distribution and administration.

Income   An increase in economic benefits during the accounting period in the form of inflows or enhancements of assets or decrease of liabilities that result in increases in equity, other than those relating to contributions from equity participants.

Income statement   Discloses a firm's earnings for a predefined period, which in the annual report is 12 months.

Liabilities   An entity's obligations to transfer economic benefits as a result of past transactions or events.

Measurement   Refers to how accounting items are measured. Typical measurement attributes include historical cost and fair value.

Nature of expense method   Operating expenses are classified according to the nature of the expense.

Recognition   Refers to when a transaction is recognised in the financial statements.

Statement of changes in owners' equity
Reconciles equity at the beginning of the period with equity at the end of the period.

Statement of comprehensive income   Includes all income and expense items recognised in the income statement and all other income and expense items, which have not been recognised in the income statement.

Chapter 3

Accounts payable   An amount due for payment to a supplier of goods or services.

Accrual-based performance measure   An accounting-based performance measure. It generally allows the recognition of a transaction before it has had its cash impact. An example is net earnings.

Cash-flow-based performance measure   A cash-flow-based performance measure. For example, cash flow from operations.

Comprehensive income   Includes net earnings plus all changes in equity except those resulting from investment by or distribution to owners.

E Net earnings.

Earnings capacity   Reflects a company's value creation with given measurement period (e.g. one year).

Earnings per share (EPS)   Net income/number of shares outstanding.

EBIT   Earnings before interests and taxes.

EBITDA   Earnings before interests, taxes, depreciation and amortisation.

EBT   Earnings before tax.

Net earnings   It is the bottom line in the income statement and reflects the accounting profit to shareholders.

Operating income   Shows the accounting profit from a company's operations. EBIT or operating earnings are alternative terms for operating income.

Shareholder value added (SVA)   A multi-period performance measure. It is defined as the difference between the present value of future cash flows at the end and at the beginning of the measurement period plus the free cash flow generated in the measurement period.

Chapter 4

Analytical balance sheet   Requires that every accounting item is classified as belonging to either 'operations' or 'financing'.

Analytical income statement   Requires that every accounting item is classified as either an 'operating' or 'financing' item.

Invested capital   Represents the amount a firm has invested in its operating activities and which requires a return.

Net financial expenses after tax   (Financial expenses − financial income) × (1 − corporate tax rate).

Net operating profit after tax (NOPAT)   EBIT × (1 − corporate tax rate).

Chapter 5

Benchmarking   A comparison of different companies – typically within the same industry.

Common-size analysis   Scales each accounting item as a percentage of a key figure. Typically, balance sheet items are measured as a percentage of total assets (or invested capital) and income statement items are measured as percentages of revenue.

Days on hand of invested capital   365/turnover rate of invested capital.

Economic Value Added   (ROIC − WACC) × invested capital.

Financial leverage   Net interest-bearing debt divided by book value of equity.

Indexing   Measure the magnitude of changes over time (for example in revenue). Because index numbers work in a similar way to percentages they make such changes easier to compare. The base equals 100 and the index number is usually expressed as 100 × the ratio to the base value.

Internal rate of return (IRR) The discount factor that results in a net present value equal to zero for a project. IRR shows what investors can expect to earn on average each year (expressed as a percentage) during the entire lifetime of a project.

Net borrowing costs (NBC) Net financial expenses after tax/net interest bearing debt.

Profit margin Operating income/revenue.

Residual income (RI) (ROE – cost of equity) × book value of equity.

Return on equity (ROE) Net income/book value of equity.

Return on invested capital (ROIC) Operating income as a percentage of invested capital.

Trend analysis A comparison of the same company across time.

Turnover rate Revenue/invested capital.

Weighted average cost of capital (WACC) Represents the average cost of equity and net interest-bearing debt.

Chapter 6

Payout ratio Dividends/net income.

Share buy-backs An alternative way of distributing profits to shareholders.

Sustainable growth rate Indicates how fast a company can grow while preserving its financial leverage.

Transitory items Earnings which are non-recurrent in nature.

Chapter 7

Capital expenditure ratio Cash flow from operations/capital expenditure.

Cash burn rate (Cash and cash equivalents + securities + receivables)/EBIT.

CFO to debt ratio Cash flow from operations/total liabilities.

CFO to short-term debt ratio Cash flow from operations divided by current liabilities.

Current ratio Current assets divided by current liabilities.

Financial leverage Total liabilities/book value of equity.

Interest coverage ratio EBIT/net financial expenses.

Interest coverage ratio (cash) Cash flow from operations/net financial expenses.

Liquidity cycle Represents the number of days it takes to convert inventory to cash. An approximate value of the liquidity cycle is 365 divided by the turnover rate of net working capital.

Long-term liquidity risk Refers to a company's ability to satisfy (pay) all long-term obligations.

Net working capital Inventory + receivables + prepaid expenses – operating liabilities.

Quick ratio (Cash + securities + receivables)/current liabilities.

Short-term liquidity risk Refers to a company's ability to satisfy (pay) all short-term obligations.

Solvency ratio Book value of equity/(total liabilities + book value of equity).

Turnover rate of net working capital Revenue/net working capital.

Chapter 8

Evidence-relevance model Gives an overview of the supporting evidence of the different forecasting assumptions.

Financial value driver A financial ratio that mirrors the company's underlying performance and is closely related to value creation.

Five forces analysis An industry analysis covering five different forces affecting an industry's attractiveness.

Free cash flow to equity holders (FCFE) FCFF minus transactions with debt holders (new debt/repayment of debt and net financial expenses).

Free cash flow to the firm (FCFF) Cash flow from operations minus cash flow from investing activities.

PEST analysis A strategic analysis of macro factors including Political, Economic, Sociocultural and Technological factors.

Pro forma statements Projected financial statements such as the income statement, balance sheet and cash flow statement.

Sales driven forecasting approach The forecasting of different accounting item such as operating expenses and investments are driven by the expected level of activity (sales).

Strategic analysis   An analysis of the strength of a business's position and understanding the important external factors that may influence that position.

Strategic value driver   Strategic or an operational initiative that can be undertaken by a company with the purpose of improving value.

SWOT analysis   An analysis of a company's Strengths, Weaknesses, Opportunities and Threats.

Value chain analysis   An assessment analysis of both primary and supporting activities of a company.

Value driver map   Illustrates the relationship between different value drivers.

Chapter 9

Adjusted present value approach   Enterprise value is estimated by discounting the free cash flows to the firm by the required rate of return on assets plus the value of the tax shield on net interest-bearing debt.

Contingent claim models   Models which price firms based on complex option models. Such models are seldom used in practice.

Enterprise value   The value of a firm's invested capital (net operating assets) or alternatively equity plus net interest-bearing debt. Determined by discounting the free cash flows to the firm by the weighted average cost of capital (WACC).

EVA-model   Enterprise value is estimated by adding the present value of future economic profit (EVA) to book value of invested capital.

Liquidation models   In law, liquidation is the process by which a company (or part of a company) is brought to an end, and the assets and property of the company redistributed. The value of a firm using the liquidation model is the difference between the amount obtained by selling the assets and settling the liabilities.

Market value of equity   Estimated by discounting the free cash flows to equity holders by the investors' required rate of return.

Multiple   A relative valuation model. For instance, an EV/EBIT = 10 tells that investors are willing to pay 10 EUR for each EUR of operating earnings.

P/E multiples (or ratios)   Price divided by EPS. P/E multiples are popular in part due to their wide availability.

Present value models   Valuation of firms by discounting future dividends, earnings or cash flows.

Relative valuation models (multiples)   Valuation using multiples is a method for determining the current value of a company by examining and comparing the financial ratios of relevant peer groups, also often described as comparable company analysis. One of the most widely used multiples is the price–earnings ratio (P/E ratio or PER) of stocks in a similar industry.

Residual income model   Market value of equity is estimated by adding the present value of future residual income (earnings in excess of investors' required rate of return) to book value of equity.

Valuation approaches   The value of firms (or any asset) may be based on a variety of different models including present value models, relative valuation models (multiples), liquidation models and contingent claim models.

Chapter 10

Capital structure   In finance, capital structure refers to the way a corporation finances its assets through some combination of equity, debt or hybrid securities. A firm's capital structure is then the composition or 'structure' of its liabilities.

Cost of capital   The price investors or bankers ask for supplying capital/cash. The price of capital depends on the risk involved in supplying funds to a firm and the time value of money.

Financial risk   Analysis of financial risk aims at assessing the effect of debt on financial risk. Since equity investors receive their claims after debt holders, they require a higher rate of return than debt holders. This implies that financial leverage affects equity investors' perception of risk.

Operational risks In assessing the operating risks focus is on company-specific factors that may affect the stability of operating earnings.

Owners' required rate of return The shareholders' required return is the minimum return that investors expect for providing capital to the company, thus setting a benchmark or hurdle rate that a new project has to meet.

Risk-free interest rate The risk-free interest rate expresses how much an investor can earn without incurring any risk. Theoretically, the best estimate of the risk-free rate would be the expected return on a zero-β portfolio.

Systematic risk (β) In finance, systematic risk, sometimes called market risk, aggregate risk or undiversifiable risk, is the risk associated with aggregate market returns.

WACC The minimum return that a company must earn on an existing asset base to satisfy its debt holders, owners and other providers of capital. Companies raise money from a number of sources: common equity, preferred equity, straight debt, convertible debt, exchangeable debt, warrants, options, pension liabilities, executive stock options, and so on. Different securities, which represent different sources of finance, are expected to generate different returns. WACC is calculated taking into account the relative weights of each component of the capital structure. The more complex the company's capital structure, the more labourious it is to calculate WACC.

Chapter 11

A credit score A credit score is a numerical expression based on a statistical analysis of a firm's (or person's) financial data and other information used to assess the firm's creditworthiness.

Altman's Z-score A credit score (Z-score) formula for predicting bankruptcy. The formula may be used to predict the probability that a firm will go into bankruptcy within one to five years.

Bonds A bond is a formal contract to repay borrowed money with interest at fixed intervals.

Corporate bonds, also referred to as notes, are debt obligations issued by the borrower directly into the public fixed income markets.

Collateral Creditors often secure their loans by requiring a pledge in the asset on which the borrowing is based. The pledge ensures that if the borrower defaults, the lender can realise the asset (collateral) to satisfy its claims against the borrower.

Convertible debt and other hybrid instruments Convertible debt is a debt instrument that can be exchanged for a specified number of shares within a specified date and at an agreed price (strike price).

Expected loss Exposure at default $\times$ probability of default $\times$ (1 − probability of recovery).

Fundamental credit analysis Analysis of a firm's credit risk using thorough financial statement analysis.

Logit analysis Logit regression is an alternative method to the multiple discriminant analysis. It has the advantage of estimating probabilities of bankruptcy.

Medium-term notes Medium-term notes, also referred to as MTNs, are a flexible form of financing available to borrowers with high credit quality.

Multiple discriminant analysis A statistical technique used to classify an observation into one of several *a priori* groupings – in this case bankruptcy versus non-bankruptcy groups. A multiple discriminant analysis attempts to derive a linear combination of financial ratios which best distinguish between the bankruptcy and non-bankruptcy firms.

Private placement Private placements are an issue of debt that is placed primarily with insurance companies. Their term is typically of longer duration and up to 30 years.

Statistical models Statistical models used to assess credit risk includes univariate analysis, multiple discriminant analysis and logit analysis.

Univariate analysis A statistical model used to predict bankruptcy based on a large sample.

Chapter 12

Absolute performance measures Measure based on absolute (financial) numbers such as EBIT or net earnings.

Bonus bank Bonus banks may be used to defer compensation, to take account of 'negative bonuses' and to create long-term incentives (extending managerial horizon).

Bonus plans Contracts which prescribe how to compensate employees for their efforts. Bonuses may be based on stock prices (options and warrants), financial performance measures and non-financial performance measures.

Congruence A crucial part of a bonus plan is to align the interests of management (agent) and owners (principal). Management should only be awarded a bonus to the extent that they act in the interest of the owners.

Modern EVA bonus plan According to the plan, bonus consists of a target bonus paid if a predetermined target is obtained plus an additional bonus for improvement in EVA in excess of expected increase in EVA.

Multi-period performance measures A performance measure which spans more than one period.

Performance measure A measure of how well a firm is run measured in financial terms (e.g. EBIT).

Performance standard This may be internal (e.g. budgets) or external (e.g. benchmarking against competitors).

Performance structure The way compensation is linked to performance. Compensation may be uncapped or there may be an upper limit ('cap') and lower limit ('floor') on the bonus.

Relative performance measures Measures such as EVA, ROIC etc.

XY bonus plan In the XY plan bonus consists of two components. A bonus calculated as a percentage of the change in EVA during a financial year (X component), no matter whether the bonus becomes negative or positive, and an additional bonus calculated as a percentage of actual EVA, but only if EVA is positive (Y component).

Chapter 13

Accounting quality Refers to the overall reasonableness of reported financial numbers.

Conservative accounting policies Prudent accounting. For example, choosing an 'accelerated' depreciation method, or one that allocates a large amount of depreciation expense at the beginning of an asset's useful life, signals conservatism.

Liberal accounting policies Aggressive accounting policies. For example, depreciating non-current assets over extended periods of time is a signal of aggressive accounting.

Red flags A signal that 'something is wrong' and accounting quality low.

Chapter 14

Accounting flexibility Within GAAP management has discretion in reporting financial numbers.

Accounting regulation The laws and rules which guide firms in how to report financial data.

Classification The way different accounting items are shown in the financial statements.

Conceptual framework A coherent system of inter-related objectives and fundamentals that should lead to consistent standards that prescribe the nature, function and limits of financial accounting and financial statements.

Definition of accounting items In order to be recognised, accounting items must meet the definition criteria. For example, an asset is a resource controlled by the entity as a result of past events and from which future economic benefits are expected to flow to the entity.

Disclosure The purpose of accounting disclosure is to inform both current and potential investors of the accounting strategies and methods used when developing periodic corporate financial statements. These financial statements include, but are not limited to, the balance sheet, the statement of cash flows, the income statement, and the statement of stockholders' equity. The full disclosure principle requires that any event that would have an impact on the financial statements should be disclosed.

Measurement   Accounting items may be measured using a number of different measurement attributes including amortised costs, historical costs, fair value etc.

Chapter 15

Contingent liabilities   Liabilities that are not recognised in the balance sheet because they depend upon some future (uncertain) event(s).

Deferred tax liabilities   The obligation to pay tax is deferred (postponed) to some future date due to differences in how earnings are determined for accounting purposes and tax purposes, respectively.

Leases   Leasing is a process by which a firm can obtain the use of a certain fixed assets for which it must pay a series of contractual, periodic payments.

Provisions   A liability where the amount to be settled and/or timing are uncertain.

Index

UNIVERSITY OF WINCHESTER
LIBRARY